WISDOM'S LAW OF WATERCOURSES

Wisdom's
LAW OF WATERCOURSES

Fifth edition

WILLIAM HOWARTH, B.A. LL.M.

Reader in Law,
University College of Wales, Aberystwyth,
and Editor of the journal *Water Law*

Shaw & Sons Limited

Crayford, Kent

Published by Shaw & Sons Limited,
Shaway House, 21 Bourne Park,
Bourne Road, Crayford,
Kent DA1 4BZ

First published — May 1962
2nd edition — October 1970
3rd edition — February 1976
4th edition — August 1979
5th edition — March 1992

ISBN 0 7219 0083 6

A CIP catalogue record for this book
is available from the British Library

Printed in Great Britain

PREFACE TO THE FIFTH EDITION

The preparation of a new edition of the late A.S. Wisdom's highly regarded work *The Law of Rivers and Watercourses* has been no easy task. The text which follows has been written with two potential readers, and critics, in mind. On one side has been the revisionist looking for a statement of the law of England and Wales relating to watercourses in which the bulk of Wisdom's words have been superseded by a more modern account of the law, and the old format abandoned unless there are overriding reasons for keeping it intact. On the other side has been a preservationist looking for an account of recent developments within the familiar structure of a standard work which should at all costs be retained. Inevitably, it is impossible to please both kinds of reader, but the new edition is my best attempt to do so.

The main objective has been to steer the difficult path between fidelity to the original author's text and style of presentation and the need to depart from it where the changes in the law and administration relating to watercourses have made reorganisation and rewriting unavoidable in order to produce an accurate account of the present law. The unrivalled standing in which Wisdom's work has long been held by all with an involvement in water law is such that modifications have not been made lightly, but the revolutions in the subject which have come about since the last edition, in 1979, have meant that the body of the earlier work has needed to be substantially reclothed.

Not least significant amongst the changes is the Water Act 1989, providing for the comprehensive reorganisation of water management and regulation of the aquatic environment. These developments are so fundamental that they have necessitated an almost total revision of the later chapters of the work. In turn, the water consolidation legislation of 1991, and particularly the Water Resources Act 1991 and the Land Drainage Act 1991, have made totally new coverage of water regulation necessary. Other legislative developments, and innumerable judicial decisions relating to diverse aspects of watercourses, may have been narrower in their consequences but have also required considerable rewriting and reordering of the work. Despite these imposed constraints, it is hoped that the end product remains faithful to Wisdom's overall aim of summarising the law relating to watercourses "within a reasonably confined but comprehensive compass", and retains some of the familiarity of structure which past readers have found so valuable. The modification of the title, from *The Law of Rivers and Watercourses* to *Wisdom's Law of Watercourses,* is not attributable to any omission or shortening of the discussion of the law relating to rivers, but rather because the term "watercourse" is now understood to encompass all kinds of flowing waters *including* rivers.

This work has been, for me, part of a continuing learning process about water law and thanks are due to all the numerous persons named in prefaces to my previous works for providing me with the general legal background which has been necessary in undertaking the project. In addition, Simon Ball, Tim Burton, Han Somsen and David Freestone, as the editorial team of the journal *Water Law*, have been first–rate in keeping me informed of recent developments in the law, as have the members of the Advisory Board of the journal. My colleagues at the University College of Wales, Aberystwyth, have humoured my preoccupation with water law and helped me greatly where it has flowed into their areas of expertise. Lillian Stevenson, the Law Librarian, has provided valuable help in tracing obscure and often imperfectly referenced sources. Most important of all, the support and encouragement of Ann Cresswell and my parents have kept me from faltering where the task seemed insuperable. To these, the publishers, and many others, I am extremely grateful.

For the most part the law is stated as at 19 September 1991, and assuming the water consolidation legislation of 1991 to have entered into force. However, where changes in the law are imminent, as in relation to waste management, in Ch.11, and land drainage rating, in Ch.12, the opportunity has been taken to anticipate forthcoming developments.

William Howarth.

Department of Law,
University College of Wales,
Aberystwyth.

CONTENTS

Page

PREFACE v
TABLE OF STATUTES xix
TABLE OF STATUTORY INSTRUMENTS xlviii
TABLE OF CASES li

Chapter 1 – GENERAL CHARACTERISTICS OF WATERCOURSES 1
DEFINITIONS OF WATERCOURSES 1
Watercourses in general 1
The statutory definition of "watercourse" 3
Statutory definitions of "inland waters" 5
Watercourses at common law 6
Water flowing in a channel 7
Waste surface water 8
Underground water 9
Artificial watercourses 10
The constituents of a watercourse 11
The bed 11
The bank 12
The flowing water 13
TIDAL AND NON–TIDAL WATERCOURSES 15
Tidal watercourses 15
Ownership of the bed of a tidal watercourse 16
Non–tidal watercourses 16
Ownership of the bed of non–tidal watercourses 17
The *medium filum* rule 17
Alteration of the channel of a watercourse 20
Stillwaters 21

Chapter 2 – THE SEA AND COASTAL WATERS 24
Introduction 24
TIDAL WATERS AND THE SEA 25
Tidal waters and the sea in domestic law 25
THE TERRITORIAL SEA 26
The territorial sea in international law 26
Territorial waters in domestic law 28
THE EXCLUSIVE ECONOMIC ZONE 32
The exclusive economic zone in international law 32
The exclusive economic zone in domestic law 33
THE CONTINENTAL SHELF 36
The continental shelf in international law 36
The continental shelf in domestic law 38
THE HIGH SEAS 39
The high seas in international law 39
The high seas in domestic law 40
THE FORESHORE 41
Limits and ownership 41
Express grant 44

Page

Grant by prescription 45
Possessory title 46
Accretion and encroachment 46
Rights over the foreshore 50
Access over the foreshore 50
Jurisdiction over the foreshore 52
The right to take seaweed, shells, sand and shingle 53
Wreck 55
Royal fish and fowl 58
COAST PROTECTION AND SEA DEFENCE 59
Sea walls and embankments 61
Repair of sea walls and river banks 62

Chapter 3 – NATURAL RIGHTS OF WATER 66
RIPARIAN RIGHTS 66
The nature of riparian rights 66
Riparian owners 69
Rights and duties of riparian owners 70
Classification of riparian rights 72
ABSTRACTION AND DIVERSION AT COMMON LAW 72
Ordinary use of water 72
Extraordinary use of water 73
Irrigation 74
Diversion in general 76
OBSTRUCTION AT COMMON LAW 78
Placing erections on the bed of a watercourse 78
Use of water for milling purposes 80
Clearing the channel of a watercourse 81
Protection against flooding 82
ESCAPE, OVERFLOW AND DISCHARGE OF WATER 84
The position of landowners 84
Discharges of water 87
POLLUTION AT COMMON LAW 89
Rights of a riparian owner as to quality of water 89
The meaning of "pollution" 91
Permissible pollution 92
Pollution and fisheries 93
Remedies for pollution 94
Damages 94
The injunction 95
Public nuisance 98

Chapter 4 – ACQUIRED RIGHTS OF WATER 100
NATURE AND CHARACTERISTICS OF WATER EASEMENTS 100
Acquisition of water easements 101
Grant 101
Prescription 103
Custom 105

Page
Statute 105
SPECIFIC EASEMENTS OF WATER 106
Easements of abstraction, diversion and obstruction 106
Easements to pollute water 107
Easements regarding underground and percolating water 110
Easements to discharge or receive water 110
Secondary easements 111
EXTINGUISHMENT OF WATER EASEMENTS 112
Operation of law 112
Release 113
Licence given to servient owner 113
Abandonment by non-use 113
Alteration in the use of the dominant tenement 114

Chapter 5 – ARTIFICIAL WATERCOURSES AND UNDERGROUND WATER 115
Introduction 115
Distinction between natural and artificial watercourses 115
Permanent artificial watercourses 116
Temporary artificial watercourses 118
Pollution of artificial watercourses 120
PERCOLATING UNDERGROUND WATER 121
The absence of riparian rights in underground percolating water 121
Abstraction of percolating water in a well or on the surface 123
Restrictions on underground abstraction 124
Springs and wells 125
Support from underground water 125
WATER FLOWING IN A DEFINED UNDERGROUND CHANNEL 126
PERCOLATING WATER ON THE SURFACE 128
Pollution of percolating water 129

Chapter 6 – NAVIGATION ON WATERCOURSES 131
THE RIGHT OF NAVIGATION 131
Navigation on tidal watercourses 131
Navigation on non–tidal watercourses 133
Incidents of the right of navigation 135
Passage and grounding 135
Anchoring, mooring and landing 136
Towing 137
Extinguishment of the right of navigation 139
Navigation and fishing 139
OBSTRUCTIONS TO NAVIGATION 140
Erections on the bed of a watercourse 141
Works causing silting 144
Works on the foreshore 145
Wreck 146
Locks, weirs and dams 147
Bridges 148

Page
Miscellaneous obstructions 149
RIPARIAN RIGHTS ON NAVIGABLE WATERCOURSES 149
The right of access 150
The right to moor 151
The right to place erections on the bank or bed of a watercourse .152
CONSERVANCY AND NAVIGATION AUTHORITIES 153
Property in watercourses 154
Maintenance of navigation 156
Regulation of navigation 158
The navigation function of the National Rivers Authority 159
Regulation of navigation by water undertakers 161

Chapter 7 – FERRIES AND BRIDGES 162
THE LEGAL CHARACTER OF FERRIES 162
RIGHTS AND OBLIGATIONS OF THE OWNER OF A FERRY 165
Tolls 165
Maintenance of a ferry 165
Liability for loss or injury 167
Disturbance of ferries 167
Extinguishment of ferries 169
BRIDGES 169
Construction of bridges 169
Maintenance of bridges 172

Chapter 8 – FISHERIES AT COMMON LAW 175
TYPES OF FISHERIES 175
PUBLIC FISHERIES 176
The right to fish in the sea and tidal waters 177
Fishing on the foreshore 177
Several fisheries in tidal waters 180
Royal fisheries 181
Limits of tidal part of a river 181
Fishing in non–tidal waters 182
PRIVATE FISHERIES 182
Several fisheries 183
Common of fishery 183
Claims to private fisheries 184
Claim by express grant 185
Lease or licence 185
Prescription 186
Evidence of title to fisheries 187
Fisheries in tidal waters 187
Fisheries in non–tidal waters 187
Documentary evidence 188
Evidence of possession 189
Presumptions as to ownership of fisheries 190
In tidal waters 190
In non–tidal waters 190

Page

Rebuttal of presumptions 191
Boundaries of fisheries 191
Fisheries in lakes and ponds 193
Fisheries in canals and reservoirs 194
Fishing paths 194
Weirs obstructing fisheries 195
Disturbance of fisheries 196

Chapter 9 – WATER REGULATION 198
RECENT DEVELOPMENTS IN WATER REGULATION 198
The background to the Water Act 1989 198
The water consolidation legislation 201
The Water Resources Act 1991 202
THE NATIONAL RIVERS AUTHORITY 204
The constitution of the National Rivers Authority 204
Principal functions of the Authority 206
Incidental functions and powers of the Authority 207
Ministerial directions to the Authority 208
COMMITTEES WITH FUNCTIONS IN RELATION TO THE AUTHORITY 209
The Advisory Committee for Wales 209
Regional rivers advisory committees 209
Fisheries advisory committees 210
Regional and local flood defence committees 210
GENERAL DUTIES 211
General duties with respect to the water industry 211
The general environmental and recreational duties 211
Sites of special scientific interest 213
Codes of practice 214
LAND AND WORKS POWERS OF THE AUTHORITY 214
Acquisition of land 214
Works and pipe–laying powers 216
Compulsory works orders 217
POWERS OF ENTRY 218
SUPPLEMENTAL PROVISIONS ON LAND AND WORKS POWERS 221
INFORMATION PROVISIONS 224
Annual report and publication of information 224
Registers to be kept by the authority 224
Abstraction and impounding licences 224
Pollution control register 225
Register for works discharges 226
Maps 226
Freshwater limits 226
Main river maps 226
Maps of waterworks 227
Provision and acquisition of information 228
Restrictions on disclosure of information and false statements 231
MISCELLANEOUS AND SUPPLEMENTAL MATTERS 233

	Page
Directions in the interests of national security	233
Civil liability for escapes of water	233
Evidence of samples and abstractions	234
Byelaws	235
Byelaw offences	236
Local inquires	237
Offences and judicial disqualification	238
FINANCIAL PROVISIONS IN RELATION TO THE AUTHORITY	239
General financial provisions	239
Revenue provisions	240
Grants and loans	241
Chapter 10 – WATER RESOURCES	243
Introduction	243
GENERAL MANAGEMENT FUNCTIONS	244
General management of water resources	244
Minimum acceptable flows	245
Directions to consider minimum acceptable flow	247
Minimum acceptable level or volume of inland waters	247
RESTRICTIONS ON ABSTRACTION AND IMPOUNDING	248
Restrictions on abstraction	248
Restrictions on impounding	251
Rights to abstract or impound	253
Navigation, harbour and conservancy authorities	253
Abstraction of small quantities	253
Curtailment of rights to abstract small quantities	255
Rights to abstract for drainage purposes	255
Notices with respect to borings	256
Miscellaneous rights to abstract	256
APPLICATIONS FOR A LICENCE	257
Regulations with respect to applications	257
Applicants for a licence	258
Combined abstraction and impounding licences	259
Licence application procedure	259
General consideration of applications	260
Reference of applications to the Secretary of State	261
Appeals to the Secretary of State	262
CONTENT AND CONSEQUENCES OF LICENCES	263
Form and content of licences	263
Revocation and variation of licences	265
Derogation from protected rights	266
Civil liability	268
Abstraction and impounding by the Authority and water undertakers	269
WATER RESOURCE CHARGES	270
Charging schemes for licences	270
Register of applications and licences	273
DROUGHT	273

Page
Ordinary and emergency drought orders 273
Provisions and duration of ordinary drought orders 274
Provisions and duration of emergency drought orders 276
Provisions, works and compensation under drought orders 277
Offences under drought orders 279
RESERVOIR SAFETY 280
The Reservoirs Act 1975 280
Registration of reservoirs by local authorities 281
Qualification of engineers 282
Certification of reservoirs 282
Inspections and monitoring 284
Discontinuance or abandonment 286
Additional powers 287
Criminal and civil liability 288

Chapter 11 – WATER POLLUTION 290
Introduction 290
Controlled waters 290
Relevant territorial waters 290
Coastal waters 291
Inland freshwaters 291
Ground waters 292
WATER QUALITY CLASSIFICATION AND OBJECTIVES 292
Classification of quality of waters 292
Water quality objectives 294
General duties to achieve and maintain objectives 295
WATER POLLUTION OFFENCES 295
Offences of polluting controlled waters 295
Prohibitions of certain discharges 298
Discharges into and from public sewers 299
Offences concerning deposits and vegetation in rivers 301
Miscellaneous defences to principal offences 301
AUTHORISED DISCHARGES 303
Defences to the principal offences for authorised discharges 303
Discharge consents 304
Generally 304
Applications for consents 305
Consideration and determination of applications 306
Notification of proposal to give consent 307
Reference of applications for consent to the Secretary of State 308
Consents without application 309
Revocation of consents and alteration and imposition of conditions 309
Restriction on variation and revocation of consents 311
Appeals 311
Charges in connection with discharge consents 312

Page

Discharge consents and powers of the authority to discharge water 313
Integrated pollution control and water pollution law 315
General nature of integrated pollution control 315
Authorisations for prescribed processes 316
Offences 317
Information provisions 318
Relationship between HMIP and the National Rivers Authority 319
Waste disposal 320
Waste management licensing 321
The duty of care 322
Deposit of waste at sea 324
POLLUTION PREVENTION 325
Anti-pollution works and operations 325
Other powers to deal with foul water and pollution 326
Requirements to take precautions against pollution 327
Water protection zones 328
Nitrate sensitive areas 330
Codes of good agricultural practice 332
Water pollution prevention and planning law 333
SUPPLEMENTAL PROVISIONS ON WATER POLLUTION 335
Application to radioactive substances 335
Civil liability, savings and limitation for summary offences 335
International obligations and transitional provisions 336
WATER POLLUTION UNDER MISCELLANEOUS LEGISLATION 337
Discharges to sewers 337
Public health law and water pollution 339
Radioactive pollution 342
Oil and other pollution from ships 346
Water supplies 350
Other miscellaneous provisions 351
Gas 351
Pipelines 352
Fisheries 352
Animal health 353
Cemeteries and Harbours Clauses Acts 353
Pesticides 354
WATER QUALITY UNDER EUROPEAN COMMUNITY LEGISLATION 355
The constitution and legislation of the European Community 355
The water quality directives 359
Directives concerned with particular pollutants 361
Directives concerned with water for particular uses 363
Directives concerned with particular polluting activities 364
The Urban Waste Water Treatment Directive 365
The Directive on Pollution by Nitrates from Diffuse Sources 367

Page
Community water law and national legislation 368

Chapter 12 – FLOOD DEFENCE AND LAND DRAINAGE 371
Introduction 371
FLOOD DEFENCE AND THE NATIONAL RIVERS AUTHORITY ...373
The flood defence and land drainage functions 373
Flood defence committees 374
Regional flood defence committees 375
Local flood defence schemes and committees 376
Main river functions of the Authority 378
Schemes for transfer of functions to the Authority 379
Structures in, over or under a main river 379
Arrangements with certain authorities 380
Flood defence and drainage works 381
Flood warning systems 382
Flood defence regulations and byelaws 383
INTERNAL DRAINAGE BOARDS 384
Supervision of drainage boards by the Authority 387
Environmental and recreational duties 389
POWERS TO FACILITATE OR SECURE THE DRAINAGE OF LAND 391
General powers of internal drainage boards and local authorities 391
Disposal of spoil 394
Exercise and supervision of drainage powers 395
Drainage of small areas 396
Arrangements as to works 397
Obligations to repair watercourses and bridges 397
Ministerial authorisation for landowners to carry out works 398
Obstructions in watercourses 398
Works for maintaining the flow of a watercourse 399
Restoration and improvement of ditches 401
Powers to modify existing obligations 402
Variation of awards 402
Commutation of obligations 402
Power to vary navigation rights 403
FINANCIAL PROVISIONS CONCERNING THE NATIONAL RIVERS AUTHORITY 404
Levies on local authorities 404
General drainage charges 404
Special drainage charges 405
Revenue from internal drainage boards 406
FINANCIAL PROVISIONS CONCERNING INTERNAL DRAINAGE BOARDS 407
Raising and apportionment of expenses 407
Levying of drainage rates 408
MISCELLANEOUS FINANCIAL PROVISIONS AND POWERS 409
Further financial provisions 409

Page

Powers to borrow 409
Navigation tolls 410
Contributions by the Authority 410
Allocation of Authority revenue 411
Ministerial grants 411
Local authority contributions and expenses 411
Miscellaneous powers of internal drainage boards 412
Powers to acquire and dispose of land 412
Powers of entry of internal drainage boards and local authorities 412
Regulations and byelaws 413

Chapter 13 – FISHERIES UNDER STATUTE 415
THE FISHERIES FUNCTION OF THE NATIONAL RIVERS AUTHORITY 415
The fisheries function 415
Ministerial powers and fisheries orders 415
Regional and local fisheries advisory committees 418
Fisheries contributions 418
Land acquisition for fisheries purposes 419
The power to make fishery byelaws 419
Fishery byelaw purposes 420
THE SALMON AND FRESHWATER FISHERIES ACT 1975 423
Prohibition of certain modes of taking or destroying fish 423
Prohibited implements 423
Roe, spawning and unclean fish 424
Nets 425
Poisonous matter and polluting effluent 426
Explosives, poisons, electrical devices and destruction of dams 427
Obstructions to the passage of fish 428
Fixed engines 428
Fishing weirs 429
Fishing mill dams 430
Duty to make and maintain fish passes 430
Power of the Authority to construct and alter fish passes 431
Minister's consents and approvals for fish passes 431
Injuring or obstructing a fish pass or free gap 431
Sluices 432
Gratings 432
Boxes and cribs in weirs and dams 433
Restrictions on taking salmon or trout above or below an obstruction 433
Times of fishing and selling and exporting fish 434
Close seasons and times: salmon 434
Close seasons and times: trout 435
Sale, export and consignment of salmon and trout 436
Close seasons: freshwater fish 437

Page
Fishing licences 438
Licences to fish 438
Limitation of fishing licences 439
Unlicensed fishing 440
Duty on licences 440
Power to require production of fishing licences 441
Introduction of fish into inland waters 441
Powers of water bailiffs 442
Powers of search 442
Power to enter lands 443
Orders and warrants to enter suspected premises 443
Power to apprehend persons fishing illegally at night 444
The water bailiff as a police constable 444
Offences and penalties 445
Punishments 445
Forfeiture 446
Licence forfeiture and disqualification 447
Magistrates' powers 448
THE SALMON ACT 1986 448
Dealer licensing 449
Handling salmon in suspicious circumstances 449
THE THEFT ACT 1968 451
Theft of fish 451
Taking or destroying fish 452
THE DISEASES OF FISH ACTS 1937 AND 1983 453
Registration of fish farms 455
THE SEA FISHERIES REGULATION ACT 1966 457
Local fisheries committees 457
Byelaws for the regulation of sea fisheries 458
Fishery officers 461
Other powers of local fisheries committees 462
Areas of local fisheries committees and the National Rivers Authority 463

INDEX 465

TABLE OF STATUTES

		Page
1225	Magna Charta, 9 Hen. III	147, 176, 180, 187, 189, 195
1289	Quia Emptores, 18 Edw. I	184
1324	De Prerogativa Regis, 17 Edw. II, st.2, c.11	56, 58
1350	25 Edw. III, st.4, c.4	147, 195
1371	45 Edw. III, c.2	195
1393	17 Rich. II, c.9	195
1399	1 Hen. IV, c.12	195
1402	4 Hen. IV, c.11	195
1427	Sewers, 6 Hen. VI, c.5	59, 372
1472	12 Edw. IV, c.7	195
1531	Statute of Sewers, 23 Hen. VIII, c.5	59, 372
1549	Sewers, 3 & 4 Edw. VI, c.8	59
1562	Sewers, 13 Eliz. 1, c.9	59
1609	7 Jac. 1, c.18	53
1832	Prescription Act	51, 108, 110, 119, 148, 187
	s.2	104
1833	Sewers Act	59
1847	Cemeteries Clauses Act	
	s.2	353
	s.22	353
1847	Harbour, Docks and Piers Clauses Act	
	s.56	147
	s.73	353–4
1858	Cornwall Submarine Mines Act	30
1859	Tweed Fisheries Amendment Act	207, 415
1861	Land Drainage Act	59
1861	Malicious Damage Act	
	s.31	141
1861	Salmon Fishery Act	423
1863	Railways Clauses Act	171
	s.3	15, 25
1865	Salmon Fishery Act	428
1866	Crown Lands Act	
	s.7	16
1868	Documentary Evidence Act	227
1868	Public Health Act	
	s.68	351
1875	Explosives Act	
	s.108	25
1875	Public Health Act	
	s.17	8, 295
	s.68	305
	s.164	51

Page

1876 Rivers Pollution Prevention Act 10
s.2 297
s.3 109
s.4 109
1878 Territorial Waters Jurisdiction Act 28, 29
s.2 28
s.7 ....28, 177
1888 Railway and Canal Traffic Act 249
1893 North Sea Fisheries Act
s.9 28
1894 Merchant Shipping Act 34, 135
s.373 34
s.418 158
s.421 158
s.510 56
s.513 51
s.523 56
s.530 147
s.531 147
s.534 147
s.742 25
Part IX 56
1906 Open Spaces Act
s.15 51
1907 Public Health Acts Amendment Act
s.82 52
s.83 52
1914 Land Drainage Act 59
1915 Fishery Harbours Act 463
1916 Larceny Act 14
1918 Land Drainage Act 59
1919 Ferries (Acquisition by Local Authorities) Act
s.1 164
(4) 164
s.2 164
1923 Salmon and Freshwater Fisheries Act 109, 423
1925 Land Registration Act 216
1926 Land Drainage Act 59
1928 Petroleum (Consolidation) Act 337
1929 Mines and Quarries (Tips) Act 280
1930 Land Drainage Act 59, 372, 393
s.36(1) 64
s.38 13
s.81 13

Page

1930 Reservoirs (Safety Provisions) Act 280, 281, 289
1932 Rights of Water Act 134
1932 Thames Conservancy Act
s.77 137
s.79 133
s.97 159
1934 Petroleum (Production) Act
s.1(2), (3) 38
1936 Public Health Act
s.27 300
s.30 4
s.231 51
s.259 82
(1)(a), (b) 340
s.262 63
s.264 63
Part III 339
1937 Diseases of Fish Act 206, 207, 415, 416, 442
s.1 453
s.2(1), (2) 454
s.2A 454
s.3(1)–(3) 455
s.4, 4A 455
s.7(1), (2), (3), (4), (8) 456
s.8(1) 455, 457
(2) 455
s.10(1) 453, 454
s.13(1) 453
1937 Factories Act
s.151(1) 14
1945 Law Reform (Contributory Negligence) Act 234
1945 Water Act
s.21 350
s.23 269
s.26 105
1947 Agriculture Act 406
s.109(3) 254
1949 Civil Aviation Act
s.51 56
1949 Coast Protection Act 55, 60, 84, 372
s.16 61
s.18 .... 31, 55, 61
s.32(1), (5) 60
s.34 .... 145, 146

1949 Coast Protection Act – *continued.* Page
s.35 146
s.36 146
s.43 146
s.49(1) 26, 42, 145
(2) 26
Part II 145
Part III 53
Sch.4 26
1949 Consolidation of Enactments (Procedure) Act 202
1949 National Parks and Access to the Countryside Act
s.27(6), (7) 137
s.53 165
s.59(2) 51
Part V 51
1951 Rivers (Prevention of Pollution) Act
s.2(1) 297
1954 Mines and Quarries Act 302
1954 Transport Charges, etc. (Miscellaneous Provisions) Act
s.6 164
1956 Crown Estate Act 53
1957 Housing Act
s.103 105
1957 Occupiers Liability Act 62, 65, 138, 157
1958 Water Act 252
1960 Radioactive Substances Act 335
s.1(3)–(5) 343
s.6 344
(1), (3), (5) 343
s.8(1), (3), (4), (7) 344
s.9(2)(a) 342
s.11A(1)–(3) 342
s.11B, s.11C 344
s.13(2), (7) 345
s.18(1), (2) 343
s.19(1) 343
Sch.1 342
Sch.3 342–3
1961 Crown Estate Act 53
1961 Public Health Act
s.76 52
1961 Rivers (Prevention of Pollution) Act
s.10(1), (2) 235
1962 Pipelines Act
s.37(1) 352

Page

1963 Water Resources Act 243, 251, 252, 267
s.23(1) 75
s.26 351
s.33 268
s.36(2), (3) 252
s.67 269
s.135(1) 250, 252
1964 Continental Shelf Act 38, 39, 41, 146
s.1(1) 38
ss.2–9 38
1964 Police Act
s.15 445
1965 Compulsory Purchase Act 215
1965 Gas Act
s.15 352
1965 Law Commission Act 201
1965 Nuclear Installations Act 342, 344
s.7 345
s.12(1), (2) 345
s.13(4)(a) 345
s.15(1), (2) 345
s.16(1) 346
s.19(1) 346
s.26(1) 345
1966 Sea Fisheries Regulation Act 177, 206, 415, 416
s.1(1) 457
s.2(1), (2) 458
s.2(5) 458
s.3 457
s.4 457
s.5 429
(1) 459
(c) 353
s.6 460
s.7(1), (2) 460
s.8 460
s.10(1) 461
(2) 462
(3) 461
(4) 462
s.11(1) 462
(2), (2A), (3) 461
(5) 460
(7) 461

		Page
1966	Sea Fisheries Regulation Act – *continued.*	
	s.13(1), (2)	462
	(3), (4), (5)	463
	s.17(1), (2)	458
	s.18(1)	463
	(2), (3)	464
	s.19	464
	s.20(1)	26, 457, 464
1967	Sea Fish (Conservation) Act	
	s.4	35
1967	Sea Fisheries (Shellfish) Act	177
	s.1	353
	s.7(4)(c)	353
	s.10	459
	s.16(2)	459
	s.17(2)	459
1968	Countryside Act	
	s.13(13)	21
1968	Firearms Act	
	s.57(1)	423
1968	Sea Fisheries Act	
	s.7	461
	s.17	56
1968	Theft Act	14
	s.1(1)	451
	s.4(4)	451
	s.12(1)	159
	Sch.1, para 2	452
	para.2(1), (2), (3), (4)	452
1968	Transport Act	
	s.112	139
	s.113	158
1969	Public Health (Recurring Nuisances) Act	339
1970	Conservation of Seals Act	462
1971	Merchant Shipping (Oil Pollution) Act	348
	s.1	349
	s.2	349
	s.4(1)	349
	s.10	349
1971	Mineral Workings (Offshore Installations) Act	38
	s.1(2)(a), (3)	39
	s.2	39
	s.3	39
	s.6	39
	s.7	39

1971 Mineral Workings (Offshore Installations) Act – *continued.* Page

s.8 39

1971 Prevention of Oil Pollution Act 38, 253, 346

s.2 347

(1) 347

s.8(2) 253

s.10 348

s.11 348

s.19(6) 463

s.29(1) 26, 253, 347

1972 European Communities Act

s.2(2) 36, 370

(4) 370

1972 Gas Act 351

1972 Land Charges Act 216

1972 Local Government Act

s.71 52

s.72 52

s.214(3) 353

s.250(2)–(5) 238

s.272(1) 457, 458

Sch.26, para.14 353

Sch.30 .... 457, 458

1972 Salmon and Freshwater Fishery Act 423

1973 Protection of Wrecks Act 31

s.1(1), (3), (5) 31

s.2 32

s.3(1) 31

(3) 32

1973 Water Act 198

s.10 243

s.30 270

s.31 270

1974 Control of Pollution Act

s.5 .... 303, 320

s.31(1) 297

s.36(4) 305

s.56(1) 25

s.100 355

Part I 320

Sch.3, para.17 235

1974 Merchant Shipping Act 348

Part I 349

1975 Reservoirs Act 243, 251, 280–9

s.1(1)–(3) 280

1975 Reservoirs Act – *continued*. Page
(4) 281
s.2 281
s.3(1), (2), (3) 282
s.4(1), (2), (3), (5) 282
s.6(1) 283
(2), (3) 283, 285
(4) 285
s.7 283
s.8(1), (2) 283
s.9(1) 283
(2) 283, 285
(7) 283
s.10(1), (2) 284
(3), (5), (6), (7) 285
(9) 284
s.11 285
(1) 285
s.12 286
s.13(1)–(3) 286
s.14(1), (2), (4) 286
s.15(1), (2) 287, 288
(5) 287
s.16 288
(1), (2), (6) 287
s.17(1), (4), (5) 288
s.18(1) 288
s.22(1) 288
(2)–(4) 289
s.28 289
Sch.2 289
1975 Salmon and Freshwater Fisheries Act 202, 206, 207, 415, 416, 420, 449
s.1 446
(1)(a) 423
(b), (c) 424
(3) 423–4
(4) 424
s.2(1) 424
(2), (3) 425
(4) 140, 425
(5) 425
s.4 304
(1) 352, 426, 427
(2) 426
s.5 446

1975 Salmon and Freshwater Fisheries Act – *continued.* Page
(1) 352, 427
(2)–(5) 427
ss.6–18 196
s.6 459
(1) 428
(2), (3) 429
s.7 429
s.8(1)–(5) 430
s.9 431
s.10 .... 215, 431
s.11 431
s.12 432
s.13 432
s.14 .... 77, 433
s.16 433
s.17 434
s.19(1) 434, 435
(2), (3) 434
(4), (5) 435
(6)–(8) 437
s.20 435
(3) 436
s.21(1), (2) 438
s.22(1)–(4) 436
s.23(1), (2) 437
s.24(1)–(3) 437
s.25(1), (2), (3) 438
(4)–(6), (7) 439
(8) 440, 441
s.26(1), (7) 439
s.27 440
s.28(6) 445
s.29 416
s.30 442
s.31(1) 442
(b), (c) 450
(2) 443
s.32(1) 443
s.33(1) 443
s.33(2) 444, 450
s.34 444
s.35 441
s.36(1) 444, 451, 461
(2) 438

1975 Salmon and Freshwater Fisheries Act – *continued*. Page

(3) 445

s.37 .... 446, 447, 448

s.39(1) 451

s.41(1) 416, 418–19, 425, 427, 428, 429, 430, 439

s.42(8) 425

s.43(2) 423

Part I 423

Part II 423

Part III 423

Part IV 423

Part V 423

Part VI 423

Sch.1 422

para.4, 5 437

para.6 .... 434, 435

Sch.2, para.1–8 440

para.9–14 447

para.13 438

para.15, 16, 17 441

Sch.3, para.39(1)(a) 451

(c) 445

Sch.4 446

Part I 446

Part II 451

para.1(2) 446

para.2, 4 448

para.5 .... 442, 446

para.7, 8, 9 447

para.10, 11, 12 448

1976 Drought Act 243

1976 Energy Act 38

1976 Fatal Accidents Act 234

1976 Fishery Limits Act 177

s.1 ....33, 34

(4) 34

(5) 33

s.2(2)–(4), (5), (6) 35

(7) 34

s.3 35

s.6(1) 34

s.8 34

s.9(1) 427

s.10(2) 33

Sch.2, para.20 427

Page

1976 Land Drainage Act ... 59, 373, 393
s.4 ... 376
s.6 ... 384
s.27(4) ... 25
s.117(1) ... 372
Sch.6, para.6, 9 ... 372
1977 Criminal Law Act
s.31(5), (6), (9) ... 354
Sch.6 ... 446
1978 Civil Liability (Contributions) Act ... 234
1978 Interpretation Act ... 268
s.18 ... 268, 335
1979 Ancient Monuments and Archaeological Areas Act
ss.35–41 ... 31
1980 Highways Act
s.10 ... 170
s.14 ... 170
s.16 ... 170
s.18 ... 170
s.20 ... 217
s.24 ... 164
(4) ... 164
s.41 ... 172
s.45 ... 55
s.52 ... 55
s.53 ... 173
s.55 ... 173
s.56 ... 173
s.57 ... 173
s.91 ... 169
s.92 ... 169
s.93 ... 172
s.94 ... 172
s.100 ... 302
s.105 ... 164
s.106(1)–(4) ... 170
s.107 ... 164, 170
s.108(4) ... 171
s.220 ... 164
s.271(1)(d) ... 164
s.329(1) ... 164
Sch.1 ... 170
1980 Limitation Act ... 234
s.15 ... 46

		Page
1980	Limitation Act – *continued.*	
	Sch.1 para 11	46
1980	Magistrates Court Act	
	s.32(2), (3)	446
	s.127	336
1981	Acquisition of Land Act	105, 214–15
1981	Animal Health Act	
	s.10(1)	453
	s.35(4)	353
1981	Fisheries Act	
	s.30(1)	35
	(2)	36
1981	Wildlife and Countryside Act	462
	s.36	31
1982	Criminal Justice Act	
	s.38	351, 460, 462
	s.46	351, 446, 460, 462
1982	Oil and Gas (Enterprise) Act	38
1983	Diseases of Fish Act	453
1984	Police and Criminal Evidence Act	
	s.24	444
	s.25	445
1985	Food and Environment Protection Act	
	s.8(1)	324
	s.9(1), (3)	325
	s.16(1), (2)	354
	(12)	355
	(15)	354
	s.21(1), (2)	325
	(3), (4)	355
	s.24(1)	324, 354
	Part II	303, 324, 355
	Part III	354
1985	Local Government Act	
	s.16	457, 458,464
	Sch.8, para.19	458, 464
	para.19(2)	457
1986	Gas Act	
	Part I	233
1986	Hovercraft Act	302
1986	Prevention of Oil Pollution Act	346
1986	Public Order Act	
	s.38	351
1986	Salmon Act	423, 429, 442
	s.20(1)	458

1986 Salmon Act – *continued.* Page
s.31(1), (2), (6) 449
s.32 .... 442, 443, 444
(1), (2)–(4), (5) 450
(6) 451
(a) 442
(b) 443, 444
(7) 450
s.33(1) 428
(2), (3) 429
s.34 442
s.35 446
(1) 446
s.37(1) 458, 459
(2), (3) 460
s.40(1) 449
Part III 448
1987 Channel Tunnel Act
s.6(2) 252
Sch.2, Pt.II, Section A, para.5(4) 252
1987 Coal Industry Act 38
1987 Territorial Sea Act
s.1(1), (3), (7) 29
1987 Territorial Waters Act
s.1 28
Sch.2 28
1988 Local Government Finance Act 375, 384, 385, 404
s.75 407
1988 Merchant Shipping Act 348
s.36(1) 145
1988 Norfolk and Suffolk Broads Act 213, 390
1988 Public Utility Transfers and Water Charges Act
s.1 200
1989 Electricity Act
s.6(1) 233
1989 Water Act 198–201, 211, 243, 336, 423
s.1(1) 204
s.3 209
s.4(1) 205
s.103(5) 292
s.104 293
s.107 300
(1) 297
s.110 328
s.136 372

1989 Water Act – *continued.* Page
(8) 206
(9) 373
s.137 372
(1), (2) 375
s.138 372
s.139 372
(1) 377
(2), (4) 376
s.140 ....372, 384
s.141 ....457, 462
s.185(2)(c)–(e) 328
Part I 202
Part II, Chapter III 59
Part III 202
Chapter I 290
Chapter III 372
Chapter V 206
Sch.2 ....205, 269
Sch.13, para.23(3) 206
Sch.15 ....59, 372
para.1(3) 206
Sch.16 375
Sch.17, para.1 462
para.1(3) 457
para.3 455
para.7 441
para.7(3) 429
para.15 447
Sch.25, para.7(4) 350
para.30 352
para.32(3) 352
para.49 280
Sch.26, para.30,31 267–8
para.36(2) 372
para.38 227
para.41(1) 269
1990 Environmental Protection Act
s.2 316
s.6 316
s.7(2)(c) 317
(3) 317
(4) 316
(7) 317
(12)(e) 317

1990 Environmental Protection Act – *continued.* Page

s.13 317
s.14 317
s.17 320
s.20 225
(1), (7) 318
(9) 320
s.21(1) 318
s.22 319
s.23(1)–(3) 318
(1)(l) 318
s.25(1) 316
s.26(1) 318
s.28(3) 319
s.29(1), (2) 321
s.30(1) 321
s.33(1), (2), (3) 322
(7)–(9) 323
s.34 322
s.35 321
s.36(2) 324
(3) 321
(4), (5), (10) 322
s.39(1)–(7) 323
s.62 323
s.74 321
s.75 321
s.79(1) 340
(11) 339
s.80(1)–(6) 340
s.81(1)–(4), (7) 341
s.82 341
s.100 343
(1) 342
s.102 344
s.105 342
s.140 355
s.146 325
(2), (3) 324
Part I 225, 303, 315, 316
Part II 303, 320, 322, 323
Part III 82, 394
Part V 342
Sch.1 316
Sch.3 341

1990 Environmental Protection Act – *continued.* Page
Sch.5 342
1990 Town and Country Planning Act 152
s.1(1), (3) 333
s.31 334
(3)(b) 334
s.36 334
(3)(b) 334
s.55 171–2
(1) 333
s.57 171–2
(1) 333
s.58 334
s.62 334
s.65 ....324, 334
s.70 334
s.90 223
s.316(1) 172
s.336(1) 233
1991 Land Drainage Act 59, 82, 84, 202, 373, 378,
s.1 384
s.2 ....374, 386
(7) 386
s.3 374
s.4 ....374, 386
s.5 ....374, 387
s.6 374
s.7 ....374, 387
s.8 ....374, 388
s.9 374
(1)–(4), (5), (6) 388
s.10 388
s.11 389
s.12 371
(1), (2) 389
(3)–(6) 390
s.13 391
(5) 390
s.14 412
(1), (2), (3) 392
(4), (5) 392, 394
(6) 392
s.15 412
(1) 394
(b) 13

1991 Land Drainage Act – *continued*. Page
(2) 394
(3)–(5) 395
s.16 .... 395, 412
s.17 .... 395, 412
s.18 ....391, 394, 396
(4), (6) 396
s.19(1)–(3) 397
s.20 397
s.21 .... 174, 398
s.22 398
s.23 ....171, 388, 399
s.24 .... 388, 399
s.25 378
(1)–(3) 399
(4)–(6) 400
s.26 400
s.27 400
s.28 401
(5) 401
s.29(1), (2) 401
(3)–(6) 402
s.30 402
s.32 402
s.33 ....64, 378, 403
s.34 .... 378, 403
s.35 404
s.36 407
s.37(1), (2) 408
s.38 .... 374, 385
(1), (2) 408
s.39 374
(1), (2) 408
s.40(1), (2) 408
s.41(1), (2), (4) 409
s.42(1), (3) 409
s.43 409
s.44 409
s.45 409
s.46 409
s.47 .... 374, 409
s.55(1)–(5) 410
s.56 410
s.57 .... 374, 410
s.58 .... 374, 411

1991 Land Drainage Act – *continued.* Page
s.59 411
s.60 411
s.61 411
s.62(1)–(3) 412
s.63 412
(4) 412
s.64(1), (2)–(6) 413
s.65 413
s.66 412
(1)–(3), (5)–(7) 414
s.72(1) 4, 13, 372, 384, 385, 394
(2) 385
s.73(1) 378
s.134 405
s.135 405
s.136 405
s.137(1)–(4) 406
s.138(1)–(3) 406
s.139 406
s.140 406
s.141 407
s.165(2) 60
Part IV 206
Chapter II 407
Sch.1 384
Sch.2 384
Sch.3 ....386, 402, 404
Sch.4 396
Sch.5 414
Sch.15 406
1991 New Roads and Street Works Act 217
s.48 279
s.78 234
1991 Planning and Compensation Act
s.13 333
s.26 334
Sch.4 334
1991 Statutory Water Companies Act 202
1991 Water Consolidation (Consequential Provisions) Act 202
s.1(1) 202
Sch.1, para.1 305
para.30(1) 305, 426
Sch.2 270
para.1 202

Page

1991 Water Industry Act ... 3, 202, 211, 221
s.2 ... 212, 389
s.3 ... 212, 390
s.18 ... 245, 277
s.37 ... 244
s.72 ... 350
(5) ... 350
s.111(1)–(4) ... 338
(5) ... 337
s.117(5)(b) ... 5
s.118 ... 338
s.120 ... 339
s.138 ... 339
s.141(1), (2) ... 338
s.155 ... 105
s.156(7) ... 212, 390
s.157(1) ... 161, 419
(2) ... 161
(3) ... 161, 419
s.165 ... 303
s.167 ... 270, 303
(6) ... 270
s.218(1) ... 350
s.219 ... 5
(1) ... 4, 5
(2) ... 4
Part II ... 211, 221
Part III ... 211
Part IV ... 11, 211, 337
Chapter III ... 339
Part VI ... 278
Sch.10 ... 161, 419
Sch.11 ... 270
para.7 ... 270

1991 Water Resources Act ... 75, 202–4, 211, 423
s.1(1), (2), (3)–(5), (6) ... 205
s.2(1) ... 206
(c) ... 373
(d) ... 415
(e) ... 159
(2) ... 207, 214, 246
(4) ... 207
(5) ... 207, 373
(6) ... 207, 415

1991 Water Resources Act – *continued*. Page
(7) 207, 415
s.3 208
s.4 419
(1) 208
s.5 .... 209, 224
s.6 209
s.7 210
s.8 210
(1), (2) 418
s.9 .... 210, 375
(2) 374
(3) 375
s.10 210
(1), (2) 214, 376
(4) 376
(6) 375
s.11 .... 210, 376
s.12 .... 210, 377
(1) 377
s.13 .... 210, 377
s.14 .... 210, 376, 377
s.15 211
s.16 .... 206, 246
(1), (2), (3) 212
(4), (5) 213
(6) 212
s.17 .... 213, 246, 371
s.19(1) 243, 244
(2) 244
s.20(1) 244
(2), (3) 245
s.21(1) 245
(2), (3) 246
(4), (5) 246, 261
(6), (7) 247
(8) 245
(9) 246
s.22(1)–(3) 247
s.23(1)–(2) 248
(3) 248, 251
s.24 .... 75, 78, 268
(1) 249
(2) 251, 254
(3), (4), (5) 251

1991 Water Resources Act – *continued.* Page
s.25 .... 78, 268
(1) 251
(2), (3) 252
(4) 251
(5)–(7), (8) 252
s.26(1) 253
s.27(1) 253
(2) 253, 258
(3) 254, 261
(4) 255, 261
(5) 254, 261
(6) 254, 255, 261
(7) 254
(8) 253
s.28 .... 4, 255
(5) 4
s.29 .... 4, 255
(5) 255
s.30 .... 4, 256, 268
(2), (3) 229
s.31 .... 4, 229
s.32 257
(1) 256
s.33 257
s.34(1), (2) 258
s.35(1)–(3) 258
(4)–(6) 259
s.36 259
s.37 265
(1)–(3), (4)–(6) 260
s.38 .... 260, 265
s.39 .... 261, 265
(1) 267
s.40 .... 261, 265
s.41 .... 262, 265
s.42 .... 262, 265
s.43 .... 262, 265
(1)(b) 263
s.44 .... 263, 265
s.45(1) 263
s.46 264
(2)(b) 235
(6) 235
s.47 264

1991 Water Resources Act – *continued*. Page

s.48 265
(1) 261
s.49 .... 224, 264
s.50 .... 224, 264
s.51(1) 265
(2) 265
(3) 265, 267
(4) 265
(5) 267
s.52 265
(1), (2) 265
s.53 265
s.54 .... 265, 268
s.55 .... 265, 268
s.56 265
s.57 266
s.58 266
s.60(1)–(3), (4) 267
s.61 268
(1) 268
s.62 268
s.63(1) 268
s.64 .... 225, 269
s.66 .... 250, 258
s.70 269
s.72(1) 254
(2) 249
(5) 254
s.73(1), (2), (3), (4) 274
s.74(1), (2) 275
(3), (4) 276
s.75(1), (2), (3), (4) 276
(5) 277
s.76(1) 277
(3) 274
s.77(1) 277
(2), (3), (5) 278
(6) 277
s.78(1), (2) 278
(3) 279
(5) 279
s.79(1), (2), (3) 279
s.80 280
s.82 369

1991 Water Resources Act – *continued.* Page

(1), (2) 293
s.83 .... 225, 369
(1), (2), (3) 294
(4)–(6) 295
s.84 369
(1), (2) 295
(2)(a) 320
s.85(1) 296, 300, 427
(2) 296, 298, 303, 320
(3) 296, 299, 303, 309, 320
(4) 296, 298, 299, 303, 320
(5) 297
(6) 297
s.86 ....296, 302, 309
(1) 299, 333
(2), (3), (4), (5), (6) 299
s.87(1) 300
(2), (3) 300, 337
s.88(1) 303
(1)(a) 304, 312
(b) 315, 319
(c) 320
(d) 324
(2) 304
(3), (4) 303, 320
s.89(1), (2), (3), (4) 302
(4)(a) 312
(5) 302
s.90 312
(1), (2)–(6) 301
s.91 313
(1) 312
(2) 312, 329
(3) 329
(5) 312
s.92 333
(1) 327
(2) 328
s.93(3) 330
(4)(a)–(d) 329
(5) 329
s.94 .... 209, 369
(1), (2) 330
(3), (5), (6) 331

1991 Water Resources Act – *continued.* Page

s.95 332
s.96(1) 329
(2) 331
s.97(1) 332
(2) 333
(3) 332
s.98(1) 335, 342
s.99 314
(1), (2) 304
s.100 336
s.101 336
s.102 336
s.103 336
s.104(1) 6, 290
(1)(a) 25, 290
(b), (c) 291
(d) 292
(2) 4
(3) ....6, 25, 226 ,291, 292
(4) 6, 292
(a) 291
(d) 4, 291
s.105(1) 374
s.106 375
(1)(b) 240
s.107 379
s.108 .... 374, 379
(9) 379
s.109 .... 78, 171, 380
s.110 .... 78, 171, 380
s.111 381
s.112 383
s.113(1) 4, 13, 373, 378, 379
s.114 415
s.115(1), (2) 416
(3)–(6), (7), (8), (9) 417
s.116 .... 370, 417
s.117 .... 239, 271
s.118 404
(1)–(3) 240
s.119 240
s.120(1), (2) 240
s.123 271
s.124 271

1991 Water Resources Act – *continued.* Page
(4) 271
s.125 272
s.126 272
s.127 273
s.128(1) 273
s.129 273
s.131 313
(1)–(3), (6) 313
s.132(1), (2), (3), (5) 313
s.133 404
s.139 374
s.140 374
s.142 418
s.143 410
(1) 159
s.144 241
s.146(1), (2) 241
s.147(1), (2), (5), (6) 241
s.148(1), (2) 241
(5) 241, 383
s.149 241
(3) 381
s.150 242
s.154 .... 215, 419
s.155 .... 50, 418
(1)–(2), (7) 215
s.156 ....215, 416, 419
s.157 216
s.158 216
s.159 ....217, 219, 314
(5) 216, 314
(6) 216
(b) 326
s.160 ....217, 219, 314
s.161 217
(1), (2), (3)–(5) 326
s.162 .... 217, 327
(1) 326
(2), (3) 219, 314
(6) 327
s.163 .... 217, 219, 226, 303, 314, 327
(1)(b) 314
(4) 314
s.164 .... 226, 315

1991 Water Resources Act – *continued*. Page

s.165 217
(1) 381
(2) 59, 207, 373, 381
(3) 207, 373, 381
(4), (5) 382
(6) 381
s.166 217
(1) 382
s.167 ....217, 382
(1)(b) 13
(4) 13
s.168 ....218, 219, 303
s.169 ....218, 220
s.170 219
(1) 219
s.171 219
s.172 220
s.173 220
s.175(1) 217
(7) 221
s.176(1), (2), (3), (4), (5), (6) 222
s.178 222
s.179(1), (2) 222
s.180 223
(1) 223
s.182 ....215, 223
s.183 223
s.184 223
s.186(1) 221
s.187 224
s.188 224
s.189 ....225, 273
s.190(1) 225, 306
(f) 320
(2) 226
s.191(1), (2), (3) 226
s.192 ....25, 226
(1), (2) 292
s.193 ....227, 378
(1), (2) 227
s.194 378
(1), (2) 227
s.195 228
s.196(1), (3) 228

1991 Water Resources Act – *continued.* Page

s.197(1) 228
(2), (3) 229
(7) 228
s.198 232
(1), (2), (5), (8) 229
s.199 229
s.200 230
s.201 230
s.202 230
s.203 231
s.204 232
s.205 232
s.206 232
s.207 ..... 233, 242
(7) 233
s.208 234
(4), (5) 234
s.209(1), (2) 234
(3) 235
(4) 234
s.210 ..... 159, 236, 383, 419, 427, 464
s.211 237
(3) 420, 446
(6) 420
s.212 ..... 237, 420
s.213 238
s.214 238
s.215 238
s.216(2), (3) 251, 252
s.217 239
s.218 239
s.221 205
(1) 3, 4, 5, 6, 228, 249, 250, 253, 254, 291, 292, 296, 373
(3) 250
s.250(2)–(5) 228
Part II 4, 206, 243
Chapter I 243
Chapter II 107, 124, 207, 208, 218, 224, 235, 238, 243, 248, 249, 250–1, 252, 260, 263, 268, 269, 270, 273, 277, 323
Chapter III 243
Part III 206, 290, 335, 336
Chapter I 246, 316–17
Chapter II 10, 225, 290, 297, 303, 304, 313, 320, 324, 326, 426
Chapter III 327, 328

1991 Water Resources Act – *continued.* Page
Part IV 59, 373
Part V 206, 207, 415, 417, 420
Part VI, Chapter II 375
Part VII 227, 278
Chapter I 217, 325
Chapter II 442, 443
Chapter III 223
Sch.1 205
Sch.2 206
para.1 159
Sch.3 375
Sch.4 .... 376, 377
Sch.5 247
para.5 247
Sch.7 268
para.4 267
para.6 268
Sch.8 274
Sch.9 279
Sch.10 .... 304, 305, 313
para.1 312
para.1(1)–(6) 305
para.1(7) 225, 306
para.2(1)–(4), (5), (6) 307, 309
para.3(1)–(4) 308
para.4(1)–(3) 308
para.4(4)–(7) 309
para.5(1), (2), (3), (4) 309
para.6(1)–(3), (4) 310
para.6(5), (6) 311
para.7(1), (2) 311, 312
para.7(3), (4) 311
Sch.11 330
Sch.12 .... 331, 332
Sch.13 336
para.4 304
Sch.14 379
Sch.15 405
Sch.16 406
Sch.17, para.1(3), (4) 416
Sch.18 215
Sch.19 218
Sch.20 220
para.2 444

1991 Water Resources Act – *continued.* Page

para.7 443

Sch.22 222

Sch.23 223

Sch.25 ....235–6, 237, 383, 419, 464

Sch.25, para.1–3 160

para.5(1), (2) 384

para.6 421

(1) 421

(2) 421

(e) 29

(3) 422

(4) 422, 427

(5) 422

(6) 421

(7) 421, 422

Sch.26 .... 235–6, 383, 419, 464

para.7 236

TABLE OF STATUTORY INSTRUMENTS

			Page
1932	No.64	(S.R. and O.) Land Drainage (General) Regulations	386
1938	No.136	(S.R. and O.) Aircraft (Wreck and Salvage) Order	56
1962	No.2648	Radioactive Substances (Phosphatic Substances, Rare Earths etc.) Exemption Order	343
	No.2712	Radioactive Substances (Geological Specimens) Exemption Order	343
1964	No.697	Continental Shelf (Designation of Areas) Order	38
1965	No.443	Land Drainage (River Authorities) General Regulations	386, 403
	No.445	Drainage Schemes (Notices) Regulations	397
	No.534	Water Resources (Licences) Regulations	224, 257, 259, 262, 263, 269, 273
	No.1010	Spray Irrigation (Definition) Order	254, 272
	No.1092	Water Resources (Miscellaneous Provisions) Regulations	229, 256
	No.1531	Continental Shelf (Designation of Additional Areas) Order	38
1966	No.944	Diseases of Fish Order	453
1967	No.212	Land Drainage (Grants) Regulations	411
1968	No.891	Continental Shelf (Designation of Additional Areas) Order	38
1971	No.594	Continental Shelf (Designation of Additional Areas) Order	38
1973	No.2093	Diseases of Fish Order	453, 454
1974	No.1489	Continental Shelf (Designation of Additional Areas) Order	38
1976	No.1153	Continental Shelf (Designation of Additional Areas) Order	38
1977	No.1871	Continental Shelf (Designation of Additional Areas) Order	38
1978	No.178	Continental Shelf (Designation of Additional Areas) Order	38
	No.272	Transfer of Functions (Wales) (No.1) Order	34, 416, 457
	No.1022	Diseases of Fish Order	453
	No.1029	Continental Shelf (Designation of Additional Areas) Order	38
1979	No.1447	Continental Shelf (Designation of Additional Areas) Order	38
1980	No.953	Radioactive Substances (Smoke Detectors) Exemption Order	343
1982	No.1072	Continental Shelf (Designation of Additional Areas) Order	38
1983	No.1398	Merchant Shipping (Prevention of Oil Pollution) Regulations	346, 348
1984	No.301	Diseases of Fish Order	453
	No.455	Diseases of Fish Regulations	453
	No.862	Prevention of Pollution (Reception Facilities) Order	347
	No.1874	Reservoirs Act 1975 (Supervising Engineers Panel) (Applications and Fees) Regulations	282
1985	No.175	Reservoirs Act 1975 (All Reservoirs Panel) (Applications and Fees) Regulations	282
	No.177	Reservoirs Act 1975 (Registers, Reports and Records) Regulations	281, 285

			Page
	No.1086	Reservoirs Act 1975 (Non–Impounding and Service Reservoirs Panels) (Applications and Fees) Regulations	282
	No.1391	Registration of Fish Farming Businesses Order	456
	No.1699	Deposits at Sea (Exemptions) Order	325
	No.1785	Sea Fisheries (Byelaws) Regulations	353, 458
	No.2040	Merchant Shipping (Prevention of Oil Pollution) (Amendment) Regulations	346
1986	No.283	Importation of Live Fish of the Salmon Family Order	453
	No.1510	Control of Pesticides Regulations	354
	No.1992	Control of Pollution (Anglers' Lead Weights) Regulations	355
	No.2265	Salmonid Viscera Order	453
	No.2300	Control of Pollution (Anti–fouling Paints) (Amendment) Regulations	355
1987	No.402	Control of Pollution (Landed Ships' Waste) Regulations	347
	No.551	Merchant Shipping (Control of Pollution by Noxious Liquid Substances in Bulk) Regulations	346–7
	No.586	Merchant Shipping (Reporting of Pollution Incidents) Regulations	346
	No.783	Control of Pollution (Anti–fouling Paints and Treatments) Regulations	355
1988	No.69	Reservoirs Act 1975 (Application Fees) (Amendment) Regulations	282
	No.195	Diseases of Fish Order	453
	No.1158	Control of Pollution (Radioactive Waste) Regulations	335
	No.1199	Town and Country Planning (Assessment of Environmental Effects) Regulations	335, 394
	No.1217	Land Drainage Improvement Works (Assessment of Environmental Effects) Regulations	394
	No.1813	Town and Country Planning General Development Order	152, 324, 335, 382, 393–4
1989	No.482	Territorial Sea (Limits) Order	29
	No.1147	Water Supply (Water Quality) Regulations	292
	No.1148	Surface Waters (Classification) Regulations	293
	No.1149	Controlled Waters (Lakes and Ponds) Order	292
	No.1151	Control of Pollution (Consents for Discharges etc.) (Secretary of State Functions) Regulations	308
	No.1152	Water and Sewerage (Conservation, Access and Recreation) (Code of Practice) Order	214
	No.1156	Trade Effluents (Prescribed Processes and Substances) Regulations	339
	No.1157	Control of Pollution (Discharges by the National Rivers Authority) Regulations	304, 314
	No.1158	Control of Pollution (Radioactive Waste) Regulations	335, 342
	No.1160	Control of Pollution (Registers) Regulations	225

			Page
	No.1186	Reservoirs (Panels of Civil Engineers) (Reappointment) Regulations	282
	No.1465	Water Authorities (Successor Companies) Order	205
	No.1530	Water Authorities (Transfer of Functions) (Appointed Day) Order	205
	No.1798	Merchant Shipping (Distress Signals and Prevention of Collisions) Regulations	158
	No.1968	Water (Consequential Amendments) Regulations	459
	No.2286	Surface Waters (Dangerous Substances) (Classification) Regulations	293
	No.2292	Merchant Shipping (Prevention of Pollution by Garbage) Regulations	347
	No.2293	Merchant Shipping (Reception Facilities for Garbage) Regulations	347
	No.2398	Continental Shelf (Designation of Additional Areas) Order	38
1990	No.72	Internal Drainage Boards (Finance) Regulations	384, 407, 408
	No.118	National Rivers Authority (Levies) Regulations	404
	No.173	Drainage Rates (Forms) Regulations	409
	No.214	Drainage Charges Regulations	405
	No.564	General Drainage Charges (Forms) Regulations	405
	No.616	Diseases of Fish Order	453
	No.1013	Nitrate Sensitive Areas (Designation) Order	332, 369
	No.1152	Drainage Rates (Appeals) Regulations	409
	No.1187	Nitrate Sensitive Areas (Designation) (Amendment) Order	332, 369
	No.1629	Trade Effluents (Prescribed Processes and Substances) (Amendment) Regulations	339
1991	No.324	Control of Pollution (Silage, Slurry and Agricultural Fuel Oil) Regulations	328
	No.472	Environmental Protection (Prescribed Processes and Substances) Regulations	316
	No.507	Environmental Protection (Applications, Appeals and Registers) Regulations	316
	No.513	Environmental Protection (Authorisation of Processes) (Determination Periods) Regulations	316
	No.523	Internal Drainage Boards (Finance) Regulations	384
	No.1597	Bathing Waters (Classification) Regulations	294
	No.2285	Water (Prevention of Pollution) (Code of Practice) Order	332

TABLE OF CASES

A

Page

Abraham v. Great Northern Ry. Co. (1851), 16 Q.B. 586; 20 L.J.Q.B. 322; 17 L.T.O.S. 16; 15 Jur.855; 117 E.R.1004 .... 143, 148
Ackroyd v. Smith (1850), 10 C.B. 164; 19 L.J.C.P. 315; 15 L.T.O.S. 395; 14 Jur.1047; 138 E.R.68 100
Acton v. Blundell (1843), 12 M. & W.324; 13 L.J. Ex. 289 1 L.T.O.S. 207; 152 E.R. 1223 122
Adinarayana v. Ramudu (1914), I.L.R. 37 Mad.304 8
Aiton v. Stephen (1876), 1 A.C.459 .... 51, 178
Alabama, State of v. State of Georgia (1859),54 U.S.427 11–12
Alcock v. Cooke (1829), 5 Bing. 340; 2 Moore & P. 625; 2 State Tr. N.S.327; 7 L.J.O.S.C.P.126; 130 E.R.1092 56
Alder v. Savill (1814), 5 Taunt. 454; 128 E.R. 766 79
Alexander v. Tonkin [1979] 1 W.L.R. 629; (1979) 123 S.J.111; [1979] 2 All E.R. 1009; Crim.L.R. 248, D.C. 426
Alford Drainage Board v. Mablethorpe [1986] 1 E.G.L.R.215; (1985) 277 E.G. 867; (1985) 26 R.V.R.29, Lands Tribunal 406
Allen v. Parker (1891) 30 L.R. Ir.87 424
Alletta, The, and the England [1966] 1 Lloyd's Rep. 573, C.A. 136
Alphacell v. Woodward [1972] A.C. 824; [1972] 2 W.L.R. 1320; 116 S.J.431; [1972] 2 All E.R. 475; 70 L.G.R. 455; [1972] Crim. L.R. 41, H.L. 426
Alston's Estate, Re (1856), 28 L.T.O.S. 337; 21 J.P.163; 5 W.R. 189 16
Anderson v. Jacobs (1905), 93 L.T.17; 21 T.L.R. 453 61
Andrew v. Cod Beck Internal Drainage Board (1983) 23 R.V.R. 270 393
Anglo–French Continental Shelf Case (1979) 18 1 L.M.397 37
Anglo–Norwegian Fisheries Case, [1952] 1 T.L.R.181; 15 M.L.R. 373; (1951) I.C.J. Rep. 116 .... 27, 177
Anns v. Merton L.B.C. [1978] A.C. 728; [1977] 2 W.L.R. 1024; (1977) 121 S.J. 377; 75 L.G.R. 555; [1977] J.P.L. 514; (1977) 243 E.G. 523, 591; [1977] L.G.C. 498; (1987) L.S. 319 .... 76, 249
Aquila, The (1798), 1 Ch.Rob. 37; 165 E.R.87 57
Argyll & Bute District Council v. Secretary of State for Scotland [1977] S.L.T.33 53
Arkwright v. Gell (1839), 5 M. & W. 203; 2 Horn. & H.17;8 L.J. Ex. 201; 151 E.R. 87 .... 3, 101, 118, 119
Ash v. Great Northern Rly. Co. (1903), 67 J.P. 417; 19 T.L.R. 639 393
Ashcroft v. Cambro Waste Products [1981] 1 W.L.R. 1349; (1981) 125 S.J. 288; [1981] 3 All E.R. 699; [1981] 79 L.G.R. 612; [1982] J.P.L. 176, D.C. 298
A.–G. v. Acton L.B. (1882), 22 Ch.D. 221; 52 L.J. Ch. 168 47 L.T. 510; 31 W.R. 153 111
A.–G. v. Basingstoke (1876), 45 L.J.Ch.726 99
A.–G. v. Birmingham Corp. (1858), 4 K. & J. 528; 22 J.P. 561; 6 W.R. 881 .... 94, 96, 97
A.–G. v. Birmingham Corp. (1880), 15 Ch.D 423; 43 L.T. 77; 29 W.R. 127 96

Page

A.–G. v. Birmingham Drainage Board, [1908] 2 Ch. 551; 77 L.J. Ch. 836; 98 L.T. 310; 72 J.P. 20; 24 T.L.R.126 .... 92, 296

A.–G. v. Birmingham Drainage Board, [1910] 1 Ch. 48; 79 L.J. Ch. 137; 101 L.T. 796; 74 J.P. 57; 26 T.L.R. 93; 54 S.J. 198 99

A.–G. v. Birmingham Drainage Board, [1912] A.C. 788; 82 L.J. Ch. 45; 107 L.T. 353; 76 J.P.481; 11 L.G.R.194 97

A.–G. v. Bristol Waterworks Co (1855), 10 Ex. 884; 3 C.L.R. 726; 24 L.J. Ex 205; 24 L.T.O.S. 311 77

A.–G. v. Burridge (1822), 10 Price 350; 147 E.R. 335 43

A.–G. v. Chambers (1854), 4 De G.M. & G 206; 23 L.T.O.S. 238; 18 Jur. 779; 2 W.R. 636; 43 E.R. 486 .... 41, 42, 178

A.–G. v. Cockermouth L.B. (1874), L.R. 18 Eq. 172; 30 L.T. 590; 38 J.P. 660; 40 W.R.619 99

A.–G. (Allen) v. Colchester Corpn. [1955] 2 All E.R. 124; 2 Q.B. 207; 99 S.J. 291; 53 L.G.R.415 .... 166, 169

A.–G. v. Colney Hatch Lunatic Asylum (1868), 4 Ch. App.146; 38 L.J. Ch. 265; 19 L.T. 708; 33 J.P. 196; 17 W.R. 240 97

A.–G. v. Copeland, [1902] 1 K.B. 690 111

A.–G. v. Cornwall County Council (1933), 97 J.P. 281; 31 L.G.R. 364 165

A.–G. v. Emerson, [1891] A.C. 649; 61 L.J.Q.B. 79; 65 L.T. 564; 55 J.P.709; 7 T.L.R.522 .... 42, 44, 45, 183, 185, 188, 190

A.–G. v. Gee (1870), L.R. 10 Eq.131; 23 L.T. 299; 34 J.P. 596 .... 91, 96

A.–G. v. Great Eastern Rly. Co. (1871), 6 Ch. App.572; 35 J.P. 788; 2 3 L.T. 344; 19 W.R. 788 .... 73, 76, 155

A.–G. v. Great Northern Rly. Co.[1909] 1 Ch. 775; 78 L.J. Ch. 577; 99 L.T. 696; 73 J.P.41 .... 104, 155

A.–G. v. Hanmer (1858) 27 L.J. Ch.837; 31 L.T.O.S. 379; 22 J.P. 543; 4 Jur.N.S. 751; 6 W.R. 804 .... 43, 44, 53

A.–G. v. Johnson (1819) 2 Wils. Ch. 87; 37 E.R. 240 .... 43, 141

A.–G. v. Jones (1862) 2 H. & C. 347; 33 L.J. Ex.249; 6 L.T. 655; 26 J.P. 518; 159 E.R. 144 45

A.–G. v. Kingston–on–Thames Corpn. (1865) 6 New Rep.248; 34 L.J. Ch.481; 12 L.T. 665; 29 J.P.515; 11 Jur. N.S. 596; 13 W.R.888 98

A.–G. v. Leeds Corpn.(1870), 5 Ch. App. 583; 39 L.J. Ch.711 34 J.P. 708; 19 W.R. 19 95

A.–G. v. Logan [1891] 2 Q.B. 100; 65 L.T. 162; 55 J.P. 615; 7 T.L.R. 279 99

A.–G. v. London Corpn. (1849) 12 Beav. 8; 18 L.J. Ch.314; 13 L.T.O.S. 521; 13 Jur. 372; 50 E.R. 962 .... 16, 42

A.–G. v. Lonsdale (1868), L.R. 7 Eq.377; 38 L.J.Ch. 335 20 L.T. 64; 33 J.P. 534 .... 68, 99, 141, 142, 153

A.–G. v. M'Carthy [1911] 2 I.R. 260 48

A.–G. v. Newcastle Corpn. (1903) 67 J.P. 155 20

A.–G. v. Parmeter, Re Portsmouth Harbour (1811) 10 Price 378 .... 44, 141

A.–G. v. Plymouth Corporation (1754) 145 E.R. 1202 22

A.–G. v. Preston Corpn. (1896) 13 T.L.R.14 96

A.–G. v. Reeve (1885), 1 T.L.R.675 49

A.–G. v. Richards (1795), 2 Anstr. 603; 3 R.R.632 .... 42, 141

Page

A.–G. v. Richmond (1866), L.R. 2 Eq.306; 35 L.J. Ch.597; 14 L.T. 398; 30 J.P. 708; 12 Jur. N.S.544; 14 W.R. 686 93
A.–G. v. Rowley Bros. & Oxley (1910) 75 J.P.81; 9 L.G.R. 121; 11 Ex. 602 68
A.–G. v. St. Ives R.D.C. [1961] 2 W.L.R. 111; 105 S.J. 87; [1961] 1 All E.R. 265 397
A.–G. v. Shrewsbury Bridge Co (1882) 21 Ch.D.752; 51 L.J. Ch.746; 46 L.T. 687; 30 W.R. 916 ....61, 99
A.–G. v. Simpson, [1901] 2 Ch. 671 165
A.–G. v. Storey (1912), 107 L.T. 430; 56 S.J.735, C.A. 42
A.–G. v. Terry (1874), 9 Ch. App. 423; 30 L.T. 215; 38 J.P. 340, 22 W.R. 395 ....141, 142, 143, 153
A.–G. v. Thames Conservators (1862) 1 Hem. & M.1; 1 New Rep.121; 8 L.T.9; 8 Jur N.S. 1203; 11 W.R.163; 71 E.R.1. ....141, 143, 151
A.–G. v. Tod Heatley, [1897] 1 Ch.560; 66 L.J.Ch.275; 76 L.T. 174; 45 W.R.394; 13 T.L.R.220; 41 S.J. 311; 61 J.P.Jo.164 63
A.–G. v. Tomline (1880) 14 Ch.D 58; 49 L.J. Ch.377; 42 L.T. 880; 44 J.P. 617; 28 W.R. 870 ....54, 59, 61, 62
A.–G. v. Wellingborough U.D.C. (1974) 72 L.G.R.507; (1974) *The Times*, March 29, 1974, C.A. 99
A.–G. v. Wilcox [1938] Ch.934; (1938) 3 All E.R. 367; 159 L.T. 212; 54 T.L.R.985; 82 S.J. 566; 36 L.G.R.593 138
A.–G. v. Wright [1897] 2 Q.B. 318; 66 L.J.Q.B. 834; 77 L.T. 295; 46 W.R. 85; 13 T.L.R. 480 ....136, 141, 179
A.–G. ex.rel Yorkshire Derwent Trust Ltd v. Brotherton [1991] 2 W.L.R.I; (1990) 134 S.J.1367; *The Independent* 8 August, 1990 C.A. 132, 134
A.–G. and Doncaster R.D.C. v. West Riding of Yorkshire County Council (1903) 67 J.P. 173; 19 T.L.R. 192; 1 L.G.R. 223 172
A.–G. for British Columbia v. A.–G. for Canada [1914] A.C. 153; 83 L.J.P.C.169; 110 L.T.484; 30 T.L.R. 144 .... 30, 175, 176, 177, 180, 181
A.–G. for Ireland v. Vandeleur [1907] A.C. 369; 76 L.J.P.C. 89; 97 L.T. 221 45
A.–G. of Southern Nigeria v. Holt & Co. Ltd. [1915] A.C.599; 84 L.J.P.C.98; 112 L.T. 955 ....46, 48, 49, 151
A.–G. of Straits Settlement v. Wemyss (1888), 13 A.C.192; 57 L.J.P.C. 62; 58 L.T. 358 ....51, 150, 151
Attwood v. Llay Main Collieries, [1926] Ch. 444; 95 L.J. Ch.221; 134 L.T. 268; 70 S.J. 265 ....68, 73, 74, 75

B

Badger v. S. Yorks Rly. (1858) 1 E. & E. 359; 28 L.J.Q.B. 118; 32 L.T.O.S. 207; 5 Jur. N.S.459; 7 W.R. 130; 120 E.R. 945 .... 137, 154
Bagott v. Orr (1801), 2 Bos. & P.472; 126 E.R.1391 .... 178, 179
Baily & Co. v. Clark, Son & Morland, [1902] 1 Ch.649; 71 L.J. Ch. 396; 86 .T.309; 50 W.R. 511; 18 T.L.R. 364; 46 S.J. 316 ....10, 72, 91, 103, 116, 118
Baird v. Fortune (1861) 5 L.T.2; 25 J.P.691; 7 Jur. N.S.926; 10 W.R. 2; 4 Macq.127 53

Page

Baird v. Williamson (1863) 15 C.B.N.S. 376; 3 New Rep 86; 33 L.J.C.P. 101; 9 L.T. 412; 12 W.R. 150; 143 E.R. 831 88
Ball v. Herbert (1789), 3 Term Rep. 253; 1 R.R.695 .... 137, 139, 195
Ballacorkish Co. v. Harrison (1873) L.R. 5 P.C. 49; 43 L.J.P.C. 19; 29 L.T.658 123
Ballard v. Tomlinson (1885) 29 Ch.D. 115; 54 L.J. Ch.454; 52 L.T.942; 49 J.P.692; 33 W.R.533; 1 T.L.R.270; 14, 90, 91, 121, 129
Balston v. Bensted (1808) 1 Camp 463; 170 E.R.462 .... 110, 125
Bank View Mills Ltd. v. Nelson Corpn, [1943] 1 K.B. 337; [1943] 1 All E.R. 299; 112 L.J.K.B. 306; 168 L.T.244; 107 J.P. 86; 41 L.G.R.119 98
Bankart v. Tennant (1870) L.R. 10 Eq. 141; 39 L.J. Ch,809; 23 L.T. 137; 34 J.P. 628; 18 W.R.639 102
Barker v. Faulkner (1898) 79 L.T.24 196
Barker v. Herbert [1911] 2 K.B. 633; 80 L.J.K.B.1329; 105 L.T.349; 75 J.P.481; 27 T.L.R.488; 9 L.G.R.1083 86
Barnacott v. Passmore (1887) 19 Q.B.D. 75; 51 J.P. 821; 35 W.R. 812 445
Barnard v. Roberts (1907) 96 L.T. 648; 71 J.P. 277; 23 T.L.R. 439; 51 Sol. Jo. 411; 21 Cox C.C. 425, D.C. 424
Barraclough v. Brown [1897] A.C. 614; 66 L.J.Q.B.672; 76 L.T.797; 62 J.P.275; 13 T.L.R.527 147
Bartlett v. Tottenham [1932] 1 Ch. 114; 45 L.T.686 .... 84, 85, 119, 128
Bateman v Welsh Water Authority (1986) 27 R.V.R. 10; [1986] 2 E.G. L.R. 213; (1986) 279 E.G. 1367, Lands Tribunal 279
Baxendale v. Instow Parish Council [1982] Ch.14; [1981] 2 W.L.R. 1055; (1981) 125 S.J. 289; [1981] 2 All E.R. 620 .... 41, 46, 48, 49
Baxendale v. McMurray (1867) 2 Ch.App 790; 31 J.P.821; 16 W.R. 32 109
Bealey v. Shaw (1805) 6 East 208; 2 Smith K.B.321; 102 E.R.1266 .... 76, 100, 104, 106, 114
Beaufort (Duke) v. Aird (John) & Co. (1904) 20 T.L.R. 602 .... 185, 190
Beaufort (Duke) v. Swansea Corpn. (1849) 3 Ex.413; 12 L.T.O.S. 453; 154 E.R. 905 .... 43, 44, 45
Beckett, Alfred F. v. Lyons [1967] Ch.449; 2 W.L.R. 421; 1 All E.R. 833; 110 S.J.925; 65 L.G.R.73 .... 50, 54
Beeston v. Weate (1856), 5 E. & B.986; 25 L.J.Q.B. 115; 26 L.T.O.S.272; 20 J.P.452; 2 Jur. N.S.540; 119 E.R.748 .... 101, 106, 112, 116
Behrens v. Richards [1905] 2 Ch.614; 74 L.J. Ch.615; 93 L.T. 623; 69 J.P.381; 54 W.R.141; 21 T.L.R.705; 41 S.J.685; 3 L.G.R. 1228 51
Belfast Ropeworks v. Boyd (1887) 21 L.R. Ir.560 .... 73, 80
Bell v. Quebec Corpn (1879), 5 A.C.84; 49 L.J.P.C. 1; 41 L.T.451 151
Bell v. Wyndham (1865) 29 J.P. 214 435
Benest v. Pipon (1829) 1 Knapp 60, 2 State Tr.N.S. App.1012; 12 E.R.243 54
Benjamin v. Storr (1874) L.R.9 C.P.400; 30 L.T.362 99
Bevins v Bird (1865) 6 New Rep.111; 12 L.T.306; 29 J.P.500 .... 180, 428
Bidder v. Croydon L.B. (1862) 6 L.T.778 .... 93, 94
Biddulph v. Arthur (1775) 2 Wils 23; 95 E.R.665 55
Bickett v. Morris (1866), L.R. 1 Sc. & Div.417; 14 L.T. 835; 30 J.P. 532; 12 Jur N.S.802 .... 17, 78, 82

Page
Bien, The [1911] P.40 140
Birch v. Ancholme Drainage Board (1958) J.P.L.257; 9 P. & C.R.268 393
Birch v. Turner (1864) 29 J.P.37 428
Bird v. Great Eastern Rly.Co. (1865) 19 C.B.N.S. 268; 34 L.J.C.P. 366;
13 L.T.365; 11 Jur. N.S.782 185
Bird v. Higginson (1837) 6 Ad. & El.824; 6 L.J. Ex. 282; 1 J.P. 322 185
Birkett v. McGlassons Ltd [1957] 1 All E.R. 369; 1 W.L.R. 269; 121 J.P. 126;
101 S.J.149 436
Black v. Ballymena Comrs. (1886) 17 L.R. Ir.459 122
Blackburne v. Somers (1879) 5 L.R. Ir. 1 ....108, 109, 117, 127
Blacketer v. Gillet (1850) 9 C.B.26; 1 L.M. &. P.88; 19 L.J.C.P.307;
14 L.T.O.S.351; 14 Jur.814; 137 E.R.800 167
Blackrod U.D.C. v. Crankshaw (John) Co, Ltd (1913), 136 L.T. Jo. 239 122
Blair & Sumner v. Deakin (1887) 57 L.T. 522; 52 J.P. 327; 3 T.L.R. 757 95
Bleachers Assocn. Ltd. v. Chapel-en-le-Frith R.D.C.[1933] Ch 356;
102 L.J. Ch.17; 148 L.T. 91; 96 J.P. 515; 49 T.L.R. 51;
76 S.J. 902; 31 L.G.R.88 127
Blewett v. Tregonning (1835) 3 Ad. & El. 554; 1 Har. & W.431;
5 Nev. & MK.B. 234; 4 L.J.K.B.223; 111 E.R. 524 54
Blissett v. Hart (1744), Willes 508; 125 E.R. 1293 .... 163, 167
Bloomfield v. Johnston (1868) I.R. 8 C.L.68 .... 22, 194
Blount v. Layard (1888), [1891] 2 Ch. 681 ....17, 182, 186
Blower v. Ellis (1886) 50 J.P. 326 23
Blundell v. Catterall (1821) 5 B. & Ald.268;
106 E.R. 1190 .... 42, 50, 51, 131, 137, 178, 195
Booth v. Ratte (1889) 15 A.C. 188; 59 L.J.P.C. 41; 62 L.T. 198; 28 W.R. 737 152
Bostock v. Sidebottom (1852) 18 Q.B. 813; 19 L.T.O.S.316; 16 Jur. 1013;
118 E.R.306 112
Boston Corpn. v. Fenwick (1923) 129 L.T. 766; 39 T.L.R.441 147
Bourke v. Davis (1889) 44 Ch.D. 110; 62 L.T.34; 38 W.R.167;
6 T.L.R.87 ....23, 133, 134
Bournemouth-Swanage Ferry Co. v. Harvey [1930] A.C.549; 99 L.J. Ch. 337;
143 L.T. 313; 46 T.L.R. 439; 28 L.G.R. 351 169
Bower v. Hill (1835) 2 Bing N.C. 339; 1 Hodg. 45; 2 Scott 535;
5 L.J.C.P. 77; 132 E.R.133 .... 113, 133
Box v. Jubb (1879) 4 Ex. D.76; 48 L.J.Q.B. 417; 41 L.T.97; 27 W.R. 415 86
Boxes v. British Waterways Board [1971] 2 Lloyd's Rep.183 C.A. 157
Brace v. South Eastern Regional Housing Association,(1984) 270 E.G. 1286 126
Bradford Corpn. v. Ferrand [1902] 2 Ch. 655; 71 L.J. Ch.859; 87 L.T. 388;
67 J.P.21; 51 W.R.122; 18 T.L.R.830 ....9, 127
Bradford Corpn. v. Pickles [1895] A.C. 587; 64 L.J. Ch. 759; 73 L.T. 353;
60 J.P. 3; 44 W.R.190; 11 T.L.R.555; 11 R.286 124
Brain v. Marfell (1879) 41 L.T. 457; 44 J.P.56; 28 W.R.130 ....102, 123, 125
Braintree D.C. v. Gosfield Hall Settlement Trustees
(unreported Chelmsford Crown Court 13 July 1977) 281
Bramlett v. Tees Conservancy (1885) 49 J.P.214 64
Brecknock and Abergavenny Canal Navigation Co. v. Pritchard (1796)
6 Term. Rep. 750; [1775-1802] All E.R. 375; 101 E.R. 807 173

Page

Brew v. Haren (1877) I.R. 11 C.L. 198 .... 43, 44, 53
Bridges' Repair Case (1609) 13 Co. Rep. 33; 77 E.R.1442 .... 81, 156
Bridges v. Highton (1865) 11 L.T.653 197
Bridges v. Saltaun (1873) 11 Macph. (Ct. of Sess) 588; 45 Sc. Jur.372 71
Bridgewater Trustees v. Bootle-cum-Linacre (1866) L.R. 2 Q.B. 4;
7 B. & S. 348; 36 L.J.Q.B. 41; 15 L.T. 351; 31 J.P.245; 15 W.R. 169 52
Briggs v. Swanwick (1883) 10 Q.B.D. 510; 52 L.J.M.C.63; 47 J.P. 564;
31 W.R. 565 438
Brighton Corpn. v. Packham (1908) 72 J.P. 318; 24 T.L.R.603; 6 L.G.R. 495 50
Brighton & Hove General Gas Co. v. Hove Bungalow Ltd. [1924] 1 Ch., 372;
93 L.J. Ch.197; 130 L.T. 248; 88 J.P.61; 68 S.J. 165; 21 L.G.R. 758 48
Brinckman v. Matley [1904] 2 Ch. 313; 73 L.J. Ch.642; 91 L.T. 429;
68 J.P. 534; 20 T.L.R. 671; 48 S.J.639; 2 L.G.R. 1057 .... 50, 51
Briscoe v. Drought (1860) Ir. R.11 C.L. 264 .... 3, 6
Bristow v. Cormican (1878) 3 A.C. 641 .... 17, 18, 22, 43, 189, 193
British Celanese Ltd v. A. H. Hunt [1969] 1 W.L.R. 959;
[1969] 2 All E.R. 1252 87
British Dredging (Services) Ltd v. Secretary of State for Wales
[1975] 2 All E.R. 845; [1975] 1 Lloyd's Rep. 569;
(1974) 73 L.G.R. 191 61
British Waterways Board v. Anglian Water Authority
(1991) *The Times* 23 April 1991 250
Broadbent v. Ramsbotham (1856), 11 Ex.602; 25 L.J. Ex.115;
26 L.T.O.S. 244; 20 J.P.486; 4 W.R.290; 156 E.R. 971 .... 14, 69, 85, 128
Brown v. Best (1747) 1 Wils.174; 95 E.R.557 .... 106, 112
Brown v. Dunstable Corpn. [1899] 2 Ch. 378; 68 L.J. Ch.498; 80 L.T.650;
63 J.P.519; 47 W.R.538; 15 T.L.R.386; 43 S.J. 508 116
Brown v. Ellis (1886), 50 J.P. 326 181
Brown v. Mallett (1848), 5 C.B. 599; 17 L.J.C.P. 227; 11 L.T.O.S. 64;
12 Jur.204; 136 E.R.1013 146
Brownlow v. Metropolitan Board of Works (1864), 16 C.B.N.S. 546;
4 New Rep. 173; 33 L.J.C.P.233; 12 W.R.871; 143 E.R. 1241 .... 143, 153
Bruce v. Willis (1840), 11 A. & E. 463 .... 137, 155
Brymbo Water Co. v. Lesters Lime Co. (1894), 8 R.329 119
Buckley v. Buckley, [1898] 2 Q.B. 608; 67 L.J.Q.B. 953 114
Bulstrode v. Hall (1663), 1 Keb.532; 1 Sid.148; 83 E.R. 1096 .... 16, 42
Bunting v. Hicks (1894), 70 L.T. 455; 10 T.L.R. 360; 7 R.293, C.A. 103, 116
Burgess v. Gwynedd River Authority Ref. 18/1970 (1972) 24 P. & C.R. 150 393
Burley Ltd v. Lloyds Ltd (1929), 45 T.L.R. 626 143
Burrows v. Lang [1901] 2 Ch.502; 70 L.J.Ch.607; 84 L.T. 623;
49 W.R.564; 17 T.L.R. 514; 45 S.J.536 .... 101, 115, 119
Burton v. Hudson [1909] 2 K.B. 564; 78 L.J.K.B. 905; 101 L.T. 233;
73 J.P. 401; 25 T.L.R. 641 61
Bury v. Pope (1586). Cro.Eliz.118; 1 Leon.168; 74 E.R.155 103
Butterworth v. West Riding of Yorkshire Rivers Board,[1909] A.C.45;
78 L.J.K.B. 203; 100 L.T.85; 73 J.P. 89; 25 T.L.R. 117;
7 L.G.R. 189 .... 109, 296, 297

Page

C

Cain v. Campbell [1978] Crim. L.R.292 D.C. 435
Calcraft v. Guest [1898] 1 Q.B. 759; 67 L.J.Q.B.505; 78 L.T. 283;
46 W.R.420; 42 S.J.343 .... 25, 182
Callaghan v. Callaghan (1897), 31 I.L.T.418 103
Calmady v. Rowe (1844), 6 C.B. 861; 4 L.T.O.S.96; 136 E.R. 1487 .... 46, 53, 55
Cambridge Water Company v. Eastern Counties Leather PLC
[1991] ENDS Report 36, Queen's Bench Division 31 July 1991 .... 87, 129
Campbell's Trustees v. Sweeney, [1911] S.C. 1319 .... 134, 136
Canham v. Fisk (1831), 2 Cr. & J. 126; 1 Tyr.155; 1 L.J.Ex.61; 149 E.R.53 112
Canvey Island Comrs. v. Preedy,[1922] 1 Ch.179; 91 L.J. Ch.203;
126 L.T.445; 86 J.P.21; 66 S.J.182; 20 L.G.R. 125 ....54, 61
Cargill v. Gotts [1981] 1 W.L.R. 441; (1980) 125 S.J.99;
[1981] 1 All E.R. 682; (1980) 41 P. & C.R.300
[1981] J.P.L. 515 C.A. 23, 73, 75, 106, 107, 248, 269
Carlisle Corpn. v. Graham (1869) L.R. 4 Ex.361; 38 L.J. Ex.226;
21 L.T.333; 18 W.R.318 ....21, 139, 193
Carlyon v. Lovering (1857) 1 H. & N. 784; 26 L.J. Ex.251;
28 L.T.O.S. 356; 5 W.R. 347 ....93, 105, 108, 110, 116
Carter v. Murcot (1768), 4 Burr. 2162 186
Case of Swans (1592), 7 Co. Rep.15b; 77 E.R.435 58
Cawkwell v. Russell (1856), 26 L.J. Ex.34 .... 111, 121
Caygill v. Thwaite (1885) 49 J.P. 614; 33 W.R. 581; 1 T.L.R. 386 452
Chad v. Tilsed (1821), 5 Moore 185; 2 Brod. & Bing.403; 23 E.R. 477 ....44, 56
Chadwick v. Marsden (1867), L.R. 2 Ex.285; 36 L.J. Ex.177; 16 L.T. 666;
31 J.P. 535; 15 W.R. 964 102
Chalk v. Wyatt (1810), 3 Mer.688; 36 E.R. 264 54
Chamber Colliery Co. v. Hopwood (1886), 32 Ch.D.549; 55 L.J. Ch.859;
55 L.T.449 116
Chamber Colliery Co. v. Rochdale Canal Co,[1895] A.C.564; 64 L.J.Q.B.645;
73 L.T.258; 11 R.264 19
Champion v. Maughan [1984] 1 W.L.R. 469; (1984) 128 S.J. 220;
[1984] 1 All E.R. 685; (1984) Crim. L.R. 291;
(1984) 81 L.S. Gaz. 586, D.C. 428
Chapman, Morsons & Co. v. Aukland Union (1889), 23 Q.B.D. 294;
58 L.J.Q.B. 504; 61 L.T.446; 53 J.P.820 96
Charles v. Finchley L.B. (1883) 23 Ch. D.767; 52 L.J. Ch.554;
48 L.T. 569; 47 J.P.791; 51 W.R. 717 111
Chasemore v. Richards (1859), 7 H.L. Cas.349; 29 L.J. Ex. 81;
33 L.T.O.S. 350; 5 Jur. N.S.873; 23 J.P. 596;
7 W.R. 685; 11 E.R. 140 ....9, 14, 66, 71, 110, 121–2, 126
Chesham (Lord) v. Chesham U.D.C. (1935),79 S.J.453 90
Chesterfield (Lord) v. Harris, [1908] 2 Ch. 397 191
Chester Mill Case (1610), 10 Co. Rep. 137 b 195
Child v. Greenhill (1639), Cro.Car.553; March 48 .... 93, 196
Cinque Ports (Lord Warden) v. R. (1831), 2 Hag.Adm.484 58
Clarke v. Mercer (1859), 1 F. & F.492 194

Page

Clarke v. Somerset Drainage Comrs. (1888), 57 L.J.M.C.96; 59 L.T. 670; 30 W.R.890; 4 T.L.R.539; 52 J.P. Jo.308 109
Claxton v. Claxton (1873), I.R. 7 C.L.23 106
Clayton v. Sale U.D.C. [1926] 1 K.B.415; 95 L.J.K.B. 178; 134 L.T. 147; 90 J.P.5; 42 T.L.R. 72; 24 L.G.R.34 63
Clowes v. Beck (1851), 13 Beav.347; 20 L.J. Ch.505; 17 L.T.O.S. 300; 51 E.R. 134 54
Cochrane v. Earl of Minto (1915), 6 Pat. App. 139 22
Cocker v. Cowper (1834), 1 Cr. M & R.418; 5 Tyr.103; 149 E.R. 1143 102
Coe v. Wise (1866) L.R. 1 Q.B. 711; 7 B. & S.831; 37 L.J.Q.B. 262; 14 L.T.891; 30 J.P.484; 14 W.R.865 393
Colbran v. Barnes (1861), 11 C.B.N.S. 246; 142 E.R. 791 149
Colchester Corpn. v. Brooke (1845) 7 Q.B. 339; 15 L.J.Q.B.59; 5 L.T.O.S. 192; 9 Jur.1090; 115 E.R.518 ....133, 135, 140, 141
Collier v. Anglian Water Authority (1983) *The Times*, 26 March 1983 ....62, 65
Collins v. Middle Level Comrs. (1869) L.R. 4 C.P.279; 38 L.J.C.P. 236; 20 L.T. 442; 17 W.R.929 64
Combridge v. Harrison (1895) 72 L.T.592; 59 J.P.198 ....439, 440
Constable's Case (1601), 5 Co.Rep.106a 56
Constable v. Nicholson (1863), 14 C.B.N.S.230; 2 New Rep.76; 32 L.J.C.P. 240; 11 W.R.698; 143 E.R.434 54
Cook v. Clareborough (1903), 75 L.J.K.B. 332; 94 L.T.550; 70 J.P. 252 426
Cooper v. Hawkins [1904] 2 K.B. 164; 73 L.J.K.B.113; 89 L.T. 476; 68 J.P.25; 52 W.R.233; 19 T.L.R.620; 1 L.G.R.833 165
Coote v. Lear (1886), 2 T.L.R. 806 167
Coppinger v. Sheehan, [1906] 1 I.R.519 51
Cory v. Bristow (1877) 2 A.C. 262; 46 L.J.M.C. 273; 36 L.T.595 155
Cory v. Yarmouth & Norwich Ry.Co, (1844), 3 Hare 593; 3 Ry. & Can. Cas.524; 67 E.R.516 169
Cosh v. Larsen [1971] 115 S.J.302; 1 Lloyds Rep. 557,D.C. 347
Costard & Wingfield's Case (1586) Godb.96; 2 Leon 44; 78 E.R. 59 18
Courtney v. Collett (1697), 1 Ld.Raym.272; 12 Mod.Rep.164; 91 E.R.1079 197
Cowes U.D.C. v. Southampton, etc. Steam Packet Co.[1905] 2 K.B.287; 74 L.J.K.B. 665; 92 L.T.658; 69 J.P.298; 53 W.R.602; 21 T.L.R.506; 49 S.J.501 162
Cowler v. Jones (1890), 54 J.P.660 445
Cowper (Earl) v. Baker (1810), 17 Ves.128; 36 E.R.264 54
Cracknell v. Thetford Corpn. (1869), L.R. 4 C.P. 629; 38 L.J.C.P. 353 ....81, 143, 156
Crompton v. Lea (1874), L.R.19 Eq.115; 44 L.J.Ch.69; 31 L.T. 469; 23 W.R.53 ..89
Crook v. Seaford Corpn. (1871) 6 Ch. App.551; 25 L.T.1; 19 W.R. 938 19
Cross v. Minister of Agricuture, [1941] I.R.55 182
Crossley & Sons v. Lightowler (1867), 2 Ch.App.478; 36 L.J. Ch.584; 16 L.T.438 ....68, 90, 91, 95, 108, 113, 116, 120
Crossman v. West (1887), 13 A.C. 160 57
Crown Estate Commissioners v. Fairlie Yacht Slip Ltd. (1977) S.L.T. 19, Ct. of Session 30, 43, 131, 136, 179

Page

Curling v. Wood (1847), 16 M. & W.628; 17 L.J.Ex.301; 11 L.T.159; 12 Jur.1055; 153 E.R.1341 153
Curtis v. Wild [1991] 4 All E.R. 172 135

D

Dakin v. Cornish (1845) 6 Ex.360; 155 E.R.582 73
Dalton v. Angus (1881), 6 A.C.740; 46 J.P.132; 30 W.R.191 103
Dalton v. Denton (1857), 1 C.B.N.S.672; 6 L.T.228 151
Dalyell v. Tyrer (1858), E.B. & E. 899; 28 L.J.Q.B. 52; 31 L.T.O.S. 214; 5 Jur.N.S.335; 6 W.R.684; 120 E.R.744 167
Davies v. Evans (1902), 86 L.T.419; 66 J.P. 392; 18 T.L.R. 355; 20 Cox C.C.177 .... 424, 426
Davies v. Marshall (1861), 10 C.B.N.S. 697; 31 L.J.C.P. 61; 4 L.T.581; 7 Jur. N.S.1247; 9 W.R. 866; 142 E.R. 627 113
Dawood Hashim Esoof v. Tuck Sein (1931), 58 Ind. App.80 P.C. 68
Daws v. M'Donald (1887), 13 V.L.R.689 8
Day & Sons v. Thames Water Authority (1984) 270 E.G. 1294; [1984] F.S.R. 596; (1984) 24 R.V.R. 216 393
Dee Conservancy Board v. McConnell [1928] 2 K.B.159; 97 L.J.K.B. 487; 138 L.T.656; 92 J.P.54; 26 L.G.R.204 147
Deed (John S.) & Sons v. British Electricity Authority & Croydon Corpn. (1950), 66 T.L.R.567; 114 J.P.533; 49 L.G.R.107 .... 111, 114
Dell v. Chesham U.D.C. (1921) 3 K.B. 427; 90 L.J.K.B. 1322; 125 L.T. 633; 85 J.P. 186; 37 T.L.R. 731; 19 L.G.R.489 295
Denaby & Cadeby Main Collieries v. Anson [1911] 1 K.B. 171; 80 L.J.K.B.320; 103 L.T.349; 26 T.L.R.667; 54 S.J.748 .... 132, 135
Devonshire v. Drohan [1900] 2 I.R. 161 432
Devonshire (Duke) v. Eglin (1851), 14 Beav.530; 20 L.J. Ex.495; 51 E.R.389 ...102
Devonshire (Duke) v. Pattinson (1887), 20 Q.B.D. 263; 57 L.J.Q.B. 189; 58 L.T.392; 52 J.P.276; 4 T.L.R.164; 19, 182, 191
Dewhirst v. Wrigley (1834). Coop. Pr.Cas.329; 47 E.R.529 102
Dexter v. Aldershot U.D.C. (1915), 79 J.P.580 97
Dibden v. Skirrow (1908), 1 Ch.41; 77 L.J. Ch.107; 97 L.T. 658; 71 J.P.555; 24 T.L.R.70; 6 L.G.R.108 168
Dickens & Kemp v. Shaw (1823), 1 L.J.O.S.K.B. 122 .... 42, 45, 56
Dickinson v. Grand Junction Canal (1852), 7 Ex.282; 21 L.J. Ex.241; 18 L.T.O.S.258; 16 Jur.200 ....10, 71, 110, 127–8
Dickinson v. Shepley Sewerage Board (1904) 68 J.P. 363 .... 94, 120
Dimes v. Petley (1850), 15 Q.B. 276; 19 L.J.Q.B.449; 16 L.T.O.S. 1; 14 J.P. 653; 14 Jur.1132; 117 E.R.462 141
Dobson v. Blackmore (1847), 9 Q.B. 991; 16 L.J.Q.B. 233; 11 J.P. 401; 11 Jur. 556; 115 E.R.1554 .... 149, 150
Dodd v. Armor (1867), 31 J.P.773 426
Doe d. Seebkristo v. East India Co (1856), 10 Moo.P.C.C.140; 6 Moo. Ind. App.267 46
Doe d. Douglas v. Lock (1835), 2 Ad. & El.705; 4 Nev. & M.K.B.807; 4 L.J.K.B.113 186

Page
Doe d. Strode v. Seaton (1834), 2 A. & E. 171; 4 N. & M.81 4 L.J.K.B. 13; 41 R.R. 412 188
Doe d. Egremont (Earl) v. Williams (1848), 11 Q.B.688; 17 L.J.Q.B. 154; 11 L.T.O.S.27; 12 Jur.455; 166 E.R.631 6
Douglas, The (1882), 51 L.J.P.55; 46 L.T.488; 30 W.R.692 146
Drewett v. Sheard (1836), 7 C. & P.465 ....11, 104, 107
Drinkwater v. Porter (1835), 7 C. & P. 181 ....134, 137
Dudden v. Clutton Union (1857), 1 H. & N.627; 26 L.J.Ex.146; 11 Ex.627; 156 E.R.1353 ....8, 123, 125
Dulverton R.D.C. v. Tracey (1921), 85 J.P.217; 19 L.G.R.693 94
Dungarven Guardians v. Mansfield [1897] 1 Ir.R.420 105
Dunwich Corpn. v. Sterry (1831), 1 B. & Ad.831; 9 L.J.O.S.K.B. 167; 109 E.R. 995 57
Durrant v. Branksome U.D.C. [1897] 2 Ch.291; 66 L.J. Ch.653; 76 L.T.739; 46 W.R.134; 13 T.L.R.482; 41 S.J.621 ....85, 295
Dwyer v. Rich (1870), I.R. 4 C.L.424 18
Dysart v. Hammerton, [1914] 1 Ch.822 104

E

East Suffolk Rivers Catchment Board v. Kent [1941] A.C.74; [1940] 4 All E.R. 527; 110 L.J.K.B.252; 165 L.T.65; 105 J.P.129; 57 T.L.R.199; 85 S.J.164; 39 L.G.R.79 ....60, 392
Eastern Counties Ry. Co. v. Dorling (1859), 5 C.B.N.S.821; 28 L.J.C.P.202, 23 J.P.470; 5 Jur.N.S.869; 141 E.R.329 152
Eaton v. Swansea Waterworks Co. (1851), 17 Q.B.267; 10 L.J.Q.B.482; 17 L.T.O.S.154; 15 Jur.675; 117 E.R.1282 104
Ecroyd v. Coulthard, [1898] 2 Ch.358; 67 L.J. Ch.458; 78 L.T.702; 14 T.L.R.462 ....19, 190
Edgar v. English Fisheries Special Comrs. (1870), 23 L.T.732; 35 J.P.822 189
Edinburgh Water Trustees v. Sommerville & Son (1906), 95 L.T.217 70
Edleston v. Crossley & Sons Ltd. (1868), 18 L.T.15 ....17, 78, 79
Edwards v. Morgan [1967] Crim. L.R. 40; 116 New L.J. 1517,D.C. 445
EEC Directive Concerning the Quality of Bathing Water, re; EC Commission v. Kingdom of the Netherlands, Case 96/81 [1982] E.C.R. 1791, 1819, European Ct. 293, 357
Ella, The [1915] P.111; 84 L.J. P.97 147
Elliot v. North Eastern Ry. Co, (1863), 10 H.L. Cas.333; 32 L.J.Ch.402 126
Elmhirst v. Spencer (1849), 2 Mac. & G.45; 14 L.T.O.S. 433; 42 E.R. 18 ....91, 92
Elwell v. Crowther (1862), 31 Beav.163; 31 L.J. Ch.763; 6 L.T.596; 8 Jur.N.S.1004; 10 W.R.615 81
Embleton v. Brown (1860), 3 E. & E.234; 30 L.J.M.C.1; 6 Jur. N.S.1298; 121 E.R.429 52
Embrey v. Owen (1851), 6 Ex.353; 20 L.J.Ex.212; 17 L.T.O.S. 79; 15 Jur.633; 155 E.R.579 ....13, 66, 67, 73, 74, 81, 89
Emerald, The, Greta Holme, [1896] P192; [1897] A.C.596; 66 L.J.P.166; 77 L.T.231; 13 T.L.R.552 147

Page

English v. Metropolitan Water Board, [1907] 1 K.B.588; 76 L.J.K.B.361; 96 L.T.573; 71 J.P.313; 23 T.L.R.313; 5 L.G.R.384 124
Ennor v. Barwell (1860), 2 Giff.410; 3 L.T.170; 25 J.P.54 .... 9, 14, 125
Epstein v. Reymes (1972), 29 D.L.R. (3rd)(Supreme Court of Canada) 117
Esso Petroleum Co. v. Southport Corpn. [1956] 2 W.L.R.81; 100 S.J.32; 120 J.P.54; [1955] 3 All E.R.864 H.L.; A.C.218 .... 90, 348
Eton R.D.C. v. Thames Conservators, [1950] Ch.540; [1950] 1 All E.R.996; 114 J.P.279; 66 T.L.R.875; 94 S.J.285; 48 L.G.R.259 402
Evans v. Godber [1974] 1 W.L.R. 1317; 118 S.J. 699; 3 All E.R. 341; 2 Lloyd's Rep. 326; Crim L.R. 551, D.C. 136
Evans v. Owen, [1895] 1 Q.B.237; 64 L.J.M.C.59; 72 L.T.54; 43 W.R. 237; 39 S.J.152 426
Ewart v. Belfast Poor Law Comrs (1881), 9 L.R. Ir.172 .... 110, 122, 127
Ewart v. Cochrane (1861), 5 L.T. 1; 25 J.P.612; 7 Jur. N.S.925; 10 W.R.3; 3 Macq.117 103

F

Factortame Ltd v. Secretary of State for Transport (No.2) (Case 213/89) [1991] 1 All E.R.70 .... 36, 359
Fagernes, The (1927) P.311, C.A. 29
Falmouth (Lord) v. George (1828), 5 Bing 286; 2 Moo. & P.457; 7 L.J.O.S.C.P.40; 130 E.R.1071 179
Falmouth (Earl) v. Penrose (1827), 6 B. & C.385; 9 Dow. & Ry. K.B.452; 5 L.J.O.S.K.B.156; 108 E.R.494 179
Farquaharson v. Farquaharson (1741), 3 Bli, N.S.421; 4 E.R.1389; Mor.12, 779 ..84
Fear v. Vickers (No.1) (1911), 27 T.L.R.558; 55 S.J.688 82
Federal Steam Navigation Co. Ltd. v Department of Trade and Industry [1974] 1 W.L.R. 505; 118 S.J. 478; 2 All E.R. 97; 59 Crim. App R. 131 ...34
Fennings v. Grenville (Lord) (1808), 1 Taunt.241; 127 E.R.825 177
Fentiman v. Smith (1805), 4 East 107; 102 E.R.770 101
Ferens v. O'Brien (1883), 11 Q.B.D.21; 52 L.J.M.C.70; 47 J.P.472; 31 W.R.643; 15 Cox C.C.332 14
Fergusson v. Malvern U.D.C. (1909), 73 J.P.361 .... 92, 120
Ferrand v. Midland Ry. Co. (1901), 17 T.L.R.427 148
Finch v. Resbridger (1700) 2 Vern 390 103
Fisheries Jurisdiction Cases (United Kingdom v. Iceland) 1974 I.C.J. Rep.3 32
Fisherrow Harbour Commissioners v. Musselborough Real Estate Co. (1903) 5 F. 387 (Scotland) 42
Fitzgerald v. Firbank, [1897] 2 Ch.96; 66 L.J. Ch.529; 76 L.T.584; 13 T.L.R.390; 41 S.J.490 .... 93, 186, 196
Fitzhardinge (Lord) v. Purcell, [1908] 2 Ch.139; 77 L.J.Ch.529; 99 L.T.154; 72 J.P.276; 24 T.L.R.564 ....16, 43, 51, 178, 181, 189
Fitzherbert Brockhole's Agreement, Re, River Wyre Catchement Board v. Miller [1939] Ch.51; 109 L.J. Ch.17; 162 L.T.43; 103 J.P.379; 56 T.L.R.62; 83 S.J.890; 37 L.G.R.606 402
Fitzwalter's (Lord) Case (1674), 1 Mod.Rep.105; 3 Keb.242 184

Page

Fletcher v. Bealey (1885), 28 Ch.D.688; 54 L.J.Ch.424; 52 L.T.541; 33 W.R.745; 1 T.L.R.233 98
Fletcher v. Birkenhead Corpn. [1907] 1 K.B.205; 76 L.J.K.B. 218; 96 L.T.287; 71 J.P.111; 23 T.L.R.195; 51 S.J.171; 5 L.G.R. 293 126
Fletcher v. Smith (1877), 2 A.C.781 ....76, 89
Fobbing Sewers Comrs. v. R.(1886), 11 A.C.449; 56 L.J.M.C.1; 51 J.P.227; 34 W.R.721; 2 T.L.R.493 63
Forbes v. Lee Conservancy Board (1879), 4 Ex.D.116; 48 L.J.Q.B. 402; 27 W.R.688 156
Ford v. Lacy (1861), 7 H. & N. 151; 30 L.J. Ex.351; 7 Jur. N.S.684; 158 E.R.429 ....20, 48
Foreman v. Free Fisheries of Whitstable (1869), L.R. 4 H.L.266 .... 30, 192
Foster v. British Gas PLC [1991] 2 W.L.R. 258; [1990] 3 All E.R. 897; [1991] I.C.R. 84; [1990] I.R.L.R. 353; *The Times* 13 July 1990, European Ct. 357
Foster v. Warblington U.D.C. [1906] 1 K.B.648; 75 L.J.K.B. 514; 94 L.T.876; 70 J.P.233; 54 W.R.575; 22 T.L.R.421; 4 L.G.R.735 .... 43, 104, 179
Foster v. Wright (1878), 4 C.P.D.438; 49 L.J.C.P.97; 44 J.P.7 .... 17, 20, 47, 193
Fotheringham v. Kerr or Passmore (1984) 48 P. & C.R. 173; 134 New L.J. 567, H.L. 192
Fowey Marine (Ensworth) Ltd. v Gafford [1968] 2 Q.B. 618; 1 All E.R. 979; 2 W.L.R. 842; 112 S.J. 114 136
Fraser v. Fear, [1912] W.N.227; 107 L.T.423; 57 S.J.29; 77, 196, 428
Frechette v. Compagnie Manufacturie de St. Hyacinthe (1883), 9 A.C.170; 53 L.J.P.C.20; 50 L.T.62 67
French Hoek Comrs. v. Hugo (1885), 10 A.C.336 113
Fuller v. Brown (1849), 3 New Mag. Cas.172; 3 New Sess. Cas. 603; 13 L.T.O.S.301; 13 J.P. 445 185

G

Gabbett v. Clancy (1845), 8 I.L.R.299 188
Gammell v. Comrs. of Woods and Forests (1859), 3 Macq.419, H.L. 29
Gann v. Free Fisheries of Whitstable (1865), 11 H.L.C. 192; 5 New Rep.432; 33 L.J.C.P.29; 12 L.T. 150; 29 J.P.243; 13 W.R.589; 11 E.R.1305 ....16, 31, 132, 136, 139, 192
Garnett v. Backhouse (1867), L.R. 3 Q.B.30; 8 B. & S.490; 37 L.J.Q.B.1; 17 L.T.170; 32 J.P.5 430
Gartner v. Kidman (1962), 36 A.L.J.R.43 117
Gaved v. Martyn (1865), 19 C.B.N.S. 732; 34 L.J.C.P.353; 13 L.T.74; 11 Jur. N.S.1017; 14 W.R.62; 144 E.R.974 .... 71, 105, 111, 115, 117, 119
Gazard v. Cooke (1890) 55 J.P.102 .... 439, 440
Geddis v. Bann Reservoir (1878), 3 A.C.430 143
General Estates Co. v. Beaver [1914] 3 K.B.918; 84 L.J.K.B. 21; 111 C.T.957; 79 J.P.41; 30 T.L.R.634; 12 L.G.R.1146; 162, 163
George v. Carpenter, [1893] 1 Q.B.505; 18 L.T.714; 57 J.P.311; 4 1 W.R.366; 37 S.J.387 426
Gerrard v. Crowe, [1921] 1 A.C.395; 90 L.J.P.C.42; 124 L.T.486; 37 T.L.R.110 ..83

Page

Gewiese and Mehlich v. Mackenzie (No.24/83)[1984] 2 All E.R. 129; E.C.R.817; 2 C.M.L.R.409, European Court 36
Gibbons v. Lenfestey (1915), 84 L.J.P.C.158; 113 L.T.55 ....85, 88
Gibson v. Ryan, [1968] 1 Q.B. 250; [1967] 3 W.L.R.997; 131 J.P. 498; 111 S.J. 601; 3 All E.R. 184, D.C. 439
Gifford v. Yarborough (Lord) (1828) 5 Bing.163 ....46, 47
Giles v. Groves (1848), 12 Q.B. 721; 6 Dow. & L.146; 17 L.J.Q.B.323; 11 L.T.O.S.433; 12 Jur.1084; 116 E.R.1041 163
Gillett v. Kent Rivers Catchment Board, [1938] 4 All E.R.810 .... 60, 392
Gipps v. Woollicot (1697), Holt K.B.323; Comb.464; Skin 677; 3 Salk 360 175
Glazebrook v. Gwynedd River Board (1964), 15 P.J.C.R.75 393
Glee v. Meadows (1911), 105 L.T.327; 75 J.P.142 52
Glossop v. Heston & Isleworth L.B. (1879), 12 Ch.D.102; 49 L.J. Ch.89; 44 J.P.36; 40 L.T.736; 28 W.R.111 96
Goldsmid v. Tunbridge Wells Comrs. (1866), 1 Ch.App.349; 35 L.J. Ch.382; 14 L.T.154; 30 J.P.419; 12 Jur.N.S. 308; 14 W.R. 562 .... 95, 97, 108
Goodhart v. Hyett (1883), 25 Ch. D.182; 53 L.J.Ch.219; 50 L.T.95; 48 J.P.293; 32 W.R.165 112
Goodman v. Saltash Corpn. (1882), 2 A.C.633; 52 L.J.Q.B.193; 48 L.T.239; 47 J.P.276; 31 W.R.293 .... 54, 103, 109, 180, 183, 187
Goolden v. Thames Conservators (1891), [1897] 2 Q.B.338 H.L. 11
Gore v. English Fisheries Comrs. (1871), L.R. 6 Q.B.561; 40 L.J.Q.B.252; 24 L.T.702; 33 J.P.405; 19 W.R.1083 428
Government of the State of Penang v. Beng Hong Oon [1972] A.C.425; [1972] 2 W.L.R. 1; 115 S.J.889; [1971] 3 All E.R.1163, P.C. 42
Granby (Marquis) v. Bakewell U.D.C. (1923); 87 J.P.105; 21 L.G.R. 329 ....94, 95, 196
Grand Junction Canal Co. v. Petty (1888), 21 Q.B.D.273; 57 L.J.Q.B.572; 59 L.T.767; 52 J.P.692 138
Grand Junction Canal Co. v. Shugar (1871), 6 Ch.App.483; 24 L.T.402; 35 J.P.660; 19 W.R.569 123
Grand Union Canal Co. v. Ashby (1861), 6 H. & N.394; 30 L.J.Ex.203; 3 L.T.673 194
Gravesham Borough Council v. British Railways Board (1977) *Law Society's Gazette* 8 March 1978, p.249 166
Gray v. Blamey [1991] 1 W.L.R. 47; 1 All E.R. 1; [1990] Crim. L.R. 746; C.O.D. 388; *The Times* 4 June 1990 .... 26, 428
Gray v. Bond (1821), 2 Brod. & Bing.667; 5 Moore C.P. 527; 129 E.R.1123 .... 179, 195
Gray v. Sylvester (1897), 61 J.P.807; 46 W.R.63; 14 T.L.R.10; 42 S.J.13 52
Gray v. Trowe (1601), Gouldsh. 129; 75 E.R.1043 451
Gray's Case (1594), Owen 20 .... 196, 451
Greatrex v. Hayward (1853), 8 Ex.291; 22 L.J. Ex.137; 155 E.R.1357 .... 85, 110, 116, 118, 119, 128
Great Torrington Commons Conservators v. Moore Stevens, [1904] 1 Ch. 347; 73 L.J.Ch. 124; 89 L.T. 667; 68 J.P. 111; 2 L.G.R. 397 19
Green v. Matthews (1930), 46 T.L.R. 206 109
Greenbank v. Sanderson (1884), 49 J.P. 40 .... 188, 190

Page
Greenock Corpn. v. Caledonian Ry, [1917] A.C. 556 76
Greenslade v. Halliday (1830), 6 Bing 379; 53 R.R.241 75
Greenwich Board of Works v. Maudslay (1870). L.R. 5 Q.B.379; 39 L.J.Q.B. 205; 23 L.T. 121; 35 J.P.8; 18 W.R. 948 62
Gridley v. Thames Conservators (1886), 3 T.L.R.108 157
Griffiths' Case (1564), Moore Rep.69 63
Grit, The [1924] P.246; 94 L.J.P.6; 132 L.T.638; 40 T.L.R.891 153
Grove v. Portal, [1902] 1 Ch. 727; 71 L.J. Ch.290; 86 L.T. 350; 18 T.L.R. 319; 46 S.J. 296 183

H

Haigh v. Deudraeth R.D.C. [1945] 2 All E.R. 661; 174 L.T. 243; 110 J.P. 97; 89 S.J. 579; 44 L.G.R. 24 89
Hale v. Oldroyd (1845), 14 M. & W. 789; 15 L.J.Ex.4; 153 E.R. 694 114
Hall v. Reid (1882), 10 Q.B.134; 52 L.J.M.C.32; 48 L.T.221 4 26
Hall v. Swift (1838), 4 Bing. N.C.381; 1 Arn.157; 6 Scott 167; 7 L.J.C.P.209; 132 E.R.834 .... 107, 114
Halse v. Alder (1874), 38 J.P.407 .... 189, 452
Hamelin v. Bannerman, [1895] A.C.237; 64 L.J.P.C.66; 72 L.T.128; 60 J.P.22; 43 W.R.639; 11 R.368 81
Hamilton v. A.–G.for Ireland (1880), 5 L.R.Ir.555; 9 L.R. Ir.271 ....45, 53
Hamilton v. Donegal (Marquis) (1795), 3 Ridg. P.R.267 .... 79, 196
Hamilton & Smyth v. Davis (1771), 5 Burr. 2733; 98 E.R.433 58
Hammerton v. Dysart (Earl), [1916] 1 A.C.57; 85 L.J.Ch.33; 113 L.T.1032; 80 J.P.97; 31 T.L.R.592; 59 S.J.665; 13 L.G.R. 1255 ....103, 162, 165, 168
Hammond v. Hall (1840), 10 Sim.551; 5 Jur.694; 59 E.R.729 122
Hanbury v. Jenkins [1901] 2 Ch.401; 70 L.J.Ch.730; 65 J.P.631; 49 W.R.615; 17 T.L.R.539; 18, 79, 175, 183, 185, 190, 191
Hancock v. York, Newcastle Ry. Co. (1850), 10 C.B.348; 14 L.T.O.S.467; 138 E.R.140 149
Hanley v. Edingburgh Corpn. [1913] A.C.488; 78 J.P.233; 29 T.L.R. 404; 57 S.J.460; 11 L.G.R.766 76
Hanna v. Pollock, [1900] 2 I.R.664 .... 104, 119
Harbottle v. Terry (1882), 10 Q.B.131; 52 L.J.M.C.31; 48 L.T.219; 47 J.P.136; 31 W.R.289 426
Hargreaves v. Diddams (1875), L.R.10 Q.B.582; 44 L.J.M.C. 178; 32 L.T.600; 40 J.P.167; 23 W.R.828 .... 182, 194
Harmond v. Pearson (1808), 1 Camp.515; 170 E.R.1041 146
Harrington, The (1888), 13 P.D.48; 57 L.J.P.45; 59 L.T.72 147
Harrington (Earl) v. Derby Corpn. [1905] 1 Ch.205; 74 L.J.Ch.219; 92 L.T.153; 69 J.P.62; 21 T.L.R.98; 3 L.G.R.321 95
Harris v. Chesterfield (Earl), [1911] A.C.623; 80 L.J.Ch.626; 105 L.T.453; 27 T.L.R.548; 55 S.J.686 .... 175, 184, 187
Harrison v. Great Northern Ry.Co. (1864), 3 H. & C.231; 5 New Rep. 93; 33 L.J.Ex.266; 10 L.T.621; 10 Jur.N.S.992; 12 W.R.1081; 159 E.R.518 ....64, 86

Page

Harrison v. Rutland (Duke), [1893] 1 Q.B.142; 62 L.J.Q.B. 117;
68 L.T.35; 57 J.P.278; 41 W.R.322; 9 T.L.R.115; 4 R.155, C.A. 195

Harrop v. Hirst (1868), L.R. 4 Ex. 43; 38 L.J. Ex.1; 19 L.T. 426; 33 J.P.103;
17 W.R.164 .... 76, 105

Harwich Harbour Conservancy Board v. Secretary of State for the Environment,
(1974) 118 S.J.755 [1974] J.P.L. 724; 233 E.G.263;
[1975] 1 Lloyd's Rep.334,C.A. 145

Hastings Corpn. v. Ivall (1874), L.R.19 Eq.558 .... 44, 45, 53

Hayes v. Bridges (1795), 1 Ridg. L. & S. 390 183

Hayes v. Hayes (1897), 31 I.L.T. Jo.392 49

Healy v. Thorne (1870), I.R. 4 C.L.495 43

Hemphill v. M'Kenna (1845), 8 I.L.R.43 162

Hereford v. Worcester County Council and Dubberley (1985) 1 P.A.D.85 334

Heseltine v. Myers (1894) 58 J.P. 689 443

Hesketh v. Willis Cruisers (1968) 19 P.J.C.R.573, C.A. 18, 185

Hewlins v. Shippam (1826), 5 B. & C.221; 7 Dow. & Ry.K.B. 783;
4 L.J.O.S.K.B.241 101

High Wycombe Corpn. v. Thames Conservators (1898) 78 L.T. 463;
14 T.L.R. 358, D.C. 298

Hill v. Cock (1872) 26 L.T.185; 36 J.P.552 .... 80, 141

Hill v. George (1880) 44 J.P.424 440

Hill v. Tupper (1863), 2 H. & C.121; 2 New Rep.201; 32 L.J.Ex.217;
8 L.T.792; 9 Jur.N.S.725; 11 W.R.784; 159 E.R.51 101

Hind v. Manfield (1614), Noy.103; 74 E.R.1068 147

Hindson v. Ashby, [1896] 2 Ch.1; 65 L.J.Ch.515; 74 L.T.327; 60 J.P.484;
45 W.R.252; 12 T.L.R.314; 40 S.J.417 ....12, 17, 19, 20, 21, 44, 47,
48, 150, 151, 183, 185, 191, 192, 193

Hix v. Gardiner (1614), 2 Bulst.195; 80 E.R.1062 165

Hodgkinson v. Ennor (1863), 4 B. & S.229; 2 New Rep.272; 32 L.J.Q.B. 231;
8 L.T.451; 27 J.P.469; 9 Jur.N.S. 1152; 11 W.R.775 .... 91, 121, 129

Hodgson v. Field (1806), 7 East 613; 3 Smith K.B.538; 103 E.R.238 112

Hodgson v. Little (1864) 16 C.B.N.S.198; 33 L.J.M.C.229; 11 L.T.136;
10 Jur. N.S.953; 12 W.R.1103; 143 E.R.1101 435

Hodgson v. York Corpn. (1873), 28 L.T.836; 37 J.P.725 .... 81, 156

Hogarth v. Jackson (1827), 2 C. & P. 595; Mood. & M.58.N.P. 177

Holford v. Bailey (1849), 13 Q.B.D. 426; 18 L.J.Q.B.109; 13 L.T.O.S.261;
13 Jur.278; 116 E.R.1325 ....175, 191, 196

Holford v. George (1868), L.R. 3 Q.B.639; 9 B. & S.815; 37 L.J.Q.B. 185;
18 L.T.817; 32 J.P.468; 16 W.R.1204 428

Holford v. Pritchard (1849), 3 Ex.793; 18 L.J.Ex.315; 13 L.T.O.S.74 185

Holien v. Tipping [1915]1 I.R.210 61

Holker v. Porritt (1875) L.R. 10 Ex.59; 44 L.J.Ex.52; 33 L.T. 125;
39 J.P.196; 23 W.R.400 ....70, 116

Holker v. Porritt (1883) 11 Q.B.D.21 14

Hollis v. Goldfinch (1823), 1 B. & C.205; 2 Dow. & Ry. K.B. 316;
1 L.J.O.S.K.B.91; 107 E.R.76 ....18, 137, 155

Home Brewery PLC v. Davis and Co. [1987] Q.B.339; 2 W.L.R.117;
1 All E.R.637; (1987) 84 L.S. Gaz.657; (1987) 131 S.J.102 ....85, 87

Page

Hopkins v. Great Northern Ry.Co. (1877), 2 Q.B.D. 224; 46 L.J.Q.B. 265; 36 L.T.898; 42 J.P.229 168

Hopton v. Thirwell (1863), 3 New Rep.70; 9 L.T.327; 27 J.P.743 424

Horne v. Mackenzie (1839), 6 Cl. & Fin.628; Mackl. & Rob. 977; 7 E.R.834 ....15, 132, 181

Hough v. Clark (1907), 23 T.L.R. 682; 5 L.G.R.1195 19

Hoveringham Gravels v. Secretary of State for the Environment [1975] Q.B.754; 2 W.L.R.897; 119 S.J.355; 2 All E.R.931; 73 L.G.R.238; 30 P & C.R.151, C.A. 333

Howard v. Ingersoll (1851), 54 U.S.381; 17 Ala.781 12

Howe v. Stawell (1833), Alc. & N.348 53

Hudson v. MacRae (1863), 4 B. & S.585; 3 New Rep.76; 33 L.J.M.C.65; 9 L.T.678; 28 J.P.436; 12 W.R.80; 122 E.R.579 182

Hudson v. Tabor (1877), 2 Q.B.D.290; 46 L.J.Q.B.463; 36 L.T.492; 42 J.P.20; 25 W.R.740 ....59, 62

Hull & Selby Ry. Co. Re.(1839), 5 M. & W.327; 8 L.J. Ex.260 ....20, 46, 47

Hulley v. Silversprings Bleaching Co. [1922] 2 Ch.268; 91 L.J.Ch.207; 126 L.T.499; 86 J.P.30; 66 Sol.Jo.195 109

Humorist, The [1944] P.28; 113 J.P.41; 171 L.T.85; 60 T.L.R.190 153

Humphries v. Cousins (1877), 2 C.P.D.239 121

Hunwick v. Essex Rivers Catchment Board (1952), 116 J.P. 217; [1952] 1 All E.R.765; 1 Lloyd's Rep.335 62

Hurdman v. North Eastern Ry. (1878), 3 C.P.D.168; 47 L.J.Q.B.368; 38 L.T.339; 26 W.R.489 88

Huzzey v. Field (1835), 2 Cr. M. & R.432; 5 Tyr.855; 4 L.J. Ex.239; 150 E.R.186 ....162, 168

I

Ilchester (Earl) v. Rashleigh (1889), 61 L.T.477; 38 W.R. 104; 5 T.L.R.739 ....15, 133, 178

Impress (Worcester) Ltd v. Rees (1971) 115 S.J.245; [1971] 2 All E.R.357; 69 L.G.R.305, D.C. 298

Ingram v. Morecroft (1863), 33 Beav. 49 71

Ingram v. Percival [1968], 3 W.L.R.663; 3 All E.R.657, D.C; 133 J.P.1; 112 S.J.722 ....15, 26, 182, 428

Ipswich (Inhabitants) v. Browne (1581), Sav.11,14; 123 E.R.984 ....162, 179, 194

Isle of Ely Case (1609), 10 Co,Rep. 141a; 77 E.R.1139 61

Iveagh (Earl) v. Martin, [1960] 2 All E.R.668; 3 W.L.R. 210; 104 S.J.567 ....134, 135, 137

Ivimey v. Stocker (1866), 1 Ch. App.396; 35 L.J.Ch.467; 14 L.T.427; 12 Jur.N.S.419; 14 W.R.743 ....105, 111, 116

J

James v. Plant (1836), 4 Ad. & El.761; 6 Nev. & M.K.B.282; 6 L.J. Ex.260; 111 E.R.967 112

Page

Jenkins v. Harvey (1835), 1 Cr. M. & R.877; 1 Gale 23; 5 Tyr.326; 5 L.J.Ex.17; 149 E.R.1336 103

Jinman v. E. Coast Insurance Co, (1878), 42 J.P.809 147

Johnston v. O'Neill [1911] A.C.552; 81 L.J.C.P.17; 105 L.T. 587; 27 T.L.R.545; 55 S.J.686 ....17, 22, 133, 182, 188, 193

Joliffe v. Wallesley L.B. (1873), L.R. 9 C.P.62; 43 L.J.C.P. 41; 29 L.T.582; 38 J.P.40 ....143, 149

Jones v. Davies (1902), 86 L.T.447; 66 J.P.439; 20 Cox C.C. 184 ....186, 424

Jones v. Llanrwst U.D.C. [1911] 1 Ch. 393; 75 J.P.68; 80 L.J. Ch.145; 103 L.T.751; 27 T.L.R. 133; 9 L.G.R.222 90

Jones v. Mersey River Board, [1958] 1 Q.B.143; [1957] 3 W.L.R.789; 121 J.P.581; 101 S.J.867; [1957] 3 All E.R. 375; 9 P. & C.R.13 ....13, 379, 393

Jones v. Owens (1870) 34 J.P. 759 442

Jones v. Williams (1837), 2 M. & W.326; Murp. & H.51; 6 L.J. Ex.107 18

Jordeson v. Sutton, Southcoates & Drypool Gas Co, [1899] 2 Ch.217 ..85, 126, 139

Juxon v. Thornhill (1628), Cro. Car.132; 79 E.R.716 156

K

Kearns v. Cordwainers' Co. (1859), 6 C.B.N.S.388; 28 L.J.C.P. 285; 33 L.T.O.S.271; 23 J.P.760; 5 Jur.N.S.1216; 141 E.R.508 143

Keighley's Case (1609) 10 Co.Rep.139a; 77 E.R.1136 63

Kena Mahomed v. Bohatoo Sircar (1863), Marsh 506 8

Kensit v. Great Eastern Ry. Co.(1884), 27 Ch.D,122; 54 L.J.Ch.19; 51 L.T.862; 32 W.R.885 69

Keppell v. Bailey (1834), 2 My. & K.517 100

Kingdon v. Hutt River Board (1905) 25 N.Z.L.R.145 12

Kingsway Furniture (Dartford) Ltd. v. Harpglow Ltd. and Kylefield Ltd., 23 March 1990 (Official Referee's Business) [1991] 2 *Water Law* 10 ....15, 182

Kinloch v. Neville (1840), 6 M. & W.795; 10 L.J.Ex.248 137

Kintore v. Forbes (1828), 4 Bli. N.S.485; 5 E.R.173 180

Kirby v. Gibbs (1667), 2 Keble 274 ....42, 43

Kirkheaton L.B. v. Ainley, [1892] 2 Q.B.274; 61 L.J.Q.B. 812; 67 L.T.209; 57 J.P.36; 8 T.L.R.663; 36 S.J.608 ....296, 297

L

Lagon Navigation Co. v. Lambeg Bleaching Co. [1927] A.C. 226; 96 L.J.P.C.25; 136 L.T.417; 91 J.P.46; 25L.G.R. 1 83

Lamb v. Newbiggin (1844), 1 Car. & Kir.549 ....18, 191

Lanarkshire County Council v. National Coal Board (1948) S.C.698; 1948 S.L.T.435 173

Lancashire, The (1874), L.R. 4 A. & E.198; 29 L.T.927; 2 Asp.M.L.C.202 167

Land Securities Co. v. Commercial Gas Co. (1902), 18 T.L.R.405 ....151, 152

Page

Langbrook Properties v. Surrey County Council, [1969] 3 All E.R.1424; 113 S.J.983 .... 124, 126
Latter v. Littlehampton U.D.C. (1909), 101 L.T.172; 73 J.P.426; 8 L.G.R.211 ...168
Lawes v. Turner & Frere (1892), 8 T.L.R.584 143
Layzell v. Thompson (1926), 91 J.P.89; 43 T.L.R.58; (1927), 96 L.J. Ch.332 163
Le Strange v. Rowe (1866), 4 F. & F.1048 .... 42, 44, 56
Lea Conservancy Board v. Bishop's Stortford U.D.C. (1906), 70 J.P. 244; 4 L.G.R.662 91
Lea Conservancy Board v. Button (1879), 6 A.C.685; 51 L.J. Ch.17; 45 L.T.385 .... 138, 154
Lea Conservancy Board v. Hertford Corpn. (1884), 48 J.P. 628; Cab. & El.299 93
Leakey v. National Trust [1980] Q.B. 485; [1980] 2 W.L.R.65; (1979) 123 S.J. 606; [1980] 1 All E.R 17; (1979) 78 L.G.R. 100, C.A. 87
Leavett v. Clark [1915] 3 K.B.9; [1914–15] All E.R.Rep.690; 79 J.P. 396; 84 L.J.K.B.2157; 113 L.T.424; 31 T.L.R.424; 25 Cox, C.C.44; 13 L.G.R.894 452
Leconfield v. Lonsdale (1870), L.R.5 C.P.657; 39 L.J.C.P. 305; 23 L.T.155 ....104, 148, 189, 195, 428
Legge (George) & Son Ltd v. Wenlock Corpn. [1936] 3 All E.R.599; 101 J.P.599; 106 L.J. Ch.71; 155 L.T.615; 53 T.L.R.11, 80 S.J.913 10
Letton v. Goodden (1866), L.R. 2 Eq.123; 35 L.J. Ch.427; 14 L.T.296; 30 J.P.677; 14 W.R.554 165
Leigh Land Reclamation Ltd v. Walsall M.B.C. (1991) 155 J.P.N.332; *The Times* November 2, 1990 D.C. 303
Leith–Buchanan v. Hogg, [1931] S.C.204 .... 134, 137
Lewis v. Arthur (1871) 24 L.T.66; 35 J.P.35 438
Liford's Case (1614), 11 Co. Rep.46b; 77 E.R. 1206 .... 63, 112
Liggins v. Inge (1831), 7 Bing 682; 5 Moo. & P.C.712; 9 L.T.O.S.C.P. 202 .... 13, 102, 113
Lillywhite v. Trimmer (1867), 36 L.J. Ch.525; 16 L.T. 318; 15 W.R.763 ....91, 96, 97
Linnane v. Nestor & McNamara, [1943] I.R.208 ....46, 53
Liverpool Corpn. v. Coghill [1918] 1 Ch.307; 87 L.J.Ch.186; 118 L.T.336; 82 J.P.129; 34 T.L.R.156; 16 L.G.R.91 .... 105, 109
Liverpool and North Wales Steamship Co. Ltd. v Mersey Trading Co. Ltd. [1908] 2 Ch. 460 136
Llandudno U.D.C. v. Woods, [1899] 2 Ch.705; 68 L.J.Ch. 623; 81 L.T.170; 63 J.P.775; 48 W.R.43; 43 S.J.189 .... 50, 178
Lockhart v. National Coal Board [1981] S.C.C.R.9; S.L.T.161 (Scot) 298
Lockwood v. Wood (1844), 6 Q.B. 50; 13 L.J.Q.B.365; 3 L.T.O.S. 139; 8 Jur.543; 115 E.R.19 179
Lomax v. Stott (1870), 39 L.J. Ch.834 89
London County Council v. Price's Candle Co. Ltd. (1911), 75 J.P.329; 9 L.G.R.660 96
London & Birmingham Ry. Co. v. Grand Junction Canal Co.(1835) 1 Rail, Cas.224 148
London & N.W. Rly. v Fobbing Sewers Comrs. (1896), 66 L.J.Q.B. 127; 75 L.T.629; 41 S.J.128 63

Page

Londonderry Bridge Comrs. v. M'Keever (1890), 27 L.R. Ir. 464 .... 163, 169
Longhurst v. Guildford, Godalming & District Water Co, [1961] 1 Q.B.408; 8 W.L.R.915; 3 All E.R.545 H.L; 105 S.J.866; 59 L.G.R.565; [1963] A.C.265 14
Loose v. Castleton (1978) *The Times*, June 21, 1978, C.A. 30, 192
Lopez v. Muddun Mohun Thakoor (1870), 13 Moo. Ind. App. 467; 20 E.R.625 ...47
Lord v. Sydney Comrs. (1859), 12 Moo. P.C. 473; 33 L.T.O.S.1; 7 W.R.267 67
Lord Advocate v. Blantyre (Lord) (1879), 4 A.C.770, H.L. 44
Lord Advocate v. Hamilton (1852), 1 Macq. 46, H.L. 16
Lord Advocate v. Lovat (1880), 5 A.C.273 .... 188, 189, 190
Lord Advocate v. Sinclair (1867), L.R. 1 H.L.Sc.176 58
Lord Advocate v. Wemyss, [1900] A.C.66 ....29, 45
Lord Advocate v. Young (1887), 12 A.C.544 ....45, 46
Loring v. Bridgewood Golf and Country Club Ltd (1974) 44 D.L.R. (3rd) 161 84
Lotus Ltd. v. British Soda Co. Ltd. [1972] Ch.123; [1971] 2 W.L.R.7; (1970) 114 S.J.885; [1971] 1 All E.R. 265; 22 P. & C.R.11 126
Loud v. Murray (1851), 17 L.T.O.S.248 80
Lovegrove v. Isle of Wight River Board (1956), J.P.L.221 393
Lovett v. Fairclough, (1990) *The Times* 10 March 1990 192
Lowe v. Govett (1832), 3 B. & Ad.863; 1 L.J.K.B.224; 110 E.R.317 ....43, 53
Luttrell's Case (1601), 4 Co. Rep. 86; 76 E.R. 1063 .... 106, 114
Lyme Regis Corpn. v. Henley (1834), 1 Bing. N.C.222; 8 Bli. N.S.690; 2 Cl. & Fin.331; 1 Scott 29; 131 E.R.1103 63
Lyne v. Leonard (1868) L.R.3 Q.B.156; 9 B.& S.65; 37 L.J.M.C.55 18 L.T.55; 32 J.P.422; 16 W.R. 562 428
Lynn Regis v. Taylor (1684), 3 Lev. 160 54
Lynn Corpn. v. Turner (1774), 1 Cowp,86; 98 E.R.980 .... 15, 133
Lyon v. Fishmongers' Co. (1876), 1 A.C.662; 46 L.J. Ch.68; 35 L.T.569; 42 J.P.163; 25 W.R.165 ....68, 69, 91, 143, 150
Lyons v. Winter (1899), 25 V.L.R.464 7

M

M'Attee v. Hogg (1903), 5 F.(Ct. of Sess.) 67 436
MacCannon v. Sinclair (1859), 2 E. & E.53, 28 L.J.M.C.247; 33 L.T.O.S.221; 23 J.P.757; 5 Jur.N.S.1302; 7 W.R.567; 121 E.R.21 18
McCartney v. Londonderry Rly. [1904] A.C.301; 73 L.J.P.C.73; 91 L.T.105; 53 W.R.385 .... 66, 72, 74
McCutcheon v. David MacBrayne Ltd. [1964] 1 W.L.R.125; 108 S.J.93; 1 Lloyd's Rep.16; 1964 S.C.(H.L.)28; S.L.T.66 167
McEvoy v. Great Northern Rly. [1910] 2 I.R.325 101
McGlone v. Smith (1888), 22 L.R. Ir.559 82
McIntyre Corp. v. McGavin [1893] A.C.268; 20 R. (Ct. of Sess.) 49; 30 Sc. L.R.941; 1 S.L.T.110 .... 109, 114
MacKenzie v. Bankes (1878), 3 A.C.1324, H.L. 22
MacKinnon v. Nicolson [1916] S.C.6 .... 444, 452
McLeod v. Buchanan [1940] 2 All E.R.179 298
M'Nab v. Robertson, [1897] A.C.129, H.L.Sc. 7, 8, 9, 127

Page
MacNaghton v. Baird, [1903] 2 I.R.731 104
MacNamara v. Higgins (1854), 4 I.C.L.R.326 54
Macey v. Metropolitan Board of Works (1864), 33 L.J.Ch.377; 10 L.T.66 151
Magor v. Chadwick (1840), 11 Ad. & El.571; 9 L.J.Q.B.159; 113 E.R.532 115
Mahoney v. Neeman & Neeman (No.2) (1966), 100 I.L.T.R.205 ....46, 53
Malcomson v. O'Dea (1863), 10 H.L.C.593; 9 L.T.93; 27 J.P. 820; 9 Jur. N.S.1135; 12 W.R.178; 11 E.R. 1155 ....16, 42, 175, 178, 180, 187, 188, 190
Maldon Corpn. v. Laurie (1933), 97 J.P. Jo. 132; 175 L.T.Jo. 320; 61
Mannal v. Fisher (1859), 5 C.B.N.S.856; 23 J.P.375; 5 Jur. N.S.389; 141 E.R.343 188
Manning v. Wasdale (1836), 5 Ad. & El.758; 44 R.R.576 ....23, 104, 105, 111
Manser v. Northern & Eastern Counties Ry. Co.(1841) 2 Rail. Cas. 380 148
Mansford v. Ross & Glendenning (1886), 5 N.Z.R.C.A.33 7
Manug Bya v. Manug Kyi Lya (1925), L.R.52 Ind.App.385 117
Margate L.B. v. Margate Harbour Co. (1869), 33 J.P.437 54
Marine Industrial Transmissions v. Southern Water Authority (1989) 29 R.V.R.221 393
Marriage v. East Norfolk Rivers Catchment Board, [1950] 1 K.B.284; 66 T.L.R.225; 114 J.P.38; 94 S.J.32; [1949] 2 All E.R.1021; 113 J.P.362 ....392, 393
Marsden & Sons Ltd. v. Old Silkstone Collieries Ltd. (1914) 78 J.P. Jo.220; 13 L.G.R.342 98
Marshall v. Richardson (1889) 60 L.T.605 440
Marshall v. Southampton Area Health Authority [1986] Q.B.401; 2 W.L.R.780; I.C.R.335; (1986) 130 S.J. 340; [1986] 2 All E.R.584; I.C.M.L.R.688; 2 E.C.R.723; I.R.L.R.140; (1986) 83 L.S.Gaz.1720 357
Marshall v. Ulleswater Steam Navigation Co. (1863), 3 B. & S.732; 1 New Rep.519; 32 L.J.Q.B.139; 8 L.T.416; 27 J.P.516; 9 Jur. N.S.988; 11 W.R.489;122 E.R.274 ....21, 23, 191, 194
Marshall v Ulleswater Steam Navigation Co. (1871), L.R. 7 Q.B. 166; 41 L.J.Q.B.413 150
Mason v. Hill (1833), 5 B. & Ad.1; 2 Nev. & M.K.B.747; 2 L.J.K.B. 118 ....13, 70, 81, 89, 113
Mason v. Shrewsbury & Hereford Rly.Co.(1871), L.R.6 Q.B.578; 40 L.J.Q.B.293; 25 L.T.239; 36 J.P.324; 20 W.R.14 ....85, 106, 114, 117
Massereene & Ferrard v. Murphy (1931), N.I.192 ....78, 79
Matthews v. Peache (1855), 5 E. & B.546; 20 J.P.244; 4 W.R.22; 119 E.R.583 ..164
Maw v. Holloway, [1914] 3 K.B.594; 84 L.J.K.B.99; 111 L.T.670; 78 J.P.347 ....424, 438
Maxey Drainage Board v. Great Northern Rly. (1912), 106 L.T.429; 76 J.P.236; 10 L.G.R.248 83
Maxwell Willshire v. Bromley R.D.C. (1917), 87 L.J. Ch.241; 82 J.P.12; 16 L.G.R.414 ....5, 8
Mayfield v. Robinson (1845), 7 Q.B.486 163
Mecca, The [1895] P.95; 64 L.J.P.40; 71 L.T. 711; 43 W.R.209; 11 T.L.R.139; 39 Sol.Jo.132; 7 Asp M.L.C.529, C.A. 41

Page

Medway Co. v. Romney (Earl) (1861), 9 C.B.N.S.575; 30 L.J.C.P.236; 4 L.T.87; 25 J.P.550; 7 Jur.N.S.846; 9 W.R.482; 142 E.R.226 ..... 14, 70, 74, 155
Mellor v. Walmesley [1905] 2 Ch.164; 74 L.J.Ch.475; 93 L.T. 574; 53 W.R.581; 21 T.L.R.591; 49 Sol.Jo.565 ..... 41, 48, 49
Menzies v. Breadalbane (1828), 3 Bli. N.S.414; 4 E.R. 1387; 32 R.R.103 ..... 11, 82
Menzies v. Breadalbane (Marquis) (1901), 4F. (Ct. of Sess.) 55 19
Menzies v. Macdonald (1856), 2 Macq.463; 2 Jur.N.S.575; 4 W.R.625 22
Mercer v. Denne [1904] 2 Ch.538; 74 L.J.Ch.723; 93 L.T.412; 70 J.P.65; 54 W.R.303; 21 T.L.R.760; 3 L.G.R 1293 ..... 43, 47, 49, 51, 179
Merricks v. Cadwallader (1881), 51L.J.M.C.20; 46 L.T.29; 46 J.P.216 426
Mersey Docks v. Gibbs (1864), L.R. 1 H.L.93; 35 L.J. Ex.225; 14 L.T.677 157
Metropolitan Board of Works v. McCarthy (1874), L.R. 7 H.L. 243; 23 L.J.C.P.385 151
Michell v. Brown (1858), 1 E. & E.267; 28 L.J.M.C.53; 23 L.T.O.S.146; 23 J.P.548; 5 Jur.N.S.707; 7 W.R.80; 120 E.R.909 149
Micklethwait v. Newlay Bridge Co, (1886), 33 Ch.D.133; 55 L.T.336; 51 J.P.132; 2 T.L.R.844 18
Micklethwait v. Vincent (1892), 67 L.T.225; 8 T.L.R.685; 23, 134, 181
Miles v. Rose (1814), 5 Taunt 705; 1 Marsh 313 15
Miller v. Little (1878), 2 L.R. Ir.304; 4 L.R.Ir.302 ..... 11, 20, 193
Millington v. Griffiths (1874), 30 L.T.65 109
Mills v. Avon and Dorset River Board [1955] Ch.341; 2 W.L.R.413; 119 J.P.199; 99 S.J.130; 1 All E.R.382 439
Mills v. Colchester Corpn. (1868), L.R.3 C.P. 575; 37 L.J.C.P. 278; 16 W.R. 987 187
Miner v. Gilmour (1859), 12 Moo. P.C.131; 33 L.T.O.S.98 ..... 66, 72, 73
Molkerei-Zentrale Westfalen/Lippe GmbH. v. Hauptzollant, 28/67 [1968] E.C.R.143; C M.L.R.187; 6 C.M.L. Rev.132, European Ct. 357
Monckton v. Wolverhampton Corpn. *The Times*, Nov.26 1960 98
Monmouth Canal & Rly. Co. v. Hill (1859), 28 L.J.Ex.283; 4 H. & N.421; 23 J.P.679 ..... 12, 138
Moorcock, The (1889), 14 P.D.64; 58 L.J.P.73; 60 L.T. 654; 37 W.R.439; 5 T.L.R.316 153
Moore v. Webb (1857), 1 C.B.N.S.673; 28 L.T.O.S.270; 140 E.R.277 109
Moorman v. Tordoff (1908), 98 L.T.416; 6 L.G.R.360; 72 J.P.142 52
Morland v. Cook (1868), L.R. 6 Eq.252; 37 L.J.Ch.825; 18 L.T.496; 16 W.R.777 63
Morgan v. Last (1886), 2 T.L.R.262 81
Moses v. Iggo, [1906] 1 K.B.516; 75 L.J.K.B.331; 94 L.T. 548; 70 J.P.251; 50 S.J.343 426
Moses v. Midland Rly.Co. (1915), 84 L.J.K.B.2181; 113 L.T. 451; 79 J.P.367; 31 T.L.R.440 ..... 297, 298, 426
Moses v. Raywood, [1911] 2 K.B.271; 80 L.J.K.B.823; 105 L.T.76; 75 J.P.263; 22 Cox C.C.516 ..... 426, 440
Mostyn v. Atherton, [1899] 2 Ch. 360; 68 L.J.Ch.629; 81 L.T.356; 48 W.R.168 123

Page
Moulton v. Wilby (1863), 2 H. & C.25; 2 New Rep.40; 32 L.J.M.C.164; 8 L.T.284; 27 J.P.536 .... 430, 434
Mouse's Case (1608), 12 Co.Rep.63; 2 Bulst.280; 77 E.R.1341 167
Mulholland v. Killen (1874), 9 I.R.Eq.471 43
Murgatroyd v. Robinson (1857), 7 E. & B.391; 26 L.J.Q.B.233; 29 L.T.O.S.63; 3 Jur.N.S.615; 5 W.R.375; 119 E.R.1292 108
Murphy v. Brentwood D.C. [1990] 3 W.L.R.414; 2 All E.R.908; (1990) 22 H.L.R.502; 134 S.J.1076; 21 Con. L.R.I.; (1991) 89 L.G.R.24; (1990)6 Const.L.J.304; 154 L.G. Rev.1010; 50 Build.L.R.I.; (1991) 3 Admin.L.R.37, H.L. 75–6, 249
Murphy v. Ryan (1868), I.R. 2 C.L.143 .... 16, 132, 182
Mussett v. Burch (1876), 35 L.T.486; 41 J.P.72 .... 182, 194

N

Nanaimo Rly Co. v. Treat (1919) 121 L.T.657 (Canada) 42
National Guaranteed Manure Co. v. Donald (1859), 4 H. & N.8; 28 L.J. Ex.185; 7 W.R.185; 157 E.R.737 .... 101, 112
National Rivers Authority v. Appletise Bottling Co.Ltd., (1991) *Water Guardians* April 1991 300
National Rivers Authority v. Newcastle and Gateshead Water Co., (1990) *The Times* 23 November 1990 270
National Rivers Authority v. Shell UK Ltd. [1990] 1 *Water Law* 40 297
Nature Conservancy Council v. Southern Water Authority (1991) *The Times* 17 June 1991 D.C. 213, 391
Nedeport (Prior) v. Weston (1443), Y.B. 22 Hen.VI fo.14, pl.23; 2 Roll Abr.140, pl.4 165
Neill v. Devonshire (Duke) (1882), 8 A.C.135; 31 W.R.622 ....176, 188, 189
Neptun, The [1938] P.21; 107 L.J.P.49; 54 T.L.R.195 158
Nesbitt v. Mablethorpe U.D.C. [1917] 2 K.B.568; 86 L.J.K.B. 1401; 81 J.P.289; 117 L.T.365; 15 L.G.R.647 48
New Moss Colliery Co. v. Manchester Corpn. [1908] A.C.117; 77 L.J.Ch.392; 98 L.T.467; 72 J.P.169; 6 L.G.R.809; 24 T.L.R.386 126
New River Co. v. Johnston (1860), 2 E. & E.435; 29 L.J.M.C. 93; 1 L.T.295; 24 J.P.244; 6 Jur.N.S.374; W.R.179; 121 E.R.164 123
New Windsor Corpn. v. Stovell (1884), 27 Ch.D.665; 54 L.J. 113; 51 L.T.626; 33 W.R.223 102
Newcastle (Duke) v. Clark (1818), 2 Moo. Rep.666; 20 R.R. 583; 8 Taunt 627 12
Newton v. Cubitt (1862), 12 C.B.N.S.32; 1 New Rep.400; 31 L.J.C.P.246; 6 L.T.860; 142 E.R.1053 .... 162, 168
Nicholls v. Ely Beet Sugar Factory Ltd. [1931] 2 Ch. 84; 100 L.J.Ch. 259; 145 L.T. 113 .... 186, 196
Nicholls v. Ely Beet Sugar Factory Ltd, [1936] Ch.343; 105 L.J.Ch.279; 154 L.T.531; 80 S.J.127 94
Nichols v. Marsland (1875), L.R.10 Ex.255; 44 L.J.Ex.134; 33 L.T.265; 23 W.R.693 86
Nield v. London & N.W.Ry.Co. (1874), L.R.10 Ex.4; 44 L.J.Ex. 15; 23 W.R.60 ....83, 86

Page

Nitro–Phosphate Co. v. London Docks Co (1878), 9 Ch.D.503; 39 L.T.433; 27 W.R.267 64
Nixon v. Tynemouth Union (1888), 52 J.P.504 94
Norbury (Lord) v. Kitchin (1863), 1 New Rep.241; 7 L.T.685; 9 Jur. N.S.132 74
Norbury (Earl) v. Kitchin (1866), 15 L.T.501 ....72, 79
Normile v. Ruddle (1912), 41 I.L.T.179 81
North Level Comrs. v. River Welland Catchment Board, [1938] Ch.379; [1937] 4 All E.R.684; 107 L.J.Ch.178; 158 L.T.107; 102 J.P.82; 54 T.L.R.263; 82 S.J.76; 36 L.G.R.77 .... 64, 397
North Sea Continental Shelf Cases (1969) I.C.J. Rep p3 37
North Shore Ry. Co. v. Pion (1889), 14 A.C.612; 59 L.J.P.C. 25; 61 L.T.525 .... 68, 150
North Staffordshire Ry. Co. v. Hanley Corpn. (1909), 73 J.P. 477; 26 T.L.R.20; 8 L.G.R.375 148
North & South Shields Ferry Co. v. Barker (1848), 2 Ex.136; 154 E.R. 437 .... 167, 169
Northam v. Hurley (1853), 1 E. & B.665; 22 L.J.Q.B.183; 17 Jur.672; 118 E.R.586 102
Northumberland (Duke) v. Houghton (1870), L.R. 5 Ex.127; 39 L.J. Ex.66; 22 L.T.491; 18 W.R.495 189
Nuttall v. Bracewell (1866), 2 L.R.2 Ex.1; 4 H. & C.714; 30 L.J. Ex.1; 15 L.T.313; 31 J.P.8; 12 Jur. N.S.989 ....66, 70, 80, 101, 117

O

Oakes v. Mersey River Board (1957), 9 P. & C.R.145; J.P.L.824 .... 13, 379, 393
Octavia Stella, The (1887), 6 Asp.M.L.C.182; 57 L.T.632 140
Oldaker v. Hunt (1855), 6 De G.M. & G.376; 19 J.P.179; 3 Eq. Rep.671; 25 L.T.O.S.26; 1 Jur.N.S.785; 3 W.R.297 ....92, 94
Olding v. Wild (1866), 14 L.T.402; 30 J.P.295 428
Onions v. Clarke (1917) 86 L.J.K.B.740; 116 L.T.335; 81 J.P.77 D.C. 434
Ormerod v. Todmorden Joint Stock Mill (1883), 11 Q.B.D. 155; 52 L.J.Q.B.445; 47 J.P.532; 31 W.R.759 ....69, 92, 94, 120
Original Hartlepool Collieries Co. v. Gibb (1877), 5 Ch.D.713; 46 L.J.Ch.311; 36 L.T.433; 41 J.P.660; 3 Asp.M.L.C.411 ....132, 140, 151
Orr Ewing v. Colquhoun (1877), 2 A.C. 839 H.L. 43, 79, 80, 132, 134, 142, 152, 155
Owen v. Davies, [1874] W.N.175 74
Owen v. Faversham Corpn. (1908), 73 J.P.33 109

P

Padwick v. Knight (1852), 7 Ex.854; 22 L.J. Ex.198; 19 L.T.O.S. 206; 16 J.P.Jo.437; 155 E.R.1196 54
Paley v. Birch (1867) 8 B. & S.336 452
Palme v. Persse (1877), 11 I.R. Eq.616 80

Page
Palmer v. Rouse (1858), 3 H. & N. 505; 22 J.P.773; 157 E.R. 1019 ....55, 57
Palmis v. Hebblethwaite (1688), 2 Show. 249; Skin 64; 89 E.R. 921 107
Parker v. Bournemouth Corpn. (1902), 86 L.T.449; 66 J.P. 440; 18 T.L.R.372 52
Parker v. Lord Advocate, [1904] A.C.364; 20 T.L.R.547,H.L. 58
Parnaby v. Lancaster Canal Co. (1839), 11 A. & E.223 157
Parrett Navigation Co. v. Robins (1842), 10M. & W.593 .... 81, 156
Parteriche v. Mason (1774), 2 Chit.658 191
Payne v. Ecclesiastical Comrs. & Landon (1913), 30 T.L.R. 167 184
Payne v. Partridge (1690), 1 Salk.12; 1 Show.255; 91 E.R.12 .... 165, 166
Pearce v. Bunting, [1896] 2 Q.B.360; 65 L.J.M.C.131; 60 J.P.695;
12 T.L.R.476; 40 S.J.601 .... 11, 20, 193
Pearce v. Croydon R.D.C. (1910), 74 J.P.429; 8 L.G.R. 909 5
Pearce v. Scotcher (1882), 9 Q.B.D. 162; 46 L.T.342; 46 J.P.248 .... 182, 194
Pelly v. Woodbridge U.D.C. (1950), 114 J.P. Jo.666 166
Pemberton v. Bright, [1960] 1 All E.R.792 76
Pennington v. Brinksop Hall Coal Co. (1877), 5 Ch.D.769; 46 L.J. Ch.773;
37 L.T.149; 25 W.R.874; 57 L.T.522 ....95, 96
Percival v. Nanson (1851), 7 Ex.1; 21 L.J.Ex.1; 155 E.R.830 188
Percival v. Stanton, [1954] 1 W.L.R.300; 118 J.P.171; 98 S.J.114;
[1954] 1 All E.R.392 428
Pery v. Thornton (1889), 23 L.R. Ir.402 .... 180, 194
Peter v. Daniel (1848), 5 C.B.568; 17 L.J.C.P.117; 12 Jur.604; 136 E.R.1001 112
Peter v. Kendal (1827), 6 B. & C.703; 5 L.J.O.S.K.B.282;
108 E.R.610 ....162, 163, 166, 169
Phillimore v. Watford R.D.C. [1913] 2 Ch.434; 82 L.J.Ch.514;
109 L.T.616; 77 J.P.453; 57 S.J.741; 11 L.G.R.980 ....8, 111
Philpot v. Bath (1905), 21 T.L.R.634; 49 S.J.618 ....46, 62
Pierce v. Lord Fauconberg (1757), 1 Burr.292 137
Pike v. Rossiter (1877), 37 L.T.635; 42 J.P.231 430
Pim v. Currell (1840), 6 M. & W.234; 151 E.R.395 163
Pirie & Sons Ltd. v. Kintore (Earl), [1906] A.C.478; 75 L.J.C.P.96 .... 77, 196, 428
Pitts v. Kingsbridge Highway Board (1871), 25 L.T.195; 19 W.R.884 54
Polden v. Bastard (1865), L.R. 1 Q.B.156; 7 B. & S. 130; 35 L.J.Q.B.92;
13 L.T.441; 30 J.P.73; 14 W.R.198 111
Pollock v. Moses (1894), 63 L.J.M.C. 116; 70 L.T.378; 58 J.P.527;
17 Cox.C.C.737 445
Pomfret v. Ricroft (1669), 1 Wms.Saund.321; 2 Keb.543,569; 1 Sid. 429;
1 Vent 26,44; 85 E.R.454 112
Popplewell v. Hodkinson (1869), L.R. 4 Ex.248; 38 L.J.Ex. 126; 17 W.R.806 126
Port of London Authority v. Canvey Island Comrs. [1932] 1 Ch.446;
101 L.J.Ch.63; 146 L.T.195; 96 J.P.28; 30 L.G.R.42 151
Portsmouth Waterworks Co. v. London, Brighton & S.C.Ry. (1909),
26 T.L.R.173; 74 J.P.61 69
Post Office v. Estuary Radio Ltd. [1968] 2 Q.B. 740; [1967] 5 All E.R.663 C.A. .28
Powell v. Butler (1871), I.R. 5 C.L.309 111
Prescott v. Hutin (1966) 110 S.J.905; [1967] Crim.L.R.55,D.C. 424
Preston Corpn. v. Fullwood L.B. (1885), 53 L.T.718; 50 J.P.228;
34 W.R.169; 2 T.L.R.134 101

Page
Price v. Bradley (1885), 16 Q.B.D.148; 53 L.T.16; 50 J.P.150; 34 W.R.165 435
Price v. Cromack [1975] 1 W.L.R.988; 119 S.J.458;
[1975] 2 All E.R.113, D.C. 298, 426
Pride of Derby Angling Assocn. Ltd. v. British Celanese Ltd. [1953] Ch.149;
117 J.P.52; 97 S.J.28; [1953] 1 All E.R. 179; 51 L.G.R.121;
16 M.L.R.241 ....89, 90, 93, 96, 97
Priestley v. Manchester & Leeds Ry. Co. (1840), 4 Y. & Coll. 63;
2 Rail.Cas.134 148
Proctor v. Avon & Dorset River Board, [1953] C.P.L.562;
162 E.G.162 ....392, 393, 425
Provinder Millers (Winchester) Ltd, v. Southampton County Council,
[1939] 4 All E.R.157; Ch.356; 161 L.T.363; 103 J.P.401;
56 T.L.R.74; 83 S.J.870 83
Putbus, The [1969] P.136; [1969] 2 W.L.R.1241; 113 S.J.223;
[1969] 1 Lloyd's Rep.253; [1969] 2 All E.R.676, C.A 31
Pyer v. Carter (1857), 1 H. & N. 916; 26 L.J.Ex.258; 28 L.T.O.S.371;
21 J.P.247; 5 W.R.371; 156 E.R.1472 103
Pyle v. Welsh Water Authority (1986)
unreported Carmarthen Crown Court 17 March 1986 425

Q

Queens of the River S.S.Co. v. Eastern Gibb & Co. and the Thames Conservators
(1907), 96 L.T.901; 23 T.L.R.478; 12 Com. Cas. 278 157

R

R. v Aire & Calder Navigation Co. (1829), 9 B. & C.820; 4 Man. & Ry. K.B.728;
8 L.J.O.S.M.C.9; 109 E.R.305 154
R. v. Alfresford (1786), 1 Term Rep.358 190
R. v. Antrim Justices, [1906] 2 I.R.298 .... 295, 427
R. v. Baker (1867), L.R. 2 Q.B.621; 36 L.J.Q.B. 242; 31 J.P.692;
15 W.R.1144 63
R. v. Bell (1822), 1 L.J.O.S.K.B.42 142
R. v. Betts (1850), 16 Q.B. 1022; 19 L.J.Q.B.531; 15 L.T.O.S. 182;
4 Cox C.C.211; 14 J.P. Jo.318; 117 E.R.1172; 43, 139, 142, 148
R. v. Bradford Navigation Co. (1865), 6 B. & S.631; 29 J.P.613; 34 L.J.Q.B.191;
11 Jur. N.S.766; 13 W.R.892 99
R. v. Brecon (Inhabitants), Re Glastonbury Bridge (1850), 15 Q.B.813;
19 L.J.M.C.203; 15 L.T.O.S.432; 14 J.P.655; 15 Jur. 351 18
R. v. Bristol Dock Co. (1810), 12 East 429 94
R. v. Bristol Dock Co. (1839), 1 Ry. & Can.Cas.548 141
R. v. Bucks Inhabitants (1810) 12 East. 192 172
R. v. Burrow (1869), 34 J.P.53 194
R. v. Cambrian Ry. Co. (1871), L.R. 6 Q.B.422; 40 L.J.Q.B. 169;
25 L.T.84; 36 J.P.4; 19 W.R. 1138 168
R. v. Clark (1702), 12 Mod. Rep. 615; 88 E.R.1558 .... 141, 147

Page

R. v. Cramp (1880) 5 Q.B.D.307 296
R. v. Dacorum Magistrates Court, *ex parte* Michael Gardiner Ltd. (1985) 149 J.P.677; [1985] Crim. L.R.394, 520 D.C. 336
R. v. Darlington L.B. (1865), 6 B. & S. 562; 6 New Rep.178; 35 L.J.Q.B.45; 29 J.P.419; 13 W.R.789; 122 E.R.1303 393
R. v. Delamere (1865), 13 W.R. 757 156
R. v. Devon Inhabitants (1825) 4 B.& C.670 172
R. v. Downing (1870), 23 L.T.398; 35 J.P.196; 11 Cox C.C.580 .... 179, 189
R. v. Essex Sewers Comrs. (1823), 1 B. & C.477; 25 R.R. 467; 2 Dow & Ry. K.B.700; 1 L.J.O.S.K.B.169; 107 E.R.177 63
R. v. Forty–Nine Casks of Brandy (1836), 3 Hag. Adm.257; 166 E.R.401 ....26, 57
R. v. Garner [1986] 1 W.L.R.73; 1 All E.R.78; (1985) 82 Cr.App.R.27; 7 Cr.App.R.(S)285; [1986] Crim. L.R.66, C.A. 297
R. v. Grosvenor (1819), 2 Stark, 511 .... 43, 142
R. v. Henley [1892] 1 Q.B. 504; 61 L.J.M.C.136; 66 L.T. 675; 56 J.P.391; 40 W.R.383; 36 S.J.233; 17 Cox C.C.518 448
R. v. Hornsea (1854), 2 C.L.R.596; 23 L.J.M.C.59; 6 Cox C.C.279 65
R. v. Howlett [1968] 112 S.J.150 179
R. v. Huggins [1895] 1 Q.B.563; 64 L.J.M.C.149; 72 L.T.193; 59 J.P.104; 43 W.R.329; 11 T.L.R.205; 39 S.J.234 448
R. v. Hundsdon (1781), 2 East P.C.611; O.B.S.P. 1781, Case 196 451
R. v. Kent Justices, *Ex parte* Lye, [1967] 2 Q.B.153; [1967] 1 All E.R.560 28
R. v. Keyn (1876), 2 Ex. D.63; 46 L.J.M.C.17 .... 29, 30, 40
R. v. Landulph (Inhabitants) (1834), 1 Mod. & R.393, N.P. 18, 65
R. v. Leigh (1839), 10 Ad. & El.398; 2 Per. & Dav.357; 113 E.R.152 63
R. v. Liverpool J.J. *Ex parte* Molyneux [1972] 2 Q.B.384; 2 W.L.R.1033; 116 S.J. 238; 2 All E.R.471; 1 Lloyd's Rep. 367; Crim. L.R.706 D.C. 41
R. v. Lordsmere (Inhabitants) (1886), 54 L.T.766; 51 J.P. 86; 2 T.L.R.623; 16 Cox C.C.65 65
R. v. Mallison (1902), 86 L.T.600; 66 J.P.503; 20 Cox C.C. 204 451
R. v. Medley (1834), 6 C. & P. 292 ....94, 99
R. v. Minister of Agriculture, Fisheries and Food, *ex parte* Graham (1988) *The Times* 16 April 1988 439
R. v. Minister of Agriculture, Fisheries and Food, *ex parte* Wear Valley District Council (1988) *Local Government Review* p.849 439
R. v. Montague (1825), 4 B. & C.598; 6 Dow. & Ry. K.B.616; 3 Dow & Ry. M.C. 292; 4 L.J.O.S.K.B.21; 107 E.R.1183 .... 133, 139
R. v. Musson (1858), 8 E. & B.900; 27 L.J.M.C.100; 30 L.T.O.S.272; 22 J.P.609; 4 Jur N.S.100; 6 W.R.246; 120 E.R.336 52
R. v. Nicholson (1810), 12 East 330; 104 E.R.129 163
R. v. Oxfordshire (Inhabitants) (1830), 1 B. & Ad.301; 35 R.R.302; 8 L.J.O.S.K.B.354; 109 E.R.794 .... 7, 8, 128, 172
R. v. Pagham Sewers Comrs. (1828), 8 B. & C.355; 2 Man. & Ry. K.B. 468; 108 E.R.1075 ....61, 83
R. v. Paul (Inhabitants) (1840), 2 Moo. & R.307 65
R. v. Pwllheli Justices, Ex p. Soane, [1948] 2 All E.R. 815; 92 S.J.634 448
R. v. Randall (1842), Car. & M. 496 .... 43, 134, 143
R. v. Recorder and Justices for Londonderry [1930] N.I.104 433

Page

R. v. Reed (1871), 12 Cox C.C. 1 50
R. v. River Weaver Navigation Trustees (1827), 7 B. & C.70; Pratt 28; 9 Dow. & Ry. K.B.788; 5 L.J.O.S.M.C.102; 108 E.R.651 154
R. v. Russell (1827), 6 B. & C.566; 9 Dow. & Ry. K.B.566; 5 L.J.O.S.M.C.80; 108 E.R.560 ....43, 140, 142, 143
R. v. Ryan (1845), 8 I.L.R.119 148
R. v. St. Mary Pembroke (1851), 15 J.P. Jo.336 162
R. v. Severn & Wye Rly. (1819), 2 B. & Ald.648 137
R. v. Shepard (1822), 1 L.J.O.S.K.B.45 142
R. v. Smith (1780), 2 Doug K.B.441; 99 E.R.283 16
R. v. South West Water Authority *ex parte* Cox (1981) *The Times* 2 January 1981 439
R. v. Southern Canada Power Co. [1937] 3 All E.R.923; 81 S.J.785 76
R. v. Steer (1704), 6 Mod.Rep.183; 3 Salk.189,291 .... 196, 451
R. v. Stephens (1866), L.R. 1 Q.B.702; 7 B. & S.710; 35 L.J.Q.B.251; 14 L.T.593; 30 J.P.822; 12 Jur.N.S.961; 14 W.R.859 149
R. v. Stimpson (1863), 4 B. & S 301; 2 New Rep.422; 10 Jur. N.S.41 .... 181, 452
R. v. Strand Board of Works (1864), 4 B. & S.526; 33 L.J.Q.B.299; 11 L.T.183; 28 J.P.532; 12 W.R.828 18
R. v. Tindall (1837), 6 Ad. & El.143; 1 Nev. & P.K.B.719; 6 L.J.M.C.97; 1 J.P.139; 112 E.R.55 .... 142, 143
R. v. Tippett (1819), 3 B. & Ald.193; 106 E.R.632 139
R. v. Trinity House (1662), 1 Sid.86; 1 Keb.331; 82 E.R.986 ....16, 19
R. v. Two Casks of Tallow (1837), 3 Hagg.Adm.294; 6 L.T.558 57
R. v. Ward (1836), 4 Ad. & El.384; 1 Har. & W.703; 5 L.J.K.B. 221; 111 E.R. 832 143
R. v. Watts (1798), 2 Esp. 675; 170 E.R.493 .... 140, 147
R. v. Wharton (1701), Holt K.B.499; 12 Mod.Rep.510; 90 E.R. 1175 17
R. v. Williams (1991) *The Times* 4 July 1991 446
Race v. Ward (1855), 4 E. & B.702; 3 C.L.R.744; 24 L.J.Q.B.153; 24 L.T.O.S.270; 19 J.P.563; 1 Jur. N.S.704; 3 W.R.240; 119 E.R.259 ....104, 105, 110, 111, 125
Rade v. K. & E. Sand and Gravel (Sarina) (1969) 10 D.L.R. (3rd) 218, Ontario High Court 126
Rameshur Pershad Narain Singh v. Koonj Behari Pattuk (1878), 4 A.C.121, P.C. 115–16, 117
Ramsgate Corpn. v. Debling (1906), 70 J.P.132; 22 T.L.R.369; 4 L.G.R.495 50
Rankin v. De Coster [1975] 1 W.L.R.606; 119 S.J.285; 2 All E.R. 303; 2 Lloyd's Rep.84; Crim. L.R.226, D.C. 347
Rawson v. Peters, *The Times*, 2 November 1972 C.A. 140, 196
Rawstorne v. Backhouse (1867), L.R.3 C.P.67; 37 L.J.C.P.26; 17 L.T.441; 32 J.P.151; 16 W.R.249 180
Rawstron v. Taylor (1855), 11 Ex. 369; 25 L.J. Ex. 33; 156 E.R. 873 ....9, 71, 85, 102, 110, 128
Read v. J. Lyons and Co. Ltd. [1947] A.C.156; [1947] L.J.R.39; 175 L.T.413; 62 T.L.R. 646; [1946] 2 All E.R.471 87
Reece v. Miller (1882), 8 Q.B.D. 626; 51 L.J.M.C.64; 47 J.P.37 ....15, 25, 132, 181, 182

Page

Reeve v. Digby (1638), Cro. Car. 495; 79 E.R.1027 195

Regents Canal and Dock Co. v. London County Council (1909) 73 J.P.276; 7 L.G.R.580, C.A. 173

Rhodes v. Airedale Drainage Comrs. (1876), 1 C.P.D.402; 45 L.J.Q.B. 861; 35 L.T.46; 24 W.R.1053 392

Rhymney Ry. Co. v. Glamorganshire Canal Co. (1904), 91 L.T. 113; 20 T.L.R.593 148

Rich v. Kneeland (1613), Cro.Jac.330; Hob 17 167

Rickards v. Lothian, [1913] A.C.263; 82 L.J.C.P.42; 108 L.T. 225; 29 T.L.R.281; 57 S.J.281 ....86, 87

Ridge v. Midland Ry. (1888), 53 J.P.55 82

Rippingale Farms Ltd. v. Black Sluice I.D.B. [1963] 1 W.L.R. 1347; 3 All E.R.726; 128 J.P.65; 107 S.J.829; 62 L.G.R.40, C.A. 393

Roberts v. Charing Cross Ry. (1903), 87 L.T.732; 19 T.L.R. 160 393

Roberts v. Fellowes (1906), 94 L.T.279 ....63, 110, 112, 128

Roberts v. Gwyrfai Rural District Council, [1899] 2 Ch.608; 68 L.J. Ch.757; 81 L.T. 465; 64 J.P.52; 48 W.R.51; 16 T.L.R. 2; 44 S.J.10. ....74, 77

Roberts v. Richards (1881), 50 L.J. Ch. 297; 44 L.T.271 .... 115, 117

Roberts v. Rose (1865), 2 B. & C.910; L.R. 1 Ex.82; 4 H. & C.103; 35 L.J. Ex. 62; 13 L.T.471 80

Robinson v. Byron (Lord) (1785), 1 Bro. C.C.588; 28 E.R.1315 ....71, 81

Robson v. Northumberland & Tyneside River Board (1952), 3 P. & C.R.150 392

Robson v. Robinson (1783), 3 Doug. K.B.306 428

Rochdale Canal Co. v. Radcliffe (1852), 18 Q.B. 287; 21 L.J.Q.B. 297; 18 L.T.O.S.163; 16 Jur.1111; 118 E.R.108 101

Rochford R.D.C. v. Port of London Authority, [1914] 2 K.B. 916; 78 J.P. 329; 83 L.J.K.B.1066; 111 L.T.207; 12 L.G.R.979 297

Rogers v. Allen (1808), 1 Camp.309 ....183, 186, 188

Rolle v. Whyte (1868), L.R. 3 Q.B. 286; 7 B. & S.116; 37 L.J.Q.B. 105; 17 L.T.560; 32 J.P.645; 16 W.R.593 ....103, 147, 148, 195, 428

Rose v. Groves (1843), 1 Dow. & L.61; 5 Man. & G.613; 6 Scott N.R.645; 12 L.J.C.P.251; 1 L.T.O.S.146; 7 Jur.951; 134 E.R.705 ....141, 149, 150

Rose v. Miles (1815), 4 M. & S. 101; 5 Taunt.705 ....99, 133, 141

Rossiter v. Pike (1878), 4 Q.B.D.24; 48 L.J.M.C.81; 39 L.T.496; 43 J.P. 157 430

Rouse v. Gravelworks Ltd. [1940] 1 K.B.489; [1940] 1 All E.R.26; 109 L.J.K.B.408; 162 L.T.230; 56 T.L.R.225; 84 S.J.112 84

Royal v. Yaxley (1872), 36 J.P.680; 20 W.R.903 169

Royal Borough of Windsor and Maidenhead v. Worton (1986) 2 P.A.D.502 152

Royal Fishery of Banne Case (1619), Dav. Ir.55 .... 58, 181

Royal Mail Steam Packet Co. v. George & Branday, [1900] A.C.480; 69 L.J.C.P.107; 82 L.T.539 114

Rugby Joint Water Board v. Walters, [1967] Ch. 397; [1966] 3 All E.R.497; 3 W.L.R. 934; 131 J.P.10; 110 S.J.635 75

Ruther v. Harris (1876) 1 Ex.D.97; 33 L.T.825; 40 J.P.454 434

Rylands v. Fletcher (1868), L.R. 3 H.L. 330; L.R. 1 Ex.265; 37 L.J. Ex.161; 19 L.T.220; 33 J.P.70 ....86, 90, 129, 289

Page

S

St. Helen's Smelting Co. v. Tipping (1865), 11 H.L. Cas.642; 29 J.P.579; 35 L.J.Q.B. 66; 12 L.T. 776; 11 Jur N.S.785; 13 W.R. 1038 95
Salt Union Ltd v. Brunner, [1906] 2 K.B. 822; 76 L.J.K.B.55; 95 L.T.647; 22 T.L.R.835 126
Sampson v. Hoddinott (1857), 1 C.B.N.S. 590; 26 L.J.C.P.148; 28 L.T.O.S.304; 21 J.P.375; 3 Jur. N.S.243; 5 W.R.230; 71, 75, 100
Sandgate U.D.C. v. Kent County Council (1898), 79 L.T.425; 15 T.L.R.59 65
Sandwich (Earl) v. Great Northern Ry. (1878), 10 Ch. D.707; 49 L.J. Ch.225; 43 J.P.429; 27 W.R.616 74
Saunders v. Newman (1818), 1 B. & Ald. 258; 106, E.R.95 .... 79, 87, 106, 114
Saxby v. Manchester & Sheffield Ry. Co. (1869), L.R. 4 C.P. 198; 38 L.J.C.P.153; 19 L.T.640; 17 W.R.293 86
Scots Mines Co. v. Leadhills Mines Co. (1859), 34 L.T.O.S.34 89
Scott v. Hanson (1826), 5 L.T.O.S. Ch.67; affirmed (1829), 1 Russ. & M. 128 L.C. 104
Scott–Whitehead v. National Coal Board (1987) 53 P. & C.R.263; [1981] 2 E.G.L.R.227 .... 74, 75, 93, 108, 249, 269
Scratton v. Brown (1825), 4 B. & C.485; 6 Dow. & Ry. 536 .... 20, 41, 46, 48, 49, 185
Scutt & Screeton v. Lower Ouse Internal Drainage Board (1953), 4 P. & C.R.71 393
Sea Fishery Restrictions, Re. EC Commission v. Ireland, [1978] 2 C.M.L.R.466, E.C.J. 35
Secretary of State for India v. Chelikani Rama Rao (1916), L.R.43 Ind. App.192; 85 L.J.P.C.222; 32 T.L.R.652 .... 31, 47
Secretary of State for India v. Foucar (1933), 50 T.L.R.241; 61 L.R. Ind. App.18 P.C. 48
Secretary of State for India v. Vizlinagaram (1921), L.R.49 Ind. App. 67 47
Sephton v. Lancashire River Board, [1962] 1 All E.R.183 60
Severn–Trent River Authority v. Express Foods Group Ltd. [1989] Crim. L.R.226 297
Seymour v. Courtenay (1771), 5 Burr 2814; 98 E.R.478 .... 175, 183
Sharp v. Waterhouse (1857), 7 E. & B.816; 27 L.J.Q.B.70; 3 Jur. N.S.1022 116
Sharp v. Wilson, Rotheray & Co. (1905), 93 L.T.155; 21 T.L.R.679 71
Sharpness New Docks and Gloucester and Birmingham Navigation Co. v. A.–G. [1915] A.C.654; [1914–15] All E.R.355; 84 L.J.K.B.907; 112 L.T.826; 79 J.P.305; 31 T.L.R. 254; 59 Sol. Jo.381; 13 L.G.R.563, H.L. 173
Sheffield City Council v. Yorkshire Water Services [1991] 1 W.L.R.58; 2 All E.R. 280; [1990] R.V.R.254; (1991) 89 L.G.R.326 (1990) *The Times* 5 June 1990 200
Short v. Bastard (1881) 46 J.P.580 440
Shuttleworth v. Le Fleming (1865), 19 C.B.N.S. 687; 34 L.J.C.P.309; 11 Jur. N.S.841 .... 187, 195

Page

Sim E. Bak v. Ang Yong Huat, [1923] A.C.429; 92 L.J.C.P. 136; 129 L.T.72 .... 15, 133
Simpson v. A.-G. [1904] A.C.476; 74 L.J. Ch.1; 91 L.T.610; 69 J.P.85; 20 T.L.R. 761; 3 L.G.R.190 ....133, 155, 156, 163, 166
Simpson v. Godmanchester Corpn. [1897] A.C.696; 66 L.J. Ch. 770; 77 L.T.409; 13 T.L.R.544 .... 83, 101
Smeaton v. Ilford Corpn. [1954] Ch.450; [1954] 2 W.L.R.668; 118 J.P.290; 98 S.J.251; [1954] 1 All E.R.923; 52 L.G.R.253 87
Smith v. Andrews, [1891] 2 Ch. 678; 65 L.T.175 ....17, 87, 134, 182, 188, 452
Smith v. Archibald (1880), 5 A.C.489 ....23, 111, 125
Smith v. Cawdle Fen Comrs. [1938] 4 All E.R. 64; 160 L.T. 61; 82 S.J.890; 37 L.G.R.22 .... 60, 392
Smith v. Cooke (1914), 84 L.J.K.B. 959; 112 L.T.864; 79 J.P.245; 24 Cox C.C.691 177
Smith v. Great Western Rly. Co. (1926), 135 L.T. 112; 42 T.L.R.391 297
Smith v. Kemp (1693), Carth 285; Holt K.B. 322; 2 Salk.637; 3 Mod.Rep.186 ..196
Smith v. Kenrick (1849), 7 C.B.515; 18 L.J.C.P. 172; 12 L.T.O.S.556; 13 Jur.362; 137 E.R.205 ....87, 88
Smith v. River Douglas Catchment Board (1949), 113 J.P. 388 ....63, 86
Snape v. Dobbs (1823), 1 Bing. 202; 8 Moore C.P.23; 1 L.J.O.S.K.B.58 194
Snark, The, [1909] P.105; 69 L.J.P.41; 82 L.T.42; 48 W.R. 279; 16 T.L.R.160; 44 S.J.209 146
Somerset (Duke) v. Fogwell (1826), 5 B. & C.875; 8 Dow. & Ry. K.B.747; 5 L.J.O.S.K.B.49 ....45, 185, 190, 191
Somerset Drainage Comrs. v. Bridgewater Corpn. (1899), 81 L.T. 729 ....6, 93, 104, 109
South Shields Water Co. v. Cookson (1845), 15 L.T.Ex.315 124
Southall-Norwood U.D.C. v. Middlesex County Council (1901), 83 L.T.742; 65 J.P.215; 49 W.R.376; 14 T.L.R.208; 45 S.J.241 297
Southcote's Case (1601), 4 Co. Rep.83b; 76 E.R.1061 167
Southern Centre of Theosophy Inc. v. State of South Australia [1982] A.C.706; 2 W.L.R. 544; (1982) 126 S.J. 80; [1982] 1 All E.R.283, P.C. 21, 42, 48, 49
Southern Water Authority v. Pegrum [1989] L.G.T.672; (1989) 153 J.P.581; [1989] Crim. L.R.442; (1989) 153 L.G.Rev.672; 153 L.G.Rev. 831 D.C. 298
Spokes v. Banbury (1865), L.R. 1 Eq.42; 30 J.P.54; 35 L.J. Ch. 105; 13 L.T.428; 11 Jur. N.S.1010; 14 W.R.128 98
Sree Eckowrie Sing v. Heeraloll Seal (1868), 12 Moo. Ind. App. 136; 20 E.R. 292 47
Staffordshire County Council v. Seisdon R.D.C. (1907), 96 L.T. 328; 71 J.P. 185; 5 L.G.R. 347 90
Staffordshire & Worcestershire Canal Co. v. Birmingham Canal Co. (1866), L.R. 1 H.L. 254; 35 L.J. Ch. 757 .... 101, 110
Staffordshire & Worcestershire Canal Navigation Co. v. Bradley, [1912] 1 Ch. 91; 81 L.J. Ch.147; 106 L.T.215; 56 S.J. 91; 75 J.P. Jo. 555 ....175, 194, 195
State of Alabama v. State of Georgia, *see* Alabama, State of v. State of Georgia

Page

Stead v. Nicholas, [1901] 2 K.B.163; 70 L.J.K.B.653; 85 L.T. 23; 65 J.P. 484; 49 W.R.522; 17 T.L.R.454; 45 S.J.467 426
Stead v. Tillotson (1900) 64 J.P. 343 .... 400, 439
Steel Stampings v. Severn Trent Water Authority (1982) 263 E.G.359 393
Stephens v. Anglian Water Authority (1987) 131 S.J.1214; [1987] 3 All E.R. 379; (1988) 55 P. & C.R.348; 86 L.G.R. 48; (1987) C. Const. L.J.321; 84 L.S.Gaz.2693,C.A. 124, 126
Stephens v. Snell (1954), *The Times*, 5 June 1954 30
Stevens v. Thames Conservators, [1958] 1 Lloyds Rep.401 .... 157, 192
Stockport Waterworks Co. v. Potter (1864), 3 H. & C.300; 4 New.Rep. 441; 10 L.T.748; 10 Jur. N.S.1005 ....68, 69, 92, 100, 120
Stollmeyer v. Trinidad Lake Petroleum Co. [1918] A.C. 485; 87 L.J.P.C.77; 118 L.T.514 .... 7, 66, 73, 128
Stoney v. Keane (1903), 37 I.L.T.212 53
Stubbs v. Hilditch (1887), 51 J.P.758 149
Suffield v. Brown (1864), 4 De G.J. & Sim.185; 3 New Rep. 340; 33 L.J.Ch.249; 9 L.T.627; 10 Jur. N.S. 111; 12 W.R.356; 46 E.R.888 103
Sutcliffe v. Booth (1863), 32 L.J.Q.B. 136; 27 J.P.613; 9 Jur. N.S. 1037 .... 91, 117, 120
Swift, The [1901] P.168; 70 L.J.P. 47; 85 L.T.346; 17 T.L.R.400; 9 Asp. M.L.C.244 .... 136, 140, 179
Swindon Waterworks Co. v. Wilts. & Berks Canal Co. (1875), L.R. 7 H.L.697; 45 L.J. Ch. 638; 33 L.T.513; 40 J.P. 804; 24 W.R. 284 .... 66, 73, 74
Symes v. Essex Rivers Catchment Board, [1937] 1 K.B.548; [1936] 3 All E.R.908; 106 L.J.K.B.279; 156 L.T. 116; 101 J.P.179; 53 T.L.R.180; 81 S.J.33; 35 L.G.R.163 .... 59, 61, 393

T

Tamur Marine Navigation Co. v. Wagstaffe (1836), 4 B. & S. 288 156
Tate & Lyle Ltd. v. Greater London Council [1983] 2 A.C. 509; 2 W.L.R. 649; 1 All E.R. 1159; 46 P. & C.R.243; (1983) 81 L.G.R.4434; [1983] 2 Lloyd's Rep.117, H.L. 79, 131, 141, 143, 144–5, 153
Taylor v. Bennett (1836), 7 C. & P. 329; 173 E.R.146 ....91, 92
Taylor v. Pritchard [1910] K.B.320 442
Taylor v. Roper, (1951) 115 J.P. 445 298
Taylor v. St. Helens Corpn. (1877), 6 Ch.D.264; 46 L.J.Ch.857; 37 L.T.253; 25 W.R. 885 .... 6, 102, 125
Temple Pier Co. v. Metropolitan Board of Works (1865) 11 Jur.N.S.337 151
Tenant v. Goldwin (1703), Salk 21 .... 121, 129
Tennent and Carroll Industries PLC v. Clancy [1988] 1 L.R.M. 214 .... 140, 196
Tetreault v. Montreal Harbour Comrs, [1926] A.C.299 151
Thakurin Ritraj Koer v. Thakurin Sarfaraz Koer (1905), 21 T.L.R. 637 20
Thames Conservators v. Kent, [1918] 2 K.B.272; 88 L.J.K.B. 537; 120 L.T.16; 83 J.P.85; 17 L.G.R.88 .... 18, 138
Thames Conservators v. Port of London Sanitary Authority, [1894] 1 Q.B. 647; 63 L.J.M.C.121; 69 L.T.803; 58 J.P.335; 10 T.L.R.160; 38 S.J.153 .... 63, 155

Page

Thames Conservators v. Smeed, Dean & Co, [1897] 2 Q.B. 334; 66 L.J.Q.B.716; 77 L.T. 325; 61 J.P.612; 45 W.R. 691; 12 T.L.R.524; 41 S.J.675 .... 11, 12, 20, 193
Thames Water Authority v. Homewood (1981) *The Times* 25 November 1981 ..437
Thameside Estates v. Greater London Council (1977) 249 E.G. 347, 448, Lands Tribunal 393
Thomas v. Birmingham Canal Co. (1879), 49 L.J.Q.B.851; 43 L.T.435; 45 J.P.21 83
Thomas v. Gower R.D.C. [1922] 2 K.B. 76; 91 L.J.K.B.666; 127 L.T. 333; 86 J.P.147; 38 T.L.R.598; 20 L.G.R.567 85
Thomas v. Jones (1864) 5 B.& S.916; 5 New Rep.121; 34 L.J.M.C.45; 11 L.T.450; 29 J.P.55; 11 Jur. N.S.306; 13 W.R.154; 122 E.R. 1071 428
Thomas v. Thomas (1835), 2 Cr. M. & R.34; 1 Gale 61; 5 Tyr.804; 4 L.J.Ex. 179; 150 E.R.15 112
Thomas & Evans Ltd. v. Mid–Rhondda Co–Operative Socy. [1940] 4 All E.R.357; 110 L.J.K.B.699; 164 L.T.303; 57 T.L.R.228; 84 S.J.682 .... 62, 84
Thompson v. Horner, [1927] N.I.191 79
Thurrock Grays, etc. Sewerage Board v. Goldsmith (1914), 79 J.P.17 112
Tighe v. Sinnott, [1897] 1 Ir, R.140 188
Tilbury v. Silva (1890), 45 Ch.D.98; 63 L.T.141 .... 17, 18, 183, 187
Tipping v. Eckersley (1855), 2 K. & J.264 91
Tisdell v. Combe (1838), 7 Ad. & El.788; 3 Nev. & P.K.B.29; 1 Will. Woll. & H.5; 7 L.J.M.C.48; 2 Jur.32; 112 E.R.667 158
Toome Eel Fishery (N.I.) v. Cardwell (1966), N.I. 1 C.A 22
Tracey Elliott v. Morley (Earl) (1907), 51 S.J.625 .... 42, 190, 192
Trafford v. The King (1832), 8 Bing.204; 34 R.R. 680 82
Trafford v. Thrower (1929), 45 T.L.R.502 .... 21, 48
Tredegar Iron & Coal Co. v. Calliope (Owners), The Calliope, [1891] A.C.11; 60 L.J.P.28; 63 L.T.781; 55 J.P. 357; 39 W.R.641 153
Trent River Board v. Wardle Ltd [1957] Crim. L.R.196; 121 J.P. Jo. 121 234
Trinidad Asphalt Co. v. Ambard, [1899] A.C.594; 68 L.J.P.C. 114; 81 L.T. 132; 48 W.R.116 126
Tripp v. Frank (1792), 4 Term Rep. 666; 100 E.R.1234 168
Trotter v. Harris (1828), 2 Y. & J.285; 148 E.R.926 163
Truro Corpn. v. Rowe, [1902] 2 K.B. 709; 71 L.J.K.B. 974;87 L.T. 386; 66 J.P. 821; 51 W.R. 68; 18 T.L.R. 820 179
Trustees of the Port and Harbour of Lerwick v. Crown Estate Commissioners [1990] S.C.L.R.484 .... 30, 43, 136
Twee Gebroeders, The (1801) 3 Ch.Rob.336; 1 Eng.Pr.Cas.323 165 E.R.485 29
Tyler v. Bennett (1836), 5 Ad. & El.377; 2 Har. & W.272; 6 Nev. & M.K.B.826; 111 E.R.1208 125

U

United Alkali Co. v. Simpson, [1894] 2 Q.B. 116; 63 L.J.M.C.141; 71 L.T.258; 58 J.P.607; 42 W.R.509; 10 T.L.R.438;38 S.J. 419; 10 R.235 149

Page

Uptopia (Owners) v. Primula (Owners), The Uptopia, [1893]A.C.492; 69 L.J.P.C.118; 76 L.T.47 146

V

Valentine v. Kennedy (1985) S.C.C.R. 88 451
Van Diemen's Land Co. v. Table Cape Marine Board [1906] A.C.92; 75 L.J.P.C.28; 93 L.T.709; 54 W.R.498; 22 T.L.R.114 44
Van Duyn, 41/74 [1974] E.C.R.1337; [1975] Ch.358; 2 W.L.R.760; (1974) 119 S.J.302; [1975] 3 All E.R.190; 1 C.M.L.R.I. European Court 357
Vance v. Frost (1894), 58 J.P.398; 10 T.L.R.186 428
Vernon v. Prior (1747), 3 Term Rep.254; 100 E.R.561 137
Vianna, The (1858), Sw.405; 166 E.R.1187 159
Vicker's Lease Re Pocock v. Vickers [1947] Ch.420; [1948] L.J.R.69; 177 L.T.637; 91 S.J.249; [1947] 1 All E.R.707 186
Ville de St. Nazaire, The (1903), 51 W.R.590 153
Vincent v. Thames Conservators (1953), 4 P. & C.R. 66 392
Vooght v. Winch (1819), 2 B. & Ald.662; 106 E.R.507 ....133, 139, 143
Voorwaats and the Khedive, The (1880), 5 A.C.876; 43 L.T. 610; 29 W.R.173; 4 Asp.M.L.C. 360 159
Vyner v. North Eastern Rly. (1898), 14 T.L.R.554 64

W

Walker v. Jackson (1843), 10 M. & W. 161; 11 L.J. Ex.346; 12 L.T. Ex.165; 152 E.R.424 167
Walton–cum–Trimley Re. Ex.p. Tomline (1873), 28 L.R.12 21 W.R.475 43
Wansford Trout Farm v. Yorkshire Water Authority, (1986) Unreported, Queen's Bench Division, 23 July 1986 234
Ward v. Cresswell (1741), Willes 265; 125 E.R.1165 ....176, 178
Ward v. Gray (1865, 6 B. & S.345; 34 L.J.M.C.146; 12 L.T. 305; 29 J.P.470; 11 Jur. N.S.738; 13 W.R.653 163
Ward v. Robins (1846), 15 M. & W. 237; 7 L.T.O.S.114; 153 E.R. 837 104
Ware v. Regent's Canal Co. (1858), 3 De G. & J.212; 28 L.J. Ch.153; 32 L.T.O.S.136; 23 J.P. 3; 5 Jur N.S.25; 7 W.R.67; 44 E.R. 1250 99
Warren v. Matthews (1703), 1 Salk 357; 6 Mod.Rep.73; 91 E.R.312 ....58, 180, 181
Waterford Conservators v. Connolly (18889), 24 I.L.T.7 ....19, 192
Watts v. Kelson (1871), 6 Ch. App. 166; 40 L.J.Ch.126; 24 L.T.209; 35 J.P.422; 10 W.R.338 ....103, 114
Watts v. Lucas (1871), L.R. 6 Q.B.226; 40 L.J.M.C.73; 24 L.T.128; 35 J.P.579; 19 W.R.470 ....428, 440
Wear River Comrs. v. Adamson (1877), 2 A.C.743; 47 L.J.Q.B. 193; 37 L.T.543; 42 J.P.244; 26 W.R.217; 3 Asp. M.L.C. 521 64
Webber v. Richards (1844), 2 L.T.O.S. 420 43
Wedderburn v. Duke of Atholl (1900) A.C.403; 16 T.L.R.413, H.L. 424
Weeks v. Heward (1862), 10 W.R.557 ....84, 85, 128

Page

Weld v. Hornby (1806), 7 East 195; 3 Smith K.B. 244; 103 E.R. 75 .... 195, 196

Wellington Corpn. v. Lower Hutt Corpn. [1904] A.C.775; 73 L.J.C.P. 80; 91 L.T.539; 20 T.L.R.712 434

Wells v. Hardy [1964] 2 Q.B. 447; [1964] 2 W.L.R.958; 128 J.P.328; 108 S.J.238; [1964] 1 All E.R.953, D.C. 182, 425, 452

Welsh National Water Development Authority v. Burgess (1974) 28 P. & C.R. 378; [1974] J.P.L. 665, C.A. 393

Welsh Water Authority v. Crowther, Unreported Chester Crown Court, 4 November 1988 .... 140, 425

Welsh Water Authority v. Williams Motors (Cwmdu) Ltd. (1988) *The Times* 5 December 1988 298

West Cumberland Iron & Steel Co. v. Kenyon (1879), 11 Ch.D. 782; 48 L.J. Ch.793; 40 L.T.703; 43 J.P.731; 28 W.R.23 84

West Riding of Yorkshire Council v. Holmworth Urban Sanitary Authority, [1894] 2 Q.B. 842; 59 J.P.213; 63 L.J.Q.B.485; 71 L.T.217 426

West Riding of Yorkshire Rivers Board v. Linthwaite U.D.C. [1915] 2 K.B.436; 79 J.P.280; 84 L.J.K.B.793; 112 L.T. 813; 31 T.L.R.154; 59 S.J.331; 13 L.G.R.301 297

West Riding of Yorkshire Rivers Board v. Reuben Grant & Sons Ltd. (1903), 67 J.P.183; 19 T.L.R. 140; 1 L.G.R.133 ....8, 10

West Riding of Yorkshire Rivers Board v. Tadcaster R.D.C. (1907), 97 L.T.436; 71 J.P.429; 5 L.G.R.1208 ....15, 26, 132, 182

Westover v. Perkins (1859), 2 E. & E.57; 28 L.J.M.C.227; 33 L.T.O.S.221; 23 J.P.727; 5 Jur. N.S.1352; 7 W.R.582; 121 E.R.22 165

Whaley v. Laing (1857), 2 H. & N.476; 26 L.J.Ex.327; 5 W.R. 834; 157 E.R.196 .... 94, 120

Whalley v. Lancashire & Yorks Rly. (1884), 13 Q.B.D. 131; 53 L.J.Q.B.285; 50 L.T.472; 48 J.P.500; 32 W.R.711 83

Wharton v. Taylor (1965) 109 S.J. 475, D.C. 439

Wheal Remfrey China Clay Co. v. Truro Corpn. [1923] 2 K.B. 594; 92 L.J.K.B.1033; 129 L.T.827; 87 J.P.201; 21 L.G.R.646 149

Whelan v. Hewson (1871), I.R. 6 C.L.283 180

White v. Crisp (1854), 10 Ex. 312; 2 C.L.R.1215; 23 L.J. Ex. 317; 23 L.T.O.S.300; 2 W.R.624; 156 E.R.463 146

White v. Phillips (1863), 15 C.B.N.S. 245; 33 L.J.C.P.33; 9 L.T.388; 10 Jur.N.S.425; 12 W.R.85; 143 E.R.778 153

White (John) & Sons v. White [1906] A.C.72; 75 L.J.P.C.14; 94 L.T.65 .... 13, 66, 72, 81

Whitmores (Edenbridge) Ltd v. Stanford [1909] 1 Ch.427; 78 L.J. Ch.144; 99 L.T.924; 25 T.L.R.169; 53 S.J.134 .... 86, 118

Whitstable Free Fishers v. Foreman (1868), L.R. 3 C.P. 578; 32 J.P.596 139

Wickham v. Hawker (1840), 7 M. & W.63; 10 L.J. Ex.153 186

Wiggins v. Boddington (1828), 3 C. & P.544; 172 E.R.539 148

Williams v. Jones (1810), 12 East 346; 104 E.R.136 162

Williams v. Long (1893) 57 J.P.217; 37 Sol.Jo.253, D.C. 439

Williams v. Morland (1824), 2 B. & C.910; 4 Dow. & Ry. K.B. 583; 2 L.J.O.S.K.B.191; 107 E.R. 420 ....13, 79

Page

Williams v. Wilcox (1838), 8 Ad. & El.314; 3 Nev. & P.K.B. 606;
1 Will,Woll. & H. 477; 7 L.J.Q.B.229 ...... 131, 134, 139, 142, 147, 195, 428
Williams & Sons Ltd. v. Port of London Authority (1933), 39 Com. Cas.77 158
Willoughby v. Horridge (1852), 12 C.B.742; 22 L.J.C.P.90; 16 J.P.761;
12 Jur.323; 138 E.R.1096 167
Wills' Trustees v. Cairngorm Canoeing and Sailing School [1976]
S.L.T. 215 .... 132, 140, 196
Wilson v. Cator (1863), 1 New Rep. 314; 7 L.T. 676; 37 J.P. 133; 11 W.R.337 ..147
Wilson v. Stewart (1748), 2 How. E.E.532 103
Wilson v. Waddell (1876) 2 A.C.95; 35 L.T.639; 42 J.P.116 88
Winch v. Thames Conservators (1874), L.R. 9 C.P.378; 43 L.J.C.P. 167;
31 L.T.128; 22 W.R.879; 36 J.P.646 .... 137, 138, 157
Wishart v. Wyllie (1853), 1 Macq. 389, H.L. 17, 70
Witham v. Wansford Trout Farm Ltd, (1991) Unreported
Queen's Bench Division 12 April 1991; [1991] 2 *Water Law* 143 98
Withers v. Purchase (1889), 60 L.T.819; 5 T.L.R.399 82
Womersley v. Church (1867), 17 L.T.190 .... 91, 121, 129
Wood v. Saunders (1875), 10 Ch. App. 583; 44 L.J. Ch.514;
32 L.T.363; 23 W.R.514 116
Wood v. Sutcliffe (1851), 2 Sim. N.S.163; 21 L.J.Ch.253; 18 L.T.O.S. 194;
16 Jur. N.S.75; 61 E.R.303 ....95, 97
Wood v. Waud (1849), 3 Ex.748; 18 L.J. Ex.305; 13 L.T.O.S. 212;
13 Jur.472; 154 E.R.1047 ....10, 89, 108, 115, 116, 118
Wright v. Howard (1823) 1 Sim. & St.190; 1 L.J.O.S.Ch.94; 57 E.R.76 .... 79, 100
Wright v. Williams (1836), 1 M. & W.77; 1 Gale 410; Tyr & Gr.375;
6 L.T. Ex.107; 150 E.R.353 ....93, 104, 108, 110
Wrothwell Ltd. v. Yorkshire Water Authority [1984] Crim. L.R.43 298
Wyatt v. Thompson (1794), 1 Esp. 252; 170 E.R.347 .... 136, 137

Y

Young & Co. v. Bankier Distillery Co. [1893] A.C.691; 69 L.T 838;
58 J.P. 100 ....76, 88, 89–90, 92
Young v. Hitchens (1844), 6 Q.B.606; Dav. & Mer.572; 2 L.T.O.S. 451
Young v. Sun Alliance and London Insurance Ltd. [1977] 1 W.L.R.104;
120 S.J.469; [1976] 3 All E.R.561; [1976] 2 Lloyd's Rep. 189, C.A. 83
Young v. Thank (1845), 6 L.T.O.S.146 168

Z

Zetland (Earl) v. Glover Incorporation of Perth (1870), L.R. 2 Sc. & D.70;
8 Macph. (Ct. of Sess) 144; 42 Sc.Jur.501, H.L. 19

Chapter 1

GENERAL CHARACTERISTICS OF WATERCOURSES

DEFINITIONS OF WATERCOURSES

Watercourses in general

The expression "watercourse" is used to refer to a range of different kinds of moving waters, encompassing estuaries, rivers, streams and their tributaries above and below ground, which are commonly but loosely distinguished by characteristics of length, breadth and depth. In law, as in ordinary language, the precise sub–category into which a particular watercourse is placed may be of limited significance. The rights and duties surrounding it will usually be those associated with watercourses in general. These will depend upon the existence of common law riparian rights of waterside landowners, and other interests in the surrounding land, and a range of matters concerning water rights which are now provided for under statute. Legal rights may be dependent upon factual categories, such as whether the watercourse is natural or artificial, percolating or in a defined channel, tidal or non–tidal, or navigable or non–navigable, but for the most part the fact that, say, a particular water is referred to as a "stream" rather than a "river" or some other term does not of itself change the legal interests associated with it. For that reason the expression "watercourse" is used in this work as a general term encompassing a range of particular descriptions of flowing water which may be at issue in individual cases.

All watercourses have a natural source of surface or underground water, and flow under the action of gravity along a reasonably well defined channel, consisting of a bed and banks, to a confluence with another watercourse or tidal waters. Although the legal status of the bed and banks of a watercourse, and the water flowing in it, are essential characteristics, it may be noted from the outset that a number of related matters may also be of considerable legal significance. First, the relationship between a watercourse and its catchment area, comprising the total extent of its natural drainage basin within which surface and subterranean water discharge, is of major importance. Increasingly the law relating to water resource management and pollution control has linked the state of watercourses with activities conducted on adjoining land, and sought to regulate land use in order to maintain water supplies for reasons of aquatic conservation.

A second focus of attention is the range of distinct legal features which may arise through the particular uses and activities pursued in relation to the watercourse. These may encompass abstraction for domestic, industrial and agricultural supply, applications related to power generation or cooling, and other commercial and recreational activities such as navigation, fisheries and a range of other amenities which are provided by watercourses. Although rather difficult to classify, water uses may be broadly distinguished according to whether they involve (a) the retention of water in its natural channel, as in navigational, fishery and general amenity uses; (b) the impoundment, abstraction or diversion of water from its natural channel, as in employment for domestic or industrial water supply applications; or (c) the supplementation of a natural flow, for example, by discharges of effluent of various kinds or through the acceleration of surface water removal from land as a consequence of drainage operations.

A third matter of importance is the connection between watercourses and water contained in underground strata. This inter-relationship is an inextricable one where the existence of sub-surface flow allows the free exchange of water to and from the defined channel of a watercourse. For this reason the regulation of both the abstraction of water from underground sources and the discharge of effluent into underground strata is closely related to the state of watercourses within the catchment areas in which abstraction and discharge operations take place. Moreover, the need for these kinds of regulation is underlined by frequent uncertainty as to the wider effects of subterranean abstraction and discharge operations upon watercourses outside the catchments in which they take place.

Given these complex relationships between watercourses and related matters, and the diverse legal issues to which they give rise, the limitations of any definition of "watercourse" must be appreciated. Nonetheless a number of noteworthy definitions of "watercourse" and related terms have been offered by legal writers in the past. Thus Angell, in his renowned text, *A Treatise on the Law of Watercourses*,[1] observed that

> "a watercourse begins *ex jure naturae*, and having taken a certain course naturally, cannot be diverted . . . water flows in its natural course, and should be permitted thus to flow, so that all through whose land it naturally flows, may enjoy the privilege of using it. The property in the water therefore, by virtue of the riparian ownership, is in its nature usu–fructuary, and consists not so much of the fluid itself, as the advantage of its impetus."

Woolrych, in his classic work, *A Treatise of the Law of Waters*,[2] noted the definition of a river as "a running stream, pent in on either side with walls and banks, and bearing that name as well where the waters flow and reflow, as where they have their current one way." Hence, the meaning of "river" includes all natural streams, however small, which have a definite and permanent course, and excludes all bodies of water, however large, which are of a temporary character, that is, which are dependent on the will or convenience of individuals for their volume or duration.[3]

The statutory definition of "watercourse"

For certain statutory purposes, the expression "watercourse" encompasses a range of subcategories of flowing water subject to explicit exclusions relating to water supply conduits. Hence s.221(1) of the Water Resources Act 1991 states that "watercourse" includes all rivers, streams, ditches, drains, cuts, culverts, dykes, sluices, sewers and passages through which water flows except mains and other pipes which belong to the National Rivers Authority or a water undertaker or are used by a water undertaker or any other person for the purposes only of providing a supply of water to any premises. Within this definition, the terms "drain" and "sewer" are stated to have the same meaning as in the Water Industry Act 1991. Accordingly, "drain" means a drain used for the drainage of one building or of any buildings or yards appurtenant to buildings within

---

[1] (3rd. 1840) p.11.

[2] (2nd ed. 1851) p.40, following *Callis on Sewers*, (1647) p.77.

[3] Coulson and Forbes, *The Law of Waters* (6th ed. 1952) p.93, citing *Briscoe v. Drought*, (1860) Ir. R.11 C.L. 264; and *Arkwright v. Gell*, (1839) 5 M. & W. 203.

the same curtilage, and includes reference to a tunnel or conduit which serves or is to serve as a drain. "Sewer" includes all sewers and drains which are used for the drainage of buildings and yards appurtenant to buildings, and also encompasses tunnels and conduits serving that purpose.[4]

Although the general definition of "watercourse" provided under the Water Resources Act 1991 serves for most statutory purposes, variations in the meaning of the phrase are to be found in particular contexts. Thus, in respect of flood defence[5] and land drainage matters[6] where, though a similar general definition of "watercourse" is to be found,[7] it is specified that for purposes relating to the restoration and improvement of ditches the definition of "ditch" includes a culverted and piped ditch but does not include a watercourse vested in or under the control of a drainage body.[8] Another variation arises in relation to the control of pollution functions of the National Rivers Authority,[9] where any reference to the waters of any watercourse includes a reference to the bottom, channel or bed of the watercourse which is for the time being dry.[10] Also in relation to the control of pollution specific powers are given to the Secretary of State to modify the definition of a "watercourse" so that a watercourse of specified description is to be treated as if it were not a relevant watercourse for pollution control purposes.[11] In other statutory contexts, such as the former s.30 of the Public Health Act 1936, which required the purification of sewage before discharge into a "watercourse", the expression was undefined and its

---

[4] s.219(1) and (2) Water Industry Act 1991.

[5] Specifically in relation to flood defence, the words in the general definition excluding mains and pipes vested in the National Rivers Authority or a water undertaker are to be replaced by "except a public sewer" (s.113(1) Water Resources Act 1991). "Public sewer" means a sewer vested for the time being in a sewerage undertaker in its capacity as such (s.221(1) Water Resources Act 1991).

[6] Generally see Ch.12 below.

[7] See s.72(1) Land Drainage Act 1991.

[8] s.28(5), and ss.28 to 31 on the restoration and improvement of ditches generally.

[9] Under Part II Water Resources Act 1991, and generally see Ch. 11 below.

[10] s.104(2) Water Resources Act 1991.

[11] s.104(4)(d).

precise meaning has been left to be ascertained by the courts.[12] Now, however, the corresponding prohibition upon water undertakers using sewers or drains for the purpose of conveying foul water into watercourses without adequate treatment is made subject to the general statutory definition of watercourse previously described.[13]

Statutory definitions of "inland waters"

Certain statutory contexts subsume the expression "watercourse" to the wider expression "inland waters". Hence within the Water Resources Act 1991 "inland waters" means the whole or any part of any of the following: (a) any river, stream or other watercourse, whether natural or artificial and whether tidal or not; (b) any lake or pond, whether natural or artificial, or any reservoir or dock, in so far as the lake, pond, reservoir or dock does not fall within paragraph (a) of this definition; and (c) so much of any channel, creek, bay, estuary or arm of the sea as does not fall within paragraph (a) or (b) of this definition.[14]

The definition of "inland waters", which is of central importance for water resource management purposes, is to be contrasted with a distinct definition of "inland freshwaters" formulated in relation to matters of pollution control. "Inland freshwaters" are defined as the waters of any relevant lake or pond or of so much of any relevant river or watercourse as is above the freshwater limit. Within this definition "relevant lake or pond" means any lake or pond which, whether it is natural or artificial or above or below ground, discharges into a relevant river or watercourse or into another lake or pond which is itself a relevant lake or pond. "Relevant river or watercourse" means any river or watercourse, including an underground river or watercourse and an artificial river or watercourse, which is neither a public sewer nor a sewer or drain which drains into a public sewer. In either case, however, variation of the categories is permissible in that the Secretary of State may by order provide that certain lakes or ponds are to be treated as relevant lakes or ponds; or that certain lakes or ponds are to be treated as

---

12 See *Pearce v. Croydon R.D.C.*, (1910) 74 J.P. 429; and *Maxwell-Willshire v. Bromley R.D.C.*, (1917) 87 L.J.Ch. 241.

13 See ss.117(5)(b) and 219 Water Industry Act 1991.

14 s.221(1) Water Resources Act 1991; see also s.219(1) Water Industry Act 1991.

if they were not relevant lakes or ponds; or that specified watercourses are to be treated as if they were not a relevant river or watercourse.[15] Subject to Ministerial variation, however, the definition of "inland freshwaters" is formulated to exclude "discrete waters" which are independently defined as inland waters so far as they comprise (a) a lake, pond or reservoir which does not discharge to any other inland waters; or (b) one of a group of two or more lakes, ponds or reservoirs, whether near to or distant from each other, and of watercourses or mains connecting them, where none of the inland waters in the group discharges to any inland waters outside the group.[16]

Watercourses at common law

As a consequence of the widely different contexts in which the term is used, a certain amount of ambivalence surrounds the meaning of "watercourse" at common law. However, some initial observations as to the essential characteristics of watercourses at common law may be made at this stage. In *Taylor v. St. Helens Corporation*,[17] the word "watercourse" in a grant was held to be capable of meaning either an easement or right to the running of water, or the channel through which the water ran, or the land over which the water flowed, but the meaning must, in each case, be determined by the context in which the word is used. Hence, in *Doe d. Egremont (Earl) v. Williams*,[18] it was held that a watercourse reserved in a lease was to be understood to be the stream and flow of water at issue, and not the channel through which it flowed, whilst in another case, in interpreting a private Act of Parliament, "watercourse" was held to encompass a tidal river.[19] In each instance, however, the question as to whether a watercourse exists or not is a matter of fact to be determined subject to the water at issue being capable of constituting a watercourse in law.[20]

---

[15] s.104(1), (3) and (4) Water Resources Act 1991.

[16] s.221(1).

[17] (1877) 6 Ch. D. 264.

[18] (1848) 11 Q.B. 688.

[19] *Somerset Drainage Comrs. v. Bridgewater Corpn.*, (1899) 81 L.T. 729.

[20] *Briscoe v. Drought*, (1860) Ir. R. II C.L. 264.

Water flowing in a channel

Although, ordinarily, the principal characteristic of a watercourse at common law is that it consists of water flowing in a channel with reasonably well defined banks, it is not essential that the flow of water should be maintained continuously in a particular channel. Accordingly, it has been held that a watercourse does not cease to exist where it occasionally dries up.[21] Likewise in *Stollmeyer v. Trinidad Lake Petroleum Co.*,[22] a stream which flowed in a permanently defined channel, fed exclusively by rainwater running off the surface of the land, ceased to flow for a considerable time each year. It was held that the fact that the river naturally ran dry for a good portion of the year did not mean that it ceased to be a river merely because of that fact.

Normally the expression "watercourse" implies the existence of defined banks between which water has a continuous flow, but this may not always be the case and an essential characteristic for a watercourse to be found is the existence of flowing as opposed to stillwaters.[23] The importance of this feature is well illustrated by observations in cases from other jurisdictions. In *Lyons v. Winter*[24] it was noted that, for there to be a watercourse, there must be a stream of water flowing in a defined channel or between something in the nature of banks. The stream may be very small and need not always run, nor need the banks be clearly or sharply defined, but there must always be a course, marked on the earth by visible signs, along which the water usually flows. In *Mansford v. Ross and Glenning*[25] it was observed that a river may, for part of its length, leave or depart from its normal defined channel without necessarily ceasing to be regarded as a river, and where a well defined natural stream empties into a swamp and all definite channel is lost, but it emerges again into a well defined channel below, it is a question of fact whether it continues to be the same stream.

The point of commencement of a watercourse is at the point at which it issues from the ground and starts to run in a defined channel, and accordingly the taking of water at a spring head has been held to be a

---

[21] *R. v. Oxfordshire*, (1830) 1 B.& Ad. 301.

[22] [1918] A.C. 485.

[23] *M'Nab v. Robertson*, [1897] A.C. 129 H.L.Sc.

[24] (1899), 25 V.L.R. 464, (an Australian case).

[25] (1886), 5 N.Z.L.R.C.A. 33, (a New Zealand case).

wrongful diversion.[26] In *West Riding of Yorkshire Rivers Board v. Reuben Grant & Sons Ltd.*,[27] it was held that the fact that a watercourse was covered in was not material unless done by a local authority in order to turn it into a sewer. Bourne flows of underground water, frequently found in chalk areas, which run periodically in times of flood across the surface of the ground in a channel, have been held not to constitute a watercourse.[28] However, it has been decided that a right to discharge water into a watercourse existed in relation to a body of water, which after following a defined natural channel, passed down into a chalk bed, where the water gradually filtered into and was absorbed in the chalk.[29]

Waste surface water

The counterpart of the requirement that the water in a watercourse must flow between reasonably defined banks, or a defined channel,[30] is that water which percolates discontinuously through or along strata will not constitute a watercourse. For that reason it has been held that water percolating from marshy ground did not constitute a stream.[31] Similarly no claim can be made, either as a natural right or as an easement by prescription, to water which does not flow in a definite course such as surface water or surface drainage.[32] Thus in *Phillimore v. Watford RDC*,[33] an agricultural channel, constructed by a landowner to carry off surface water from his land, but in which there was no constant flow of water, was held not to be a natural stream or watercourse. Similarly, waste water which is allowed to flow from a canal has been held not to be a watercourse, where the water in the canal was not itself flowing water.[34] In the same way, water which squanders itself over an undefined area, such as surface water the supply of which is intermittent and its flow

---

[26] *Maxwell Willshire v. Bromley R.D.C.*, (1917) 87 L.J. Ch. 241.

[27] (1903) 67 J.P. 183.

[28] *R. v. Oxfordshire*, (1830) 1 B. & Ad. 301.

[29] *Dudden v. Clutton Union*, (1857) 11 Ex. 627.

[30] *Daws v. M'Donald*, (1887) 13 V.L.R. 689, (an Australian case).

[31] *M'Nab v. Robertson*, [1897] A.C. 129 H.L.Sc.

[32] *Kena Mahomed v. Bohatoo Sircar*, (1863) Marsh 506; *Adinarayana v. Ramudu*, (1914) L.L.R. 37 Mad. 304.

[33] [1913] 2 Ch. 434, dealing with the meaning of a watercourse within s.17 Public Health Act 1875.

[34] *M'Nab v. Robertson*, [1897] A.C. 129 H.L.Sc.

following no regular or definite course, has been held not to be a watercourse.[35] Rights may be acquired by long use to the natural flow of water from surface springs providing the water flows in a sufficiently well defined channel.[36]

Underground water

In principal, at least, the legal position concerning underground water flowing in a channel is the same as that which applies to surface watercourses.[37] This proposition needs to be qualified, however, by the proviso that the subterranean water at issue is contained within a defined channel and that the channel is *known*. This requirement is authoritatively stated in a series of decisions commencing with *Chasemore v. Richards*,[38] where it was noted that "the principles which apply to flowing water in streams and rivers . . . are wholly inapplicable to water percolating through underground strata, which has no certain course, no defined limits, but which oozes through the soil in every direction in which the rain penetrates." Accordingly, in *Bradford Corporation v. Ferrand*,[39] it was decided that there could be no riparian rights existing in respect of water in an underground channel where the existence of the channel was not known and could not be ascertained except by excavation. Similarly, in *M'Nab v. Robertson,*[40] Lord Watson stated:

> "I see no reason to doubt that a subterraneous flow of water may in some circumstances possess the very same characteristics as a body of water running on the surface; but in my opinion, water, whether falling from the sky or escaping from a spring which does not flow onward with any continuity of parts, but becomes dissipated in the earth's strata, and simply percolates through or along those strata, until it issues from them at a lower level, through dislocation of the strata or otherwise, cannot with any propriety be described as a stream."

---

35 *Rawstron v. Taylor*, (1855) 11 Ex. 369.

36 *Ennor v. Barwell*, (1860) 3 L.T. 170.

37 Generally see Ch.5 below on underground water.

38 (1859) 7 H.L.C. 349.

39 [1902] 2 Ch. 655.

40 [1897] A.C. 129 H.L.Sc.

By contrast, however, it has been held that a watercourse which sinks underground and pursues a well known subterranean course for a short length and then emerges again does not cease to be a stream.[41]

Artificial watercourses

In relation to natural watercourses, normally the riparian owners are entitled to exercise all those rights which attach to and are co-extensive with their ownership. However, the position of an owner of land through which an artificial watercourse passes may not be the same.[42] In particular, the extent of his interest will depend upon the character of the watercourse concerned and specifically whether it is of a permanent or temporary nature, the circumstances under which it was created and the mode in which it has been used and enjoyed. In general, if an artificially constructed watercourse is of a permanent character and its origin is unknown, the inference to be drawn from its use is that the channel was originally constructed with the intention that all riparian owners should have the same rights as they would have had if the watercourse had been of natural origin.[43] Alternatively, riparian rights will not arise where, from the nature of the circumstances, it is evident that the enjoyment of the artificial watercourse is dependent upon temporary circumstances and is not of a permanent character.[44]

Although formerly it may have been possible for a natural stream to become an artificial one through a stream becoming a sewer through the discharge of sewage thereto,[45] this possibility no longer exists. It was established in *George Legge & Son Ltd. v. Wenlock Corpn.*,[46] that since the coming into operation of the Rivers Pollution Prevention Act 1876 [47] the status of a natural stream cannot be altered to that of a sewer, now

---

[41] *Dickinson v. Grand Junction Canal*, (1852) 7 Ex. 282.

[42] Generally see Ch.5 below on artificial watercourses.

[43] *Baily & Co. v. Clark Son & Morland*, [1902] 1 Ch. 649.

[44] *Wood v. Waud*, (1849) 3 Ex. 748.

[45] *West Riding of Yorkshire Rivers Board v. Reuben Grant and Sons Ltd.*,(1903) 67 J.P. 183.

[46] [1936] 2 All E.R. 1367.

[47] Providing water pollution offences analogous to those now provided for under Chapter II of Part III of the Water Resources Act 1991, see Ch. 11 below.

provided for under the Water Industry Act 1991,[48] merely by the fact of discharging of sewage into it.

The constituents of a watercourse

For legal purposes the constituent parts of a watercourse have traditionally been the subject of a threefold distinction: (1) the bed or *alveus;* (2) the bank or shore; and (3) the water flowing therein.[49]

The bed

Following ordinary language, the bed of a watercourse is that part of the subaquatic land which constitutes the channel between its banks and which accommodates the flow of water at its ordinary levels. The precise extent of this area has been the subject of several decisions. In *Menzies v. Breadalbane,*[50] the bed or *alveus* of a river was stated to consist of the course taken by the river at ordinary times, that is, excluding times of extraordinary flooding. Likewise in *Thames Conservators v. Smeed, Dean & Co.,*[51] a right to dredge "the bed of the Thames", as applied to the tidal portion of the river, meant the soil between the ordinary high water mark on one side and the ordinary high water mark on the other. It is notable, however, that this opinion involved disapproval of earlier decisions in which the "bed" of a tidal river had been contrasted with the "shore" by limiting the meaning of the term "bed" to that part of the river bounded by the low–water lines.[52]

In *Goolden v. Thames Conservators,*[53] the bed of a non–tidal part of the Thames was taken to mean the soil underneath the waters of the river between its banks. A more explicit definition of the bed of a non–tidal river was provided in the American case of *State of Alabama v.*

---

[48] Generally see Part IV Water Industry Act 1991.

[49] *Drewett v. Sheard,* (1836) 7 Car. & P. 465.

[50] (1828) 32 R.R. 103.

[51] [1897] 2 Q.B. 334.

[52] *Pearce v. Bunting,* [1896] 2 Q.B. 360; and *Miller v. Little,* (1878) 4 L.R.Ir. 302.

[53] (1891), [1897] 2 Q.B. 338.

State of Georgia,[54] and has been cited with approval in subsequent British decisions:[55]

> "The bed of a river is that portion of its soil which is alternatively covered and left bare as there may be an increase or diminution in the supply of water, and which is adequate to contain it at its average and mean stage during the entire year without reference to the extraordinary freshets of the winter or spring, or the extreme droughts of the summer or autumn."

The bank

An explicit statement of the meaning of the phrase "bank", which assimilates its meaning to a part of the bed, is to be found in the American case of *Howard v. Ingersoll*,[56] where it was said that:

> "The banks are the elevations of land which confine the waters in their natural channel when they rise the highest and do not overflow the banks; and in that condition of the water the banks and the soil which is permanently submerged form the bed of the river. The banks are part of the river bed, but the river does not include lands beyond the banks."

By contrast, however, other indications as to the meaning of the phrase have suggested that the extent of the banks should be distinguished from the bed of a watercourse. Hence it has been stated in a New Zealand decision that "the bed of the river (in law) extends from bank to bank", implying that the bank is not to be construed as a part of the bed.[57]

Amongst the British authorities clear distinctions have been drawn between river banks and walls.[58] In *Monmouth Canal & Railway Co. v. Hill*,[59] the banks of a canal were characterised as the substantial soil which confines the water on either side of the canal and the view was expressed that the banks of the canal encompassed the towpath. The issue

---

[54] (1859) 54 U.S. 427.

[55] *Hindson v. Ashby*, [1896] 2 Ch. 1; and *Thames Conservators v. Smeed, Dean and Co.*, [1897] 2 Q.B. 334.

[56] (1851) 17 Ala. 781.

[57] *Kingdon v. Hutt River Board*, (1905) 25 N.Z.L.R. 145.

[58] *Newcastle (Duke) v. Clark*, (1818) 8 Taunt. 627.

[59] (1859) 28 L.J. Ex. 283.

was directly confronted in *Jones v. Mersey River Board*,[60] in relation to s.38 of the former Land Drainage Act 1930, which empowered a drainage board to deposit any matter removed during dredging any watercourse on the *banks* of the watercourse. Under the former s.81 of the 1930 Act,[61] unless the context required otherwise, the expression "banks" meant banks, walls, or embankments adjoining or confining, or constructed for the purposes of or in conjunction with, any channel or sea front, and included all land between the bank and low–water mark. In construing this definition it was noted that its meaning must depend to a great extent on the particular facts of each case, including the character of the river and its surroundings, but it was resolved that the word "bank" was not to be limited to the actual slope or vertical face of the bank and also encompassed so much of the land adjoining the river as performed or contributed to the function of containing the river. Similarly in *Oakes v. Mersey River Board*,[62] the Lands Tribunal held that an artificially constructed bank will come within the definition of "banks" provided for in land drainage legislation.

The flowing water

Although riparian owners are entitled, as a matter of common law, to the ordinary use of water flowing past their land,[63] the general position is that there can be no ownership or right of property in the flowing water of a watercourse. Flowing water is *publici juris* in the sense that all may reasonably use it who have a right of access to it, and none can have any property in the water itself, except in a particular portion that he may choose to abstract and take into his possession, and that this right extends only for the duration of possession.[64] Once the abstraction or appropriation is abandoned the water again becomes *publici juris.*[65]

[60] [1957] 3 All E.R. 375, the statutory provision at issue corresponds with s.15(1)(b) Land Drainage Act 1991 and s.167(1)(b) Water Resources Act 1991.

[61] Now see s.72(1) Land Drainage Act 1991 and ss.167(4) and 113(1) Water Resources Act 1991.

[62] (1957) J.P.L. 824.

[63] *White (John) & Sons v. White*, [1906] A.C. 72, but see Ch.10 below on the position under statute as to the abstraction of water.

[64] *Embrey v. Owen*, (1851) 6 Ex. 353; *Mason v. Hill*, (1833) 5 B. & Ad. 1; *Williams v. Morland*, (1824), 2 B & C. 910.

[65] *Liggins v. Inge*, (1831) 7 Bing. 682.

Similarly, there is no property in water percolating through the subsoil until it has been the subject of appropriation.[66]

In addition to the common law right of a landowner to appropriate water from a natural watercourse, he will be entitled to appropriate water from an artificial channel unless the right of abstraction has been reserved by other owners.[67] A landowner is also entitled to appropriate surface water where the water flows in no defined channel, despite appropriation preventing the water reaching a watercourse for which it has previously constituted a source of supply.[68]

The element of appropriation required to secure the ownership of water may be brought about simply by the abstraction and containment of the water concerned. It has also been held to exist where a watercourse rises and remains within a particular property and no one is entitled to share the use of the water with the owner of the property.[69] Appropriation may arise by the conferral of a proprietary interest in a watercourse by statute.[70] When once appropriated, the existence of a property right in the water has the consequence that it is capable of being the subject of theft.[71] Thus water supplied by a water undertaking to a consumer and standing in his pipes was held under the former law to be the subject of larceny.[72] Similarly water has been held to be "an article" for the purposes of factories legislation.[73]

---

[66] *Ballard v. Tomlinson*, (1885) 29 Ch. D. 115.

[67] *Ennor v. Barwell*, (1860) 2 Giff. 410.

[68] *Broadbent v. Ramsbotham*, (1856) 11 Ex. 602; *Chasemore v. Richards*, (1859) 7 H.L. Cas. 349.

[69] *Holker v. Porritt*, (1875) 33 L.T. 125.

[70] *Medway Co. v. Romney (Earl)*, (1861) 9 C.B. 575.

[71] Generally, see Theft Act 1968.

[72] *Ferens v. O'Brien*, (1883) 11 Q.B.D. 21, and see Larceny Act 1916, now repealed.

[73] *Longhurst v. Guildford, Godalming and District Water Co.*, [1961] 3 All E.R. 545, H.L., interpreting s.151(1) Factories Act 1937, now repealed.

TIDAL AND NON-TIDAL WATERCOURSES

Tidal watercourses[74]

The essential characteristic of a tidal watercourse is that of tidal ebb and flow. Beyond that, *prima facie*, the bed of the watercourse belongs to the Crown and the public have a right to use it for purposes of navigation and fishing. The extent of a tidal watercourse is determined by the extent of the regular ebb and flow of the highest tides.[75] The expression "tidal waters" includes those waters not merely where there is a horizontal ebb and flow, but also any waters where the tide flows or reflows so as to cause a vertical rise and fall by the effect of an ordinary sea tide.[76] Consequently, it is irrelevant whether the waters are saline or not.[77] In relation to navigation,[78] the flow of the tide is strong *prima facie* evidence of a public navigable river, but whether a particular water is or is not of that character depends upon the situation and the nature of the channel. Clearly, not every ditch or cutting forms part of a public navigable watercourse, even though it may be large enough to allow the passage of a boat: the question is one of degree to be determined by having regard to all the facts.[79]

---

[74] Several matters relating to tidal watercourses are considered in greater detail later in this work, see in particular the discussion of rights in the sea and coastal waters in Ch. 2, navigation on tidal waters in Ch.6, and fisheries in tidal waters in Ch.8.

[75] *Reece v. Miller*, (1882) 8 Q.B.D. 626; *Lynn Corpn. v. Turner*, (1774) 1 Cowp. 86; *Horne v. Mackenzie,* (1839) 6 Cl. & Fin. 628; see also definition given in s.3 Railways Clauses Act 1863.

[76] *West Riding of Yorkshire Rivers Board v. Tadcaster R.D.C.*, (1907) 97 L.T. 436; *Ingram v. Percival*, [1969] 1 Q.B. 548.

[77] *Kingsway Furniture (Dartford) Ltd. v. Harpglow Ltd. and Kylefield Ltd.*, 23 March 1990 (Official Referee's Business) [1991] 2 *Water Law* 10.

[78] On navigation generally, see Ch.6 below. In relation to the limits of a tidal part of a river for fisheries purposes, see p.181 below.

[79] *Sim E Bak v. Ang Yong Huat*, [1923] A.C. 429; *Ilchester (Earl) v. Rashleigh*, (1889) 61 L.T. 477; *Miles v. Rose*, (1814) 5 Taunt. 705.

Ownership of the bed of a tidal watercourse

The right to the soil of a tidal navigable watercourse is not by presumption of law vested in the owners of the adjoining lands,[80] but lies, *prima facie*, in the Crown so far as the tide flows and reflows,[81] unless another person can sustain a stronger title.[82] In earlier cases it was held that the Crown was the owner of the soil of "public navigable rivers",[83] "navigable rivers",[84] and "tidal navigable rivers".[85] It was eventually established in *Murphy v. Ryan*,[86] however, that the Crown had no such rights, and the public had no right to fish, in a navigable river beyond the point where the tide ebbed and flowed. The ownership of the Crown is for the benefit of the subjects, who have the public right of fishing and navigation and ancillary rights, and the Crown can only grant the bed of the sea or a tidal river subject to such rights.[87] The right of the Crown to the bed of a tidal river is limited to the ordinary high water mark along the shore and extends as far up the watercourse as the tide flows.[88]

Non–tidal watercourses

The main difference between a non–tidal watercourse and its tidal counterpart is that, usually, neither the Crown nor the public have any rights or privileges in relation to a non–tidal watercourse, though many of the more important non–tidal watercourses are subject to public rights of navigation. As a consequence of this, the bed of a non–tidal watercourse is *prima facie* in private ownership and the public have no

---

[80] *R. v. Smith,* (1780) 2 Doug. K.B. 441.

[81] *Fitzhardinge (Lord) v. Purcell*, [1908] 2 Ch. 139; *Gann v. Free Fishers of Whitstable*, (1865) 11 H.L.C. 192; *Malcomson v. O'Dea*, (1863) 10 H.L.C. 593; *Lord Advocate for Scotland v. Hamilton*, (1852) 1 Macq. 46 H.L.; *Bulstrode v. Hall*, (1663) 1 Sid. 148; *R. v. Trinity House*, (1662) 1 Sid. 86.

[82] *Re Alston's Estate*, (1856) 21 J.P. 163; *Attorney–General v. London Corpn.*, (1849) 12 Beav 8.

[83] *Lord Advocate for Scotland v. Hamilton*, (1852) 1 Macq. 46, H.L.

[84] *R. v. Smith,* (1780) 2 Doug. K.B. 441.

[85] *R. v. Trinity House*, (1662) 1 Sid. 86; *Bulstrode v. Hall*, (1663) 1 Sid. 148.

[86] (1868) I.R. 2 C.L. 143.

[87] *Fitzhardinge (Lord) v. Purcell*, [1908] 2 Ch. 139; *Malcomson v. O'Dea*, (1863) 10 H.L.C. 593.

[88] s.7 Crown Lands Act 1866.

right to fish therein. Subject to differences in the public right of navigation, riparian owners of non–tidal watercourses possess similar rights and natural easements to those which belong to riparian owners below the flow of the tide.

Ownership of the bed of non–tidal watercourses

The Crown is not normally entitled to the soil of the bed of non–tidal inland waters.[89] In the ordinary case, *prima facie* the proprietors on each side of a non–tidal watercourse are respectively entitled to the soil *usque ad medium aquae*.[90] Hence, in *Blount v. Layard*[91] it was stated that the natural presumption is that a person whose land abuts a watercourse owns the bed up to the middle of the stream.[92] If land on both sides of the watercourse is owned, the presumption is that the whole bed of the watercourse belongs to the owner of the land, unless it is a tidal watercourse. These presumptions apply to land of any tenure, whether freehold, leasehold or former copyhold,[93] and apply whether the watercourse is navigable or non–navigable.[94] However, the right to the bed of a watercourse is not inseparably bound to the right to the bank since it is possible for an owner of both to retain one and to part with the other.[95]

The *medium filum* rule

As previously noted, the general rule in relation to the ownership of the bed of non–tidal rivers is that the riparian owners of the banks are presumed each to own half the bed of the river *usque ad medium filum*

---

[89] *Johnston v. O'Neill*, [1911] A.C. 522; *Smith v. Andrews*, [1891] 2 Ch. 678; *Bristow v. Cormican*, (1878) 3 A.C. 641.

[90] *R. v. Wharton*, (1701) Holt K.B. 499; *Wishart v. Wyllie*, (1853) 1 Macq. 389, H.L.; *Bickett v. Morris*, (1866) 30 J.P. 532; *Edleston v. Crossley & Sons Ltd.*, (1868) 18 L.T. 15; *Bristow v. Cormican*, (1878) 3 A.C. 641. See also the discussion of presumptions as to ownership of fisheries at p.190 below.

[91] (1888) [1891] 2 Ch. 681.

[92] See the discussion of the *medium filum* rule below.

[93] *Tilbury v. Silva*, (1890) 45 Ch. D. 98.

[94] *Foster v. Wright*, (1878) 44 J.P. 7; *Hindson v. Ashby*, [1896] 2 Ch. 71.

[95] *Smith v. Andrews*, [1891] 2 Ch. 678.

aquae.[96] Accordingly, the general rule of conveyancing is that where a piece of land is conveyed, which is bounded by a non–navigable watercourse, the conveyance passes the bed of the stream up to the middle line or *medium filum.*[97] This general rule is, however, subject to there being nothing in the language of the deed, or the nature of the subject matter of the grant, or the surrounding circumstances, which is sufficient to rebut the presumption. The rule applies despite the fact that the measurement of the property can be satisfied without including the half of the bed of the river, and despite the fact that though the land is described as bounded by a river the map which is referred to in the grant does not include the bed of the river.[98] The rule also applies where land is conveyed by Act of Parliament.[99] Acts of ownership exercised on the bed and banks of a river sufficient to prove possession by a claimant are admissible in evidence.[100] The fact that a river is of more than ordinary breadth does not prevent a conveyance of premises bounded by the river from operating to convey the portion of the bed and soil of the river abutting thereon up to midstream.[101] Where two parishes are separated by a watercourse, the *medium filum* is the presumptive boundary between them.[102] In the case of two counties separated by a river, in the absence of any words in an Act determining the boundary between them, the *medium filum* rule applies similarly and the middle of the river continuously forms the boundary line between them.[103]

The presumption that a conveyance of land adjoining a watercourse passes half of the soil of the river without explicit mention

---

[96] *Lamb v. Newbiggin*, (1844) 1 Car. & Kir. 549; and *Bristowe v. Cormican*, (1877) 3 App. Cas. 641.

[97] *Tilbury v. Silva*, (1890) 45 Ch. D. 98.

[98] *Micklethwait v. Newlay Bridge Co.*, (1886) 51 J.P. 132; *Tilbury v. Silva*, (1890) 45 Ch. D. 98; *Thames Conservators v. Kent*, [1918] 2 K.B. 272; *Hesketh v. Willis Cruisers*, (1968) 19 P & C.R. 573, C.A.

[99] *R. v. Strand Board of Works*, (1863) 4 B. & S. 526.

[100] *Costard and Wingfield's Case*, (1586) 2 Leon. 44; *Hollis v. Goldfinch*, (1823) 1 B. & C. 208; *Jones v. Williams*, (1837) 2 M. & W. 326; *Hanbury v. Jenkins*, [1901] 2 Ch. 401.

[101] *Dwyer v. Rich*, (1870) I.R. 4 C.L. 424.

[102] *R. v. Landulph (Inhabitants)*, (1834) 1 Mood. & R. 393 N.P.; *MacCannon v. Sinclair*, (1859) 23 J.P. 757.

[103] *R. v. Brecon (Inhabitants), Re Glastonbury Bridge*, (1850) 14 J.P. 655.

does not apply unless the bed is in the disposition of the grantor. An award under an Inclosure Act of waste bordering a river does not carry with it the river bed to the *medium filum*.[104] Nor does the rule apply in the case of canals[105] or tidal waters.[106] A conveyance of riparian land fronting a river will not be construed as passing any portion of the bed of the river if the fishing in such waters is vested in another person.[107]

The *medium filum* rule, in the absence of evidence to the contrary, applies to situations where an island is formed in the watercourse by drawing a *medium filum* as a boundary through each arm of the stream.[108] However, in a Scottish decision, it was held that when the bed of a river is divided by an island into main and subsidiary channels, the latter being dry at times, the *medium filum* of the river is the centre line of the bed from bank to bank, and not the centre line of the main channel.[109] A shifting sand–bank in the bed of a river has been held to be a portion of the bed and not to affect the rights of the riparian owners, which continued to extend from the shore to the *medium filum*.[110]

For the purposes of riparian boundaries and fishery limits, it would seem that the position of the *medium filum* in a non tidal watercourse is represented by a line running down the middle of the bed at the ordinary state of the stream. That is, the *medium filum* is drawn as the midline of the usual flow of the watercourse without regard to periods of flood water or drought.[111] It is not clearly established how the boundaries of land abutting the banks of a watercourse are to be extended to the middle of the stream where a boundary lies at an obtuse angle to the bank. Of some bearing upon this problem, however, is the decision in *Crook v. Seaford Corp.*[112] where it was decided that the boundaries of a sea beach

---

104 *Ecroyd v. Coulthard*, [1898] 2 Ch. 358; *Hough v. Clark*, (1907) 23 T.L.R. 682.
105 *Chamber Colliery Co. v. Rochdale Canal Co.*, [1895] A.C. 564.
106 *R. v. Trinity House*, (1662) 1 Sid. 86.
107 *Devonshire (Duke) v. Pattison*, (1887) 20 Q.B.D. 263; *Waterford Conservators v. Connolly*, (1889), 24 I.L.T. 7.
108 *Great Torrington Commons Conservators v. Moore Stevens*, [1904] 1 Ch. 347.
109 *Menzies v. Breadalbane*, (1901) 4 F. (Ct. of Sess.) 55.
110 *Zetland (Earl) v. Glover Incorporation of Perth*, (1870) 8 Macph. (Ct. of Sess.) 144.
111 *Hindson v. Ashby*, [1896] 2 Ch. 71, and see Moore, *History and Law of Fisheries*, (1903) pp.114 to 118.
112 (1871) 6 Ch. App. 551.

above the high water mark fronting onto the defendant's field were to be determined by two lines drawn from the extremities of the field perpendicular to the sea coast towards the sea and continued to the high water mark.

Some uncertainty exists as to whether the middle line of a tidal river, termed the *medium filum aquae*, should be drawn in the middle of the channel at ordinary low tide or by the centre line of the river between ordinary high water mark on each side of the river. Support for the more likely view that the boundary line is the centre of the channel at low water is to be found in commentaries by Hale.[113]

Alteration of the channel of a watercourse

Where a tidal or non–tidal watercourse shifts its channel gradually and imperceptibly, the ownership of the bed remains with the former owners and the *medium filum* remains the boundary between the riparian properties. Similarly, in the case of a tidal watercourse ownership remains with the Crown.[114] In this respect there is no difference between tidal and non–tidal or navigable and non–navigable watercourses.[115] However, if the change in the course is sudden and perceptible and the original boundary is reasonably ascertainable, the right to the soil remains as before.[116] Thus, if by the irruption of the waters of a tidal watercourse a new channel is formed in the land of a subject, though the rights of the Crown and the public may come into existence and be exercised in what has become a portion of the tidal watercourse, the right to the soil remains with the owner. Consequently, if at any time thereafter the waters recede and the watercourse again changes its course, leaving the channel dry, the soil becomes the exclusive property of the owner once again and is free from all rights of the Crown and the

---

[113] Hale, *De Jure Maris*, First Treatise, p.354; Moore, *Law of Fisheries*, (1903) pp.118 to 123; *Pearce v. Bunting*, (1896) 60 J.P. 695; *Thames Conservators v. Smeed*, [1897] 2 Q.B. 334; *Miller v. Little*, (1878) 4 L.R. Ir. 302; *Attorney–General v. Newcastle Corpn.*, (1903) 67 J.P.155.

[114] *Scratton v. Brown*, (1825) 4 B. & C. 485; *Re Hull & Selby Rly Co.*, (1839) 5 M. & W. 527.

[115] *Foster v. Wright*, (1878) 44 J.P. 7; *Hindson v. Ashby*, [1896] 2 Ch. 1.

[116] *Ford v. Lacy*, (1861) 30 L.J. Ex. 351; *Thakurin Ritraj Koer v. Thakurin Sarfaraz Koer*, (1905) 21 T.L.R. 637.

public.[117] Whether a strip of land has ceased to be part of a watercourse is a question of fact which is to be determined by having regard to all the material circumstances of the case, including the fluctuations of the watercourse and the nature of the land and its growth and use.[118]

A counterpart of the movement of riparian boundaries as a result of gradual alterations in the channel of a watercourse is that land which is added to the bank of one riparian owner becomes the property of that owner. This rule, termed "the doctrine of accretion", is similarly applicable to the boundaries of tidal, non–tidal and coastal land. Detailed discussion of the principles which apply to the acquisition of land by accretion is provided later in this work.[119]

Stillwaters

In most respects, the law relating to flowing water applies to stillwaters such as lakes[120] and ponds. Formerly it was thought that the doctrine of accretion did not apply to standing waters,[121] but this view has been overruled by the decision in *Southern Centre of Theosophy Inc. v. State of South Australia*[122] where it was held that the doctrine applied to an inland lake where the land in respect of which the accretion was claimed, and that covered by the waters of the lake, were the property of the Crown.

At common law there are relatively few authorities concerning the status of stillwaters, and these are almost invariably concerned with the ownership of lake beds. A leading decision is *Marshall v. Ulleswater Steam Navigation Co.*,[123] where it was decided that the plaintiff was the owner of the bed and soil of Lake Ulleswater upon proof that he held a grant of a several and exclusive fishery in the lake. The court was in doubt, however, whether the soil in lakes, like that in fresh–water watercourses, *prima facie* belonged to the riparian owners on either side

[117] *Carlisle Corpn. v. Graham*, (1869) 21 L.T. 333.
[118] *Hindson v. Ashby*, [1896] 2 Ch. 1.
[119] See the discussion of accretion and encroachment at p.46 below.
[120] For statutory purposes a "lake" has been defined to include any expanse of water other than a river or canal (s.13(13) Countryside Act 1968).
[121] *Trafford v. Thrower*, (1929) 45 T.L.R. 502.
[122] [1982] 1 All E.R. 283.
[123] (1863) 3 B. & S. 732.

in accordance with the *medium filum* rule, or whether the soil belonged to the Crown by virtue of the royal prerogative. Subsequently, it was decided that a grant from the Crown of land adjacent to a large non–tidal Irish lake did not pass the soil of the lake *ad medium filum* to the owner of the adjoining land.[124] The uncertainty concerning the ownership of the beds of stillwaters was resolved in later decisions. In *Bristow v. Cormican*,[125] it was held that the Crown had no legal right to the soil of fishery in an inland non–tidal lake, and *Johnston v. O'Neill*[126] determined that this principle applied irrespective of the size of the lake. The inference to be drawn from these decisions is that the Crown has no *prima facie* interest in the soil of a non–tidal lake, unless the Crown is the actual owner of the bed or the adjoining land.[127] The ownership of the bed of stillwaters belongs to the owner or owners of the adjacent banks in accordance with the *medium filum* rule.

The question as to the extent of a lake arose in *Mackenzie v. Bankes*[128] where two lakes were joined by a narrow and shallow channel, which was not a river and was divided by a causeway. It was held that, in the circumstances, the waters concerned were to be regarded as separate and distinct lakes. Because the Crown has no right to the fisheries in inland non–tidal stillwaters,[129] and the public have no common law right to fish therein,[130] irrespective of the size of the lake, the right of fishery in such waters belongs *prima facie* to the riparian owners *ad medium filum aquae*.[131]

As in the case of non–tidal watercourses, the public do not have a right to navigate on non–tidal lakes, but a right to navigate thereon may

---

[124] *Bloomfield v. Johnston*, (1868) Ir. 8 C.L. 68.
[125] (1878) 3 A.C. 641, H.L.
[126] [1991] A.C. 552.
[127] *Attorney–General v. Plymouth Corporation* (1754) 145 E.R. 1202.
[128] *MacKenzie v. Bankes*, (1878) 3 A.C. 1324; *Cochrane v. Earl of Minto*, (1915) 6 Pat. App. 139.
[129] *Bristow v. Cormican*, (1878) 3 A.C. 461.
[130] *Johnston v. O'Neill*, [1911] A.C. 552; *Toome Eel Fishery (N.I.) v. Cardwell*, [1963] N.I. 92.
[131] On the rights of joint owners of a lake see *Menzies v. Macdonald*, (1856) 2 Macq. 463; on rights of fisheries on stillwaters see p.193 below.

be acquired by dedication, immemorial use or under statute.[132] In *Bourke v. Davis*,[133] a lake in private grounds was touched at one point only by a public road and it was held that this did not entitle a person to launch boats from the road and boat on the lake for pleasure. Likewise the use of a private lake for other purposes will only be lawful where it is the subject of an established right. Hence, it has been decided that the privilege of washing and watering cattle at a pond or taking and using water for culinary and other domestic purposes can be maintained where it is established as an easement.[134]

---

132 *Marshall v. Ulleswater Steam Navigation Co.*, (1863) 3 B. & S. 732; *Micklethwait v. Vincent*, (1892) 67 L.T. 225; *Blower v. Ellis*, (1886) 50 J.P. 326.

133 (1889) 62 L.T. 34.

134 *Manning v. Wasdale*, (1836), 5 Ad. & El. 758; *Smith v. Archibald*, (1880) 5 A.C. 489; *Cargill v. Gotts*, [1981] 1 All E.R. 68.

Chapter 2

THE SEA AND COASTAL WATERS

Introduction

This Chapter deals with the general legal status of the sea and coastal land and waters. Specifically, the objective is to consider the legal significance of a number of key expressions including (1) "tidal waters" and "the sea", (2) "territorial waters", (3) the "exclusive economic zone", (4) the "continental shelf", (5) "the high seas", (6) "the foreshore", and (7) "tidal rivers". Several of these terms represent distinct concepts of international law which have a direct bearing upon the national, or domestic, law of England and Wales.

Many of the key principles of international law relating to coastal waters and the sea were established by the Geneva Convention on the Law of the Sea. Separate Conventions adopted by the 1958 Conference were the Convention on the Territorial Sea and Contiguous Zone;[1] the Convention on the High Seas;[2] the Convention on the Continental Shelf;[3] and the Convention on Fishing and Conservation of Living Resources of the High Seas.[4] The principles set out in these conventions have to some extent been re–stated in the Third United Nations Conference on the Law of the Sea of 1982, termed "UNCLOS".[5] Although UNCLOS has not yet received the ratifications of a sufficient number of nations for it to come into force, it is likely that many of its provisions reflect customary international law. To that extent it provides the basis for a number of measures within the domestic law of England and Wales considered in the following discussion. Where concepts relating to the sea and coastal waters possess distinct meanings in international and national law, the contrast between the two levels of regulation is indicated in the following account by the use of subheadings indicating whether it is primarily international or domestic law that is under consideration.

---

[1] (1965) Cmnd.2511.

[2] (1963) Cmnd.1929.

[3] (1964) Cmnd.2422.

[4] (1966) Cmnd.3208.

[5] (1983) Cmnd.89941.

TIDAL WATERS AND THE SEA

Tidal waters and the sea in domestic law

In the law of England and Wales the expression "tidal waters" has previously been defined by statute, for a range of different purposes, in many instances as waters within the ebb and flow of ordinary spring tides.[6] However, in relation to the control of water pollution, the expression "tidal waters" is now replaced by the related expressions "territorial waters"[7] and "coastal waters".[8] Hence, s.104(1)(a) of the Water Resources Act 1991 defines "coastal waters" as any waters which are within the area which extends landwards from the baselines, from which the breadth of the territorial sea adjacent to England and Wales is measured,[9] as far as the limit of the highest tide or, in the case of the waters of any relevant river or watercourse, as far as the fresh–water limit of the river or watercourse, together with the waters of any enclosed dock which adjoins waters within that area. In relation to this definition it is envisaged that the Secretary of State will deposit maps with the National Rivers Authority showing the fresh–water limits of every relevant river or watercourse, and will revise those maps when necessary.[10]

As a matter of common law, the courts have construed the expression "tidal waters" to mean waters which are subject to the regular ebb and flow of the ordinary highest tides, irrespective of what occurs under unusual circumstances.[11] This definition includes those waters not only where there is a horizontal ebb and flow, but also where there is a vertical rise and fall caused by the ordinary sea tide.[12] The meaning of

---

[6] See, for example, s.3 Railway Clauses Act 1863, s.108 Explosives Act 1875, s.742 Merchant Shipping Act 1894 and s.27(4) of the Land Drainage Act 1976 (now repealed). See also p.181 below for further discussion of the meaning of "tidal waters".

[7] Considered at p.290 below.

[8] Contrast s.56(1) Control of Pollution Act 1974, now repealed.

[9] See p.26 below on the meanings of "baselines" and "territorial sea".

[10] ss.104(3) and 192 Water Resources Act 1991; and see p.226 below.

[11] *Reece v. Miller*, (1882) 8 Q.B.D. 626.

[12] *Calcraft v. Guest*, [1898] 1 Q.B. 759, considered in Moore *The History and Law of Fisheries*, (1903) p.102; *West Riding of Yorkshire Rivers Board v. Tadcaster RDC*,

"tidal waters", encompassing waters where there is a vertical rise and fall of water level caused by tides, is sufficiently wide to include the sea at a distance from the coast. Nonetheless, in some legal contexts the expression "the sea" is used. "The sea" has been defined by statute to include an estuary or arm of the sea,[13] the coast up to the high water mark[14] and the waters of any channel, creek, bay or estuary and of any river so far up that river as the tide flows.[15] As a matter of common law it has been noted that the coast, as the land which bounds the sea, is properly to be distinguished from the sea itself.[16] Within the general meaning of "the sea" a number of distinct zones are characterised for legal purposes and discussed in the following sections.

THE TERRITORIAL SEA

The territorial sea in international law

A basic principle of the international law of the sea is that the sovereignty of a coastal state extends beyond its land territory and internal waters to an adjacent belt of sea described as the "territorial sea". This sovereignty extends to the air space over the territorial sea as well as to its bed and subsoil.[17] Every coastal state has the right to establish the breadth of its territorial sea up to a limit not exceeding 12 nautical miles measured in accordance with requirements set out in United Nations Conference on the Law of the Sea.[18] Although normally the baseline for measuring the breadth of the territorial sea is the low–water line along the coast, as marked on large–scale charts officially recognised by the state concerned,[19] specific exceptions are allowed for in relation to islands, deeply indented coastlines, internal waters, mouths of rivers,

---

(1907) L.T. 436; *Ingram v. Percival*, [1968] 3 All E.R. 657; and *Gray v. Blamey*, (1990) *The Times* 4 June D.C.

[13] s.29(1) Prevention of Oil Pollution Act 1971.

[14] s.20(1) Sea Fisheries Regulation Act 1966.

[15] s.49(1) Coast Protection Act 1949, but see also s.49(2) and Sch. 4.

[16] *R. v. Forty–nine Casks of Brandy*, (1836) 3 Hag. Adm. 257.

[17] Art.2 UNCLOS Convention (1982).

[18] Art.3.

[19] Art.5.

bays and other coastal features justifying a departure from the low–water line.[20]

Whilst a coastal state possesses sovereignty over its territorial sea in international law, a right of innocent passage through the territorial sea is possessed by ships of all states, for the purpose of traversing the sea, or proceeding to or from internal waters.[21] The exercise of this right is regarded as innocent only so long as it is not prejudicial to the peace, good order or security of the coastal state, and providing it takes place in conformity with UNCLOS and other rules of international law.[22] Hence, the coastal state may not hamper the innocent passage of foreign ships through the territorial sea except in accordance with the terms of the Convention.[23]

The duty of a coastal state not to interfere with the right of innocent passage of foreign ships involves a limitation upon the criminal jurisdiction of a coastal state in relation to foreign ships. Accordingly, the criminal jurisdiction of a coastal state may not be exercised on board a foreign ship passing through the territorial sea to arrest any person or to conduct any investigation in connection with any crime committed on board the ship during its passage with certain exceptions. The exceptions are (a) if the consequences of the crime extend to the coastal state; (b) if the crime is of a kind to disturb the peace of the country or the good order of the territorial sea; (c) if the assistance of the local authorities has been requested by the master of the ship or by a diplomatic agent or consular officer of the flag state; or (d) if such measures are necessary for the suppression of illicit traffic in narcotic drugs or psychotropic substances.[24]

Whilst in the area of its territorial sea a coastal state has the same law–making power as for its land territory, a more limited legislative jurisdiction arises in relation to a band of water beyond the territorial sea known as the "contiguous zone". Specifically, certain powers are given to coastal states under UNCLOS in relation to the contiguous zone, which may not extend beyond 24 nautical miles from the baselines from which

---

[20] Arts.6 to 16; and see *Anglo–Norwegian Fisheries Case*, (1951) I.C.J. Rep 116.

[21] Arts. 17 and 18.

[22] Art.19.

[23] Art.24.

[24] Art 27.

the breadth of the territorial sea is measured. Within the contiguous zone the coastal state may exercise the control necessary to prevent infringement of its customs, fiscal, immigration or sanitary laws and regulations within its territory or territorial sea, and to punish infringement of laws and regulations committed within its territory or territorial sea.[25]

Territorial waters in domestic law

In the law of England and Wales "territorial waters" are generally acknowledged to be those coastal waters over which a state declares exclusive sovereignty.[26] Accordingly, the jurisdiction of the Crown was statutorily provided for in the preamble to the Territorial Waters Jurisdiction Act 1878. This declared that territorial waters are to extend, "over the open seas adjacent to the coasts of the United Kingdom and of all other parts of Her Majesty's dominions to such a distance as is necessary for the defence and security of such dominions". Beyond this, the 1878 Act provided that an offence committed by a person, whether a subject or not, within territorial waters is an offence within the jurisdiction of the admiralty though it may have been committed on board or by means of a foreign ship.[27] "Territorial waters" were defined under the Act as such part of the sea adjacent to the coast of the United Kingdom or any part of Her Majesty's dominions as is deemed by international law to be within the territorial sovereignty of Her Majesty, and for the purposes of the Act any part of the open sea within one marine league of the coast measured from low–water mark was deemed to be open sea within territorial waters of Her Majesty's dominions.[28]

The territorial waters of the United Kingdom were traditionally subject to a three nautical mile limit.[29] This distance was established

---

[25] Art.33.

[26] *R. v. Kent Justices ex parte Lye*, [1967] 2 Q.B. 153; and *Post Office v. Estuary Radio Ltd.*, [1968] 2 Q.B. 740.

[27] s.2 Territorial Waters Jurisdiction Act 1878; now see s.1 Territorial Waters Act 1987.

[28] s.7 Territorial Waters Jurisdiction Act 1878, repealed by Sch.2 Territorial Waters Act 1987. See also s.9 North Sea Fisheries Act 1893.

[29] *Post Office v. Estuary Radio Ltd.*, [1967] 5 All E.R. 663, C.A.; *R. v. Kent Justices, ex parte Lye*, [1967] 1 All E.R. 560.

according to the principle that territorial sovereignty extended only so far as the power of arms carried, and three miles was customarily considered to be the maximum range of cannon shot fired from shore batteries.[30] It was recognised, however, that a court would treat as conclusive a statement by the appropriate officer of the Crown as to the extent of territorial waters.[31] Accordingly, it has now been provided for under the Territorial Sea Act 1987 that the breadth of the territorial sea adjacent to the United Kingdom will for all purposes be 12 nautical miles. The baselines from which the breadth of the territorial sea is to be measured are to be those established by Her Majesty by Order in Council. In any legal proceedings a certificate issued by or under the authority of the Secretary of State stating the location of any baseline established in accordance with this procedure is to be conclusive of what is stated in the certificate.[32]

A problematic issue relating to property rights in the sea bed below the low water mark surrounds the extent of the Crown's ownership of areas of subterranean land. In the important, if somewhat inconclusive, decision in *R. v. Keyn*,[33] the minority of the court held that the sea within three miles of the coast of England was part of the territory of that country. However, a strong minority of the court took the contrary view. It was in response to this uncertainty that the matter was explicitly provided for under the Territorial Waters Jurisdiction Act of 1878.

The issue of Crown ownership of the sea bed had also been considered prior to *R. v. Keyn* in *Gammel v. Commissioners of Woods and Forests*[34] and *Gann v. Free Fishers of Whitstable*,[35] and was reconsidered in the later Scots decision in *Lord Advocate v. Wemyss.*[36] In each of these cases support was expressed for the principle of Crown ownership of the sea bed within three miles of the low water mark. It was

[30] Bynkershoek, *Essay on Sovereignty over the Sea* (1702); and *The Twee Gebroeders*, (1801) 165 E.R. 485.

[31] *The Fagerness*, (1927), P.311, C.A.

[32] s.1(1) and (3) Territorial Sea Act 1987. "Nautical miles" is defined to mean international nautical miles of 1,852 metres (s.1(7)). See Territorial Waters Order in Council 1964; Territorial Sea (Limits) Order 1989, S.I. 1989 No.482.

[33] (1876) 2 Ex.D. 63; and generally see Marston, *The Marginal Seabed* (1981).

[34] (1859), 3 Macq. 419, H.L.

[35] (1865), 11 H.L.C. 192.

[36] [1900] A.C. 66.

stated in *Attorney–General for British Columbia v. Attorney–General for Canada*,[37] however, that the question whether the shore below low water mark within three miles of the coast formed part of the territory of the Crown, or was merely subject to special powers for protective and police purposes, was not one which belonged to municipal law alone and that it was not desirable that any municipal court should pronounce upon it.

Support can be found for the majority decision in *R. v. Keyn*, to the effect that the Crown has no right to the soil below the low water mark. Hence, in *Stephens v. Snell*,[38] it was held that land below the low water mark is not any part of the Kingdom, though in a later case[39] it was stated that the Crown claimed property in the soil of the sea under the territorial waters within one marine league of the coast measured from low water mark and also claimed entitlement to the mines and minerals under the soil. However, in the recent decision in *Trustees of the Port and Harbour of Lerwick v. Crown Estate Commissioners*, it was held that the right of the Crown in the sea bed in internal waters and within the limits of the territorial sea around Scotland is a right of property derived from its sovereignty. As a consequence of this, a grant or licence from the Crown Estate Commissioners was required before salmon farming operations affecting the sea bed around the Shetland Islands could lawfully be engaged in.[40]

These uncertainties concerning Crown ownership of the sea bed do not detract from the power of the Crown to establish a title to the sea bed below low water mark against a subject,[41] or, conversely, that a subject may establish such a title against the Crown.[42] Similarly unaffected is the principle that islands which arise from the sea within the

---

[37] [1914] A.C. 153.

[38] (1954) *The Times* 5 June 1954.

[39] *The Putbus, Owners, etc. of Ship Zenetia v. Owners of Ship Putbus*, [1969] 2 All E.R. 676 at p.683.

[40] [1990] S.C.L.R. 484; and see also *Crown Estate Commissioners v. Fairlie Yacht Slip Ltd.*, [1979] S.C. 156.

[41] See the Cornwall Submarine Mines Act 1858.

[42] For example, as regards oyster beds extending below low water mark: *Gann v. Free Fishers of Whitstable*, (1865) 11 H.L.C. 192; *Foreman v. Free Fishers of Whitstable*, (1869) L.R. 4 H.L. 266; *Loose v. Castleton*, (1978) *The Times*, 21 June 1978.

limits of territorial waters are presumed to be the property of the Crown and the onus of establishing title to such land by adverse possession lies upon the person asserting such possession.[43]

The difficulties surrounding Crown ownership of the territorial sea bed do not prevent the exercise of legislative jurisdiction in relation to it, and a number of enactments illustrate this form of control over sea bed activities in this area.[44] In particular, the Protection of Wrecks Act 1973 was enacted to secure the protection of wrecks, and the sites of wrecks, in territorial waters from interference by unauthorised persons. This protection is provided by means of a power of the Secretary of State to make an order designating an area around the site of a wreck in United Kingdom waters[45] as a "restricted area". The power is not to be exercised in relation to any area unless he is satisfied that it is, or may prove to be, the site of a vessel lying wrecked on or in the sea bed, and that on account of the historical, archaeological or artistic importance of the vessel, or of any objects contained or formerly contained in it which may be lying on the sea bed in or near the wreck, the site ought to be protected from unauthorised interference. Within a restricted area it is an offence to tamper with, damage or remove any part of a vessel or any object formerly contained in it; to carry out diving or salvage operations directed to the exploration of the wreck or remove objects from it or from the sea bed; or to deposit anything which would obliterate the site, obstruct access to it or damage any part of the wreck. This offence is made subject to a licensing power whereby the Secretary of State may authorise persons who are competent and properly equipped to carry out salvage operations, or authorise other activities to be undertaken by persons who have a legitimate reason for requiring a licence.[46]

---

[43] *Secretary of State for India v. Chelikani Rama Rao*, (1916) L.R. 43 Ind. App. 192.

[44] For example, see s.18 Coast Protection Act 1949, prohibiting the excavation of minerals on or under the sea shore; s.36 Wildlife and Countryside Act 1981, concerning marine nature reserves; ss.35 to 41 Ancient Monuments and Archaeological Areas Act 1979, concerning areas of archaeological importance.

[45] "United Kingdom waters" means any part of the sea within the seaward limits of the United Kingdom, and includes any part of a river within the ebb and flow of ordinary spring tides. "The sea" includes any estuary or arm of the sea (s.3(1) Protection of Wrecks Act 1973).

[46] s.1(1), (3) and (5).

A power to designate an area as a "prohibited area" under the 1973 Act may be exercised by the Secretary of State where a wrecked vessel is a potential danger to life or property because of anything contained in it, and on that account ought to be protected from unauthorised interference. Accordingly, it is an offence for a person, without written consent granted by the Secretary of State, to enter a prohibited area either on the surface or under the water.[47] The penalties provided for under the Act are that a person found guilty of an offence relating to a designated or prohibited area will be liable, on summary conviction, to a fine of not more than £2,000 or, on conviction on indictment, to a fine of unlimited amount. These offences are subject to general exception in that they are not committed where action is taken for the sole purpose of dealing with an emergency, or by a body exercising statutory powers, or out of necessity due to stress of weather or navigational hazards.[48]

THE EXCLUSIVE ECONOMIC ZONE

The exclusive economic zone in international law

The idea of a band of the sea beyond territorial waters in which a coastal state possess jurisdictional powers has been recognised in relation to fisheries for some time.[49] It was not until the United Nations Conference on the Law of the Sea in 1982, however, that the idea became clearly defined. Under UNCLOS, the "exclusive economic zone" is defined as an area of sea beyond and adjacent to the territorial sea,[50] in which the rights and jurisdiction of the coastal state and the rights and freedoms of other states are subject to the specific legal regime established under Part V of the Convention.[51] Amongst other things, this regime provides that the zone is not to extend beyond 200 nautical miles from the baselines from which the breadth of the territorial sea is measured.[52]

---

47 s.2.

48 s.3(3).

49 *Fisheries Jurisdiction Cases (United Kingdom v. Iceland)*, 1974 I.C.J. Rep. 3.

50 See p.26 above.

51 Art.55 UNCLOS.

52 Art.57.

Within the exclusive economic zone the coastal state possesses: (a) sovereign rights for the purpose of exploring and exploiting, conserving and managing the natural resources, whether living or non-living, of the water superjacent to the sea-bed and of the sea-bed and subsoil, and with regard to other activities for the economic exploitation and exploration of the zone, such as the production of energy from the water, currents and winds; (b) jurisdiction as provided for in the relevant provision of the convention with regard to, (i) the establishment and use of artificial islands, installations and structures, (ii) marine and scientific research, (iii) the protection and preservation of the marine environment; and (c) other rights and duties provided by the UNCLOS Convention.[53]

Notably, the rights possessed by coastal states in relation to the exclusive economic zone fall short of complete sovereignty over the area and remain subject to the basic freedoms of the high seas,[54] including the freedom of navigation. More generally the coastal state is bound to pay due regard to the rights and duties of other states in relation to the zone.[55] Rights over the exclusive economic zone also entail certain duties in relation to it. Amongst these are the obligations of the coastal state to conserve and utilise the natural living resources of the zone at the maximum sustainable yield and to determine the allowable catch of such resources.[56]

The exclusive economic zone in domestic law

A key application of the concept of the Exclusive Economic Zone in the law of England and Wales arises in relation to fishery limits. In accordance with the international regime for coastal jurisdiction, the Fishery Limits Act 1976 provides that British fishery limits[57] extend to 200 nautical miles[58] from the baselines from which the territorial sea adjacent to the United Kingdom, the Channel Islands and the Isle of Man

[53] Art.56(1).
[54] See p.39 below.
[55] Art.56(2) UNCLOS.
[56] Arts.61 and 62.
[57] Subject to s.10(2) Fishery Limits Act 1976, references to British fishery limits in any enactment relating to sea fishing or whaling are to the limits set by or under s.1 of the Act (s.1(5) Fishery Limits Act 1976).
[58] "Miles" means international nautical miles of 1,852 metres (s.8).

is measured. This general limit is subject to the express proviso that Her Majesty may by Order in Council declare that British fishery limits may extend to any other specified line for the purpose of implementing any international agreement or the arbitral award of an international body. Where the median line[59] is less that 200 miles from the baselines for territorial waters, and no other line is specified by an Order in Council, British fishery limits extend to the median line.[60]

The Ministers[61] may by order[62] designate any country outside the United Kingdom, Channel Islands and the Isle of Man and, in relation to it, areas within British fishery limits in which, and descriptions of sea fish[63] for which, fishing boats[64] registered in that country may fish. A foreign fishing boat[65] not registered in a country for the time being designated under the Fishery Limits Act 1976 must not enter British fishery limits except for a purpose recognised by international law or by a convention for the time being in force between the United Kingdom and the government of the country to which the boat belongs. A boat entering those limits for such a purpose must return outside these limits as soon as the purpose has been fulfilled and must not fish or attempt to fish while within the limits. A foreign boat which is registered must not

---

[59] The median line is a line every point of which is equidistant from the nearest points of, on the one hand, the baselines mentioned above and, on the other hand, the corresponding baselines of other countries (s.1(4)).

[60] s.1.

[61] "The Ministers" means the Minister of Agriculture, Fisheries and Food and the Secretaries of State concerned with sea fishing in Scotland and Northern Ireland respectively, and in Wales the Secretary of State for Wales acting jointly (s.8, as amended by the Transfer of Functions (Wales)(No.1) Order 1978, S.I. 1978 No.272).

[62] Such orders are subject to annulment pursuant to a resolution of either House of Parliament (s.2(7) Fishery Limits Act 1976) and orders are made by statutory instrument (s.6(1)).

[63] "Sea fish" includes shellfish, salmon and migratory trout, and "sea fishing" has a corresponding meaning (s.8).

[64] "Fishing boat" means any vessel employed in fishing operations or any operations ancillary thereto (s.8).

[65] "Foreign fishing boat" means a fishing boat which is not (a) registered in the United Kingdom, the Channel Islands or the Isle of Man; or (b) exempted from registration by regulations under s.373 of the Merchant Shipping Act 1894; or (c) owned wholly by a person who is (within the meaning of the Merchant Shipping Act 1894) qualified to own a British ship (s.8 Fishery Limits Act 1976).

fish or attempt to fish within British fishery limits except in an area and for descriptions of fish for the time being designated in relation to that country. At any time when a foreign fishing boat is in an area within British fishery limits and whether it is prohibited from fishing in that area at all, or it is permitted to fish only for certain descriptions of fish, then its fishing gear, or so much of it as is not required for permitted fishing, must be stowed in accordance with an order made by the Ministers.[66]

Contravention of any of the provisions relating to access to British fisheries will, on summary conviction, make the master of the boat liable to a fine not exceeding £50,000 or, on conviction on indictment, liable to a fine of an unlimited amount. In addition the court may on convicting him make an order for the forfeiture of any fish or fishing gear found in the boat or taken or used by any person from the boat. These measures do not prohibit or restrict fishing by fishing boats registered in a country outside the United Kingdom in an area with respect to which special provision is made by arrangements between the United Kingdom government and the government of that country for fishing for the purpose of scientific research.[67] The Ministers may by order license fishing by British or foreign fishing boats in any specified area within British fishery limits.[68]

The general prohibitions and restrictions upon activities of fishing boats registered outside the United Kingdom are subject to a major exception in relation to fishing rights within the European Economic Community. Within the Community the fishing industry is subject to a common structural policy, whereby equality of access to maritime fishing grounds under the sovereignty of the member states is to be secured, allowing fishermen common access to Community waters.[69] However, if any fishing boat fishes within British fishery limits in contravention of an enforceable Community restriction, the master, owner and charterer are each guilty of an offence.[70] The fisheries

---

[66] s.2(2) to (4).

[67] s.2(5) and (6).

[68] s.4 Sea Fish (Conservation) Act 1967, as substituted by s.3 Fishery Limits Act 1976.

[69] See EEC Council Regulation 101/76 preamble; and see *Re Sea Fishery Restrictions: EC Commission v. Ireland*, [1978] 2 C.M.L.R. 466, E.C.J.

[70] s.30(1) Fisheries Act 1981.

Ministers may make whatever legal provision is necessary for the enforcement of Community restrictions or obligations in relation to sea fishing.[71]

THE CONTINENTAL SHELF

The continental shelf in international law

In geographical terms, the "continental shelf" refers to the gently sloping ledge covered by relatively shallow water projecting from the coastline which occurs before the steep decline into ocean waters. It is an area of sea bed which varies considerably in its extent in different parts of the world. For example, off parts of the west coast of the United States the continental shelf extends less than five miles, whilst, by comparison, the entire bed of the North Sea constitutes continental shelf.

For the purposes of international law, UNCLOS defines the continental shelf of a coastal state as: "the sea–bed and subsoil of the submarine areas that extend beyond its territorial sea throughout the natural prolongation of its land territory to the outer edge of the continental margin, or to a distance of 200 nautical miles from the baselines from which the breadth of the territorial sea is measured where the outer edge of the continental margin does not extend up to that distance". Hence the continental shelf extends to 200 nautical miles for all states, but may extend considerably further for some states, depending upon coastal geography, up to a general outer limit of 350 nautical miles.[72]

The rights of a coastal state in relation to the continental shelf consist of a collection of functional sovereign rights concerning the exploration and exploitation of natural resources. Specifically, the natural resources concerned consist of mineral and other non–living resources of the sea bed and subsoil together with living organisms belonging to sedentary species. Along with the power of the coastal state to undertake and regulate the exploration for, and exploration of, these resources

---

[71] s.30(2); see also s.2(2) European Communities Act 1972; Case 34/83 *Gewise v. Mackenzie*, [1984] 2 All E.R. 129, E.C.J.; and Case 213/89 *Factortame Ltd. v. Secretary of State for Transport (No.2)*, [1991] 1 All E.R. 70.

[72] Art.76(1) and (6) UNCLOS.

itself, it may grant consents to others to do so.[73] The rights of the coastal state over the continental shelf do not affect the legal status of the superjacent waters or the status of the air space above the waters. Moreover, the exercise of the rights of the coastal state over the continental shelf must not infringe or result in any unjustifiable interference with navigation and other rights and freedoms of other states as provided for in the Convention.[74]

Clearly the geography of the continental shelf does not always place it within the jurisdiction of a single coastal state. Accordingly, as with the determination of the boundaries of exclusive economic zones, it is necessary to determine rights to the geographical continental shelf between states which share a land border running to the sea, termed "adjacent states", and states which share a continental shelf which runs under the area of sea between them, termed "opposite states". The strict legal principles relating to the determination of the exclusive economic zone and the continental shelf are essentially the same: delimitation of the areas between states with opposite or adjacent coasts is to be effected by agreement on the basis of international law in order to achieve an equitable solution.[75]

The practice of determining the extent of the continental shelf, as illustrated in the *North Sea Continental Shelf Cases*,[76] stressed the need for delimitation to be effected by agreement in accordance with equitable principles taking into account all the relevant circumstances. These circumstances may take cognisance of the "equidistance principle" of dividing the continental shelf by a median line drawn equidistant from the nearest points of the baselines of the territorial sea of each state.[77] This rule is not to be applied, however, where it leads to an inequitable result, or where it defeats the ultimate objective of determining the "natural prolongation" of the land territory of the states concerned.[78]

---

[73] Art.77.

[74] Art.78.

[75] Art.74 relating to the exclusive economic zone; and Art.83 relating to the continental shelf.

[76] (1969) I.C.J. Rep p.3.

[77] Previously provided for by Art.6 Convention on the Continental Shelf (1964) Cmnd.2422.

[78] *Anglo–French Continental Shelf Case*, (1979) 18 I.L.M. 397.

The continental shelf in domestic law

Within the domestic law of England and Wales the Continental Shelf Act 1964 was passed to give effect to the Convention on the High Seas of 1958,[79] allowing coastal states to exercise sovereign rights over the continental shelf, defined according to international law, for the purposes of exploring and exploiting its natural resources. The Act enables Orders in Council to be made designating areas of the sea within which any rights exercisable by the United Kingdom outside territorial waters with respect to the sea bed and subsoil and their natural resources become vested in the Crown.[80] An exception to this principle arises in relation to deposits of coal where rights to this resource are exercisable by the British Coal Corporation, and in relation to petroleum where the licensing and other provisions of the Petroleum (Production) Act 1934 are applicable.[81] The Continental Shelf Act 1964 also provides for the designation of areas for the safety of navigation, wireless telegraphy, radioactive substances, and submarine cables and pipe–lines.[82]

Another example of regulation extending to the continental shelf is the Mineral Workings (Offshore Installations) Act 1971,[83] which was enacted to provide for the safety, health and welfare or persons on installations concerned with the underwater exploitation and exploration of mineral resources in the waters surrounding the United Kingdom, and generally for the safety of offshore installations and the prevention of accidents on or near them. The Act empowers the Secretary of State to

---

[79] Cmnd.584.

[80] s.1(1) Continental Shelf Act 1964. See Continental Shelf (Designation of Areas) Order 1964, S.I. 1964 No.697, and further orders S.I. 1965 No.1531; S.I. 1968 No.891; S.I. 1971 No.594; S.I. 1974 No.1489; S.I. 1976 No.1153; S.I. 1977 No.1871; S.I. 1978 No.178; S.I. 1978 No.1029; S.I. 1979 No.1447; S.I. 1982 No.1072; and S.I. 1989 No.2398.

[81] s.1(2) and (3) Petroleum (Production) Act 1934; and see also Coal Industry Act 1987.

[82] ss.2 to 9 Continental Shelf Act 1964. Other matters originally provided for under the 1964 Act, relating to the protection of installations, the discharge of oil and the supply of natural gas, are now provided for under Oil and Gas (Enterprise) Act 1982, Prevention of Oil Pollution Act 1971 and the Energy Act 1976 respectively.

[83] As amended by the Oil and Gas (Enterprise) Act 1982.

make regulations for the registration of offshore installations[84] and their construction and survey,[85] and for the safety, health and welfare of persons on offshore installations in waters to which the Act applies.[86] There are also provisions regarding the appointment and duties of managers of such installations, and for the application of the criminal law to installations in territorial waters and designated areas.[87]

THE HIGH SEAS

The high seas in international law

As a matter of international law, the meaning of the phrase the "high seas" is confined to those parts of the sea that are not included in the exclusive economic zone, the territorial sea or the internal waters of a state.[88] Following a classical doctrine of the Law of the Sea expressed by Grotius,[89] the high seas are free, or *res communis*, and not subject to appropriation by, or the sovereignty of, any nation.

The principle of freedom of the seas is stated in the United Nations Conference on the Law of the Sea of 1982 to comprise, *inter alia*, both for coastal and landlocked states: (a) freedom of navigation; (b) freedom of overflight; (c) freedom to lay submarine cables and pipelines, subject to Part VI of the Convention; (d) freedom to construct artificial islands

---

[84] "Offshore installation" means any installation which is maintained, or is to be established, for underwater exploitation or exploration; "exploration" means exploration with a view to exploitation; "underwater exploitation" or "underwater exploration" means exploitation or exploration from or by means of any floating or other installation which is maintained in the water, or on the foreshore or other land intermittently covered with water, and is not connected with dry land by a permanent structure providing access at all times and for all purposes (s.1(3) Mineral Workings (Offshore Installations) Act 1971).

[85] ss.2, 3 and 7 Mineral Workings (Offshore Installations) Act 1971.

[86] "Waters to which the Act applies" means the waters in or adjacent to the United Kingdom up to the seaward limits of territorial waters, and the waters in any designated area within the meaning of the Continental Shelf Act 1964 (ss.1(2)(a), 6 and 7 Mineral Workings (Offshore Installations) Act 1971).

[87] s.8.

[88] Art.86 UNCLOS.

[89] *Mare Liberum* (1609).

and other installations permitted under international law, subject to part VI of the Convention; (e) freedom of fishing, subject to conditions laid down by s.2 of Part VII of the Convention; (f) freedom of scientific research, subject to Parts VI and XIII of the Convention. These freedoms are to be exercised by all states with due regard to the interests of other states in their exercise of the freedom of the high seas, and also with regard to rights under the Convention with respect to activities in the area concerned.[90] It is specifically provided, however, that the freedoms relating to the high seas are to be reserved for peaceful purposes.[91]

In relation to state jurisdiction over ships on the high seas, the flag state, that is, the state in which the ship is registered, will under most circumstances have exclusive jurisdiction over the vessel. Within the terms of UNCLOS, the right of the state of nationality to exercise exclusive civil and criminal jurisdiction over it is subject to specified exceptions. The exceptions are: (a) cases of "hot pursuit" from the territorial sea or contiguous zone; (b) as a residual right in cases of collisions on the high seas; (c) cases of piracy; (d) cases in respect of unauthorised sound and television broadcasting; (e) under the right of visit in cases of ships of unknown nationality; and (f) cases in respect of certain pollution matters.[92] In these exceptional situations jurisdiction is shared by the flag state and other states which consist, generally, of those states specifically interested or harmed by the actions of the ship concerned. In relation to piracy, however, this is a crime of universal jurisdiction in international law in which all states share jurisdiction.

The high seas in domestic law

Under the law of England and Wales the "high seas" traditionally commence at low water mark,[93] and comprise all the sea beyond the low water mark. This is in accordance with the customary view of the jurisdiction of the Court of Admiralty, that the "high seas" encompass all water below low water mark where great ships can go, except such parts

---

[90] Art.87 UNCLOS.

[91] Art.88.

[92] The six exceptions are provided for under Arts.11, 97, 100, 109, 110 and 221 respectively.

[93] *R. v. Keyn*, (1856), 2 Ex. D. 63.

of the sea as are within the body of a county, for the realm of England extends only to the low–water mark and all beyond that constitutes the high seas.[94] This is in notable contrast to the position in international law, which, as previously stated, defines the "high seas" as commencing outside the limits of the territorial waters of coastal states, and consequently the expression extends to all parts of the sea that are not included in the territorial waters or internal waters of a state.[95]

Following international law, the law of England and Wales regards the high seas as open to all for navigation,[96] commerce and fishery,[97] and also for aviation and the laying of submarine cables and pipe lines.[98] The soil of the bed of the sea beyond territorial waters does not belong to the Crown or to any individual. However, the Crown may exercise certain rights over areas of the sea bed and subsoil outside territorial waters as designated by Order in Council made pursuant to the Continental Shelf Act 1964.[99]

THE FORESHORE

Limits and ownership

In the law of England and Wales, the expressions "foreshore" and "seashore" have the same meaning.[100] Both refer to that portion of land which lies between high and low water mark at ordinary tides,[101] or

---

[94] *The Mecca*, [1895] P. 95; and *R. v. Liverpool JJ, ex parte Molyneux*, [1972] 2 All E.R. 471.

[95] See the Report of the First United Nations Conference on the Law of the Sea (1958) (Cmnd. 584), Art.1 Convention on the High Seas.

[96] Generally on rights of navigation see Ch.6 below.

[97] Generally on rights of fishery see Ch.8 below.

[98] See the Report on the Law of the Sea (1958) (Cmnd. 584), Art.2 Convention on the High Seas.

[99] See p.38 above.

[100] *Mellor v. Walmesley*, [1905] 2 Ch. 164; and see the definition of "seashore" under s.49(1) Coast Protection Act 1949.

[101] *Attorney–General v. Chambers*, (1854) 23 L.T.O.S. 238; *Scratton v. Brown*, (1825) 4 B. & S. 485. *Scratton v. Brown* was distinguished in *Baxendale v. Instow Parish Council*, [1981] 2 All E.R. 620.

between the ordinary flux and reflux of the sea.[102] Ordinary high tide is taken as the line of medium high tide between the spring and neap tides, and is ascertained by the average of the medium tides during the year,[103] that is, the point on the shore which is about four days in each week for the most part of the year reached and covered by the tides.[104] Notably, in Scotland the bounds of the "foreshore" are differently drawn with the area of the foreshore circumscribed by the lines of high and low water marks of *ordinary spring tides*.[105]

Although ordinarily the expression "sea beach" may be used to describe an area of land extending beyond the foreshore, and perhaps only washed by exceptionally high tides, in law it has been held that, *prima facie*, "sea beach" should be attributed the same meaning as "foreshore". That is to say, land described as a "sea beach" normally extends landward only so far as the boundary line of medium high tide.[106] Similarly the expression "coastline" has been construed to be limited by the upper boundary of the foreshore.[107]

The soil of the foreshore and the bed of arms and estuaries of the sea, and of tidal navigable rivers, so far as the tide ebbs and flows, lies *prima facie* in the ownership of the Crown.[108] This principle is, however, subject to exceptions where ownership is excluded by a stronger title,[109] or where the Crown has parted with ownership.[110] The Crown's right of ownership in tidal waters is subject to the public rights of fishery and

---

[102] *Blundell v. Catterall*, (1821) 5 B. & Ald. 268. See also the definition of "seashore" under s.49(1) Coast Protection Act 1949, cited at p.145 below.

[103] *Tracey Elliot v. Morley (Earl)*, (1907) 51 S.J. 625.

[104] *Attorney-General v. Chambers*, (1854) 23 L.T.O.S. 238.

[105] *Fisherrow Harbour Commissioners v. Mussleborough Real Estate Co.*, (1903) 5 F. 387 (Scotland).

[106] *Government of the State of Penang v. Beng Hong Oon*, [1971] 3 All E.R. 1163; and *Southern Centre of Theosophy Inc. v. State of South Australia*, [1982] 1 All E.R. 283.

[107] *Nanaimo Rly Co. v. Treat*, (1919) 121 L.T. 657 (Canada).

[108] *Malcomson v. O'Dea*, (1863) 27 J.P. 820; *Bulstrode v. Hall*, (1663) 1 Sid. 148; *Kirby v. Gibbs*, (1667) 2 Keble 274; *Dickens and Kemp v. Shaw*, (1823) 1 L.J.O.S.K.B. 122; *Attorney-General v. Emerson*, [1891] A.C. 649; *Attorney-General v. Richards*, (1795) 2 Anst. 603; *Attorney-General v. Storey*, (1912) 109 L.T. 430.

[109] *Attorney-General v. London Corpn.*, (1849) 13 Jur. 372.

[110] *Le Strange v. Rowe*, (1866) 4 F. & F. 1048.

navigation and rights ancillary thereto.[111] Land above the foreshore is presumed to belong to the owner of adjoining land,[112] but there is no legal presumption that the foreshore between high and low water mark belongs to the adjacent land owner.[113] Any encroachment on the soil of the foreshore held by the Crown has been held to be a public nuisance to the Queen's subjects either in relation to their right of navigation or right of way.[114] Hence, the placing of an unauthorised erection on the bed of the foreshore by a person who is not the owner may be restrained by an injunction at the suit of the Attorney General whether it amounts to a nuisance or not, and may be abated by a private owner.[115] Likewise the Crown Estate Commissioners, as the administrators of the Crown's estate in the sea bed, have the exclusive right to permit the laying of fixed moorings on the sea bed, and the laying of such moorings is not justified as an incident of the public right of navigation.[116]

In many instances the foreshore is owned by the lord of the manor,[117] or a local authority[118] or a private individual,[119] and may be part of an adjoining manor,[120] town[121] or land.[122] Title to the foreshore may be held in gross[123] and may be freehold or leasehold.[124] Ownership of the

---

[111] *Fitzhardinge (Lord) v. Purcell*, (1908) 72 J.P. 276.

[112] *Lowe v. Govett*, (1832) 1 L.J.K.B. 224.

[113] *Webber v. Richards*, (1844) 2 L.T.O.S. 420.

[114] *R. v. Betts*, (1850) 16 Q.B. 1022; *R. v. Randall*, (1842) Car. & M. 496; *R. v. Russell*, (1827) 6 B. & C. 566.

[115] *R. v. Grosvenor*, (1819) 2 Stark. 511; *Attorney-General v. Johnson*, (1819) 2 Wils. Ch. 87; *Orr Ewing v. Colquhoun*, (1877) 2 A.C. 839.

[116] *Crown Estate Commissioners v. Fairlie Yacht Slip Ltd.*, [1979] S.C. 156 (Scotland); *Trustees of the Port and Harbour of Lerwick v. Crown Estate Commissioners*, (1990) S.C.L.R. 484.

[117] *Attorney-General v. Hanmer*, (1858) 22 J.P. 543.

[118] *Attorney-General v. Burridge*, (1822) 10 Price 350.

[119] *Bristow v. Cormican*, (1878) 3 A.C. 641.

[120] *Re Walton-cum-Trimley, ex p. Tomline*, (1873) 28 L.R. 12; *Beaufort (Duke) v. Swansea Corp.*, (1849) 3 Ex. 413; *Kirby v. Gibbs*, (1667) 2 Keble 294.

[121] *Foster v. Warblington U.D.C.*, [1906] 1 K.B. 648.

[122] *Brew v. Haren*, (1877) Ir. R. 11 C.L. 198.

[123] *Mulholland v. Killen*, (1874) Ir. R. 9 Eq. 471; *Healy v. Thorne*, (1870) Ir. R. 4 C.L. 495.

[124] *Mercer v. Denne*, [1904] 2 Ch. 534.

foreshore may pass to a subject by three means: (1) express grant; (2) prescription; or (3) possessory title.

Express grant

A subject may be the owner of part of the foreshore by express grant from the Crown, but the grant will be construed strictly in favour of the Crown *pro publico bono* and against the grantee.[125] Nonetheless, the foreshore will pass from the Crown providing that the grant contains sufficient description of the soil between high and low water mark.[126] Thus a grant of "lands within the flux and reflux of the sea" has been held to be a clear recognition that the foreshore between the land boundary of a manor and low water mark was vested in the lord of the manor.[127] In each instance, however, the question of whether a grant of a manor by the sea coast includes the foreshore will depend on the language of the grant. In particular, ownership will depend on whether it can be presumed from the grant that the landward boundary is formed by the high water mark, in which case the foreshore will be excluded from the grant, or, alternatively, whether the boundary extends to low water mark, in which case the foreshore will be within the grant.[128]

In an instance of doubt as to whether a particular grant by the Crown includes the foreshore, as where the limits of an ancient grant of a manor are inadequately defined, evidence of acts of use antecedent to the grant may be given to clarify the extent of the grant.[129] Also evidence of modern acts of ownership are admissible to show that the foreshore is a part of the manor.[130] In particular, acts of continuous ownership which may have a bearing on the extent of a grant include rights of anchorage, groundage and taking wreck, royal fish and seaweed, constructing jetties, and licences to take shingle, sand and gravel.[131] In each case, however,

---

[125] *Attorney–General v. Parmeter, Re Portsmouth Harbour*, (1811) 10 Price 378.
[126] *Attorney–General v. Hanmer*, (1858) 22 J.P. 543.
[127] *Attorney–General v. Emerson*, [1891] A.C. 649; *Hindson v. Ashby*, [1896] 2 Ch. 1.
[128] *Hastings Corpn. v. Ivall*, (1874) L.R. 19 Eq. 558.
[129] *Van Diemens' Land Co. v. Table Cape Marine Board*, [1906] A.C. 92.
[130] *Beaufort (Duke) v. Swansea Corpn.*, (1849) 3 Ex. 413.
[131] *Chad v. Tilsed*, (1821) 5 Moore 185; *Le Strange v. Rowe*, (1866) 4 F. & F. 1048; *Brew v. Haren*, (1877) Ir. R. 11 C.L. 198; *Lord Advocate v. Blantyre*, (1879) 4 A.C. 770.

the overriding question of fact to be determined is that of whether the grant, coupled with the evidence of acts of ownership, show that, on the balance of probabilities, the foreshore in question was passed by the grant.[132]

Grant by prescription

In the absence of an express grant of the foreshore by the Crown, acts of ownership by the claimant may be regarded as evidence of ownership, and taken into account along with other circumstances, in determining whether the claimant has acquired a prescriptive title to the foreshore.[133] In a situation where an action is brought by the claimant against a trespasser, sufficient title to the foreshore can be established against the trespasser without the need for the claimant to produce evidence sufficient to displace the title of the Crown.[134]

Evidence of long use, coupled with a grant, may be sufficient to satisfy a court of the claimant's title to part of the foreshore.[135] A very strong case for a prescriptive right will be required to persuade a court to accept that there has been a grant of part of the foreshore, and it is difficult to state definitive requirements with regard to the character and length of possession necessary to provide prescriptive entitlement to the foreshore.[136] Consequently, each case must depend upon its own particular circumstances.[137] However, proof by the lord of an adjoining manor of the ownership of a several fishery over part of the foreshore has been held to raise a presumption of ownership against the Crown that the freehold of that part of the foreshore is vested in the owner of the fishery.[138] Similarly, evidence of a custom to take "wreck of the sea, flotsam and jetsam",[139] building a retaining wall on the foreshore and

---

[132] *Attorney-General v. Jones*, (1862) 2 H. & C. 347.

[133] *Lord Advocate v. Wemyss*, [1900] A.C. 48.

[134] *Hastings Corpn. v. Ivall*, (1874) L.R. 19 Eq. 558.

[135] *Beaufort (Duke) v. Swansea Corpn.*, (1849) 3 Ex. 413; *Attorney-General for Ireland v. Vandeleur*, [1907] A.C. 369.

[136] *Dickens and Kemp v. Shaw*, (1823) 1 L.J.O.S.K.B. 122.

[137] *Lord Advocate v. Young*, (1887) 12 A.C. 544.

[138] *Attorney-General v. Emerson*, [1891] A.C. 649; *Somerset (Duke) v. Fogwell*, (1826) 5 B. & C. 875.

[139] *Hamilton v. Attorney-General for Ireland*, (1880) 5 L.R. Ir. Ch. 555.

taking sand, stone and seaweed from the shore,[140] have been held admissible in proving title to the seashore.

Possessory title

A person may obtain title to the foreshore where it has been held against the Crown for more than sixty years, or more than twelve years against a subject who was the previous owner.[141]

Accretion and encroachment

"Accretion" is the natural addition of soil to waterside land, whilst "dereliction" is the retreat of water to expose new land, and the legal principles relating to these processes apply to changes to the foreshore in the same way as to changes in the boundaries of inland waters. In general, where either accretion or dereliction has the result of adding land above the foreshore "slowly, gradually and by imperceptible increase", the new land belongs to the owner of the land above high water mark, and not to the Crown. Where the foreshore is owned by a subject, land added to the foreshore belongs to the owner of the foreshore.[142] Conversely where encroachment of the sea takes place with the same imperceptible progress, due either to erosion of waterside land or the advancement of the sea, land which was formerly above high water mark becomes the property of the owner of the foreshore to the detriment of the owner of the adjacent land.[143] Foreshore which is encroached upon by the sea passes either to the private ownership of the soil in the tidal water,[144] or becomes a part of the sea bed which is in the ownership of the Crown. Public rights of navigation and fishing over the foreshore follow

[140] *Lord Advocate v. Young*, (1887) 12 A.C. 544; *Calmady v. Rowe*, (1844) 6 C.B. 861; *Linnane v. Nestor and McNamara*, [1943] I.R. 208.

[141] s.15 and Sch.1 para.11 Limitation Act 1980. See *Attorney-General of Southern Nigeria v. Holt & Co. Ltd.*, [1915] A.C. 599; *Philpot v. Bath*, (1905) 21 T.L.R. 634.

[142] *Gifford v Lord Yarborough*, (1828) 5 Bing. 163; *Doe d. Seebkristo v. East India Co.*, (1856) 10 Moo. P.C.C. 140.

[143] *Re Hull and Selby Rly Co.*, (1839) 5 M. & W. 327; *Mahoney v. Neenan and Neenan*, (No.2) (1966) 100 I.L.T.R. 205.

[144] *Scratton v. Brown*, (1825) 5 B. & C. 485; distinguished in *Baxendale v. Instow Parish Council,* [1981] 2 All E.R. 620.

the extent of the foreshore, as it alters by accretion and encroachment from time to time.[145]

The application of the doctrine of accretion to the ownership of coastal land is subject to the requirement that the changes which take place are "imperceptible". This term is understood to mean that the changes which take place are imperceptible in their progress, and not necessarily that they are imperceptible after a long lapse of time.[146] The requirement that deposition takes place "slowly, gradually and by imperceptible increase" only defines the test of accretion relative to the conditions to which it is applied.[147]

The doctrine of accretion is based on the impracticality of identifying an old boundary line from time to time where it is obscured due to the gradual and imperceptible addition of alluvium to land.[148] Thus, where acquisition from the sea or a river is slow, gradual and imperceptible, the necessity of the situation, and the difficulties of any other means of determining ownership, cause the law to regard the alluvium as belonging to the owner of the adjoining land.[149] Although the eventual amount of land which is acquired by accretion may be considerable "that which cannot be perceived in its progress is taken as if it never had existed at all".[150] The title to the alluvial land follows that of the land to which it adheres.[151]

The doctrine of accretion applies to the seashore and land abutting flowing watercourses, including both tidal and non–tidal waters, whether navigable or not.[152] Accretion applies to islands which arise within the territorial limit of the sea, which become the property of the Crown, subject to the possibility of a person establishing a title by adverse possession where the onus of establishing this lies upon the person asserting adverse possession.[153] Until recent times it was thought that the doctrine did not apply to stillwaters such as canals, lakes and other areas

---

[145] *Mercer v. Denne*, [1905] 2 Ch. 538.

[146] *Gifford v. Lord Yarborough*, (1828) 5 Bing. 163.

[147] *Secretary of State for India v. Vizlinagaram*, (1921) L.R. 49 Ind. App. 67.

[148] *Hindson v. Ashby*, (1896) 60 J.P. 454; *Foster v. Wright*, (1878) 44 J.P. 7.

[149] *Lopez v. Muddum Mohum Thaokoor*, (1870) 13 Moo. Ind. App. 467.

[150] *Re Hull and Selby Railway Co.*, (1839) 5 M. & W. 328.

[151] *Sree Eckowrie Sing v. Heeraloll Seal*, (1868) 12 Moo. Ind. App. 136.

[152] *Foster v. Wright*, (1878) 44 J.P. 7.

[153] *Secretary of State for India v. Chelikani Rama Rao*, (1916) 85 L.J.P.C. 222.

of stillwater, but it has now been established that there is no reason in principle to prevent the application of accretion to these waters.[154]

The doctrine of accretion has long been recognised to be a convenient rule for the adjustment of the boundaries of property, but a rather "rough–and–ready" solution to particular problems which may vary significantly in their special facts.[155] For that reason it has been thought that it should be subject to exceptions to take account of the individual circumstances to which it is applied. In particular, some uncertainty has previously surrounded the question as to whether the doctrine of accretion applied to situations where the original boundary line of a property was clear and fixed so that the extent of the alluvial land was readily determined in relation to it.[156] The uncertainty was resolved in *Brighton and Hove General Gas Co. v. Hove Bungalows Ltd.*,[157] where it was held that the general law of accretion applied irrespective of the former boundary of the land being well known and readily ascertainable.[158]

In general, a conveyance of land which includes a portion of the foreshore will entitle those claiming under the grantee to an increase in the land which has been brought about by accretion.[159] Likewise, a conveyance of land which is bounded by the sea shore will pass any land which is subsequently added as a result of accretion.[160] Land added by accretion in consequence of gradual and imperceptible recession of the sea assumes the legal characteristics of the adjoining land and may,

---

[154] *Southern Centre of Theosophy Inc. v. State of South Australia*, [1982] 1 All E.R. 283; contrast the previous authority of *Trafford v. Thrower*, (1929) 45 T.L.R. 502.

[155] See Moore *The History and Law of Fisheries* (1903) p.133.

[156] This doubt was expressed in *Ford v. Lacy*, (1861) 30 L.J. Ex. 351; and in *Hindson v. Ashby*, (1896) 60 J.P. 454.

[157] [1924] 1 Ch. 372; see also *Attorney–General. v. M'Carthy*, [1911] 2 I.R. 260; *Secretary of State for India v. Foucar*, (1933) 61 L.R. Ind. App. 18.

[158] See also *Attorney–General Southern Nigeria v. John Holt and Co. Ltd.*, [1924] A.C. 599.

[159] *Mellor v. Walmesley*, (1905) 93 L.T. 574.

[160] *Scratton v. Brown*, (1825) 4 B. & C. 485, distinguished in *Baxendale v. Instow Parish Council*, [1981] 2 All E.R. 620; *Nesbitt v. Mablethorpe U.D.C.*, (1917) 81 J.P. 289.

accordingly, become freehold or leasehold, or subject to customary rights.[161]

The general rules relating to operation of the doctrine of accretion are, however, subject to displacement where clear words are used.[162] Although there is a presumption that a conveyance of foreshore will convey a movable piece of land consisting of the foreshore as it is from time to time, this is a matter of construction.[163] Specifically, it must be considered in each case whether what is conveyed is the "movable freehold" of the foreshore as it is from time to time, or the "fixed freehold" of an immovable piece of land as it was at the time of the conveyance.[164] Hence, despite the doctrine of accretion being founded on justice and convenience, it is now established that it may be qualified by the express intention of the parties to a conveyance of waterside land.[165]

Other qualifications to the operation of the doctrine of accretion exclude its operation where accretions of land on the seashore are shown to have been perceptible in their progress, by reference to marks and measures, for example where accretions of land are due to the erection of harbour works or the removal of shingle under licence, the land which is gained as a consequence belongs to the Crown and not the adjacent owner.[166] Similarly, where property on the original foreshore is suddenly altered by artificial work upon it, the bounds of the property concerned remain in their original position and the reclaimed land is vested in the Crown.[167] Also, where land is suddenly overrun by the sea and marks remain by which its limit may be identified, or where there is only a temporary encroachment, the property remains that of the owner of the land encroached upon.[168] Finally, special provision is made under statute

---

161 *Mercer v. Denne*, [1904] 2 Ch. 538.

162 *Mellor v. Walmesley*, [1905] 2 Ch. 164.

163 *Scratton v. Brown*, [1824–34] All E.R. Rep. 59; distinguished in *Baxendale v. Instow Parish Council,* [1981] 2 All E.R. 620.

164 *Baxendale v. Instow Parish Council*, [1981] 2 All E.R. 620.

165 *Southern Centre of Theosophy Inc. v. State of South Australia*, [1982] 1 All E.R. 283.

166 *Attorney–General v. Reeve*, (1885) 1 T.L.R. 675.

167 *Attorney–General of Southern Nigeria v. Holt*, [1915] A.C. 599.

168 *Hayes v. Hayes*, (1897) 31 I.L.T. 392.

for the acquisition by the National Rivers Authority of certain accretions of land resulting from drainage work.[169]

Rights over the foreshore

At common law there exist a collection of rights which may be exercised in relation to the sea and the foreshore. First, there are the public rights of navigation and fishery which are dealt with elsewhere in this work.[170] Second, there are other miscellaneous rights which may be exercisable either by the public in general or by the owner of the foreshore by virtue of his proprietary interest: these include the right of access to and passage over the foreshore, bathing, taking shells, seaweed, sand, gravel and shingle. Third, there are the prerogative rights of the Crown relating to wreck and royal fish.

Access over the foreshore

The public rights over the foreshore are, at common law, limited to those of fishing, navigation and ancillary rights. Although walking, bathing and beachcombing may be tolerated by the Crown, they are not exercised by virtue of any legal rights possessed by the public. Thus, it has been observed that "it is notorious that many things are done on the foreshore by the public which they have no right to do".[171] In law there is no public entitlement to venture upon the foreshore for bathing or other amusement, or to hold public or religious meetings there, without the consent of the owner, unless these rights may be justified by custom or prescription.[172] Where bathing is generally permitted at a certain place it may be a criminal offence of indecent exposure to bathe uncovered at that place.[173] A local authority is empowered to make byelaws regulating

---

[169] s.155 Water Resources Act 1991; and see p.215 below.

[170] On navigation generally see Ch.6; and on rights of fishery see Ch.8.

[171] *Alfred F. Beckett v. Lyons*, [1966] 2 W.L.R. 421.

[172] *Llandudno U.D.C. v. Woods*, [1899] 2 Ch. 705; *Brighton Corpn. v. Packham*, (1908) 72 J.P. 318; *Brinckman v. Matley*, [1904] 2 Ch. 313; *Blundell v. Catterall*, (1821), 5 B. & Ald. 268.

[173] *R. v. Reed*, (1871) 12 Cox C.C. 1; and see *Ramsgate Corp. v. Debling*, ((1906) 70 J.P. 132) on the right to place deckchairs on the seashore.

public bathing in the sea under s.231 Public Health Act 1936, or by means of a private Act.

Other alleged public rights over the foreshore have been found not to be substantiated by common law. Hence there is no general right for the public to shoot over the foreshore, though the owner of the foreshore may do so.[174] The right to place deckchairs on the seashore for hire cannot be claimed by prescription under the Prescription Act 1832, since it is a right in gross, and an owner of the foreshore has been held to be able to bring an action for an injunction to restrain trespass thereon.[175]

Despite the general limitations upon public access to the foreshore at common law, access is permissible in a number of particular cases. (1) Access is permitted by the public in a case of peril or necessity.[176] (2) Access is allowed by an owner of land adjoining the sea, who has the same right of access as a riparian owner in respect of a tidal river,[177] and this access extends from every part of the frontage over every part of the foreshore and includes a right of access to the sea across the foreshore left bare by the receding tide.[178] (3) Access may be provided for by Part V of the National Parks and Access to the Countryside Act 1949, which provides that the public may enjoy access for open air recreation to open country, which includes the foreshore.[179] (4) The inhabitants of a parish or local fishermen may by immemorial custom acquire a right over the foreshore.[180] (5) In many instances the public are admitted to parts of the seashore vested in local authorities subject to any local regulations or byelaws in force.

A range of particular powers of local authorities to regulate activities on the foreshore is provided for under statute. (1) Where a local authority owns or leases the foreshore, byelaws may be made under s.164 of the Public Health Act 1875, or s.15 of the Open Spaces Act 1906. (2) Powers exist for a local authority to make byelaws for the prevention of danger, obstruction or annoyance to persons using the seashore or

---

[174] *Fitzhardinge (Lord) v. Purcell*, [1908] 2 Ch. 139.

[175] *Behrens v. Richards*, [1905] 2 Ch. 614.

[176] *Blundell v. Catterall*, (1821) 5 B. & Ald. 268; *Brinckman v. Matley*, [1904] 2 Ch. 313; see also s.513 Merchant Shipping Act 1894.

[177] *Attorney–General of Straits Settlement v. Wemyss*, (1888) 13 A.C. 192.

[178] *Coppinger v. Shean*, [1906] 1 Ir. R. 519.

[179] s.59(2) National Parks and Access to the Countryside Act 1949.

[180] *Mercer v. Denne*, [1904] 2 Ch. 534; *Aiton v. Stephen*, (1876) 1 A.C. 459.

promenades under ss.82 and 83 of the Public Health Acts Amendment Act 1907. (3) Byelaws to regulate the speed and use of pleasure boats, including hovercraft, and requiring the use of effectual silencers on boats propelled by internal combustion engines may be made under s.76 of the Public Health Act 1961. (4) Under local Acts some seaside authorities are empowered to make byelaws, and regulations for sea beaches and foreshore vested in them.[181]

Jurisdiction over the foreshore

Formerly, in the absence of evidence to the contrary, the foreshore below high water mark was excluded from the limits of the adjoining parish or town[182] and, accordingly, the occupiers of a pier were only liable for rates in respect of that part of the pier covering land above high water mark.[183] Now, by s.72 of the Local Government Act 1972, every accretion from the sea, whether natural or artificial, and every part of the seashore to low water mark which did not form part of a parish on the 26 October 1972 is annexed to and incorporated with the parish or parishes which the accretion of seashore adjoins in England, or in Wales the community or communities which the accretion of seashore adjoins, in proportion to the extent of the common boundary. The land is consequently annexed and incorporated with the district and county within which that parish or community is situated. The part of the seashore comprised between high and low water mark forms part of the body of the adjoining county and enables cognisance to be taken of offences committed there, whether or not committed when the shore is covered with water.[184] A mechanism is provided for the modification of the seaward boundaries of local government areas through a review commission making proposals to the Secretary of State.[185] The foreshore belonging to the Crown and under the management of the Minister of

---

[181] See *Gray v. Sylvester*, (1897) 61 J.P. 807; *Parker v. Bournemouth Corpn.*, (1902) 66 J.P. 440; *Moorman v. Tordoff*, (1908) 72 J.P. 142; *Glee v. Meadows*, (1911) 75 J.P. 142.

[182] *Bridgewater Trustees v. Bootle-cum-Linacre*, (1866) 7 B. & S. 348.

[183] *R. v. Musson*, (1858) 22 J.P. 609.

[184] *Embleton v. Brown*, (1860) 3 E. & E. 234.

[185] s.71 Local Government Act 1972.

Transport immediately before the 1 April 1950 is now managed by the Crown Estate Commissioners.[186]

The right to take seaweed, shells, sand and shingle

A consequence of the limited common law right of access to the foreshore, for the purposes of navigation, fishing and ancillary matters, is that there is no general public right to take things from the foreshore. Hence the general position in relation to natural products found on the foreshore, such as seaweed, shells, sand and shingle, is that they belong to the owner of the foreshore and cannot lawfully be removed without his permission.[187] Exceptions to this principle, however, arise where a right to take sand, shells, shingle and seaweed exists under statute,[188] or where it is claimed by prescription.[189]

In accordance with the general principle regarding the removal of things from the foreshore, seaweed cast or growing on the foreshore is the property of the foreshore owner,[190] who may bring an action in trespass for its wrongful removal.[191] The owner of land adjoining the foreshore is entitled to seaweed deposited above high water mark by the tides.[192] The public are entitled to take floating seaweed as an incident of the right of navigation or fishing,[193] but the lord of the manor cannot claim an exclusive right to cut seaweed below low water mark except by

---

186 Part III Coast Protection Act 1949 (now repealed); see Crown Estate Acts 1956 and 1961. On the inapplicability of planning law to developments below the limit of the foreshore, see *Argyll and Bute District Council v. Secretary of State for Scotland* ([1977] S.L.T.33).

187 *Howe v. Stawell*, (1833) Alc. & N. 348; *Lowe v. Govett*, (1832) 6 C.B. 681; *Hamilton v. Attorney-General*, (1880) 9 L.R. Ir. 271.

188 For example, 7 Jac. 1, c.18 (1609).

189 *Hamilton v. Attorney-General*, (1880) 9 L.R. Ir. 271; *Attorney-General v. Hanmer*, (1858) 22 J.P. 543.

190 *Howe v. Stawell*, (1833) Alc. & N. 348; *Lowe v. Govett*, (1832) 3 B. & Ad. 863; *Hamilton v. Attorney-General*, (1880) 9 L.R. Ir.271.

191 *Brew v. Haren*, (1877) I.R. 11 CL 198; Calmady v. Rowe, (1844) 6 C.B. 681; *Hastings Corpn. v. Ivall*, (1874) L.R. 19 Eq. 558; *Stoney v. Keane*, (1903) 37 I.L.T. 212; *Linnane v. Nestor and McNamara*, [1943] I.R. 208.

192 *Mahoney v. Neenan and Neenan (No.2)*, (1966) 100 I.L.T.R. 205.

193 *Baird v. Fortune*, (1861) 5 L.T. 2.

grant or prescription.[194] The owner of land on which decomposed seaweed accumulates and becomes a nuisance may be liable to remove it.[195]

A claim to take shingle and sand by the inhabitants of a town cannot be founded on custom, since the claim relates to a *profit a prendre* in the soil of another person, which may arise only by grant or prescription.[196] Despite this, a custom of allowing the freemen of an ancient borough and ship owners to dig ballast has been upheld,[197] and the taking of stones from waste land, whether adjoining the foreshore or otherwise, for the purpose of repairing highways may be pleaded as a prescriptive right by the inhabitants of a parish.[198] A custom to take shingle above high water mark for highway repairs will not be upheld in relation to parts of a beach which are private property.[199] Moreover, a custom will not extend to the removal of shingle in such a manner as to cause injury to adjoining property or to expose land to the inroads of the sea,[200] and an injunction may be obtained against taking valuable stones found on the foreshore.[201] Likewise, the claim to a custom for the inhabitants of a parish who are landowners to take sand which had drifted from the shore to adjoining closes was not upheld since the deposited sand had become part of the soil of the close and became the property of the owner of the close.[202] Similarly, it has been found that the inhabitants of a county have no right to take sea–washed coal from the foreshore, because a fluctuating body of persons cannot acquire a prescriptive right of that character.[203]

---

[194] *Benest v. Pipon*, (1829) 1 Knapp 60.

[195] *Margate L.B. v. Margate Harbour Co.*, (1869) 33 J.P. 437.

[196] *Constable v. Nicholson*, (1863) 14 C.B.N.S. 230; *Pitts v. Kingsbridge Highway Board*, (1871) 25 L.T. 195; *MacNamara v. Higgins*, (1854) 4 I.C.L. 326.

[197] *Lynn Regis v. Taylor*, (1684) 3 Lev. 160.

[198] *Padwick v. Knight*, (1852) 7 Ex. 854; *Clowes v. Beck*, (1851) 13 Beav. 347.

[199] *Pitts v. Kingsbridge Highway Board*, (1871) 25 L.T. 195.

[200] *Attorney–General v. Tomline*, (1880) 14 Ch.D. 58; *Cowper (Earl) v. Baker*, (1810) 17 Ves. 128; *Chalk v. Wyatt*, (1810) 3 Mer. 688; *Canvey Island Comrs. v. Preedy*, [1922] 1 Ch. 179.

[201] *Cowper (Earl) v. Baker*, (1810)17 Ves.128.

[202] *Blewett v. Tregonning*, (1835) 3 Ad. & El. 554.

[203] *Alfred F. Beckett Ltd. v. Lyons*, [1966] 2 W.L.R. 421; *Goodman v. Saltash Corpn.*, (1882) 7 A.C. 633; *Blewitt v. Tregonning*, (1835) 3 Ad. & El. 554.

In addition to common law rulings, a number of statutory provisions regulate the exploitation of minerals found on the foreshore. A highway authority is empowered to dig and carry away gravel, sand, stone and other material from waste or common land, including the bed of any river or brook flowing through the land, and may gather and carry away stones, but in doing so must not remove such quantity of stones or other materials from the sea beach as to cause danger by inundation or increased danger of encroachment by the sea.[204] Under s.18 of the Coast Protection Act 1949 it is an offence to excavate any materials, including minerals and turf, on, under or forming part of the seashore except under licence from a coast protection authority.[205] Planning permission is not required for operations involving the removal of sand and gravel from the sea bed taking place below low water mark in areas outside the limits of jurisdiction of the county, but the provisions of Town and Country Planning legislation apply in relation to operations in areas beyond the low water mark which fall within the administrative boundaries of a local planning authority.[206]

Wreck

Wreck is a royal franchise belonging to the Crown and entitling it to various kinds of unclaimed property found at sea or on the foreshore, unless the right has been granted to a subject. In order to constitute wreck, in the strict sense, goods must come to land. Whilst they remain at sea they are distinguished in law as "flotsam", "jetsam", "lagan" and "derelict".[207]

A subject may gain title to wreck by charter or prescription. In many parts of the country wreck belongs to lords of the manors, or may be claimed as part or parcel of a hundred or town.[208] The right of a subject to wreck may be presumed by long use, unless there is sufficient evidence to the contrary to rebut this.[209] The right to wreck will not pass

---

[204] ss.45 and 52 Highways Act 1980.

[205] On the Coast Protection Act 1949 generally see p.59 below.

[206] (1949) J.P.L. 421.

[207] *Palmer v. Rouse*, (1858) 3 H. & N. 505.

[208] *Palmer v. Rouse*, (1858) 3 H. & N. 505; *Calmady v. Rowe*, (1844) 6 C.B. 861.

[209] *Biddulph v. Arthur*, (1755) 2 Wils. 23.

under the general terms of a grant.[210] Similarly, it will not pass by a grant of the seashore by itself. Whilst a royal grant of wreck to the lord of a manor gives him, as an incident, the right to pass over the foreshore to take wreck, it does not pass any right to the soil of the foreshore.[211] However, where there is a grant of a manor with rights of anchorage, groundage, wreck, etc., this is a strong presumption that the soil of the foreshore was intended to pass under the grant.[212]

By the statute *De Prerogativa Regis* (1324)[213] the King was entitled to wreck of the sea throughout the realm. The modern rights relating to wreck and salvage are now contained in Part IX of the Merchant Shipping Act 1894. This provides that the Crown is entitled to all unclaimed wreck found in any part of Her Majesty's dominions, except where this right has been granted to another person.[214] "Wreck", for these purposes, includes jetsam, flotsam, lagan and derelict found in or on the shores of the sea or any tidal water,[215] and also fishing boats or fishing gear lost or abandoned at sea and found or taken possession of within territorial waters of the United Kingdom, or found or taken possession of beyond such waters and brought within such waters.[216] The provisions of the Merchant Shipping Act 1894, and various other statutes relating to wreck and salvage have been applied, with necessary modifications, to aircraft in the same way as they apply to vessels.[217]

Traditionally, the definitions of the main categories of wreck were established in *Constables Case.*[218] This defined "flotsam" as items which float on the sea when a ship is sunk or otherwise perishes; "jetsam" as items which are cast into the sea to lighten a ship which is in danger of being sunk and afterwards the ship perishes; "lagan" as items which are jettisoned from a ship, which afterwards perishes, attached to a buoy or

---

210 *Alcock v. Cooke*, (1829) 2 M. & P. 625.

211 *Dickens and Kemp v. Shaw*, (1823) 1 L.J.O.K.S.B. 122.

212 *Le Strange v. Rowe*, (1866) 4 F. & F. 1048; *Chad v. Tilsed*, (1821) 2 Brod. & Bing. 403.

213 17 Ed. II, Stat.1, c.11.

214 s.523 Merchant Shipping Act 1894.

215 s.510.

216 s.17 Sea Fisheries Act 1968.

217 s.51 Civil Aviation Act 1949; Aircraft (Wreck and Salvage) Order 1938 S.R.& O. 1938 No.136.

218 (1601) 5 Co. Rep. 106a.

cork by mariners with the intention that they may be recovered. Strictly, none of these categories of goods are properly called "wreck" for so long as they remain in or upon the sea, but they become wreck as soon as the action of the sea places them upon land. "Derelict" is a term applied to a ship which is abandoned or deserted at sea[219] without any hope of recovery.[220]

In order for items to constitute wreck they must have touched the ground, though they need not have been left dry.[221] It is not necessary that a vessel must be lost with all hands for items to constitute wreck.[222] Floating timber which has drifted from the shore and is found at sea without an apparent owner is not wreck.[223] Items floating between high and low water mark, which have not touched the ground are not wreck. Where items have touched land between high and low water mark but again become afloat their legal category depends upon their state at the time they are seized and taken into possession, and in particular whether the person who seized them as salvor was in a boat, wading or swimming.

Property which comes ashore is wreck and belongs to the Crown or to a grantee of wreck. Whilst at sea property belongs to the Queen in her office of Admiralty as flotsam, jetsam, lagan or derelict. Above the high water mark the property belongs to the lord of the manor as the Crown grantee, but below low water mark the lord of the manor has no claim, since at common law it is on the high seas and belongs to the Admiralty. If property is not claimed by its original owner within a year it belongs to the Crown so long as it is afloat or surrounded by water.[224] If property in goods can be proved, the lord of the manor is not entitled to them as wreck.[225]

---

[219] *Crossman v. West*, (1887) 13 A.C. 160.
[220] *The Aquila*, (1798) 1 Ch. Rb. 37.
[221] *R. v. Forty-nine Casks of Brandy*, (1836) 3 Hag. Adm. 257.
[222] *Dunwich Corpn. v. Sterry*, (1831) 1 B. & Ad. 831.
[223] *Palmer v. Rouse*, (1858) 22 J.P. 773.
[224] *R. v. Two Casks of Tallow*, (1837) 6 L.T. 558.
[225] *Hamilton and Smyth v. Davis*, (1771) 5 Burr 2732.

Royal fish and fowl

The statute *De Prerogativa Regis*[226] enacted that the King is entitled to whales and sturgeons taken in the sea or elsewhere within the realm, except in certain places privileged by the King. The Statute applied to royal fish found on the shore or caught near the coasts, presumably within territorial waters, but such fish found and taken within the precincts of jurisdiction of the Cinque Ports belong to the Lord Warden. Claims by the Crown of the right to take dolphin, grampuses and other large fish and mammals have not been recognised.[227] Hale, in *De Jure Maris,*[228] noted three types of royal fish: the sturgeon, porpoise and whale. Notably, his list excluded the salmon and lamprey, and he also stated that whales "taken in the wide sea or out of the precincts of the sea belonging to the Crown" belong to the taker. In Scotland fisheries for oysters, mussels and salmon are amongst the patrimonial rights of the Crown and, therefore, not part of the public right of fishery.[229]

White swans are "fowl royal", and those which are wild and unmarked and found swimming in an open and common river belong to the Crown as a matter of royal prerogative. A subject may have property in white swans not marked and in his private waters, and if they escape out of his waters into an open and common river he is entitled to claim them back.[230] It is notable that swans on the Thames belong either to the Crown or to the Dyers and Vintners Companies, and these guilds have enjoyed the privileges from time immemorial to own and mark swans there. Ownership is indicated by the marking of cygnets claimed by the two Companies at an annual ceremony of "swan upping".

---

[226] 17 Ed. II st. 1, c.11 (1324) see also *Royal Fishery of Banne Case*, (1619) Dav. Ir. 35; *Warren v. Matthews*, (1703) 1 Salk. 357.

[227] *Cinque Ports (Lord Warden) v. R.*, (1831) 2 Hag. Ad. 484.

[228] Ch.VII.

[229] *Lord Advocate v. Sinclair*, (1867) L.R. 1 H.L. Sc. 176; *Parker v. Lord Advocate*, [1904] A.C. 364.

[230] *Case of Swans*, (1592) 7 Coke 15b.

COAST PROTECTION AND SEA DEFENCE

At common law it is part of the prerogative and duty of the Crown to preserve the realm from the inroads of the sea and to protect land from inundation by water for the benefit, not of an individual, but of the commonwealth.[231] Over the years, however, the prerogative rights and duties in relation to coast protection and sea defence have been entrusted to various statutory authorities.[232] Commissioners of sewers were established for that purpose in 1427,[233] and later, in a more permanent form, under the Bill of Sewers in 1531.[234] The latter Act provided for the appointment of commissioners of sewers with powers to make surveys of sea defences and obstructions to rivers, to maintain and repair existing walls and sewers, to remedy nuisances and to levy rates for payment of the expenses so incurred. The Sewers Act 1833 empowered commissioners to erect new works and restricted their jurisdiction to the coast and navigable rivers.

A series of enactments relating to land drainage and flood defence[235] have been replaced by the Land Drainage Act 1991, which, in conjunction with the flood defence powers given to the National Rivers Authority under Part IV of the Water Resources Act 1991, are now the principal statutory measures concerning flood prevention in relation to inland waters. Although these provisions are mainly concerned with inland flood prevention and the control of flow in inland waters to keep floodwater from farm lands, it is notable that powers are also provided to enable works to be carried out by the National Rivers Authority in defence against sea water.[236] The powers of drainage boards, local authorities and the National Rivers Authority under the Acts are

---

231 Per Fry, J. in *Attorney-General v. Tomline*, (1880) 14 Ch. D. 58; see also *Hudson v. Tabor*, (1877) 2 Q.B.D. 290.

232 *Symes v. Essex Rivers Catchment Board*, [1936] 3 All E.R. 908.

233 Under 6 Hen. 6, c.5.

234 23 Hen. 8, c.5, as amended by later statutes, including 3 & 4 Edw. 6, c.8, and 13 Eliz. 1. c.9; and generally see Callis *On the Statute of Sewers* (1662).

235 In particular, the Land Drainage Acts of 1861, 1914, 1918, 1926, 1930 and 1976, and Part II Chapter III, and Sch.15 Water Act 1989. On flood defence and land drainage generally see Ch.12 below.

236 s.165(2) Water Resources Act 1991; and see *Symes v. Essex Rivers Catchment Board*, (1937) 101 J.P. 179.

permissive rather than imperative in character, and the National Rivers Authority cannot be required to repair a sea wall,[237] though a duty to maintain sea banks may be imposed under a local Act.[238]

The principal enactment dealing specifically with the prevention of erosion and encroachment by the sea is the Coast Protection Act 1949. Broadly, this Act provides for the appointment of maritime district councils as coast protection authorities for their area to carry out construction, repairs, maintenance, and improvement work for protecting land against erosion and encroachment by the sea. The Act also makes provision for the establishment of coast protection boards or joint committees of coast protection authorities. The Act is binding upon the Crown and applies in relation to Crown land as it applies in relation to any other land.[239]

Coast protection authorities are concerned with protecting the coast against destruction, including built–up areas, and preventing erosion caused by wave and tidal action. By contrast the powers of the National Rivers Authority to maintain and improve existing works and construct new works for flood prevention, though generally limited to operations on "main rivers", extend beyond the low water mark in relation to defence against sea or tidal water and are exercisable irrespective of whether they are in connection with a main river.[240] In addition to the functions of the National Rivers Authority and coast protection authorities, various dock, port, harbour and navigation authorities possess statutory powers in relation to sea defence within their particular areas.

---

[237] *Smith v. Cawdle Fen Commissioners*, (1938) 82 S.J. 890; *Gillett v. Kent Rivers Catchment Board*, [1938] 4 All E.R. 810; *East Suffolk Rivers Catchment Board v. Kent*, (1940) 105 J.P. 129.

[238] *Sephton v. Lancashire River Board*, [1962] 1 All E.R. 183.

[239] s.32(1) Coast Protection Act 1949. "Crown land" means land an interest in which belongs to her Majesty in right of the Crown or the Duchy of Lancaster, or to the Duchy of Cornwall, or to a government department, or land held in trust for Her Majesty for the purposes of a government department (s.32(5)).

[240] s.165(2) Land Drainage Act 1991; and see p.378 below on the meaning of "main river".

Sea walls and embankments

A consequence of the duty of the Crown to protect the realm from the inroads of the sea, by maintaining the natural barriers and erecting artificial barriers, is that a subject who owns part of the foreshore will be restrained by an injunction from removing a natural barrier of shingle if the effect of the removal would be to expose neighbouring land to the inroads of the sea.[241] Similarly, a person who is responsible for a sea wall is entitled to an injunction to restrain others from removing shingle from the foreshore so as to expose the wall and the lands protected thereby to a greater risk of inundation by the sea.[242] The Attorney–General may maintain an action on behalf of the public to restrain the commission of an act of this kind,[243] and a coast protection authority may by order prohibit the excavation or removal of materials on, under or forming part of the foreshore.[244] In *Symes v. Essex Rivers Catchment Board*[245] it was held that an owner of land outside a sea wall, erected to prevent the incursion of the sea into the land within the wall, had no right to convey sea water through the wall onto the land behind, or to make a breach in the wall which would expose the land within the wall to the risk of sea flooding.

Persons occupying land adjoining the sea may erect such defences as are necessary for the protection of their land though such erections may render it necessary for their neighbours to do the same.[246] The consent of the coast protection authority is required, however, for coast protection works other than works involving maintenance or repair of existing works.[247] A person who, in order to protect his house from the sea, places rocks and piles on the foreshore belonging to his neighbour

---

[241] *Attorney–General v. Tomline*, (1880) 14 Ch. D. 58; *Isle of Ely Case*, (1609) 10 Co. Rep. 141a; *Maldon Corpn. v Laurie*, (1933) 97 J.P.Jo. 132.

[242] *Canvey Island Comrs. v. Preedy*, [1922] 1 Ch. 179; *Holien v. Tipping*, [1915] 1 I.R. 210.

[243] *Attorney–General v. Shrewsbury Bridge Co.*, (1882) 46 L.T. 687.

[244] s.18 Coast Protection Act 1949; see also *Anderson v. Jacobs*, (1905) 93 L.T. 17; *Burton v. Hudson*, [1909] 2 K.B. 564; *British Dredging (Services) Ltd. v. Secretary of State for Wales*, [1975] 2 All E.R. 845.

[245] [1936] 3 All E.R. 908.

[246] *R. v. Pagham Sewers Commisioners*, (1828) 8 B. & C. 355.

[247] s.16 Coast Protection Act 1949.

may acquire an easement over that land for the purpose of protecting his house from the sea.[248]

Nothing prevents a public right of way existing along the surface of a sea wall or embankment erected to protect the neighbouring lands, and where the public have had uninterrupted and open use of the right of way a dedication of a public highway by the owner of the soil may be presumed.[249] The authority responsible for the repair of a sea wall with a public footpath along the top is required to repair the wall so as to restrain the sea water. In relation to a sea wall which is also used as a footpath the authority responsible for its repair may owe a duty of care to those using the footpath and become liable where injury is sustained because of its state of disrepair.[250]

Repair of sea walls and river banks

At common law there is no general duty, in the absence of some specific legal obligation to the contrary, for a riparian owner to keep his portion of a bank in repair. *Hudson v Tabor*[251] decided that a landowner was not under any common law liability to repair his sea wall for the protection of his neighbours. It appears that the same principle extends to the bank of a river, whether it is tidal or non–tidal. Clearly it is prudent in many circumstances for a river frontager to maintain his bank, but where this is done it is through an individual's own volition rather than as a matter of legal duty.

However, a legal obligation to maintain or repair a bank may arise by prescription, custom, tenure, covenant or under statute.[252] In most circumstances the maintenance of a sea wall is at issue. An example of

---

[248] *Philpot v. Bath*, (1905) 21 T.L.R. 634.

[249] *Greenwich Board of Works v. Maudslay*, (1870) 35 J.P. 8.

[250] *Collier v. Anglian Water Authority*, (1983) *The Times* 26 March 1983, and see Occupiers Liability Act 1957; contrast the decision in *Hunwick v. Essex Rivers Catchment Board*, (1952) 116 J.P. 217.

[251] (1877) 2 Q.B.D. 290; *Attorney–General v. Tomline*, (1880) 14 Ch. D. 58; *Thomas & Evans Ltd. v. Mid–Rhondda Co–operative Society*, [1940] 4 All E.R. 357.

[252] Before *Hudson v. Tabor*, the grounds for an obligation to repair also included frontage, ownership and *per usum rei*, see Callis *On the Law of Sewers* (1622), pp. 115 to 122.

prescriptive liability is to be found in *R. v. Leigh*,[253] where it was said that a landowner might by prescription be obliged to maintain a sea wall not only against ordinary weather and tides, but also against an extraordinary tempest.[254] Where a corporation are liable to repair sea walls, for example under the terms of a grant from the Crown, a person who suffers damage by the decay of the walls may sue the corporation for damages.[255] In relation to this liability, in *London and N.W. Rly. v. Fobbing Sewers Commissioners*[256] it was held that where a farm had been subject to a duty to repair a sea wall by reason of its tenure, that liability attached to every part of the farm, though it had been sold and become vested in several different purchasers. In *Morland v. Cook*[257] a covenant provided for the expenses of maintaining a sea wall to be met by the owners of certain lands despite the fact that the purchasers of those lands had no notice of the covenant.

Liability to repair a sea wall may also arise where want of repair has caused it to become a public nuisance.[258] A landowner may be required to abate a nuisance due to the flooding of his land by a breach in the bank.[259] A right to go onto another riparian owner's land in order to repair the banks of a river to make it available for working a mill may be claimed as an easement.[260]

The common law position regarding obligations to repair the banks of a watercourse has been affected by a number of statutory provisions. For example, under ss.262 and 264 of the Public Health Act 1936, a pipe, drain or culvert may be substituted for a watercourse and a duty to repair, maintain or cleanse it imposed upon the landowner on

---

[253] (1839) 10 Ad. & El. 398.

[254] See also *Keighley's Case*, (1609) 10 Co. Rep. 139a; *Fobbing Sewers Commissioners v. R.*, (1886) 51 J.P. 227; *R. v. Essex Sewers Commisioners*, (1823) 1 B. & C. 477; *Griffith's Case*, (1564) Moore Rep. 69.

[255] *Lyme Regis Corpn. v. Henley*, (1834) 1 Scott 29.

[256] (1896) 75 L.T. 629. and see *R. v. Baker*, (1867) L.R. 2 Q.B. 621.

[257] (1868) 18 L.T. 496; see also *Smith v. River Douglas Catchment Board*, (1949) 113 J.P. 388.

[258] *Attorney–General v. Tod Heatley*, [1897] 1 Ch. 560; *Thames Conservators v. London Port Sanitary Authority*, [1894] 1 Q.B. 647.

[259] *Clayton v. Sale U.D.C.*, (1926) 90 J.P.5.

[260] *Roberts v. Fellowes*, (1906) 94 L.T. 279; *Liford's Case*, (1614) 77 E.R. 1206.

whose land it is situated.[261] Section 33 of the Land Drainage Act 1991 provides for the commutation of obligations, imposed by reason of tenure, custom, prescription or otherwise, to do any work by way of repairing banks or walls, maintaining watercourse or otherwise.[262] Despite the possibility of commutation of obligations relating to the repair of banks and walls, it has been held that land drainage legislation does not affect any existing obligations to repair by reason of tenure, custom, prescription or otherwise. Thus in *North Level Commissioners v. River Welland Catchment Board*[263] it was decided that the general wording of the former Land Drainage Act 1930, or any scheme made under it, did not transfer an obligation to repair an artificial bank from the plaintiffs to a catchment board established under the Act.

In *Harrison v. Great Northern Railway*[264] a company who undertook to maintain a channel for conveying water neglected to do so and was held responsible for the injury arising from the banks of the channel giving way in a period of extraordinary rainfall as a consequence of the outlet not being of sufficient width. In *Vyner v. North Eastern Railway*[265] a company which was statutorily responsible for maintaining a river navigation was held not to be liable to maintain flood banks behind the natural river banks, since these banks were not constructed to keep the water within the *alveus* of the river.

Navigation commissioners who are under a statutory duty to maintain sea walls will be liable for damage caused by an overflow not only to land reclaimed by them, but also property adjoining that land.[266] Where there is a statutory obligation to maintain a river wall at a certain height, failure to do so will render those responsible liable to an action for negligence, and an act of God, such as an extraordinarily high tide, will not excuse them from liability.[267]

---

[261] On the duties of public authorities in relation to statutory nuisances generally see p.339 below.

[262] See p.402 below.

[263] [1937] 4 All E.R. 684; and see s.36(1) Land Drainage Act 1930, now repealed.

[264] (1864) 3 H. & C. 231.

[265] (1898) 14 T.L.R. 554.

[266] *Bramlett v. Tees Conservancy*, (1885) 49 J.P. 214; *Collins v. Middle Level Commissioners*, (1869) 20 L.T. 442.

[267] *Nitro–Phosphate Co. v. London Docks Co.*, (1878) 9 Ch. D. 503; *Wear Rivers Commissioners v. Adamson*, (1877) 2 A.C. 750.

A number of decisions have concerned responsibilities for sea walls that also function as a highway. Hence, in the past a parish council was not convicted for failing to rebuild a sea wall washed away by the sea, over the top of which an alleged highway formerly passed,[268] nor for failing to repair part of a highway washed away by the sea.[269] A highway authority, which was under an obligation to keep up a road, was held to be chargeable with the cost of works needed for the preservation of the road, though the works at issue, concerning a sea wall and groynes necessary to prevent a road running along the foreshore from being periodically injured by the inroads of the sea, did not actually form part of the road. The fact that a footpath along the top of a sea wall is, as well as being part of the highway, used as a promenade for purposes of pleasure does not affect the liability to repair.[270] Liability to users of the footpath who suffer injury due to its disrepair may arise under the Occupiers Liability Act 1957.[271]

[268] *R. v. Inhabitants of Paul*, (1840) 2 Moo. & R. 307.

[269] *R. v. Hornsea*, (1854) 2 C.L.R. 596; *R.v. Landulph (Inhabitants)*, (1834) 1 Moo. & R. 393.

[270] *Sandgate U.D.C. v. Kent C.C.*, (1898) 79 L.T. 425; *R. v. Lordsmere (Inhabitants)*, (1886) 51 J.P. 86.

[271] *Collier v. Anglian Water Authority*, (1983) *The Times* 26 March 1983.

Chapter 3

NATURAL RIGHTS OF WATER

RIPARIAN RIGHTS

The nature of riparian rights

The proprietor of land on the banks of a natural watercourse is entitled to the enjoyment of the collection of legal interests that are commonly known as "riparian rights". An authoritative statement as to the meaning of this expression was provided by Lord Wensleydale in *Chasemore v. Richards* decided in 1859:[1]

> "The subject of rights to streams of water flowing on the surface has been of late years fully discussed, and, by a series of carefully considered judgments,[2] placed upon a clear and satisfactory footing. It has been settled that the right of enjoyment of a natural stream of water on the surface *ex jure naturae* belongs to the proprietor of the adjoining land as a natural incident to the right of the soil itself; and that he is entitled to the benefit of it, as he is to all the other advantages belonging to the land of which he is the owner. He has the right to have it come to him in its natural state, in flow, quantity and quality, and to go from him without obstruction, upon the same principle that he is entitled to the support of his neighbour's soil for his own in its natural state. His right in no way depends on prescription or the presumed grant of his neighbour, nor from the presumed acquiescence of the proprietors above and below."

Lord Wensleydale's observations about the right to the enjoyment of water in its natural state of quantity and quality have now to be read subject to a range of statutory provisions dealing with abstraction,[3]

---

[1] (1859) 7 H.L. Cas. 349.

[2] For example, Parke, B. in *Embrey v. Owen*, (1851) 6 Ex. 353, 369; Lord Kingsdown in *Miner v. Gilmour*, (1859) 12 Moo. P.C.C.131. Later cases in point include *Swindon Waterworks Co. v. Wilts. & Berks. Canal Co.*, (1875) 33 L.T. 513; *McCartney v. Londonderry Rly.*, [1904] A.C. 301; *Nuttall v. Bracewell*, (1866) 4 H. & C. 714; *White (John) & Sons v. White*, [1906] A.C. 72; *Stollmeyer v. Trinidad Lake Petroleum Co.*, [1918] A.C. 485.

[3] On water abstraction under statute see Ch.10 below.

pollution control[4] and various other matters which have extensively modified the traditional conception of riparian rights. Whilst recognising these statutory inroads, the purpose of this chapter is to describe the fundamental common law principles relating to riparian ownership in their unmodified form, and to defer for later consideration an account of the ways in which legislation has modified the operation of riparian law.

In the first instance the right to *use* water and the right of *ownership* in that water are properly distinguished. Hence it was stated by Parke B. in *Embrey v. Owen* that,

> "the right to have a stream flow in its natural state, without diminution or alteration is an incident of property in the land through which it passes; but flowing water is *publici juris*, not in the sense that it is *bonum vacans*, to which the first occupant may acquire an exclusive right, but that it is public and common in the sense only, that all may reasonably use it who have a right of access to it, and that none can have any property in the water itself, except in the particular portion which he may choose to abstract from the stream and take into his possession, and that during the time of his possession only."[5]

Accordingly, riparian rights are generally concerned with the right to *use* water, rather than the ownership or actual use of the water concerned, and the right to resist interference with a natural flow of water may be established without it needing to be shown that there is any impairment of the actual use of the water at issue.[6]

Although rights to use flowing water do not necessarily depend upon the ownership of the soil covered by the water,[7] riparian rights are founded on the right of access to the watercourse, and for that reason a riparian tenement must be in reasonable proximity to the water in which the rights are claimed.[8] Hence, a site which is some distance from a watercourse though connected to it by a strip of land, may be held in law to be too remote to sustain the character of a riparian tenement. The requirement that a riparian tenement must be reasonably proximate to a

---

[4] On statutory provisions relating to water pollution see Ch.11 below.

[5] Per Parke, B., in *Embrey v. Owen*, (1851) 6 Ex. 353.

[6] *Frechette v. Compagnie Manufacturie de St. Hyacinthe*, (1883) 9 A.C. 170.

[7] *Lord v. Sydney Commissioners*, (1859) 12 Moo. P.C. 473.

[8] Although on acquired easements of water see Ch.4 below.

watercourse will prevent a large estate being a riparian tenement merely because some part of it is bounded by a watercourse. In each instance, however, the question whether a particular piece of land sustains the character of a riparian tenement is a question of fact and must be determined according to the particular circumstances.[9]

For riparian rights, properly so called, to arise the land must be in actual contact with the watercourse. In this respect lateral contact with the watercourse is as good as vertical, and thus riparian rights arise equally where water flows past land where only the bank is owned as where it flows over land where the bed is owned. In the case of a tidal watercourse, where the foreshore is left uncovered by water at times of low water, it has been held that the intermittent lack of contact between the land and the water at certain states of the tide does not prevent riparian rights being established.[10]

A riparian owner of the banks of a navigable or tidal river has similar rights to those enjoyed by other riparian owners. In relation to ownership of navigable rivers, however, riparian ownership does not permit the owner to cause any interference with the public right of navigation.[11] Whilst the rights of a riparian owner to the banks of a tidal river exist *jure naturae*, it is essential to the existence of these rights that the land is in contact with the flow of the watercourse, at least at times of ordinary high tides.[12] Hence, land which is separated from a watercourse by a strip of land in separate ownership will not be held to abut the watercourse for these purposes.[13] A consequence of this is that if a person wishes to exercise riparian rights, for example by bringing an action to stop pollution of a watercourse, it will be necessary for him to acquire an interest in at least a small portion of the bank of the watercourse before he will be entitled to do so.[14] The rights of a riparian owner in relation to lateral tributaries of a main watercourse extend only to water which

---

[9] *Attwood v. Llay Main Colleries*, [1926] Ch. 444.

[10] *North Shore Rly. v. Pion*, (1889) 14 A.C. 612; *Stockport Waterworks Co. v. Potter*, (1864) 10 L.T. 748.

[11] *North Shore Rly. Co. v. Pion*, (1889) 61 L.T. 525; *Lyon v. Fishmongers' Co.*, (1876) 35 L.T. 569; *Attorney-General v. Lonsdale*, (1868) 20 L.T. 64; and see Ch.6 below on navigation.

[12] *Dawood Hashim Esoof v. Tuck Sein*, (1931) 58 Ind. App. 80, P.C.

[13] *Attorney-General v. Rowley Bros. and Oxley*, (1910) 11 Ex. 602.

[14] *Crossley v. Lightowler*, (1867) 16 L.T. 438.

flows in defined natural channels and will not encompass water flowing over or through land before entering a definite channel.[15]

Riparian owners

The rights of a riparian owner do not necessarily depend on ownership of the soil under the watercourse,[16] and may be derived entirely from the possession of land abutting the watercourse. Consequently, if the owner grants any portion of land so abutting, the grantee becomes a riparian owner and acquires corresponding rights. If the owner grants away any part of an estate not abutting a watercourse the grantee acquires no riparian rights merely by virtue of his occupation. Neither can the grantee acquire such rights by express grant, except against the grantor, so as to bring actions against other persons for infringement of those rights.[17]

Riparian rights are not easements to be granted or reserved as appurtenant to what is respectively sold or retained, but are parts of the fee simple and inheritance of the land sold or retained. Hence, where a riparian owner sells part of his estate including land on the banks of a natural stream, it is not necessary to make any express provision as to the grant or reservation of the ordinary rights of a riparian proprietor.[18] A riparian owner cannot, except against himself, confer on a person who is not a riparian owner any right to use the water of the watercourse, and any use by a non–riparian owner, even under a grant from a riparian owner, is wrongful if it sensibly affects the flow of the water to the land of other riparian owners.[19] In one decided case,[20] the owner of land not abutting on a river with the licence of a higher riparian owner took water from the river and, after using it for cooling certain apparatus, returned it to the river unpolluted and undiminished. It was held that a lower

---

[15] *Broadbent v. Ramsbottom*, (1856) 11 Ex. 602.

[16] *Lyon v. Fishmongers' Co.*, (1876) 1 A.C. 662.

[17] *Stockport Waterworks Co. v. Potter*, (1864) 10 L.T. 748.

[18] *Portsmouth Waterworks Co. v. London Brighton and South Coast Ry.*, (1909) 26 T.L.R. 175.

[19] *Ormerod v. Todmorden Joint Stock Mill*, (1883) 11 Q.B.D. 155.

[20] *Kensit v. G.E. Ry. Co.*, (1884) 27 Ch.D. 122.

riparian owner could not obtain an injunction against the person taking the water, or against the riparian owner through whose land it was taken.

Where there are riparian proprietors on both sides of a non–tidal river, ordinarily, they are entitled to the soil of the bed *usque ad medium aquae*.[21] In some instances, however, where the same person owns both banks he will then be entitled to change the channel as he pleases, provided he restores the water to the old channel before it leaves his land and provided it flows from his land into the land below without increase or diminution in quantity, quality or direction.[22]

Rights and duties of riparian owners

The respective rights and duties of riparian proprietors were incisively stated by Lord Denman in *Mason v. Hill*[23] in 1833.

> "The possessor of land though which a natural stream runs, has a right to the advantage of that stream flowing in its natural course, and to use it when he pleases for any purpose of his own not inconsistent with the similar rights in the proprietors of the land above and below. A proprietor above cannot diminish the quantity or injure the quality of water which would otherwise descend, nor can a proprietor below throw back the water without his licence or consent."

It follows that riparian proprietors are entitled, subject to any statutory modification of their rights, to require that nothing is done to affect or prejudice either the quality or quantity of the watercourse as it flows in its natural state. Where an Act of Parliament has authorised interference with the natural flow, the original rights of the riparian proprietors are impaired only so far as the reasonable exercise of statutory rights have that consequence.[24]

Proprietors of waterside land possess riparian rights whether or not they choose to exercise those rights, and are not prevented from

---

21 *Wishart v. Wyllie*, (1853) 1 Macq. 389, H.L. On the *medium filum* rule generally see p.17 above.

22 *Nuttall v. Bracewell*, (1866) 15 L.T. 313; *Holker v. Porritt*, (1875) 39 J.P. 196.

23 (1833) 5 B. & A. 1.

24 *Edinburgh Water Trustees v. Sommerville & Son*, (1906) 95 L.T. 217; see also *Medway Co. v. Romney (Earl)*, (1861) 4 L.T. 87.

exercising them through not having done so previously.[25] A riparian owner who has acquired a right to divert water from a watercourse is not bound to continue to exercise that right, but if he abandons it and restores water to its original channel, he may be bound to do so in such a manner as not to expose the servient tenement to injury.[26]

The flow of a natural watercourse creates riparian rights and duties between all the riparian owners along the whole of its course, and subject to exercising reasonable use, each proprietor is bound to allow the water to flow on without altering its quality or quantity.[27] Correspondingly, apart from a use authorised by statute, grant or prescription, any unreasonable and unauthorised interference with the use of the water to the prejudice of other riparian owners may become the subject of an action from damages,[28] and may be restrained by an injunction,[29] even though there may be no actual damage to the plaintiff.[30] In the case of waterside land which is the subject of a lease, it will not be necessary for the plaintiff to show damage to a reversionary interest, it is enough to show obstruction of his right from which the law will infer damage. However, in one instance the defendant purchaser sold part of his land to the plaintiff, covenanting for quiet enjoyment, and afterwards the defendant raised by three inches the level of a brook running past the plaintiff's property. It was held that in these circumstances the court would not intervene.[31]

The rights of riparian proprietors apply only to watercourses flowing in known and defined channels either upon or below the surface of the ground. Thus, riparian rights will have no application to situations where a flow of water squanders itself over an undefined area,[32] or in relation to underground water which merely percolates through the strata in no known channel.[33] Similarly, riparian rights will not arise in relation

---

[25] *Sampson v. Hoddinott*, (1857) 1 C.B.N.S. 590.

[26] *Bridges v. Saltaun*, (1873) 45 Sc. Jur. 372.

[27] *Gaved v. Martyn*, (1865) 19 C.B.N.S. 732.

[28] *Dickinson v. Grand Junction Canal*, (1852) 21 L.J. Ex. 241.

[29] *Robinson v. Byron (Lord)*, (1785) 1 Bro. C.C. 588.

[30] *Sampson v. Hoddinott*, (1857) 1 C.B.N.S. 590; *Sharp v. Wilson, Rotheray & Co.*, (1905) 93 L.T. 155.

[31] *Ingram v. Morecroft*, (1863) 33 Beav. 49.

[32] *Rawstron v. Taylor*, (1855) 11 Ex. 369.

[33] *Chasemore v. Richards*, (1859) 7 H.L.C. 349.

to an artificial watercourse unless, taking into account its character and in particular whether it is temporary or permanent, the circumstances under which it was presumed to have been created and the mode in which it has been used and enjoyed, the inference can be drawn that the watercourse has acquired the status of a natural watercourse.[34]

Classification of riparian rights

In considering the natural rights of riparian owners in detail it is convenient to classify them as follows: (1) Rights as to the natural quantity of waters relating to abstraction, diversion, obstruction and overflow, considered in the following section; (2) Rights concerning the natural quality of water relating to water purity and pollution, considered later in this chapter; and (3) Rights of riparian owners on the banks of navigable rivers, considered later in this work.[35]

ABSTRACTION AND DIVERSION AT COMMON LAW

Ordinary use of water

A riparian proprietor has the right to make "ordinary" use of the water flowing in the watercourse. This encompasses the reasonable use of the water for domestic purposes and for the watering of livestock and, where these uses of the water are made, abstraction can be undertaken without regard to the effect which they may have upon downstream proprietors.[36] Thus, ordinary or "primary" uses of water are not subject to restriction at common law and, if their effect is to exhaust the water altogether, a downstream proprietor will have no legal basis for redress.[37] "Domestic purposes" have been held to include drinking and culinary purposes, cleansing and washing, and feeding and supplying the ordinary quantity of water for cattle. If a riparian owner does not use the water for

---

[34] *Baily & Co. v. Clark Son & Morland*, [1902] 1 Ch. 649; and on artificial watercourses generally see Ch.5 below.

[35] On rights of navigation generally see Ch.6 below.

[36] *Miner v. Gilmour*, (1859) 12 Moo. P.C.C. 131; *Norbury (Lord) v. Kitchin*, (1863) 7 L.T. 685; *White & Sons v. White*, [1906] A.C. 72.

[37] *McCartney v. Londonderry Ry. Co.*, [1904] A.C. 301.

these purposes he is not entitled to appropriate to other purposes the amount which he would be entitled to take for domestic purposes.[38] Although common law rights of water abstraction have been substantially amended by statute, it is notable that certain exceptions from the operation of statutory provisions remain in relation to certain domestic and agricultural water uses.[39]

Extraordinary use of water

In addition to the ordinary use of flowing water, a riparian proprietor has the right to use the water for any other purpose provided that this does not interfere with the rights of other proprietors above or below. This "extraordinary", or "secondary", use of the water will allow a proprietor to dam up the stream for the purposes of a mill, or divert the water for irrigation providing that by so doing no sensible injury is inflicted upon other riparian owners.[40] The limits of extraordinary water use have never been precisely defined, and are probably incapable of definition, but it is clear that they are subject to significant restrictions. Specifically, the use of the water must be reasonable, the purpose for which it is taken must be connected with the abstracter's tenement and the water must be restored to the watercourse substantially undiminished in volume and unaltered in character.[41]

In particular instances extraordinary use has been held to extend to manufacturing purposes,[42] irrigation, providing that the running stream was not exhausted,[43] and damming a river for milling.[44] Alternatively it has been decided that extraordinary use will not allow water to be taken for purposes such as supplying a town with water,[45] or supplying a

---

[38] *Attorney–General v. Great Eastern Ry.*, (1871) 23 L.T. 344.

[39] Generally see Ch.10 below on water abstraction under statute; and see *Cargill v. Gotts,* [1981] 1 All E.R. 68.

[40] *Miner v. Gilmour*, (1859) 12 Moo. P.C.C. 131.

[41] *Swindon Waterworks Co. v. Wilts. & Berks. Canal*, (1875) 33 L.T. 513; *Stollmeyer v. Trinidad Lake Petroleum Co.*, [1918] A.C. 485; *Attwood v. Llay Main Collieries*, [1926] Ch. 444.

[42] *Dakin v. Cornish*, (1845) 6 Ex. 360.

[43] *Embrey v. Owen*, (1851) 6 Ex. 353.

[44] *Belfast Ropeworks v. Boyd*, (1887) 21 L.R. Ir. 560.

[45] *Swindon Waterworks Co. v. Wilts. & Berks. Canal*, (1875) 33 L.T. 513.

lunatic asylum and prison.[46] Thus in *Swindon Waterworks Co. v. Wilts. and Berks. Canal,*[47] water undertakers who owned riparian land and collected water in a reservoir, sought to use the water to supply a nearby town with water. It was held that this was not a reasonable use of the water and a canal company who were downstream riparian proprietors were entitled to an injunction to restrain this use. The question whether a particular extraordinary use is reasonable is an issue of fact which must be determined by reference to all the circumstances.[48]

In *McCartney v. Londonderry Ry. Co.*[49] a railway company wanted to abstract water from a stream at a point at which the stream was crossed by the railway and to use the water for the working of their engines along the whole length of the line. It was held that this was impermissible since the purpose for which the water was to be used was unconnected with the land at the point from which it was to be abstracted. In *Attwood v. Llay Main Collieries*[50] the defendants abstracted river water for their colliery without returning it to the river, and it was held that this was an unjustified use since it amounted to a complete diversion of part of the river and an infringement of the rights of lower riparian owners. Moreover, it was not necessary for the plaintiff, who was a lower riparian owner, to prove damage or the future possible acquisition of prescriptive rights by the defendants in order to secure relief.

Irrigation

A riparian owner may use the water of a stream for purposes of irrigation provided that the diversion is not continuous and that water is returned to the stream with no greater diminution than that caused by the evaporation and absorption attendant on irrigation.[51] However, if water is diverted for irrigation and delays the passage of the water so as to infringe the riparian rights of lower riparian owners, an action will be

---

46 *Medway Co. v. Romney (Earl),* (1861) 9 C.B.N.S. 575.

47 (1875) 33 L.T. 513.

48 *Norbury (Lord) v. Kitchin,* (1863) 7 L.T. 685.

49 [1904] A.C. 503 (overruling *Sandwich (Earl) v. Great Northern Ry.*, (1878) 10 Ch. D. 707). See also *Owen v. Davies,* [1874] W.N. 175; *Roberts v. Gwyrfai District Council,* [1899] 2 Ch. 608.

50 [1926] Ch. 444.

51 *Embrey v. Owen,* (1851) 6 Ex. 353; *Scott-Whitehead v. National Coal Board,* (1987) 53 P. & C.R. 263.

available against the abstractor.[52] Where a right to irrigate exists it is immaterial what means are taken to transfer the water onto the irrigated land, provided that no more than the lawful quantity of water is diverted,[53] but the common law does not recognise ordinary or extraordinary rights to take water for spray irrigation since the water is not returned to the river.[54] The precise quantity of water which may be taken for irrigation depends upon the circumstances of each case.[55]

The use of water for irrigation pursuant to common law rights of abstraction is subject to specific licensing provisions and special regulations relating to spray irrigation provided for under the Water Resources Act 1991 considered later in this work.[56] However, in *Cargill v. Gotts* it was held that despite the fact that abstraction of water to spray crops and water cattle was unlawful under statute,[57] the plaintiff had established a prescriptive easement to do so at common law. Consequently, the defendant had no right to exercise self–help to prevent the abstraction taking place and damages were awarded against the defendant for interference with the right.[58] In *Scott–Whitehead v. National Coal Board* an action in negligence was brought against the Coal Board for contaminating a water supply used for spray irrigation and also against a water authority who had issued a licence to authorise the abstraction under statutory provisions. It was held that although both defendants owed the plaintiff a duty of care, the Coal Board were not liable because they did not know of the harm which would be caused to the plaintiff's crops by the contamination. In relation to the water authority, however, it was held that they were in breach of the duty of care by failing to warn the abstractor of the danger posed by the contamination and were found liable in negligence for failing to do so.[59]

---

[52] *Sampson v. Hoddinott*, (1857) 21 J.P. 375.

[53] *Greenslade v. Halliday*, (1830) 6 Bing. 379.

[54] *Rugby Joint Water Board v. Walters*, [1966] 3 All E.R. 497.

[55] *Attwood v. Llay Main Collieries*, [1926] 3 All E.R. 497.

[56] See p.254 below.

[57] Under s.23(1) Water Resources Act 1963, now see s.24 Water Resources Act 1991, discussed at p.249 below.

[58] [1981] 1 All E.R. 682.

[59] (1987) 53 P. & C.R. 263. However, this decision may now need to be reconsidered in the light of the subsequent ruling in *Murphy v. Brentwood D.C.*, ([1990] 2 All

Diversion in general

A person who diverts a watercourse into a new artificial channel for his own convenience must make it capable of carrying off all the water which may reasonably be expected to flow into it, irrespective of the capacity of the natural channel.[60] Thus, it is the duty of anyone who interferes with the course of a stream to see that the works which are substituted for the natural channel are adequate to carry off the water brought down by extraordinary rainfall, and if damage results from the deficiency of the modified channel that has been provided then the person who modified the original channel will be liable.[61]

An upper riparian owner who has the right to take water by a channel of a certain size cannot enlarge the channel so as to divert more water to the prejudice of a lower owner,[62] and where a riparian owner is entitled to abstract water from a stream for a particular purpose he cannot use the water for other purposes.[63] A person who diverts water from a watercourse in large quantities so as to leave insufficient for other users may be restrained from so doing without the plaintiff having to prove actual damage or inconvenience because the defendant's act, if repeated sufficiently, may ripen into an adverse right.[64]

The duty upon riparian owners who divert a watercourse is to return the water substantially undiminished in both quantity and quality. Hence where water is added to the diverted stream this may give rise to an action by a downstream riparian owner if the added water brings about a sensible alteration to the natural quality of the water in the watercourse.[65] However, in every case the ultimate issue is whether the diversion has significant effects upon the natural state of the watercourse. Thus in an instance where the defendant placed a dam across a stream,

---

E.R. 908) which restricts the liabilities of public authorities in negligence by overruling *Anns v. Merton L.B.C.* ([1978] A.C.728).

[60] *Fletcher v. Smith*, (1877) 2 A.C. 781; *Hanley v. Edinburgh Corpn.*, [1913] A.C. 488.

[61] *Greenock Corpn. v. Caledonian Ry. Co.*, [1917] A.C. 556; *R. v. Southern Canada Power Co.*, [1937] 3 All E.R. 923; see also *Pemberton v.Bright*, [1960] 1 All E.R. 792.

[62] *Bealey v. Shaw*, (1805) 6 East 208.

[63] *Attorney-General v. Great Eastern Ry. Co.*, (1871) 6 Ch. App. 572.

[64] *Harrop v. Hirst*, (1868) 19 L.T. 426.

[65] *Young & Co. v. Bankier Distillery Co.*, [1893] A.C. 691.

this gave rise to a complaint that the operation of the plaintiff's downstream mill was impaired by the water being prevented from running its natural course. It was held, however, that the water had returned to its former course before it reached the mill and there was, therefore, no significant detriment to the mill and the action should fail.

Another feature of diversions which is capable of giving rise to common law actions, as well as criminal proceedings under statute,[66] is interference with the movements of migratory fish. The applicable common law principle is that a lower riparian owner must not divert the flow of water in a river to such an extent as to interfere with the free passage of fish up the river, and an upper riparian owner has a remedy if a diversion materially obstructs the passage of fish.[67]

Riparian rights may be abrogated in certain cases by local statutes facilitating operations upon a particular watercourse, but in every instance the powers provided by statute must not be exceeded to the detriment of riparian owners. Where a public body was empowered by statute to divert or interfere with a stream, subject to the consent of each riparian owner being obtained in a manner prescribed by the statute, it was held that it would be restrained from altering the stream without the need for proof of sensible injury to any riparian owner where it had failed to obtain the consent of a riparian owner in accordance with the statutory provisions.[68]

Other matters concerning riparian rights in respect of diversions of watercourses are considered elsewhere in this work. Of special significance may be issues arising from the abstraction and diversion of percolating and underground water,[69] and restrictions on the abstraction of water from navigable rivers.[70]

---

[66] Under Part II Salmon and Freshwater Fisheries Act 1975, see p.428 below.

[67] *Pirie & Sons Ltd. v. Kintore (Earl)*, [1906] A.C. 478; *Fraser v. Fear*, (1912) 107 L.T. 423.

[68] *Roberts v. Gwyrfrai R.D.C.*, [1899] 2 Ch. 608; *Attorney-General v. Bristol Waterworks Co.*, (1855) 10 Ex. 884.

[69] See Ch.5 generally.

[70] See Ch.10 generally.

OBSTRUCTION AT COMMON LAW

The rights and obligations of a riparian owner with respect to obstruction or alteration of the natural flow of water in a watercourse may be considered under the following heads: (1) placing erections on the bed of a watercourse; (2) use of water for milling purposes; (3) clearing the channel of a watercourse; and (4) providing protection against flooding. Initially it may be noted, however, that these matters of common law have been extensively modified by statute and, for a complete statement of the law, the discussion which follows must be read alongside certain statutory provisions. In particular, it should be noted that the construction or alteration of impounding works, such as a dam or weir, in an inland water will require a licence from the National Rivers Authority in accordance with the Water Resources Act 1991.[71] Also, the erection, alteration or repair of a structure in, over or under a main river needs the consent of the Authority.[72] The discussion which follows is confined to matters of common law relating to obstruction, and statutory qualifications which may have a bearing upon the topic are dealt with elsewhere in this work.

Placing erections on the bed of a watercourse[73]

It follows from the basic principles of riparian ownership discussed previously that, in relation to a non–tidal watercourse, each riparian proprietor *prima facie* has the property in the soil of the bed or *alveus* from his own side to the *medium filum flumen.*[74] Riparian owners are not entitled to use the *alveus* in such a manner as to interfere with the natural flow of the watercourse or abridge the width of the stream, or to interfere with its natural course. However, anything done *in alveo* which produces no sensible effect on the watercourse will be permissible.[75]

---

[71] See ss.24 and 25 Water Resources Act 1991, considered at p.251 below.

[72] See ss.109 and 110 Water Resources Act 1991, considered at p.379 below.

[73] See also p.141 below.

[74] On the *medium filum* rule generally see p.17 above.

[75] *Bickett v. Morris,* (1866) 30 J.P. 532; *Masserenne and Ferrard v. Murphy,* (1931) N.I. 192; *Edleston v. Crossley & Sons Ltd.,* (1868) 18 L.T. 15.

In accordance with these principles, it has been held that the construction of an embankment which narrows a watercourse, but does not obstruct it, will not give rise to any action without proof of damage.[76] Similarly, a riparian owner will be permitted to place stakes and wattles on the soil of a river to prevent erosion by floods or to make pens to prevent cattle from straying.[77] A riparian owner may build an erection on his land though covered by water, so long as it does not interfere with any public rights of navigation,[78] or with the rights of other riparian owners.[79] Thus an obstruction cannot be erected in a watercourse so as to throw back the water on to an upper riparian owner's land causing flooding of his land and injury to his mill,[80] though it is possible that a right of this kind may be acquired as an easement.[81] The erection of piers in the bed of a river to support a building, which results in the flooding of adjoining banks without causing actual damage, will constitute an unlawful obstruction and diversion of the water for which an injunction will be granted.[82] Subject to the general right of fishery possessed by riparian owners, it will not be permissible to erect obstructions which interfere with the free passage of fish and prevent fish from reaching the upper parts of a watercourse to the detriment of upper riparian owners.[83]

In an action for obstruction it is not necessary for the plaintiff to prove either that damage has been sustained or that it is likely to be sustained.[84] In addition to remedies of damages and an injunction the erection of an illegitimate obstruction may give rise to a right to abate the nuisance by those whose rights are infringed as a consequence of it. However, when abating an obstruction the least injurious means must be

---

[76] *Thompson v. Horner*, [1927] N.I. 191.

[77] *Hanbury v. Jenkins*, [1901] 2 Ch. 401.

[78] *Tate & Lyle Ltd. v. Greater London Council*, [1983] 1 All E.R. 1159, see p.141 below.

[79] *Orr Ewing v. Colquhoun*, (1877) 2 A.C. 839, H.L.

[80] *Saunders v. Newman*, (1818) 1 B. & Ald. 258.

[81] *Alder v. Savill*, (1814) 5 Taunt. 454; *Wright v. Howard*, (1823) 1 Sim. & St. 190.

[82] *Masserenne and Ferrard v. Murphy*, (1931) N.I. 192.

[83] *Hamilton v. Donegal (Marquis)*, (1795) 3 Ridg. P.R. 267.

[84] *Edleston v. Crossley & Sons Ltd.*, (1868) 18 L.T. 15; *Norbury (Earl) v. Kitchen*, (1866) 15 L.T. 501; *Williams v. Morland*, (1824) 2 B. & C. 910.

employed causing the minimum interference with the wrongdoer's property and avoiding injury to innocent third parties or the public.[85]

The exercise of the right to place erections on the bed of a watercourse is also capable of giving rise to a range of other legal issues which the riparian owner will be obliged to take into account. Specifically, the erection may involve an obstruction to navigation,[86] a drainage obstruction to the watercourse,[87] or an obstruction to the passage of migratory fish.[88] Each of these matters is dealt with elsewhere in this work.

Use of water for milling purposes

The reasonable uses which a riparian owner may lawfully make of the water passing his land include turning its natural gravitation into water power, by weirs and other devices, erected in *alveo fluminis*, providing that the effect of this use does not cause sensible injury to downstream proprietors.[89] Thus, a riparian proprietor may erect a mill on the banks of a watercourse and take the water from the stream to work the mill, so long as he does not hold back the water upon his upstream neighbours, nor injuriously affect the volume and flow of the water to his neighbours downstream, unless a prescriptive right has been acquired to do so.[90] Similarly with the construction of a dam in a watercourse and the diversion of water for milling purposes, no need for consent from other riparian owners will be required provided that the dam is situated sufficiently far below the lands of upstream owners as not to impede the flow of water from their land, and providing the flow of water is restored to its natural channel by the time it enters the property of downstream owners.[91]

A riparian owner who constructs works to harness the power of a flow of water can thereby acquire an interest in the water power and sell

---

[85] *Hill v. Cock*, (1872) 26 L.T. 185; *Roberts v. Rose*, (1865) 4 H. & C. 103.

[86] See p.140 below.

[87] See p.398 below.

[88] See p.428 below.

[89] *Belfast Ropeworks Co. Ltd.*, v. Boyd (1888) 21 L.R.Ir. 560; *Loud v. Murray*, (1851) 17 L.T.O.S. 248; *Palme v. Persse*, (1877) 11 I.R.Eq. 616.

[90] *Nuttall v. Bracewell*, (1866) L.R. 2 Ex. 1.

[91] *Orr Ewing v. Colquhoun*, (1877) 2 A.C. 839, H.L.

that interest along with his land notwithstanding that the watercourse concerned is navigable.[92] Ownership of an artificial dam does not convert the flowing stream into a pond so as to give the owner an exclusive right to use the whole of the running water.[93] Where a licence is required to erect a dam at a particular location this will be strictly construed not to authorise the licensee to erect the dam at another spot.[94]

A mill owner may bring an action for infringement of water rights although he has not enjoyed those rights precisely in the same state for a prescriptive period of twenty years,[95] but an action for diverting water from a mill will not succeed unless sensible diminution of the water arising from the diversion can be shown.[96] In an action of this kind the onus will lie upon the plaintiff to prove that damage has occurred as a result of diminution of water flow to his mill.[97] If shown, a court may require the defendant to give an undertaking not to use his land in such a manner as to obstruct or interfere with the passage and flow of water to the plaintiff's mill.[98] A court may also grant an injunction to restrain the defendant from preventing water flowing to a mill in regular quantities.[99]

Clearing the channel of a watercourse

A riparian owner is under no common law duty to clear the channel of a watercourse where the stream becomes silted up or choked with weeds due to natural causes, or to compensate adjoining owners whose land is flooded as a consequence.[100] The course of a watercourse which a riparian owner is entitled to have preserved is the natural and apparently permanent course existing when the right is asserted or called

---

[92] *Hamelin v. Bannerman*, [1895] A.C. 237.
[93] *White & Sons v. White*, [1906] A.C. 72.
[94] *Mason v. Hill*, (1833) 5 B. & Ad. 1.
[95] *Saunders v. Newman*, (1818) 15 Jur. 633.
[96] *Embrey v. Owen*, (1851) 15 Jur. 633.
[97] *Morgan v. Last*, (1886) 2 T.L.R. 262.
[98] *Elwell v. Crowther*, (1862) 31 Beav. 163.
[99] *Robinson v. Byron (Lord)*, (1785) 1 Bro. C.C. 588.
[100] *Bridges' Repair Case*, (1609) 12 Co. Rep. 33; *Parrett Navigation Co. v. Robins*, (1842) 10 M. & W. 593; *Cracknell v. Thetford Corpn.*, (1869) L.R. 4 C.P. 629; *Hodgson v. York Corpn.*, (1873) 37 J.P. 725; *Normile v. Ruddle*, (1912) 47 I.L.T. 179.

into question, and a riparian owner cannot remove a long established natural accretion of gravel or a shoal in a river bed so as to restore the flow of water to its former state as to velocity, direction and height.[101] Neither may he alter the level of a river by removing obstructions which by lapse of time have become embedded and consolidated in and form a part of the river bed, if the effect of so doing is to diminish or increase the flow of water which a mill owner lower down has been enjoying owing to the diversion of the watercourse or the alteration in its level by the obstructions.[102] It may be noted, however, that this type of situation may be the subject of remedies provided for by statute under the Land Drainage Act 1991[103] or the Public Health Act 1936.[104]

Protection against flooding

At common law a riparian owner with land on the banks of a non-tidal watercourse has the right to raise the river banks from time to time as it becomes necessary to confine flood water within the banks and prevent it from overflowing onto his land. This work may only be done provided that it can be accomplished without actual injury to the property of others,[105] and in particular without injury to property on the other side of the watercourse as well as land above or below the riparian property.[106] Hence in *Menzies v. Breadalbane*,[107] it was decided that a proprietor of the bank of a river had no right to build a mound which would, if completed, throw the water of the river on to the ground of an owner of the opposite bank, so as to overflow and injure them, in times of ordinary flood. Whilst a riparian owner is entitled to protect his property from flooding, he may not execute works of alteration to the bed of the watercourse which have the effect of increasing its normal flow and

---

101 *Withers v. Purchase*, (1889) 60 L.T. 819.

102 *Fear v. Vickers*, (1911) 27 T.L.R. 558; *McGlone v. Smith*, (1888) 22 L.R.Ir. 554.

103 See p.399 below.

104 See s.259 Public Health Act 1936, and see the discussion of statutory nuisance, now provided for under Part III Environmental Protection Act 1990, at p.339 below.

105 *Trafford v. The King*, (1832) 8 Bing. 204; *Ridge v. Midland Ry.*, (1888) 53 J.P. 55.

106 *Bickett v. Morris*, (1866) 30 J.P. 532.

107 (1828) 3 Bli. N.S. 414.

diminishing the flow past a nearby mill.[108] This right applies in relation to inland waters, whether tidal or non tidal, but should be contrasted with the broader rights of an owner of the seashore, who is entitled to protect himself from the inroads of the sea by erecting appropriate works in a *bona fide* manner, without regard to damage thereby caused to his neighbours.[109]

In relation to the protection of land against flooding, the precise meaning of the word "flood" is a matter of some difficulty, but it is thought to mean a large and sudden movement of water which arises in some abnormal and violent situation. Consequently, it has been held that a gradual seepage of water did not involve a flood.[110] By contrast to the principles relating to the prevention of flooding, in the actual event of an extraordinary flood, a riparian owner may enclose his land and divert the water without regard to the consequences of that action for his neighbours.[111] If a flood embankment is placed some distance from a watercourse the person erecting it is not liable if, during heavy floods, water flows from the embankment and onto his neighbour's land.[112] In these instances, however, the action taken by the riparian owner must be in respect of warding off a common danger and not merely to transfer to another person's land a danger which exists on his own land.[113]

A right to discharge flood water on to another person's land, for example, by opening sluice gates to prevent damage to one's own lands, may be acquired as an easement.[114] Further, a riparian owner may erect a bank on his land to prevent the old course of a river being gradually altered, providing the bank was built on old foundations and it is established to be a local custom for owners to embank under these

---

108 *Provinder Millers (Winchester) Ltd. v. Southampton County Council*, [1939] 4 All E.R. 157.

109 *R. v.* Pagham Sewers Commissioners, (1828) 8 B. & C. 355.

110 *Young v. Sun Alliance and London Insurance Ltd.*, [1976] 3 All E.R. 561.

111 *Nield v. London & N.W. Rly.*, (1874) 44 L.J. Ex. 15; *Lagon Navigation Co. v. Lambeg Bleaching Co.*, [1927] A.C. 226.

112 *Gerrard v. Crowe*, [1921] 1 A.C. 395.

113 *Whalley v. Lancashire & Yorks Rly.*, (1884) 50 L.T. 472; *Thomas v. Birmingham Canal Co.*, (1879) 43 L.T. 435; *Maxey Drainage Board v. Great Northern Rly.*, (1912) 106 L.T. 429.

114 *Simpson v. Godmanchester Corpn.*, [1897] A.C. 696.

circumstances.[115] Where a riparian owner erects a wall along the side of a watercourse to prevent flooding of his land, and after many years demolishes part of the wall in connection with building operations, with the result that a neighbour's property is damaged by flood, the neighbour has no right to the protection of the wall and cannot maintain an action for damages on the ground of negligence, nuisance or other common law actions.[116]

As a concluding comment to this section it is to be noted that many of the common law rights and duties in relation to flood protection are now to be read alongside statutory provisions. Of particular relevance amongst these are matters provided for under the Land Drainage Act 1991, and the Coast Protection Act 1947, considered elsewhere in this work.[117]

ESCAPE, OVERFLOW AND DISCHARGE OF WATER

The position of landowners

No liability arises from the action of water which is naturally present on land. Thus, where excavated gravel workings became filled with water which eroded the adjoining land and deprived it of natural support, the owner of the gravel pit was held not liable.[118] Similarly, in another case, a court declined to restrain the draining of gravel pits into a stream to the injury of watercress beds which were supplied by the stream.[119] An owner of land who uses it in a natural manner and without negligence or wilfulness, will not be liable for escapes of water which cause damage on a neighbour's land,[120] since the proprietor of the higher

---

[115] *Farquharson v. Farquharson*, (1741) 3 Bli. N.S. 421.

[116] *Thomas & Evans Ltd. v. Mid-Rhondda Co-operative Society*, [1940] 4 All E.R. 357. On other common law actions, see the discussion of *Rylands v. Fletcher* at p.86 below.

[117] On the Land Drainage Act 1991 see Ch.12 below; and on the Coast Protection Act 1949 see p.59 above.

[118] *Rouse v. Gravelworks Ltd.*, [1940] 1 K.B. 489.

[119] *Weeks v. Heward*, (1862) 10 W.R. 557.

[120] *West Cumberland Iron & Steel Co. v. Kenyon*, (1879) 11 Ch. D. 782; *Bartlett v. Tottenham*, [1932] 1 Ch. 114. Contrast the position where an owner deliberately

ground has the right to have the water which falls on to his land discharge on to the contiguous lower land of his neighbour.[121] This principle applies even though an improved system of drainage has allowed the higher proprietor to increase the flow of water to the lower land.[122]

In a Canadian case,[123] it was held that the defendant, who was the owner of higher land, was not under a duty to take positive steps to ensure that surface water on his land did not run off to the possible injury of the plaintiff, who occupied adjoining lower land, and the defendant was not liable in negligence for failing to keep catch basins and drains clear. The defendant was, however, liable for diverting flood waters by removing a stone barrier bounding his land, so that substantial quantities of water which would not otherwise have overflowed the boundary wall, flowed onto the plaintiff's land and caused damage. The plaintiff may have acquired an easement by prescription in order that water might be diverted from his land.

At common law an owner has an unqualified right to drain his land for agricultural purposes in order to remove surface water which follows no definite course, and where this is done a neighbour cannot complain that he is thereby deprived of water which would have otherwise come onto his land.[124] Similarly, it is permissible for persons to drain their land and to allow the water to run into a stream, though the consequence is to swell the flow of water in the stream to a greater extent than would otherwise be the case.[125] Hence, it has been held that a riparian owner has no remedy where a stream overflowed and damaged his land unless he is able to show that the injury was due to an unlawful act of another riparian owner above or below him.[126] Alternatively, a

---

drains his land on to that of adjoining owners, see *Thomas v. Gower R.D.C.*, [1922] 2 K.B. 76.

[121] *Gibbons v. Lenfestey*, (1915) 84 L.J.P.C. 158; but contrast the discussion of *Home Brewery PLC v. Davis and Co.*, ([1987] 1 All E.R. 637) at p.87 below.

[122] *Jordeson v. Sutton, Southcotes & Drypool Gas Co.*, [1899] 2 Ch. 217.

[123] *Loring v. Bridgewood Golf and Country Club Ltd.*, (1974) 44 D.L.R. (3rd) 161.

[124] *Rawstron v. Taylor*, (1855) 11 Ex. 369; *Greatrex v. Hayward*, (1853) 8 Ex. 291; *Broadbent v. Ramsbotham*, (1856) 11 Ex. 602; *Weeks v. Heward*, (1862) 10 W.R. 557; *Bartlett v. Tottenham*, [1932] 1 Ch. 114.

[125] *Durrant v. Branksome U.D.C.*, (1897) 76 L.T. 739.

[126] *Mason v. Shrewsbury & Hereford Ry. Co.*, (1871) 25 L.T. 239.

remedy might be available where it can be shown that some other person or body that was responsible for maintaining the channel has neglected to do so.[127]

In relation to accumulations of water on land a notable authority is the rule in the case of *Rylands v. Fletcher*. This provides that where an owner, for his own purposes, brings onto his land and keeps anything which is likely to do mischief if it escapes, such as the accumulation of water in a reservoir, he must keep it at his peril, and if he does not do so he will be liable for all the damage which is the natural consequence of its escape.[128] The rule is, however, subject to a number of exceptions and qualifications. A person who stores water on his own land, and uses all reasonable care to keep it safely there, will not be liable in an action brought by a neighbour who suffers injury as a consequence of its escape if it can be shown that the escape was caused by an agent which is beyond the control of the person who accumulates the water. Thus, no liability would arise as a consequence of a storm which amounts to *vis major*, or to an act of God, in the sense that it is practically, though not physically, impossible to resist it.[129] Nor will a person be liable for the consequences of water being collected or impounded upon his land for the purposes of another person.[130] Similarly, liability will not arise under the principle if it is shown that the defendant had no control over the reservoir or knowledge of the circumstances which caused the overflow.[131] Likewise, the owner will not be liable if a trespasser is responsible for allowing the escape of water collected in an artificial pond on the owner's land.[132]

More generally, the rule in *Rylands v. Fletcher* has been the subject of a series of decisions restricting its effect and emphasising that liability under the principle will only arise in relation to "non–natural"

---

[127] *Harrison v. Great Northern Ry. Co.*, (1864) 3 H. & C. 231; *Smith v. River Douglas Catchment Board*, (1949) 113 J.P. 388.

[128] *Rylands v. Fletcher*, (1868) 19 L.T. 220.

[129] *Nichols v. Marsland*, (1875) 33 L.T. 265.

[130] *Whitmores (Edenbridge) Ltd. v. Stanford*, [1909] 1 Ch. 427; *Saxby v. Manchester & Sheffield Ry. Co.*, (1869) L.R. 4 C.P. 198.

[131] *Box v. Jubb*, (1879) 3 Ex. D. 76; *Nield v. London & N.W. Rly. Co.*, (1874) L.R. 10 Ex. 4.

[132] *Barker v. Herbert*, [1911] 2 K.B. 633; *Rickards v. Lothian*, [1913] A.C. 263.

uses of land.[133] This expression has been narrowly defined so that many purposes for which water is accumulated upon land will fall outside the ambit of the principle. It has been held that the accumulation of water in a property for domestic use is not a non–natural use of land since that use of water is desirable and in the interests of the community,[134] and it has been doubted whether provision for sewage disposal by a local authority constituted a non–natural use of land.[135] Most recently, in *Cambridge Water Company v. Eastern Counties Leather PLC*, it was held that although an industrial solvent was a substance likely to cause damage if it escaped, the storage of the chemical at premises in an industrial area was a natural use of the land and for the general benefit of the community. Accordingly, the plaintiffs were not entitled to recover where spillage of the solvent over a period of time resulted in contamination of the underground water from which they abstracted for water supply purposes.[136]

Discharges of water

The occupier of land is under no obligation to prevent water that has come naturally onto his land, and has not been artificially retained there, from passing onto his neighbour's lower land.[137] However, the lower occupier is under no obligation to receive the water and may put up barriers or otherwise pen back the flow of water even if this causes damage to the higher occupier, but the right to do so is not an absolute one and must be exercised reasonably. Thus in *Home Brewery PLC v. Davis and Co.* the defendant raised the level of his land by filling in clay pits and an osier bed which had previously received water from the plaintiffs' adjoining land, thereby causing flooding of the plaintiffs' land and forcing them to install pumps to overcome the flooding. It was held that the defendant was entitled only to take reasonable steps to prevent water entering his land, and although the filling of the clay pits was

---

[133] *British Celanese Ltd. v. A.H. Hunt*, [1969] 1 W.L.R. 959; *Read v. J. Lyons and Co. Ltd.*, [1947] A.C. 156.

[134] *Rickards v. Lothian*, [1913] A.C. 263.

[135] *Smeaton v. Ilford Corporation*, [1954] 1 All E.R. 179.

[136] [1991] *ENDS Report* 36, Queen's Bench Division 31 July 1991.

[137] *Smith v. Kendrick*, (1849) 7 C.B. 515; *Leakey v. National Trust*, [1980] Q.B. 485.

reasonable in view of the development of the land, the additional flooding of the plaintiffs' land caused by the filling of the osier bed was reasonably foreseeable and the defendant was liable, in either nuisance or trespass, for the cost of pumping and maintenance work to prevent flooding due to this cause.[138]

Much of the law relating to the escape and overflow of water derives from the problem of water discharging from one mine to an adjoining mine. The owner of a mine at a higher level is entitled to work the whole of his property in the usual and proper manner for the purposes of mineral extraction. In doing so he will not be liable for any water which, in consequence of his works, flows by gravitation or natural means into an adjoining mine,[139] provided that his works are conducted with due skill.[140]

By application of this principle, a mine owner will not be liable if in the ordinary course of mining he taps a spring from which the water by gravitation rises to the surface and floods an adjoining mine.[141] Also, since the right to work mines is a right of property, which when duly exercised gives rise to no responsibility, where mineral workings cause a subsidence of the surface and a consequent flow of rainfall into an adjacent lower coal–field, the injuries are regarded as being from gravitation and percolation, and do not constitute a valid ground for a claim for damages.[142] Hence in *Smith v. Kendrick*,[143] the owner of a mine on a higher level removed a barrier of coal between his mine and a mine on a lower level, so that water percolated through and inundated the lower mine. It was held that the owner of the higher mine was not liable for the injury so occasioned.

By way of exception to the general principle, however, if a mine owner does not merely suffer the water to flow through his mine, but employs some purposive activity to redirect the water then this may give rise to liability on his part. Thus, where activities are undertaken such as

---

[138] [1987] 1 All E.R. 637; contrast *Gibbons v. Lenfestey*, (1915) 84 L.J.P.C. 158.

[139] *Baird v. Williamson*, (1863) 15 C.B.N.S. 376.

[140] *Hurdman v. North Eastern Ry.*, (1878) 38 L.T. 339.

[141] *Young & Co. v. Bankier Distillery Co.*, [1893] A.C. 691.

[142] *Wilson v. Waddell*, (1876) 35 L.T. 639.

[143] (1849) 7 C.B. 515.

pumping,[144] or sinking or boring,[145] or tapping a river bed,[146] or diverting the course of a stream,[147] which have the effect of conveying the water into an adjacent mine which would not otherwise have occurred, or only would have done so more gradually or in much smaller volume, then the mine owner will be liable for any resultant damage, though this was done in the ordinary course of working and without negligence.[148]

POLLUTION AT COMMON LAW

Rights of a riparian owner as to quality of water

The principles of riparian ownership as they apply to water pollution were authoritatively reaffirmed by Lord Macnaghten in *John Young and Co. v. Bankier Distillery Co.*[149] in 1893.

> "A riparian proprietor is entitled to have the water of the stream, on the banks of which his property lies, flow down as it has been accustomed to flow down to his property, subject to the ordinary use of the flowing water by upper proprietors, and such further use, if any, on their part in connection with their property as may be reasonable under the circumstances. Every riparian owner is thus entitled to the water of his stream in its natural flow, without sensible diminution or increase, and without sensible alteration in its character or quality. Any invasion of this right causing actual damage, or calculated to found a claim which may ripen into an adverse right, entitles the party injured to the intervention of the court."

Thus, unless an upstream proprietor has gained the right to pollute through long enjoyment or grant, the general right of a riparian owner is to receive the flow of water without sensible alteration in character or

---

[144] *Lomax v. Stott*, (1870) 39 L.J. Ch. 834.
[145] *Scots Mines Co. v. Leadhills Mines Co.*, (1859) 34 L.T.O.S. 34.
[146] *Crompton v. Lea*, (1874) 31 L.T. 469.
[147] *Fletcher v. Smith*, (1877) 2 A.C. 781.
[148] *Young & Co. v. Bankier Distillery Co.*, [1893] A.C. 691.
[149] *Young v. Bankier Distillery Co.*, [1893] A.C. 691; and see also *Wood v. Waud*, (1849) 3 Ex. 748; *Mason v. Hill*, (1833) 5 B. & Ald. 1; *Embrey v. Owen*, (1851) 6 Ex. 353; *Haigh v. Deudraeth R.D.C.*, [1945] 2 All E.R. 661; *Pride of Derby Angling Association v. British Celanese Ltd.*, [1953] 1 All E.R. 179.

quality. On the facts of the case itself, the defendants discharged water which had been pumped from the lower strata of their mine into a stream which was used by the plaintiffs for the purposes of their distillery and the discharge, which though not impure was hard in quality, and made water from the stream less suitable for the plaintiff's use. It was held that the plaintiffs were not bound to receive the discharge.

Anyone who contaminates the water of a natural stream causing sensible alteration in character or quality infringes the rights of lower riparian owners, who can maintain an action against the discharger, without the need to prove actual damage, and obtain an injunction to prevent the continuation of the injury.[150] Similarly, if there is discharged a quantity of polluting matter which exceeds the minimum of which the law will take account, the plaintiff is entitled to an order of the court to prevent the continuation of the discharge.[151] This principle is to be contrasted with the position in relation to non–riparian owners of artificial watercourses which is considered elsewhere in this work.[152] It is also to be noted that, as a matter of criminal law, water pollution is the subject of extensive statutory regulation which is dealt with in a separate chapter.[153] The following discussion is confined to exposition of the common law principles relating to the subject.

In an action for pollution the plaintiff may claim an injunction and damages for nuisance and trespass.[154] In certain circumstances proceedings may be brought on the principle of *Rylands v. Fletcher*, whereby the polluter is strictly liable for an escape of polluting matter from his land.[155] Alternatively, an action may be brought on the basis of an allegation of negligence against the polluter.[156] A person other than a riparian owner, such as a fishery owner in tidal or non–tidal waters,[157] or

---

[150] *Jones v. Llanrwst U.D.C.*, [1911] 1 Ch. 393; *Crossley & Sons v. Lightowler*, (1867) 16 L.T. 438; *Chesham (Lord) v. Chesham U.D.C.*, (1935) 79 S.J. 453.

[151] *Staffordshire County Council v. Seisdon R.D.C.*, (1907) 96 L.T. 328.

[152] See Ch.5 below.

[153] See Ch.11 below.

[154] *Pride of Derby Angling Association v. British Celanese Ltd.*, [1953] 1 All E.R. 179.

[155] *Jones v. Llanrwst U.D.C.*, [1911] 1 Ch. 393.

[156] *Esso Petroleum Co. Ltd. v. Southport Corp.*, [1956] A.C. 218.

[157] *Ballard v. Tomlinson*, (1885) 29 Ch.D. 115.

the owner of a well which is polluted,[158] can bring an action for pollution on similar bases.

The principles relating to pollution of natural watercourses also apply to certain other types of water: (1) tidal waters;[159] (2) water which percolates discontinuously either on the surface or through underground strata;[160] (3) artificial watercourses of a permanent character which, by the circumstances of their origin and use are deemed to be natural;[161] (4) wells supplied by water percolating through the earth and not flowing in any defined channel;[162] and (5) ponds and inland lakes.[163]

The meaning of "pollution"

Whilst a riparian owner can maintain an action to restrain the pollution of a watercourse without having to show that the fouling was actually injurious to him,[164] it must be proved that the contamination involved is of more than a trifling or insubstantial nature.[165] Hence, no action will lie if the damage is temporary, or too minute, or too trivial to support a case,[166] so that in one instance where a waste discharge merely made water temporarily muddy it was held that this was not sufficiently substantial to be actionable.[167] However, actionable pollution will encompass changes to the physical character of the watercourse, such as raising the temperature by the discharge of heated water,[168] and changes to the character of the water such as the addition of hard water to a

---

[158] *Tipping v. Eckersley*, (1855) 2 K. & J. 264.

[159] *Lyon v. Fishmongers' Co.*, (1876) 1 A.C. 662.

[160] *Ballard v. Tomlinson*, (1885) 29 Ch.D. 115; *Hodgkinson v. Ennor*, (1863) 4 v. B. & S. 229; and on the pollution of percolating water see p.129 below.

[161] *Sutcliffe v. Booth*, (1863) 27 J.P. 613; *Baily v. Clark, Son & Morland*, [1902] 1 Ch. 649. Contrast the position in relation to artificial watercourses which are not of a permanent character and do not give rise to riparian rights, see p.115 below.

[162] *Womersley v. Church*, (1867) 17 L.T. 190; *Ballard v. Tomlinson*, (1885) 29 Ch.D. 115.

[163] On stillwaters generally see p.21 above.

[164] *Crossley & Sons Ltd. v. Lightowler*, (1867) 16 L.T. 438.

[165] *Elmhirst v. Spencer*, (1849) 2 Mac. & G. 45.

[166] *Lillywhite v. Trimmer*, (1867) 16 L.T. 318; *Attorney-General v. Gee*, (1870) 23 L.T. 299; *Lea Conservancy Board v. Bishop's Stortford U.D.C.*, (1906) 70 J.P. 244.

[167] *Taylor v. Bennett*, (1836) 7 C. & P. 329.

[168] *Tipping v. Eckersley*, (1855) 2 K. & J. 264.

stream where the water is naturally of a soft character.[169] Pollution will also be found to have occurred where a waste discharge renders the water unsuitable for the purposes of lower riparian owners such as sheep washing[170] or cattle drinking.[171]

In each case pollution will be considered as something which changes the natural quality of the watercourse.[172] In determining this it will not be necessary to show a general deterioration of the stream, it will be sufficient to prove that something has been added to the water which causes deterioration of the quality of the water at the point where the offending matter enters the watercourse.[173]

Permissible pollution

Despite the general common law rights of riparian owners in relation to water pollution there are a range of circumstances in which legal action may be precluded either because the person causing the pollution has acquired a legal right to do so or otherwise. Thus, if a riparian owner of a watercourse causes pollution which is confined to his own property so that the stream is free from noxious matter at the point where it leaves his land no action may be brought by downstream riparian owners.[174] Similarly, if the pollution affects only the land of a person who is not entitled to complain of the nuisance[175] then no action will be available.

In a range of circumstances a person may gain the legal right to cause, and continue causing, pollution of a watercourse. A right of this kind may arise where there is proof of an immemorial custom, for example, to win minerals from a mine and to wash impurities in the minerals in an adjacent stream, provided that the claim is not indefinite

---

[169] *John Young and Co. v. Bankier Distillery Co.*, [1893] A.C. 691, H.L.
[170] *Taylor v. Bennett*, (1836) 7 C. & P. 329.
[171] *Oldaker v. Hunt*, (1855) 3 W.R. 297.
[172] *John Young and Co. v. Bankier Distillery Co.*, [1893] A.C. 691, H.L.
[173] *Attorney-General v. Birmingham, Tame & Rea District Drainage Board*, [1908] 2 Ch. 551.
[174] *Elmhirst v. Spencer*, (1849) 15 L.T.O.S. 433.
[175] *Ormerod v. Todmorden Mill Co.*, (1883) 11 Q.B.D. 155; *Stockport Waterworks Co. v. Potter*, (1864) 3 H. & C. 300; *Ferguson v. Malvern U.D.C.*, (1908) 72 J.P. 101.

and unreasonable and the use is confined to the necessary working of the mine.[176] However, a custom cannot authorise actions which are illegal in character, such as the discharge of sewage matter into a river in concentrations which do not allow for sufficient dilution.[177] A right to pollute may also arise under an Act of Parliament which has the effect of overriding common law rights,[178] or of preserving existing rights to pollute.[179] In each case where this is claimed though it will be necessary to show that the proper interpretation of the statute at issue provides the authorisation claimed by the polluter.[180] In addition, rights to pollute may arise at common law by an express or implied grant[181] or by prescription.[182] In relation to a claim to a prescriptive right to pollute, however, it has recently be reaffirmed that the burden of establishing the right to an easement to pollute lies upon the party claiming it, so that where certainty and uniformity over the prescriptive period were lacking the claim failed.[183]

Pollution and fisheries

A riparian owner, or any other person who is entitled to a right of fishery in a watercourse, has a right of action against anyone who unlawfully does any act which disturbs the enjoyment of the fishery. This right has been held to be available where matter is discharged into a watercourse which has the effect of driving away fish and interfering with their breeding.[184] Similarly, where crude sewage was discharged into a river and immediately afterwards fish died in large numbers, it was held that the proper inference to be drawn, in the absence of an

---

176 *Carlyon v. Lovering*, (1857) 1 H. & N. 784; *Wright v. Williams*, (1836) 1 M. & W. 77.

177 *Attorney-General v. Richmond*, (1866) 14 L.T. 398.

178 *Lea Conservancy Board v. Hertford Corpn.*, (1884) 48 J.P. 628.

179 *Somerset Drainage Comrs. v. Bridgwater Corpn.*, (1899) 81 L.T. 729.

180 *Pride of Derby Angling Association Ltd. v. British Celanese Ltd.*, [1953] 1 All E.R. 179.

181 *Lea Conservancy Board v. Hertford Corpn.*, (1884) 48 J.P. 628.

182 See p.107 below.

183 *Scott-Whitehead v. National Coal Board*, (1987) 53 P. & C.R. 263.

184 *Fitzgerald v. Firbank*, [1897] 2 Ch. 96; *Bidder v. Croydon L.B.*, (1862) 6 L.T. 778; *Child v. Greenhill*, (1639) Cro. Car. 553.

alternative cause for the incident, was that the fish died from deoxygenation of the water caused by the sewage and the owner of the fishery was entitled to damages[185] and an injunction.[186] In less extreme circumstances, interference with a several fishery is the invasion of a private right and an action may be maintained without proof of special damage.[187]

A range of statutory provisions apply specifically to the protection of fisheries under criminal law and these are described later in this work.[188] As a matter of common law, it has been held that an indictment would lie against a gas company for a nuisance arising from the discharge of gas refuse into water which destroyed fish and rendered the water unfit for drinking.[189] A remedy for pollution by indictment may, however, be removed by statute.[190]

Remedies for pollution

Damages

Where an injury has been caused to a person's private right in a watercourse, whether freehold or leasehold, he is entitled to damages of either a nominal or substantial character. In addition, where further damage to the interest is reasonably apprehended an injunction may be granted against the party in default.[191] In exceptional situations a party who is merely licensed by a riparian owner to use water may maintain an action for fouling the water,[192] but normally a person who is not a riparian owner, and has no easement or right to use the water, cannot maintain an action for pollution.[193] Where damages are recoverable the

---

[185] *Dulverton R.D.C. v. Tracy*, (1921) 85 J.P. 217; *Granby (Marquis) v. Bakewell U.D.C.*, (1923) 87 J.P. 105.

[186] *Attorney–General v. Birmingham Corpn.*, (1858) 22 J.P. 561; *Bidder v. Croydon L.B.*, (1862) 6 L.T. 778; *Oldaker v. Hunt*, (1855) 19 J.P. 179.

[187] *Nicholls v. Ely Beet Sugar Factory Ltd.*, (1936) 154 L.T. 531.

[188] See p.352 below.

[189] *R. v. Medley*, (1834) 6 C. & P. 292.

[190] *R. v. Bristol Dock Co.*, (1810) 12 East 429.

[191] *Nixon v. Tynemouth Union*, (1888) 52 J.P. 504.

[192] *Whaley v. Laing*, (1857) 2 H. & N. 476.

[193] *Ormerod v. Todmorden Mill Co.*, (1883) 47 J.P. 532; *Dickinson v. Shepley Sewerage Board*, (1904) 68 J.P. 363.

amount awarded will represent the loss suffered by the plaintiff as the natural result of the injury caused by the acts of the defendant.[194] Accordingly, damages have been awarded for injury to the plaintiff's house and fishing and for procuring a new water supply and engine, but damages are not normally awarded for loss of amenity.[195]

The injunction

Where a right exists to use a watercourse flowing through land, and polluting matter is discharged into it so as to cause injury of a kind that is likely to continue or increase so as to become serious and permanent, the court will grant an injunction to restrain the continuation of the discharge. In determining whether an injury is sufficiently serious for an injunction to be granted, the court will have regard to all the circumstances and, in particular, the effect of the nuisance upon the value of an estate and the prospect of dealing with it to advantage.[196] In an action for an injunction against a polluter, it is no defence for the defendant to claim that the water was also fouled by other manufacturers,[197] or that the share he contributed to the nuisance is infinitesimal and inappreciable,[198] or that the injunction, if granted, would result in unemployment[199] or inconvenience a large body of the public.[200]

Despite the general principles as to availability of injunctions to prevent water pollution, a person who has established that a sensible deterioration of the quality of the water will take place may not always be entitled to an injunction as a matter of course. In particular, an injunction may be declined where it would not serve to restore the plaintiff to the right he has established, or where the act complained of could be adequately compensated by an award of pecuniary damages.[201] The court will not grant an injunction if the nuisance has been to a great

---

[194] *Granby (Marquis) v. Bakewell U.D.C.*, (1923) 87 J.P. 105.

[195] *Harrington (Earl) v. Derby Corpn.*, [1905] 1 Ch. 205.

[196] *Goldsmid v. Tunbridge Wells*, (1866) 14 L.T. 154.

[197] *St. Helens Smelting Co. v. Tipping*, (1865) 12 L.T. 776; *Crossley v. Lightowler*, (1867) 2 Ch. App. 478.

[198] *Blair & Sumner v. Deakin*, (1887) 57 L.T. 522.

[199] *Pennington v. Brinsop Hall Coal Co.*, (1877) 57 L.T. 522.

[200] *Attorney–General v. Leeds Corpn.*, (1870) 5 Ch. App. 583.

[201] *Wood v. Sutcliffe*, (1851) 21 L.J. Ch. 253.

extent abated since the institution of the proceedings,[202] or where the defendant has taken steps to remedy the injury since the commencement of the action.[203] Also an injunction will be refused if the injury complained of is too trivial,[204] or if the pollution is unlikely to recur.[205]

An injunction restraining a local authority from polluting a river by sewage will not apply to another authority to whom the functions of the former authority are transferred.[206] If a local authority do not act themselves to cause a nuisance, but neglect to perform their duty of providing a satisfactory and healthy drainage system, this is not a ground of action by an individual for damages or an injunction, and the remedy lies by way of prerogative writ of *mandamus*.[207] When granting an injunction to restrain pollution from sewage matter, it is a common practice to grant an immediate injunction restraining any new connections with the river but to suspend the operation of the order for a period of time in respect of existing sewers to enable the defendants to improve their sewage works so as to be able to comply with the order.[208]

An injunction will be declined where damages are an adequate remedy. Thus, where an action was brought to prevent a sanitary authority from continuing to discharge sewage into a stream, the court declined to give an injunction, because it was unlikely that the discharge would recur, but gave damages.[209] Conversely, in another action to restrain the discharge of effluent containing acid into a stream where the defendants requested that damages, in lieu of an injunction, should be given, the court ruled that an injunction should be granted. Amongst other reasons, the injunction was ordered to prevent the inconvenience to the plaintiff of having to bring repeated actions in relation to a continuing source of pollution.[210]

---

[202] *Lillywhite v. Trimmer*, (1867) 16 L.T. 318.

[203] *London C.C. v. Price's Candle Co. Ltd.*, (1911) 75 J.P. 329.

[204] *Attorney-General v. Preston Corpn.*, (1896) 13 T.L.R. 14; *Attorney-General v.Gee*, (1870) 23 L.T. 299.

[205] *Chapman, Morsons & Co. v. Aukland Union*, (1889) 23 Q.B.D. 294.

[206] *Attorney-General v. Birmingham Corpn.*, (1880) 15 Ch.D. 423.

[207] *Glossop v. Heston and Isleworth L.B.*, (1879) 12 Ch.D. 102.

[208] *Attorney-General v. Birmingham Corpn.*, (1858) 4 K. & J. 528; *Pride of Derby Angling Association v. British Celanese Ltd.*, [1953] 1 All E.R. 179.

[209] *Chapman, Morsons and Co. v. Aukland Union*, (1889) 23 Q.B.D. 294.

[210] *Pennington v. Brinksop Hall Coal Co.*, (1877) 37 L.T. 149.

Once the plaintiff has proved his right to an injunction it is no part of the court's duty to enquire as to how the defendant can best remove the nuisance. The plaintiff is entitled to an injunction immediately, unless the removal of the nuisance is physically impossible, and the defendant must find his own way out of the difficulty, whatever the inconvenience or cost of so doing may be.[211] By way of exception to this, however, there have been exceptional instances where courts have been prepared to recognise the effect of restrictions upon improvement works imposed as a matter of wartime exigency, and have allowed an injunction to be suspended to the end of the war.[212]

Where the difficulty of rectifying the state of an offending discharge is great the court will suspend the operation of the injunction for a period of time, with liberty given to the defendant to apply for an extension of time.[213] Where important public interests are involved, such as the improvement of drainage of a town, the court will protect the private rights of the individual if these are infringed in any material degree, but will at the same time have regard to the nature and extent of the injury involved and to the balance of inconvenience between the parties in granting or declining the injunction.[214] An injunction, once granted, may be discharged by the court if the circumstances which existed at the date of the judgment no longer apply.[215]

The fact that a person has submitted to an injury by pollution for some time, trusting to the assurance of a local authority that they were carrying out works which would eventually rectify the problem, does not preclude a person from applying for an injunction on grounds of *laches*, or delay, from applying for an injunction.[216] Where this is not shown, however, a person may become guilty of acquiescence to continuation of a discharge of pollution to such an extent that he may become disentitled to an injunction.[217]

---

[211] *Goldsmid v. Tunbridge Wells*, (1866) 14 L.T. 154.

[212] *Dexter v. Aldershot U.D.C.*, (1915) 79 J.P. 580; *Pride of Derby Angling Association v. British Celanese Ltd.*, [1953] 1 All E.R. 179.

[213] *Attorney-General v. Colney Hatch Lunatic Asylum*, (1868) 19 L.T. 708.

[214] *Lillywhite v. Trimmer*, (1967) 16 L.T. 318.

[215] *Attorney-General v. Birmingham Drainage Board*, [1912] A.C. 788.

[216] *Attorney-General v. Birmingham Corpn.*, (1858) 4 K. & J. 528.

[217] *Wood v. Sutcliffe*, (1851) 21 L.J. Ch. 253.

A *quia timet* action may be maintained to restrain an imminent danger of pollution of a substantial kind, or where the apprehended injury, if it transpires, will cause damage of an irreparable kind.[218] For an action of this kind to be sustained there must be an actual present danger or the immediate probability of a nuisance.[219] An injunction will not be granted in a *quia timet* action if there is merely the *possibility* that the ground for an injunction may be established in the future. Hence, it will not be sufficient to show, hypothetically, that if the defendant does or fails to do some act, a case for an injunction would be established.[220]

Where an order of the court is granted restraining a local authority from discharging their sewage into a river to the injury of the plaintiff, it is no excuse for a breach of the injunction that the authority has attempted to deodorise the sewage so as to make it innocuous and have failed to do so. It is their duty, if they are unable to obey the order by other means, not to discharge the sewage into the river at all, and as a final sanction a court may order sequestration of their property.[221] In an action for sequestration of assets for a breach of an undertaking given against further pollution, the court instead of making a sequestration order, may grant an injunction in the terms of the undertaking and penalise the defendants by ordering them to pay all costs of the application.[222] A writ of sequestration against a local authority for its failure to comply with an undertaking not to pollute a river will not lie for an accidental breach of the undertaking.[223]

Public nuisance

If pollution of water is caused to such an extent as to constitute a public nuisance, the Attorney–General may institute proceedings on

---

[218] *Fletcher v. Bealey*, (1885) 28 Ch.D. 688.

[219] *Attorney–General v. Kingston–on–Thames Corpn.*, (1865) 12 L.T. 665.

[220] *Bank View Mills Ltd. v. Nelson Corpn.*, [1943] 1 K.B. 337.

[221] *Spokes v. Banbury*, (1865) 13 L.T. 428.

[222] *Marsden & Sons Ltd. v. Old Silkstone Collieries Ltd.*, (1914) 13 L.G.R. 342; *Witham v. Wansford Trout Farm Ltd.*, (1991) Unreported Queen's Bench Division 12 April 1991, [1991] 2 *Water Law* 143.

[223] *Monckton v. Wolverhampton Corpn.*, (1960) *The Times*, 26 November 1960.

behalf of the public by indictment,[224] or he may commence civil proceedings on his own motion by an information,[225] but more commonly a relator action will be pursued by an aggrieved individual with the sanction of the Attorney–General.[226] Where the Attorney–General proceeds on his own behalf, the court may grant an injunction to restrain the continuation of the nuisance,[227] and in a relator action, where the relator may be a private individual[228] or a corporation,[229] his claim may be joined with the claim for an injunction.[230] A private person may maintain an action in respect of a public nuisance, without the need for the support of the Attorney–General, if he can show that he has sustained particular damage beyond that suffered by the public generally and that the damage is direct and substantial.[231] The Attorney–General is entitled to apply for an injunction in respect of an anticipated offence, for example, where a public authority proposes to breach a statute without excuse.[232]

---

224 *R. v. Medley*, (1834) 6 C. & P. 292; *R. v. Bradford Navigation Co.*, (1865) 6 B. & S. 631.

225 *Ware v. Regent's Canal Co.*, (1858) 23 J.P. 3.

226 *Attorney–General v. Basingstoke*, (1876) 45 L.J. Ch. 726.

227 *Attorney–General v. Shrewsbury Bridge Co.*, (1882) 21 Ch.D. 752; *Attorney–General v. Birmingham Drainage Board*, (1910) 26 T.L.R. 93.

228 *Attorney–General v. Lonsdale*, (1868) 33 J.P. 534.

229 *Attorney–General v. Logan*, (1891) 55 J.P. 615.

230 *Attorney–General v. Cockermouth L.B.*, (1874) 30 L.T. 590.

231 *Benjamin v. Storr*, (1874) 30 L.T. 362; *Rose v. Miles*, (1815) 4 M. & S. 101.

232 *Attorney–General v. Wellingborough U.D.C.*, (1974) *The Times*, 29 March 1974.

Chapter 4

ACQUIRED RIGHTS OF WATER

NATURE AND CHARACTERISTICS OF WATER EASEMENTS

In addition to the natural riparian rights enjoyed by owners of waterside land, a riparian owner may acquire additional rights in the nature of easements. A riparian owner may gain an additional right to use water beyond his natural rights, but an acquired right of this kind will have no operation against the natural rights of other riparian owners unless it is the subject of a grant or the exercise of the right raises the presumption of a grant. If this is the case the tenement in respect of which it is used becomes the dominant tenement and the tenement to the detriment of which it is used becomes the servient tenement,[1] since easements of water must be connected with the enjoyment of a dominant tenement and cannot exist in gross.[2]

As has been described, the general rule of law is that each riparian owner has the right to the advantages of a flow of water to his land without sensible alteration to the quantity and quality. However, an adverse right may be founded on the occupation of land and, though the watercourse is either diminished in quantity or quality, if the occupation of the person making use of it has existed for a sufficient length of time to raise a presumption of a grant, other riparian owners must take the flow of water subject to the adverse right.[3] *Prima facie*, therefore, each riparian owner has an equal collection of natural riparian rights and cannot acquire additional rights, such as the right to dam back the water upon the proprietor above or divert it from the proprietor below, without a grant of the right or twenty years' enjoyment which is taken to be evidence of a grant.[4]

Easements of water must be distinguished from other rights such as restrictive covenants,[5] mere licences or covenants for a person to do a

---

[1] *Sampson v. Hoddinott*, (1857) 1 C.B.N.S. 570.

[2] *Ackroyd v. Smith*, (1850) 10 C.B. 164; *Stockport Waterworks Co. v. Potter*, (1864) 3 H. & C. 300.

[3] *Bealey v. Shaw*, (1805) 6 East 208.

[4] *Wright v. Howard*, (1823) 1 Sim. & St. 190.

[5] *Keppell v. Bailey*, (1834) 2 My. & K. 517.

particular thing,[6] and an easement cannot be acquired in respect of a temporary watercourse constructed for a specific purpose.[7] Although easements depend upon the existence of a dominant and servient tenement, an easement will not be invalid merely because it confers some benefit upon persons other than the owner of the dominant tenement. Thus in one instance, a corporation which owned land had, for more than 200 years, owned the right to use gates of certain locks on a river belonging to another person in times of flood in order to prevent flood damage to certain lands. It was held that this right constituted an easement despite the fact that it benefited land belonging to other persons.[8]

An easement cannot be acquired if it is not within the power of the presumed grantor to grant it.[9] Thus in one case the right of a company to the flow of water in a canal ceased upon the stopping up of the canal and the conversion of the canal into a railway.[10] In another case it was held that the defendant's claim to draw off surface water from a canal was invalid since the canal company did not have any statutory power to grant water for that purpose.[11]

Acquisition of water easements

An easement of water may be acquired on either of four legal bases: (1) by grant; (2) by prescription; (3) by custom; or (4) by statute.

Grant

A legal easement of water as an incorporeal hereditament may only be created or transferred by deed,[12] and a verbal licence is not

---

[6] *Hill v. Tupper*, (1863) 2 H. & C. 121.

[7] *Burrows v. Lang*, [1901] 2 Ch. 502; *Beeston v. Weate*, (1856) 20 J.P. 452; *Arkwright v. Gell*, (1839) 5 M. & W. 203.

[8] *Simpson v. Godmanchester Corpn.*, [1897] A.C. 696.

[9] *Preston Corpn. v. Fullwood L.B.*, (1885) 53 L.T. 718.

[10] *National Guaranteed Manure Co. v. Donald*, (1859) 4 H. & N. 8.

[11] *Rochdale Canal Co. v. Radcliffe*, (1852) 18 Q.B. 287. See also *McEvoy v. Great Northern Rly.*, [1900] 3 Ir. R. 325; *Staffordshire Canal Co. v. Birmingham Canal Co.*, (1866) L.R. 1 H.L. 254.

[12] *Hewlins v. Shippam*, (1826) 5 B. & C. 221; *Fentiman v. Smith*, (1805) 4 East 107; *Nuttall v. Bracewell*, (1866) 15 L.T. 313.

sufficient to confer an easement.[13] Despite the lack of a formal agreement, a court acting on the equitable doctrine of acquiescence may, in certain cases, recognise the existence of an easement. Hence, where the owner of the servient tenement granted permission for the enjoyment of an easement, or did not object to its enjoyment, and the dominant owner or others incurred expense in executing works, it was held that the dominant owner had acquired a right over a watercourse and the court restrained the servient owner from interfering with the flow of water by an injunction.[14]

Where an easement is created by express deed of grant the extent of the easement must be construed according to the wording of the grant.[15] A grant of an easement in a watercourse may relate to either the right to the running water, or the land over which the water flows, or the channel through which the water flows.[16] Where rights of water are created by deed, the court cannot take into consideration the rights which the parties would have had as riparian owners or otherwise, and the nature and extent of their interest must be regulated entirely by the deed.[17] Whether it is to be presumed that a grant has been executed is a question of fact.[18]

Where part of a property is sold, all continuous and apparent easements over the other part of the property which are necessary for the enjoyment of the part sold will pass to the purchaser. Therefore, where the owner of two or more adjoining houses sells one of them, that house is entitled to the benefit of, and is subject to the burden of, all existing drains communication with the other house, without any express reservation or grant for that purpose.[19]

---

[13] *Cocker v. Cowper*, (1834) 5 Tyr. 103.

[14] *Devonshire (Duke) v. Eglin*, (1851) 14 Beav. 530; *Liggins v. Inge*, (1831) 7 Bing. 682; *Bankart v. Tennant*, (1870) 23 L.T. 137.

[15] *New Windsor Corpn. v. Stovell*, (1884) 51 L.T. 626.

[16] *Taylor v. St. Helens Corpn.*, (1877) 6 Ch.D. 264; *Brain v. Marfell*, (1879) 41 L.T. 457.

[17] *Northam v. Hurley*, (1853) 1 E. & B. 665; *Chadwick v. Marsden*, (1867) 16 L.T. 666; *Rawstron v. Taylor*, (1855) 11 Ex. 369.

[18] *Dewhirst v. Wrigley*, (1834) 47 E.R. 529.

[19] *Pyer v. Carter*, (1857) 1 H. & N. 916; *Ewart v. Cochrane*, (1861) 5 L.T. 1; *Watts v. Kelson*, (1871) 24 L.T. 209; *Bunting v. Hicks*, (1894) 70 L.T. 455. On continuous easements see *Suffield v. Brown*, (1864) 9 L.T. 627.

Prescription

On the principle that a right to an incorporeal hereditament may be acquired by lapse of time, a prescriptive grant of a particular right to a watercourse may be claimed on proof of long use without interruption.[20] Where there has been a long continued and exclusive enjoyment of a right of property, the courts will presume that the enjoyment is a right or property of lawful origin.[21] For example, after long enjoyment of a watercourse running to a house and garden through the ground of another, it was presumed that the owner of the house had the right to the watercourse, and an injunction would be granted to prevent interference with the watercourse unless the defendant could show that the right was the subject of a special licence or agreement.[22] As a matter of common law, the enjoyment of the right must be shown to have continued since time immemorial, a date which is set at the limit of legal memory fixed at 1189. The inevitable difficulties of proving the enjoyment of a right since this date led to courts presented with evidence of enjoyment for as long as anyone could remember allowing a presumption that enjoyment had existed for the required period.[23]

The presumption of enjoyment of right since time immemorial could, however, be defeated by proof that the actual origin of the right was of a more recent date,[24] and accordingly the courts introduced a modification of the doctrine, namely, the presumption of lost modern grant. This allowed, on evidence of enjoyment of a right for a period of between twenty and sixty years, for the court to presume an actual grant of the easement had been made at some time after 1189, and before the period of enjoyment supporting the claim, but that the grant had been lost in modern times.[25] By application of this presumption, twenty years' exclusive enjoyment of a right to water will provide a conclusive

---

[20] *Goodman v. Saltash Corpn.*, (1882) 48 L.T. 239.

[21] *Foster v. Warblington U.D.C.*, [1906] 1 K.B. 648; *Hammerton v. Dysart (Duke)*, [1916] 1 A.C. 57.

[22] *Callaghan v. Callaghan*, (1897) 31 I.L.T. 418; *Wilson v. Stewart*, (1748) 2 How. E.E. 532; *Finch v. Resbridger,* (1700) 2 Verm. 390.

[23] *Jenkins v. Harvey*, (1835) 1 Cr. M. & R. 877.

[24] *Bury v. Page*, (1586) Cro. Eliz. 118.

[25] *Dalton v. Angus*, (1881) 6 A.C. 740; *Baily v. Clark*, [1902] 1 Ch. 649; *Rolle v. Whyte*, (1868) L.R. 3 Q.B. 303.

presumption of the existence of a right of the person enjoying the use.[26] In particular instances, the presumption of lost modern grant has allowed courts to presume grants for a corporation to discharge sewage into a tidal river,[27] for the operation of a franchise ferry,[28] and for the abstraction of water to irrigate a mill meadow.[29]

In addition to claims based upon prescription at common law and the principle of lost modern grant, an alternative means of establishing a prescriptive right to water use is provided for under the Prescription Act 1832. Under s.2 of the Act a claim lawfully made at common law, by custom, prescription or grant of any watercourse[30] or the use of any water[31] which has been actually enjoyed by the claimant without interruption for a full period of twenty years can be defeated only by proof that the right has not been enjoyed for the period of twenty years. Where the right has been enjoyed for a full period of forty years, the right is deemed absolute and indefeasible unless enjoyed by a consent or agreement given or made for that purpose by deed or writing. The 1832 Act does not replace the other methods of establishing prescriptive rights at common law or under the doctrine of lost modern grant and the three methods may be pleaded alternatively.

The enjoyment of an easement established by prescription must be shown not to have been interrupted and to involve use as of right.[32] The prescriptive right must be limited and defined by the user, and where the use is unlimited, and water is taken without regard to the needs of the servient owner, a prescriptive right cannot be obtained.[33] Also the actual enjoyment of a prescriptive right which must be established must not be secret, unknown and unsuspected by the servient owner. In one instance a noxious discharge from a factory into the plaintiff's sewers was made

---

[26] *Bealey v. Shaw*, (1805) 6 East. 208; *Hanna v. Pollock*, [1900] 2 I.R. 664.

[27] *Somerset Drainage Comrs. v. Bridgwater Corpn.*, (1899) L.T. 729.

[28] *Dysart v. Hammerton*, [1914] 1 Ch. 822.

[29] *Scott v. Hanson*, (1829) 1 Russ. & M. 128.

[30] *Wright v. Williams*, (1836) 1 M. & W. 77; *Ward v. Robins*, (1846) 15 M. & W. 237.

[31] *Race v. Ward*, (1855) 4 E. & B. 702; *Manning v. Wasdale*, (1836) 5 Ad. & El. 758; *Macnaghten v. Baird*, [1903] 2 Ir.R. 731; *Leconfield v. Lonsdale*, (1870) L.R. 5 C.P. 657; *Drewitt v. Sheard*, (1836) 7 C. & P. 465.

[32] *Eaton v. Swansea Waterworks Co.*, (1851) 17 Q.B. 267.

[33] *Attorney-General v. Great Northern Rly.*, [1909] 1 Ch. 775.

intermittently and mainly at night without the knowledge of the plaintiffs, and it was held to be of such a character as not to establish an easement.[34]

Custom

An easement may be claimed as a particular custom by the inhabitants of a district, for example, for the flow of water from a spring, well or pond for domestic purposes or the watering of cattle,[35] and the inhabitants can maintain an action without having suffered individual damage for any infringement of the right.[36] Such a claim will not be upheld if it is too wide to be the subject of a custom, as where a claim is made on behalf of the public at large and is not confined to any particular class of persons.[37] A claim by tin miners to use a natural stream for washing ore and carrying away river washing was held to be a valid custom since it was sufficiently definite and reasonable and the use was limited to the necessary working of the mine.[38]

Statute

Easements relating to water may arise through the exercise of powers conferred upon a body by a general or private statute. Hence statutory water undertakers have been held to be entitled to acquire by agreement, or compulsorily, rights to take water from a stream or other source,[39] and a local authority or county council has been formerly held to be authorised to abstract water from a river, stream or lake in order to afford a water supply for houses provided by them.[40]

---

[34] *Liverpool Corporation v. Coghill*, [1918] 1 Ch. 307.

[35] *Race v. Ward*, (1855) 4 E. & B. 702; *Manning v. Wasdale*, (1836) 5 Ad. & El. 758.

[36] *Harrop v. Hirst*, (1868) 19 L.T. 426.

[37] *Dungarven Guardians v. Mansfield*, [1897] 1 I.R. 420.

[38] *Carlyon v. Lovering*, (1857) 1 H. & N. 784; *Ivimey v. Stocker*, (1866) 1 Ch. App. 396; *Gaved v. Martyn*, (1865) 13 L.T. 74.

[39] Formerly under s.26 Water Act 1945 (repealed), and now see s.155 Water Industry Act 1991 and Acquisition of Land Act 1981.

[40] s.103 Housing Act 1957 (repealed).

SPECIFIC EASEMENTS OF WATER

Easements of abstraction, diversion and obstruction

The right to divert water, which in its natural course would pass over or along the land of a riparian owner, and of conveying it to the land of the party diverting it is a recognised water easement.[41] Ordinarily an easement of this kind can only be created by grant or by continuous enjoyment over a long period from which the existence of a former grant may reasonably be presumed.[42] Alternatively, a right of this kind may also be created by statute.[43] Where a prescriptive right to discharge surface water across adjacent property by a specific channel has been acquired, the obstruction of the channel on the servient tenement, by the tenant of the latter, is an invasion of a legal right for which an action is maintainable without proof of actual perceptible damage.[44]

Once an easement to divert or obstruct a watercourse has been established, the diversion or obstruction cannot subsequently be altered or increased so as to increase the burden to the servient tenement. Thus were a court found that a mill owner had acquired a prescriptive right to divert water from a stream to his mill, it was held that he was not entitled to alter his sluices so as to divert more water to the mill.[45] By contrast it has been held that an alteration to the dimensions of a mill wheel will not destroy an easement,[46] nor will a change in the character of the property to which a prescriptive right is annexed such as a change from a fulling mill to a mill for grinding corn, providing this causes no additional injury to the servient tenement.[47] In more recent times it has been decided that an easement to abstract water from a pond for the purpose of spray irrigation and watering cattle may be a continuation of a previous use despite the fact that it involves fluctuations in the amount and application

---

[41] See *Cargill v. Gotts*, [1981] 1 All E.R. 682.

[42] *Beeston v. Weate*, (1856) 5 E. & B. 986.

[43] *Mason v. Shrewsbury Ry. Co.*, (1871) 25 L.T. 239.

[44] *Claxton v. Claxton*, (1875) I.R. 7 C.L. 23.

[45] *Bealey v. Shaw*, (1805) 6 East 208; and see also *Brown v. Best*, (1747) 1 Wils. 174.

[46] *Saunders v. Newman*, (1818) 1 B. & A. 258.

[47] *Luttrell's Case*, (1601) 4 Co. Rep. 86.

of water drawn due to changes in the type and methods of farming undertaken.[48]

A slight alteration in the course of a stream does not destroy any right annexed to it,[49] and it has been held that prescriptive right to a watercourse supplying an ancient mill is not destroyed by the old mill being pulled down and a new mill being built on the same stream.[50] However, where the owner of a mill changed his milling method to revert back to a method which had been used more than twenty years previously, and which required a higher head of water than that used during the intervening period, it was held that the discontinuance of the former method during the twenty year period would cause the mill owner to lose his right to the higher head of water.[51]

It is also pertinent to note at this point that the easements relating to abstraction, diversion and obstruction of watercourses as a matter of common law must be read alongside various statutory restrictions which may effectively limit the operation of water easements by making their exercise unlawful.[52] Specifically, subject to specified exceptions, a person may only abstract water from an inland water or underground strata, or construct or alter impounding works in an inland water, in pursuance of a licence granted by the National Rivers Authority under Chapter II of Part II of the Water Resources Act 1991.[53]

Easements to pollute water

A riparian owner has a right to the flow of the watercourse passing through his land in its natural state of quantity and quality, and where there is sensible deterioration in the quality of the water arising from the activities of an upstream owner normally this will be actionable as a matter of common law. By way of exception to this, however, no action will be possible where a riparian owner has gained a right to pollute

---

[48] *Cargill v. Gotts*, [1981] 1 All E.R. 682.

[49] *Hall v. Swift*, (1838) 6 Scott 167.

[50] *Palmis v. Hebblethwaite*, (1688) 2 Show. 249.

[51] *Drewett v. Sheard*, (1836) 7 C. & P. 465.

[52] *Cargill v. Gotts*, [1981] 1 All E.R. 682.

[53] See p.257 below.

through long enjoyment or otherwise.[54] Hence it has been held that the privilege of washing away rubble dislodged in the working of a tin mine and transmitting it down a natural stream running through another person's land may be claimed as a local custom or pleaded as a prescriptive right under the Prescription Act 1832.[55] Similarly a claim to be entitled to discharge water from a copper mine, which has been impregnated with metallic substances, into a neighbour's watercourse is a claim which may be brought under the 1832 Act.[56] However, rights of this kind may only be acquired by continued perceptible injury to the servient tenement over a period of twenty years,[57] and variation in the certainty and uniformity of a discharge may be sufficient to defeat a claim to a prescriptive right to pollute.[58]

Where a prescriptive right to pollute a watercourse has been acquired, the level of pollution must not be significantly increased to the prejudice of other riparian owners. The fact that a watercourse is polluted by another person is no defence to an action to restrain the pollution caused by a particular discharger.[59] Even assuming a prescriptive right to pollute a watercourse has been established, that right must be confined to its extent at the time of commencement of the prescriptive period, and if the pollution is substantially increased, whether gradually or suddenly, the court will grant an injunction to prevent the excess. If it is impossible to separate the unlawful excess from the legal exercise of the easement the wrongdoer must bear the consequences of any restriction which is necessary in order to prevent the excess even if this involves a total prohibition of the discharge.[60] A riparian owner who has a prescriptive right to take water from a watercourse, in a particular manner and at a particular place, and to return it in a polluted condition, is not entitled to take the water in any other manner or from any other place, nor to

---

[54] *Wood v. Waud*, (1849) 3 Ex. 748.

[55] *Carlyon v. Lovering*, (1857) 1 H. & N. 784.

[56] *Wright v. Williams*, (1836) 1 M. & W. 77.

[57] *Goldsmid v. Tunbridge Wells Commissioners*, (1866) 1 Ch. App. 349; *Murgatroyd v. Robinson*, (1857) 7 E. & B. 391.

[58] *Scott–Whitehead v. National Coal Board*, (1987) 53 P. & C.R. 263.

[59] *Crossley v. Lightowler*, (1867) 15 L.T. 438.

[60] *Blackburne v. Somers*, (1879) 5 L.R. Ir. 1.

exercise his common law rights in such a manner as to add to the pollution of the watercourse.[61]

The claim to a prescriptive right to foul a well has been defeated by variation and excess in the degree of fouling during the prescriptive period.[62] A mere change in the nature of the polluting matter which does not increase the pollution to any substantial extent, as against the servient tenement, does not necessarily destroy an easement.[63] However, a complete change of business to that originally carried on by a person having a prescriptive right to pollute a watercourse, even though the alteration actually decreases the level of pollution, will not be permissible.[64] Where a prescriptive right is claimed to pollute a river, the question to be considered by the court is whether the claim is for an immemorial right to pollute not limited to the purposes of the business, or for a more limited right to pollute for the purposes of the business as carried on for more than twenty years.[65]

Prescription may only be claimed for something which can have a lawful origin at common law.[66] Accordingly, an easement cannot be claimed in respect of anything which would be injurious to public health,[67] or which would cause a nuisance, such as the discharge of untreated sewage into tidal water so as to pollute oyster beds.[68] Nor can prescription be claimed to pollute waters in a manner which is forbidden by statute, for example by ss.3 or 4 of the former Rivers Pollution Prevention Act 1876,[69] or s.8 of the former Salmon and Freshwater Fisheries Act 1923.

---

[61] *McIntyre Corpn. v. McGavin*, [1893] A.C. 268.

[62] *Millington v. Griffiths*, (1874) 30 L.T. 65.

[63] *Baxendale v. McMurray*, (1867) 31 J.P. 821; *Somerset Drainage Comrs. v. Bridgwater Corpn.*, (1899) 81 L.T. 670.

[64] *Clarke v. Somerset Drainage Comrs.*, (1888) 59 L.T. 670.

[65] *Moore v. Webb*, (1857) 1 C.B.N.S. 673.

[66] *Goodman v. Saltash Corpn.*, (1882) 48 L.T. 239.

[67] *Blackburne v. Somers*, (1879) 5 L.R. Ir. 1.

[68] *Liverpool Corpn. v. Coghill*, [1918] 1 Ch. 307.

[69] *Owen v. Faversham Corpn.*, (1908) 73 J.P. 33; *Butterworth v. West Riding of Yorkshire Rivers Board*, [1909] A.C. 45; *Hulley v. Silversprings Bleaching Co.*, [1922] 2 Ch. 268; *Green v. Matthews*, (1930) 46 T.L.R. 206.

Easements regarding underground and percolating water

Easements of water may be acquired in respect of water flowing in an underground stream through a known and defined channel since the principles which regulate the rights of landowners to watercourses are similarly applicable to all water flowing in a natural and defined course whether above ground or in a known subterranean channel.[70] However, there can be no express grant or reservation of water which percolates through underground strata, which has no defined course and no defined limits, since the principles relating to easements of water will not apply to percolating underground water.[71]

Underground water which does not flow in a channel cannot be the subject of property or be capable of being conveyed.[72] Similarly, an easement cannot be created in respect of mere surface water, the supply of which is irregular and the flow of which follows no regular or definite course.[73] Likewise, a claim to have water percolate through the banks of a river cannot be acquired by prescription,[74] though a prescriptive right can be acquired in water issuing from a spring or well above ground.[75] Nor can a claim be established under the Prescription Act 1832 to waste water from a canal.[76]

Easements to discharge or receive water

A claim to empty and discharge polluted water from a mine into a watercourse of a neighbour may be established under the Prescription Act 1832.[77] Similarly, it has been held that a right can be established to

---

[70] *Chasemore v. Richards*, (1859) 7 H.L.C. 349.

[71] *Dickinson v. Grand Junction Canal*, (1852) 7 Ex. 282.

[72] *Ewart v. Belfast Poor Law Comrs.*, (1881) 9 L.R.Ir. 172. On underground and percolating water generallly see Ch.5 below.

[73] *Rawstron v. Taylor*, (1855) 11 Ex. 369; *Greatrex v. Hayward*, (1853) 18 Ex. 291.

[74] *Roberts v. Fellowes*, (1906) 94 L.T. 281.

[75] *Balston v. Bensted*, (1808) 1 Camp. 463; *Race v. Ward*, (1855) 19 J.P. 563.

[76] *Staffordshire Canal Co. v. Birmingham Canal Co.*, (1866) L.R. 1 H.L. 254. On easements of artificial watercourses generally see Ch.5 below.

[77] *Wright v. Williams*, (1836) 1 M. & W. 77; *Carlyon v. Lovering*, (1857) 1 H. & N. 784.

discharge ordinary refuse water into another person's drain.[78] A prescriptive right may be acquired to transmit sewage from one sanitary district into the sewers of another district,[79] and for a highway authority to discharge surface water from a highway onto adjoining land.[80] However, the right of a corporation to discharge effluent into a river will not create an easement or grant in favour of the riparian owner which prevents the corporation from discontinuing the discharge.[81]

A right to receive the flow of water from another person's land may be acquired as an easement. Thus in one decided case,[82] tin workers had from before the time of living memory used the water of an artificial watercourse arising from the land of another person, and when the tin workers abandoned the mine, which came into the possession of the plaintiffs, the owner of the land on which the watercourse arose sought to divert the watercourse. On these facts, it was held that the plaintiffs had, either by prescription or custom, acquired a right to the continued use of the water.

In addition to the rights concerning easements to make use of the flow of water in a watercourse, rights may also arise to take water by manual means. Hence past cases have established easements allowing persons to go onto the land of another to take water from a pump,[83] pond,[84] spring or well.[85]

Secondary easements

When an easement is granted or otherwise acquired, it includes all secondary rights as are necessary for its proper enjoyment. Thus where

---

[78] *Cawkwell v. Russell*, (1856) 26 L.J. Ex 34; *Charles v. Finchley L.B.*, (1883) 47 J.P. 791.

[79] *Attorney-General v. Acton L.B.*, (1882) 22 Ch.D. 221; but see *Phillimore v. Watford R.D.C.*, [1913] 2 Ch. 434.

[80] *Attorney-General v. Copeland*, [1902] 1 K.B. 690.

[81] *Deed (John S.) & Sons Ltd. v. British Electricity Authority and Croydon Corporation*, (1950) 114 J.P. 533.

[82] *Ivimey v. Stocker*, (1866) 14 L.T. 427; *Gaved v. Martyn*, (1865) 13 L.T. 74; *Powell v. Butler*, (1871) I.R. 5 C.L. 309.

[83] *Polden v. Bastard*, (1865) L.R. 1 Q.B. 156.

[84] *Manning v. Wasdale*, (1836) 4 Ad. & El. 758.

[85] *Race v. Ward*, (1855) 4 E. & B. 702; *Smith v. Archibald*, (1880) 5 A.C. 489.

there is a prescriptive right to lay pipes across another person's property, a right will be implied for the purpose of entering the land and mending pipes.[86] Similarly, a prescriptive right to a watercourse includes the right to enter on the land of the servient tenement for the purpose of cleansing and scouring the watercourse,[87] or to repair the banks.[88] However, a privilege granted by deed to make a goit across another person's land will not include the subsequent right to enter the land to widen the goit.[89] If the principal easement ceases, secondary easements relating to it will also be extinguished.[90]

EXTINGUISHMENT OF WATER EASEMENTS

An easement of water may be extinguished by operation of law or by release.

Operation of law

When an easement is granted for a specific purpose, it will cease when that purpose has been accomplished. Thus, an easement to take water to fill a canal was held to cease when the canal was converted into a railway and so ceased to exist.[91] If the dominant and servient tenements become vested in a single person the easement is extinguished by unity of ownership, but it will only be suspended if there is merely unity of possession.[92]

---

[86] *Pomfret v. Ricroft*, (1669) 1 Sid. 429; *Goodhart v. Hyett*, (1883) 25 Ch.D. 182; *Thurrock Grays, etc., Sewerage Board v. Goldsmith*, (1914) 79 J.P. 17; *Brown v. Best*, (1747) 1 Wils. 174.

[87] *Peter v. Daniel*, (1848) 5 C.B. 586; *Liford's Case*, (1614) 11 Co. Rep. 46b.

[88] *Roberts v. Fellowes*, (1906) 94 L.T. 279; *Hodgson v. Field*, (1806) 7 East 613.

[89] *Bostock v. Sidebottom*, (1852) 18 Q.B. 813.

[90] *Beeston v Weate*, (1856) 5 E. & B. 986.

[91] *National Manure Co. v. Donald*, (1859) 4 H. & N. 8.

[92] *Canham v. Fisk*, (1831) 1 Tyr. 155; *Thomas v. Thomas*, (1835) 1 Gale 61; *James v. Plant*, (1836) 4 Ad. & El. 761.

Release

Release of an easement may be express or implied. An easement of water may be expressly released by deed, but in equity an easement may become extinguished by consent or acquiescence.[93] An implied release may arise in three different ways: by a licence given by the servient owner; by abandonment through non–use; and by an alteration of the use of the dominant tenement.

Licence given to servient owner

A verbal or written licence may have the effect of extinguishing an easement, as where the owner of the dominant tenement gives his permission to the servient owner to use his land in a way which is incompatible with the future enjoyment of the easement.[94]

Abandonment by non–use

Once a water easement has been acquired it cannot be lost by a subsequent act which does not amount to a surrender, even though that act would have, before the acquisition of the right, rendered the use precarious.[95] The mere suspension of the exercise of a prescriptive right is not sufficient to destroy the right without some evidence of an intention to abandon it, for example, where a factory has not been in use for more than twenty years and has gone to ruin. However, a long continued suspension may render it necessary for the person claiming the right to show that some indication was given during the period of non–use of the intention to preserve the right. The question of abandonment of an easement is one of intention to be decided on the facts of each particular case.[96] Mere non–use of a right to water over ten years,[97] or the obstruction by weed of a navigable drain for sixteen years,[98] will not be taken by themselves as presumptions of abandonment. Where a corporation had the right to discharge sewage effluent into a watercourse,

---

[93] *Davies v. Marshall*, (1861) 4 L.T. 581.

[94] *Liggins v. Inge*, (1831) 7 Bing. 682; *Davies v. Marshall*, (1861) 4 L.T. 581.

[95] *French Hoek Comrs. v. Hugo*, (1885) 10 A.C. 336.

[96] *Crossley v. Lightowler*, (1867) 16 L.T. 438.

[97] *Mason v. Hill*, (1833), 5 B. & Ad. 1.

[98] *Bower v. Hill*, (1835) 1 Hodg. 45.

this was held not to create a right in the riparian owner to any continuance of the discharge where the corporation wished to abandon it.[99]

Alteration in the use of the dominant tenement

A substantial extension or alteration in the use of a prescriptive right may destroy that right,[100] but if the alteration of the dominant tenement does not impose any additional burden on the servient tenement, the easement will not be extinguished, as was held to be the case where a fulling mill was converted to the grinding of corn,[101] or the dimensions of a mill wheel were altered,[102] or where there was a minute change in the course of a stream.[103] However, an easement will be destroyed if there is an encroachment by the dominant owner which renders the easement necessarily more injurious to the servient owner. Hence, a mill owner having a right to divert water was held to be unable to divert more water by altering his sluices,[104] and a riparian owner who had an easement to pollute water was held not to be entitled to increase the level of pollution.[105]

An easement exists for the benefit of the dominant tenement alone, and a servient owner acquires no right to insist on its continuance or to seek damages for its abandonment.[106] However, a person who constructs for his own use an artificial watercourse, whether on his own land or on another person's, is in the absence of agreement to the contrary, bound to keep the watercourse in a such a state of repair as will prevent damage to the servient tenement, and if he fails to do so he will be liable for any damage which may result.[107]

---

[99] *Deed (John S.) & Sons Ltd. v. British Electricity Authority and Croydon Corporation*, (1950) 114 J.P. 533.

[100] *Royal Mail Steam Packet Co. v. George & Branday*, [1900] A.C. 480.

[101] *Luttrell's Case*, (1601) 4 Co. Rep. 86.

[102] *Saunders v. Newman*, (1818) 1 B. & Ald. 258.

[103] *Hall v. Swift*, (1838) 4 Bing. 381; see also *Hale v. Oldroyd*, (1845) 14 M. & W. 789; *Watts v. Kelson*, (1871) 6 Ch. App. 166.

[104] *Bealey v. Shaw*, (1805) 6 East 208.

[105] *McIntyre v. McGavin*, [1893] A.C. 268.

[106] *Mason v. Shrewsbury Rly. Co.*, (1871) 25 L.T. 239.

[107] *Buckley v. Buckley*, [1898] 2 Q.B. 608.

Chapter 5

ARTIFICIAL WATERCOURSES AND UNDERGROUND WATER

Introduction

The general principles of riparian ownership which have been previously described do not apply to artificial watercourses which are governed by significantly different legal rules. The most frequently encountered examples of artificial watercourses arise where spring water is conveyed through a specially constructed open channel to a farmhouse for domestic and agricultural use;[1] or where an artificial cut is made to a natural watercourse for drainage purposes or for the discharge of waste;[2] or where water is diverted from a watercourse through a goit to work a mill wheel;[3] and in canals, sewers and water mains where artificial watercourses are usually constructed under statutory powers.

Distinction between natural and artificial watercourses

Although formerly the legal principles applicable to artificial watercourses had been assimilated to those applicable to natural watercourses,[4] it was subsequently clarified that this view was too broad.[5] The present position was authoritatively expressed by Sir Montague Smith delivering judgment in *Rameshur Pershad Narain Singh v. Koonj Behari Pattuk* in 1878.[6]

> "The right to the water of a river flowing in a natural channel through a man's land, and the right to water flowing to it through an artificial watercourse constructed on his neighbour's land, do not rest on the same principle. In the former case each successive riparian owner is *prima facie* entitled to the unimpeded flow of the water in its natural course, and to its reasonable enjoyment as it passes through his land, as a natural right of his ownership of it. In

---

[1] *Roberts v. Richards*, (1881) 44 L.T. 271.

[2] *Gaved v. Martyn*, (1865) 13 L.T. 74.

[3] *Burrows v. Lang*, [1901] 2 Ch. 503.

[4] *Magor v. Chadwick*, (1840) 11 Ad. & El. 571.

[5] *Wood v. Waud*, (1849) 3 Ex. 748.

[6] (1876) 4 A.C. 121.

> the latter case any right to the flow of the water must rest on some grant or arrangement, either provided or presumed, from or with the owners of the lands from which the water is artificially brought, or on some other legal origin."

Accordingly, the right to an artificial watercourse does not arise as a natural right of property, but must be established as an easement, except where an artificial stream is constructed by an owner solely on his own land.[7] An easement relating to an artificial watercourse may arise either by grant,[8] long continued enjoyment or under statute. In either case, the character and extent of the right so acquired, and the rights of the parties concerned, are governed by the terms of the grant, the nature of the use, or the provisions of the statute giving rise to the right.[9]

Essentially, two kinds of easements arise in relation to the enjoyment of artificial watercourses.[10] The first is the right to continued enjoyment of a discharge onto land from an artificial channel constructed by the owner of higher land.[11] The second is the right to discharge water through an artificial channel onto another person's land below.[12] In either case the right to an artificial watercourse, as against the person creating it, depends upon the character of the watercourse, and in particular whether it is permanent or temporary, the circumstances under which it was created or is presumed to have been created, and the manner in which it has in fact been enjoyed.[13]

Permanent artificial watercourses

Riparian rights, which are identical to those attaching to natural streams, may be acquired by prescription in artificial watercourses of a

---

[7] *Bunting v. Hicks*, (1894) 70 L.T. 455; *Holker v. Porritt*, (1875) 33 L.T. 125; *Beeston v. Weate*, (1856) 5 E. & B. 986.

[8] *Wood v. Saunders*, (1875) 10 Ch. App. 583.

[9] *Sharp v. Waterhouse*, (1857) 7 E. & B. 816; *Crossley v. Lightowler*, (1867) 16 L.T. 438.

[10] *Chamber Colliery Co. v. Hopwood*, (1886) 55 L.T. 449.

[11] *Ivimey v. Stocker*, (1866) 1 Ch. App. 396; *Greatrex v. Hayward*, (1853) 8 Ex. 291.

[12] *Carlyon v. Lovering*, (1857) 1 H. & N. 784; *Brown v. Dunstable Corpn.*, [1899] 2 Ch. 378.

[13] *Wood v. Waud*, (1849) 3 Ex. 748; *Baily & Co. v. Clark, Son & Morland*, [1902] 1 Ch. 649.

permanent character where those rights can be shown to arise from grant, prescription or implication of law.[14] The precise nature of the rights depend in each case upon the character of the watercourse and the purpose for which it was constructed. Providing the watercourse is constructed for lasting purposes, and for the general benefit of those in its vicinity, and not merely with the temporary and private object of benefiting the property of those by whom it was constructed, riparian rights may be acquired in its waters in the same way as in a natural stream.[15]

A watercourse, though artificial, may have been originally constructed, and subsequently used, under circumstances and in a manner which served to give all the rights of riparian owners in a natural stream to persons owning land adjoining the channel.[16] Similarly, if a watercourse is partly natural and partly artificial, but it cannot be discerned when the artificial portion was constructed, the watercourse may be deemed to be natural, or if in part artificial, to have been constructed so as to allow all the rights of riparian owners to the proprietors of the banks.[17]

Easements to the flow of water in an artificial channel on the land of another may be acquired if the circumstances under which it was created show that it was intended to be of a permanent character.[18] However, in no case can the owner of the servient tenement acquire, by the mere existence of the easement, a right against the owner of the dominant tenement to the continued diversion of a stream, since the easement exists for the benefit of the dominant tenement alone and the servient owner acquires no right to insist on its continuance or to seek damages for its abandonment.[19]

---

[14] *Gartner v. Kidman*, [1962] A.L.J.R. 620.

[15] *Blackburne v. Somers*, (1879) 5 L.R.Ir. 1.

[16] *Sutcliffe v. Booth*, (1863) 27 J.P. 613; *Nuttall v. Bracewell*, (1866) L.R. 2 Exch. 1; *Rameshur Pershad Narain Singh v. Koonj Behar Pattak*, (1878) 4 App. Cas. 121, P.C.; *Baily & Co. v. Clark, Son & Morland*, [1902] 1 Ch. 649; *Manug Bya v. Manug Kyi Lyo*, (1925) L.R. 52 Ind. App. 385, P.C.; *Epstein v. Reymes*, (1972), 29 D.L.R. (3rd), (Supreme Court of Canada).

[17] *Roberts v. Richards*, (1881) 44 L.T. 271.

[18] *Gaved v. Martyn*, (1865) 13 L.T. 74.

[19] *Mason v. Shrewsbury Rly.*, (1871) 25 L.T. 239.

In one instance it was held that, in the case of an artificial watercourse the origin of which was unknown, the proper inference to be drawn from the use of the water and other circumstances was that the channel was originally constructed on the understanding that all riparian proprietors should have the same rights. These included a right to use the water for manufacturing purposes, as they would have done had the stream been a natural one.[20] In a case of that kind it will follow that an owner of land adjoining the channel will be entitled to all the natural rights of riparian owners along with any additional prescriptive rights which may arise in relation to the watercourse. Hence, where the plaintiffs and the predecessors in title had constantly used the water of an artificial channel for nearly 250 years, and where water flowed through an artificial channel past the land of several owners to serve the purpose of an owner lower down, the conditions upon which the channel was originally constructed would include a grant of an easement to the running water and *prima facie* every owner on the banks of the channel would be entitled to half of the bed of the channel adjoining his land.[21]

Temporary artificial watercourses

Some significant differences arise in relation to the rights which exist in temporary artificial watercourses. In one such instance the watercourse at issue was an artificial stream which drained certain mines but was of only a temporary character continuing in existence solely for the object of draining the mines. It was held that, under these circumstances, the owners of the banks of the stream could not compel the mine owners to continue the discharge.[22] Similarly, no action was held to lie for injury caused by the diversion of an artificial watercourse where it was clear from the nature of the circumstances that the enjoyment of the watercourse depended upon temporary circumstances and the interruption was by a person who stood in the nature of a grantor.[23]

---

[20] *Baily and Co. v. Clark, Son and Morland*, [1902] 1 Ch. 649.

[21] *Whitmores (Edenbridge) Ltd. v. Stanford*, [1909] 1 Ch. 427.

[22] *Arkwright v. Gell*, (1839) 5 M. & W. 203.

[23] *Wood v. Waud*, (1849) 18 L.J. Ex. 305; see also *Greatrex v. Hayward*, (1853) 8 Ex. 291.

A right to a flow of water along an artificial channel cannot be acquired under the Prescription Act 1832 unless the circumstances under which the channel was constructed show that it was intended to be of a permanent character.[24] In one case where an ancient watercourse was diverted from a natural stream and constructed and maintained solely for the purposes of a mill, it was held to be constructed for a special temporary purpose, and a purchaser of the mill acquired no right either by implied grant or by statute to the continued use of the water in the watercourse.[25] In another decision it was held that a flow of water for twenty years from a drain made for agricultural improvements did not give rise to a right of a neighbour to preclude the owner from altering the level of the drain. In that case the drain was found to be of a temporary character and dependent upon the manner which the defendant might adopt in draining his land.[26]

A number of other decisions have been reached against claims that artificial watercourses have been intended to be of a permanent character. In one instance a claim to an artificial drain was held only to be permissive in character since the drain was open to alteration or removal at the will of the person who had constructed it.[27] In another instance where a person made an artificial channel to bring water to a stream it was held that *prima facie* he could cut it off it he chose to do so.[28] Likewise, it was held that no prescriptive right could be acquired to receive water overflowing from a tank along an artificial stream which had been found to be constructed for temporary purposes only.[29] It follows from these decisions that the meaning of "temporary purpose" is not confined to purposes that happen to last for only a few years, but include purposes that are temporary in the sense that they are capable of coming to an end within the reasonable contemplation of the parties.[30]

---

[24] *Gaved v. Martyn*, (1865) 13 L.T. 74.
[25] *Burrows v. Lang*, [1901] 2 Ch. 503.
[26] *Greatrex v. Hayward*, (1853) 8 Ex. 291.
[27] *Hanna v. Pollock*, [1900] 2 I.R. 664.
[28] *Brymbo Water Co. v. Lesters Lime Co.*, (1894) 8 R. 329.
[29] *Bartlett v. Tottenham*, (1932) 45 L.T. 686.
[30] *Arkwright v. Gell*, (1839) 5 M. & W. 203; *Burrows v. Lang*, [1901] 2 Ch. 503.

Pollution of artificial watercourses

In general terms, the pollution of water which flows in an artificial channel can be likened to the rights which arise in respect of diversion or obstruction of an artificial watercourse, that is, that only a riparian owner can sue in respect of injury caused by pollution of the watercourse. If this is the case, and an artificial watercourse has been constructed with the intention that the owners of the banks should acquire riparian rights, they will have the same remedies against pollution as have the riparian owners of a natural stream.[31]

However, where the circumstances of the owners of banks of an artificial watercourse are not assimilated to that of riparian owners the position is significantly different. Thus, in one instance a mere licensee using water from a canal was held to be unable to sue another person who polluted the canal water since it was held that the licensee had no legal right to the water.[32] In another case where the plaintiffs possessed certain non–riparian land bordering a natural stream, and were without riparian lands with respect to the stream, it was held that they could not sue a riparian owner of the stream who polluted the water so that the supply which the plaintiffs abstracted through conduits was also polluted.[33] Similarly, it was held that the owner of a mill which received water from a natural stream by means of an artificial goit, could not sue in respect of the stream being polluted since he was not a riparian owner of the goit.[34]

Despite the basic principle that only a riparian owner is entitled to sue another riparian owner for the pollution of water flowing past his land, at common law no one is entitled to use his land so as to send foul water, by an artificial channel or otherwise, on to the property of his neighbour. In consequence of this it was held, in an early case, that if filth is created on a person's land, then he whose it is must keep it there

---

[31] *Sutcliffe v. Booth*, (1863) 27 J.P. 613; and see p.94 above on common law remedies for water pollution.

[32] *Whaley v. Laing*, (1857) 2 H. & N. 476.

[33] *Stockport Waterworks Co. v. Potter*, (1864) 3 H. & C. 300; and *Ormerod v. Todmorden Mill Co.*, (1883) 47 J.P. 532.

[34] *Crossley v. Lightowler*, (1867) 16 L.T. 638; see also *Dickinson v. Shepley Sewerage Board*, (1904), 68 J.P. 363; *Fergusson v. Malvern U.D.C.*, (1908) 72 J.P. 273.

and the failure to do so will be a trespass.[35] Thus it has been held that a person would be restrained from using a cesspool in such a manner as to cause water percolating through his property to pollute a well on adjoining land.[36] The same conclusion was reached where water and sewage came onto the defendant's land by an artificial drain, made for the defendant's convenience, and flooded the plaintiff's adjoining premises, and liability was found despite the fact that the defendant was unaware of the existence of the drain or of his liability to repair it.[37]

Similar issues arose in *Ballard v. Tomlinson*,[38] where the plaintiff and the defendant were adjoining landowners and each had a deep well in his own land, with the plaintiff's land being at a lower level than the defendant's. The defendant turned sewage into his well and polluted the water which percolated underground from his property to the plaintiff's land, and consequently the water which came into the plaintiff's well from the percolating water became contaminated by the defendant's sewage. It has held that the plaintiff had a right of action against the defendant for polluting the source of supply, despite the fact that, until he appropriated it by pumping, the plaintiff had no property in the percolating water under his land. It may, however, be possible to establish a right to discharge dirty water which might serve as a defence to an action of this kind.[39]

PERCOLATING UNDERGROUND WATER

The absence of riparian rights in underground percolating water

A succinct statement as to the law relating to underground or subterranean water is provided in the speech of Lord Chelmsford in *Chasemore v. Richards*, decided in 1859.[40]

> "The law as to water flowing in a certain and definite channel has been conclusively settled in a series of decisions, in which the

---

[35] *Tenant v. Goldwin*, (1703) Salk. 21.

[36] *Womersley v. Church*, (1867) 17 L.T. 190.

[37] *Humphries v. Cousins*, (1877) 2 C.P.D. 239.

[38] (1885) 29 Ch. D. 115; see also *Hodgkinson v. Ennor*, (1863) 4 B. & S. 229.

[39] *Cawkwell v. Russell*, (1856) 26 L.J. Ex. 34.

[40] (1859) 7 H.L. Cas. 349.

> whole subject has been fully and satisfactorily considered, and the relative rights and duties of riparian owners have been carefully adjusted and established. The principles of these decisions appear to me to be applicable to all water flowing in a certain and defined course, whether in an open visible stream or in a known subterranean channel. But it appears to me that the principles which apply to flowing water in streams and rivers . . . are wholly inapplicable to water percolating through underground strata, which oozes through the soil in every direction in which the rain penetrates."

The owner of land through which water percolates through subterranean strata has no right or interest in it which enables him to maintain an action against another landowner whose actions interfere with the supply of water. So, for example, the owner of a well was unable to maintain an action against a landowner who, in conducting mining operations in his land in the usual manner, had drained away all the water from the well and caused it to dry up.[41] Similarly in *Chasemore v. Richards*,[42] an owner of land who had for more than sixty years enjoyed the use of a stream which was mainly supplied by percolating underground water, lost the use of the stream after an adjoining landowner had dug an extensive well for supplying water for the use of local inhabitants, many of whom had no title as landowners to the use of the water. It was held that, despite this, the first owner had no right of action.

An important contrast, however, lies between water flowing in a defined channel and undefined flows of water percolating through the soil. Hence, it has been held in otherwise similar cases that underground water not flowing in a known channel was not the subject of property or capable of being the subject of a grant[43] and that subterranean water can only be the subject of riparian rights when flowing in a known and defined channel.[44] Hence, a landowner was held not to be entitled to compensation under statute for the abstraction of water from

---

[41] *Acton v. Blundell*, (1843) 12 M. & W. 324; *Hammond v. Hall*, (1840) 10 Sim. 551.

[42] (1859) 7 H.L. Cas. 349.

[43] *Ewart v. Belfast Poor Law Commissioners*, (1881) 9 L.R.Ir. 172.

[44] *Black v. Ballymena Commissioners*, (1886) 17 L.R.Ir. 459; *Blackrod U.D.C. v. Crankshaw (John) Co. Ltd.*, (1913) 136 L.T.Jo. 239.

underground springs, which rose in his land and fed his ponds, through a sewer constructed under statutory powers on neighbouring land, since the underground percolating water which had been abstracted was not the subject of any property rights which had been appropriated. Where a landowner granted the surface of land to another person, but retained the ownership of the minerals beneath it, lessees of the mineral rights were held not to be liable when, as a consequence of mineral working, they caused the water to be drained from the surface of the land.[45]

Abstraction of percolating water in a well or on the surface

It follows from the general absence of rights to protect a percolating water source that no action will be available where the water is intercepted before it reaches a well.[46] The issue remains, however, at what point after entering a well or on reaching the surface will water become the subject of legal protection? In relation to wells it has been held that where water had actually percolated into a well, and had then been abstracted from the well as a consequence of workings on adjacent property, no action would lie.[47] In another case where water arose from a spring which served the plaintiff's well and the defendants sank a well at the spring head, it was held that this was not taking underground percolating water, but water after it had arrived at the spring head and the defendants were, therefore, guilty of a wrongful diversion.[48] The same reasoning was adopted where the source of the spring at issue had been built around and formed into a well, thus resulting in an artificial channel for a short distance.[49]

Although a landowner will not in general be restrained from drawing off the subterranean water in the adjoining land, he will be restrained if, in so doing, he draws off water which flows in a defined surface channel through adjoining land.[50] That outcome may be contrasted with another situation where the defendants, in pumping a

---

[45] *Ballacorkish Co. v. Harrison*, (1873) 29 L.T. 658.

[46] *Brain v. Marfell*, (1879) 41 L.T. 455.

[47] *New River Co. v. Johnson*, (1860) 24 J.P. 244.

[48] *Dudden v. Clutton Union*, (1857) 1 H. & N. 627.

[49] *Mostyn v. Atherton*, (1899) 81 L.T. 356.

[50] *Grand Junction Canal Co. v. Shugur*, (1871) 24 L.T. 402.

well, lowered the general level of the water in a neighbouring land so that the stream became dry. The effect of this was to cause the water in a nearby stream to leak through the bed and sides, and the supply of water to a lower riparian owner was thereby seriously diminished. It was held that the riparian owner had no right of action against the defendants because the injury was caused by withdrawal of support rather than by abstraction from the stream.[51]

Restrictions on underground abstraction

An overriding common law principle is that a landowner is entitled to sink a borehole or well on his land to intercept water percolating underground through his property, though the effect of this is to interfere with the supply of underground water to nearby springs, providing that no interference takes place to water flowing in a defined channel. Moreover, providing the landowner's act is a lawful one, it is immaterial what his motives may be for doing so, and the presence of an improper motive will not render him liable to others who are deprived of water as a consequence of his actions.[52]

As with other common law rights to water which have been considered, the exercise of these rights has become the subject of detailed statutory regulation. In this instance it may be noted that it is an offence to construct or extend a well, borehole or other work for the abstraction of water from underground strata, or to install or modify machinery where additional quantities of water may be abstracted, unless the abstraction is authorised by a licence granted by the National Rivers Authority under Chapter II of Part II of the Water Resources Act 1991, and the abstraction takes place in accordance with the terms of that licence.[53]

---

[51] *English v. Metropolitan Water Board*, [1907] 1 K.B. 588.

[52] *Bradford Corpn. v. Pickles*, [1895] A.C. 587; *South Shields Water Co. v. Cookson*, (1845) 15 L.J. Ex. 315; *Langbrook Properties v. Surrey County Council*, (1969) 113 S.J. 983; *Stephens v. Anglian Water Authority*, [1987] 3 All E.R. 379 .

[53] See Ch.10 below.

Springs and wells

A spring of water is characterised as a natural source of water of a definite and well marked extent,[54] or as has been judicially stated, "a spring is not an artificial space, but a natural chasm in which water has collected, and from which it is either lost by percolation or rises in a defined channel".[55] At the point at which water from a spring issues from the ground and forms a defined channel it constitutes a watercourse,[56] and water as it issues from a spring or well is not considered as the produce of the soil so as to make the right to take it for domestic purposes a *profit a prendre.* The right to do so can only exist as an easement which may be claimed by custom.[57] A right to take water from a well for the benefit and more convenient occupation of a dwelling-house has been held to be an interest in land of this kind.[58] Similarly, after twenty years uninterrupted enjoyment of a spring of water, an absolute right to it was gained by the owner of the land in which it issued from the ground and it was held that an adjoining owner could not lawfully construct a drain whereby the supply of water from the spring was diminished.[59] Nor may a person cut trenches in his land so as to interrupt the natural flow of water from surface springs to his neighbour's property.[60]

Support from underground water

Whilst at common law an owner cannot withdraw from his neighbour the support of adjacent soil,[61] there is no right to the support of adjacent subterranean water. In one case where the defendant, by excavations on his own land, drained the plaintiff's land so that the soil subsided and cottages on the land became cracked and damaged it was held that the plaintiff had no right of action, because the defendant was

---

[54] *Taylor v. St Helens Corpn.*, (1877) 6 Ch. D. 264.
[55] *Brain v. Marfell*, (1879) 41 L.T. 457.
[56] *Dudden v. Clutton Union*, (1857) 1 H. & N. 627.
[57] *Race v. Ward*, (1855) 19 J.P. 563; *Smith v. Archibald*, (1880) 5 A.C. 489.
[58] *Tyler v. Bennett*, (1836) 5 Ad. & El. 377.
[59] *Balston v. Bensted*, (1808) 1 Camp. 463.
[60] *Ennor v. Barwell*, (1860) 3 L.T. 170.
[61] *New Moss Colliery v. Manchester Corpn.*, [1908] A.C. 117.

entitled to drain his soil without legal hindrance if for any reason it became necessary or convenient for him to do so.[62] Most recently this principle was reaffirmed in *Stephens v. Anglian Water Authority*,[63] where abstraction of percolating water caused subsidence of the plaintiff's land and damage to a house. In the claim for negligence, it was reasserted that a landowner is entitled to exercise his right to abstract subterranean water flowing in undefined channels under his land regardless of the consequences, whether physical or pecuniary, to his neighbours and regardless of his motive or intention or whether he anticipated damage, and accordingly the action failed. This principle does not apply to the loss of support due to the removal of wet sand, running silt, or dissolved rock salt.[64] The lack of a legal right to the support of underground water contrasts with principles which have been applied in other jurisdictions.[65]

WATER FLOWING IN A DEFINED UNDERGROUND CHANNEL

Water which flows in a known and definite underground channel is placed in the same legal category as water flowing in a similarly definite channel on the surface.[66] Hence it was stated by Baron Pollock in the case of *Dickinson v. Grand Junction Canal Co.*,[67] decided in 1852, that,

---

[62] *Popplewell v. Hodkinson*, (1869) L.R. 4 Ex. 248; *Elliot v. North Eastern Ry. Co.*, (1863) 10 H.L.C. 333.

[63] [1987] 3 All E.R. 379; *Langbrook Properties Ltd. v. Surrey C.C.*, [1969] 3 All E.R. 1424.

[64] *Jordeson v. Sutton, etc., Gas Co.*, [1899] 2 Ch. 217; *Lotus Ltd. v. British Soda Co. Ltd.*, [1972] Ch.123. See also *Salt Union v. Brunner*, [1906] 2 K.B. 822; *Fletcher v. Birkenhead Corpn.*, [1907] 1 K.B. 205; *Trinidad Asphalt Co. v. Ambrad*, [1899] A.C. 594; *Brace v. South Eastern Regional Housing Association*, (1984) 270 E.G. 1286.

[65] In Canada it has been held that a right of support from subsurface waters exists where the land is in its natural state and the water has been performing the duties of natural support, or where a building which obviously depended upon the support of the water has been severed from the ownership of the land, or where the claim is for a building which had for twenty years enjoyed the support of the water (*Rade v. K & E. Sand and Gravel (Sarina)*, (1969) 10 D.L.R. (3d) 218, Ontario High Court).

[66] *Chasemore v. Richards*, (1859) 7 H.L. Cas. 349.

[67] (1852) 7 Ex. 282.

> "if the course of a subterranean stream were well known, as is the case with many which sink underground, pursue for a short space a subterranean course, and then emerge again, it could never be contended that the owner of the soil under which the stream flowed, could not maintain an action for the diversion of it, if it took place under such circumstances as would have enabled him to recover had the stream been wholly above ground."

This principle follows from the fact that an underground flow of water in many circumstances possesses the same characteristics as a body of water flowing on the surface.[68]

It must be stressed, however, that in order to apply the principles relating to riparian rights to subterranean water, it must flow not only in a defined channel but also in a channel which is *known* in a sense which extends beyond that watercourse being merely defined. This point was emphasised in a case where water was only discovered by deep excavations made in the land under which the water flowed, and even then it was a matter of controversy whether any defined channel existed.[69] A "defined" channel has been stated to mean "a contracted and bounded channel, although the course of the stream may be undefined by human knowledge". Whilst a "known" channel implies "the knowledge by reasonable inference from existing and observed facts in the natural or pre–existing conditions of the surface of the ground" this is not synonymous with "visible", and not restricted to knowledge derived from exposure of the ground by excavation.[70] If underground water flows in a defined channel into a well supplying a stream above ground, but the existence and course of that channel are not known and cannot be ascertained except by subsequent excavation, the lower riparian owners on the banks of the stream have no right of action for the abstraction of the underground water.[71]

---

[68] *M'Nab v. Robertson*, [1897] A.C. 129.

[69] *Ewart v. Belfast Poor Law Guardians*, (1881) 9 L.R.Ir. 172.

[70] *Black v. Ballymena Commissioners*, (1886) 17 I.R.Ir. 459.

[71] *Bradford Corpn. v. Ferrand*, [1902] 2 Ch. 655, as considered in *Bleachers Assocn. Ltd. v. Chapel–en–le–Frith R.D.C.*, [1933] 1 Ch. 356.

PERCOLATING WATER ON THE SURFACE

Water flowing on the surface in a reasonably defined channel usually constitutes a natural watercourse, despite the fact that it may occasionally run dry,[72] but water which squanders itself over an undefined area and has no certain supply and no definite course is not a watercourse,[73] and does not give rise to riparian rights or acquired rights. The owner of land has an unqualified right to drain it for agricultural purposes in order to remove surface water, and a neighbouring proprietor will be unable to sustain any legal action because he is thereby deprived of water that would otherwise have come onto his land. Similarly a right to water percolating through the banks of a stream cannot be claimed as an easement.[74]

The absence of riparian rights to surface water which flows over land without a definite channel has the consequence that the owner of the land over which the water flows has the right to appropriate the flow of water, despite the fact that this may prevent the water reaching a watercourse in which others have riparian rights.[75] Moreover, it has been held that receiving the flow of water from a drain made for the purposes of agricultural improvement did not give the recipient, through whose land it flowed, the right to the continuing flow so as to preclude the owner of the drained land from altering the level of the drain for further improvement of the land so as to cut off the supply.[76] Similarly, a land owner has been held not to be entitled to the overflow from a tank set up to supply water for cattle where the overflow was of only a temporary character.[77] In the absence of a prescriptive right to the flow of water, a court has declined to restrain the draining of gravel pits into a stream to the injury of watercress beds supplied by the stream.[78]

---

[72] *R. v. Oxfordshire*, (1830) 1 B. & A. 301; *Stollmeyer v. Trinidad Lake Petroleum Co.*, [1918] A.C. 485.

[73] *Rawstron v. Taylor*, (1855) 11 Ex. 254.

[74] *Roberts v. Fellowes*, (1906) 94 L.T. 279.

[75] *Broadbent v. Ramsbotham*, (1856) 11 Ex. 602.

[76] *Greatrex v. Hayward*, (1853) 8 Ex. 291.

[77] *Bartlett v. Tottenham*, [1932] 1 Ch. 114.

[78] *Weeks v. Heward*, (1862) 10 W.R. 557.

Pollution of percolating water

Whilst the abstraction or diversion of percolating water is not actionable as a matter of common law, a person who pollutes underground percolating water is liable and may be restrained from so doing by an injunction. It may be noted also that an act of this kind may give rise to criminal proceedings provided for by statute and considered elsewhere in this work.[79]

In one instance the plaintiff owned a paper mill and had an immemorial right to the supply of water from a cavern which was fed by rainwater running through underground passages. The defendant, an adjoining owner, in the process of lead working, discharged polluted water from pits through natural passages in the rock leading to the cavern. It was held here that a right of action arose on the principle that a landowner must not use his land in such a manner as to injure the property of his neighbour.[80] In another instance the defendant was restrained from using his cesspool in such a manner as to pollute water percolating through his land and supplying an adjacent well.[81]

In the recent decision in *Cambridge Water Company v. Eastern Counties Leather PLC*,[82] the use of a polluting solvent at industrial premises resulted, over a period of years, in spillages which caused the contamination of underground water from which the plaintiffs abstracted water for water supply purposes. Arguments based upon the principle in *Rylands v. Fletcher* failed for the reason that, though the substance was likely to cause damage if it escaped, the storage of the chemical at premises in an industrial area was a natural use of the land and for the general benefit of the community.[83] In relation to claims based upon nuisance and negligence, it was recognised that these torts rested upon the reasonable foreseeability of the damage arising and, because a reasonable supervisor of the operations concerned would not have

---

[79] See Ch.12 below.

[80] *Hodgkinson v. Ennor*, (1863) 4 B. & S. 229; and see *Tenant v. Goldwin*, (1703) Salk. 21.

[81] *Womersley v. Church*, (1867) 17 L.T. 190; and see *Ballard v. Tomlinson*, (1885) 29 Ch.D. 115. considered at p.121 above.

[82] [1991] *ENDS Report* 36, Queen's Bench Division 31 July 1991.

[83] See p.86 above on the principle in *Rylands v. Fletcher*.

appreciated the environmental hazard constituted by the spillages at the time when they happened, no liability was found against the defendants.

Chapter 6

NAVIGATION ON WATERCOURSES

THE RIGHT OF NAVIGATION

The right of navigation has been defined by Lord Cameron in *Crown Estates Commissioners v. Fairlie Yacht Slip,*[1] in the following terms:

> "the basic concept of the word 'navigation' is the passage or transit through navigable waters whether they be tidal or non–tidal, of communication by sea, and, in principle, it would appear to follow that it is those activities which are necessarily subservient to that essential purpose which may be exercised as of right by virtue of the recognised and undoubted right of navigation."

The circumstances under which the right of navigation may lawfully be exercised are dependent upon whether the waters concerned are tidal or non–tidal. The right of navigation exists as a general right of way in all tidal waters and in those inland waters that are subject to a particular right of navigation.[2]

Navigation on tidal watercourses

In tidal waters the right of navigation is a right of way of all the public for all purposes of navigation, trade and intercourse,[3] and at common law the public have always had a right paramount to the rights of property of the Crown and its grantees to navigate over every part of a common navigable river.[4] For that reason, if the Crown grants a portion of the bed and soil of an estuary or tidal water, the grantee takes subject to the public right of navigation and cannot, as owner of the soil, in any

---

[1] [1979] S.C. 156, at p.182. Similarly, it has been described as "a right to pass and re–pass over the whole width and depth of water [in a watercourse] and the incidental right of loading and unloading" by Lord Templeman in *Tate & Lyle Ltd. v. Greater London Council*, [1983] 1 All E.R. 1159.

[2] On tidal and non–tidal waters generally see p.15 above.

[3] *Blundell v. Catterall*, (1821) 5 B. & Ald. 268.

[4] *Williams v. Wilcox*, (1838) 8 Ad. & El. 314.

way interfere with the enjoyment of the public right.[5] The public right to the free use of the sea for the purposes of navigation has been unchallenged from the earliest times. Frequently the principle has been expressed as the maxim that the sea is a public highway and that ships have the right *eundi redeundi et morandi* over every part of it, no matter to whom the soil lying under it may belong.[6]

A tidal navigable watercourse is a watercourse which is subject to the vertical flow and reflow of the ordinary tides and navigable as such. It includes the navigable parts of the watercourse where fresh water is arrested by the horizontal flow of the tide. Parts of a watercourse which are only affected by extraordinary tides do not constitute part of the navigable watercourse.[7] The navigable mouth of a watercourse encompasses the whole area between the lowest ebb and the highest flood mark.[8] Essentially the word "navigable", when applied to a watercourse in which the soil *prima facie* belongs to the Crown and fishing to the public, imports that the watercourse is one in which the tide ebbs and flows.[9]

The right of navigation has been conceived of as a right of way, though different in certain respects from a right of way over land.[10] Accordingly, the public have a right to use a watercourse for the purposes of navigation which is analogous to the public right to pass along a public road or footpath which passes through a private estate.[11] Hence, a navigable watercourse constitutes a public highway navigable by all members of the public providing that they do so in a reasonable manner and for a reasonable purpose.[12] The right extends, *prima facie*, over the entire space over which the tide flows, and is not suspended

---

[5] *Gann v. Free Fishers of Whitstable*, (1864) 11 H.L.C. 192.

[6] *Denaby and Cadeby Main Colliers v. Anson*, [1911] 1 K.B. 171.

[7] *Reece v. Miller*, (1882) 8 Q.B.D. 626; *West Riding of Yorkshire Rivers Board v. Tadcaster R.D.C.*, (1907) 97 L.T. 436.

[8] *Horne v. MacKenzie*, (1839) 6 Cl. & Fin. 628.

[9] *Murphy v. Ryan*, (1868) Ir. R. 2 C.L. 143.

[10] For a discussion of the contrasts see *Wills' Trustees v. Cairngorm Canoeing and Sailing School*, [1976] S.L.T. 162. See *Attorney-General ex rel. Yorkshire Derwent Trust Ltd. v. Brotherton*, 2 W.L.R. 1.

[11] *Orr Ewing v. Colquhoun*, (1877) 2 A.C. 839.

[12] *Original Hartlepool Collieries Co. v. Gibb*, (1877) 5 Ch. D. 713.

when the tide is out or too low for vessels to float.[13] Whilst the flow of the ordinary tide is strong *prima facie* evidence of the existence of a public navigable watercourse, and its actual use for the purpose of navigation is the strongest evidence of its navigability,[14] ultimately the question of whether a particular water is navigable or not is a question of fact.[15]

It has been held that the question as to whether a particular water is navigable depends upon the character and nature of the channel, and that not every ditch or cutting forms part of a public navigable river, though it may be large enough to admit the passage of a boat.[16] Every creek or river into which the tide flows is not for that reason necessarily a public navigable channel, despite the fact that it may be sufficiently large for that purpose.[17] If there is a broad deep channel, calculated to serve for the purposes of commerce, it will be natural to conclude that it constitutes an area of public navigation, but a small stream intermittently navigated by very small boats is not necessarily navigable.[18]

Navigation on non–tidal watercourses

In general the public have no right at common law to navigate on non–tidal inland waters,[19] but a right to do so may be acquired by immemorial usage by the public,[20] by dedication of riparian owners,[21] or under statute.[22] A claim to a public right of navigation over a non–tidal watercourse must be treated similarly as if it were a claim for a right of way on dry land,[23] in that the public who have acquired the right to

---

[13] *Colchester Corpn. v. Brooke*, (1845) 7 Q.B.D. 339.

[14] *Rose v. Miles*, (1815) 5 Taunt. 705; *Ilchester v. Rashleigh*, (1889) 61 L.T. 477; *Lynn Corpn. v. Turner*, (1774), 1 Cowp. 86.

[15] *Vooght v. Winch*, (1819) 2 B. Ald. 662.

[16] *Sim E Bak v. Ang Yong Huat*, [1923] A.C. 429.

[17] *R. v. Montague*, (1825) 4 C. & C. 598.

[18] Ilchester v. Rashleigh, (1889) 61 L.T. 477; see also *Bower v. Hill*, (1835) 2 Scott 535.

[19] *Bourke v. Davis*, (1889) 44 Ch. D. 110; *Johnston v. O'Neill*, [1911] A.C. 552.

[20] *Bower v. Hill*, (1835) 2 Scott 535.

[21] *Simpson v. Attorney–General*, [1904] A.C. 476.

[22] See, for example, s.79 Thames Conservancy Act 1932.

[23] *Bourke v. Davis*, (1889) 44 Ch. D. 110.

navigate on an inland water have no right of property in the land over which they pass.[24] It has recently been held that a right of navigation on a non–tidal water is capable of being acquired by long use under the Rights of Water Act 1932.[25]

The principles in relation to rights of navigation applicable to tidal waters differ from those pertaining to non–navigable waters in a number of respects. First, the right of navigation on tidal waters is unlimited, in that all vessels are entitled to use the whole of the channel at all times,[26] whereas the right of navigation on non–tidal waters is confined to the extent of the use or grant on which it depends and may be restricted to a particular part of the watercourse.[27] Second, the banks of a non–tidal river belong, *prima facie*, to the riparian owners, and the right of navigation does not generally extend to landing or mooring on the banks,[28] except where this facility is established by custom, grant or statute, or where it is exercised at places which are established to be public landing places.[29] Thus, it has been decided that a public right of navigation in a non–tidal loch did not include a right to beach or moor boats on private ground for carrying on the business of a boat–hirer, and that a public right to embark and disembark on private ground could not be acquired by prescription.[30]

A public right of navigation on inland waters does not encompass any public right to fish[31] or to shoot wild–fowl.[32] The riparian owners of a non–tidal watercourse may establish a private right of way, or a private right to use boats for recreation, by custom, but the existence of private rights of this kind will not entitle the public at large to boat on the water, or support any claim that it is a public highway.[33]

---

[24] *Orr Ewing v. Colquhoun*, (1877) 2 A.C. 839.

[25] *Attorney–General ex rel. Yorkshire Derwent Trust Ltd. v. Brotherton*, [1991] 2 W.L.R. 1, Court of Appeal (a decision of the House of Lords is pending).

[26] *R. v. Randall*, (1842) Car. & M. 496.

[27] *Williams v. Wilcox*, (1838) 8 A. & E. 314.

[28] But see *Campbell's Trustees v. Sweeney*, [1911] S.C. 1319.

[29] *Drinkwater v. Porter*, (1835) 7 C. & P. 181.

[30] *Leith–Buchanan v. Hogg*, [1931] S.C. 204; see also *Iveagh (Earl) v. Martin*, [1960] 2 All E.R. 668.

[31] *Smith v. Andrews*, [1891] 2 Ch. 678.

[32] *Micklethwait v. Vincent*, (1892) 67 L.T. 225.

[33] *Bourke v. Davis*, (1889) 44 Ch.D. 110.

In the recent case of *Curtis v. Wild*[34] it was held that the question whether an enclosed sheet of water, such as a reservoir, is water which can be used by vessels or ships for "navigation", within the purposes of the Merchant Shipping Act 1894, depends not on the size of the water but on the purpose of the vessel concerned. Where a vessel is proceeding from an originating place A to a terminus B for the purpose of discharging people or cargo at a destination point there is navigation. However, where the water is simply used for pleasure boating there is no navigation for the purposes of the Act.

Incidents of the right of navigation

Passage and grounding

The public right to navigate includes all those rights upon the waterway as, in relation to the circumstances of each particular watercourse, are necessary for the full and convenient passage of vessels along its channel. For example, it may encompass a right of grounding whereby a vessel may remain aground upon the bed of the waterway until the tide permits her to continue if she cannot reach her destination in a single tide. In those circumstances no toll can be demanded by the owner of the soil other than where the grounding takes place in a harbour.[35] Thus, a vessel is entitled to remain temporarily in one place until the wind or weather, or possibly a change of season, permits her to leave. Likewise, temporary immobility may extend until a cargo has been obtained, or repairs completed. In no case, however, may a vessel become permanently moored, for example, for the purpose of supplying commodities required by ships for use whilst being navigated because permanent occupation in that manner by one vessel, to the exclusion of the public, is an infringement of the right of free passage of others.[36]

Notably, the rights of different vessels on a particular navigable watercourse are not co-extensive. Whilst a small boat may be entitled to go up to the furthest point she can reach so as to make full use of the public way, the same right does not exist in respect of large vessels. A

---

[34] [1991] 4 All E.R. 172.

[35] *Colchester Corpn. v. Brooke*, (1845) 7 Q.B. 339.

[36] *Denaby and Cadeby Main Collieries Ltd. v. Anson*, [1911] 1 K.B. 171; *Iveagh (Earl) v. Martin*, [1960] 2 All E.R. 668.

large vessel will not be entitled to proceed to a place beyond the point to which vessels of that size are accustomed to go and where there is accommodation for loading or unloading them.[37]

Anchoring, mooring and landing

The right to anchor or moor a vessel is a necessary part of the right to navigate in tidal waters.[38] The general proprietary right of the Crown to the sea bed has the consequence that private persons are not permitted to lay down fixtures on the sea bed for the purpose of facilitating anchorage for vessels without the permission of the Crown.[39] It is possible, however, that the right to fix moorings in the soil of the foreshore of tidal navigable waters may be claimed on the presumption of legal origin by grant from the Crown of the foreshore for that purpose, or by a concession from an owner of the foreshore.[40]

In relation to non–tidal navigable watercourses, the right to anchor or moor may be one of the incidents of navigation but it may only be exercised reasonably in the course of navigation,[41] or exercised by grant, custom or statute. Consequently, there is no common law right to lay or maintain permanent moorings on another person's land without permission, and this cannot be claimed as an ordinary incident of navigation other than where the right arises by custom or statute.[42] Whether a vessel has actually "moored" or not is a question of fact, but it has been held that the term is capable of encompassing a situation where a vessel was anchored.[43] Where a public right of navigation in tidal waters includes the right to use a quay on payment of a fee, this extends only to the use in the course of embarking, loading or unloading a vessel,

---

[37] *The Swift*, [1901] P.168.

[38] *Gann v. Free Fishers of Whitstable*, (1865) 11 H.L.C. 192.

[39] *Crown Estate Commissioners v. Fairlie Yacht Slip Ltd.* [1979] S.C. 156; *Trustees of the Port and Harbour of Lerwick v. Crown Estate Commissioners*, (1990) S.C.C.L. 484.

[40] *Attorney–General v. Wright*, [1897] 2 Q.B. 318; *Wyatt v. Thompson*, (1794) 1 Esp. 252.

[41] *Campbells' Trustees v. Sweeney*, [1911] S.C.1319.

[42] *Fowey Marine (Ensworth) Ltd. v. Gafford*, [1968] 1 All E.R. 979.

[43] *Evans v. Godber*, [1974] 1 W.L.R. 1317. See also *The Alletta and The England*, [1925] 2 Lloyd's Rep. 479; *Liverpool and North Wales Steamship Co. Ltd. v. Mersey Trading Co. Ltd.*, [1908] 2 Ch. 460.

or in the course of carrying out repairs to a vessel as is necessary or desirable before she can resume her voyage, and the public right does not extend to using the quay as a place of business for repairing vessels.[44]

There is no general right of landing or embarkation, for either passengers or goods, on the foreshore or the land adjoining thereto, other than at places appropriated by usage, grant or statute for those purposes,[45] or with the consent of the owner. Since the banks of a non–tidal navigable watercourse are privately owned, the consent of the riparian owner is necessary to land or moor a vessel to the bank, except at a public landing stage.[46] The right for the public to embark or disembark on private ground, or to beach or moor vessels there for carrying on the business of a boat hirer cannot be acquired by prescription.[47]

Towing

Where the banks of navigable watercourses are in private ownership they will not be subject to a common law right of the public to tow, but a right of towing may exist by custom,[48] use or prescription,[49] dedication or statute.[50] A towpath may be either a private path by a canal, or a public right of way subject to a right of towing,[51] or a highway restricted to be used only by horses employed in towing barges.[52] The soil of the towpath may be vested by statute in the navigation authority,[53] but in other cases, a navigation authority may have only a statutory use or easement of the soil sufficient for the purposes of navigation.[54] Although conservators may have no ownership of property in the soil of

---

44 *Iveagh (Earl) v. Martin*, [1960] 2 All E.R. 668.

45 *Blundell v. Catterall*, (1821) 5 B. & Ald. 268.

46 *Drinkwater v. Porter*, (1835) 7 C. & P. 181.

47 *Leith–Buchanan v. Hogg*, [1931] S.C. 204.

48 *Wyatt v. Thompson*, (1794) 1 Esp. 252.

49 *Ball v. Herbert*, (1789) 3 Term Rep. 253; *Pierce v. Lord Fauconberg*, (1757) 1 Burr. 292; *Vernon v. Prior*, (1747) 3 Term. Rep. 254; *Kinloch v. Neville*, (1840) 6 M. & W. 795.

50 See s.77 Thames Conservancy Act 1932.

51 s.27(6) and (7) National Parks and Access to the Countryside Act 1949.

52 *Winch v. Thames Conservators*, (1874) 36 J.P. 646; *R. v. Severn and Wye Rly.*, (1819) 2 B. & Ald. 648.

53 *Bruce v. Willis*, (1840) 11 A. & E. 463.

54 *Badger v. South Yorks Rly.*, (1858) 7 W.R. 130; *Hollis v. Goldfinch*, (1823) 1 B. & C. 205.

the towpath, they will be entitled to restrain by injunction an adjoining landowner from using the towpath so as to obstruct its free use for navigation.[55] Where the freehold interest in a towpath is vested in the riparian owners, subject to a right of towing, they may use the towpath as they wish, provided that no interference, injury or obstruction is caused to it.[56] An owner of land adjoining the towpath may erect a wharf on his own land and take goods across the towpath to the wharf.[57]

In *Winch v. Thames Conservators*,[58] conservators who kept open a towpath, and took an aggregate toll for the use of the whole navigation, were held to be under a duty to those using the towpath to take reasonable care that the whole towpath was kept in such state as not to expose users to undue danger. The conservators were held to be liable to any person who sustained loss as a result of a portion of the towpath being out of repair, unless the defective condition was a latent one the existence of which the conservators were ignorant despite the exercise of reasonable care on their part.

The banks of a canal have been held to include the towpath,[59] and a towpath is not confined to the beaten track but includes so much of the bank as may ordinarily be used by horses towing barges.[60] A navigation authority, though empowered to make byelaws in relation to a towpath, have been held not to be entitled to exercise this power in relation to parts of the towpath not vested in them where the activities which are regulated cause no damage to the towpath or interference with navigation.[61] A prescriptive right to a public towpath on the banks of a navigable river has been held not to be extinguished as a consequence of part of the river adjoining the towpath becoming converted into a floating harbour by statute, though as a consequence the towpath became

---

[55] *Lea Conservancy Board v. Button*, (1879) 45 L.T. 385; *Attorney-General v. Wilcox*, (1938) 82 S.J. 566.

[56] *Thames Conservators v. Kent*, (1918) 83 J.P. 85.

[57] *Monmouthshire Canal & Rly. Co. v. Hill*, (1859) 23 J.P. 679.

[58] (1874) 36 J.P. 646; now see Occupiers Liability Act 1957.

[59] *Monmouthshire Canal & Rly. Co. v. Hill*, (1859) 23 J.P. 679.

[60] *Winch v. Thames Conservators*, (1874) 36 J.P. 646.

[61] *Thames Conservators v. Kent*, (1918) 83 J.P. 85; and see *Grand Junction Canal v. Petty*, (1888), 52 J.P. 692.

subject to use at all times of the tide, whereas previously it was only used when the tide was sufficiently high for purposes of navigation.[62]

Extinguishment of the right of navigation

A public right of navigation may be extinguished by statute,[63] or restricted under certain circumstances by the National Rivers Authority,[64] or it may cease as a result of natural causes such as the recession of waters or the accumulation of silt.[65] In the event of a navigable watercourse becoming choked with silt, the public have no right to cut another passage through adjoining lands.[66] In the event of a navigable watercourse gradually shifting its course to follow an entirely new channel distinguishable from the old one, it is likely that the right of navigation will follow to the new channel, though the bed of the soil and the right of fishing may be vested in the owner of the adjoining land. A consequence of this may be to exclude the right of the Crown to the bed and that of the public to the fishery.[67] In a decided case where navigation commissioners restored a silted channel to its former course, the right of navigation was held to be reinstated in the restored channel.[68]

Navigation and fishing

In general, the right of navigation takes precedence over the right of fishery in tidal waters and navigable rivers. Thus in *Gann v. Free Fishers of Whitstable*[69] the grant of an oyster bed in the sea below low water mark was held to have been taken by the grantee subject to the public right of navigation. Accordingly, the grantee's ownership of the soil did not permit him to make a claim of an anchorage due or undertake

---

[62] *R. v. Tippett*, (1819) 3 B. & Ald. 193.

[63] See, for instance, s.112 Transport Act 1968.

[64] On the general powers of the National Rivers Authority in relation to navigation see p.159 below.

[65] *R. v. Montague*, (1825) 4 B. & C. 598.

[66] *Ball v. Herbert*, (1789) 3 T.R. 253.

[67] *Carlisle Corpn. v. Graham*, (1869) L.R. 4 Ex. 366; *Williams v. Wilcox*, (1838) 8 Ad. & El. 314.

[68] *R. v. Betts*, (1850) 16 Q.B. 1022; *Vooght v. Winch*, (1819) 2 B. & Ald. 662.

[69] (1864) 11 H.L. 192; *Whitstable Free Fishers v. Foreman*, (1868) 32 J.P. 596.

activities which in any way interfered with the public right of navigation. The general precedence of navigation over fishery rights is, however, subject to certain qualifications. The right of navigation must be exercised reasonably, and where it conflicts with a right of fishery the right of navigation must not be abused so as to cause injury to the fishing.[70] Where a vessel grounds on an oyster bed and does damage, it has been held that the master will be liable if he was aware of the existence of the bed, or if the grounding was due to improper navigation, or if after grounding and receiving notice of the existence of the bed he failed to take reasonable steps to remove the vessel as speedily as possible.[71]

Where no right of navigation exists in relation to inland waters, the use of those waters for the purposes of navigation will amount to a trespass which will be actionable in respect of any interference which it causes to rights of fishery in the waters. Thus, where a canoeist disturbed fish in a river and interfered with an incorporeal fishery, nominal damages were awarded and permission given for an application for an injunction to prevent further trespass, despite the fact that no damage was shown to have been caused to the fishery and that no anglers were fishing at the time.[72] It is also possible that a person acting in this manner, at certain times of the year, may commit the offence of wilfully disturbing spawning fish.[73]

OBSTRUCTIONS TO NAVIGATION

The obstruction of a public navigable river is a public nuisance at common law and may be the subject of indictment,[74] or an information

---

70 *Original Hartlepool Collieries Co. v. Gibb*, (1877) 41 J.P. 660.

71 *Colchester Corpn. v. Brooke*, (1845) 7 Q.B. 339; *The Octavia Stella*, (1887) 57 L.T. 632; *The Swift*, [1901] P. 168; *The Bien*, [1911] P.40.

72 *Rawson v. Peters*, (1972) *The Times* 2 November 1972 C.A.; *Wills' Trustees v. Cairngorm Caoeing and Sailing School*, [1976] S.L.T. 162; *Tennent and Carroll Industries PLC v. Clancy*, [1988] I.L.R.M. 214.

73 Under s.2(4) Salmon and Freshwater Fishery Act 1975, discussed at p.424 below; *Welsh Water Authority v. Crowther*, Unreported Chester Crown Court 4 November 1988.

74 *R. v. Watts*, (1798) 2 Esp. 675; *R. v. Russell*, (1827) 6 Ad. & El. 143.

filed by the Attorney-General against the person responsible.[75] In an appropriate case an obstruction to navigation may be the subject of an application to the court for the order of *mandamus*,[76] or the nuisance may be abated by a decree of the court.[77] Similarly, an obstruction which constitutes a private nuisance may be directly abated in a reasonable manner, provided the least injurious means are employed,[78] but a private person cannot abate an obstruction in a navigable channel unless he suffers some special injury beyond that suffered by the rest of the public.[79] In that case the plaintiff is entitled to bring an action on proof of special damage.[80] By contrast, an obstruction which interferes with a right of access is an injury to private property and is actionable without proof of special damage.[81] Under s.31 of the Malicious Damage Act 1861 it is an offence to do any injury or mischief so as to obstruct the navigation of a navigable river or canal.

In the account which follows, the various kinds of obstructions which may arise in navigable watercourses are dealt with under seven headings: (1) Erections on the bed of a watercourse; (2) Works causing silting; (3) Works on the foreshore; (4) Wreck; (5) Bridges; (6) Locks, weirs and dams; and (7) Miscellaneous obstructions.[82]

Erections on the bed of a watercourse

As a general principle, a riparian owner is entitled to construct an erection on his land though covered with water, provided that it does not

[75] *R. v. Clark*, (1702) 12 Mod. Rep. 615; *Attorney-General v. Richards*, (1795) 2 Anst. 603; *Attorney-General v. Johnson*, (1819) 2 Wils. Ch. 87; *Attorney-General v. Lonsdale*, (1868) 20 L.T. 64; *Attorney-General v. Terry*, (1874) 30 L.T. 215; *Attorney-General v. Wright*, [1897] 2 Q.B. 318; *Tate & Lyle Ltd. v. Greater London Council*, [1983] 1 All E.R. 1159.

[76] *R. v. Bristol Dock Co.*, (1839) 1 Ry. & Can. Cas. 548.

[77] *Attorney-General v. Parmeter*, (1811) 10 Price 412.

[78] *Hill v. Cock*, (1872) 36 J.P. 552.

[79] *Colchester Corpn. v. Brooke*, (1845) 7 Q.B. 339; *Dimes v. Petley*, (1850) 15 Q.B. 276; *Attorney-General v. Thames Conservators*, (1862), 1 Hem. & M. 1.

[80] *Rose v. Miles*, (1815) 4 M. & S. 101; *Tate & Lyle Ltd. v. Greater London Council*, [1983] 1 All E.R. 1159.

[81] *Rose v. Groves*, (1843) 5 Man. & G. 613.

[82] See also the discussion of the natural right of a riparian owner to place an erection on the bed of a watercourse at p.78 above.

interfere with public rights of navigation or with the rights of other riparian owners.[83] On the other hand, any structure on the bed of a navigable watercourse may amount to an obstruction to navigation. Hence in the case of *Attorney-General v. Terry*[84] a wharf which extended three feet into a river, which had a navigable width of sixty feet, was, nonetheless, held to constitute a tangible and substantial interference with the public right of navigation.

Whether an obstruction in a navigable river amounts to an actionable nuisance is a question of fact. An encroachment is not necessarily a nuisance and it is for the court to determine on the particular facts of the case whether the public have been in any way inconvenienced.[85] Normally an obstruction must be a nuisance at the time of erection.[86] Whilst an anticipated injury is generally not sufficient to support an action,[87] an erection which was not an obstruction at the time it was erected may become one owing to the river silting up or otherwise.[88] If the encroachment is of a trifling nature the courts will not interfere and, for example, no action will be sustained if the erection is in a reasonable situation and a reasonable space is left for the passage of vessels on the river,[89] or where the consequences of the encroachment are only slight and uncertain.[90]

To constitute a nuisance there must be some actual obstruction of a navigable watercourse[91] which produces inconvenience to the public in the use of the watercourse for the purposes of navigation.[92] Thus, where some obstruction is shown, the question to be addressed is whether it occasions hindrance to the navigation of the watercourse by vessels of any description and not whether the obstruction provides a benefit to

---

[83] *Orr Ewing v. Colquhoun*, (1877) 2 A.C. 839.
[84] (1874) 30 L.T. 315.
[85] *R. v. Shepard*, (1822) 1 L.J.O.S.K.B. 45.
[86] *R. v. Bell*, (1822) 1 L.J.O.S.K.B. 42.
[87] *Orr Ewing v. Colquhoun*, (1877), 2 A.C. 839; but see *Attorney-General v. Lonsdale*, (1868) 20 L.T. 64.
[88] *Williams v. Wilcox*, (1838) 8 Ad. & El. 314.
[89] *R. v. Russell*, (1827) 6 B. & C. 566.
[90] *R. v. Tindall*, (1837) 6 Ad. & El. 143.
[91] *R. v. Betts*, (1850) 16 Q.B. 1022.
[92] *R. v. Shepard*, (1822) 1 L.J.O.S.K.B. 45; *R. v. Grosvenor*, (1819) 2 Stark. 511.

navigation in general.[93] It is no defence to an action to show that the inconvenience occasioned is counter-balanced by some benefit to the public.[94] Thus, where a person causing an obstruction did so for the purpose of his own trade, this was held to be too remote a benefit to the public generally and did not provide any justification for the obstruction.[95]

Whilst a right to obstruct a navigable river cannot be acquired by prescription,[96] it is clear that statutory authorisation will provide a defence to an action for obstruction of navigation. Thus, where the owners of a wharf on a navigable river were granted a licence by river conservators to construct a jetty under an Act of Parliament, they were held not liable in an action for obstruction of the free navigation by adjoining owners since the Act contemplated some interference with navigation.[97] Similarly, in another instance a railway company were held to be authorised to conduct works which had the effect of obstructing part of the bed of a navigable river.[98] If a statute permits obstruction of navigation, no action will lie for damage caused by the execution of the authorised works,[99] unless the works are carried out negligently or are outside the statutory powers.[100] Despite the justification which a statutory licence may provide for actions of a licensee, so far as the public right of navigation is concerned, it will not authorise the licensee thereby to affect injuriously another riparian owner's land.[101]

---

93 *R. v. Randall*, (1842) Car. & M. 496.

94 *R. v. Ward*, (1836) 4 Ad. & El. 395; *R. v. Tindall*, (1837) 6 Ad. & El. 143; *Attorney-General v. Terry*, (1874) 30 L.T. 315 (overruling *R. v. Russell*, (1827) 6 B. & C. 566).

95 *Attorney-General v. Terry*, (1874) 30 L.T. 315.

96 *Vooght v. Winch*, (1819) 2 B. & Ald. 662.

97 *Kearns v. Cordwainers' Co.*, (1859) 6 C.B.N.S. 388; *Attorney-General v. Thames Conservators*, (1862) 8 L.T. 9.

98 *Abraham v. Great Northern Ry. Co.*, (1851) 16 Q.B. 586.

99 *Cracknell v. Thetford Corpn.*, (1869) L.R. 4 C.P. 629.

100 *Geddis v. Bann Reservoir*, (1878) 3 A.C. 430; *Brownlow v. Metropolitan Board of Works*, (1864) 16 C.B.N.S. 546; *Joliffe v. Wallasey L.B.*, (1873) L.R. 9 C.P.62; *Tate & Lyle Ltd. v. Greater London Council*, [1983] 1 All E.R. 1159, see p.144 below.

101 *Lyon v. Fishmongers' Co.*, (1876) 1 A.C. 662; *Lawes v. Turner and Frere*, (1892) 8 T.L.R. 584; *Joliffe v. Wallasey L.B.*, (1873) L.R. 9 C.P. 62; *Burley Ltd. v. Lloyd Ltd.*, (1929) 45 T.L.R. 626.

Works causing silting

The problem of an obstruction which has a consequent effect upon the bed of a public navigable watercourse through causing silting was the subject of extensive discussion in *Tate & Lyle Industries Ltd. v. Greater London Council.*[102] The facts were that the defendants had constructed ferry terminals adjoining the tidal River Thames, in accordance with a licence granted by the Port of London Authority, but because of their inappropriate design excessive silting the bed of the River occurred. This made it necessary for the plaintiffs to carry out extensive dredging work in order for vessels to gain access to their jetties. The plaintiffs' claim that they had a right to the maintenance of the depth of water which had existed before the defendants' terminals had been constructed was based upon three grounds: (1) on their rights as riparian owners; (2) as a contractual right against the Port of London Authority; and (3) as members of the public suffering particular damage from interference with the public right of navigation.

On the first ground, it was found that the plaintiffs could not sue as riparian owners because, as such, they had no right to object to an alteration to the depth of water adjacent to their land which did not cause damage or interfere with acknowledged riparian rights or amount to a private nuisance to them as occupiers of the land. Moreover, their jetties, to which access had been restricted due to the siltation, were only chattels which did not form part of the bank belonging to them as owners of the land and were not, therefore, capable of attracting riparian rights.

On the second ground, it was held that the plaintiffs had no cause of action in contract against the Port of London Authority, who had authorised the construction of the plaintiffs' jetties, because the authorisation which had been granted did not confer any right to the maintenance of a particular depth of water around the jetties to enable the plaintiffs to enjoy the benefit of them. In addition, however, the authorisation which the Port of London Authority had granted to the defendants to construct the ferry terminals did not provide the defendants with any defence of statutory authority for the silting which had occurred, since the authorisation extended only to the degree of siltation

---

[102] [1983] 1 All E.R. 1159.

which was inevitable and not to additional siltation which was due to the particular design of the terminals which had been chosen by the defendants.

On the third ground of public nuisance, it was found that the public right of navigation encompassed a right to pass and repass over the whole width and depth of water in the river and the incidental rights of loading and unloading, and the construction of the ferry terminals interfered with that right over the river bed between the main shipping channels and the plaintiffs' jetties. Furthermore, because the interference with the public right of navigation caused particular damage to the plaintiffs, since vessels of requisite dimensions were unable to pass to their jetties, they were entitled to maintain a claim for public nuisance and to recover the cost of dredging which was attributable to the inappropriate design of the defendants' ferry terminals.

Works on the foreshore

Part II of the Coast Protection Act 1949 contains provisions intended to restrict certain types of works detrimental to navigation.[103] Section 34 of the Act requires that specified operations may not be carried out without the consent of the Minister of Transport where obstruction or danger to navigation is caused or is likely to result, while the operation is being carried out or subsequently, by reason of the use of the works undertaken.[104] The operations concerned are the following: (a) the construction, alteration or improvement of any works on, under or over any part of the seashore[105] lying below high water mark of ordinary spring tides; (b) the deposit of any object or any materials[106] on any part of the seashore lying below high water mark of ordinary spring tides; or

---

103 On the Coast Protection Act 1949 generally see p.59 above.

104 As amended by s.36(1) Merchant Shipping Act 1988; and see *Harwich Harbour Conservancy Board v. Secretary of State for the Environment,* [1974] 1 Lloyd's Rep 140.

105 "Seashore" means the bed and shore of the sea, and of every channel, creek, bay, or estuary, and of every river as far up that river as the tide flows and any cliff, bank, barrier, dune, beach, flat or other land adjacent to the shore (s.49(1) Coast Protection Act 1949).

106 "Materials" includes minerals and turf but not seaweed (s.49(1) Coast Protection Act 1949).

(c) the removal of any object or materials from any part of the seashore lying below low water mark of ordinary spring tides. In relation to operations under (a) and (b), the Ministerial consent required applies in relation to any part of the sea bed in a designated area under the Continental Shelf Act 1964. The Minister can refuse consent or give it subject to such conditions as are thought fit, having regard to the nature and extent of the obstruction or danger which appears would otherwise be caused or be likely to result.[107]

Certain operations are exempt from the restrictions upon works detrimental to navigation provided for under the 1949 Act. Exempt operations include the carrying out of approved coast protection work, dredging operations including the deposit of dredged material authorised by a local Act, and the removal of sunken vessels or obstructions or dangers to navigation by a conservancy, harbour or navigation authority.[108] Subject to these exceptions, any person who carries out any operation in contravention of the restriction upon works detrimental to navigation, or fails to comply with the conditions subject to which consent for works is given, is guilty of an offence under the Act.[109]

Wreck

The owner of a vessel sunk in the fairway of a navigable watercourse is under a duty, so long as he retains possession, management and control of her, to take reasonable precautions to prevent other vessels from striking the wreck and to warn other vessels of its position. Consequently, the owner will be liable for damage to another vessel if the damage could have been prevented by reasonable skill and care on his part.[110] This duty may be transferred with the transfer of possession and control of the wreck to another person.[111]

---

[107] s.34 Coast Protection Act 1949.

[108] See, more particularly, s.35 Coast Protection Act 1949.

[109] ss.36 and 43 Coast Protection Act 1949.

[110] *The Douglas*, (1882) 46 L.T. 488; *The Snark*, [1900] P.105; *Brown v. Mallett*, (1848) 5 C.B. 599; *Harmond v. Pearson*, (1808) 1 Camp. 515.

[111] *White v. Crisp*, (1854) 10 Ex. 312; *Uptopia (Owners) v. Primula (Owners), The Uptopia*, [1893] A.C. 492.

Where a vessel is sunk in a navigable watercourse by misfortune or accident, the owner cannot be compelled by indictment to remove it.[112] If a vessel sinks in a navigable channel owing to the negligence of the owners of the vessel and obstructs the navigation or blocks the approaches to a wharf, the owners are liable at common law for the damage caused by the obstruction and cannot escape liability by abandoning the wreck.[113] Under statute, conservancy and harbour authorities have the power to remove or destroy vessels sunk, stranded or abandoned in waters under their jurisdiction and to sell the wreck and recover their expenses from the proceeds of sale.[114]

Locks, weirs and dams

In early cases concerning the River Thames it was established that hindering the course of a navigable watercourse by causing locks to be constructed was contrary to Magna Charta.[115] Similarly, diversion of part of the Thames, so as to weaken the current for carrying barges, was impermissible without statutory authority.[116]

Weirs on navigable watercourses which impede navigation have long been declared by statute to be a nuisance. Magna Charta, in 1225, stated that all weirs except on the coast should be put down, and a later enactment[117] ordered the destruction of all weirs, mills and other fixed engines for fishing which had been constructed during the reign of Edward I. A weir appurtenant to a fishery which obstructs the whole or part of a navigable watercourse is legal, therefore, if granted by the Crown before that reign.[118] In an Irish case,[119] it was held that the erection

---

[112] *R. v. Watts*, (1798) 2 Esp. 675.

[113] *Dee Conservancy Board v. McConnell*, [1928] 2 K.B. 159; for other cases on recovery of expenses, see *The Harrington*, (1888) 59 L.T. 851; *The Ella*, [1915] P.111; *Boston Corpn. v. Fenwick*, (1923) 129 L.T. 766; *Barraclough v. Brown*, [1897] A.C. 614; *Wilson v. Cator*, (1863) 1 New Rep. 314; *Jinman v. East Coast Insurance Co.*, (1878) 42 J.P. 809; *The Emerald, The Greta Holme*, [1896] P.192.

[114] For example, ss.530, 531 and 534 Merchant Shipping Act 1894; s.56 Harbour, Docks and Piers Clauses Act 1847.

[115] *R. v. Clark*, (1702) 12 Mod. Rep. 615.

[116] *Hind v. Manfield*, (1614) Noy. 103.

[117] 25 Edward III st. 4 c.4 (1350).

[118] *Williams v. Wilcox*, (1838) 8 Ad. & El. 314; *Rolle v. Whyte*, (1868) 7 B. & S. 116.

of weirs in a tidal river was a nuisance to the navigation and an indictable offence at common law, but a claim to a weir in a non–navigable river may be within the Prescription Act 1832.[120] As a consequence of the general statutory prohibition, however, most locks and weirs are now erected under statutory authority.[121]

Bridges[122]

A bridge across a navigable watercourse, the construction of which is not authorised, is not necessarily an obstruction,[123] though unnecessary delay in opening a swing bridge carrying a public highway across a dock may amount to an obstruction of navigation.[124] Although statutory authorisation to construct a bridge will normally provide a defence to any action for the obstruction of navigation on a watercourse, the terms of the statutory authority may limit the scope of this defence. Hence, where a railway company was required by statute to carry a bridge across a canal at a certain height, the company was responsible for an obstruction to canal traffic caused by the bridge being at a lower elevation because of ground subsidence due to causes beyond the control of either the railway company or the canal company.[125]

---

119 *R. v. Ryan*, (1845) 8 I.L.R. 119.

120 *Rolle v. Whyte*, (1868) 7 B. & S. 116; *Leconfield v. Lonsdale*, (1870) L.R. 5 C.P. 657.

121 Also in relation to locks, weirs and dams, see the discussion of obstructions to watercourses in relation to land drainage and flood prevention at p.398 below; obstructions to the passage of fish at p.428 below; and weirs obstructing fisheries at p.429 below.

122 On bridges generally see Ch.7 below; and in relation to structures over watercourses in relation to land drainage and flood defence see p.379 below.

123 *R. v. Betts*, (1850) 16 Q.B. 1022.

124 *Wiggins v. Boddington*, (1828) 3 C. & P. 544.

125 *Rhymney Ry. Co. v. Glamorganshire Canal Co.*, (1904) 91 L.T. 113; see also *North Staffordshire Ry. Co. v. Hanley Corpn.*, (1909) 73 J.P. 477. For other decisions on railway bridges across a navigation see; *London and Brimingham Ry. Co. v. Grand Junction Canal Co.*, (1835) 1 Ry. & Can. Cas. 224; *Priestley v. Manchester and Leeds Ry. Co.*, (1840) 4 Y. & C. Ex. 63; *Manser v. Northern and Eastern Counties Ry. Co.*, (1841) 2 Ry. & Can. Cas. 380; *Ferrand v. Midland Ry. Co.*, (1901) 17 T.L.R. 427; and *Abraham v. Great Northern Ry. Co.*, (1851) 16 Q.B. 586.

Miscellaneous obstructions

In addition to the previous categories that have been listed, a range of miscellaneous matters may constitute obstructions to navigation. For example, in one instance it was held that the removal of a mooring anchor, which had been fixed in a known part of a navigable river, to another part of the river which was covered by ordinary tides, so that a vessel ran foul of it, amounted to an obstruction.[126] The continued mooring of a boat across a public navigable creek, preventing a person from navigating barges and causing goods to be conveyed by a longer land route, amounted to special damage suffered by the inconvenienced carrier and provided ground for an action for the obstruction.[127] Mooring several vessels in a river in breach of a local byelaw so as to prevent other vessels passing has also been held to constitute an obstruction.[128] Stacking colliery refuse so that it falls into a navigable river and causes an obstruction has been held to be an indictable offence,[129] as also has the casting of ballast from a ship into navigable waters to the prejudice of navigation.[130]

RIPARIAN RIGHTS ON NAVIGABLE WATERCOURSES

The rights of proprietors on the banks of a watercourse are founded upon the right of access which they have to the water.[131] In this respect a riparian owner on the banks of a tidal navigable watercourse has natural rights and easements similar to those which are possessed by

---

126 *Hancock v. York, Newcastle Ry. Co.*, (1850) 10 C.B. 348; *Joliffe v. Wallasey Local Board*, (1873) 38 J.P. 40.

127 *Rose v. Groves*, (1843) 5 Man. & G. 613; *Dobson v. Blackmore*, (1847) 9 Q.B. 991.

128 *Stubbs v. Hilditch*, (1887) 51 J.P. 758.

129 *R. v. Stephens*, (1866) 14 L.T. 593.

130 *Michell v. Brown*, (1858) 23 J.P. 548; see also *United Alkali Co. v. Simpson*, [1894] 2 Q.B. 116; *Wheal Remfrey China Clay Co. v. Truro Corpn.*, [1923] 2 K.B. 594; *Colbran v. Barnes*, (1861) 11 C.B.N.S. 246.

131 Generally see the discussion of riparian rights in Ch.3 above.

a riparian owner above the flow of the tide. In each case the rights of the riparian owners are subject to the public right of navigation.[132]

Of particular importance to navigation amongst the rights possessed by riparian owners on the banks of navigable watercourses are three matters: (1) the right of access to the watercourse for the purpose of navigation; (2) the right to moor boats; and (3) the right to place erections on the bank and bed of the watercourse.

The right of access

A public navigable watercourse is a public highway, and the owners of land on the banks are entitled to gain access to the watercourse from any point on their own land.[133] The position is the same whether access is required by a land owner to or from the sea, or tidal or non-tidal watercourses or stillwaters.[134] The owner of land at a point of access, or a wharf, on the bank of a public navigable watercourse, has the same right of navigation as is enjoyed by other members of the public. This right is enjoyed in common with other members of the public irrespective of riparian ownership of the land adjoining the watercourse.

Where a right of navigation is connected with an exclusive right of access to and from a particular point, it ceases to be a right held in common with the rest of the public and constitutes a right which is exclusive to those holding riparian land. In that case an encroachment upon the exclusive right may be the subject of a legal action for damages or an injunction against those responsible for the encroachment.[135] Any interference with a right of access to a navigable river is actionable without proof of special damage,[136] but whether an obstruction amounts to an interference with a riparian owner's private right of access to his

[132] *Lyon v. Fishmongers' Co.*, (1876) 1 A.C. 683; *North Shore Ry. Co. v. Pion*, (1889) 14 A.C. 612.

[133] *Marshall v. Ulleswater Navigation Co.*, (1871) L.R. 7 Q.B. 166.

[134] *Hindson v. Ashby*, [1896] 2 Ch. 1; *Attorney-General of Straits Settlements v. Wemyss*, (1888) 13 A.C. 192.

[135] *Lyon v. Fishmongers' Co.*, (1876), 1 A.C. 683.

[136] *Rose v. Groves*, (1843) 6 Scott N.R. 645; *Dobson v. Blackmore*, (1847), 9 Q.B. 991.

frontage is a question of fact to be determined in accordance with the circumstances of the particular case.[137]

A riparian owner's right of access is not necessarily affected by the fact that a highway[138] or a sea wall[139] intervenes between his land and the watercourse. Where, due to accretion or works of reclamation, the water has receded from the bank or foreshore, a riparian owner continues to be entitled to have access over the land which has been added.[140] The right of access includes a right of the riparian owner to land and to cross any intervening shore at all states of the tide even where private property is involved.[141]

The right to moor

A riparian owner may moor vessels of ordinary size alongside his frontage or wharf for the purposes of loading or unloading at reasonable times, for a reasonable duration, and the owner of adjoining premises will be restrained by injunction from interfering with the access of a vessel though it overlaps with the adjoining premises.[142] A vessel will not, however, be allowed to obstruct the proper access to neighbouring premises used as a wharf, nor to obstruct the free access to premises if used as a dock by other vessels.[143] If a vessel is moored alongside a wharf, and access is required to a neighbouring wharf, the vessel must

137 *Bell v. Quebec Corpn.*, (1879) 5 A.C. 84; *Attorney-General v. Thames Conservators*, (1862) 1 Hem. & M. 1; *Attorney-General of Staits Settlements v. Wemyss*, (1888), 13 A.C. 192.

138 *Tetreault v. Montreal Harbour Comrs.*, [1926] A.C. 299.

139 *Port of London Authority v. Canvey Island Comrs.*, [1932] 1 Ch. 446.

140 *Hindson v. Ashby*, [1896] 2 Ch. 1; *Attorney-General of Southern Nigeria v. John Holt & Co.*, (Liverpool) Ltd., [1915] A.C. 599.

141 *Metropolitan Board of Works v. McCarthy*, (1874) L.R. 7 H.L. 243; *Macey v. Metropolitan Board of Works*, (1864) 10 L.T. 66.

142 *Attorney-General v. Thames Conservators*, (1862) 1 Hem. & M. 1; *Dalton v. Denton*, (1857) 6 L.T. 228; *Temple Pier Co. v. Metropolitan Board of Works*, (1865) 11 Jur. N.S. 337.

143 *Original Hartlepool Collieries v. Gibb*, (1877) 5 Ch. D. 713; *Land Securities Co. Ltd. v. Commercial Gas Co.*, (1902) 18 T.L.R. 405.

move to give that access immediately.[144] If the moored vessel is secured in position, a person entitled to access may pass over the vessel.[145]

A riparian owner may moor a floating wharf or boathouse alongside his premises, providing that navigation is not obstructed as a result.[146] The question of whether planning permission is required for the mooring of a vessel or floating structure in a navigable channel depends upon the particular circumstances. Specifically, if a vessel is moored or anchored to the bank or shore for a purpose which is incidental to the ordinary course of navigation, planning consent will not normally be required. If, however, work is needed for the construction of a landing stage, pile or jetty for mooring purposes, this will constitute an operation in, on or over the land covered by water and planning permission will be required. The mooring of a houseboat for residential purposes, or the placing of some permanent structure alongside the frontage of a watercourse, or other activities which involve operations or material change of use of the waterside land may constitute developments for which planning consent will be required.[147]

The right to place erections on the bank or bed of a watercourse[148]

As a general principle, a riparian owner can place erections on the bed and banks of a natural watercourse in much the same way as he is entitled to do so on other parts of his land not covered by water. This principle is stated with the proviso, however, that a riparian owner must not interfere with any public rights of navigation or encroach upon the rights of other riparian owners upstream or downstream.[149] Another qualification is that a riparian owner who is also the owner of the soil of

---

[144] *Land Securities Co. v. Commercial Gas Co.*, (1902) 18 T.L.R. 405.

[145] *Eastern Counties Ry. Co. v. Darling*, (1859) 5 C.B.N.S. 821.

[146] *Booth v. Ratte*, (1889) 62 L.T. 198.

[147] However, planning permission may be deemed under certain circumstances where the use of moorings is incidental to the enjoyment of a dwelling house, see Art.2 Part I of Sch.2 to Town and Country Planning General Development Order 1988, S.I 1988 No.1813, and *Royal Borough of Windsor and Maidenhead v. Worton*, (1986) 2 P.A.D. 502. Generally see Town and Country Planning Act 1990, and discussion of planning law at p.333 below.

[148] See also p.78 above.

[149] *Orr Ewing v. Colquhoun*, (1877) 2 A.C. 839.

a navigable watercourse has no greater right to the use of the *alveus*, or bed, of a tidal watercourse than of a non–tidal watercourse.[150] The erection of works, such as wharfs, jetties, or piles on the bed of a navigable watercourse is normally permissible unless there is some actual interference with the navigation, in which case the obstruction will amount to a public nuisance.[151] An erection which has previously not been a nuisance may become one by a change in circumstances.[152] The placing of an unauthorised erection on the bed or foreshore of tidal waters by a person who is not the owner is liable to abatement by the Crown or the owner of the soil.

The owner of a structure on the shore of a navigable watercourse which, either from its original defective construction or from want of repair, presents a dangerous hidden obstruction to navigation on the watercourse, is responsible for any injury occasioned by the structure. The obligation upon the owner of the structure is either to keep it in repair, or to give proper notice of the danger to those who might suffer injury as a consequence of it.[153] A wharf must be kept in a fit and proper condition to receive vessels,[154] and a wharfinger must take reasonable care to ensure that the bed of the watercourse adjoining the jetty will not cause injury to vessels using the jetty.[155] However, a wharfinger will not be liable in negligence if the river bed is in its normal state and the nature of the river is known to those in charge of the vessel.[156]

CONSERVANCY AND NAVIGATION AUTHORITIES

As a matter of common law, the monarch as Lord High Admiral was conservator of all ports, havens, rivers, creeks and arms of the sea

---

[150] *Attorney–General v. Lonsdale*, (1868) L.R. 7 Eq. 377.

[151] *Tate & Lyle Ltd. v. Greater London Council*, [1983] 1 All E.R. 1159, see p.144 above.

[152] *Attorney–General v. Terry*, (1874) 30 L.T. 215.

[153] *White v. Phillips*, (1863) 9 L.T. 388; *Brownlow v. Metropolitan Board of Works*, (1864) 16 C.B.N.S. 546; *Curling v. Wood*, (1847) 16 M. & W. 628; *The Grit*, (1924) 132 L.T. 638.

[154] *The Ville de St. Nazaire*, (1903) 51 W.R. 590.

[155] *The Moorcock*, (1889) 14 P.D. 64.

[156] *Tredegar Iron and Coal Co. v. Calliope (Owners), The Calliope*, [1891] A.C. 11; *The Humorist*, [1944] P.28.

and protector of the navigation thereof, and the Crown under the royal prerogative exercised jurisdiction over the "royal rivers". In the course of time, however, the conservancy in many rivers has been devolved to various public bodies. These include commissioners, conservators, municipal corporations, navigation authorities and companies, port or harbour boards and certain other corporate bodies.

The precise powers, duties and other rights of a conservancy or navigation authority are defined in each case by reference to the particular statute to which it owes its origin. Generally, each statute providing for the constitution and rights of an authority contains provisions for the restoration, maintenance and improvement of a navigable watercourse by means of locks and weirs, dredging and clearing the channel of obstructions, allows for the regulation of navigation by means of byelaws, and empowers the authority to charge tolls on traffic, and occasionally to license erections and works on the river bed. Although it is to be stressed that the powers and duties of any particular conservancy or navigation authority rest upon the interpretation of its enabling enactment, some broad indication of the scope of rights possessed by authorities of this kind can be gathered from a general examination of the case law.

Property in watercourses

Where the navigation of a watercourse is placed under the jurisdiction of trustees or a board of conservators by statute, the ownership of the bed and banks does not normally vest in them, unless explicit vesting is provided for in the statute.[157] If the language of the enactment is uncertain as to whether the soil of the watercourse is to be vested in the authority, a court is likely to infer that the authority have only the use of the soil or an easement necessary for the purpose of navigation.[158] For example, in one decided case it was held that the proprietors of a navigation did not necessarily acquire an interest in the

---

[157] *R. v. River Weaver Navigation Trustees*, (1827) Pratt 28; *Lea Conservancy Board v. Button*, (1879) 12 Ch. D. 383.

[158] *Badger v. S. Yorks Rly. Co.*, (1858) 1 E. & E. 359; *R. v. Aire and Calder Navigation Co.*, (1829) 9 B. & C. 820.

soil of the river bank to maintain an action for trespass.[159] However, there are instances where the wording of an Act will bring about the statutory transfer of land having the effect of vesting the land in the authority without the need for a deed of conveyance.[160] An authority will not normally have any proprietary interest in the water contained in a watercourse by virtue of their founding enactment,[161] but again a proprietary interest in the water is capable of being conveyed by statute where clear words show that intention.[162]

The Conservators of the River Thames, who have no proprietary interest in the bed and soil of the non–tidal part of the river, have been held to be the guardians of the navigation of the river, the protectors of the bed and soil of the river for navigation purposes, and to have certain conservancy rights in connection with the maintenance and improvement of the navigation. Accordingly they may dredge and grant licences for landing places, wharfs and jetties irrespective of the ownership of the soil.[163]

In no case will members of the public who have acquired a right to navigate in inland waters gain any right of property in those waters by virtue of the right of navigation.[164] It has been accepted in the past that statutory authorities entrusted with powers and duties for a public purpose are often in a better position than private individuals to judge what is in the best interests of that purpose. Hence in *Attorney–General v. Great Eastern Railway Co.*,[165] where there was a conflict of evidence as to whether the removal of water by a railway company, from a river which was under the control of conservators, would impede navigation, the court held that the conservancy authority were the best judges of what was needed for their purpose and restrained the railway company from taking water from the river.

[159] *Hollis v. Goldfinch*, (1823) 1 B. & C. 205.
[160] *Bruce v. Willis*, (1840) 11 A. & E. 463.
[161] *Attorney–General v. Great Northern Ry. Co.*, [1909] 1 Ch. 775.
[162] *Medway Co. v. Romney*, (1861) 25 J.P. 550.
[163] *Cory v. Bristow*, (1877) 2 A.C. 262; *Thames Conservators v. Port of London Sanitary Authority*, (1894) 58 J.P. 335.
[164] *Orr Ewing v. Colquhoun*, (1877) 2 A.C. 839.
[165] (1871) 35 J.P. 788.

Maintenance of navigation

At common law the owner of the bed of a navigable watercourse was not bound to maintain the channel in a state clear of natural obstructions such as weed or silt. Consequently, he would not be liable for damage arising through the silting of the channel, such as the overflow of the river causing damage to adjoining land.[166] Likewise, a navigation authority, empowered by statute to protect navigation and to take tolls for the use of the navigation, has been held not to be under a duty to cut weeds and dredge the channel unless this is required for the benefit of navigation.[167]

In *Forbes v. Lee Conservancy Board*[168] the court held that unpaid trustees appointed for public purposes in aid of the common law right of navigation in an ancient navigable river were not liable to remove obstructing piles, since the duty imposed upon them by statute in this respect was discretionary rather than mandatory. Similarly, a landowner who was authorised by Act of Parliament to improve the navigation of a river running through his land was held not to be bound to maintain or repair locks on the river. In this case there was no evidence that the locks had been dedicated to the public as a highway, and it was held that the owner was justified in closing them down altogether if the tolls taken from navigation were insufficient to defray the cost of maintaining them.[169] A person who is empowered to make a river navigable is entitled to take tolls for the carriage of goods in barges over the river where it has been made navigable.[170] Some navigation Acts provide for the payment of compensation in cases of damage sustained by reason of the navigation.[171]

Although there may be no initial obligation to do so, where a navigation authority elect to keep the navigation on a watercourse open

---

[166] *Hodgson v. York Corpn.*, (1873) 287 L.T. 836; *Bridge's Repair Case*, (1609) 3 Co. Rep. 33.

[167] *Parrett Navigation Co. v. Robins*, (1842) 10 M. & W. 593; *Cracknell v. Thetford Corpn.*, (1869) 38 L.J.C.P. 353.

[168] (1879) 4 Ex. D. 116.

[169] *Simpson v. Attorney-General*, [1904] A.C. 476.

[170] *Tamar Marine Navigation Co. v. Wagstaffe*, (1863) 4 B. & S. 288; *Juxon v. Thornhill*, (1628) Cro. Car. 132.

[171] *R. v. Delamere*, (1865) 13 W.R. 757.

to the public, and to take tolls for its use, they are under a common law duty to take reasonable care to ensure that the public may navigate without danger to their lives or property.[172] This duty has been held to encompass a duty to regulate traffic.[173] The principle on which liability of navigation authorities is founded has been held to apply whether the tolls concerned are taken for the profit of the authority or are applied exclusively for the maintenance of navigation work.[174]

In *Winch v. Thames Conservators*,[175] concerned with an injury arising from a defective towpath, the defendants were held to be liable for the damage caused on the ground that so long as they kept the towpath open, and took tolls for its use, they were under an obligation to take reasonable care to see that it was in such a state as not to expose persons using it to undue danger. It was also held that the defendant conservators would not have been held liable if the defective state of the towpath was a latent one, the existence of which they were ignorant after reasonable care on their part, or if they had given notice of it to those who paid tolls or had informed them that they must take the towpath as they found it.[176] It has also been held that the duty to take reasonable care does not extend so as to render a conservancy authority responsible for damage caused by hazardous obstructions in a navigable river where there is no evidence that they knew or ought to have known of a possible danger and there is no negligence on their part.[177]

The provision of information by a conservancy board as to the minimum depth of water in a navigable watercourse does not give rise to any actionable warranty that the minimum depth is to be found on any particular date where the bed of the watercourse is constantly changing. Accordingly, it has been held that the provision of information of this kind which turns out to be incorrect does not amount to a breach of duty to exercise reasonable care in the performance of a conservancy board's

---

[172] *Parnaby v. Lancaster Canal Co.*, (1839) 11 A. & E. 223.

[173] *Boxes v. British Waterways Board*, [1971] 2 Lloyd's Rep. 183, C.A.

[174] *Mersey Docks v. Gibbs*, (1864) 14 L.T. 677.

[175] (1874) 31 L.T. 128.

[176] Now see Occupiers Liability Act 1957.

[177] *Gridley v. Thames Conservators*, (1886) 3 T.L.R. 108; *Queens of the River S.S. Co. v. Eastern Gibb & Co. and Thames Conservators*, (1907) 96 L.T. 901; *Stevens v. Thames Conservators*, [1958] 1 Lloyd's Rep. 401.

navigation functions.[178] Likewise, a port authority who provided moorings in a river for vessels were held not to be under any absolute duty to keep the mooring buoys fit for the purpose for which they were used, but only under a duty to take all reasonable steps to see that the buoys were fit for that purpose.[179]

Regulation of navigation

Conservancy, navigation, harbour, and other authorities with an interest in navigation are frequently empowered under their private Acts of Parliament to make byelaws or rules for regulating navigation on waters under their jurisdiction. Where no specific powers exist enabling byelaws of this kind to be made, Her Majesty in Council, on the application of any person having authority over the waters concerned or any person interested in the navigation thereof, may make rules for the regulation of navigation. Where rules of this kind are made, as regards vessels navigating the waters, they have the same force as if they were part of the "collision regulations".[180] The "collision regulations" are regulations for preventing collisions at sea, made in pursuance of s.418 of the Merchant Shipping Act 1894.[181] The Regulations must be observed by all vessels, including seaplanes and hovercraft, upon the high seas and connected waters which are navigable by seagoing vessels. The Regulations are overridden where local rules have been made for the navigation of a harbour, inland watercourse or stillwater. The Secretary of State may by order confer on certain bodies who own or manage an inland waterway, such as navigation authorities or local authorities, the power to make byelaws regulating navigation on the waterway, subject to confirmation by the Secretary of State.[182]

Typically, navigation byelaws may impose a specific speed limit in respect of vessels navigating inland waters.[183] Alternatively, more

---

[178] *The Neptun*, [1938] P.21.

[179] *Williams & Sons Ltd. v. Port of London Authority*, (1933) 39 Com. Cas. 77.

[180] s.421(1) Merchant Shipping Act 1894.

[181] See also the International Regulations for Preventing Collisions at Sea 1972 as amended by S.I. 1989 No.1798, which apply to the high seas and other waters connected with them and navigable by sea-going vessels.

[182] s.113 Transport Act 1968.

[183] *Tisdell v. Combe*, (1838) 7 Ad. & El. 788.

general provision may be made making it an offence to fail to navigate a vessel with care and caution and at such a speed or in such a manner as to endanger life or cause injury to persons or property.[184] In addition to adhering to byelaws, it is the common law duty of a person in charge of a vessel to use reasonable skill to prevent the vessel from doing injury.[185] Negligence in exercising this duty amounts to a breach of good seamanship, or a breach of the international or local regulations for preventing collisions. Vessels may also be subject to generally applicable legal provisions. Hence, for example, a person who takes a vessel without the consent of the owner or other lawful authority commits a specific offence under the Theft Act.[186]

The navigation function of the National Rivers Authority

Amongst the functions of the National Rivers Authority are certain duties to act as a navigation, harbour or conservancy authority.[187] Accordingly, the Authority has conferred upon it specific powers to make byelaws with respect to its navigation function.[188] In addition, where any navigable waters in England and Wales, or in so much of the adjacent territorial sea as is included in the area of a regional flood defence committee,[189] are not subject to the control of any navigation, harbour or conservancy authority,[190] the Authority may apply to the Secretary of State for an order imposing tolls in respect of the navigation of vessels in those waters.[191] The Authority may also, in pursuance of a Ministerial order, have any of the functions or property of a navigation, harbour or conservancy authority transferred to it.[192]

---

184 For example, s.97 Thames Conservancy Act 1932.

185 *The Vianna*, (1858) Sw. 405; *The Voorwaats and The Khedive*, (1880) 5 A.C. 876.

186 s.12(1) Theft Act 1968.

187 s.2(1)(e) Water Resources Act 1991; on the functions of the Authority generally see Ch.9 below.

188 s.210 Water Resources Act 1991; and see p.235 below on the byelaw–making powers of the Authority generally.

189 On regional flood defence committees see p.375 below.

190 On the definitions of these terms see p.253 below.

191 s.143(1) Water Resources Act 1991.

192 Sch.2 para.1.

In relation to the power of the Authority to make byelaws in respect of navigation, it may make byelaws prohibiting specified inland waters from being used for boating, whether with mechanically propelled boats or otherwise, or regulating the way in which the waters may be used for that purpose. However, byelaws for this purpose are not to apply to tidal or discrete waters, inland waters subject to a navigation, harbour or conservancy authorities, or any reservoir belonging to, and operated by, a water undertaker. Byelaws may include provision prohibiting the use of the waters by boats which are not registered with the Authority and authorise the Authority to impose reasonable charges in respect of the registration of boats in pursuance of byelaws.[193]

In respect of inland waters in which there is a public right of navigation, and which are not subject to the control of any navigation, harbour or conservancy authority, unless that authority is prescribed as unable to carry out its functions, the National Rivers Authority may make byelaws for a range of specified purposes. These are: (a) for the preservation of order on the waters or associated land; (b) for the prevention of damage to anything in or on the waters or land; and (c) for securing that persons resorting to the waters or land behave so as to avoid undue interference with the enjoyment of the waters or land by others. These powers allow byelaws to be made for the regulation of sailing or boating, prohibiting the use of inland waters by boats which are not registered with the Authority, requiring the provision of sanitary appliances for the purposes of preventing pollution and authorising the imposition of reasonable charges for registration of boats.[194] In relation to waterways and associated land owned or managed by the National Rivers Authority, similar powers are provided for to allow the Authority to make byelaws for the preservation of order, the prevention of damage and to secure that persons resorting to waterways behave so as to avoid undue interference with the enjoyment of the waterway by others.[195]

---

193 Sch.25 para.1.
194 Sch.25 para.2.
195 Sch.25 para.3.

Regulation of navigation by water undertakers

Under the Water Industry Act 1991, water and sewerage undertakers have analogous powers to regulate navigation by byelaws to those possessed by the National Rivers Authority. Thus, it is provided that undertakers are to have the power to make byelaws with respect to any waterway owned or managed by them and with respect to any land held or managed with the waterway. Specifically, byelaws may be made for the preservation of order on the waterway or land, the prevention of damage to anything on or in the waterway or land, and securing that persons resorting to the waterway or land behave as to avoid undue interference with the enjoyment of the waters or land by others. In particular, byelaws may be made regulating sailing, boating and other forms of recreation; prohibiting the use of boats which are not registered with the undertaker; requiring the provision of sanitary appliances necessary for preventing pollution; providing for contravention of byelaws to constitute a summary offence punishable by a fine not exceeding £1,000; and authorising the making of reasonable charges in respect of the registration of boats for the purposes of the byelaws.[196]

---

[196] s.157(1) to (3) Water Industry Act 1991. The detailed provisions with respect to the making of byelaws of these kinds are provided for under Sch.10 Water Industry Act 1991.

Chapter 7

FERRIES AND BRIDGES

THE LEGAL CHARACTER OF FERRIES

A public ferry is a public highway of a special kind,[1] consisting of an exclusive right to carry passengers across a river or arm of the sea from one place to another, or to connect a line of road leading from one place to another. It is not a servitude imposed upon a district or area of land, and is wholly unconnected with the ownership or occupation of land. A ferry exists in respect of persons using a right of way over water coming down to a landing stage on the water's edge, or where the ferry is between towns, or "vills", from or to one or more landing places at one vill to one or more landing places at the other.[2] Hence, franchise ferries are of two types: from point to point or from vill to vill. In the more common case of a point to point ferry, the exclusive right is only to ferry passengers coming along a public right of way to a landing place and desiring to cross to a landing place on the opposite bank and continue their journey along another public way.[3] A vill to vill ferry is an exclusive right of ferriage from one vill to another throughout the area of the vills.[4] Thus a point to point ferry has fixed termini which cannot be varied to any substantial extent, whilst a vill to vill ferry may have more than one termini on either side and can be varied within the limits of the vills.[5]

The owner of a ferry must have a right to use land on both sides of the water for the purpose of embarking and disembarking passengers, but he need not have any property in the soil on either side.[6] The ferry owner thus possesses the right to make a special use of the highway, but this

---

[1] *Huzzey v. Field*, (1835) 5 Tyr. 855.

[2] *Newton v. Cubitt*, (1862) 12 C.B.N.S. 32; *Ipswich (Inhabitants) v. Browne*, (1581) Sav. 11. Ex.Ch.

[3] *Hammertson v. Dysart (Earl)*, [1916] 1 A.C. 57; *Cowes U.D.C. v. Southampton, etc., Steam Packet Co.*, [1905] 2 K.B. 287.

[4] *General Estates Co. v. Beaver*, [1914] 3 K.B. 918.

[5] *Hammertson v. Dysart (Earl)*, [1916] 1 A.C. 57; *Hemphill v. M'Kenna*, (1845) 8 I.L.R. 43.

[6] *Peter v. Kendal*, (1827) 6 B. & C. 703; *Williams v. Jones*, (1810) 12 East 346; *R. v. St. Mary Pembroke*, (1851), 15 J.P. Jo. 336.

right falls short of ownership of the highway, or occupation of the highway other than during passage between the termini.[7] By contrast, a floating bridge, consisting of a vessel propelled by steam from one side of a river to the other and kept on its course by a chain laid across the bed of the river, is in legal substance a ferry and not a bridge.[8] A ferry may exist over a tidal creek which at low water could be traversed on foot,[9] and a ferry may be a one–way ferry, where the owners of opposite manors each have a ferry taking passengers only in one direction.[10]

Traditionally, a ferry is *publici juris* and a franchise which no one can establish without a licence from the Crown, and once a ferry has been established, another competing ferry cannot be established without authorisation. If a second ferry is established without a licence, the Crown formerly had a remedy by a *quo warranto*, and the former grantee had a remedy by action.[11] All ancient ferries have their origin in a royal grant, or in prescription, which presumes a royal grant,[12] or by statute.[13] It may be presumed as a point of fact that a ferry has a legal origin from a period of thirty–five years of operation, and a variation in the amount of ferriage will not avoid the franchise.[14] A charter from the Crown granting rights of ferriage over certain rivers only covers ferries existing at the date of the grant and does not confer on the grantee the right to create new ferries over those rivers.[15] A ferry, as an incorporeal hereditament, must be transferred by deed.[16] A ferry may be granted in more or less extensive terms and where it is clear from the terms of the grant that it was intended to grant the ferriage only from one definite place to another definite place, the ferry owner cannot apply his franchise to another

---

[7] *R. v. Nicholson*, (1810) 12 East 330.

[8] *Ward v. Gray*, (1865) 12 L.T. 305.

[9] *Layzell v. Thompson*, (1926) 91 J.P. 89.

[10] *General Estates Co. v. Beaver*, [1914] 3 K.B. 918; *Giles v. Groves*, (1848) 12 Q.B. 721.

[11] *Blissett v. Hart*, (1744) Willes 508.

[12] *Simpson v. Attorney–General*, [1904] A.C. 476.

[13] See *Pim v. Curell*, (1840) 6 M. & W. 234, on a grant of ferry rights by the Crown.

[14] *Trotter v. Harris*, (1828) 2 Y. & J. 285; *Layzell v. Thompson*, (1926) 91 J.P. 89.

[15] *Londonderry Bridge Commissioner v. M'Keever*, (1890) 27 L.R.Ir. 464.

[16] *Mayfield v. Robinson*, (1845) 7 Q.B. 486; *Peter v. Kendal*, (1827) 6 B. & C. 703.

landing place, some way distant from the original place, merely because it is more convenient to do so.[17]

Many of the more important modern ferries are established and worked under local Acts of Parliament, and by the Ferries (Acquisition by Local Authorities) Act 1919. This Act enables a local authority to purchase by agreement or accept the transfer of an existing ferry[18] which is within the area of the authority or which serves the inhabitants of that area.[19] The local authority is empowered to work, maintain and improve the ferry acquired under these provisions, to charge tolls or to free the ferry from tolls, and must make regulations, subject to confirmation by the Secretary of State for the Environment, as to the working of the ferry for the protection from injury of passengers and the general public.[20] New road–ferries[21] may be provided and maintained by the Secretary of State, or, with the Secretary of State's approval, by a local highway authority,[22] who are empowered to improve a road–ferry provided by them,[23] and to acquire by agreement or compulsorily purchase land required by them for the purpose of providing or improving a road–ferry.[24] A ferry undertaking, other than one acquired under the Ferries (Acquisition by Local Authorities) Act 1919, may have their statutory charges revised by an order made by the Secretary of State.[25]

Under s.24 of the Highways Act 1980, the Secretary of State for Transport or a local highway authority may provide and maintain a new road ferry connecting the end of one highway maintainable at public expense with the end of another highway. Provision is also made for the improvement of ferries and the Secretary of State may make loans to the authority for that purpose.[26] Where proposals have been approved by the Secretary of State relating to a long–distance route in accordance with

---

[17] *Matthews v. Peache*, (1855) 20 J.P. 244.

[18] "Existing ferry" is defined by s.1(4) Ferries (Acquisition by Local Authorities) Act 1919.

[19] s.1 Ferries (Acquisition by Local Authorities) Act 1919.

[20] ss.1 and 2.

[21] "Road–ferry" is defined in s.329(1) Highways Act 1980.

[22] s.24(4) Highways Act 1980.

[23] s.107.

[24] s.220.

[25] s.6 Transport Charges, etc. (Miscellaneous Provisions) Act 1954.

[26] See ss.105 and 271(1)(d) Highways Act 1980.

the National Parks and Access to the Countryside Act 1949, including proposals for the provision and operation of a ferry, the highway authority for either or both of the highways to be connected by the ferry has power to provide and operate the ferry and to do all things which appear to them expedient for that purpose. The highway authority may, with the approval of the Secretary of State, make arrangements with any person to provide and operate the ferry and make such contributions as may be agreed with that person.[27]

RIGHTS AND OBLIGATIONS OF THE OWNER OF A FERRY

Tolls

A franchise of ferry is a toll franchise allowing the owner to take a reasonable toll,[28] unless by custom the inhabitants of a particular district have a right to pass a certain ferry free of toll.[29] The Crown has a general prerogative of exemption from payment of tolls,[30] even in respect of tolls created by statute.[31]

Maintenance of a ferry

A ferry owner is under the obligation always to provide proper boats with competent boatmen and all other things necessary for the maintenance of the ferry in an efficient state for use by the public, and failure to do this may result in proceedings brought by way of indictment.[32] A right of ferry is in derogation of common right, for by common right any person entitled to cross a river in a boat is entitled to carry passengers. Within the limits of an ancient ferry no one is permitted to convey passengers across other than the ferry owner, and no one may

---

[27] s.53 National Parks and Access to the Countryside Act 1949.

[28] *Attorney-General v. Simpson*, [1901] 2 Ch. 671; *Hammerton v. Dysart (Earl)*, [1916] 1 A.C. 57; *Hix v. Gardiner*, (1614), Bulst. 195.

[29] *Payne v. Partridge*, (1690) 1 Salk. 12.

[30] *Westover v. Perkins*, (1859) 2 E. & E. 57; *Cooper v. Hawkins*, [1904] 2 K.B. 164.

[31] *Attorney-General v. Cornwall County Council*, (1933) 97 J.P. 281.

[32] *Letton v Goodden*, (1866) 14 L.T. 296; *Nedeport (Prior) v. Weston*, (1443) 2 Roll. Abr. 140, pl.4.

disturb the ferry. Hence, traditionally the ferry carries with it an exclusive right or monopoly and in consideration of that monopoly the ferry owner is bound always to have his ferry ready for service.[33]

As a matter of common law, if the ferry owner fails to maintain the ferry and keep it in repair, he will be liable on indictment, and the Crown may on the ground of neglect repeal the franchise, or a private person who has suffered special damage may bring an action.[34] It is no excuse for the neglect that a ferry owner has erected a bridge across the river for common passage, which is more convenient that the ferry, because an owner is not entitled to suppress the ferry and put up a bridge in its place without licence. However, an action will not lie against the ferry owner for not keeping a boat for the ferry unless some special damage ensues.[35]

It is likely that the present position is that the courts will not grant an injunction to require the owner of a ferry to continue to operate it, as where an interlocutory mandatory injunction was refused against a local authority for discontinuing a public ferry.[36] Thus, where a corporation ceased to work their franchise ferry because it operated at a loss, a mandatory injunction was not granted because the court considered that it could not compel the performance of personal services or the doing of a continuous act requiring the continuous employment of people. In addition, where the ferry could only be continued at a loss it was considered inequitable to compel the defendants to continue working it, and hence the declaration sought was declined because no useful purpose would be achieved by it.[37] In a later case it was stated that an injunction in such cases would only be granted in the most exceptional instances.[38]

---

[33] *Simpson v. Attorney-General*, [1904] A.C. 476.

[34] *Peter v. Kendal*, (1827) 6 B. & C. 703.

[35] *Payne v. Partridge*, (1690) 1 Salk. 12.

[36] *Pelly v. Woodbridge U.D.C.*, (1950) 114 J.P.Jo. 666.

[37] *Attorney-General v. Colchester Corporation*, [1955] 2 All E.R. 124.

[38] *Gravesham Borough Council v. British Railways Board*, (1977) *Law Society's Gazette*, 8 March, 1978 p.249.

Liability for loss or injury

The owner of a ferry is liable for any injury caused by negligence to passengers,[39] goods[40] or animals[41] carried on the ferry boat, and the owner of a ferry for carriages is bound to convey carriages and their contents.[42] A ferry owner is liable as a common carrier in respect of goods carried by him.[43] If a ferry operator overloads a barge, a passenger may cast the goods out of the barge in case of necessity for the safety of the passengers, and the owners of the things will have a remedy for their loss against the ferry operator. If there is no overloading and the danger accrued only by act of God, with no default on the ferry operator, passengers and the owners of goods will have to bear their own loss.[44]

Disturbance of ferries

Where a franchise of ferry exists, it confers an exclusive and absolute right of ferry and of taking tolls between fixed points. The counterpart of this is that if another person sets up a new ferry upon the same river near to the first ferry so as to impair it, the first owner will have a right of action.[45] The mere act of the defendants in carrying passengers in another boat who would otherwise be likely to use the original ferry has been held to be a disturbance of the franchise.[46] The owner of a ferry has a cause of action against anyone who sets up a new ferry either in the line of the old one or in another line so near as to make it an alternative means of carrying passengers between substantially the same points. However, where a new ferry is set up in proximity to an old one, the question to be addressed by the court is whether the new traffic is in fact taking customers from the old ferry or whether it is really new

---

[39] *Dalyell v. Tyrer*, (1858) E.B. & E. 899.

[40] *Coote v. Lear*, (1886) 2 T.L.R. 806; *McCutcheon v. David MacBrayne Ltd.*, [1964] 1 All E.R. 430.

[41] *Willoughby v. Horridge*, (1852) 16 J.P. 761.

[42] *Walker v. Jackson*, (1843) 10 M. & W. 161. On the liability of a ferry boat in collision, see *The Lancashire*, (1874) 29 L.T. 927.

[43] *Southcote's Case*, (1601) 4 Co.Rep. 83; *Rich v. Kneeland*, (1613) Cro. Jac. 330.

[44] *Mouse's Case*, (1608) 12 Co.Rep. 63.

[45] *Blissett v. Hart*, (1774) Willes 508; *Blacketer v.Gillett*, (1850) 9 C.B. 26.

[46] *North & South Shields Ferry Co. v. Barker*, (1848) 2 Ex. 136.

traffic requiring new facilities and as such would not naturally use the highway served by the old ferry. If the latter is found to be the case, the owner of the old ferry will have no cause of action. Increased traffic in consequence of the growth of population or of a change in character of the district served by the old ferry will not be considered to be "new traffic" for these purposes, and will not entitle a person to set up a new ferry near the old one.[47]

Where an exclusive ferry connects two points, a person is not prevented from using another boat from one point of the old ferry to a different point on the other side, provided that it is not done fraudulently and as a pretext for avoiding the regular ferry.[48] A new ferry which has the effect of taking away passengers from a regular ferry must be shown to be injurious,[49] but where the public convenience requires a new passage at such a distance from the old ferry as makes it a real convenience to the public, the proximity of the new ferry from the old one may be such that it is not actionable.[50]

The owner of a ferry cannot maintain an action for loss of traffic caused by a new highway by bridge or ferry made to provide for new traffic. Thus in one instance a railway company constructed a railway bridge and a foot bridge across a river under statutory powers a half mile above an ancient ferry, so that traffic using the ferry declined. It was held that the ferry owner could not claim for compensation since he did not have the exclusive right to carry passengers and goods across the river by any means whatever, but only an exclusive right to carry them across by means of the ferry.[51] Also, where a bridge was constructed by private enterprise connecting the same highway as a ferry, so that the ferry owner lost part of the income derived from tolls, it was held that the bridge was not a disturbance of the ferry and the ferry owner had no remedy.[52] In an action for disturbance of a ferry, it is sufficient for the plaintiff to prove that he was in possession of the ferry at the time when

---

[47] *Hammerton v. Dysart (Earl)*, [1916] 1 A.C. 57.

[48] *Tripp v. Frank*, (1792) 4 T.R. 666.

[49] *Huzzey v. Field*, (1835) 5 Tyr. 855.

[50] *Newton v Cubitt*, (1862) 6 L.T. 860.

[51] *Hopkins v. Great Northern Ry. Co.*, (1877) 2 Q.B.D. 224; overruling *R. v. Cambrian Ry. Co.*, (1871) 25 L.T. 84.

[52] *Dibden v. Skirrow*, [1908] 1 Ch. 41; *Latter v. Littlehampton U.D.C.*, (1909) 73 J.P. 426; *Young v. Thank*, (1845) 6 L.T.O.S. 146.

the cause of action arose, and it is not necessary for him to allege or prove the payment of a specified sum for passage money.[53] A corporation empowered by statute to establish and work a steam–ferry, but on whom no obligation to maintain the ferry had been imposed, had no right to an action for an injunction to restrain a person who, without any title, has established a ferry which interfered with the profits of the steam–ferry.[54]

Extinguishment of ferries

A franchise of public ferry could formerly be repealed by the Crown,[55] or the ferry owner could surrender his interest in the ferry by giving up his lease.[56] A ferry may also be extinguished under statute, whereby a bridge or modern ferry is authorised to be substituted for an ancient ferry.[57]

BRIDGES

Construction of bridges

The construction of bridges, and tunnels, is provided for under the Highways Act 1980, which allows a highway authority to construct a bridge to carry a highway maintainable at public expense, but the appropriate Minister may not construct a bridge without the approval of the Treasury. In addition, a highway authority is empowered to reconstruct a bridge which is a highway maintainable at the public expense by them, either on the same site or on a new site within 200 yards of an old one.[58]

Under the 1980 Act, the construction of bridges, and tunnels, in relation to specified navigable waters is the subject of a range of

---

[53] *Peter v. Kendal*, (1827) 6 B. & C. 703.

[54] *Londonderry Bridge Commissioners v. M'Keever*, (1890) 27 L.R.Ir. 464; *Bournemouth–Swanage Ferry Co. v. Harvey*, [1930] A.C. 549.

[55] *Attorney–General v. Colchester Corpn.*, [1955] 2 All E.R. 124.

[56] *Peter v. Kendal*, (1827) 6 B. & C. 703.

[57] *Cory v. Yarmouth & Norwich Ry. Co.*, (1844) 3 Hare 593; *North & South Shields Ferry Co. v. Barker*, (1848) 2 Ex. 136; *Royal v. Yaxley*, (1872) 36 J.P. 680.

[58] ss.91 and 92 Highways Act 1980.

provisions for different orders for this purpose. Accordingly, the Minister of Transport or the Secretary of State for Wales may provide for the construction of a bridge as a part of a trunk road, or under a special road scheme.[59] A local highway authority may, by a scheme confirmed by the appropriate Minister, provide for the construction of a bridge as part of a highway, or proposed highway, which is to be maintained at public expense by that authority. In addition, a highway authority may, by orders relating to side roads or special roads,[60] provide for the construction of a bridge as a part of a highway where the order authorises the authority to provide access to premises from a highway by the construction of a bridge.[61]

Before making or confirming an order or scheme providing for the construction of a bridge over, or tunnel under, navigable waters, the Minister is to take into consideration the reasonable requirements of navigation over the waters affected by the order or scheme. A scheme providing for the construction of a bridge is to include plans indicating the position and dimensions of the proposed bridge, including its spans, headways and waterways, and in the case of a swing bridge a scheme is to contain conditions which the Minister considers expedient for regulating its operation. Specifically, copies of documents relating to the scheme are to be served on every navigation authority having jurisdiction over the waters concerned, and the National Rivers Authority. If objections are sustained by either of these bodies that the bridge is likely to obstruct or impede the performance of their functions under any enactment, or interfere with the reasonable requirements of navigation over the waters affected, the making of the order will be subject to special Parliamentary procedure.[62] An order or scheme which provides for the construction of a bridge over, or tunnel under, any navigable waters may also authorise the highway authority by whom it is to be constructed to divert such part of any specified navigable watercourse if

[59] On Ministerial orders relating to trunk roads and special roads see, respectively, ss.10 and 16 Highways Act 1980.

[60] Side roads and special roads orders are provided for under ss.14 and 18.

[61] s.106(1) to (4).

[62] s.107 and Sch.1.

that diversion is necessary or desirable for purposes connected with the bridge or tunnel or its construction.[63]

In addition to the general matters relating to the construction of bridges provided for under the Highways Act 1980, particular powers to construct bridges may arise under special or local Acts. For example, where an Act authorises the construction of a railway bridge across a navigable river, provisions from the Railways Clauses Act 1863 may be incorporated into the enabling Act, requiring the bridge to be constructed in accordance with certain specifications and to be subject to inspection by the Secretary of State. Where a railway bridge is constructed in accordance with these provisions, and is subsequently abandoned or falls into decay, the Secretary of State may remove all or part of it and restore the site to its original condition, and recover the expenses of so doing from the railway undertaker.[64]

The construction of a bridge over a main river will require the consent of the National Rivers Authority, and no person may, without the consent of the Authority, carry out alteration or repair work on a main river bridge which is likely to affect the flow of water in the watercourse or to impede drainage work. If work is carried out in contravention of these provisions the Authority may remove or alter it or pull it down, and recover the cost of so doing from the person who carried out the work. However, it is expressly stated that none of these provisions affect any enactment requiring the consent of any government department for the erection of a bridge, or any powers exercisable by any government department in relation to a bridge.[65] In addition, the erection or alteration of an obstruction to the flow of a watercourse which is not a main river will require the consent of the internal drainage board for the district in which the work is to be conducted, other than where the work is conducted in pursuance of an Act of Parliament.[66]

A private person constructing a bridge on private land will require planning permission to do so under the Town and Country Planning Act

---

[63] s.108(4).

[64] Generally see Railways Clauses Act 1863.

[65] s.109 Water Resources Act 1991, see p.379 below; and see s.110 on applications for consents and approvals in relation to this. On the meaning of "main river" see p.378 below.

[66] s.23 Land Drainage Act 1991, see p.398 below.

1990.[67] However, planning consent for the building of bridges is ordinarily deemed to be granted if the highway authority is the local planning authority and the work is carried out within its own area.[68]

Maintenance of bridges

In most circumstances a bridge will be a part of a highway which is maintained out of public funds by the highway authority.[69] However, a private duty to maintain a bridge may arise where it was constructed with the intention that it would be privately maintained. Private liability for bridges may be founded upon tenure or prescription or arise under statute. Alternatively, although as a matter of common law there may have been no initial obligation to construct a bridge,[70] once constructed and used as a public highway, a bridge may become the obligation of the inhabitants of the county to maintain,[71] unless it was established that it was maintainable by another body or person.[72]

Under the Highways Act 1980 provision is made for orders for the reconstruction and improvement of privately maintained bridges.[73] In addition, a highway authority may enter into an agreement with the owners of a bridge for the payment by the highway authority of contributions towards the cost of the reconstruction, improvement or maintenance of the bridge, or for the transfer to the highway authority of the highway carried by the bridge, or the property in the bridge, highway and approaches and all or any rights and obligations attaching to them.[74] Alternatively, a power is given for a magistrates' court to issue an order extinguishing a person's liability to maintain privately a bridge and

---

[67] See, in particular, ss.55 and 57 Town and Country Planning Act 1990, and see p.333 below on planning law generally.

[68] s.316(1).

[69] s.41 Highways Act 1980.

[70] *R. v. Devon Inhabitants*, (1825) 4 B. & C. 670.

[71] *R. v. Bucks Inhabitants*, (1810) 12 East. 192; *Attorney-General and Doncaster R.D.C. v. West Riding of Yorkshire County Council*, (1903) 67 J.P. 173.

[72] *R. v. Oxfordshire Inhabitants*, (1812) 16 East 223.

[73] s.93 Highways Act 1980.

[74] s.94.

making it a highway maintainable at public expense.[75] Ultimately, the duty to maintain a highway or bridge can be compelled by an order to do so,[76] or by the exercise of the default powers of a highway authority enabling it to conduct repair works and recover the cost from the person liable for its repair.[77]

Where a bridge has been constructed under statutory authority the enabling Act will set out responsibility for its maintenance.[78] In some instances continuing liability will be imposed to preserve the original character and condition of the bridge.[79] A highway bridge constructed under statutory authority may be required to be maintained by the undertaker even if a different bridge has been substituted for that originally provided.[80] The undertakers will be responsible for repairing any damage to a bridge even if caused by an extraordinary flood, unless other provision is made in the covenant or Act under which the duty to maintain was imposed.[81] Where liabilities of these kinds are imposed, the undertaker constructing the bridge will be liable in the same way as a private owner in relation to the maintenance of the bridge. Similarly, the duty of the undertaker to maintain the bridge may be enforced or extinguished in accordance with the powers under the Highways Act 1980.

Otherwise than in relation to a main river, where any person is liable, by reason of custom, prescription or otherwise, to do any repair work, maintenance or other work in relation to a bridge, and fails to do that work, the internal drainage board concerned, or if none the National Rivers Authority, may serve a notice on that person requiring him to do the necessary work with all reasonable dispatch. If a person fails, within seven days, to comply with a notice served for this purpose, the drainage

---

[75] s.53, this consequence may also arise where liability to maintain or improve a bridge is extinguished where a highway comprising a bridge becomes a trunk road under s.55.

[76] Under s.56.

[77] Under s.57.

[78] *Sharpness New Docks and Gloucester and Birmingham Navigation Co. v. Attorney-General*, [1915] A.C. 654.

[79] *Lanarkshire County Council v. National Coal Board*, (1948) S.C. 698.

[80] *Regents Canal and Dock Co. v. London County Council*, (1909) 73 J.P. 276.

[81] *Brecknock and Abergavenny Canal Navigation Co. v. Pritchard*, (1796) 3 R.R.335.

board concerned, or the Authority, may do all the necessary work, and any expenses incurred in so doing may be recovered from the person liable to repair the bridge.[82]

[82] s.21 Land Drainage Act 1991, and see p.398 below.

Chapter 8

FISHERIES AT COMMON LAW

TYPES OF FISHERIES

Although a number of distinct sub-categories of the right of fishery may be identified, the essential characteristic of the right is the entitlement to fish in one's own, or another person's water, which may exist either as an incident to the ownership of the soil over which the water flows or independently of the ownership of that soil.[1] Generally, the right of fishery constitutes a profit of the soil over which the water flows and the title to the fishery arises from the ownership of the soil,[2] and where the soil and the right to fish are in the same ownership the fishery is referred to as a *corporeal* or *territorial* fishery. Where, however, the right of fishery is severed from the ownership of the soil as an *incorporeal hereditament* the right amounts to a *profit a prendre* or a *profit of piscary*.[3]

A person who has the sole and exclusive right of fishing, either with or without ownership of the soil over which the right is exercised, is said to have an *exclusive*, *several* or *free* right of fishery, with these expressions being regarded in law as synonyms.[4] "Exclusive" in this context means that the owner has the right of fishing independently of all others and that no other person has a co-extensive right to the fishery.[5] By contrast, the term *common fishery* indicates the right of the public to fish in tidal waters and *common of fishery* refers to a right of one or more persons to fish in common with the owner of the fishery.

Although the distinctions between corporeal and incorporeal and several and common fisheries may be of importance in particular cases, an overriding classificatory distinction between rights of fishery is that drawn between *public* and *private* fisheries. Broadly, a public right of

---

[1] *Hanbury v. Jenkins*, [1901] 2 Ch. 401.

[2] *Attorney-General for British Columbia v. Attorney-General for Canada*, [1914] A.C. 153.

[3] *Staffordshire and Worcestershire Canal Navigation v. Bradley* [1912] 1 Ch.91; *Harris v. Earl of Chesterfield* [1911] A.C. 623.

[4] *Holford v. Bailey*, (1849), 13 Q.B. 426; *Gipps v. Woollicot*, (1697) 3 Salk. 360; *Malcomson v. O'Dea*, (1863) 10 H.L.C. 593.

[5] *Seymour v. Courtenay,* (1771) 98 E.R. 478.

fishery will exist in the sea and tidal waters unless the right of fishery has been appropriated through the creation of a private several fishery in these waters, whilst private rights of fishery exist in all fresh waters in the form or either a several fishery or a common of fishery.

The basis of the distinction between public and private fisheries lies in the original vesting of all tidal and non tidal fisheries in the Crown as the ultimate owner of all land. Ownership of the right of fishery in tidal waters formerly enabled the Crown to grant private rights of several fishery to individuals as parcels of manors.[6] Where this was done the grantee of the right was then able to convey the land and fishery to another or create incorporeal rights of fishery for the benefit of others. Although these private rights of fishery in tidal waters remain in private ownership to this day, the right of the Crown to grant such rights was abolished by Magna Charta in 1225. It follows, therefore, that private rights of fishery in tidal waters can only exist in the relatively small number of private fisheries where rights of this kind were granted before 1225. By contrast, rights of fishery in non–tidal waters are invariably private rights of fishery.

PUBLIC FISHERIES

In addition to the public right of navigation,[7] all citizens of the Crown are entitled, as a matter of public right, to exercise a right to fish in tidal waters including the high seas, estuaries and tidal watercourses and from the foreshore. Moreover, as indicated above, the provisions of Magna Charta prohibit the exercise of the Crown prerogative to grant private rights of fishery in these waters to the exclusion of the public.[8] Hence, because the right of fishing in the sea is common to all, a prescription for such a right annexed to a tenement will be invalid.[9]

---

[6] *Neill v. Duke of Devonshire,* (1882) 8 A.C. 135.

[7] See Ch.6 above on rights of navigation.

[8] *Attorney–General for British Columbia v. Attorney–General for Canada*, [1914] A.C. 153.

[9] *Ward v. Creswell,* (1741) Willes 265.

The right to fish in the sea and tidal waters

The right of the public to fish in the sea and tidal waters is enjoyed by all persons subject to limitations which arise from the special custom or usage of the country,[10] and restrictions arising through Acts of Parliament[11] or as a result of conventions with other nations confirmed by statute.[12] Formerly, the public had the right to fish in territorial waters, to a distance of three nautical miles from the low water mark,[13] to the exclusion of subjects of other states. Now, under the Fishery Limits Act 1976,[14] British fishery limits extend to 200 miles from the baselines from which the breadth of the territorial sea adjacent to the United Kingdom is measured. Generally, foreign fishing boats registered in a country designated by order may fish in areas within British fishery limits designated in the order and for descriptions of fish so registered. Foreign fishing boats not so registered cannot enter British fishery limits except for a purpose recognised by international law or in accordance with a convention between the United Kingdom and the government of the country to which the boat belongs.[15] As has been noted previously, however, a major exception to this general principle is the common fisheries policy of the European Community enabling fishing in Community waters to be undertaken by fishery vessels of all the Member States subject to a common system of regulation.[16]

Fishing on the foreshore

The public right of fishery in tidal water includes the right to fish upon the foreshore between high and low water mark, unless the area

---

[10] *Hogarth v. Jackson*, (1827) 2 C. & P. 595; *Fennings v. Grenville (Lord)*, (1808) 1 Taunt. 241.

[11] See Sea Fisheries Regulation Act 1966; Sea Fisheries (Shellfish) Act 1967, and Ch.13 below.

[12] *Attorney-General for British Columbia v. Attorney-General for Canada*, [1914] A.C. 153; *Smith v. Cooke*, (1914) 112 L.T. 864.

[13] s.7 Territorial Waters Jurisdiction Act 1878; see also *Anglo-Norwegian Fisheries Case*, [1952] 1 T.L.R. 181.

[14] See p.33 above.

[15] See p.34 above.

[16] See p.35 above.

concerned is subject to a private and exclusive right of fishery vested in an individual as described previously.[17] The ownership of the foreshore is *prima facie* vested in the Crown, subject to the public rights of fishing and navigation, but these are the only public rights recognised by the common law in the sea or foreshore. Specifically, the public have no rights over the foreshore when not covered by the tide except those which are ancillary to their rights of fishing and navigation in the sea. Similarly, when the foreshore is covered by the tide and becomes a part of the sea bed the only rights of the public over it are the rights of fishing and navigation and rights ancillary thereto.[18]

The public common law rights with respect to the sea are rights over the water, rather than upon land, and these allow for passage and fishing in the sea and on the foreshore when covered by water. Ancillary rights allow for the exercise of the rights of navigation and fishery by virtue of a right to have access to and upon the water only by and from those places which have been appointed by necessity and usage. Hence, persons exercising a right of navigation possess no general right of lading, unlading, landing or embarking wherever they please upon the foreshore or adjoining land except in cases of peril or necessity,[19] or where such rights are specifically provided for by statute. Persons lawfully exercising a right of fishery are not at liberty to use the soil above high water mark for approaching or leaving their boats, transporting fish or other purposes.[20] In general, the public are entitled to enter upon the foreshore when the tide has receded for the purposes of navigation and fishing, but have no other rights of entry without the consent of the Crown or its lessees.[21]

It has been held that an immemorial use of the foreshore in tidal and navigable waters by the owners of fishing boats and other craft, by fixing moorings in the soil for the purpose of attaching their boats to them, may be supported either as an ordinary incident of the navigation

---

[17] *Bagott v. Orr*, (1801) 2 Box. & P. 472.

[18] *Fitzhardinge (Lord) v. Purcell*, [1908] 2 Ch. 139; *Malcomson v. O'Dea*, (1863) 10 H.L.C. 593; *Attorney-General v. Chambers*, (1854) 23 L.T.O.S. 238.

[19] *Blundell v. Catterall*, (1821) 5 B. & Ald. 268.

[20] *Ilchester (Earl) v. Rashleigh*, (1889) 61 L.T. 477; *Ward v. Cresswell*, (1741) Willes 265; *Aiton v. Stephen*, (1876) 1 A.C. 459.

[21] *Llandudno U.D.C. v. Woods*, [1899] 2 Q.B. 318.

of such waters, or on a presumption of a legal origin by grant from the Crown of the foreshore subject to that use, or as concession by a former owner of the foreshore to all persons navigating the waters to use it for fixing moorings.[22] The general principle remains, however, that no fixture may be attached to the sea bed without the permission of the Crown.[23]

The right of fishery extends to allow members of the public to take shell fish found on the foreshore,[24] unless the shell fish concerned have been reduced into the possession of another person through cultivation in a shell fish bed.[25] The right to take shell fish does not carry any incidental right to appropriate a portion of the foreshore for the storage of oysters, or other shell fish, to the exclusion of other members of the public.[26] Where, however, oysters which were stored in ponds on the foreshore became polluted with sewage discharged to the sea by a local authority, and rendered unfit for consumption, the owner of the ponds was able to maintain an action for trespass against the local authority.[27]

It has been held to be a valid immemorial custom for persons from a particular parish exercising a right of fishery to spread their nets to dry on private land adjoining the foreshore,[28] though the use of different kinds of nets varied from time to time.[29] Special duties may arise from the use of land bordering the foreshore as an adjunct to the right of fishery, and a claim has been established to take fish by way of a toll from fishermen landing on a beach in consideration of the claimant furnishing and maintaining a capstan and windlass on the beach for drawing fishing boats from the water.[30] In all instances the common right

---

[22] *Attorney–General v. Wright*, [1897] 2 Q.B. 318.

[23] *Crown Estate Commissioners v. Fairlie Yacht Slip*, (1977) S.L.T.19, and see p.23 above.

[24] *Bagott v. Orr*, (1801) 2 Bos. & P. 472.

[25] *R. v. Downing*, (1870) 23 L.T. 298; *The Swift*, (1901) 85 L.T. 346; and contrast *R. v. Howlett*, (1968) 112 S.J. 150.

[26] *Truro Corpn. v. Rowe*, [1902] 2 K.B. 709.

[27] *Foster v. Warblington U.D.C.*, [1906] 1 K.B. 648.

[28] *Lockwood v. Wood*, (1844) 6 Q.B. 50; *Ipswich (Inhabitants) v. Browne*, (1581) Sav. 11, 14; *Gray v. Bond*, (1821) 2 B. & B. 667.

[29] *Mercer v. Denne*, [1905] 2 Ch. 538.

[30] *Falmouth (Earl) v. Penrose*, (1827) 6 B. & C. 385; *Falmouth (Lord) v. George*, (1828) 5 Bing. 286.

of fishery must be exercised in a reasonable and lawful manner[31] and may be carried on with the use of lines and lawful nets,[32] but not with fixed engines placed on the margins of the shore,[33] since the right to erect devices of this kind indicates ownership of the soil and of a several fishery in the waters concerned.[34]

Several fisheries in tidal waters

To the general principle that the public have a "liberty of fishing in the sea and creeks or arms thereof", Hale noted the exception, "unless in such places or creeks or navigable rivers where either the King or some other particular subject has granted a propriety exclusive of that common liberty."[35] This passage acknowledges the existence of special cases in which instances are to be found of several and exclusive rights of fishery in tidal waters which have been recognised to be the property of the owner of the soil. In all such cases, however, the proof of the existence and enjoyment of the right must be shown to extend further back that the date of Magna Charta in 1225.[36] The right to exclude the public from tidal waters and to create a several fishery may lawfully have been exercised by the Crown before that date, in which case the several fishery concerned could lawfully be made the subject of subsequent grants by the Crown to private persons, either together with or separately from the soil.[37] However, the public cannot maintain a claim to any right to fish in such a several fishery for the reason that a fluctuating and uncertain body of persons cannot claim the benefit of a *profit a prendre*.[38] Since Magna Charta, however, no grant by the Crown of part of the bed of the sea or

---

[31] *Whelan v. Hewson*, (1871) I.R. 6 C.L. 283.

[32] *Warren v. Matthews*, (1703) 1 Salk. 357; *Kintore v. Forbes*, (1828) 4 Bli. N.S. 485.

[33] *Pery v. Thornton*, (1889) 23 L.R.Ir. 402; *Bevins v. Bird*, (1865) 12 L.T. 306; and see p.428 below on the meaning of "fixed engines".

[34] *Rawstorne v. Backhouse*, (1867) 17 L.T. 441.

[35] *De Jure Maris* Chapter IV.

[36] *Attorney-General for British Columbia v. Attorney-General for Canada*, [1914] A.C. 153.

[37] *Malcomson v. O'Dea*, (1863) 10 H.L.C. 593.

[38] *Goodman v. Saltash Corpn.*, (1882) 7 A.C. 633; *Murphy v. Ryan*, (1868) I.R. 2 C.L.143.

of a tidal navigable river can operate to the detriment of the public right of fishing.[39]

Royal fisheries

The public right to fish in tidal waters does not extend to taking Royal fish,[40] whales, sturgeon and porpoise, which are caught in the water or found on the shore. These belong to the Crown and no subject can have them without special grant from the Crown.[41]

Limits of tidal part of a river

The right of fishing in a tidal river is *prima facie* a public right,[42] whilst the right of fishing in a non–tidal river is the subject of private ownership and cannot be vested in the public generally.[43] It follows that the exact location of the tidal limit in a watercourse will be of particular significance in determining the existence of public and private rights of fishery in particular waters. It has been suggested that the test for determining whether waters are tidal or not is the prevalence of fresh water and the tidal limit is where the fresh water prevails.[44] Alternatively it has been held that a river could not be considered to be tidal at a point where the water was not salt and at ordinary tides was unaffected by any tidal influence, though on occasions of very high tides the rising of salt water dammed back the fresh water and caused it to rise and fall with the flow and ebb of the tide.[45] More recently a preference has been expressed for the view that the tidal waters are those waters where the tide

---

[39] *Fitzhardinge (Lord) v. Purcell*, [1908] 2 Ch. 139.

[40] On Royal fish generally see p.58 above.

[41] *Royal Fishery of Banne Case*, (1610) Dav. Ir. 35; *Warren v. Matthews*, (1703) 1 Salk. 357.

[42] *R. v. Stimpson*, (1863) 4 B. & S. 301.

[43] *Attorney–General for British Columbia v. Attorney–General for Canada*, [1914] A.C. 153.

[44] *Horne v. Mackenzie*, (1839) 6 Cl. & Fin 628.

[45] *Reece v. Miller*, (1882) 8 Q.B.D. 626; see also *Brown v. Ellis*, (1886) 50 J.P. 326; and *Micklethwait v. Vincent* (1892) 67 L.T. 225.

ordinarily flows or reflows regardless of whether the flow could be observed by lateral or vertical motion.[46]

Fishing in non–tidal waters

The Crown is not ordinarily entitled to the soil of non–tidal waters,[47] and where the Crown is both owner of the bed of a non–tidal river and of the right of fishing, the right of fishing would be a proprietary and not a prerogative right.[48] On a similar basis no public right of fishery can legally exist in non–tidal waters.[49] This principle also applies to non–tidal navigable rivers,[50] though rendered navigable by artificial means.[51] Moreover, a legal right for the public to fish in a non–tidal river cannot be obtained by custom,[52] prescription or otherwise.[53] Hence, although members of the public may fish by licence or by the indulgence of the owner of the fishery, they have no public right of fishery in non–tidal waters.[54]

PRIVATE FISHERIES

As has been previously observed, private fisheries fall into two principal categories: the several fishery and the common of fishery.

---

[46] *Re Kingsway Furniture Ltd.*, [1991] 1 *Water Law* 10; *Ingram v. Percival*, [1968] 3 All E.R. 657; *Cross v. Minister of Agriculture*, [1941] I.R. 55; *West Riding of Yorkshire Rivers Board v. Tadcaster RDC*, (1907) 97 L.T. 436; *Calcraft v. Guest*, [1898] 1 Q.B. 759; and see also Moore *The History and Law of Fisheries* (1903) pp.102 to 107.

[47] *Johnson v. O'Neill*, [1911] A.C. 552.

[48] *Devonshire (Duke) v. Pattison*, [1887] 20 Q.B.D. 263.

[49] *Hudson v. MacRae*, (1863) 4 B. & S. 585; *Reece v. Miller*, (1882) 8 Q.B.D. 626; *Murphy v. Ryan*, (1868) I.R. 2 C.L. 143; *Wells v. Hardy*, [1964] 1 All E.R. 953.

[50] *Pearce v. Scotcher*, (1882) 46 L.T. 342.

[51] *Mussett v. Burch*, (1876) 35 L.T. 486; *Hargreaves v. Diddams*, (1875) 32 L.T. 600.

[52] *Pearce v. Scotcher*, (1882) 9 Q.B.D. 162.

[53] *Smith v. Andrews*, [1891] 2 Ch. 678.

[54] *Blount v. Layard*, [1891] 2 Ch. 681.

Several fisheries

A several fishery means an exclusive right to fish at a determined place existing either apart from or as an incident to the ownership of the soil over which the water flows. In order to constitute a several fishery it is necessary that the person claiming it should possess a right of fishing which is independent of all others, so that no other person has a co-extensive right in the fishery.[55] Where a several fishery is proved to exist, the owner of the fishery is presumed, in the absence of evidence to the contrary, to be the owner of the soil, whether it is a navigable or a non-navigable river.[56]

A several fishery need not be an exclusive right for the owner to take all the kinds of fish which may be present in the fishery. Hence the right is divisible so that the owner may reserve for himself the right to take all floating fish and grant to another the right to fish for oysters.[57] Similarly, a several fishery will not cease to exist where it is divided so that another person is entitled to fish at certain periods of the year.[58]

A several fishery may be leasehold or freehold and may be appurtenant to or parcel of a manor,[59] or appurtenant to a tenement or land.[60] In accordance with general principles of conveyancing, where a riparian owner of the soil under a river *ad medium filum* makes a freehold or leasehold grant of his land on the banks of the river, the soil to the middle line of the river passes with the grant, and so also the several fishery.[61]

Common of fishery

A common of fishery or common piscary is an incorporeal right of fishing where the owner of the right fishes in common with the owner of

---

55 *Seymour v. Courtenay*, (1771) 5 Curr. 2814.

56 *Hanbury v. Jenkins*, [1901] 2 Ch. 401; *Hindson v. Ashby*, [1896] 2 Ch. 1.

57 *Seymour v. Courtenay*, (1771) 5 Curr. 2814; *Rogers v. Allen*, (1808) 1 Camp. 309.

58 *Goodman v. Saltash Corpn.*, (1882) 7 A.C. 633.

59 *Attorney-General v. Emerson*, [1891] A.C. 649; *Rogers v. Allen*, (1808) 1 Camp. 309.

60 *Hayes v. Bridges*, (1795) 1 Ridg. L. & S. 390.

61 *Tilbury v. Silva*, (1890) 45 Ch. D. 98; *Grove v. Portal*, [1902] 1 Ch. 727; and see p.17 above on the *medium filum* rule generally.

the bed of the water or in common with other persons who enjoy the same right. Rights of common of fishery may be either a common appendant, common appurtenant or a common in gross. A common appendant is a right in respect of arable land granted to a freehold tenant prior to the Statute *Quia Emptores* in 1289. A common of piscary appurtenant is a right of fishing attached to a particular tenement or premises and may be claimed by grant, custom or prescription and arises by act of the parties and does not usually attach by tenure. The right cannot normally be severed or enjoyed apart from the dominant tenement and passes with the dominant tenement to each successive owner. A common of piscary appurtenant is limited to the needs of the occupants of the tenement.[62] A common in gross may be claimed by grant or prescription and is not connected with the ownership of land.

Claims to private fisheries

A person who claims entitlement to a private right of fishery must establish a clear legal foundation for that right which is stronger than that of any other person and, in particular, overrides that of the owner of the soil over which the right of fishery is exercised. In relation to a private watercourse the ownership of the soil will provide good evidence of a right of fishery and puts the onus of proof upon any other person who disputes the claim to ownership. Conversely, in the case of a tidal fishery, the general presumption that a public right of fishery exists in tidal waters means that the onus of proof of private ownership lies upon the person who seeks to appropriate the privilege of fishery as an exclusive right.[63] Broadly, claims to the private ownership of fisheries may rest upon three bases: express grant, lease or licence and prescription.

---

[62] *Payne v. Ecclesiastical Comrs. and Landon*, (1913) 30 T.L.R. 167; *Harris v. Chesterfield (Earl)*, [1991] A.C. 623.

[63] *Fitzwalter's (Lord) Case*, (1674) 1 Mod. Rep. 105.

Claim by express grant

The explicit use of the word "several" is not necessary to create a several fishery by express grant,[64] but it has been held that the use of the word "soil" in a grant is not adequate to pass a right of fishery.[65] The owner of a corporeal fishery may dispose of it by conveyance or lease in the ordinary way, and an incorporeal fishery must be conveyed by deed under seal.[66] A corporeal fishery comprising the freehold in the bed of the watercourse at a specified place and the right to take fish in the water above that bed is land, not a right appurtenant to land, and cannot be transferred merely by a conveyance of other land and rights appurtenant to that land.[67] *Prima facie*, the grant of a fishery passes with it the soil of the watercourse, since the owner of a fishery, in the absence of evidence to the contrary, is presumed to be the owner of the soil.[68] The owner of a several fishery in ordinary cases and where the terms of the grant are unknown, is presumed to be the owner of the soil, but where the terms of the grant are known and convey no more than an incorporeal hereditament the presumption is inapplicable.[69]

Lease or licence

A lease of a fishery may be granted with the soil of the watercourse as a corporeal hereditament or as an incorporeal right without the soil. A lease or licence of a fishery must be granted by deed,[70] but if a fishery is let by an agreement not under seal, the landlord may still recover the rent for the use and occupation of the fishery.[71] An incorporeal hereditament can only be conveyed by deed.[72] In a lease of agricultural or other land through which a watercourse runs, the right of

---

[64] *Hanbury v. Jenkins*, [1901] 2 Ch. 401; *Beaufort (Duke) v. Aird (John) and Co.*, (1904) 209 T.L.R. 602.

[65] *Scratton v. Brown*, (1825) 4 B. & C. 485.

[66] *Bird v Higginson*, (1837) 6 Ad. & El. 824.

[67] *Hesketh v. Willis Cruisers*, (1968) 19 P. & C.R. 573, C.A.

[68] *Attorney–General v. Emerson*, [1891] A.C. 643; *Hindson v. Ashby*, [1896] 2 Ch. 1.

[69] *Somerset (Duke) v. Fogwell*, (1826) 5 B. & C. 875.

[70] *Fuller v. Brown*, (1849) 13 J.P. 445; *Bird v. Great Eastern Ry. Co.*, (1865) 13 L.T. 365.

[71] *Holford v. Pritchard*, (1849) 3 Ex. 793.

[72] *Somerset (Duke) v. Fogwell*, (1826) 5 B. & C. 875; *Bird v. Higginson*, (1837) 6 Ad. & Ed. 824.

fishing, unless expressly reserved to the lessor, passes to the tenant and consequently the lessor cannot prosecute a person for unlawfully taking fish from the river.[73]

In strict terms a reservation and exception in a lease of a right of fishing operates as a re–grant by the lessee to the landlord of that right.[74] A grant by deed of the right of fishing is not a mere licence to fish, but a right to fish and carry away the fish caught, and the grantees of a right of this kind have a right of action against anyone who wrongfully interferes with their right.[75] Not all the terms of a fishery lease will necessarily convey a proprietary interest in the subject matter of the lease, hence it was decided that a clause in a fishing lease allowing the freehold owner to retain a rod on the fishery should be construed merely as a contractual right which came to an end upon the death of the owner.[76]

Prescription

In the case of non–tidal watercourses it is presumed that the owner of the bed has the right to fish in the waters.[77] In the sea and tidal watercourses the right of fishing is public and common to all and, whilst a proprietor of land may have an exclusive right of fishing, this right is not presumed. Indeed the presumption is to the contrary, that no private right of fishery exists in tidal waters. Despite this, the fact that the Crown has in the past had the capacity to grant rights of several fishery in tidal waters has the consequence that rights of this kind may be the subject of prescription since prescription implies the existence of a former grant. Nonetheless, the absence of any presumption of ownership of private fisheries in tidal waters means that rights of this kind must be proved.[78] Moreover, a prescriptive right of private fishery in tidal water must be proved as extensively as it is claimed.[79]

A prescriptive right to a several fishery in a tidal watercourse cannot be supported by custom as a claim to a *profit a prendre*, nor can it

---

[73] *Jones v. Davies*, (1902) 86 L.T. 447.

[74] *Doe d. Douglas v. Lock*, (1835) 2 Ad. & El. 705.

[75] *Fitzgerald v. Firbank*, [1897] 2 Ch. 96; *Wickham v. Hawker*, (1840) 7 M. & W. 63; *Nicholls v. Ely Beet Sugar Factory Ltd.*, [1931] 2 Ch. 84.

[76] *Re Vickers' Lease, Pocock v. Vickers*, [1947] Ch. 420.

[77] *Blount v. Layard*, [1891] 2 Ch. 681.

[78] *Carter v. Murcot*, (1768) 4 Burr. 2162.

[79] *Rogers v. Allen*, (1808) 1 Camp. 309.

be claimed by the inhabitants of ancient tenements in a borough for the reason that a fluctuating and uncertain body cannot claim a *profit a prendre*.[80] Neither can a *profit a prendre* be claimed by prescription on behalf of a large and indefinite class described as "owners and occupiers".[81] A prescriptive right may be claimed as common law or under the Prescription Act 1832, but rights in gross are not within that Act.[82]

Evidence of title to fisheries

Fisheries in tidal waters

Because Magna Charta, in 1225, made all grants by the Crown of several fisheries in tidal waters illegal, evidence of title to a several fishery in tidal waters must be shown to have existed prior to that date. This can be shown by means of an express grant or charter from the Crown, but otherwise establishing title will depend upon prescriptive rights. Hence if evidence is given of long enjoyment of a fishery, to the exclusion of others, and this enjoyment is of such a character as to establish that it has been dealt with as a right, as distinct from separate property, and there is nothing in the circumstances to show that the grant is of modern origin, a reasonable presumption is that the entitlement was created before the date of legal memory, 1189.[83]

Fisheries in non–tidal waters

Title to the ownership of a fishery in non–tidal waters may be proved in the same way as ownership of a fishery in tidal waters. Evidence of the early history of a fishery may be useful or necessary in defining the boundaries of the fishery, or showing that the fishery is attached to the soil and other issues. However, it is generally the case that the title to a fishery in non–tidal waters need not be proved any further back in time than would title to any other kind of real property.[84]

---

[80] *Goodman v. Saltash Corpn.*, (1882) 48 L.T. 239; *Mills v. Colchester Corpn.*, (1868) L.R. 3 C.P. 575.

[81] *Tilbury v. Silva*, (1890) 45 Ch. D. 98; *Harris v. Chesterfield (Earl)*, [1911] A.C. 623.

[82] *Shuttleworth v. Le Fleming*, (1865) 19 C.B.N.S. 687.

[83] *Malcomson v. O'Dea*, (1863) 10 H.L.C. 593.

[84] See Moore *The History and Law of Fisheries* (1903) p.143.

Documentary evidence

In providing evidence of title to a fishery the claimant is required to produce the grant or charter and all other documents relating to the fishery along with evidence of possession and actual use of the fishery for a period sufficient to establish the right claimed. In one instance a corporation claimed the exclusive right to a fishery in a haven and their lessees brought an action against two fishermen for an invasion of that right.[85] The plaintiffs offered as evidence a charter from the reign of Elizabeth I confirming former charters of the corporation and providing them with powers to make byelaws for the preservation of the fish in the haven. In addition to a statute for the preservation of the haven, records of an action brought by the corporation in 1792 against fisherman for dredging for oysters in the water and entries of payments to the corporation for licences to fish in the haven were produced in support of the claim. On the basis of this evidence it was held that a finding that the corporation possessed the right they claimed was justified.

A range of different kinds of documents coming out of proper custody and purporting to show the existence of ownership may be admitted by a court to prove rights of fishery. Such documents have included old leases and counterparts,[86] old licences or court rolls,[87] collectors' accounts showing receipt of rent,[88] proceedings and decrees of former suits in respect of the fishery,[89] entries in rate books,[90] and land tax assessments.[91] Similarly it has been held that proof of payment of rent under a lease is sufficient evidence of a private right of fishing.[92]

---

[85] *Mannall v. Fisher* (1859) 23 J. P. 375; and see also *Neill v. Devonshire (Duke)*, (1882) 8 A.C. 135; *Lord Advocate v. Lovat*, (1880) 5 A.C. 273; *Tighe v. Sinnott*, [1897] 1 Ir.R. 140; *Johnston v. O'Neill*, [1911] A.C. 552.

[86] *Malcomson v. O'Dea*, (1863) 10 H.L.C. 593.

[87] *Rogers v. Allen*, (1808) 1 Camp 309; *Attorney-General v. Emerson*, [1891] A.C. 649.

[88] *Percival v. Nanson*, (1851) 7 Ex. 1.

[89] *Neill v. Devonshire (Duke)*, (1882) 8 A.C. 135; *Johnston v. O'Neill*, [1911] A.C. 552.

[90] *Smith v. Andrews*, [1891] 2 Ch. 678.

[91] *Doe d. Strode v. Seaton*, (1834) 2 A. & E. 171.

[92] *Gabbett v. Clancy*, (1845) 8 I.L.R. 299; *Greenbank v. Sanderson*, (1884) 49 J.P. 40.

Evidence of possession

Evidence of actual use and enjoyment of a several fishery by a plaintiff for a long period of time is sufficient evidence to presume that the right of fishery had existed since before Magna Charta and was based upon a valid grant of the fishery by the Crown. If this is shown then it falls to the defendant to establish either that the right was actually created after Magna Charta, or that at some time after Magna Charta no private fishery was in existence in the waters at issue.[93] In the absence of evidence to the contrary, proof of enjoyment of a fishery for fifty years[94] and, in another case, twenty years[95] have been held to be sufficient to establish ownership.

In the absence of evidence of possession and enjoyment, even the clearest apparent title to a several fishery, on paper only, will not exclude a public right of fishing in tidal waters. Recitals in documents as to grant by the Crown alone are no evidence of what is there recited, though actual possession in conformity with them will constitute a *prima facie* title to the fishery.[96] Possession must be considered in every case with reference to the particular circumstances, thus acts which might imply possession in one case may be wholly inadequate to prove it in another.[97] However, in relation to an identified fishery, evidence of acts of ownership in respect of any part of it will be taken to apply to the whole of the fishery.[98] In actions involving trespass where an individual fishes in a non–tidal river, it is only necessary to prove actual possession.[99]

Evidence of possession to support a claim of ownership of a several fishery may include the use of fixed engines on the foreshore and bed of a tidal navigable river,[100] the taking of fish with nets in a river by

---

[93] *Northumberland (Duke) v. Houghton*, (1870) 22 L.T. 491; see also *Leconfield v. Lonsdale*, (1870) 23 L.T. 155.

[94] *R. v. Downing*, (1870) 23 L.T. 398.

[95] *Halse v. Alder*, (1874) 38 J.P. 407.

[96] *Bristow v. Cormican*, (1878) 3 A.C. 641.

[97] *Lord Advocate v. Lovat*, (1880) 5 A.C. 273.

[98] *Neill v. Devonshire (Duke)*, (1882) 8 A.C. 135.

[99] *Bristow v. Cormican*, (1878) 3 A.C. 641.

[100] *Fitzhardinge (Lord) v. Purcell*, [1908] 2 Ch. 139; *Edgar v. English Fisheries Special Commissioners*, (1870), 23 L.T. 732; and see p.428 below on the meaning of "fixed engine".

the claimant,[101] granting or taking a lease in a fishery,[102] or receiving rent under a fishery lease.[103] Similarly acts by riparian owners, such as the placing of stakes and wattles on the soil of a river to prevent erosion by flood, cutting weeds, taking gravel and making cattle pens in the stream have also been taken to be *prima facie* acts of ownership.[104]

Presumptions as to ownership of fisheries

In tidal waters

Prima facie the Crown is entitled to every part of the foreshore of the sea between high and low water mark and to soil of tidal rivers so far as the tide flows and reflows and the right of fishery thereover is *prima facie* vested in the public.[105] However, where proof of ownership of a several fishery over part of the foreshore or tidal waters can be shown, this raises a presumption against the Crown that the freehold ownership of the soil beneath those waters is vested in the owner of the private fishery.[106] Accordingly, where a person is established to be the owner of a several fishery in tidal waters he may be presumed to be the owner of the soil.[107]

In non–tidal waters

In relation to the right of fishing in non–tidal waters or inland watercourses, it is presumed that the ownership is vested in the several riparian owners *ad medium filum aquae*, and if the same person is the owner of both banks of a watercourse then he has the entire fishing to the extent of the length of his land.[108] In the case of a private watercourse flowing through a manor, the presumption is that each owner of land within the manor on the bank of the watercourse has the right of fishing

[101] *Lord Advocate v. Lovat*, (1880) 5 A.C. 273.

[102] *R. v. Alfresford*, (1786) 1 T.R. 358; *Ecroyd v. Coulthard*, [1898] 2 Ch. 358.

[103] *Greenback v. Sanderson*, (1884) 49 J.P. 40.

[104] *Hanbury v. Jenkins*, [1901] 2 Ch. 401.

[105] *Malcomson v. O'Dea*, (1863) 10 H.L.C. 593.

[106] *Attorney–General v. Emerson*, [1891] A.C. 649; *Beaufort (Duke) v. Aird (John) & Co.*, (1904) 20 T.L.R. 602.

[107] *Somerset (Duke) v. Fogwell*, (1826) 5 B. & C. 875.

[108] *Tracey Elliott v. Morley (Earl)*, (1907) 51 S.J. 625; and see p.17 above on the *medium filum* rule generally.

in front of his land, and if the lord of the manor claims ownership of the fishery he must produce evidence to support that contention.[109] Where a watercourse divides two properties, there is a presumption that the precise line of division is the middle of the watercourse.[110]

The converse of these presumptions is that, if a several fishery is proved to exist in a watercourse, the owner of the fishery is presumed, in absence of evidence to the contrary, to be the owner of the soil over which his fishery extends whether the watercourse is navigable or non navigable.[111] Despite this presumption, however, it is clear that a several fishery is capable of existing independently of the ownership of the soil of the watercourse.[112]

Rebuttal of presumptions

The presumptions which apply in relation to the ownership of fisheries and the soil of fisheries are capable of rebuttal on proof of surrounding circumstances in relation to the particular property which negative the claimant's exclusive right to the bed of the watercourse or the fishery therein.[113] Thus, where it was attempted to raise a presumption that a right of several fishery within a manor passed to the lord by a deed as appurtenant to the manor, that presumption was rebutted by proof that, before the date of the deed, owners of the land within the manor and on the bank of the river had been entitled to the right of fishery therein.[114]

Boundaries of fisheries

As a general principle, the extent in length of a right of fishery along the course of a watercourse is determined by the length of riparian land belonging to the owner of the fishery, or by the limits assigned to the fishery by the particular conveyance, grant, lease or licence, or by its use and enjoyment in the case of a presumed grant. Hence in the case of a

---

[109] *Lamb v. Newbiggin*, (1844) 1 Car. & Kir. 549.

[110] *Chesterfield (Lord) v. Harris*, [1908] 2 Ch. 397.

[111] *Hanbury v. Jenkins*, [1901] 2 Ch. 401; *Hindson v. Ashby*, [1896] 2 Ch. 1; *Holford v. Bailey*, (1849) 13 Q.B.D. 426; *Somerset (Duke) v. Fogwell*, (1826) 5 B. & C. 875; *Partheriche v. Mason*, (1774) 2 Chit. 658.

[112] *Marshall v. Ulleswater Steam Navigation Co.*, (1863) 3 B. & S. 732.

[113] *Devonshire (Duke) v. Pattison*, (1887) 20 Q.B.D. 263.

[114] *Lamb v. Newbiggin*, (1844) 1 Car. & Kir. 549.

manorial fishery, it was held that the extent of the fishery was determined by the boundaries of the manor.[115] Likewise, fisheries on the foreshore are usually limited to the foreshore of the manors, though occasionally a sea fishery, such as an oyster bed, will be held to extend for some distance below the low water mark.[116]

In respect of the width of a fishery in a non–tidal watercourse, the respective riparian owners are presumed to be the owners of the soil of one half of the stream and are entitled to fish the watercourse *ad medium filum*. This principle is applicable unless the same person owns both banks, in which case that person will *prima facie* own the fishing over the entire bed of the watercourse to the extent of his ownership of the riparian land.[117] In relation to a Scottish river where the opposite banks were in different ownership, it has been held that each proprietor was entitled to stand on his own bank, or to wade out to the *medium filum* limit of his property in the bed of the river, and to fish as far across the river as he could reach by normal casting, and was not restricted to casting up to the limit of the medium filum.[118]

Normally, the *medium filum* of a non–tidal watercourse is defined as a line running down the centre of the watercourse at the ordinary state of flow, that is, without regard to periods of flood water or drought.[119] Ascertaining the *medium filum* of a tidal watercourse containing fish may be a matter of some difficulty. In the case of certain wide estuaries, the riparian manors, which include the fisheries, are limited to their respective foreshores and, therefore, the extent of the width of their fisheries may be determined without too much difficulty. However, in certain tidal rivers with narrow estuaries, the manors and fisheries extend

---

115 *Stephens v. Snell*, [1939] 3 All E.R. 622.

116 *Gann v. Free Fishers of Whitstable*, (1865), 11 H.L.C. 192; *Foreman v. Free Fishers of Whitstable*, (1869), L.R. 4 H.L. 266; *Loose v. Castleton*, (1978) *The Times*, 21 June (1978).

117 *Tracey Elliott v. Morley (Earl)*, (1907) 51 Sol. Jo. 625; *Waterford Conservators v. Connolly*, (1889) 24 I.L.T. 7; and see p.17 above concerning the *medium filum* rule generally.

118 *Fotheringham v. Kerr*, (1984) *The Times* 25 May 1984; but see *Lovett v. Fairclough*, (1990) *The Times* 10 March 1990.

119 *Hindson v. Ashby*, [1896] 1 Ch. 78; and see Moore *The History and Law of Fisheries*, (1903) pp.114 to 118.

to midstream and different views may be taken as to the width of those fisheries.

On one view, the *medium filum* is taken to be the middle of the river at its state of low water, with the low water channel of fresh water defining the boundary between riparian manors and fisheries. On another view, the *medium filum* is taken to be a line drawn along the centre of the river at times of high water when the flow is at the ordinary high water mark on each side. Clearly there may be particular instances where the two approaches lead to widely discrepant results, and yet the issue as to which of these methods of determination is the correct one has not been the subject of any authoritative judicial resolution.[120]

Additional difficulties may arise in relation to watercourses that undergo a change in course over a period of time. It has been held that in a several fishery in a tidal river, the waters of which permanently receded from one channel and started to flow in another, the fishery could not be followed from the old to the new channel.[121] However, where a river channel gradually and imperceptibly changed its course over a period of years, it was held that an exclusive right of fishery over the whole bed of the river would follow the change in the course of the river.[122] Similarly, where two persons each had an exclusive right to fish in an estuary, each to the middle line of the river flowing through it, and the river changed its course through the estuary, the limit of each fishery continued to be the middle line of the new channel of the river.[123]

Fisheries in lakes and ponds

The Crown is not ordinarily entitled to the soil of fisheries of an inland non–tidal lake, irrespective of its size, and no public right of fishery can exist in these waters,[124] whether they are navigable or not.[125] If

---

120 See Moore *The History and Law of Fisheries*, (1903) Ch.XX; Hale's First Treatise, *De Jure Maris*, in Moore A History of the Foreshore (3rd ed. 1888) at p.354; *Pearce v. Bunting*, (1896) 60 J.P. 695; *Thames Conservators v. Smeed Dean & Co.*, [1897] 2 Q.B. 334; *Miller v. Little*, (1879) 4 L.R. Ir. 304.

121 *Carlisle Corpn. v. Graham*, (1869) 21 L.T. 333.

122 *Foster v. Wright*, (1878) 44 J.P. 7; *Hindson v. Ashby*, [1896] 2 Q.B. 1.

123 *Miller v. Little*, (1879) 4 L.R. Ir. 304.

124 *Johnston v. O'Neill*, [1911] A.C. 552; *Bristow v. Cormican*, (1878) 3 A.C. 641.

a pond is situated in land which has a single owner then, *prima facie*, the right of fishing is vested in the owner,[126] and where a lake lies between a number of manors it appears that the rights of fishery are divided *ad medium filum aquae*.[127] Although a person may construct a fish pond on his own land, he may not do so on a common if this disturbs the commoners' rights.[128]

Fisheries in canals and reservoirs

The right of fishery in a canal or reservoir is usually regulated by the provisions of the statute under which the canal or reservoir is constructed. Accordingly, the owners of land on either side may have the sole, exclusive and several right of fishing in so much of the canal as was made over or through their land,[129] together with the right to use the towpath and banks of the canal in exercise of their rights.[130] The public have no right to fish in a canal,[131] nor, if a non–tidal watercourse is rendered statutorily navigable, do the public acquire any right to fish therein.[132]

Fishing paths

A fishery owner has no right to land and deposit nets or walk along the bank of a watercourse for purposes of fishing unless he is the owner of the bank or has the consent of the owner of the soil,[133] but a prescriptive right to do so may be presumed depending upon the

---

125 *Bloomfield v. Johnston*, (1868) I.R. 8 C.L. 68; *R. v. Burrow*, (1869) 34 J.P. 53; *Pery v. Thornton*, (1889), 23 L.R. Ir. 402.

126 *Clarke v. Mercer*, (1859) 1 F. & F. 492.

127 *Marshall v. Ulleswater Steam Navigation Co.*, (1863) 3 B. & S. 732.

128 *Reeve v. Digby*, (1638) Cro. Car. 495.

129 *Grand Union Canal Co. v. Ashby*, (1861) 6 H. & N. 394; *Snape v. Dobbs*, (1823) 1 Bing. 202.

130 *Staffordshire & Worcestershire Canal Navigation v. Bradley*, [1912] 1 Ch. 91.

131 *Mussett v. Birch*, (1876) 35 L.T. 486.

132 *Hargreaves v. Diddams*, (1875) 32 L.T. 600; *Peace v. Scotcher*, (1882) 9 Q.B.D. 162.

133 *Ipswich v. Browne*, (1581) Savil. 11, 14.

evidence of use.[134] The public have no right to fish from river banks which are in private ownership, although they may have a right to fish in the river.[135] Similarly, there is no public right to fish from a public highway beside a river,[136] nor from a canal towpath.[137] In tidal waters the public may use the foreshore for fishing[138] and fishermen may in some circumstances be presumed to have a right to land nets on the shore above the ordinary high water mark.[139]

Weirs obstructing fisheries

The erection of weirs in navigable rivers was forbidden from early times by statute. Magna Charta, in 1225, enacted that "all weirs from henceforth shall be utterly put down in Thames and Medway and throughout all England except by the sea coast", and similar declarations were made in later statutes.[140] These provisions have been held to apply only to navigable rivers,[141] and a weir is not illegal if it can be shown to have been granted by the Crown before the reign of Edward I.[142] Also, fishing weirs may exist in non-navigable rivers although constructed more recently than the reign of Edward I, and a right to such weirs in private waters may be acquired by grant from other riparian owners, or by enjoyment or by any other means by which such rights may be constituted.[143] Once the right to an ancient weir has been proved, it must not be raised, altered or enlarged, and not converted from a brushwood to a stone weir.[144] In addition, it may be noted, fishing weirs are subject to

---

134 *Gray v. Bond*, (1821) 2 B. & B. 667; *Shuttleworth v. Le Fleming*, (1865) 19 C.B.N.S. 687.

135 *Ball v. Herbert*, (1789) 3 T.R. 253.

136 *Harrison v. Rutland (Duke)*, [1893] 1 Q.B. 142.

137 *Staffordshire and Worcestershire Canal Navigation v. Bradley*, [1912] 1 Ch. 91.

138 *Blundell v. Catterall*, (1821) 5 B. & Ald. 268.

139 *Gray v. Bond*, (1821) 2 B. & B. 667.

140 25 Edward III, st. 4, c.4 (1350); 45 Edward III, c.2 (1371); 17 Richard II, c.9 (1393); 1 Henry IV, c.12 (1399); 4 Henry IV, c.11 (1402); 12 Edward IV, c.7 (1472).

141 *Leconfield v. Lonsdale*, (1870) 23 L.T. 155.

142 *Williams v. Wilcox*, (1838) 8 Ad. & El. 314.

143 *Rolle v. Whyte*, (1868) 7 B. & S. 116.

144 *Chester Mill Case*, (1610) 10 Co. Rep. 137b; *Weld v. Hornby*, (1806) 7 East 195.

regulation under the provisions of the Salmon and Freshwater Fisheries Act 1975.[145]

Disturbance of fisheries[146]

An action will lie at common law for the disturbance of a fishery,[147] and similarly the act of stealing fish from a private pond was, at common law, an indictable offence.[148] A right to fish and to take away any fish caught is a *profit a prendre* and an incorporeal hereditament and the owner of this interest has a right of action for an injunction and damages against anyone who unlawfully does any act which disturbs the exercise or enjoyment of the right.[149] Disturbance of a several fishery is an invasion of a private right and it is not necessary to prove pecuniary loss in order to sustain an action. Injury to the legal right carries with it the right to damages.[150] Hence, where a canoeist disturbed fish in a river and interfered with an incorporeal fishery, the plaintiff was awarded nominal damages and given liberty to apply to the county court for an injunction despite the fact that no damage was caused and no person was actually fishing at the time of the incident.[151]

Damaging a fishery by interfering with the free passage of fish up a river by the erection of weirs across a river which have the effect of preventing fish from reaching the upper reaches of a river constitutes an injury to the owners of the upper waters and gives rise to an action for damages and will be restrained by an injunction.[152] The courts will grant

[145] ss.6 to 18 Salmon and Freshwater Fisheries Act 1975; see p.428 below.

[146] See also the discussion of navigation and fisheries at p.139 above.

[147] *Child v. Greenhill*, (1639) Cro. Car. 553; *Smith v. Kemp*, (1693) 2 Salk. 637; *Holford v. Bailey*, (1849) 13 Q.B. 426.

[148] *Gray's Case*, (1594) Owen 20; *R. v. Steer*, (1704) 6 Mod. Rep. 183; and see p.451 below on the theft of fish.

[149] *Fitzgerald v. Firbank*, [1897] 2 Ch. 96; *Granby (Marquis) v. Bakewell U.D.C.*, (1923) 87 J.P. 105.

[150] *Nicholls v. Ely Beet Sugar Factory Ltd.*, [1931] 2 Ch. 84.

[151] *Rawson v. Peters*, (1972) *The Times* 2 November 1972, C.A; *Wills' Trustees v. Cairngorm Canoeing and Sailing School Ltd.*, (1976) S.L.T. 162; *Tennent and Caroll Industries PLC v. Clancy*, [1988] I.L.R.M. 214.

[152] *Hamilton v. Donegal (Marquis)*, (1795) 3 Ridg. P.R. 267; *Weld v. Hornby*, (1806) 7 East 195; *Barker v. Faulkner*, (1898) 79 L.T. 24; *Pirie & Sons Ltd. v. Kintore (Earl)*, [1906] A.C. 478; *Fraser v. Fear*, (1912) 107 L.T. 423.

an injunction to restrain a person from enclosing the bed of a river where this has the effect of destroying the fishery.[153] Likewise causing water to overflow into another person's fishery will be actionable as a trespass although done by an action on the defendant's own soil.[154] Similarly, in a wide range of circumstances, causing pollution of watercourses will be actionable by downstream fishery owners due to the consequences of such activities upon fisheries.[155]

---

153 *Bridges v. Highton*, (1865) 11 L.T. 653.

154 *Courtney v. Collet*, (1697) 12 Mod. Rep. 164.

155 See Ch.11 on water pollution generally.

Chapter 9

WATER REGULATION

RECENT DEVELOPMENTS IN WATER REGULATION

The background to the Water Act 1989

Before 1 September 1989 both the management of the water industry and the protection of the aquatic environment had been the responsibility of water authorities provided with powers under the Water Act 1973. The 1973 Act had established a system of integrated water management whereby regional water authorities had comprehensive responsibility for all aspects of the water cycle involving duties with respect to water supply and sewage treatment along with pollution control, water resources, land drainage and a range of other matters relating to the management of watercourses. The system of integrated water management was entirely reformed by the Water Act 1989.

The Water Act 1989 was preceded by a series of legislative proposals and consultative documents which provide an indication as to the objectives behind the eventual legislation. Initially, the intention to repeal the Water Act 1973, which provided for the constitution, powers and duties of water authorities, and to transfer water management to the private sector was set out in the Government's 1986 White Paper, *Privatisation of Water Authorities in England and Wales*.[1] The White Paper proposed the retention of the philosophy of integrated management of the water cycle, which had underpinned the 1973 Act, with complete responsibility for water passing to privately owned Water Service Public Limited Companies. The privatised water companies would assume comprehensive responsibility for all the functions previously undertaken by water authorities, subject to regulation of certain services by a Director General of Water Services and representation by consumer committees. Ministers would retain ultimate responsibility for environmental policy.

Difficulties with the initial proposals for re-organisation of the water industry soon became evident as a consequence of the consultation process following the issue of the 1986 White Paper. Essentially, two

---

[1] Cmnd.9734.

problems underlay the plan to entrust unified water management responsibilities to private water companies. First, an unavoidable commercial conflict of interests was anticipated in allowing privately owned concerns to exercise a regulatory role over other private concerns, as would be necessary if implementation of the proposals meant, for example, that one private discharger would become responsible for granting discharge consents[2] to other industrial dischargers. Secondly, doubts were expressed as to whether the water companies which were proposed would, as private bodies, be legally capable of acting as "competent authorities" for the purpose of implementing European Community water legislation.[3]

The difficulties inherent in the original 1986 White Paper proposals were eventually recognised, and the Government came to accept the objections to private water companies acting as both "poachers and gamekeepers" in policing the aquatic environment. Modified proposals for the restructuring of water management were set out in a Department of the Environment's discussion paper of 1987, *The National Rivers Authority: the Government's Proposals for a Public Regulatory Body in a Privatised Water Industry*. The revised basis for water privatisation limited the extent of private ownership to the utility functions of water supply and sewerage services. The environmental and regulatory functions previously exercised by water authorities were to remain within the public sector and to be exercised by a National Rivers Authority.

Within the overall division between the administration of utility and regulatory functions of the re–organised water industry, the opportunity was taken to bring about a number of reforms directed towards improvement in the state of the aquatic environment. The Department of the Environment's 1986 consultation paper, *The Water Environment: the Next Steps*, set out a number of general objectives for protection of the aquatic environment which were to be accomplished alongside the re–structuring of water management. These requirements were stated as follows: (a) the need for a clearer framework of national environmental policy within which local decisions and local action on matters such as the protection of particular stretches of river could be

---

[2] On discharge consents see p.304 below.

[3] On European Community water legislation see p.355 below.

taken; (b) the need for regulatory systems to be simple, clear, justifiable and affordable, with firm safeguards against abuse; (c) the need for the public to have adequate access to information; and (d) the need for financing and charging systems to allocate costs effectively to those whose actions give rise to those costs.

More specifically in relation to the environmental functions of the National Rivers Authority, a number of objectives are set out in relation to the protection of water quality. These are: (a) the setting of quality objectives and standards for all waters on a statutory basis; (b) the provision of a power to ensure the implementation of specific national policies for environmental protection, including European Community directives on the discharge of certain substances; (c) the charging for those whose acts or omission which make the use of controls necessary; and (d) further measures for the avoidance of pollution such as the designation of protection zones.

The Public Utility Transfers and Water Charges Act 1988 provided public utilities, including the former water authorities, with the powers needed to prepare for privatisation. The 1988 Act provided that where the Secretary of State proposed that any property or functions of a public utility were to be transferred to another corporate body, the functions of that utility were to include the power to do anything appropriate to facilitate the implementation of transfer and related proposals by the Secretary of State.[4]

The Water Act 1989, which gained royal assent on 6 July 1989, transferred water supply and sewage treatment functions to the private sector in the hands of the Water Utility Companies, leaving the National Rivers Authority with responsibility for monitoring and regulating the water environment. The preamble to the Act listed the range of principal objectives and subsidiary reforms to be accomplished by the legislation in the following manner.

> "An Act to provide for the establishment and functions of a National Rivers Authority and of committees to advise that Authority; to provide for the transfer of the property, rights and liabilities of water authorities to the National Rivers Authority and to companies nominated by the Secretary of State and for the

[4] s.1 Public Utility Transfers and Water Charges Act 1988. See *Sheffield City Council v. Yorkshire Water Services*, (1990) *The Times* 5 June 1990.

dissolution of those authorities; to provide for the appointment and functions of a Director General of Water Services and of customer services committees; to provide for companies to be appointed to be water undertakers and sewerage undertakers and for the regulation of the appointed companies; to make provision with respect to, and the finances of, the nominated companies, holding companies of the nominated companies and statutory water companies; to amend the law relating to the supply of water and the law relating to the provision of sewers and the treatment and disposal of sewage; to amend the law with respect to pollution of water and the law with respect to its abstraction from inland waters and underground strata; to make new provision in relation to flood defence and fisheries; to transfer functions with respect to navigation, conservancy and harbours to the National Rivers Authority; and for connected purposes."

Accordingly, the key elements in the new organisational structure for water management and the protection of the aquatic environment are the National Rivers Authority, Water Services Public Limited Companies, referred to in the Act as "water and sewerage undertakers", the Director General of Water Services and customer services committees and the Secretary of State.

The water consolidation legislation

The enactment of the Water Act 1989, bringing about the privatisation of the water industry and establishing the National Rivers Authority with the principal duty of regulating the aquatic environment, was thought to have left the body of enactments relating to water law in a relatively untidy state, with provisions located in a large number of Acts often without clear functional divisions between them. Accordingly, a consolidation process dealing with water law was instigated by the Law Commission acting under the Law Commission Act 1965. The process of consolidation involved the repeal of diverse Acts dealing with water law and the replacement of those provisions by a relatively small number of Acts allowing for a rationalisation in the presentation of the law. This process allowed for enactments making only minor substantive changes, and of a non–controversial character, to be subject to the special

Parliamentary procedure provided for under the Consolidation of Enactments (Procedure) Act 1949. Although the consolidation exercise introduced a number of amendments to the law, discussed in the Law Commission's *Report on the Consolidation of Certain Enactments Relating to Water*,[5] these were relatively minor in their effect and introduced primarily for the purpose of ensuring consistency in the new legislation.

The outcome of the consolidation process was the passage of five Acts on 25 July 1991: the Water Resources Act 1991; the Water Industry Act 1991; the Land Drainage Act 1991; the Statutory Water Companies Act 1991; and the Water Consolidation (Consequential Provisions) Act 1991. These are referred to as "the consolidation Acts",[6] and came into force on 1 December 1991.

The Water Resources Act 1991

Although important matters in relation to watercourses are provided for under the Land Drainage Act 1991 and the Salmon and Freshwater Fisheries Act 1975, in relation to the law concerning watercourses, the most significant of the new enactments is the Water Resources Act 1991. This re-enacts provisions for the establishment of the National Rivers Authority and the principal functions of the Authority which were previously provided for under Parts I and III of the Water Act 1989. In addition, a range of transitional provisions and savings from the 1989 Act continue to have effect for the purpose of the 1991 Act. Hence, it is stated that any subordinate legislation, application or appointment made, consent or approval given, licence or certificate issued or other thing done under or for the purposes of repealed enactments, including the Water Act 1989, is to have effect for the purpose of preserving continuity as if done under the corresponding provision of the consolidation Acts.[7]

The overall structure of the Water Resources Act 1991 is as follows:

Part I: Preliminary

---

[5] (1991) Cm.1483.

[6] s.1(1) Water Consolidation (Consequential Provisions) Act 1991.

[7] Sch.2 para.1 Water Consolidation (Consequential Provisions) Act 1991.

Chapter I: The National Rivers Authority
Chapter II: Committees with Functions in Relation to the Authority
Chapter III: General Duties

Part II: Water Resources Management
Chapter I: General Management Functions
Chapter II: Abstraction and Impounding
Chapter III: Drought

Part III: Control of Pollution of Water Resources
Chapter I: Quality Objectives
Chapter II: Pollution Offences
Chapter III: Powers to Prevent and Control Pollution
Chapter IV: Supplemental Provisions with respect to Water Pollution

Part IV: Flood Defence

Part V: General Control of Fisheries

Part VI: Financial Provisions in relation to the Authority
Chapter I: General Financial Provisions
Chapter II: Revenue Provisions
Chapter III: Grants and Loans

Part VII: Land and Works Powers
Chapter I: Powers of the Authority
Chapter II: Powers of Entry
Chapter III: Provisions Supplemental to Land and Works Powers

Part VIII: Information Provisions

Part IX: Miscellaneous and Supplemental
Schedule 1: The National Rivers Authority
Schedule 2: Orders and Agreements for transfer of Navigation, Harbour and Conservancy Functions
Schedule 3: Boundaries of Regional Flood Defence Areas
Schedule 4: Membership and Proceedings of Regional and Local Flood Defence Committees
Schedule 5: Procedure relating to Statements on Minimum Acceptable Flow
Schedule 6: Orders providing for Exemption from Restrictions on Abstraction
Schedule 7: Licences of Right

Schedule 8: Proceedings on Applications for Drought Orders
Schedule 9: Compensation in respect of Drought Orders
Schedule 10: Discharge Consents
Schedule 11: Water Protection Zone Orders
Schedule 12: Nitrate Sensitive Areas
Schedule 13: Transitional Water Pollution Provisions
Schedule 14: Orders transferring Main River Functions to the Authority
Schedule 15: Supplemental provisions with respect to Drainage Charges
Schedule 16: Schemes imposing Special Drainage Charges
Schedule 17: Orders with respect to Navigation Tolls
Schedule 18: Modification of Compensation Provisions etc. in relation to the Creation of New Rights
Schedule 19: Orders conferring Compulsory Works Powers
Schedule 20: Supplemental Provisions with respect to Powers of Entry
Schedule 21: Compensation etc. in respect of certain works powers
Schedule 22: Protection for particular Undertakings
Schedule 23: Mineral Rights
Schedule 24: Disclosure of Information
Schedule 25: Byelaw–making powers of the Authority
Schedule 26: Procedure relating to Byelaws made by the Authority.

THE NATIONAL RIVERS AUTHORITY

The constitution of the National Rivers Authority

The Water Act 1989 provided that there was to be a body corporate to be known as the National Rivers Authority for the purpose of carrying out the functions assigned or transferred to it under that Act.[8]

---

[8] s.1(1) Water Act 1989. On the "transfer date" appointed by the Secretary of State, the functions of the former water authorities became functions of the National Rivers Authority or of water or sewerage undertakers. This reallocation of functions took place alongside schemes for the division of property, rights and liabilities of the

The Water Resources Act 1991 provides for the continuation of the Authority for the purpose of carrying out specified functions.[9] Accordingly, the Authority is to consist of not less than eight nor more than fifteen members, of whom two are to be appointed by the Minister, and the others are to be appointed by the Secretary of State.[10] The Secretary of State is to designate one of the members appointed by him as the chairman of the Authority, and may designate another member as the deputy chairman. In appointing members of the Authority, the Secretary of State and the Minister are to have regard to the desirability of appointing persons who have experience of, and have shown capacity in, some matter relevant to the functions of the Authority. The Authority is not to be regarded as the servant or agent of the Crown, or as exempt from any tax, duty, rate, levy or other charge whether general or local. The property of the Authority is not to be regarded as property of, or property held on behalf of, the Crown.[11]

The detailed matters on the organisation and financial provisions concerning the National Rivers Authority are set out in Schedule 1 to the Water Resources Act 1991.[12] In relation to membership of the Authority, this provides for re–appointment, resignation and removal of members, and the provision of remuneration and pensions to members. The Authority is empowered, with the approval of the Secretary of State, to appoint officers and employees and, with the exception of certain flood defence functions being carried out exclusively by regional flood defence committees, anything authorised or required to be done by the Authority may be done by an authorised member, officer or employee. The Authority may regulate its own proceedings, of which minutes are to be

---

former water authorities between the Authority and the successor companies taking over responsibility for water supply and sewage treatment, provided for under s.4(1) and Sch.2 to the Water Act 1989 (see Water Authorities (Successor Companies) Order 1989, S.I. 1989 No.1465). The "transfer date" appointed for the purposes of these transitions was 1 September 1989 (see Water Authorities (Transfer of Functions) (Appointed Day) Order 1989, S.I. 1989 No.1530).

[9] s.1(1) Water Resources Act 1991.

[10] s.1(2). The general interpretation section of the Water Resources Act 1991 (s.221) provides that "the Minister" means the Minister of Agriculture, Fisheries and Food, and "the Ministers" means the Secretary of State and the Minister.

[11] s.1(3) to (5).

[12] Sch.1 takes effect under s.1(6).

kept. Documents issued by the Authority, and executed under its seal or signed by an authorised person, are to be treated as being issued by the Authority unless the contrary is shown.

Principal functions of the Authority

The principal functions of the National Rivers Authority are (a) functions with respect to water resources under Part II of the Water Resources Act 1991; (b) functions with respect to water pollution under Part III; (c) functions with respect to flood defence and land drainage under Part IV, the Land Drainage Act 1991 and other specified provisions;[13] (d) functions with respect to fisheries under Part V of the Water Resources Act 1991, the Diseases of Fish Act 1937, the Sea Fisheries Regulation Act 1966, the Salmon and Freshwater Fisheries Act 1975 and other enactments relating to fisheries;[14] (e) the functions as a navigation, harbour or conservancy authority which were transferred to the Authority;[15] (f) functions assigned to the Authority by any other enactment.[16] These matters are dealt with in following Chapters of this work in relation to the specific topics to which they relate.

Without prejudice to the general environmental and recreational duties imposed upon the Authority,[17] it is the duty of the Authority, to such an extent as it considers desirable, generally to promote, (a) the conservation and enhancement of the natural beauty and amenity of inland and coastal waters and of land associated with those waters; (b) the conservation of flora and fauna which are dependent on an aquatic environment; and (c) the use of those waters for recreational

---

[13] Specifically, functions transferred under s.136(8) and Sch.15 para.1(3) Water Act 1989 relating to local statutory provisions and subordinate legislation.

[14] Generally see Ch.13 below on fisheries under statute.

[15] Transfer of these functions took place by virtue of Ch.V of Part III Water Act 1989, of Sch.13 para.23(3) to that Act, and may be transferred to the Authority by an order or agreement under Sch.2 Water Resources Act 1991.

[16] s.2(1) Water Resources Act 1991. It is also the duty of the Authority to make arrangements for the carrying out of research and related activities, whether by the Authority or others, in respect of matters to which the functions of the Authority relate (s.2(3)).

[17] Under s.16, considered at p.211 below.

purposes. In relation to (c) it is the duty of the Authority to take into account the needs of persons who are chronically sick or disabled.[18]

Broadly, the Authority has regulatory responsibility for inland and coastal waters in England and Wales, but the precise area within which the Authority is to exercise its functions differs according to the different functions. Hence, in relation to restrictions upon abstraction and impounding, under Chapter II of Part II of the Water Resources Act 1991, and other water resources provisions, it is stated that these are not to apply to inland waters which are part of the River Tweed or are part of the River Esk or River Sark, or any tributary stream at a point where the banks of the river or stream is in Scotland. The functions of the Authority in relation to flood defence and land drainage extend to the territorial sea adjacent to England and Wales so far as the area of any regional flood defence committee includes any area of the territorial sea or provision is made for the exercise of any power in the territorial sea.[19] The area in respect of which the Authority is to carry out its functions in relation to fisheries is stated to be the whole of England and Wales, together with the adjacent territorial sea for a distance of six miles from the baselines from which the breadth of that sea is measured, and in relation to the general control of fisheries, under Part V of the Act, the Diseases of Fish Act 1937 and the Salmon and Freshwater Fisheries Act 1975, so much of the River Esk, with its banks and tributary streams up to their source, as is situated in Scotland.[20]

Incidental functions and powers of the Authority

In addition to the principal functions of the Authority, a range of other matters are provided for by way of incidental functions. Thus, the functions of the Authority are to be taken to include the protection

---

[18] s.2(2).

[19] s.165(2) and (3) allow for the exercise of flood defence and land drainage powers in the territorial sea. On the meaning of "territorial sea" see p.26 above. On the meaning of "regional flood defence committee" see p.375 below.

[20] s.2(4) to (6). The reference to "miles" means international nautical miles of 1,852 metres, and "the River Tweed" means "the river" within the meaning of the Tweed Fisheries Amendment Act 1859, as amended by byelaws (s.2(7) Water Resources Act 1991). In relation to the area of the Authority for the purpose of the control of pollution see p.290 below.

against pollution (a) of any waters, whether on the surface or underground, which belong to the Authority or any water undertaker or from which the Authority or any water undertaker is authorised to take water; (b) any reservoir which belongs to or is operated by the Authority or any water undertaker or which the Authority or any water undertaker is proposing to acquire or construct for the purpose of being so operated; and (c) any underground strata from which the Authority or any water undertaker is authorised to abstract water in pursuance of a licence under the abstraction and impounding provisions of the Water Resources Act 1991, contained in Chapter II of Part II of the Act. Additional incidental functions relate to the furtherance of research into functions conferred upon the Authority or water or sewerage undertaker; the carrying out of works or the acquisition of land jointly or on behalf of a water or sewerage undertaker; the provision of water supplies in bulk; and the provision of houses and recreation grounds for the use of persons employed by the Authority.[21]

The incidental general powers of the Authority enable it to do anything which, in the opinion of the Authority, is calculated to facilitate, or is conducive or incidental to, the carrying out of the Authority's functions. Without prejudice to the generality of this, the Authority has the power, for the purposes of, or in connection with, the carrying out of its functions, to institute criminal proceedings, to acquire and dispose of land and other property, and to carry out engineering or building operations.[22]

Ministerial directions to the Authority

Provision is made for general or specific Ministerial directions to be given to the Authority, and where a direction of either kind is given it is the duty of the Authority to comply with the direction. Specifically, directions may be given to the Authority by the Ministers (a) with respect to the carrying out of its principal functions relating to water resources, water pollution and as a navigation, harbour or conservancy authority, by the Secretary of State; (b) with respect to the designation of land as a

---

[21] s.3.

[22] s.4(1).

nitrate sensitive area,[23] in relation to flood defence and land drainage and fisheries, by either of the Ministers; and (c) with respect to anything not falling under (a) or (b) which is connected with the carrying on of the Authority's activities generally. Ministerial directions may include directions by the Secretary of State or the Minister of Agriculture, Fisheries and Food, or both, to enable the Government of the United Kingdom to give effect to any European Community obligations, or to any international agreement to which the United Kingdom is a party. However, the power to give a Ministerial direction is to be exercisable only after consultation with the Authority except in an emergency.[24]

COMMITTEES WITH FUNCTIONS IN RELATION TO THE AUTHORITY

The Advisory Committee for Wales

Provision was made under the Water Act 1989 for the maintenance of a committee to advise the Secretary of State on matters affecting or otherwise connected with the carrying out in Wales of the Authority's functions.[25] The Advisory Committee for Wales is to continue to be maintained and to consist of persons appointed by the Secretary of State.[26]

Regional rivers advisory committees

Although the National Rivers Authority is a national body, it is bound to operate in conjunction with regional rivers advisory committees acting initially in relation to the areas of the former water authorities. A threefold duty is imposed in relation to these committees requiring the Authority (a) to establish and maintain advisory committees, consisting of persons who are not members of the Authority, for the different regions of England and Wales; (b) to consult the advisory committee for any region as to any proposals of the Authority relating generally to the

---

[23] Under s.94, and see p.330 below.

[24] s.5.

[25] Under s.3 Water Act 1989.

[26] s.6 Water Resources Act 1991.

manner in which the Authority carries out its functions in that region; (c) to consider any representation made to it by the advisory committee for any region (whether in response to (b) or otherwise) as to the manner in which the Authority carries out its functions in that region. The Authority is to ensure that the persons appointed to each regional rivers advisory committee are persons who appear to have an interest in matters likely to be affected by the manner in which the Authority carries out its functions in the region concerned.[27]

Fisheries advisory committees

An additional duty is imposed upon the Authority in relation to regional and local fisheries advisory committees. This requires the Authority to establish and maintain advisory committees of persons who are not members of the Authority but are interested in salmon fisheries, trout fisheries, freshwater fisheries or eel fisheries in the different parts of the controlled area, and to consult those committees as to the manner in which the Authority is to perform its duty to maintain, improve and develop those fisheries. This duty requires the establishment and maintenance of a regional fisheries advisory committee for each region of the Authority's area and such local advisory committees as are necessary to represent the interests of fisheries within different parts of each region.[28]

Regional and local flood defence committees

Provision is made for the continuation of regional flood defence committees, the composition of those committees and changes in their composition.[29] Further provision is made for local flood defence schemes and local flood defence committees, the composition of these committees and their membership and proceedings.[30] The powers and duties of

---

[27] s.7.

[28] s.8.

[29] ss.9 to 11.

[30] ss.12 to 14.

regional and local flood defence committees are considered later in this work.[31]

GENERAL DUTIES

General duties with respect to the water industry

It is the duty of the Authority, in exercising any of its powers, to have particular regard to the duties imposed, by virtue of the provisions of Parts II to IV of the Water Industry Act 1991, on any water undertaker or sewerage undertaker, which appears to the Authority to be or to be likely to be affected by the exercise of the power in question. It is the duty of the Ministers, in exercising any power conferred under the Water Resources Act 1991, the Water Industry Act 1991 or the Water Act 1989 in relation to, or to decisions of, the Authority, to take into account the duty imposed upon the Authority. Similarly, in exercising any power which, but for any direction given by one of the Ministers, would fall to be exercised by the Authority, account is to be taken of the duty imposed upon the Authority.[32]

The general environmental and recreational duties

It is the duty of the Authority, in formulating or considering any proposals relating to its functions, so far as may be consistent with any enactment relating to its functions, (a) to exercise any power conferred upon it with respect to proposals so as to further the conservation and enhancement of natural beauty and the conservation of flora, fauna and geological or physiographical features of special interest; (b) to have regard to the desirability of protecting and conserving buildings, sites and objects of archaeological, architectural or historic interest; and (c) to take into account any effect which the proposals would have on the beauty or amenity of any rural or urban area or on any flora, fauna, features, buildings, sites or objects. The same duty is imposed on each of the Ministers with the qualification that this is to be exercised, in the case

[31] Generally see Ch.12 below.

[32] s.15 Water Resources Act 1991.

of the Secretary of State, so far as may be consistent with his general duties with respect to the water industry.[33]

Subject to this general statement of the environmental duty, it is the recreational duty of the Authority, and each of the Ministers, in formulating or considering any proposals relating to its functions, to adhere to the following matters: (a) to have regard to the desirability of preserving for the public any freedom of access to areas of woodland, mountain, moor, heath, down, cliff or foreshore and other places of natural beauty; (b) to have regard to the desirability of maintaining the availability to the public of any facility for visiting or inspecting any building, site or object of archaeological, architectural or historic interest; and (c) to take into account any effect which the proposals would have on any such freedom of access or on the availability of any such facility. However, neither the general recreational duty nor other provisions require the Authority to make recreational facilities available free of charge.[34]

The matters provided for under the environmental and recreational duties of the Authority also apply so as to impose duties upon the Authority in relation to (a) any proposals relating to the functions of a water or sewerage undertaker; (b) any proposals relating to the management of any land held by an undertaker for any purposes whatever; and (c) any proposal relating to the disposal of protected land which falls to be treated, in accordance with the general environmental and recreational duties imposed upon undertakers, as a proposal relating to the functions of an undertaker.[35] In respect of these matters, proposals relating to undertakers are to be treated as if they are proposals relating to the functions of the Authority for the purpose of requiring the Authority to adhere to the general environmental and recreational duties.[36]

Subject to obtaining the consent of any navigation, harbour or conservancy authority before navigation under their jurisdiction is

[33] s.16(1). On the general duties of the Secretary of State with respect to the water industry see s.2 Water Industry Act 1991.

[34] s.16(2) and (6).

[35] On the disposal of protected land by a water undertaker see s.156(7) Water Industry Act 1991. On the general environmental and recreational duties imposed upon water and sewerage undertakers see s.3 Water Industry Act 1991.

[36] s.16(3) Water Resources Act 1991.

obstructed, it is the duty of the Authority to take steps which are reasonably practicable and consistent with purposes of enactments relating to its functions to secure that rights associated with the use of water or land are exercised so as to ensure that the water or land is made available for recreational purposes and is so made available in the best manner. In determining what steps to take in accordance with this duty, it is the duty of the Authority to take into account the needs of persons who are chronically sick or disabled.[37]

Sites of special scientific interest

Where the Nature Conservancy Council for England or the Countryside Council for Wales are of the opinion that an area of land is of special interest by reason of its flora, fauna or geological or physiographical features, and may at any time be affected by schemes, works, operations or activities of the Authority, or an authorisation given by the Authority, the Council are to notify that fact to the Authority. Analogous provisions allow for notification in respect of land in a National Park or in the Broads by a National Park authority or the Broads Authority provided for under the Norfolk and Suffolk Broads Act 1988. In either case, where notification takes place, the Authority is to consult the notifying body before carrying out or authorising any works, operations or activities which are likely to have a detrimental effect upon certain features of the land. Specifically, consultation is required where the activities envisaged are likely to destroy or damage any of the flora, fauna, or geographical or physiographical features, or significantly to prejudice anything the importance of which is one of the reasons why the land is of special interest. These requirements do not apply, however, in relation to anything done in an emergency where particulars of what is done are notified to the appropriate authority as soon as practicable after the emergency action is taken.[38]

---

[37] s.16(4) and (5), and see Ch.6 above on navigation.

[38] s.17. See *Nature Conservancy Council v. Southern Water Authority*, (1991) *The Times* 17 June 1991 D.C.

Codes of practice

Each of the Ministers is empowered, after consultation, to approve any code of practice giving practical guidance to the Authority with respect to the promotion of conservation and recreation,[39] the general environmental and recreational duties, and responsibilities in relation to sites of special interest, and promoting desirable practices with respect to those matters. Contravention of a code of practice is not of itself to constitute a contravention of the environmental or recreation duties or the duty in relation to sites of special interest, or to give rise to any criminal or civil liability. However, the Ministers are under a duty to take into account contraventions of the code in determining how to exercise their powers under the Act.[40] In exercise of the power to approve a code of practice of this kind, the relevant Ministers have approved a *Code of Practice on Conservation, Access and Recreation*.[41]

LAND AND WORKS POWERS OF THE AUTHORITY

Acquisition of land

The Authority is granted extensive powers of compulsory purchase over land, subject to Ministerial permission being obtained,[42] and may purchase compulsorily any land in England and Wales which is required for the purposes of, or in connection with, the carrying out of any of its functions. The Ministerial power to authorise compulsory purchase includes the power to authorise the acquisition of interests and rights over land by the creation of new interests and rights or by the extinguishment of rights. Land acquired compulsorily in this manner may include land required for the purpose of exchange for land which, under the Acquisition of Land Act 1981, forms part of a common, open space or a fuel or field garden allotment. Subject to certain provisions on

---

[39] Under s.2(2).

[40] s.10(1) and (2).

[41] See Water and Sewerage (Conservation, Access and Recreation) (Code of Practice) Order 1989, S.I. 1989 No.1152.

[42] Ministerial permission may be given by either the Secretary of State or the Minister of Agriculture, Fisheries and Food.

mineral rights,[43] the 1981 Act is to apply to compulsory purchases of land by the Authority, and detailed provisions of that Act are to apply to the acquisition of rights and creation of new rights. Specified matters of detail concerning compensation are made subject to provisions of the Compulsory Purchase Act 1965. Schedule 18 to the Water Resources Act 1991 makes certain modifications to the provisions of the Compulsory Purchase Act 1965 in relation to compulsory purchase of land by the Authority.[44]

If the relevant Minister[45] certifies that, as a result of drainage works carried out by the Authority in connection with the tidal waters of a main river, or any drainage works transferred from a drainage body to the Authority, there has been or is likely to be an accretion of land, the compulsory purchase powers of the Authority are to include the power to acquire that land.[46] Specifically, the land concerned is to include the accretion of land together with any right to reclaim or embank the accretion and any other land which is reasonably required for the purposes of reclamation of the accretion or the enjoyment of it when reclaimed.[47]

The powers conferred upon the Authority are expressly stated to include the power to purchase or lease, by agreement or compulsorily, any dam, fishing weir, fishing mill dam, fixed engine or other artificial obstruction attached to or worked in connection with the obstruction; so much of the bank adjoining a dam as may be necessary for making or maintaining a fish pass;[48] and for the purposes of erecting and working a fixed engine, any fishery land or foreshore together with any easement of adjoining land necessary for securing access. The exercise of these powers allows the Authority either to alter or remove the obstruction, or to work, in any lawful manner, the obstruction for fishery purposes.[49]

---

43 Under s.182 Water Resources Act 1991.

44 s.154.

45 "The relevant Minister" means, in relation to England, the Minister of Agriculture, Fisheries and Food, and in relation to Wales, the Secretary of State for Wales (s.155(7)).

46 On accretion generally see p.46 above.

47 s.155(1) and (2).

48 Fish passes are provided for under s.10 Salmon and Freshwater Fisheries Act 1975, see p.430 below and Ch.13 below generally.

49 s.156 Water Resources Act 1991.

Where land has been compulsorily acquired, subsequent disposal of that land requires Ministerial authorisation and must be in accordance with that authorisation. Accordingly, a consent or authorisation for these purposes is to be set out in a notice served by the Secretary of State or the Minister of Agriculture, Fisheries and Food on the Authority, and may include a requirement that, before any disposal, an opportunity of acquiring the land, or an interest in it, is made available to a specified person.[50]

Works and pipe-laying powers

The powers of the Authority are to include the power to enter into an agreement with any water or sewerage undertaker, or local authority or joint planning board, or with the owner or occupier of any land, to carry out works which are necessary or expedient in connection with the carrying out of any of the water resource management functions. The power to make works agreements for water resource purposes extends to the maintenance of works carried out in pursuance of an agreement; provision for the Authority to use, or have access to any land for water resource purposes; and agreements as to the manner in which any reservoir is to be operated. Provision is made for agreements of this kind to be registered as land charges.[51]

Powers are provided for the Authority to lay a relevant pipe in, under or over any street;[52] to inspect, maintain, adjust, repair or alter any

---

[50] s.157.

[51] s.158, provision for land charges is made under Land Charges Act 1972 and Land Registration Act 1925.

[52] "A relevant pipe" means a resource main or discharge pipe, and references to laying such a pipe are to include laying drains or sewers and the construction of watercourses for certain purposes (s.159(5) Water Resources Act 1991). The purposes are those of (a) intercepting, treating or disposing of any foul water arising or flowing upon any land; or (b) otherwise preventing the pollution of any waters belonging to the Authority or any water undertaker from which the Authority is authorised to take water; and any reservoir which belongs to or is operated by the Authority or any water undertaker or which the Authority or any water undertaker is proposing to acquire or construct for the purpose of being so operated; or (c) any underground strata from which the Authority or any water undertaker is for the time being authorised to abstract water in pursuance of an abstraction licence (s.159(6)). Subject to any provision contained in an agreement with the Authority and the

relevant pipe; and to carry out works requisite for, or incidental to, these matters including breaking up or opening, or tunnelling or boring under, a street, breaking up or opening a sewer, drain or tunnel, and moving or removing earth and other materials. The exercise of powers is subject to legislation relating to street works.[53]

Similarly, in relation to the laying of pipes in other land, the Authority has the power to lay a relevant pipe, to inspect, maintain, adjust, repair or alter the pipe, and to carry out any works requisite for, or incidental to, any such works. These powers are exercisable only after reasonable notice has been given to the owner and occupier of the land, and the minimum period of notice is to be forty–two days in relation to the alteration of an existing pipe, and three months where a pipe is to be laid otherwise than in substitution of an existing pipe.[54] Additional powers are also made available to the Authority to undertake anti–pollution works and operations, to deal with foul water and to discharge water for works purposes, and also to carry out flood defence and drainage works.[55] These matters are considered elsewhere in this work.[56]

Compulsory works orders

Where the Authority is proposing to carry out any engineering or building operations, or to discharge water into any inland water or underground strata, it may apply to either of the Ministers for an order providing for compulsory powers in relation to the carrying out of works. Where an application of this kind has been made to the Minister concerned, he may grant an order conferring compulsory powers necessary or expedient for the purpose of enabling any engineering or

---

person in whom an interest in a pipe is or is to be vested, every relevant pipe which has been laid, in exercise of any power conferred by Chapter I of Part VII of the Water Resources Act 1991 or otherwise, by the Authority, is to vest in the Authority (s.175(1)).

[53] s.159. The relevant legislation on street works is s.20 Highways Act 1980 until the coming into force of the New Roads and Street Works Act 1991.

[54] s.160 Water Resources Act 1991.

[55] Anti–pollution works are provided for under ss.161 to 163, and flood defence and drainage works under ss.165 to 167.

[56] See p.325 below on anti–pollution works, and p.381 on flood defence and drainage works.

building operations or discharges of water to be carried out or made. The detailed procedure relating to Ministerial orders conferring compulsory works powers is set out in Schedule 19 to the Water Resources Act 1991. This states the requirements in relation to applications for orders, service of notice of orders, publicity, consideration of objections, giving of notice of any order made and the payment of compensation to persons whose interests are injuriously affected by the grant of an order. Nothing in an order providing compulsory powers for carrying out works is to exempt the Authority from any restrictions imposed in relation to the abstraction and impounding under Chapter II of Part II of the Act. An order of this kind may, however, grant authority for an abstraction or discharge to be made by the Authority where no alternative power of abstraction or discharge exists.[57]

POWERS OF ENTRY

Any person designated in writing for the purpose by either the Secretary of State or the Minster of Agriculture, Fisheries and Food or by the Authority may enter any premises or vessel for the purpose of ascertaining whether any provision of the Water Resources Act 1991 and other enactments under which the Authority carries out its functions, or subordinate legislation or byelaws, is being or has been contravened. Similarly, a person so designated may carry out such inspections, measurements and tests on any premises or vessel entered by that person or on any articles found on the premises or vessel, and take away samples of water or effluent or of any land or articles as the Minister or Authority has authorised. The exercise of these powers for the purpose of enabling the Minsters or the Authority to determine whether any of the water pollution provisions of the Water Resources Act 1991 has been, or is being, contravened include the power to carry out experimental borings or other works and to install and keep monitoring and other apparatus on premises in order to obtain information on which that determination may be made.[58]

---

[57] s.168 Water Resources Act 1991.

[58] s.169.

Persons designated in writing by the Authority may enter any premises for the purpose of carrying out any survey or tests to determine whether it is appropriate and practicable for the Authority to exercise any relevant works power[59] and to ascertain how that power should be exercised, and to exercise the power. This power of entry also allows an authorised person to carry out experimental borings and other works for the purpose of ascertaining the nature of the sub–soil, and to take away and analyse samples of water, effluent, land or articles considered necessary in relation to the exercise of the works powers of the Authority.[60]

Persons designated by the Authority may also enter premises in relation to its power to carry out surveys and to search for water. Thus, entry is allowed for the purpose of determining whether it would be appropriate for the Authority to acquire any land, or interest or right over land, or to apply for a compulsory works order,[61] and what compulsory powers it would be appropriate to apply for. A person is allowed to enter premises for the purpose of carrying out any survey or tests and the power to do so includes, amongst other things, powers to carry out experimental borings or works, to install and keep monitoring or other apparatus and to take away and analyse samples of water, land or other articles. However, these powers are not to be exercised in connection with the determination of whether, where or how a reservoir should be constructed, or a borehole sunk for the purpose of abstracting or discharging water into underground strata without the written authorisation of the Secretary of State. This authorisation is not be given unless notice of the proposal has been given to the owner and occupier of the premises and consideration has been given to any representation or objections with respect to the proposal.[62]

In addition, any person designated by the Minsters or the Authority may enter any premises or vessel for the purpose of determining whether, and in what manner, any power or duty imposed on either of the Ministers or the Authority by virtue of enactments under

---

[59] "Relevant works power" means any power conferred by the provisions of ss.159, 160, 162(2) and (3) and 163 (s.170(1)).

[60] s.170.

[61] Under s.168.

[62] s.171.

which the Authority carries out its functions should be exercised or performed, or the person may enter for the purpose of exercising or performing that power or duty. Similarly, authorised persons may carry out inspections, measurements and tests on any premises or vessel entered or on any articles found on premises or vessels entered and take away samples of water, effluent, land or other articles. Where these powers are exercised in relation to water pollution functions they are to include the power to carry out experimental borings or other works on the premises and to install and keep monitoring or other apparatus there.[63]

Detailed provisions with respect to powers of entry are set out in Schedule 20 to the Water Resources Act 1991.[64] Notably, this includes the stipulation that, otherwise than by virtue of a warrant, no person may make an entry into any premises or vessel by virtue of the powers of entry described above except in an emergency, or at a reasonable time and after the required notice of the intended entry has been given to the occupier of the premises or vessel. The required notice is a period of seven days' notice, however, this period is not required in relation to the powers of entry for enforcement purposes, and for certain other purposes,[65] except where the premises or vessel in question are used for residential purposes or the entry in question is to be with heavy equipment. Provision is also made for entry to be made under a warrant issued by a Justice of the Peace where there are reasonable grounds for the exercise of the power of entry and certain conditions are fulfilled. These are, that the exercise of the power in relation to premises or a vessel has been refused; that a refusal is reasonably apprehended; that the premises or vessel are unoccupied; that the occupier is temporarily absent from the premises or vessel; that the case is one of urgency; or that an application for admission to the premises or vessel would defeat the object of the proposed entry.

Additional matters specified under Schedule 20 include the requirement that a person who exercises a power of entry is to produce evidence of his designation or other authority before he exercises the power. A person who enters the premises is bound to leave them as

---

[63] s.172.

[64] Effective under s.173.

[65] Under ss.169 and 172.

effectually secured against trespassers as he found them. Compensation is payable where a person sustains loss or damage by reason of the exercise of a power of entry or the failure to leave premises effectually secured, unless the loss or damage is due to the default of the person who sustained it. Intentional obstruction of a person acting in the exercise of these powers of entry is an offence punishable, on summary conviction, by a fine not exceeding £400.[66]

SUPPLEMENTAL PROVISIONS ON LAND AND WORKS POWERS

Subject to specified exceptions, a range of offences arise in relation to interference with works. Thus, an offence is committed if any person without the consent of the Authority, intentionally or recklessly interferes with any resource main[67] or other pipe vested in the Authority or with any structure, installation or apparatus belonging to the Authority, or by any act or omission negligently interferes with any main or other pipe or with any structure, installation or apparatus so as to damage it or so as to have an effect on its use or operation. A person committing the offence will be liable, on summary conviction, to a fine not exceeding £400. Exceptions to these provisions state that a person will not be guilty of the offence by reason of anything done in an emergency to prevent loss or damage to persons or property, and that no offence will be committed by reason of opening or closing a stopcock fitted to a service pipe[68] by means of which water is supplied to any premises by a water undertaker if he has obtained the consent of every

---

[66] On powers of entry of water bailiffs in relation to fishery offences see p.443 below.

[67] "Resource main" means any pipe, not being a trunk main within the meaning of the Water Industry Act 1991, which is or is to be used for the purpose of conveying water from one source of supply to another, from a source of supply to a regulating reservoir or from a regulating reservoir to a source of supply; or giving or taking a supply of water in bulk (s.186(1) Water Resources Act 1991).

[68] "Service pipe" and "stopcock" have the same meanings as in the Water Industry Act 1991, and "consumer" has the same meaning as in Part II of that Act (s.175(7) Water Resources Act 1991).

consumer whose supply is affected, or in the case of opening a stopcock, the stopcock was closed otherwise than by the undertaker.[69]

Any person who, without the consent of the Authority, attaches any pipe or apparatus to any resource main or other pipe vested in the Authority, or who uses a pipe or apparatus which has been so attached or altered will be guilty of an offence and liable, on summary conviction, to a fine not exceeding £400. However, it will be a defence for the person to show that he did not know, and had no grounds for suspecting, that the pipe or apparatus in question had been so attached or altered.[70]

The offences of interfering with resource mains and attaching pipes or apparatus to mains are specified to constitute a breach of a duty owed to the Authority, and any breach of this kind which causes the Authority to sustain loss or damage will be actionable at the suit of the Authority. The amount recoverable by the Authority is to include an amount which is reasonable in respect of any water wasted, misused or improperly consumed in consequence of the commission of the offence.[71]

In certain cases protection is provided for particular undertakings in connection with the carrying out of works and other activities by the Authority under Schedule 22 to the Water Resources Act 1991.[72] In addition protective provisions are provided in respect of flood defence works and watercourses. These state that, except with consent, no power is conferred by the Act to interfere with any sluices, floodgates, groynes, sea defences or other works used by any person for draining, preserving or improving any land under any local statutory provision, or with such works used by any person for irrigating land. Where the Authority proposes, otherwise than in the exercise of any compulsory powers, to construct or alter any inland waters in any internal drainage district which do not form part of a main river, or to construct or alter any works in inland waters, the Authority is bound to consult the internal drainage board for that district before doing so.[73]

---

[69] s.176(1) and (2) Water Resources Act 1991.

[70] s.176(3) and (4).

[71] s.176(5) and (6).

[72] Effective under s.178.

[73] s.179(1) and (2). On the meaning of "internal drainage district" and "internal drainage board" see p.384 below. On the meaning of "main river" see p.378 below.

Certain powers are given to navigation, harbour and conservancy authorities to divert the Authority's watercourses. These provide that where any watercourse under the control of the Authority passes under or interferes with, or with the improvement or alteration of, any river, canal, dock, harbour, basin or other work, including any adjacent towing path, which belongs to or is under the jurisdiction of any navigation, harbour or conservancy authority, the authority may undertake certain works. Specifically, the relevant authority may, at their own expense, and on substituting for the watercourses under the control of the Authority other equally effective watercourses, take up, divert or alter the level of those watercourses and do all such things as may be necessary in connection with the works.[74]

A number of other miscellaneous provisions supplemental to the land and works powers of the Authority are provided for in Chapter III of Part VII of the Water Resources Act 1991. In relation to works in tidal lands, none of the provisions authorising the Authority to carry out works authorise works below the place to which the tide flows at mean high water springs, except in accordance with plans and subject to such restrictions, as may, before the works are commenced, have been approved by the Secretary of State.[75] Matters relating to the acquisition of mineral rights by the Authority, and the working of mines and minerals where pipes, sewers or other related works are affected, are provided for under Schedule 23 to the Act.[76] Without prejudice to the provision for deemed planning permission to be granted in certain cases,[77] nothing in the Act is to be construed as authorising the carrying on of any development without the grant of planning permission.[78] Specific provision is made in relation to a duty of the Authority to make recreational facilities available in relation to works in connection with the construction or operation of certain reservoirs in Wales.[79]

---

[74] s.180.

[75] s.181(1).

[76] s.182.

[77] Under s.90 Town and Country Planning Act 1990. On planning law generally see p.333 below.

[78] s.183 Water Resources Act 1991.

[79] s.184.

INFORMATION PROVISIONS

Annual report and publication of information

As soon as reasonably practicable after the end of each financial year the Authority is bound to prepare a report on its activities during that financial year and send a copy of the report to the Secretary of State and the Minister of Agriculture, Fisheries and Food. The report is to set out any Ministerial directions given to the Authority during the year,[80] and is to be in a form and contain information specified in any direction given to the Authority by the Ministers.[81] In addition, it is the duty of the Authority to collate and publish information from which assessments can be made of the actual and prospective demand for water, and of actual and prospective water resources in England and Wales. The Authority is also to collaborate with others in collating and publishing this information or similar information in relation to places outside England and Wales.[82]

Registers to be kept by the authority

Abstraction and impounding licences

The Authority is bound to keep, in a prescribed manner,[83] registers containing prescribed information with respect to applications made for the grant, revocation or variation of abstraction and impounding licences, provided for under Chapter II of Part II of the Water Resources Act 1991, including information as to the way in which those applications have been dealt with, and information with respect to persons becoming holders of such licences.[84] The register of abstraction and impounding licences kept by the Authority is also to contain prescribed information with respect to applications for abstraction and impounding licences by

---

[80] Ministerial directions may be given under s.5, see p.208 above.

[81] s.187.

[82] s.188.

[83] See the Water Resources (Licences) Regulations 1965, S.I. 1965 No.534.

[84] Persons may become holders of abstraction or impounding licences by virtue of s.49 or under regulations made under s.50 Water Resources Act 1991, generally, see p.264 below.

the Authority,[85] and information with respect to licences granted or deemed to be granted, and licences revoked or varied, in accordance with regulations. The contents of every register kept for these purposes is to be available, at prescribed places, for inspection by the public at all reasonable hours.[86]

Pollution control register

It is the duty of the Authority to maintain in accordance with regulations,[87] prescribed particulars of the following matters on a pollution control register: (a) any notice of water quality objectives and notice of review of water quality objectives;[88] (b) applications made for consents under Chapter II of Part III of the Water Resources Act 1991;[89] (c) consents given under that Chapter and the conditions to which the consents are subject; (d) certificates issued by the Secretary of State in relation to certain applications or discharges;[90] (e) (i) samples of water or effluent taken by the Authority for the purposes of any of the water pollution provisions of the Act, (ii) information produced by analyses of those samples, (iii) such information with respect to samples of water or effluent taken by any other person, and the analyses of those samples, as is acquired by the Authority from any person under arrangements made by the Authority for the purpose of any of those provisions, and (iv) the steps taken in consequence of any of the information mentioned in (i) to (iii); and (f) any matter concerning particulars about authorisations for prescribed processes required to be kept by the chief inspector in any register under Part I of the Environmental Protection Act 1990.[91]

It is the duty of the Authority to secure that the contents of registers maintained under these provisions are available, at all

---

[85] Under s.64.

[86] s.189.

[87] See The Control of Pollution (Registers) Regulations 1989, S.I. 1989 No.1160.

[88] Served under s.83 Water Resources Act 1991.

[89] Chapter II of Part III is entitled "Pollution Offences".

[90] That is, certificates issued under Sch.10 para.1(7), to the effect that the inclusion of certain information in the register would be contrary to the public interest, or would disclose information about a trade secret to an unreasonable degree.

[91] s.190(1) Water Resources Act 1991. Registers under the Environmental Protection Act 1990 are provided for under s.20 of that Act. Generally see the discussion of integrated pollution control at p.315 below.

reasonable times, for inspection by the public free of charge. In addition, members of the public are to be afforded reasonable facilities by the Authority for obtaining, on payment of a reasonable charge, copies of entries in the registers.[92]

Register for works discharges

The Authority is to keep a register of persons and premises in relation to consents for discharges for works purposes.[93] In this register the Authority is to enter the name and address of a person in respect of any premises which abut on any watercourse if that person has requested to be so registered and is either the owner or occupier of those premises, or an officer of an association of owners or occupiers of premises which abut on that watercourse and include those premises. If the Authority contravenes, without reasonable excuse, any of these requirements it will be guilty of an offence and liable, on summary conviction, to a fine not exceeding £400.[94]

Maps

Freshwater limits

The Secretary of State is to deposit maps with the Authority showing the fresh–water limits of every relevant watercourse,[95] and may from time to time, if appropriate to do so by reason of any change of the fresh–water limit of any river or watercourse, deposit a map showing a revised limit for that river or watercourse. It is the duty of the Authority to keep maps deposited with it by the Secretary of State available, at all reasonable times, for inspection by the public free of charge.[96]

Main river maps

The Authority is bound to keep the main river map for the area of a regional flood defence committee at the principal office of the Authority for that area, and provide reasonable facilities for inspecting

---

[92] s.190(2) Water Resources Act 1991.

[93] s.191(1). Works discharges and consents thereto are provided for under ss.163 and 164 respectively.

[94] s.191(2) and (3).

[95] "Relevant watercourse" has the same meaning as in s.104(3), see p.291 below.

[96] s.192.

that map and taking copies of and extracts from it. Any local authority whose area is wholly or partly within the area of a regional flood defence committee is, on application to the Authority, entitled to be furnished with copies of the main river map for the area of that committee on payment of sums agreed between the Authority and the local authority.[97]

A "main river map" is a map relating to the area of a regional flood defence committee which shows by a distinctive colour the extent to which any watercourse in that area is to be treated as a main river, or part of a main river, and indicates which of those watercourses are designated in a special drainage scheme.[98] A main river map is conclusive evidence for all purposes as to what is a main river, and is to be taken for the purposes of the Documentary Evidence Act 1868, as it applies to either of the Ministers, to have been issued by that Minister.[99] Either of the Ministers may send the Authority one or more new maps to be substituted for the whole or any part of a main river map along with a statement to that effect specifying the date on which the substitution is to take effect.[100]

Maps of waterworks

It is the duty of the Authority to keep records, in the form of a map, of the location of every resource main or discharge pipe[101] which is for the time being vested in the Authority, and any other underground works which are for the time being vested in the Authority. The contents of these records are to be made available, at all reasonable times, for inspection by the public free of charge at an office of the Authority. Modification of the records is to be made as soon as reasonably practicable after the completion of works which make modification of the records necessary. However, this duty does not require the Authority

[97] s.193(1).

[98] Special drainage schemes are provided for under s.137. References to a "main river map" are to include so much of any map as, by virtue of Sch.26 para.38 Water Act 1989, has effect at the coming into force of the Water Resources Act 1991 (s.193(2)).

[99] s.193.

[100] s.194(1) and (2).

[101] "Discharge pipe" and "resource main" have the same meanings as in Part VII of the Water Resources Act 1991.

to keep records of any pipe which was laid before 1 September 1989 or any underground works which were completed before that date.[102]

Provision and acquisition of information

It is the duty of the Authority to furnish the Secretary of State or the Minister of Agriculture, Fisheries and Food with all the information that he may reasonably require relating to the Authority's property, the carrying out and proposed carrying out of its functions and its responsibilities generally. The information to be provided may include information which, though not in the possession of the Authority, it is reasonable to require the Authority to obtain.[103]

The Authority is also under a duty to provide a water undertaker with all specified information about water flow which is in the possession of the Authority and which is reasonably requested by the undertaker for purposes connected with the carrying out of its functions. The information specified relates to the flow, level or volume of any inland water or any water contained in underground strata, about rainfall or any fall of snow, hail or sleet or about the evaporation of any water. The Authority is also to provide reasonable facilities to all persons for the inspection of the contents of any records kept by the Authority containing this information, and for the taking of copies of, or extracts from, these records.[104]

Every water undertaker is bound to provide the Authority with specified information about water flow which is in the possession of the undertaker and reasonably requested by the Authority for purposes connected with the carrying out of any of its functions. Where records of the flow, level or volume of any inland waters, other than discrete waters,[105] are kept by a person other than a water undertaker, the Authority has the right, at all reasonable times, to inspect the contents of

[102] s.195.

[103] s.196(1) and (3).

[104] s.197(1) and (7).

[105] "Discrete waters" means inland waters so far as they comprise a lake, pond or reservoir which does not discharge to any other inland waters, or one of a group of two or more lakes, ponds or reservoirs, whether near to or distant from each other, and of watercourses or mains connecting them, where none of the inland waters in the group discharges to any inland waters outside the group (s.221(1)).

those records and to take copies of, or extracts from, the records. Any person who, without reasonable excuse, refuses or fails to permit the Authority to exercise its right to do so will be guilty of an offence and liable, on summary conviction, to a fine not exceeding £50.[106]

Any person who, for the purpose of searching for or abstracting water, proposes to sink a well or borehole intended to reach a depth of more than fifty feet below the surface must, before he begins to do so, give notice to the Natural Environment Research Council of his intention to do so. In addition, the person sinking the well or borehole is bound to keep a journal of the progress of the work and tests made on completion of the flow of water and send these to the Council. A person authorised by the Council must be allowed to have access to the well or borehole and to take specimens of material or water abstracted. Failure to comply with these obligations is an offence and a person found guilty will be liable, on summary conviction, to a fine not exceeding £400, and to a further daily fine of £20 for every day during which the offence continues.[107]

Where a person proposes to construct or extend a boring for searching for or extracting minerals he must, before he commences the work, give the Authority notice of his intention to do so in a prescribed form.[108] Contravention of this requirement, or the failure to comply with a conservation notice[109] in relation to mining operations, is an offence for which a person will be liable, on summary conviction, to a fine not exceeding £2,000 and, on conviction on indictment, to a fine of unlimited amount.[110]

Any person, other than the Authority, who proposes to install a gauge for measuring or recording the flow, level or volume of any inland waters other than discrete waters is to give notice to the Authority of his proposal to install the gauge, and is not to begin the work of installing it before the end of a period of three months beginning with the date of

---

[106] s.197(2) and (3).

[107] s.198(1), (2), (5) and (8).

[108] See Water Resources (Miscellaneous Provisions) Regulations 1965, S.I. 1965 No.1092.

[109] Conservation notices are provided for under ss.30(2) and (3) and 31 Water Resources Act 1991, see p.256 below.

[110] s.199.

service of the notice, or a shorter period allowed by the Authority. Not more than one month after the work is completed the person installing the gauge is to give notice to the Authority stating where the records obtained from the gauge are kept. Contravention of these provisions is an offence and a person guilty of the offence will be liable, on summary conviction, to a fine not exceeding £50. However, the requirements will not apply to gauges installed for the sole purpose of indicating the level of inland waters for the benefit of persons fishing those waters, or to any gauge which is removed not later than twenty–eight days after it was installed.[111]

The Authority may give directions requiring any person who is abstracting water from a source of supply to give specified information to the Authority concerning the abstraction. Subject to provision for representations to be made to the Secretary of State with respect to a direction of this kind, a person who fails to comply with a direction will be guilty of an offence and liable, on summary conviction, to a fine not exceeding £50.[112]

It is the duty of the Authority, when requested to do so by either of the Ministers, to provide appropriate advice and assistance to enable the Minister to carry out his functions in relation to water pollution under the Water Resources Act 1991. Either of the Ministers or the Authority may serve a notice on any person requiring that person to furnish him, or it, with information required for the purposes of carrying out water pollution functions. Failure, without reasonable excuse, to comply with the requirements of a notice served for this purpose is an offence and a person found guilty will be liable, on summary conviction, to a fine not exceeding £2,000.[113]

The Authority is under a duty to provide a water undertaker with specified information with respect to pollution incidents which is reasonably requested by the undertaker for purposes connected with the carrying out of its functions. Conversely, it is the duty of every water undertaker to provide the Authority with similar information where reasonably requested by the Authority for the purpose of carrying out any of its functions. Specifically, the information concerned relates to the

---

[111] s.200.

[112] s.201.

[113] s.202.

quality of controlled waters or any other waters, or about any incident in which poisonous, noxious or polluting matter or any solid waste matter has entered any controlled waters or other waters.[114]

Restrictions on disclosure of information and false statements

Subject to specified exceptions, no information with respect to any particular business which has been obtained by virtue of any of the provisions of the Water Resources Act 1991 and relates to the affairs of any individual or particular business may, during the lifetime of the individual or so long as the business continues to be carried on, be disclosed without the consent of the individual or the person for the time being carrying on the business. This general prohibition upon disclosure is made subject to a range of exceptions for particular purposes. Amongst the exceptions are disclosures, for the purpose of facilitating the carrying out by either the Ministers, the Authority, the Director General of Water Services, the Monopolies Commission or a local authority of any functions under the water consolidation legislation; for the purpose of facilitating the preference by a water or sewerage undertaker of any of the duties imposed upon it under that legislation; for the purpose of facilitating the carrying out of certain functions of the Health and Safety Commission or the Health and Safety Executive; in connection with the investigation of any criminal offence or for the purposes of any criminal proceedings; for the purpose of any civil proceedings brought under certain Acts; and in pursuance of a European Community obligation. In addition, the prohibition upon disclosure of information is not to limit matters which may be made public as part of a report of the Authority and certain other bodies, or disclosure of information relating to the functions of a water or sewerage undertaker by one Minister or government department to another, or for the purposes of assisting a designated public authority to discharge specified functions. Any person who discloses information in contravention of the prohibition will be guilty of an offence and liable, on summary conviction, to a fine not

---

[114] s.203. On the meaning of "controlled waters" see p.290 below; and generally see Ch.11 below on water pollution.

exceeding £2,000 or, on conviction on indictment, to imprisonment for a term not exceeding two years or to a fine or both.[115]

Where a person sinking a well or borehole is required to provide certain information to the Natural Environment Research Council,[116] he may require the Council to treat as confidential information provided or details of specimens taken and, where so required the Council may not, without the consent of the person, allow the information to be published or shown to any person who is not an officer of the Council or of a department of the Secretary of State. Subject to certain rights of appeal against the person withholding consent for disclosure, and an exception relating to information as to water resources and supplies, failure to comply with the confidentiality obligation is an offence and a person found guilty will be liable, on summary conviction, to a fine not exceeding £400 and, where the offence continues after conviction, to a daily fine of £20. Where a person authorised by the Council is admitted to premises and subsequently discloses information with respect to a manufacturing process or trade secret, unless the disclosure is in performance of his duty, he will be guilty of an offence punishable, on summary conviction, by imprisonment for a term not exceeding three months or to a fine not exceeding £2,000 or both and, on conviction on indictment, to imprisonment for a term not exceeding three months or to a fine or both.[117]

Offences involving the making of false statements arise in relation to furnishing information or making an application under, or for the purposes of, a range of provisions under the Water Resources Act 1991. Generally, these offences arise where any person makes any statement which he knows to be false in a material particular, or recklessly makes any statement which is false in a material particular. Penalties provided for in relation to these offences vary according to the nature of the information provided.[118]

---

[115] s.204.

[116] Under s.198, see p.229 above.

[117] s.205.

[118] s.206.

MISCELLANEOUS AND SUPPLEMENTAL MATTERS

Directions in the interests of national security

The Secretary of State may, after consultation with the Authority, give it such directions of general character as are requisite or expedient in the interests of national security for the purposes of mitigating the effects of any civil emergency[119] which may occur. If requisite or expedient to do so in the interests of national security, or for the purpose of mitigating the effects of any civil emergency, the Secretary of State may, after consultation with the Authority, give the Authority a direction requiring it to do, or not to do, a particular thing specified in the direction. It is then the duty of the Authority to comply with the direction notwithstanding any other duty imposed upon it.[120]

Civil liability for escapes of water

Except as otherwise provided for, where an escape of water, however caused, from a pipe vested in the Authority causes loss or damage, the Authority will be liable for the loss or damage. This liability is subject to the exceptions that the Authority will not be liable if the escape was due wholly to the fault of the person who sustained the loss or damage or of any servant, agent or contractor of that person, and that liability will not arise in relation to loss or damage sustained by water, sewerage or statutory undertakers,[121] any public gas or electricity supplier,[122] highway authority, or a person entitled to compensation

---

[119] "Civil emergency" is a reference to any natural disaster or other emergency which is, or may be likely, in relation to any area, so to disrupt water supplies or sewerage services, or to involve such destruction of or damage to life or property in that area, as seriously and adversely to affect the inhabitants of that area, or a substantial number of them, whether depriving them of any of the essentials of life or otherwise (s.207(7)).

[120] s.207.

[121] Undertakers, that is, within the meaning of s.336(1) Town and Country Planning Act 1990.

[122] That is, a "public gas supplier" within Part I of the Gas Act 1986 or the holder of a licence under s.6(1) of the Electricity Act 1989.

under specified street works legislation.[123] Liability of the Authority is subject to the modified operation of certain general enactments concerning civil liability.[124]

Evidence of samples and abstractions

The result of the analysis of any sample of effluent taken on behalf of the Authority in exercise of any power conferred under the Water Resources Act 1991 will not be admissible in any legal proceedings in respect of any effluent passing from any land or vessel unless the person who took the sample: (a) on taking the sample notified the occupier of the land or the owner or master of the vessel of his intention to have it analysed; (b) there and then divided the sample into three parts and caused each part to be placed in a container which was sealed and marked; and (c) delivered one part to the occupier of the land or the owner or master of the vessel and retained one part, apart from the one he submitted to be analysed, for future comparison. The tripartite sampling procedure for effluent is subject to the proviso that if it is not reasonably practicable for a person taking the sample to comply with these requirements, the requirements will be treated as having been complied with if they were complied with as soon as reasonably practicable after the sample was taken. In relation to any proceedings in respect of effluent passing from a public sewer or other outfall belonging to a sewerage undertaker into any water, references to the occupier of land are to be taken as references to the sewerage undertaker in which the sewer or outfall is vested.[125]

---

123 That is, s.78 new Roads and Street Works Act 1991.

124 s.208 Water Resources Act 1991. The Law Reform (Contributory Negligence) Act 1945, Fatal Accidents Act 1976 and Limitation Act 1980 are to apply in relation to loss or damage for which the Authority is liable under these provisions, which is not due to the fault of the Authority, as if it were due to its fault. The Authority may be entitled to recover contributions under the Civil Liability (Contributions) Act 1978 for any loss for which the Authority is liable (s.208(4) and (5) Water Resources Act 1991).

125 s.209(1) (2) and (4). On the interpretation of previous provisions on tripartite sampling by the courts see *Trent River Board v. Wardle Ltd.*, [1957] Crim L.R. 196; *Wansford Trout Farm v. Yorkshire Water Authority*, (1986) unreported, Queen's Bench Division, 23 July 1986.

Where, in accordance with the provisions contained in an abstraction licence,[126] it has been determined what quantity of water is to be taken to have been abstracted during any period from a source of supply by the holder of the licence, or to have been abstracted at a particular point or by particular means, or for use for particular purposes, that determination will, for the purpose of any proceedings relating to abstraction and impounding[127] or any related water resources provisions, be conclusive evidence of the matters to which it relates.[128]

Other provisions which are of relevance to sampling of effluent survive from earlier legislation. These provide that in any legal proceedings it is to be presumed, unless the contrary is shown, that any sample of effluent taken at an inspection chamber or manhole or other place provided in compliance with a condition imposed under a discharge consent is a sample of what was passing from the land or premises to those waters.[129] A second presumption in relation to effluent samples applies in the absence of any condition requiring the provision of a sampling facility, and provides that where an agreement has been made by the Authority and the occupier of any land or premises from which effluent is being discharged as to a sampling point, it is to be presumed in any legal proceedings, unless the contrary is shown, that any sample of effluent taken at the agreed point is a sample of what was passing from the land or premises to those waters.[130]

Byelaws

The Authority has diverse powers to make and enforce byelaws in relation to its functions, and the detailed provisions relating to these matters are provided for under Schedule 25 to the Water Resources Act 1991, concerned with the byelaw-making powers of the Authority, and Schedule 26, concerned with the procedure relating to byelaws made by

---

126 Under s.46(2)(b) and (6) Water Resources Act 1991.

127 That is, as provided for under Chapter II of Part II Water Resources Act 1991.

128 s.209(3).

129 s.10(1) Rivers (Prevention of Pollution) Act 1961, as amended by Sch.3 para.17 Control of Pollution Act 1974.

130 s.10(2) Rivers (Prevention of Pollution) Act 1961.

the Authority.[131] Schedule 25 provides that byelaws may be made by the Authority for a range of specified purposes: regulating the use of inland waters; regulating the use of navigable waters; regulating the use of the authority's waterways; controlling certain forms of pollution; flood defence and drainage purposes; and for certain purposes relating to fisheries functions.

Schedule 26 provides that no byelaw made by the Authority is to have effect until confirmed by the relevant Minister.[132] Detailed provision is made in relation to the publication of proposed byelaws to persons likely to be affected. The Minister may refuse to confirm a byelaw made by the Authority, or may confirm the byelaw either with or without modifications, and with or without a local inquiry, unless no objections are made and sustained in which case no inquiry need be held. If it appears to the relevant Minister that the revocation of a byelaw is necessary or expedient he may, after giving notice to the Authority and considering any representations or objections made by the Authority, and if required by the Authority, after holding a public inquiry, revoke the byelaw.

Byelaw offences

Contravention of an Authority byelaw is an offence which is punishable to an extent which depends upon the nature of the byelaw concerned. Thus, in relation to byelaws prohibiting specified inland waters being used for boating, swimming or other recreational purposes, or regulating their use, offences are punishable, on summary conviction, by a fine not exceeding £50 and a £5 daily fine for each day on which the offence continues. In relation to byelaw offences dealing with the regulation of certain waters on which there is a public right of navigation and waterways owned or managed by the Authority, offences are punishable, on summary conviction, by a fine not exceeding £2,000 or any smaller sum specified. Byelaw offences relating to the control of

---

131 Both Schedules are effective under s.210 Water Resources Act 1991.

132 In general terms, "the relevant Minister" means the Minister of Agriculture, Fisheries and Food in relation to land drainage and flood defence matters, that Minister or the Secretary of State in relation to the fisheries functions of the Authority, and the Secretary of State in relation to other byelaws (Sch.26 para.7).

pollution and prohibiting the use of waters for washing or cleaning purposes and keeping vessels with sanitary appliances, and byelaws for the better protection, preservation and improvement of fisheries for salmon, trout, freshwater fish and eels, are summarily punishable by a fine not exceeding £1,000 or any smaller sum specified. Byelaws for securing the efficient working of any drainage system, including the proper defence of any land against the sea or tidal water, are punishable, on summary conviction, by a fine not exceeding £2,000 and a daily fine not exceeding £40 for each day on which the contravention continues after conviction. In relation to offences against byelaws regulating the use of inland waters and byelaws for flood defence and drainage purposes, the Authority is empowered to take necessary action to remedy the contravention and recover the expenses reasonably incurred from the person in default.[133]

Special provision is made for compensation in relation to fishery byelaws where the owner or occupier of the fishery claims that the fishery is injuriously affected by a byelaw made for specified purposes and that claim is made within twelve months of the confirmation of the byelaw. In such a case the claim and amount of compensation to be paid for the damage to the fishery is to be determined, in default of agreement, by an arbitrator appointed by one of the Minsters. The byelaw purposes, in relation to which compensation claims of this kind may be made, are the prohibiting of any instrument other than a fixed engine for taking salmon, trout or freshwater fish, the specification of nets and other instruments which may be used for taking salmon, trout, freshwater fish and eels, and the imposition of requirements as to the construction, design, material and dimensions of nets or other instruments.[134]

Local inquires

Without prejudice to express provisions for the holding of public inquiries under the Water Resources Act 1991, each of the Ministers has the power to cause a local inquiry to be held in connection with any matter arising in relation to the abstraction and impounding provisions of

---

[133] s.211 and Sch.25.

[134] s.212.

the Act,[135] or the related water resource provisions, or otherwise in connection with any of the Authority's functions. Without prejudice to the generality of this, the Secretary of State may cause an inquiry to be held for the purposes of establishing or reviewing water quality objectives[136] or otherwise in relation to any of the water pollution provisions of the Act, with a view to preventing or dealing with pollution of any controlled waters,[137] or in relation to any other matter relevant to the quality of those waters.[138]

Each of the Ministers has the power to cause a local inquiry to be held in relation to the flood defence provisions of the Water Resources Act 1991, and where this power is exercised the person appointed to hold the inquiry may summons persons to attend to give evidence or produce documents, and evidence may be taken on oath. Any person who refuses or deliberately fails to attend in disobedience to a summons or who deliberately alters, suppresses, conceals, destroys, or refuses to produce any book or document which he is required to produce will be guilty of an offence and liable, on summary conviction, to imprisonment for a term not exceeding six months or to a fine not exceeding £400 or both.[139]

Offences and judicial disqualification

Where a body corporate is guilty of an offence under the Act and that offence is proved to have been committed with the consent or connivance of, or to be attributable to any neglect on the part of, any director, manager, secretary or other similar officer of the body corporate or any person who was purporting to act in any such capacity, then he, as well as the body corporate, will be guilty of that offence and will be liable to be proceeded against and punished accordingly. Where the affairs of a body corporate are managed by its members, this provision will apply in relation to the acts and defaults of a member in connection with his functions of management as if he were a director of the body

---

[135] Under Chapter II of Part II.

[136] Water quality objectives are provided for under s.63, see p.294 below.

[137] On the meaning of "controlled waters" see p.290 below.

[138] s.213.

[139] s.214. Otherwise, procedure at local inquiries is to be subject to s.250(2) to (5) Local Government Act 1972 (s.215 Water Resources Act 1991).

corporate. Where the commission by any person of an offence under the water pollution provisions of the Act is due to the act or default of some other person, that other person may be charged with and convicted of the offence whether or not proceedings for the offence are taken against the first–mentioned person.[140]

No judge of any court or Justice of the Peace will be disqualified from acting in relation to any proceedings to which the Authority is a party by reason only that he is or may become liable to pay a charge to the Authority in respect of any services of facilities that are not the subject–matter of the proceedings.[141]

FINANCIAL PROVISIONS IN RELATION TO THE AUTHORITY

General financial provisions

The Secretary of State and the Minister of Agriculture, Fisheries and Food may, after consultation with the Authority and with the Treasury's approval, determine the financial duties of the Authority, and different determinations may be made for different functions and activities of the Authority. Where the Authority has a surplus, whether on its capital or revenue account, the Secretary of State may, after consultation with the Treasury and Authority, direct the Authority to pay him an amount not exceeding the amount of the surplus.[142]

Special duties are imposed upon the Authority with respect to flood defence revenue, in that this revenue may only be spent in the carrying out of the Authority's flood defence functions in or for the benefit of the local flood defence district in which it is raised, and this revenue is to be disregarded for the purpose of determining any surplus of the Authority. However, flood defence revenue may be set aside towards research and related activities or towards meeting the Authority's administrative expenses or be paid by way of contributions towards expenses incurred by the Authority or any regional flood defence

---

[140] s.217.

[141] s.218.

[142] s.117.

committee under special arrangements[143] made for the purposes of carrying out flood defence functions involving the area of more than one regional flood defence committee.[144] Where funds are held for particular purposes under local statutory provisions these are to be used only for the particular purposes concerned, and are to be disregarded in determining any surplus of the Authority.[145]

Provision is made for contributions between the Authority and certain other authorities in relation to specified works. Thus, where on the application of navigation, harbour or conservancy authority, any works constructed or maintained by that authority have a beneficial contribution towards the Authority's water resource functions, the Authority is to contribute towards the expenditure incurred in constructing or maintaining the works. Conversely, where any works constructed or maintained by the Authority make a beneficial contribution towards the carrying out of the functions of a navigation, harbour or conservancy authority, that authority must contribute towards the expenditure incurred by the Authority in constructing or maintaining the works.[146]

Revenue provisions

The revenue provisions relating to the Authority provide for a range of different charges to be imposed in relation to its various functions. Specifically, charges are provided for in relation to water resources, the control of pollution, drainage, fisheries contributions and navigation tolls. These are considered in the Chapters in this work to which they relate. In addition to the express provisions made in respect of charges relating to the particular functions of the Authority, an incidental general power is provided for the Authority to impose charges. This provides the Authority with the power to fix and recover charges for

---

143 Provided for under s.106(1)(b).

144 s.118(1) to (3).

145 s.119.

146 s.120(1) and (2). On the meanings of "navigation, harbour or conservancy authority" see p.253 below.

services and facilities provided in the course of carrying out any of its functions.[147]

Grants and loans

The most general and important provision in relation to grants and loans to the Authority is the power of the Secretary of State, with the approval of the Treasury, to make grants to the Authority of such amounts as he thinks fit, on terms approved by the Treasury.[148] In addition, a range of particular powers to make grants is provided for in relation to specified purposes. Hence, in relation to the improvement of existing drainage works or the construction of new drainage works, the relevant Minister may make grants towards the expenditure incurred by the Authority of an amount sanctioned by the Treasury and subject to any conditions which it may approve, and advances may be made towards expenditure on future drainage works.[149] The relevant Minister may also make grants of amounts sanctioned by the Treasury towards expenditure incurred by the Authority in providing or installing apparatus, or carrying out engineering or building operations, for the purpose of a flood warning system approved by the Minister.[150] The Secretary of State, with the approval of the Treasury, may make grants to the Authority for the purpose of defraying or contributing towards any

---

[147] s.144 Water Resources Act 1991.

[148] s.146(1) and (2).

[149] s.147(1), (2) and (5). "The relevant Minister" for these purposes means, in relation to Wales, the Secretary of State, and in relation to England, the Minister of Agriculture, Fisheries and Food (s.147(6)). On other grants in respect of powers in relation to drainage purposes see s.149.

[150] s.148(1) and (2). "Flood warning system" means any system whereby, for the purpose of providing warning of any danger of flooding, information with respect to (a) rainfall, as measured at a particular place within a particular period; or (b) the level or flow of any inland water, or part of an inland water, at a particular time; or (c) other matters appearing to the Authority to be relevant for that purpose, is obtained and transmitted, whether automatically or otherwise, with or without provision for carrying out calculations based on such information and for transmitting the results of those calculations (s.148(5)).

losses it may sustain by reason of compliance with a direction given in the interests of national security.[151]

[151] s.150. Directions in the interests of national security are provided for under s.207, see p.233 below.

Chapter 10

WATER RESOURCES

Introduction

Previous provision for the management of water resources was contained in the Water Resources Act 1963, the object of which had been to promote measures for the conservation, augmentation and proper use of water resources in England and Wales, amongst other things, by the imposition of controls upon the abstraction of water. Administrative responsibility for these controls was originally entrusted to river authorities, but was later transferred to water authorities,[1] and now rests with the National Rivers Authority. Further provision for the management of water resources in times of drought was made under the Drought Act 1976. The Water Resources Act 1963 has now been substantially repealed and the Drought Act 1976 has been completely repealed and, along with modifications of the law brought about by the Water Act 1989, the present law is now contained in Part II of the Water Resources Act 1991. Accordingly, it is now the general duty of the National Rivers Authority, in accordance with directions from the Secretary of State for the Environment, to take all such actions as it considers to be necessary or expedient for the purpose of conserving, redistributing or otherwise augmenting water resources, and securing the proper use of water resources, in England and Wales.[2] This Chapter considers the general management functions of the Authority in relation to water resources, provided for under Chapter I of Part II of the 1991 Act, provisions relating to abstraction and impounding of water, under Chapter II, and controls which may be imposed under conditions of drought, under Chapter III. In addition, consideration is given to restrictions upon the impoundment of large quantities of water arising under the Reservoirs Act 1975 and, for the most part, subject to the supervision of local authorities.

---

[1] s.10 Water Act 1973.

[2] s.19(1) Water Resources Act 1991.

GENERAL MANAGEMENT FUNCTIONS

General management of water resources

It is the general duty of the Authority to take all such action as it may from time to time consider, in accordance with any directions of the Secretary of State, to be necessary or expedient for the purpose of conserving, redistributing or otherwise augmenting water resources in England and Wales, and securing the proper use of water resources in England and Wales. Nothing under this general duty is, however, to relieve any water undertaker of the obligation to develop water resources for the purpose of performing any duty imposed upon it to maintain a water supply system.[3]

So far as reasonably practicable, the Authority is to enter into and maintain such arrangements with water undertakers for securing the proper management or operation of the waters which are available to be used by water undertakers for the purposes of, or in connection with, the carrying out of their functions. This duty extends also to any reservoirs, apparatus or other works which belong to, are operated by or are otherwise under the control of, water undertakers for the purposes of, or in connection with, the carrying out of their functions. In either case the agreements entered into by the Authority with water undertakers are to be such as the Authority considers appropriate for the purpose of carrying out its function in relation to the general management of water resources.[4]

Agreements of this kind may make provision with respect to the construction or installation of any reservoirs, apparatus or other works which will be used by the undertaker in the carrying out of its functions and requiring payments to be made by the Authority to the undertaker. Arrangements between the Authority and water undertakers may require the reference to, and determination by, the Secretary of State or the Director General of Water Services of questions arising under the arrangements. The Authority is to send a copy of any arrangements it enters into in accordance with these provisions to the Secretary of State,

---

[3] s.19(1) and (2). The general duty of a water undertaker to maintain a water supply system is provided for under s.37 Water Industry Act 1991.

[4] s.20(1) Water Resources Act 1991.

and the obligations of a water undertaker by virtue of the arrangements will be enforceable by the Secretary of State.[5]

Minimum acceptable flows

The Authority may, if it thinks it appropriate to do so, submit a draft statement to the Secretary of State containing, in relation to inland waters that are not discrete waters,[6] provision for determining the minimum acceptable flow for those waters. Alternatively, where any provision for determining the minimum acceptable flow is for the time being in force in relation to those waters, provision may be submitted to the Secretary of State for amending that provision or for replacing it with different provisions for determining the minimum acceptable flow.[7]

The provisions contained in any statement for determining the minimum acceptable flow for any inland waters must, in relation to the inland waters to which it relates, set out the control points at which the flow of the water is to be measured, the method of measurement which is to be used, and the flow which is to be the minimum acceptable flow at each point for the times or periods specified in the statement. Before preparing a draft statement as to minimum acceptable flow, the Authority is bound to consult (a) any water undertaker having the right to abstract from those waters; (b) any other water undertaker having the right to abstract water from any related underground strata;[8] (c) the drainage board for any internal drainage district from which water is discharged into those waters or in which any part of the waters is situated; (d) any navigation, harbour or conservancy authority having functions in relation

---

[5] s.20(2) and (3) Water Resources Act 1991. Enforcement by the Secretary of State is by an enforcement order under s.18 Water Industry Act 1991.

[6] On the meaning "discrete waters" see p.228 above.

[7] s.21(1) Water Resources Act 1991.

[8] Underground strata are "related underground strata" in relation to any inland waters for these purposes if a water undertaker has a right to abstract water from the strata, and it appears to the Authority, having regard to the extent to which the level of water in the strata depends on the flow of those waters, that the exercise of that right may be substantially affected by so much of the draft statement in question as relates to those waters. Inland waters are "related inland waters" in relation to any other inland waters, where it appears to the Authority that changes in the flow of the other waters may affect the flow of the first–mentioned inland waters (s.21(8)).

to those waters or any related inland waters;[9] (e) if those waters or any related inland waters are tidal waters in relation to which there is no navigation, harbour or conservancy authority, the Secretary of State for Transport; and (f) any person authorised by a licence under Part I of the Electricity Act 1989 to generate electricity.[10]

In determining the flow to be specified in relation to inland waters, the Authority is to have regard (a) to the flow of water in inland waters from time to time; (b) in the light of its duties in relation to conservation, its general environmental and recreational duties and its environmental duties with respect to sites of special scientific interest,[11] to the character of the inland waters and their surroundings; and (c) to any water quality objectives[12] in relation to the inland waters or any other inland waters which may be affected by the flow in the inland waters in question.[13]

The flow which is to be the minimum acceptable flow at any control point is not to be less than the minimum which is needed for safeguarding the public health and for meeting, in respect of both quantity and quality of water, the requirements of existing lawful users of the inland water whether for agriculture, industry, water supply or other purposes. The flow must also meet the requirements of navigation, fisheries or land drainage[14] in relation to both those waters and other inland waters whose flow may be affected by changes in the flow of those waters.[15] However, the Authority will be entitled to treat any existing use of any inland waters as lawful unless, by a decision given in any legal proceedings, it has been held to be unlawful and that decision has not been quashed or reversed.[16]

Detailed provisions with respect to the submission and approval of draft statements relating to minimum acceptable flows are provided for

---

[9] On the definitions of "navigation authority", "harbour authority" and "conservancy authority" see p.253 below.

[10] s.21(2) and (3).

[11] These matters are provided for under ss.2(2), 16 and 17, discussed at p.211 above.

[12] Under Chapter I of Part III of the Water Resources Act 1991, see p.294 below.

[13] s.21(4).

[14] "Land drainage" for these purposes includes defence against water (including sea water), irrigation other than spray irrigation, warping and the provision of flood warning systems (s.21(9)). On land drainage generally see Ch.12 below.

[15] s.21(5).

[16] s.21(9).

under Schedule 5 to the Water Resources Act 1991,[17] and allow the Secretary of State to approve a draft statement in the form submitted or to alter it in such a manner as he thinks fit. The approval under that Schedule of a draft statement will bring into force, on the date specified in the approval, so much of that statement as is approved, and contains provision for determining, amending or replacing the minimum acceptable flow for any inland waters.[18] The Authority is bound to publish notice of the approval and to keep a copy of the approved statement which must be available at its offices for inspection by the public, free of charge, at all reasonable times.[19]

Directions to consider minimum acceptable flow

If the Authority is directed by the Secretary of State to consider whether the minimum acceptable flow for any particular inland waters ought to be determined or reviewed, the Authority will be bound to consider that matter as soon as reasonably practicable after being directed to do so. After considering the minimum acceptable flow for the waters as directed, the Authority must submit to the Secretary of State either a draft statement of minimum acceptable flow, or a statement that no minimum acceptable flow ought to be determined for those waters or, as the case may require, that the minimum acceptable flow for those waters does not need to be changed. Thereafter, the provisions relating to submission and approval of draft statements will apply. The powers of the Secretary of State to alter a draft statement of minimum acceptable flow before approving it will also allow him to do similarly in relation to a draft statement submitted to him as a consequence of a direction to the Authority to do so.[20]

Minimum acceptable level or volume of inland waters

Where it appears to the Authority, in the case of any particular inland waters, that it would be appropriate to measure the level or

---

[17] Schedule 5 is operative under s.21(6).
[18] s.21(7).
[19] Sch.5 para.5.
[20] s.22(1) to (3).

volume, either instead of or in addition to the flow, the Authority may determine that the provisions relating to minimum acceptable flow are to apply as if reference to the flow included a reference to the level or the volume of the waters. Where this is done any draft statement relating to the waters is to state whether the level or volume of the water is to be measured and whether it is to be measured instead of, or in addition to, the flow. The provisions relating to abstraction and impounding[21] in relation to inland waters with respect to which a minimum level or volume is to apply are applicable as if the flow were to include a reference to the level or volume.[22]

RESTRICTIONS ON ABSTRACTION AND IMPOUNDING

Restrictions on abstraction

Chapter II of Part II of the Water Resources Act 1991 provides for control of the abstraction and impounding of water from inland waters and underground strata through criminal offences of unlicensed abstraction and impounding, and by means of a system of licensing operated by the National Rivers Authority and the Secretary of State. Although, in some instances these provisions must be considered alongside the common law rights to abstract water which have been previously discussed, for the most part the provisions under the 1991 Act override former rights to abstract water. However, the possibility remains that civil actions may be brought between individuals for infringement of riparian rights to abstract.[23] Moreover, it has been held that the fact that an abstraction is unlawful under statutory provisions will not prevent an action being brought by one individual for the interference by another with a common law right to abstract.[24] In addition, the common law has,

---

[21] Under Chapter II of Part II of the Water Resources Act 1991, discussed below.

[22] s.23(1) to (3).

[23] On the common law relating to the abstraction and impounding of water see Chs.3, 4 and 5 above.

[24] *Cargill v. Gotts*, [1981] 1 All E.R. 68.

in the past, provided a remedy for an abstractor against a water authority authorising an abstraction of water contaminated by a third party.[25]

In relation to abstraction, subject to certain exceptions discussed later, it is provided that no person may abstract from any source of supply or cause or permit[26] any other person so to abstract any water, except in pursuance of a licence granted by the National Rivers Authority and in accordance with the provisions of that licence.[27] "Source of supply" means any inland waters except discrete waters and any underground strata in which water is or at any time may be contained. For the purposes of this definition "inland waters" means the whole or any part of (a) any river, stream or other watercourse,[28] whether natural or artificial and whether tidal or not; (b) any lake or pond, whether natural or artificial, or any reservoir or dock, so far as it does not fall within (a); and (c) so much of any channel, creek, bay, or estuary or arm of the sea as does not fall within (a) or (b). "Discrete waters" means inland waters so far as they comprise a lake, pond or reservoir which does not discharge to any other inland waters, or one of a group of two or more such waters, whether near to or distant from each other, and watercourses or mains connecting them, where none of the inland waters in the group discharges to any inland waters outside the group. "Underground strata" means strata subjacent to the surface of any land.[29]

---

[25] *Scott–Whitehead v. National Coal Board*, (1987) 53 P. & C.R. 263. However, this decision may now need to be reconsidered in the light of the subsequent ruling in *Murphy v. Brentwood D.C.*, ([1990] 2 All E.R. 908) which restricts the liabilities of public authorities in negligence by overruling *Anns v. Merton L.B.C.* ([1978] A.C.728).

[26] On the similar expression "cause or knowingly permit" see p.297 below.

[27] s.24(1) Water Resources Act 1991.

[28] On the general meaning of "watercourse" see p.1 above. In relation to water resources under Chapter II of Part II of the Water Resources Act 1991 this definition is qualified so that "a watercourse" is stated not to include (a) any sewer or part of a sewer vested in (i) a sewerage undertaker, (ii) a local authority or joint planning board, (iii) the Commission for the New Towns or a development corporation for a new town, (iv) a harbour board within the meaning of the Railway and Canal Traffic Act 1888; or any adit or passage constructed in connection with a well, borehole or other similar work for facilitating the collection of water in the well, borehole or work (s.72(2) Water Resources Act 1991).

[29] s.221(1). References to water contained in underground strata is a reference to water so contained otherwise than in a sewer, pipe, reservoir, tank or other

For the purposes of the offence of unlicensed abstraction, "abstraction" is defined to include doing anything whereby water contained in a source of supply is removed from the source of supply, whether temporarily or permanently, including where it is transferred to another source of supply, and "abstract" is to be construed accordingly.[30] The question as to what constitutes an abstraction was recently considered in *British Waterways Board v. Anglian Water Authority*,[31] where an abstraction licence was granted to allow the removal of water from an outfall channel which received water from a canal vested in the plaintiffs. Although the removal of the water from the outfall would inevitably result in a lowering of the canal by the effect of gravitation, it was held that the abstraction took place from the outfall rather than the canal itself, and since the outfall rather than the canal constituted the source of supply the plaintiffs had no grounds to object to the granting of the abstraction licence.[32]

Where the abstraction of water contained in underground strata is prohibited except in pursuance of a licence, no person may cause or permit any other person to begin to construct or extend any well, borehole or other work whereby water may be abstracted from those strata, or install or modify any machinery or apparatus, whereby additional quantities of water may be abstracted from those strata by means of a well, borehole or other work unless certain conditions are satisfied. These conditions require that the abstraction of the water, or additional abstraction, is authorised by a licence under Chapter II of Part

---

underground works constructed in underground strata, but water contained in (a) any well, borehole or similar work, including any adit or passage constructed in connection with the well, borehole or work for facilitating the collection of water in the well, borehole or work, or (b) any excavation into underground strata, where the level of water in the excavation depends wholly or mainly on water entering it from those strata, is to be treated as water contained in underground strata into which the well, borehole or work was sunk, or as the case may be, the excavation was made (s.221(3)).

[30] s.221(1) Water Resources Act 1991.

[31] (1991) *The Times* 23 April 1991. Although this case concerned the definition of "abstraction" provided under s.135(1) Water Resources Act 1963, this definition was in all material respects the same as now provided under s.221(1) Water Resources Act 1991.

[32] On abstraction from inland waters owned or managed by British Waterways Board see s.66.

II of the Act, and the well, borehole or work as constructed or extended, or the machinery or apparatus as installed or modified, fulfils the requirements of the licence as to the means whereby water is authorised to be abstracted.[33]

Subject to specified exceptions, a person is guilty of an offence by contravention of the general restriction upon abstraction from a source of supply or underground strata. Similarly, an offence is committed in circumstances not constituting a contravention, if a person fails to comply with a condition or requirement imposed by the provisions of an abstraction licence of which he is the holder. A person guilty of an offence will, on summary conviction, be liable to a fine which may not exceed £2,000 and, on conviction on indictment, to a fine of an unlimited amount.[34] The restrictions provided for in relation to abstraction apply notwithstanding any provisions in enactments passed before the Water Resources Act 1963, on 31 July 1963, and provisions made by virtue of earlier or later enactments.[35]

Restrictions on impounding[36]

No person may begin, or cause or permit any other person to begin, to construct or alter any impounding works at any point in an inland water, other than discrete waters, unless certain requirements are complied with. The requirements are (a) that a licence under Chapter I of Part II of the Water Resources Act 1991 granted by the Authority to obstruct or impede the flow of the inland water at that point is in force; (b) that the impounding works will not obstruct or impede the flow of the water except to the extent, and in the manner, authorised by the licence; and (c) any other requirements of the licence, whether as to the provision of compensation water or otherwise, are complied with.[37] "Impounding

---

[33] s.24(2) and (3) Water Resources Act 1991.

[34] s.24(4) and (5) Water Resources Act 1991. No proceedings may be instituted for this offence or others under Chapter II of Part II of the Act, and related water resource provisions, except by the Authority or by, or with the consent of, the Director of Public Prosecutions (s.216(2) and (3)).

[35] s.23(3). The same qualification also applies in relation to impounding (s.25(4)).

[36] For further restrictions on impounding see the discussion of Reservoirs Act 1975 at p.280 below.

[37] s.25(1) Water Resources Act 1991.

works" are defined to mean any dam, weir or other works in any inland water whereby water may be impounded, and any works for diverting the flow of an inland water in connection with the construction or alteration of any dam, weir or other works.[38] Any person who contravenes the prohibition upon unauthorised impounding of water or, in circumstances not constituting a contravention, the holder of a licence who fails to comply with a condition or requirement of a licence for the time being in force, will be guilty of an offence. On summary conviction the person will be liable to a fine not exceeding £2,000, and on indictment to a fine of unlimited amount.[39]

By way of exception to the general prohibition upon unlicensed impounding, the restrictions will not apply under specified circumstances. These arise if the construction or alteration of the impounding works, or the obstruction or impeding of the flow of water resulting from the works is authorised by virtue of an alternative statutory provision.[40] Where an alternative statutory provision is in force, allowing a water or sewerage undertaker or any other person to obstruct or impede the flow of inland waters by impounding works, references to the revocation or variation of impounding works are to apply as if references to an impounding licence included a reference to the alternative statutory provision.[41]

---

[38] s.25(8).

[39] s.25(2) and (3). No proceedings may be instituted for this offence or others under Chapter II of Part II of the Act, and related water resource provisions, except by the Authority or by, or with the consent of, the Director of Public Prosecutions (s.216(2) and (3)).

[40] s.25(5). "Alternative statutory provision" means a statutory provision which is not contained in, or made or issued under the Water Resources Act 1963 or the Water Act 1958 (s.36(2) and (3) Water Resources Act 1963). "Statutory provision" means a provision, whether of a general or a special nature, contained in, or in any document made or issued under, any Act, whether of a general or a special nature (s.135(1) Water Resources Act 1963). For example, under s.6(2) and Sch.2, Pt.II, Section A, para.5(4) Channel Tunnel Act 1987 the authorisation by that Act of the formation of a drainage lagoon in pursuance of that Act is to be treated for the purpose of the Water Resources Acts 1963 and 1991, as if it contained a licence to construct impounding works.

[41] s.25(5) to (7) Water Resources Act 1991.

Rights to abstract or impound

Navigation, harbour and conservancy authorities

Further exceptions to the general restrictions upon abstraction and impounding apply to navigation, harbour and conservancy authorities,[42] so that the restrictions on abstraction do not apply to any transfer of water from one area of inland waters to another in the course of, or resulting from, operations carried out by these authorities in carrying out their functions. Similarly, the restrictions upon impounding do not apply to the construction or alteration of impounding works in the course of these authorities performing their functions.[43]

Abstraction of small quantities

The restrictions imposed upon abstraction do not apply to abstractions of a quantity of water not exceeding five cubic metres if this does not form part of a continuous operation, or a series of operations, whereby in aggregate more than five cubic metres are abstracted. Similarly, abstractions of not more than twenty cubic metres are excepted with the consent of the Authority.[44]

The restrictions upon abstraction do not apply to abstractions from inland waters by or on behalf of an occupier of contiguous land[45] unless the quantity of water abstracted exceeds twenty cubic metres, in

---

42 "Navigation authority" means any person who has a duty or power under any enactment to work, maintain, conserve, improve or control any canal or other inland navigation, navigable river, estuary, harbour or dock. "Harbour authority" for these purposes, means a person who is a harbour authority within the meaning of the Prevention of Oil Pollution Act 1971 and is not a navigation authority. The 1971 Act defines a "harbour authority" to mean a person or body of persons empowered by an enactment, including a local enactment, to make charges in respect of vessels entering a harbour in the United Kingdom or using facilities therein (ss.29(1) and 8(2) Prevention of Oil Pollution Act 1971). "Conservancy authority" means any person who has a duty or power under any enactment to conserve, maintain or improve the navigation of a tidal water and is not a navigation authority or harbour authority (s.221(1) Water Resources Act 1991).

43 s.26(1).

44 s.27(1) and (2).

45 "Contiguous land", in relation to the abstraction of any water from inland waters, means land contiguous to those waters at the place where the abstraction is effected (s.27(8)).

aggregate, in any period of twenty–four hours. However, this exception applies only in relation to water abstracted on a holding consisting of the contiguous land, and other land held with it, and where the water is abstracted for domestic purposes of the occupier's household or for agricultural[46] purposes other than spray irrigation.[47] A person who abstracts within this exception is taken to have a right to do so for the purposes of Chapter II of Part II of the 1991 Act.[48]

In addition, the restrictions on abstraction from underground strata do not apply in so far as the water is abstracted by or on behalf of an individual as a supply of water for the domestic purposes of his household. This exception will not apply if the quantity of water abstracted from the strata exceeds twenty cubic metres, in aggregate, in any period of twenty–four hours. A person who abstracts within this exception is taken to have a right to do so for the purposes of Chapter II of Part II of the 1991 Act.[49] In relation to an abstraction within this exception, the general restrictions upon construction and extension of a well, borehole or other work and the installation of abstraction machinery or apparatus[50] will not apply.[51]

---

[46] "Agriculture" includes horticulture, fruit growing, seed growing, dairy farming, the breeding and keeping of livestock (including any creature kept for the production of food, wool, skins or fur, or for the purpose of its use in the farming of land), the use of land as grazing land, meadow land, osier land, market gardens and nursery grounds, and the use of land for woodlands where such use in ancillary to the farming of land for other agricultural purposes, and "agricultural" is to be construed accordingly (s.221(1) Water Resources Act 1991 and s.109(3) Agriculture Act 1947).

[47] "Spray irrigation" means the irrigation of land or plants, including seeds, by means of water or other liquid emerging, in whatever form, from apparatus designed or adapted to eject liquid into the air in the form of jets or spray (s.72(1) Water Resources Act 1991). The Ministers may by order direct that references to "spray irrigation" are to be given the same meaning as in the order (s.72(5)). See also the Spray Irrigation (Definition) Order 1965, S.I. 1965 No.1010, which specifies that methods of spray irrigation carried out in connection with weed or pest control and the spreading of nutrients are excepted from abstraction licensing.

[48] s.27(3) and (6) Water Resources Act 1991.

[49] s.27(5) and (6).

[50] Under s.24(2).

[51] s.27(7).

Curtailment of rights to abstract small quantities

Where an occupier is entitled to a protected right to abstract in respect of domestic and agricultural abstractions in relation to a holding,[52] the Authority may curtail the right if that right, as against other occupiers of land contiguous to the inland waters, extends to the use of the water on only part of the holding. This is done by the service by the Authority of a notice specifying the relevant part of the holding, in relation to which abstraction may take place, and having effect so that the right of abstraction applies only in relation to the specified part of the holding. In the event of an objection by the occupier to a notice of this kind, the dispute may be determined by the county court for the district in which the holding is situated.[53]

Rights to abstract for drainage purposes

The restrictions upon abstraction from a source of supply do not apply to any abstractions in the course of, or resulting from, any operations for purposes of land drainage. Similarly, the restrictions will not apply where an abstraction is necessary to prevent interference with any mining, quarrying, engineering, building or other operations, whether underground or on the surface, or to prevent damage to works resulting from such operations. This exception applies where water is abstracted, in the course of any of the operations mentioned, from an excavation into underground strata, where the level of water therein depends wholly or mainly on water entering it from such strata, and the abstraction is necessary to prevent damage to the works, notwithstanding that the water is used for the purposes of the operations. However, the exception does not apply to the construction or extension of any well, borehole or other work, or to the installation or modification of machinery or other apparatus, if the work is done for the purpose of abstracting water.[54]

---

[52] Under s.27(4) and (6).

[53] s.28.

[54] s.29. For these purposes "land drainage" is defined to include the protection of land against erosion or encroachment by water, whether from inland waters or from the sea, and also includes warping and irrigation other than spray irrigation (s.29(5)). On land drainage generally see Ch.12 below.

Notices with respect to borings

Where any person proposes to construct or to extend a well, borehole or other work which is to be used solely for the purpose of abstracting water contained in underground strata, to the extent necessary to prevent interference with the carrying out or operation of any underground works, he must, before the work is commenced, give to the Authority notice of his intention in the prescribed form.[55] The Authority may require the person, in connection with the construction, extension or use of the work, to take reasonable measures for conserving water as specified in the notice, providing that the measures specified will not interfere with the protection of the underground works in question. Contravention of the duty to notify the Authority, or failure to comply with a notice served by the Authority, is an offence punishable, on summary conviction, by a fine not exceeding £2,000 or, on conviction on indictment, by a fine of unlimited amount.[56] Provision is made for a person on whom a notice of this kind is served by the Authority to appeal to the Secretary of State on the ground that the measures required by the conservation notice served by the Authority are not reasonable, or that those measures would interfere with the protection of the underground works in question, or to appeal on both of these grounds.[57]

Miscellaneous rights to abstract

In addition to the rights to abstract which have been previously mentioned, a range of miscellaneous rights to abstract water are provided for. These allow for abstraction by machinery or apparatus on a vessel where the water is abstracted for use on that, or any other, vessel. Similarly exempted from the restriction upon abstraction are activities which involve doing anything for fire–fighting purposes or for the purpose of testing apparatus used for those purposes or training or practice in the use of the apparatus. The abstraction restriction does not apply to the abstraction of water, the construction or extension of any well, borehole to other work or the installation or modification of

---

[55] Water Resources (Miscellaneous Provisions) Regulations 1965, S.I.1965 No.1092.

[56] s.30 Water Resources Act 1991.

[57] s.32(1).

machinery or other apparatus if these things are done with the consent of the Authority, and in compliance with any conditions imposed by the Authority and for particular purposes. The particular purposes are those of ascertaining the presence of water in any underground strata, or the quantity or quality of that water, and ascertaining the effect of abstracting water from the well, borehole or other work on the abstraction of water from, or the level of water in, any other well, borehole or other work, or from any inland waters.[58]

In addition to the specific exemptions to the requirement of abstraction licensing which have been described, a general Ministerial power is given to create further exceptions. This provides that any of the "relevant authorities" may, after consultation with other authorities, apply to the Secretary of State for an order exempting any one or more sources of supply from the restriction on abstraction, on the grounds that the restriction is not needed in relation to that source, or sources, of supply. An application of this kind may be made in respect of one or more inland waters, or any class of inland waters, or any underground strata described by reference to their formation or location. For these purposes the National Rivers Authority is a relevant authority in relation to every source of supply and a navigation, harbour or conservancy authority is a relevant authority in relation to inland water in which it has functions. Detailed matters relating to orders of this kind are provided for under Schedule 6 of the Water Resources Act 1991.[59]

APPLICATIONS FOR A LICENCE

Regulations with respect to applications

Applications for an abstraction or impounding licence are to be made in a prescribed manner including particulars verified by evidence as may be prescribed.[60] The Secretary of State may make provision as to the manner in which applications for the grant of licences under Chapter II of Part II of the Water Resources Act 1991 are to be dealt with,

---

[58] s.32.

[59] s.33.

[60] See generally Part II Water Resources (Licences) Regulations 1965, S.I. 1965 No.534, as amended.

including provision requiring the giving of notices of, and information relating to, the making of applications or decisions on applications.[61]

Applicants for a licence

The provisions relating to applications for abstraction and impounding licences are exclusively formulated, so that no application for a licence may be entertained by the Authority unless it is made by a person entitled to make the application in accordance with provisions specified under the Act.[62] The provisions specify that a person may apply for a licence to abstract from an inland water if, at the place where the proposed abstraction is to be effected, he is the occupier of contiguous land, or he satisfies the Authority that at the time when the licence is to take effect he will have a right of access to that land. In relation to abstractions from underground strata, a person will be entitled to make an application if he is the occupier of the land consisting of or comprising the underground strata. Alternatively, in a case where the level of water contained in an excavation into underground strata is dependent upon water entering it from those strata, he must satisfy the Authority that he has, or at the time when the proposed licence is to take effect, will have, a right of access to the land consisting of or comprising those strata.[63]

In either of the cases where eligibility to apply for a licence depends upon the occupation of land, an occupier will be a person who satisfies the Authority that he has entered into negotiations for the acquisition of an interest in the land, such that, if the interest is acquired by him, he will be entitled to occupy the land. Alternatively, a person will be an occupier for these purposes if the person concerned is, or can be, authorised to acquire land compulsorily by virtue of any enactment. In that case the person will have to satisfy the Authority that the compulsory acquisition of the land either has been authorised, or can be

---

[61] s.34(1) and (2) Water Resources Act 1991.

[62] In relation to abstraction from inland waters owned or managed by the British Waterways Board, no person other that the Board, or a person authorised by the Board, may give a consent for the abstraction of a small quantity (under s.27(2)) and no person other than the Board is entitled to apply for a licence (s.66).

[63] s.35(1) to (3).

authorised and has been initiated. The initiation of compulsory acquisition of land by a person is a reference to the submission to the appropriate Minister of a draft order or an order which, if made or confirmed by the Minister, will authorise the compulsory acquisition of the land.[64]

Combined abstraction and impounding licences

Where a licence is required for the construction or alteration of impounding works at a point in inland waters for the purpose of abstracting water from those waters at or near that point, an application may be made to the Authority for a combined licence to obstruct or impede the flow of those waters by means of impounding works and to abstract the water. In respect of an application of this kind the Authority has the power to grant a combined abstraction and impounding licence.[65]

Licence application procedure

The Authority may not entertain an application for an abstraction, impounding or combined licence unless a specified procedure for publication of the application is complied with. The procedure requires the applicant to submit a copy of the notice and any supporting evidence in a prescribed form,[66] and publish a notice of his proposal in a prescribed form in the *London Gazette* and at least once in each of two successive weeks in one or more newspapers circulating in the relevant locality of the proposed abstraction. In addition, where the licence applied for is for abstraction from an inland water, a copy of the notice must be served on any navigation authority, harbour authority or conservancy authority having functions in relation to the waters at the proposed point of abstraction unless the source of supply does not form a part of any inland waters. In addition, notice must be served on the

---

[64] s.35(4) to (6).

[65] s.36.

[66] See Part II Water Resources (Licences) Regulations 1965, S.I. 1965 No.534, as amended.

internal drainage board and any water undertaker within whose area the proposed point of abstraction is situated.[67]

The notice, in addition to giving details of the intended abstraction, must name a place within the relevant locality where a copy of the application and any map, plan or other document submitted with it, will be open to inspection by the public, free of charge, at all reasonable hours. The notice must also state that any person may make written representations to the Authority with respect to the application. The period during which written representations may be made is to be a period of not less than twenty-eight days from the date on which the notice is first published in a newspaper, and not less than twenty-five days from the date on which it is published in the *London Gazette*. Where an application for an abstraction licence proposes that the quantity of water abstracted should not in any period of twenty-four hours exceed, in aggregate, twenty cubic metres or any lesser amount, the Authority may dispense with these requirements.[68]

General consideration of applications

The Authority is not to determine an application for an abstraction, impounding or combined licence before the end of the twenty-eight day period during which written representations may be made in relation to the application. Thereafter, it may grant a licence containing appropriate provisions or, if necessary or expedient to do so, it may refuse to grant a licence. In dealing with an application, the Authority is bound to have regard to any representations made in relation to it and the reasonable requirements of the applicant.[69]

The Authority is not to grant a licence authorising the abstraction of water, or for the flow of any inland waters to be obstructed or impeded by impounding works, so as to derogate from any rights which at the time when the application is determined are protected rights, without the consent of the person entitled to those rights. For the purposes of Chapter II of Part II of the 1991 Act, the expression "protected rights" is a reference to a right which a person may have in relation to certain

---

[67] s.37(1) to (3) Water Resources Act 1991.

[68] s.37(4) to (6).

[69] s.38.

abstractions of small quantities of water,[70] or in respect of abstractions by the holder of an abstraction licence.[71] References to derogation from protected rights, means abstracting water or obstructing or impeding the flow of waters in such a way, and to such an extent, as to prevent a person with a protected right from exercising that right to the extent of his entitlement. In a case where an application for a licence relates to abstraction from underground strata, the Authority, in dealing with the application, is also to have regard to the requirements of existing lawful users of water abstracted from those strata, whether for agriculture, industry, water supply or other purposes.[72]

In relation to an application for an abstraction, impounding or combined licence with respect to inland waters where no minimum acceptable flow for those waters has been determined, the Authority, in dealing with the application, is to have regard to the considerations by reference to which a minimum acceptable flow would be determined.[73] Where the application is made after a minimum acceptable flow has been determined, the Authority is to have regard to the need to secure the minimum acceptable flow. Similarly, regard has to be had to these considerations in relation to abstractions from underground strata where the proposed abstraction is likely to affect the flow, level or volume of any inland waters which are not discrete waters nor exempted by a Ministerial order.[74]

Reference of applications to the Secretary of State

The Secretary of State may give directions to the Authority, relating either to a particular application or to applications of a specified class, requiring that applications for licences be referred to him instead of being dealt with by the Authority. A direction of this kind may also be

---

[70] Under s.27(6), relating to abstractions by an occupier of contiguous land for domestic or agricultural purposes or abstraction from underground strata for domestic purposes (see s.27(3) to (5), described above at p.253).

[71] Under s.48(1).

[72] s.39.

[73] Minimum acceptable flow is determined under s.21(4) and (5), see p.245 above.

[74] s.40.

given exempting from determination by the Authority classes of application specified in the direction.[75]

Before determining an application referred to him, the Secretary of State may, and must if so requested by the applicant or the Authority, hold a local inquiry or hearing at which the applicant and the Authority have the opportunity to appear. The decision of the Secretary of State on an application referred to him is final, and where the decision is that a licence is to be granted, the direction is to include a direction to the Authority to grant a licence containing provisions specified in the direction.[76]

Appeals to the Secretary of State

Provision is made for appeal to the Secretary of State where an applicant for a licence is dissatisfied with the decision of the Authority in respect of a licence application.[77] Notice of appeal to the Secretary of State is to be served within a prescribed period of not less than twenty-eight days from the date when the decision to which it relates was notified to the applicant, and within that time the applicant must serve a copy of the notice on the Authority. Where written representations with respect to the application have been made, the Secretary of State must require the Authority to serve a copy of the notice of appeal on each of the persons who made those representations.[78]

Where an appeal is made to the Secretary of State he may allow or dismiss the appeal or vary any part of the decision of the Authority, and may deal with the application as if it had been made to him in the first instance. Before determining an appeal, he may, and must if a request is made by the applicant or the Authority, cause a local inquiry or hearing to be held or afford the applicant and the Authority an opportunity of appearing before, and being heard by, a person appointed by the Secretary of State for that purpose. The Secretary of State is to take into account any further representations made to him and the reasonable

---

[75] s.41.

[76] s.42.

[77] Generally, see Reg.12 Water Resources (Licences) Regulations 1965, S.I. 1965 No.534, as amended.

[78] s.43 Water Resources Act 1991.

requirements of the applicant, and also the derogation from any protected rights. His decision on the appeal is final, and where the decision is that a licence is to be granted or to be varied or revoked, it is to include a direction to the Authority to grant a licence containing, or vary the licence so as to contain, provisions specified in the direction, or revoke the licence as the case may be.[79]

Rights of appeal to the Secretary of State also arise in default of a decision by the Authority. Where an application for a licence is made to the Authority, then unless within a prescribed period, or within an extended period agreed in writing, the Authority either give notice to the applicant of its decision or give notice that the application has been referred to the Secretary of State, the provisions relating to appeals to the Secretary of State are similarly applicable.[80]

The Secretary of State may make provision by regulations as to the manner in which appeals against decisions on applications for the grant, revocation or variation of licences under Chapter II of Part II of the 1991 Act are to be dealt with. These Regulations may include provision requiring the giving of notices of, and information relating to, the making of appeals or decisions on appeals.[81]

CONTENT AND CONSEQUENCES OF LICENCES

Form and content of licences

Although particular matters relating to the form of licences may be provided for in regulations, any regulations made are to have effect subject to express provisions under the Water Resources Act 1991 for matters to be provided for in licences under Chapter II of Part II of the Act. Accordingly, every licence to abstract water is to make provision as to the quantity of water authorised to be abstracted in pursuance of the licence from the source of supply during a period, or periods, specified in the licence including provision as to the way in which that quantity is to be measured or assessed. Provision is to be made for determining, by

---

[79] s.44.

[80] s.43(1)(b).

[81] s.45(1), and generally see Reg.12 Water Resources (Licences) Regulations 1965, S.I. 1965 No.534.

measurement or assessment, what quantity of water is to be taken to have been abstracted, during any period, by the holder from the source of supply to which the licence relates. Indication is to be given in the licence as to the means whereby water is authorised to be abstracted in pursuance of the licence, by reference either to specified works, machinery or apparatus or to works, machinery or apparatus fulfilling specified requirements. Specification is to be given of the land on which, and the purposes for which, water abstracted in pursuance of the licence is to be used other than where the licence is granted to a water undertaker or sewerage undertaker or to any person who proposes to abstract the water for the purpose of supplying it to others. Every licence is to include a statement whether the licence is to remain in force until revoked or is to expire at a specified time. The same licence may make different provision with respect to the abstraction of water during different periods, abstraction from the same source of supply but at different points or by different means, or for the use of water for different purposes. Two or more licences may be granted to the same person to be held concurrently in respect of the same source of supply if the licences authorise the abstraction of water at different points or by different means.[82] Every licence is also to specify the person to whom it is granted, but this is to have effect subject to express provisions in the Act relating to succession to licences in the event of the death of the holder or where another person becomes the occupier of the land to which the licence relates.[83]

The general effect of a licence to abstract water is that the holder is to be taken to have the right to abstract water to the extent authorised by the licence and in accordance with the provisions contained in it. Where an action is brought against a person in respect of water abstracted from a source of supply, it will be a defence for him to prove that the abstraction was in pursuance of a licence and that the provisions of the licence were complied with. Similarly, where an action is brought against a person in respect of any obstruction or impeding of the flow of an inland water by impounding works, it will be a defence for him to prove that the flow was obstructed or impeded in pursuance of a licence, in the manner specified in the licence and to an extent not exceeding that specified, and

---

[82] s.46 Water Resources Act 1991.

[83] s.47. On succession to licences see s.49 and 50.

that the other requirements of the licence were complied with. However, these defences will not exonerate a person from an action for negligence or breach of contract.[84]

Revocation and variation of licences

The holder of an abstraction licence may apply to the Authority to revoke the licence, and thereupon the Authority is bound to revoke it.[85] Alternatively, the holder of a licence may apply to the Authority to vary the licence, in which case the provisions of the Act relating to publication and determination of licences, and referrals and appeals to the Secretary of State,[86] apply with the necessary modifications as they apply to an application for, and a grant of, a licence. However, if the proposed variation is limited to reducing the quantity of water authorised to be abstracted, publication of the notice of variation and the consideration of written representations by the Authority will not apply.[87]

Where it appears to the Authority that a licence should be revoked or varied, the Authority may formulate proposals to that effect. Similarly, where it appears to the Secretary of State that a licence ought to be reviewed, he may direct the Authority to formulate proposals for revoking the licence or varying it in such a manner as may be specified in the direction.[88] Where either of these procedures are followed, requirements as to publication, service of notice on relevant authorities, and provision for the making of representations apply, and where the holder of the licence objects to the proposals they must be referred to the Secretary of State for determination.[89]

If it appears necessary to the Authority, by reason of exceptional shortage of rain or other emergency, to impose a temporary restriction on the abstraction of water used for the purpose of spray irrigation, or for that purpose together with other purposes, the Authority may serve a

---

[84] s.48.

[85] s.51(1).

[86] That is, ss.37 to 44.

[87] s.51(2) to (4).

[88] s.52(1) and (2).

[89] Generally, see ss.52 and 53. On reference of modification proposals to the Secretary of State see s.54. On applications for modification of a licence by the owner of fishing rights see ss.55 and 56.

notice on the holder of a licence which authorises abstraction for that purpose reducing, during a specified period, the quantity of water authorised to be abstracted. A notice of this kind may not be served in respect of abstraction from underground strata unless that abstraction is likely to affect the flow, level or volume of an inland water. Where two or more licences authorise abstraction from the same source of supply, either at the same point or at points which are not far distant from each other, like notice must be served on all the licence holders in respect of the same period and the reductions imposed by the notices must represent as nearly as practicable the same proportion of the quantity of water authorised by the licences to be abstracted for spray irrigation.[90]

If charges payable in respect of a licence under Chapter II of Part II of the Water Resources Act are not paid within twenty–eight days after the notice demanding them has been served on the holder of the licence, the Authority may revoke the licence by the service of a notice of revocation on the holder of the licence.[91] A notice demanding the payment of charges, served for these purposes, is to state that the licence in question may be revoked if the charges are not paid within twenty–eight days after the service of the notice, set out the effect of revocation and state that no compensation is payable in respect of the revocation. Revocation of a licence is to take effect at a time specified in the notice, which is not less than twenty–eight days after the notice has been served, and will take effect only if the charges are not paid before the expiry of that period. A notice of revocation is to set out the reason for the revocation and state that the revocation will take effect only if the charges in question are not paid before the time specified in the notice.[92]

Derogation from protected rights

As has been noted, the Authority is prohibited from granting a licence authorising abstraction or impounding so as to derogate from any rights which, at the time when the application is determined, are protected rights. This means that a licence must not be granted so as to allow its holder to abstract water in such a manner, or to such an extent,

[90] s.57. On spray irrigation see p.254 above.

[91] On water resource charges generally see p.270 below.

[92] s.58.

as to prevent a person entitled to a protected right from abstracting water to the extent permitted in accordance with the protected right.[93]

A breach of the duty imposed on the Authority not to grant licences which derogate from protected rights does not invalidate the grant or modification of a licence, but any person entitled to a protected right may seek enforcement of his right by bringing a civil action against the Authority for damages for breach of statutory duty. Infringement of protected rights cannot be enforced by criminal proceedings or by prohibition or injunction, and neither can proceedings be brought against persons other than the Authority. Where the Authority is directed by the Secretary of State to grant or vary a licence which authorises derogation from protected rights, this will be treated as a breach of statutory duty on the part of the Authority. The duty of the Authority to comply with the Secretary of State's direction will not afford a defence in an action brought against it for breach of statutory duty.[94]

In an action brought against the Authority for breach of statutory duty, it is a defence to prove that the abstraction licence granted or varied by the Authority, in derogation from the protected right, was wholly or mainly attributable to exceptional shortage of rain or to an accident or other unforeseen act or event not caused by, and outside the control of, the Authority.[95] A second defence open to the Authority arises where the plaintiff is entitled to a protected right as the holder of, or the applicant for, a licence of right, and where the plaintiff could have carried out permissible alterations in the means whereby he abstracted water, and if those alterations had been carried out the abstraction of impounding authorised by the licence to which the action relates would not have derogated from his protected right.[96] For these purposes a "licence of right" is a reference to the mechanism for the statutory continuation of certain common law rights to abstract water which were made subject to the licensing system provided for under the Water Resources Act 1963, and the subsequent extension of licensing under the Water Act 1989.[97]

---

[93] s.39(1), and see ss.51(3) and 53(5) concerned with modification of licences.

[94] s.60(1) to (3).

[95] s.60(4).

[96] Sch.7 para.4.

[97] Accordingly, a reference to a licence of right is a reference to (a) any 1989 Act licence of right, that is to say, a licence granted under para.30 or 31 of Sch.26 Water

Where a licence is revoked or varied in pursuance of a modification proposal referred to the Secretary of State or an application for modification by the owner of fishing rights,[98] a duty to pay compensation arises. Specifically, where it is shown that the holder of the licence has incurred expenditure in carrying out work which is rendered abortive by the revocation or modification, or has otherwise sustained loss or damage which is directly attributable to the revocation or modification, the Authority is bound to pay him compensation in respect of that expenditure, loss or damage.[99] Where the Authority is liable to pay damages to any person in consequence of the grant or variation of a licence in compliance with a direction given by the Secretary of State, and the Authority pays to that person any sum in satisfaction of that liability, then, whether an action for the recovery of those damages has been brought or not, the Secretary of State may pay the Authority the whole or an appropriate part of the amount paid.[100]

Civil liability

Except in so far as express provision is made,[101] and subject to the provisions of the Interpretation Act 1978 relating to offences under two or more laws,[102] the restrictions imposed upon abstraction, impounding and notices with respect to borings not requiring licences,[103] are not be construed as affecting certain other legal rights. Hence, these provisions do not confer any right of action in any civil proceedings, other than for recovery of a fine, where contravened. Neither do they affect any

---

Act 1989; or (b) any licence which, having been granted in pursuance of an application under s.33 Water Resources Act 1963, has effect after the coming into force of the Water Resources Act 1991 and continues in effect as a licence under Chapter II of Part II of that Act (Sch.7 para.6 Water Resources Act 1991). Licences of right are provided for under Sch.7 Water Resources Act 1991, introduced under s.66.

[98] Under ss.54 and 55 respectively.

[99] s.61(1), and see s.62 on compensation for the owner of fishing rights making an application for the modification of a licence under s.55.

[100] s.63(1).

[101] See ss.61 and 62.

[102] See s.18 Interpretation Act 1978.

[103] Under ss.24, 25 and 30 Water Resources Act 1991 respectively.

restriction imposed by or under any other enactment, whether contained in a public general Act or in a local or private Act, or derogate from any right of action or other civil or criminal remedy in proceedings instituted otherwise than under Chapter II of Part II of the Water Resources Act 1991.[104]

Abstraction and impounding by the Authority and water undertakers

The National Rivers Authority may be authorised to abstract water in accordance with its water resource function,[105] and accordingly the provisions of Chapter II of Part II of the Water Resources Act 1991 have effect in relation to the abstraction of water and the construction or alteration of impounding works by the Authority, subject to prescribed exceptions and modifications. Regulations may provide for securing that any licence required by the Authority is granted, or deemed to be granted, by the Secretary of State rather than the Authority.[106] Detailed provisions regarding the procedure for determination of licence applications by the Authority are provided for under the Water Resources (Licences) Regulations 1965, as amended.[107]

Originally, water companies acquired the right to abstract water for supply purposes and impound water for so doing under local enactments, but subsequent statutory measures made more general provision for the construction of works to enable water to be taken for supply purposes and for land to be acquired for this purpose.[108] Despite the repeal of these provisions, any orders made under previous statutory provisions continue to be effective to authorise water undertakers to abstract within the terms of the order.[109]

---

[104] s.70. On civil proceedings generally see *Cargill v. Gotts*, [1981] 1 All E.R. 682; and *Scott-Whitehead v. National Coal Board*, (1987) 53 P. & C.R. 263.

[105] See p.206 above on the water resources function of the Authority.

[106] s.64 Water Resources Act 1991.

[107] S.I. 1965 No.534, see Regs.13 to 15.

[108] See s.23 Water Act 1945 (repealed) and s.67 Water Resources Act 1963 (repealed).

[109] Sch.26 para.41(1) Water Act 1989. Abstraction licences were transferred to water undertakers under transfer schemes provided for under Sch.2 Water Act 1989. On

For the future, where a water undertaker wishes to conduct engineering or building operations in connection with water abstraction, and to exercise compulsory powers in relation to those works, it will require an order from the Secretary of State in order to do so.[110] Where an order is granted by the Secretary of State to enable a water undertaker to conduct works, nothing in the order may exempt the undertaker from any restriction imposed by Chapter II of Part II of the Water Resources Act 1991 in respect of the abstraction and impounding of water.[111] However, in connection with any engineering or building operations to which a compulsory works order relates, and an abstraction or impounding licence is granted or deemed to be granted, no compensation will be payable in respect of any land or interest injuriously affected by the carrying out of the operations in so far as the abstraction or impounding is conducted in accordance with the provisions of the licence.[112]

WATER RESOURCE CHARGES

Charging schemes for licences

In relation to water resources, the National Rivers Authority may require the payment to it of charges specified or determined under a scheme made by it.[113] Charges are payable, first, where an application is made for any licence under Chapter II of Part II of the Water Resources Act 1991, concerned with abstraction or impounding, or for the variation of, or of the conditions of, any licence; second, where a licence to abstract water is granted to any person or there is a variation of a licence or of the conditions of a licence; and, third, where a licence is for the time being in force. The person liable to pay charges under the scheme will be, in the first case, the person who makes the application, and, in

---

the continuation of these provisions see Sch.2 Water Consolidation (Consequential Provisions) Act 1991.

[110] Under s.167 and Sch.11 Water Industry Act 1991.

[111] s.167(6).

[112] Sch.11 para.7.

[113] On the operation of a scheme for water resources charges provided for under former legislation (ss.30 and 31 Water Act 1973), see *National Rivers Authority v. Newcastle and Gateshead Water Co.*, (1990) *The Times* 23 November 1990.

the other cases, the person to whom the licence is granted or, as the case may be, the person holding the licence which is varied or is in force. Where a charge is imposed in respect of an abstraction licence which is for the time being in force, the scheme may impose a single charge in respect of the whole period for which a licence is in force or separate charges in respect of different parts of that period, or both. A charging scheme may make provision concerning the times and methods of payment, different provisions for different cases including different circumstances and localities, and contain supplemental, consequential and transitional provisions. The Authority may not make a scheme of this kind until it has been approved by the Secretary of State, and it is the duty of the Authority to bring a scheme which is in force to the attention of persons likely to be affected by it.[114]

Before submitting a scheme to the Secretary of State for approval, the Authority must publish a notice setting out its proposals, in a manner appropriate for bringing it to the attention of persons likely to be affected, and specifying the period within which representations or objections with respect to the proposals may be made to the Secretary of State. It is the duty of the Secretary of State, in determining whether or not to approve the scheme or to approve it subject to modifications, to have regard to three considerations. These are, first, he must consider any representations or objection duly made to him and not withdrawn. Second, he is to have regard to the desirability of ensuring that the amounts recovered by way of charges are the amounts which, taking one year with another, are amounts appropriate to attribute to the expenses of the Authority in relation to its water resources functions.[115] Third, he is to have regard to the need to ensure that no undue preference is shown, and that there is no undue discrimination in fixing the charges. Finally, the consent of the Treasury is required for the giving of approval by the Secretary of State to a charging scheme.[116]

---

[114] s.123 Water Resources Act 1991.

[115] In this matter he is to take into account any determinations under s.117, concerning the amounts which he considers it appropriate to attribute to the expenses incurred by the Authority in carrying out its water resource functions (s.124(4)).

[116] s.124.

No charges other than the administrative expenses of the Authority are to be levied in respect of water authorised to be abstracted for use in the production of electricity, or any other form of power, by a generating station or apparatus of a capacity of not more than five megawatts. No charges are to be levied in respect of water authorised to be abstracted from underground strata, in so far as the water is authorised to be abstracted for use for agricultural purposes other than spray irrigation, and the quantity of water authorised to be abstracted from the strata in any period of twenty–four hours does not exceed twenty cubic metres in aggregate.[117]

Provisions relating to exemptions from, and reduction of, charges allow the Authority, on the application of a person who is liable to pay charges for the abstraction of water under a licence, to make an agreement either exempting him from payment of charges, or providing for charges to be levied at a reduced rate. In exercising its power to enter into an agreement of this kind, the Authority is to have regard to the extent to which any works constructed by the person liable to pay charges make a beneficial contribution towards the fulfilment of any function of the Authority. Also, the Authority is to have regard to any financial assistance the person has rendered, or agreed to render, towards the carrying out of works by the Authority in performance of its functions, and any other material considerations. The Secretary of State may give directions to the Authority as to its powers to exempt or reduce charges in accordance with these provisions, and certain disputes as to the exercise of the powers may be referred to the Secretary of State for determination.[118]

Where a person is the holder of a licence to abstract water for spray irrigation[119] and the water is to be used on land of which he is the occupier, he may apply to the Authority to enter into an agreement concerning the payment of special charges in respect of spray irrigation. Agreements of this kind allow for charges to be payable partly in respect of basic charges calculated on the quantity of water authorised to be abstracted and partly on the quantity measured or assessed as being

117 s.125.

118 s.126.

119 On spray irrigation generally, see Spray Irrigation (Definition) Order 1965, S.I. 1965 No.1010, and p.254 above.

abstracted.[120] The period for which an agreement in relation to special charges for spray irrigation is to apply is not to be less than five years.[121] If the Authority refuses to make an agreement of this kind, or if the licence holder objects to the terms of the agreement as proposed by the Authority, either party may refer the question in dispute to the Secretary of State whose decision on the matter will be final.[122]

Register of applications and licences

The National Rivers Authority is bound to keep registers, in a manner prescribed by regulations,[123] containing information with respect to applications made to the Authority for the grant, revocation or variation of licences under Chapter II of Part II of the Water Resources Act 1991. The registers are to include information as to the way in which applications have been dealt with, and information with respect to persons becoming holders of licences by way of succession. The registers are also to contain prescribed information with respect to licences granted, or deemed to be granted, and licences revoked or varied. The contents of registers kept in accordance with these provisions are to be available at a prescribed place for inspection by the public at all reasonable hours.[124]

DROUGHT

Ordinary and emergency drought orders

If the Secretary of State is satisfied that, by reason of an exceptional shortage of rain, a serious deficiency of supplies of water in any area exists or is threatened, he may by an ordinary drought order make such provision as appears to him to be expedient with a view to meeting the deficiency. If, beyond this, he is satisfied that, by reason of

---

[120] s.127 Water Resources Act 1991.
[121] s.128(1).
[122] s.129.
[123] See Reg.17 Water Resources (Licences) Regulations 1965, S.I. 1965 No.534, as amended.
[124] s.189 Water Resources Act 1991.

an exceptional shortage of rain, a serious deficiency of supplies of water in any area exists or is threatened, and is further satisfied that the deficiency is likely to impair the economic or social well–being of persons in the area, he may by order make such provision by an emergency drought order as appears to him to be expedient with a view to meeting the deficiency.[125]

Subject to certain powers of the Secretary of State to vary or revoke ordinary drought orders,[126] the power to make a drought order of either kind in relation to any area is not to be exercisable except where an application is made to him by the Authority or a water undertaker which supplies water to premises in that area. The power to make a drought order is to be exercisable by statutory instrument and the detailed provisions with respect to the procedure on application for such an order are provided for under Schedule 8 to the Water Resources Act 1991.[127]

Provisions and duration of ordinary drought orders

An ordinary drought order made on the application of the Authority may contain any of the following provisions: (a) provision authorising the Authority, or persons authorised by it, to take water from any source specified in the order subject to specified conditions or restrictions; (b) provision authorising the Authority to discharge water to any place specified in the order subject to any specified conditions or restrictions; (c) provision authorising the Authority to prohibit or limit the taking by any person, including a water undertaker, of water from a source specified in the order if the Authority is satisfied that the taking of water from that source will seriously affect the supplies available to the Authority, any water undertaker or any other person; (d) provision suspending or modifying, subject to any specified conditions, any restrictions or obligation to which the Authority, any water or sewerage undertaker or any other person is subject as respects the taking of water from any source, the discharge of water, the supply of water, or the filtration or other treatment of water; (e) provision authorising the Authority to suspend or vary, or attach conditions to, any consent

125 s.73(1) and (2).
126 Under s.76(3).
127 s.73(3) and (4).

specified in the order for the discharge of any effluent by any person, including any sewerage or water undertaker.[128]

Where the ordinary drought order is made on the application of a water undertaker it may contain the following provisions: (a) provision authorising the water undertaker to take water from any source specified in the order subject to specified conditions or restrictions; (b) provision authorising the water undertaker to prohibit or limit the use of water for any specified purpose set out in a direction given by the Secretary of State to water undertakers generally; (c) provision authorising the water undertaker to discharge water to any place specified in the order subject to any specified conditions or restrictions; (d) provision authorising the Authority to prohibit or limit the taking by any person, including a water undertaker, of water from a source specified in the order if the Authority is satisfied that the taking of water from that source will seriously affect the supplies available to the Authority, any water undertaker or any other person; (e) provision prohibiting or limiting the taking by the Authority of water from a specified source if the taking of water from that source is determined seriously to affect the supplies available to the water undertaker; (f) provision suspending or modifying, subject to any specified conditions, any restrictions or obligation to which the water undertaker or any sewerage undertaker or any other person is subject as respects the taking of water from any source, the discharge of water, the supply of water, or the filtration or other treatment of water; (g) provision authorising the Authority to suspend or vary, or attach conditions to, any consent specified in the order for the discharge of any effluent by any person, including the company which applied for the order in any capacity.[129]

An authorisation, prohibition or limitation, or a suspension or modification, imposed under an ordinary drought order is to expire before the end of six months beginning with the day on which it comes into force, unless the period is extended in relation to that order by virtue of the power of the Secretary of State to extend the order. His power to amend an ordinary drought order is not to be exercised so as to extend

[128] s.74(1).

[129] s.74(2).

the period of six months beyond the end of one year from the day on which the order came into force.[130]

Provisions and duration of emergency drought orders

An emergency drought order made on the application of the Authority may contain any of the provisions which could be included in an ordinary drought order made on the application of the Authority. Where an emergency drought order is made on the application of a water undertaker, it may contain any of the provisions which could be included in an ordinary drought order made on the application of a water undertaker except provision (b), which authorises the water undertaker to prohibit or limit the use of water for any purpose specified in the order as a direction to water undertakers generally. In addition to the provisions which may be made in ordinary drought orders, an emergency drought order made on the application of a water undertaker may contain provision authorising the undertaker to prohibit or limit the use of water for such purposes as the undertaker thinks fit, provision authorising the undertaker to supply water by means of stand–pipes or water tanks, and to erect or set up and maintain stand–pipes or water tanks in any street.[131]

The period for which an authorisation, prohibition or limitation, or a suspension or modification under an emergency drought order is to have effect is to expire before the end of three months beginning with the day on which the order comes into force unless the period is extended by the Secretary of State. His power to amend an emergency drought order is not to be exercised so as to extend the initial period of three months beyond five months beginning with the day on which the order came into force.[132]

Where powers have been conferred on any person by an emergency drought order, the Secretary of State may give to that person such directions as he considers necessary or expedient as to the manner in which, or the circumstances in which, any of those powers are to be exercised. It will then be the duty of the person to comply with the direction, and where the person is a water or sewerage undertaker, the

---

[130] s.74(3) and (4).
[131] s.75(1) and (2).
[132] s.75(3) and (4).

duty to comply will be enforceable by further direction by the Secretary of State.[133]

Provisions, works and compensation under drought orders

Where a drought order contains a provision authorising a water undertaker to prohibit or limit the use of water, the power may be exercised in relation to consumers generally, in relation to a class of consumers or a particular consumer. The water undertaker is bound to take such steps as it thinks fit for bringing the prohibition or limitation to the attention of the persons to whom it will apply by publishing notice of it in local newspapers or sending notice of it to the persons concerned. The prohibition or limitation will not come into operation until the end of a period of seventy–two hours beginning with the day on which the notice was published or sent.[134]

Special provisions may be included in a drought order to authorise the taking of water from a source from which water is supplied to an inland navigation,[135] or to suspend or modify a restriction upon taking water from a source which is supplied to an inland navigation, or suspend or modify an obligation to discharge compensation water[136] into a canal, river or stream which is part of, or supplies, an inland navigation. The special provisions which may be included also allow for prohibiting or limiting the taking of water from the inland navigation, or for suspension or modification of any obligation to which a navigation authority is subject in respect of the discharge of water from the inland navigation.[137]

A prohibition or limitation under a drought order on a person taking water from any source may be imposed so as to have effect in relation to a source from which the person, to whom the prohibition or

---

133 s.75(5). Directions by the Secretary of State are enforceable under s.18 Water Industry Act 1991.

134 s.76(1) Water Resources Act 1991.

135 "Inland navigation" includes any canal or navigable river (s.77(6)).

136 "Compensation water" means water which a water undertaker or the Authority is under an obligation to discharge under Chapter II of Part II of the Water Resources Act 1991, or under any local statutory provision, into any river stream or brook or other running water or into a canal (s.77(6)).

137 s.77(1).

limitation applies, has a right to take water whether by virtue of an enactment or instrument, an agreement or the ownership of land. Where a drought order made on the application of a water undertaker confers a power on the Authority to prohibit or limit the taking of water from any source, or to suspend or vary, or attach conditions to, any consent for the discharge of effluent, the Authority is bound to exercise that power in a manner which ensures, so far as reasonably practicable, that the supplies of water available to the water undertaker are not seriously affected. Where a drought order confers powers on the Authority to suspend or vary, or attach conditions to, any consent for the discharge of any effluent, and the Authority exercises that power so as to restrict the discharge of effluent by a sewerage undertaker, the sewerage undertaker may modify any consent or agreements relating to the discharge by other persons of trade effluent so as to enable it to comply with requirements or conditions imposed on it under the order.[138]

A drought order may authorise the Authority or a water undertaker, subject to conditions and restrictions specified in the order, to carry out any works required for the performance of any duty or the exercise of any power which is imposed or conferred under the order.[139] For the purpose of carrying out authorised works, the Authority or the undertaker may enter upon any land specified in the order and occupy and use the land to such an extent and in such a manner as may be requisite for carrying out and maintaining the works. The order may also apply specified statutory provisions,[140] in relation to the works as they appear to the Secretary of State to be appropriate and subject to any modifications specified in the order.[141] The Secretary of State is to include in a drought order authorising the Authority or a water undertaker to enter land, provisions requiring the Authority or undertaker to give the occupier of the land, and specified other persons concerned

---

[138] s.77(2), (3) and (5).

[139] s.78(1).

[140] That is, Part VII Water Resources Act 1991 (see p.214 above) or Part VI of the Water Industry Act 1991.

[141] s.78(2) Water Resources Act 1991.

with the land, not less than twenty-four hours' notice of any intended entry.[142]

Where a drought order has been made, compensation is payable to the owners or occupiers of land, and all other persons interested in the land or injuriously affected by the entry upon or occupation or use of land, for damage sustained by that reason. In addition compensation is payable, under specified circumstances, in respect of restrictions upon abstraction and discharge of water in pursuance of an ordinary drought order.[143] However, other than in the situations explicitly provided for, neither the Authority nor any water or sewerage undertaker will incur any liability to any person for loss or damage sustained by reason of anything done, or any omission, in pursuance of any drought order. Nothing in a drought order will affect the right of the Authority, or a water or sewerage undertaker, in the event of an interruption or diminution of the supply of water, to recover any fixed or minimum charge which might have been recovered from any person.[144]

Offences under drought orders

A range of criminal offences arise in relation to drought orders. If a person takes or uses water in contravention of a prohibition or limitation imposed under a drought order, or does so otherwise than in accordance with any condition or restriction under an order, or discharges water otherwise than in accordance with any conditions or restrictions imposed under an order, he will be guilty of an offence. If a person fails to construct or maintain a gauge, weir or other apparatus for measuring the flow of water which he is required to do under a drought order, or fails to allow an authorised person under an order to inspect or examine the apparatus or any records made by the apparatus or kept by the person or to take copies of those records, he will be guilty of an

---

[142] s.78(3). However, any works to be carried out under the authority of an emergency drought order are to be included in the definition of emergency works in s.48 of the New Roads and Street Works Act 1991 (s.78(5)).

[143] s.79(1) and Sch.9 Water Resources Act 1991. See *Bateman v. Welsh Water Authority*, [1987] R.V.R. 10 on remoteness of damage suffered as a consequence of a drought order.

[144] s.79(2) and (3).

offence. In any proceedings, however, it will be a defence for the person to show that he took all reasonable precautions and exercised all due diligence to avoid the commission of the offence. A person who is guilty of an offence will be liable, on summary conviction, to a fine not exceeding £2,000 and, on conviction on indictment, to a fine.[145]

RESERVOIR SAFETY

The Reservoirs Act 1975

In addition to the general restrictions upon unlicensed impounding, previously described, impoundment of water in certain categories of reservoir may give rise to criminal liability under the provisions of the Reservoirs Act 1975 administered and enforced by local authorities. The controls operative under the 1975 Act apply to "large raised reservoirs" for water, an expression which does not include a mine or quarry lagoon which is otherwise provided for,[146] or any canal or inland navigation. A reservoir is a "raised reservoir" if it is designed to hold, or capable of holding, water above the natural level of any part of the land adjoining the reservoir, and a raised reservoir is a "large" raised reservoir if it is designed to hold more than 25,000 cubic metres of water above the level of the adjoining land. The provisions made in relation to large raised reservoirs extend to any place where water is artificially retained to form or enlarge a lake or loch, whether or not use is, or is intended to be, made of the water. The provisions also extend to large raised reservoirs constructed under statutory powers.[147] In relation to any reservoir, the expression "undertakers" means, in the case of a reservoir that is, when constructed, to be managed by the National Rivers Authority or a water undertaker, that Authority or, as the case may be, that undertaker.[148] In any other case "undertaker" means, if the reservoir is used or intended to be used for the purposes of any undertaking, the

---

[145] s.80.

[146] Mine and quarry lagoons are covered by the Mines and Quarries (Tips) Act 1929.

[147] s.1(1) to (3) Reservoirs Act 1975, previously Reservoirs (Safety Provisions) Act 1930.

[148] Amended by Sch.25 and para.49 Water Act 1989.

person for the time being carrying on that undertaking or if the reservoir is not so used, the owners or lessees of the reservoir.[149]

Registration of reservoirs by local authorities

It is the duty of each local authority in England and Wales, the councils of counties, metropolitan districts and London boroughs, to establish and maintain for their area a register showing the large raised reservoirs situated wholly or partly in their area. The register is to give prescribed information[150] about each of them and is to be kept at the principal offices of the local authority where it is to be available for inspection by any person at all reasonable times. It is the duty of the local authority, in whose area a reservoir is situated, to secure that the undertakers observe and comply with the requirements of the Reservoirs Act 1975. Accordingly, the "enforcement authority", charged with securing that undertakers observe and comply with the requirements of the Act, means the local authority in whose area a reservoir is situated.[151]

Each local authority is bound, at prescribed intervals,[152] to make to the Secretary of State a report giving prescribed information as to the steps taken by them as enforcement authority to secure that undertakers observe and comply with the requirements of the Act, or as to the steps taken by them to observe and comply with those requirements as undertakers for any reservoir situated in their area. If it appears to the Secretary of State that a local authority has failed to perform its functions under the Act, he may cause a public inquiry to be held, and if the failure to perform any function is established by the inquiry then the Secretary

---

149 s.1(4) Reservoirs Act 1975. In *Braintree D.C. v. Gosfield Hall Settlement Trustees*, (unreported Chelmsford Crown Court 13 July 1977) it was held that under the Reservoirs (Safety Provisions) Act 1930 settlement trustees as owners, and a lessee of a reservoir, were "undertakers", but an angling association with an under-lease of fishing rights were not "undertakers" for the purposes of a reservoir safety order under that Act.

150 See the Reservoirs Act 1975 (Registers, Reports and Records) Regulations 1985, S.I. 1985, No.177.

151 s.2 Reservoirs Act 1975.

152 Under the Reservoirs Act 1975 (Registers, Reports and Records) Regulations 1985, S.I. 1985 No.177.

of State may make an order directing the authority to perform the function in a specified manner.[153]

Qualification of engineers

There is to be a panel, or panels, of civil engineers for the purposes of the Act, and any reference to a "qualified civil engineer" is a reference to a civil engineer who is a member of the appropriate panel. Any civil engineer may apply in the prescribed manner to be placed on any panel and if the Secretary of State is satisfied that the applicant is qualified and fit to be placed on the panel the Secretary of State is to appoint him to be a member of the panel.[154] Initially, appointment to the panel is to be for a term of five years, with provision for re–appointment, but the Secretary of State may remove an engineer from the panel if, after consultation with the engineer, he is satisfied that the engineer is not fit to remain on the panel.[155]

Certification of reservoirs

No large raised reservoir may be constructed, whether as a new reservoir or by the alteration of an existing reservoir, or shall be altered so as to increase its capacity, unless a qualified civil engineer, termed the "construction engineer", is employed to design and supervise the construction or alteration. Where the use of a reservoir has been abandoned and the reservoir is to be brought back into use after being altered so as to increase its capacity, this is to be treated as the construction of a new reservoir. Where a large reservoir is constructed as

---

[153] ss.3(1), (2) and (3) Reservoirs Act 1975.

[154] s.4(1) and (2). Detailed provisions relating to panels of civil engineers for the purpose of the Act are prescribed under Reservoirs Act 1975 (All Reservoirs Panel) (Applications and Fees) Regulations 1985, S.I. 1985 No.175; Reservoirs Act 1975 (Non–Impounding and Service Reservoirs Panels) (Applications and Fees) Regulations 1985, S.I. 1985 No.1086; Reservoirs Act 1975 (Supervising Engineers Panel) (Applications and Fees) Regulations 1984, S.I. 1984 No.1874; Reservoirs Act 1975 (Application Fees) (Amendment) Regulations 1988, S.I. 1988 No.69; and Reservoirs (Panels of Civil Engineers) (Reappointment) Regulations 1989, S.I. 1989 No.1186.

[155] ss.4(3) and (5) Reservoirs Act 1975.

a new reservoir, or by the alteration of an existing reservoir, it may not be used for the storage of water, or be filled wholly or partially with water, otherwise than in accordance with the certificate of the construction engineer.[156]

Proceedings may be taken where it appears to the enforcement authority that a large raised reservoir is being constructed, whether as a new reservoir or by alteration of an existing reservoir so as to increase its capacity, or that a large raised reservoir has been constructed or altered and no final certificate has been given for the construction or alteration, and no construction engineer is responsible for the construction or alteration. In such circumstances the authority may serve on the undertakers a notice requiring them, within twenty–eight days, to appoint a qualified civil engineer, unless an appointment has already been made. An engineer appointed for these purposes must inspect the reservoir and make a report on the construction or alteration, and supervise the reservoir until a final certificate that he is satisfied with it is given.[157]

Where the use of a large raised reservoir has been abandoned, the reservoir may not be used as a reservoir again unless a qualified civil engineer has been employed to inspect the reservoir and make a report on it, and to supervise the reservoir until he gives a final certificate for it. If an abandoned reservoir is brought back into use for the storage of water, or filled wholly or partly with water, it may not be used otherwise than in accordance with the certificate of the engineer. Where it appears to the enforcement authority that a large raised reservoir has been brought back into use after being abandoned but a report has not been obtained, or that the report includes recommendations as to measures to be taken in the interests of safety that have not been carried out, the authority may serve notice on the undertakers requiring them within twenty–eight days after the notice is served to appoint a qualified civil engineer, or require them to carry out the recommendations within a time specified in the notice.[158]

---

[156] ss.6(1), (2) and (3). Provision for preliminary and interim certificates to be issued is provided for under s.7.

[157] s.8(1) and (2).

[158] s.9(1), (2) and (7).

Inspections and monitoring

The undertakers of any large raised reservoir are bound to have the reservoir inspected from time to time by an independent qualified civil engineer and obtain from him a report of the results of his inspection.[159] Other than where the reservoir is presently under the supervision of a construction engineer, large raised reservoirs must be inspected within the following periods: (a) within two years from the date of any final certificate for the reservoir given by the construction engineer responsible for the construction or alteration of the reservoir; (b) as soon as practicable after carrying out any alterations to the reservoir which do not increase its capacity but are such as might affect its safety and which have not been designed and supervised by a qualified civil engineer; (c) at any time when the supervising engineer so recommends; or (d) within ten years from the last inspection or within any lesser interval that may have been recommended in the report of the inspecting engineer on the last inspection.[160]

As soon as practicable after an inspection, the inspecting engineer is to make a report of the results of the inspection, including in it any recommendations he sees fit to make as to the time of the next inspection, or as to any measures that should be taken in the interests of safety. An inspecting engineer is to give a certificate stating whether the report includes recommendations as to measures to be taken in the interests of safety, and if it includes a recommendation as to the time of the next inspection, a statement as to the period within which he recommends the inspection should be made. Where recommendations are included in the report as to measures to be taken in the interests of safety, the undertakers must carry the recommendations into effect as soon as practicable under the supervision of a qualified civil engineer, and the

---

[159] "Independent" means a civil engineer who is not in the employment of the undertakers otherwise than in a consultant capacity, and who was not the engineer responsible for the reservoir or any addition to it as the construction engineer, nor connected with any such engineer as a partner, employer, employee or fellow employee in a civil engineering business (s.10(9)).

[160] s.10(1) and (2).

engineer must give a certificate as soon as he is satisfied that the recommendations have been carried into effect.[161]

Where it appears to the enforcement authority that, in relation to a large raised reservoir, an inspection and report have not been made as required, or that the latest report of the inspecting engineer includes a safety recommendation that has not been carried into effect, the authority may serve notice on the undertakers requiring them, within twenty–eight days from the date on which the notice is served, to appoint an independent civil engineer to carry out an inspection, or require them to carry out the recommendation within a time specified in the notice.[162]

For every large raised reservoir, the undertakers are to keep a record in a prescribed form[163] of (a) water levels and depth of water, including the flow of water over the waste weir or overflow; (b) leakages, settlements of walls or other works, and repairs; and (c) such other matters as may be prescribed. In order to do this the undertakers must install and maintain such instruments as may be needed to provide the information to be recorded.[164]

At all times when a large raised reservoir is not under the supervision of a construction engineer, "a supervising engineer" is to be employed to supervise the reservoir and keep the undertakers advised of its behaviour in any respect that might affect safety and to ensure that the provisions of the Act relating to construction or enlargement, re–use of abandoned reservoirs, and periodic inspection[165] are complied with and draw the attention of the undertakers to any breach of those provisions. It is the duty of the supervising engineer, so long as matters that need to be overseen by him are noted in the final certificate for the reservoir, or the latest report of the inspecting engineer, to pay attention to those matters and to give the undertakers not less often than once a year a written statement of the action he has taken to do so. In addition, the supervising engineer is to recommend to the undertakers that the reservoir should be inspected if at any time he thinks an inspection is called for. Where it

[161] s.10(3), (5) and (6).

[162] s.10(7).

[163] See the Reservoirs Act 1975 (Registers, Reports and Records) Regulations 1985, S.I. 1985 No.177.

[164] s.11(1) Reservoirs Act 1975.

[165] Provided for, respectively, under ss.6(2) to (4), 9(2) and 11.

appears to the enforcement authority that a large raised reservoir is not for the time being either under the supervision of a construction engineer or a supervising engineer, the authority may by written notice served on the undertakers require them, within twenty–eight days from the date when the notice is served, to appoint a supervising engineer.[166]

Discontinuance or abandonment

No large raised reservoir may be altered to render it incapable of holding more than 25,000 cubic metres of water above the natural level of any part of the land adjoining the reservoir, unless a qualified civil engineer is employed to design or approve and to supervise the alteration. The engineer appointed for these purposes must give a certificate as soon as he is satisfied that the alteration has been complete and has been efficiently executed. When the certificate, or a copy of it, is received by the local authority they must remove the reservoir from their register of large raised reservoirs, but until the certificate is received the reservoir remains a large raised reservoir for the purposes of the Act, despite any alterations which have been executed.[167]

Where the use of a large raised reservoir is to be abandoned, the undertakers are to obtain from a qualified civil engineer a report as to the measures that ought to be taken in the interests of safety to secure that it is incapable of filling accidentally or naturally with water above the natural level of any adjoining land, or is only capable of doing so to an extent that does not constitute a risk. Where the report makes any recommendations as to measures to be taken in the interests of safety, then the undertakers must, before the use of the reservoir is abandoned, or as soon as practicable afterwards, carry the recommendations into effect. If the report has not been obtained, or it includes a safety recommendation that has not been carried into effect, the authority may serve on the undertakers a notice requiring them, within twenty–eight days, to appoint a qualified civil engineer or to carry the recommendations into effect within a time specified in the notice.[168]

---

[166] s.12.

[167] s.13(1) to (3).

[168] s.14(1), (2) and (4).

Additional powers

Where undertakers are required by a notice from the enforcement authority to appoint an engineer for any purpose under the Act, and the undertakers fail to make the appointment, the authority may appoint an engineer for that purpose and the provisions of the Act will apply to that person as if he had been duly appointed by the undertakers. Where the undertakers are required by a notice from the enforcement authority to carry a safety recommendation into effect and the undertakers fail to comply with that requirement, the authority may cause the recommendation to be carried into effect under the supervision of a qualified civil engineer appointed by them. Where the enforcement authority make any appointment of this kind, or exercise powers to carry safety recommendations into effect, the undertakers will be bound to pay the authority the amount of the expenses reasonably incurred.[169]

Where it appears to the enforcement authority that a large raised reservoir is unsafe and that immediate action is needed to protect persons or property against an escape of water from the reservoir, it may take such measures as it considers proper to remove or reduce the risk or to mitigate the effects of an escape. Likewise, where a large raised reservoir has been abandoned, but from time to time there is an undue accumulation of water and immediate action is needed to protect persons or property against an escape of water, the authority may take such measures as it considers proper to remove or reduce the risk, or to mitigate the effects, of an escape. Where an enforcement authority exercises these powers, the undertaker will be bound to pay it the amount of expenses reasonably incurred by it in the exercise of the powers.[170]

A person duly authorised in writing by an enforcement authority may, at any reasonable time, enter upon land on which a reservoir is situated for any of the following range of purposes: (a) for the purpose of carrying out any survey or other operation needed to determine whether the reservoir is a large raised reservoir, or is being constructed or altered so as to be one, whether the reservoir being a large raised reservoir is being altered so as to increase its capacity, or whether the reservoir is or is not in use as a reservoir; (b) for the purpose of carrying out any survey

---

[169] s.15(1), (2) and (5).
[170] s.16(1), (2) and (6).

or other operation needed to determine whether any recommendation as to measures to be taken in the interests of safety has been carried out, or what period should be specified in a notice requiring the undertakers to carry such a recommendation into effect; (c) for the purpose of carrying out any inspection of the reservoir under the reserve powers of the authority to appoint an engineer,[171] or any survey or other operation needed to make a report; (d) for any purpose connected with the carrying into effect by the authority[172] of a recommendation as to measures to be taken in the interests of safety; and (e) for the purpose of carrying out any survey or other operation needed to determine whether any or what measures should be taken for any purpose connected with the emergency powers of the authority,[173] or with the carrying into effect of any emergency measures. Except in relation to the exercise of a right of entry under (e), in relation to the exercise of emergency powers, no entry may be demanded unless at least seven days' notice in writing of the intended entry has been given to the occupier or the entry is authorised by a warrant.[174] Compensation is payable by the enforcement authority where, in the exercise of any of the powers of entry, any land on which entry is made and which is not in the occupation of the undertakers is damaged, or any person is disturbed in his enjoyment of that land.[175]

Criminal and civil liability

If by the wilful default of the undertakers any of the main provisions of the Act described are not observed or complied with in relation to a large raised reservoir, or the undertakers fail to comply with a notice from the enforcement authority as provided for by the Act then, unless there is reasonable excuse for the default or failure, the undertakers will be guilty of an offence and liable on conviction on indictment, or on summary conviction, to a fine, which on summary conviction is not to exceed £2,000.[176] Lesser penalties are provided for,

---

[171] Under s.15(1).
[172] Under s.15(2).
[173] Under s.16.
[174] s.17(1) and (4). Entry under warrant is provided for by s.17(5).
[175] s.18(1).
[176] s.22(1).

however, in relation to failure to give notice required under the Act, failure to furnish information, or furnishing false information.[177]

Despite the repeal of previous reservoir safety legislation,[178] provision is made for the continuation of liability in respect of an escape of water from a reservoir. Accordingly, where damage or injury is caused by the escape of water from a reservoir constructed after the year 1930, under statutory powers granted after July 1930, the fact that the reservoir was so constructed will not exonerate the persons for the time being having the management and control of the reservoir from any indictment, action or other proceedings to which they would otherwise be liable.[179] Implicitly, therefore, conformity with the Reservoirs Act 1975 or previous legislation will not serve as a defence to civil proceedings arising from an escape of water.[180]

---

177 Provided for under ss.22(2) to (4).

178 Reservoirs (Safety Provisions) Act 1930.

179 s.28 and Sch.2 Reservoirs Act 1975.

180 On civil liability for an escape of water from a reservoir see *Rylands v. Fletcher*, (1868) L.R. 3 H.L. 330, and p.86 above.

Chapter 11

WATER POLLUTION

Introduction

The key statutory provisions relating to the pollution of water are now provided for under Part III of the Water Resources Act 1991.[1] The four Chapters of Part III of the 1991 Act deal respectively with quality objectives, pollution offences, powers to prevent and control pollution, and supplemental provisions. In addition, a number of miscellaneous statutory provisions deal with specific kinds of pollution or the pollution of particular kinds of waters. Increasingly, however, the domestic law established by these provisions must be seen as a mechanism for the implementation of European Community water pollution legislation, and the final sections of this Chapter outline the relationship between Community Law and national water pollution legislation.

Controlled waters

Under Chapter II of Part III of the Water Resources Act 1991, the principal water pollution offences, and the powers and duties of the National Rivers Authority, arise in relation to "controlled waters". This term encompasses four subcategories of water, "relevant territorial waters", "coastal waters", "inland freshwaters" and "ground waters". These expressions are defined in the following manner.[2]

Relevant territorial waters

"Relevant territorial waters" means waters which extend seaward for three miles[3] from the baselines from which the breadth of the territorial sea[4] adjacent to England and Wales is measured.[5] This definition is subject to the power of the Secretary of State to provide by

---

[1] Previously the corresponding measures were set out in Chapter I of Part III of the Water Act 1989.

[2] s.104(1) Water Resources Act 1991.

[3] "Miles" means international nautical miles of 1,852 metres (s.104(3)).

[4] On the territorial sea generally see p.26 above.

[5] s.104(1)(a) Water Resources Act 1991.

order that any particular area of territorial sea adjacent to England and Wales is to be treated as if it were an area of relevant territorial waters.[6]

Coastal waters

"Coastal waters" means waters which are within the area which extends landward from the baselines of the territorial sea so far as the limit of the highest tide or, in the case of the waters of any relevant river or watercourse, so far as the fresh–water limit of the river or watercourse, together with the waters of any enclosed dock which adjoins waters within that area.[7] Within this definition "watercourse" includes all rivers, streams, ditches, drains, cuts, culverts, dykes, sluices, sewers and passages through which water flows except mains and other pipes which belong to the Authority or a water undertaker or are used by a water undertaker or any other person for the purpose only of providing a supply of water to any premises.[8] "Relevant river or watercourse" means any river or watercourse, including an underground river and an artificial river or watercourse, which is neither a public sewer nor a sewer or drain which drains into a public sewer.[9] The Secretary of State is empowered to provide by order that a watercourse of a specified description is to be treated for these purposes as if it were not a relevant river or watercourse.[10]

Inland freshwaters

"Inland freshwaters" means the waters of any relevant lake or pond or of so much of any relevant river or watercourse as is above the fresh–water limit.[11] "Lake or pond" is stated to include a reservoir of any description, and "relevant lake or pond" means any lake or pond which, whether it is natural or artificial or above or below ground, discharges into a relevant river or watercourse or into another lake or pond which is itself a relevant lake or pond.[12] The Secretary of State is empowered to provide by order that any lake or pond which does not discharge into a

---

[6] s.104(4)(a).
[7] s.104(1)(b).
[8] s.221(1).
[9] s.104(3).
[10] s.104(4)(d).
[11] s.104(1)(c).
[12] s.104(3).

relevant river or watercourse or into a relevant lake or pond is to be treated as a relevant lake or pond, or to be treated as if it were not a relevant lake or pond, as the case may be.[13]

The distinction between coastal waters and inland freshwaters is drawn, in the case of relevant rivers or watercourses, at the "fresh–water limit" of the waters concerned. The fresh–water limit for these purposes means the place for the time being shown as such in the latest map deposited by the Secretary of State for that river or watercourse.[14] This relates to the duty of the Secretary of State to deposit maps with the Authority showing what appear to him to be the fresh–water limits of every relevant river or watercourse. He may also, by reason of any change in the fresh–water limit, deposit a map showing a revised limit for the river or watercourse concerned. In relation to the definitive maps showing fresh–water limits, it is the duty of the Authority to keep any maps deposited with it available, at all reasonable times, for inspection by the public free of charge.[15]

Ground waters

"Ground waters" are defined as any waters which are contained in underground strata, meaning strata subjacent to the surface of any land.[16]

WATER QUALITY CLASSIFICATION AND OBJECTIVES

Classification of quality of waters

It has long been recognised that purposeful management of water resources involves, first, a determination of the objective for which a particular source is to be used and, second, an associated standard of

---

[13] s.104(4). In exercise of this power, as provided for under previous legislation (s.103(5) Water Act 1989), the Controlled Waters (Lakes and Ponds) Order 1989, S.I. 1989 No.1149, has been made. This Order states that reservoirs which do not discharge into a relevant river or watercourse or a relevant lake or pond are to be treated as a relevant lake or pond unless they contain water which had been treated with a view to complying with regulation 23 of the Water Supply (Water Quality) Regulations 1989, S.I. 1989 No.1147.

[14] s.104(3).

[15] s.192(1) and (2), and see p.226 above.

[16] ss.104(1)(d), and 221(1) Water Resources Act 1991.

purity acceptable for waters designated for that purpose.[17] This general approach to water quality planning has, however, become of increasing importance in view of the need for a legal, rather than merely administrative, obligation to ensure that the requirements of European Community water Directives are complied with.[18] The means by which a legal obligation to ensure water quality meets specified objectives consists of, first, a classification scheme for water quality, second, the specification of quality objectives for particular waters by reference to the classification scheme and, third, a duty upon the Secretary of State and the Authority to use their powers to ensure that quality objectives are achieved at all times.

Provisions for water quality classification authorise the Secretary of State to make regulations prescribing a system of classifying the quality of controlled waters according to criteria specified in the regulations. The specified criteria are general requirements as to the purposes for which the waters are to be suitable, specific requirements as to the substances that are to be present in or absent from the water and their concentrations, and specific requirements as to other characteristics of those waters. The question whether prescribed requirements are satisfied may be determined by reference to prescribed samples.[19]

---

[17] See report of the National Water Council, *River Water Quality, the Next Stage. Review of Consent Conditions* (1978).

[18] See *Re the EEC Directive Concerning the Quality of Bathing Water: EC Commission v. Kingdom of the Netherlands*, Case 96/81 [1982] E.C.R. 1791, and generally see discussion of European Water Directives at p.359 below.

[19] s.82(1) and (2) Water Resources Act 1991. In accordance with the Secretary of State's power to make regulations prescribing a system of classifying water quality under previous legislation (s.104 Water Act 1989), the Surface Waters (Classification) Regulations 1989, S.I. 1989 No.1148, have been made. These Regulations classify waters according to their suitability for abstraction by water undertakers for supply, after treatment, as drinking water. Specifically, the Regulations provide for classifications DW1, DW2 and DW3, reflecting the mandatory values assigned by the European Community Directive concerned with the quality of drinking water (75/440/EEC). Likewise, the Surface Waters (Dangerous Substances) (Classification) Regulations 1989, S.I. 1989 No.2286, classify waters according to the categories DS1 and DS2, relating to inland and coastal waters respectively, reflecting concentrations of "dangerous substances" for the purposes of the European Community Dangerous Substances Directive (76/464/EEC) and other Directives. Also in exercise of the Secretary of State's

Water quality objectives

For the purpose of maintaining and improving the quality of controlled waters, the Secretary of State may serve a notice upon the Authority establishing the water quality objectives for any particular waters under the water quality classification system. Hence the Secretary of State may specify, for any particular controlled waters, one or more of the classifications, and a date at which the water quality objective is established. The achievement of the water quality objectives specified for any waters amounts to the satisfaction of the corresponding requirements under the water quality classification system.[20]

Water quality objectives for particular waters may be reviewed by the Secretary of State five years after service of the last notice establishing objectives or specifying that objectives are to remain unchanged. Alternatively, the Authority may instigate a review if, after consultation with appropriate water undertakers and other persons, it requests a review. The Secretary of State may only exercise his power to establish objectives by varying the existing objectives as a consequence of a review of this kind.[21]

Where the Secretary of State intends to exercise his power to establish or vary the objectives for any waters, he is obliged, first, to publish a notice setting out his proposal and specifying a period, of at least three months from the date of publication, during which representations or objections may be made. Second, he must consider any representations or objections which are duly made and not withdrawn. If he decides to establish or vary the objectives he may do so either in accordance with the original proposal or with that proposal modified in a manner he considers appropriate. The notice must be published so as to bring it to the attention of persons likely to be affected

---

power to make regulations for classifying water quality are enacted the Bathing Waters (Classification) Regulations 1991, S.I. 1991 No.1597, which prescribe a system of classifying the quality of relevant territorial waters, coastal waters and inland waters which are bathing waters. Under these Regulations the prescribed classification BW1 reflects the mandatory standards laid down for bathing waters under the European Council Directive concerning the quality of bathing water (76/160/EEC).

[20] s.83(1) and (2) Water Resources Act 1991.

[21] s.83(3).

by it, and a copy of the notice must be served on the Authority. If the Secretary of State decides that the quality objectives for any water should remain unchanged, he is to serve notice of that decision on the Authority.[22]

General duties to achieve and maintain objectives

The system of water quality classification, and the power to specify water quality objectives, together with other powers and obligations in relation to water pollution, forms the basis of the important general duty of the Secretary of State and the Authority to exercise their water pollution control powers to ensure, so far as it is practicable, that the water quality objectives specified for any waters are achieved at all times. Associated with this is the duty imposed upon the Authority, for the purpose of its pollution control functions, to monitor the extent of pollution in controlled waters and to consult, in appropriate cases, with river purification authorities in Scotland.[23]

WATER POLLUTION OFFENCES

Offences of polluting controlled waters

The principal offences concerning pollution of controlled waters are committed where a person causes or knowingly permits the pollution of water in particular circumstances. Specifically, it is an offence to cause or knowingly permit: (a) any poisonous, noxious or polluting[24] matter or

---

22 s.83(4) to (6).

23 s.84(1) and (2). On the significance of the duty of the Authority to achieve water quality objectives in relation to its status as the competent authority for the purpose of European Community water Directives see p.368 below.

24 The phrase "poisonous, noxious or polluting" is not defined under the Act. In *Dell v. Chesham U.D.C.* ((1921) 85 J.P. 186) it was held that surface water from a tarmac road containing tar acid was a "noxious" liquid within the meaning of s.17 Public Health Act 1875, but in *Durrent v. Branksome U.D.C.* ([1897] 2 Ch. 291) it was held that the discharge of surface water conveyed by surface sewers to a watercourse was not "noxious" though containing some sand and silt. In *R. v. Justices of Antrim* ((1906) 2 I.R. 298) where a firm of mill owners were prosecuted for having caused "deleterious or poisonous liquid" to flow from their works, it was held that the time

solid waste matter to enter[25] any controlled waters;[26] (b) matter, other than trade effluent or sewage effluent,[27] to enter controlled waters by being discharged from a drain or sewer in contravention of a notice of prohibition of the discharge;[28] (c) trade effluent or sewage effluent to be discharged into controlled waters, or from land in England and Wales, through a pipe, into the sea outside the seaward limits of controlled waters;[29] (d) trade effluent or sewage effluent to be discharged, in contravention of a notice of prohibition, from a building or from fixed plant on to or into land or waters of a lake or pond which are not inland waters;[30] and (e) any matter whatever to enter inland waters so as to tend

---

at which the deleterious character or the matter was to be ascertained was the moment it entered the river, and that the effect of the action of the river upon it was immaterial (similarly see *R. v. Cramp*, (1880) 5 Q.B.D. 307). In relation to "noxious" matter, it was held in *Attorney-General v. Birmingham, Tame and Rea District Drainage Board* ([1908] 2 Ch. 551), where the drainage board was charged with having conveyed into a stream water "not freed from noxious matter", that it was "impossible to conclude that there was an offence against the prohibition unless the special purity and quality of the watercourse had been shown to be deteriorated". A tentative conclusion which may be drawn from these decisions is that "poisonous" is a reference to an intrinsic quality of the matter discharged, whereas "noxious" or "polluting" refer to the effect of the matter upon the watercourse into which it is discharged.

[25] Under previous legislation it has been held that "enter" includes polluting matter discharged into a sewer or channel which passes into a stream: *Kirkheaton L.B. v. Ainley*, [1892] 2 Q.B. 274; and *Butterworth v. West Riding of Yorkshire Rivers Board*, [1909] A.C. 45.

[26] s.85(1) Water Resources Act 1991.

[27] "Effluent" means any liquid, including particles of matter and other substances in suspension in the liquid. "Substance" includes micro-organisms and any natural or artificial substance or other matter, whether it is in solid or liquid form or in the form of gas or vapour. "Sewage effluent" includes any effluent from the sewage disposal or sewerage works of a sewerage undertaker but does not include surface water. "Trade effluent" includes any effluent which is discharged from premises used for carrying on any trade or industry, other than surface water and domestic sewage; however, any premises wholly or mainly used, whether for profit or not, for agricultural purposes or for the purposes of fish farming or for scientific research or experiment are deemed to be premises used for carrying on a trade (s.221(1)).

[28] s.85(2). Notices of prohibition of discharges are provided for under s.86 and discussed below.

[29] s.85(3).

[30] s.85(4).

(either directly or in combination with other matter which he or another person causes or permits to enter those waters) to impede the proper flow of the waters in a manner leading or likely to lead to a substantial aggravation of pollution due to other causes, or the consequences of such pollution.[31]

These principal offences are subject to the various authorisations and defences, considered later, by which an otherwise unlawful emission into the aquatic environment may be permitted. A person who commits any of these offences, or contravenes the conditions of any consent given under Chapter II of Part III, relating to pollution offences,[32] will be guilty of an offence and liable, on summary conviction, to imprisonment for a term not exceeding three months or to a fine not exceeding £20,000 or to both or, on conviction on indictment, to imprisonment for a term not exceeding two years or to a fine or both.[33]

Significantly, the principal water pollution offences are formulated, as in previous legislation,[34] in terms of actions which "cause or knowingly permit" pollution under various circumstances. It has been held that the phrase contemplates two distinct things: *causing*, which involves an active operation which results in pollution, and *knowingly permitting*, which involves a failure to prevent pollution accompanied by

---

[31] s.85(5).

[32] On the position under previous law in relation to multiple breaches of conditions in a single discharge consent, see *Severn-Trent River Authority v. Express Foods Group Ltd.*, [1989] Crim. L.R. 226.

[33] s.85(6). The power of the Crown Court to fine on indictment is limited only by the capacity of the offender to pay, see *R. v Garner,* [1986] 1 All E.R. 78. In relation to this offence a fine of £1 million has recently been imposed, see *National Rivers Authority v. Shell UK Ltd.,* [1990] 1 *Water Law* 40.

[34] See s.2 Rivers Pollution Prevention Act 1876, s.2(1) Rivers (Prevention of Pollution) Act 1951, s.31(1) Control of Pollution Act 1974, and s.107(1) Water Act 1989 (all now repealed). For earlier cases on "cause or knowingly permit" see *Kirkheaton L.B. v. Ainley*, [1892] 2 Q.B. 283; *Southall-Norwood U.D.C. v. Middlesex County Council*, (1901) 83 L.T. 742; *Butterworth v. West Riding of Yorkshire Rivers Board*, [1909] A.C. 45; *Rochford R.D.C. v. Port of London Authority*, [1914] 2 K.B. 916; *West Riding of Yorkshire Rivers Board v. Linthwaite U.D.C.*, [1915] 2 K.B. 436; *Moses v. Midland Railway Co.*, (1915) 79 J.P. 367; and *Smith v. Great Western Railway Co.*, (1926) 135 L.T. 112.

knowledge.[35] In the leading decision of *Alphacell Ltd. v Woodward*,[36] it was held that "cause" does not require an intention to pollute waters or negligence to be shown and the offence of causing water pollution is an offence of strict liability.[37] It has been established, however, that an offence will not be committed where the behaviour of the accused is "passive".[38] Similarly, causation will be lacking where it is shown that there was a distinct and independent cause of the pollution apart from the activities of the accused, as where pollution was caused by the malicious act of a trespasser,[39] or by an act of God.[40] The same conclusion was reached in relation to the activities of an independent contractor delivering diesel fuel oil to premises where it was held that the owner of the premises had not caused pollution which arose through a spillage which was apparently due to the act of the delivery driver.[41]

Prohibitions of certain discharges

As has been noted, principal offences are committed in relation to the entry of matter, other than trade or sewage effluent, from a drain or sewer into controlled waters, or from a building or fixed plant onto any land or into any water of a lake or pond which are not inland waters,[42] where this is done in contravention of a prohibition. Contravention of a prohibition by a person takes place where the Authority has given that person notice prohibiting him from making or continuing the discharge, or the Authority has given notice prohibiting him from making or

---

[35] Generally see *McLeod v. Buchanan*, [1940] 2 All E.R. 179, at p.187. On "knowingly permitting" see *High Wycombe Corpn. v. Thames Conservators*, (1898) 78 L.T. 463; *Taylor v. Roper*, (1951) 115 J.P. 445; and *Ashcroft v. Cambro Waste Products*, [1981] 1 W.L.R. 1349.

[36] [1972] 2 All E.R. 475.

[37] *Wrothwell Ltd. v. Yorkshire Water Authority*, [1984] Crim. L.R. 43.

[38] *Price v Cromack*, [1975] 2 All E.R. 113; *Moses v. Midland Railway Co.*, (1915) 113 L.T. 451; and *Lockhart v. National Coal Board*, [1981] S.C.C.R. 9.

[39] *Impress (Worcester) Ltd. v Rees*, [1971] 2 All E.R. 357.

[40] *Alphacell Ltd. v. Woodward*, [1972] 2 All E.R. 475, at p.490, but on the limitations of this defence see *Southern Water Authority v. Pegrum*, [1989] L.G.T. 672.

[41] *Welsh Water Authority v Williams Motors (Cwmdu) Ltd.*, (1988) *The Times* 5 December 1988.

[42] Under ss.85(2) and (4) Water Resources Act 1991 respectively.

continuing the discharge unless specific conditions are observed, and those conditions are not observed. More generally, for the same purposes, a discharge is taken to be in contravention of a prohibition if the effluent or matter discharged contains a prescribed substance or a prescribed concentration of a substance, or derives from a prescribed process or from a process involving the use of prescribed substances or the use of substances in quantities which exceed prescribed amounts. In no case, however, may a prohibition notice be issued by the Authority, or regulations be made concerned with prescribed substances, requiring a discharge from a vessel to be treated as a discharge in contravention of a prohibition.[43]

A prohibition notice is to expire at a time specified in the notice.[44] The time specified is not to be before the end of the period of three months beginning with the day on which the notice was given, except in a case where the Authority is satisfied that there is an emergency which requires the prohibition to come into force at a specified time before the end of the three month period. Where a prohibition notice would expire at or after the end of the three month period, and an application is made before that time for a discharge consent in respect of the discharge, the notice is deemed not to expire until the grant or withdrawal of the application or the expiration of any period prescribed for an appeal or, if an appeal is made, on withdrawal or determination of the appeal.[45]

Discharges into and from public sewers

For the purposes of the principal water pollution offences in relation to the discharge of trade or sewage effluent into controlled waters or from land into the sea outside controlled waters, or in contravention of a relevant prohibition,[46] a special stipulation applies to the activities of sewerage undertakers. Where sewage effluent is discharged from any sewer or works vested in a sewerage undertaker, and the undertaker did not cause or knowingly permit the discharge but was bound to receive the matter included in the discharge, either

---

[43] s.86(1) to (3).

[44] s.86(4).

[45] s.86(5) and (6). On discharge consents generally see p.304 below.

[46] Under ss.85(3) and (4).

unconditionally or subject to conditions that were observed, the undertaker is deemed to have caused the discharge.[47] In effect, therefore, sewerage undertakers will be strictly liable in relation to pollution caused by discharges of inadequately treated effluent of a kind which they are bound to receive into a sewer or works.[48]

However, a sewerage undertaker will not be liable for any of the principal water pollution offences by reason only of the fact that a discharge from a sewer or works vested in it contravenes a condition of a consent relating to the discharge if three conditions are satisfied: (a) the contravention is attributable to a discharge which another person caused or permitted to be made into the sewer or works; (b) the undertaker either was not bound to receive the discharge into the sewer or works or was bound to receive it there subject to conditions which were not observed; and (c) the undertaker could not reasonably have been expected to prevent the discharge into the sewer or works.[49]

In relation to the position of a person who discharges into a sewer or works vested in a sewerage undertaker, that person will not be guilty of any of the principal water pollution offences in respect of a discharge that he caused or permitted to be made if the undertaker was bound to receive the discharge there either unconditionally or subject to conditions that were observed.[50] Conversely, however, where an unlawful discharge is made into a public sewer of matter which the sewerage undertaker is not bound to receive, and subsequently causes pollution of a watercourse into which effluent is discharged, the discharger will commit the principal water pollution offence and also an offence in relation to the unlawful discharge into the sewer.[51]

---

[47] s.87(1).

[48] On controls which apply in relation to discharges to sewers and consents in respect of these see p.337 below.

[49] s.87(2).

[50] s.87(3).

[51] See *National Rivers Authority v. Appletise Bottling Co. Ltd.*, (1991) *Water Guardians* April 1991, where a leak of apple juice concentrate which passed into a watercourse via a public sewer resulted in successful prosecutions before magistrates under both s.107 Water Act 1989 (see now s.85(1) Water Resources Act 1991) and s.27 Public Health Act 1936 (see now the discussion of discharges to sewers at p.337 below).

Offences concerning deposits and vegetation in rivers

In addition to the principal offences of polluting controlled waters, described above, separate and less serious offences are provided for in relation to unauthorised deposits and the disposal of vegetable matter in rivers. Hence, an offence is committed if, without the consent of the Authority, a person removes from any part of the bottom, channel or bed of any inland freshwaters a deposit accumulated by reason of any dam, weir or sluice holding back the waters, and does so by causing the deposit to be carried away in suspension in the waters.[52] Also an offence is committed if, without the consent of the Authority, a person causes or permits a substantial amount of vegetation to be cut or uprooted in any inland freshwaters, or to be cut or uprooted so near to any such waters that it falls into them, and he fails to take all reasonable steps to remove the vegetation from those waters. In giving a consent for the purposes of these provisions, the Authority may make the consent subject to such conditions as it considers appropriate. The Secretary of State may by regulations provide that any reference to inland freshwaters for these purposes is to be construed as including a reference to prescribed coastal waters. A person found guilty of either of the offences will be liable, on summary conviction, to a fine not exceeding £1,000.[53]

Miscellaneous defences to principal offences

The most important defences to the principal water pollution offences, in practical terms, are the defences which arise in relation to authorised discharges, considered in the following sections. However, in addition to the range of defences provided by statutory authorisations, a number of other miscellaneous defences are provided to the principal water pollution offences. The first of these provides that a person will not be guilty of an offence of polluting controlled waters in respect of an entry of any matter or discharge into waters in respect of certain kinds of emergency. Specifically, this exception applies where the entry of matter,

---

[52] s.90(1) Water Resources Act 1991. This provision does not apply to anything done in exercise of any power conferred by or under any enactment relating to land drainage, flood prevention or navigation (s.90(4)).

[53] s.90(2) to (6).

or discharge, is caused or permitted in order to avoid danger to life or health, where all reasonably practicable steps are taken for minimising the extent of the entry or discharge and its polluting effects, and particulars of the matter are furnished to the Authority as soon as reasonably practicable after it occurs.[54]

Other exceptions are provided for so that no offence of polluting waters is committed by reason of causing or permitting any discharge of trade or sewage effluent from a vessel.[55] A person will not be guilty of the principal offences in respect of his permitting water from an abandoned mine to enter controlled waters.[56] An exception is also provided, otherwise than in respect of the entry of any poisonous, noxious or polluting matter to enter controlled waters, in relation to the deposit of solid refuse of a mine or quarry on any land so that it falls or is carried into inland waters.[57] This exception arises only if the deposit was with the consent of the Authority, no other site for the deposit was reasonably practicable and all reasonably practicable steps were taken to prevent the entry.[58] Finally, where a highway authority or other person is entitled to keep open a drain,[59] no offence of polluting controlled waters will be committed by reason of causing or permitting a discharge to be made from the drain unless the discharge is made in contravention of a notice of prohibition,[60] as described above.[61]

---

[54] s.89(1).

[55] s.89(2). "Vessel" is defined to include a hovercraft within the meaning of the Hovercraft Act 1986 (s.221(1) Water Resources Act 1991).

[56] s.89(3).

[57] The meanings of "mine" and "quarry" are defined under the Mines and Quarries Act 1954. "Mine" means an excavation or system of excavations made for the purpose of, or in connection with, the getting, wholly or substantially by means involving the employment of persons below ground, of minerals (whether in their natural state or in solution or in suspension) or products of minerals (s.180(1)). "Quarry" means an excavation or system of excavations made for the purpose of, or in connection with, the getting of minerals (whether in their natural state or in solution or in suspension) or products of minerals, being neither a mine nor merely a well or borehole or a well and borehole combined (s.180(2)).

[58] s.89(4) Water Resources Act 1991.

[59] Under s.100 of the Highways Act 1980.

[60] Under s.86 Water Resources Act 1991.

[61] s.89(5).

AUTHORISED DISCHARGES

Defences to the principal offences for authorised discharges

A person will not be guilty of any of the principal water pollution offences in respect of the entry of matter into any waters or any discharge, if the entry occurs or the discharge is made under and in accordance with, or as a result of, any act or omission made under and in accordance with specified kinds of authorisation. Accordingly, an entry of matter or a discharge may be authorised by the following: (a) a discharge consent given under Chapter II of Part III of the Water Resources Act 1991; (b) an authorisation for a prescribed process designated for central control granted under Part I of the Environmental Protection Act 1990;[62] (c) a waste management or disposal licence;[63] (d) a licence granted under Part II of the Food and Environment Protection Act 1985;[64] (e) specified statutory authorisations relating to works purposes;[65] (f) any local statutory provision or statutory order which expressly confers power to discharge effluent into water;[66] or (g) any prescribed enactment.[67] The defences arising under (a) to (d) are considered in the following sections.

---

[62] See p.315 below on this.

[63] A "waste management licence" means a licence granted under Part II of the Environmental Protection Act 1990 (s.88(4)). A "disposal licence" means a licence issued in pursuance of s.5 Control of Pollution Act 1974. However, a disposal licence will not be treated as authorising an entry or discharge as mentioned in s.85 (2) to (4) Water Resources Act 1991 or any act or omission so far as it results in any such entry or discharge (ss.88(3) and (4) Water Resources Act 1991). Generally, see *Leigh Land Reclamation Ltd. v. Walsall M.B.C.,* (1990) *The Times* 2 November 1990.

[64] Part II of the Food and Environment Protection Act 1985 provides for the authorisation of deposits of waste at sea and related matters. See p.324 below.

[65] Provided for under s.163 Water Resources Act 1991 and s.165 Water Industry Act 1991.

[66] "Statutory order" means any order under s.168 Water Resources Act 1991 or s.167 Water Industry Act 1991, relating to compulsory works, or any order, byelaw, scheme or award made under any other enactment, including an order or scheme confirmed by Parliament or brought into operation in accordance with special parliamentary procedure (s.88(4)).

[67] s.88(1) Water Resources Act 1991.

Discharge consents

Generally

In practical terms, the single most important exception to the principal water pollution offences arises where a discharge is made under and in accordance with a consent granted under Chapter II of Part III of the Water Resources Act 1991,[68] termed a "discharge consent". The detailed provisions concerning discharge consents are set out in Schedule 10 to the Act.[69]

Although the provisions of Schedule 10 apply to individuals who apply for discharge consents, the Secretary of State is empowered to make regulations modifying the provisions of the Act where consents are required by the Authority. In particular he may provide for discharge consents required by the Authority to be given, or deemed to be given, by the Secretary of State rather than the Authority itself.[70] Provision is made, in respect of applications for discharge consents by water undertakers, for these applications to be treated as having been transmitted to the Secretary of State for determination. In that case, analogous provisions apply in relation to publicity, consideration of representations and objections, to those described below, and in addition the Secretary of State has the power to direct the Authority to give a temporary consent for the discharge.[71]

A discharge consent also serves as an exception to water pollution offences arising under other legislation. Specifically, no offence will be committed under s.4 of the Salmon and Freshwater Fisheries Act 1975,[72]

---

[68] Under s.88(1)(a).

[69] Effective under s.88(2).

[70] ss.99(1) and (2). The power of the Secretary of State to make Regulations has been exercised in the creation of the Control of Pollution (Discharges by the National Rivers Authority) Regulations 1989, S.I. 1989 No.1157.

[71] Generally see Sch.13 para.4 Water Resources Act 1991.

[72] s.4 Salmon and Freshwater Fisheries Act 1975 provides for an offence of causing or knowingly permitting liquid or solid matter to enter waters containing fish so as to cause the waters to be poisonous or injurious to fish or the spawning grounds, spawn or food of fish. See p.426 below.

or s.68 of the Public Health Act 1875[73] in respect of entry of matter into controlled waters where this is the subject of a discharge consent.[74]

Applications for consents

Schedule 10 to the Water Resources Act 1991 provides that applications for discharge consents are to be made to the Authority and are to be accompanied or supplemented by all reasonably required information, though failure to provide information will not invalidate an application. Where an application is made to the Authority, it is to publish notice of the application in successive weeks in a newspaper circulating in the locality of the proposed discharge and in the localities of controlled waters likely to be affected by the discharge. In addition, a copy of the notice is to be published in the *London Gazette* no earlier than the later publication in the local newspapers. A copy of the application is to be sent by the Authority to every local authority or water undertaker within whose area the proposed discharge is to occur. In the case of an application which relates to a discharge into coastal waters outside the seaward limits of relevant territorial waters, a copy is to be served on the Secretary of State and the Minister of Agriculture, Fisheries and Food. Where the notice of application is published by the Authority, it is entitled to recover the expenses of publication from the applicant.[75]

By way of exception to the general publication requirement in respect of applications for discharge consents, the provisions relating to publicity and notification which are imposed upon the Authority may be disregarded where the Authority proposes to give the consent applied for and considers that the discharge will have "no appreciable effect" on the waters into which it is to be made.[76] Under previous legislation,[77] it was suggested that the "no appreciable effect" exemption from publicity would be available where three criteria are met: first, the discharge does

[73] s.68 of the Public Health Act 1875 provides for the offence of polluting water by matter produced by persons engaged in the manufacture of gas.

[74] Sch.1 para.1 and para.30(1) Water Consolidation (Consequential Provisions) Act 1991.

[75] Sch.10 para.1(1) to (6) Water Resources Act 1991.

[76] Sch.10 para.1(5).

[77] s.36(4) Control of Pollution Act 1974, now repealed.

not affect an area of amenity or environmental significance (a beach, marine nature reserve, shell fishery, fish spawning area, or site of special scientific interest); second, the discharge does not result in a major change in the flow of receiving waters; and, third, taken together with previously consented discharges, the discharge does not result in such a change to water quality as to damage existing or future uses of the waters (whether or not resulting in a change of water quality classification), or alter by 10% or more the concentration in the receiving waters of any substance which is of importance for the quality of the water and the well being of its flora and fauna, for example, dissolved oxygen, biochemical oxygen demand, suspended solids, ammonia, nitrates, phosphates and dissolved metals.[78]

Exemption from publicity, and the exclusion of information from registers kept by the Authority,[79] may also be provided through a certificate issued by the Secretary of State. The procedure involved in issuing a certificate of this kind requires the person proposing to make an application for discharge consent to apply to the Secretary of State for certification that the provisions relating to publicity and notification are not to apply in relation to the application. Exemption of a discharge application from publicity will only be granted where the Secretary of State is satisfied that disclosure of information would be contrary to the public interest, or would prejudice some private interest to an unreasonable degree by disclosing information about a trade secret.[80]

Consideration and determination of applications

It is the duty of the Authority to consider any written representations or objections which are made during a period of six weeks beginning on the date of publication of the notice in the *London Gazette* and not withdrawn. If the requirements relating to applications are complied with, the Authority is then under a duty to consider whether to give the consent applied for, either unconditionally or subject to conditions, or to refuse it. A consent will be deemed to have been refused

---

[78] Department of the Environment, Departmental Circular No.17/84, *Water and the Environment* (1984) Annex 3 para.3.

[79] Provided for under s.190(1) Water Resources Act 1991, see p.224 above on registers kept by the Authority.

[80] Sch.10 para.1(7).

if it is not given within the period of four months beginning with the day on which the application is received or within a longer period agreed in writing between the Authority and the applicant, unless the applicant has failed to supplement the application with information required by the Authority, in which case the Authority may delay the determination for a reasonable period after the information is provided.[81]

The conditions subject to which a consent may be given are stated to be "such conditions as the Authority may think fit" and, in particular, it is explicitly stated that conditions may be included as to the following matters: (a) as to the places at which the discharges may be made and as to the design and construction of any outlets; (b) as to the nature, origin, composition, temperature, volume and rate of the discharges and as to the periods during which the discharges may be made; (c) as to the steps to be taken, in relation to the discharges or by way of subjecting any substances to treatment or any other process, for minimising the polluting effects of the discharges on any controlled waters; (d) as to the provision of facilities for taking samples of the matter discharged and as to the provision, maintenance and use of manholes, inspection chambers, observation wells and boreholes in connection with the discharges; (e) as to the provision, maintenance and testing of meters for measuring or recording the volume and rate of the discharges and apparatus for determining the nature, composition and temperature of the discharges; (f) as to the keeping of records of the nature, origin, composition, temperature, volume and rate of the discharges and records of readings of meters and other recording apparatus provided in accordance with the consent; and, (g) as to the making of returns and the giving of other information to the Authority about the nature, origin, composition, temperature, volume and rate of the discharges. A consent may be given subject to different conditions in respect of different periods, and is not limited to discharges by a particular person and, accordingly, extends to discharges which are made by any person.[82]

Notification of proposal to give consent

Where it is proposed to give a consent in relation to which representations or objections have been made, it is the duty of the

---

[81] Sch.10 para.2(1) to (4).

[82] Sch.10 para.2(5) and (6).

Authority to serve notice of the proposal to grant consent on every person who made a representation or objection. Notices of this kind are to inform persons who have made representations or objections that they may, within a twenty–one day period, request the Secretary of State to give a direction that the application is to be transmitted to him for determination. The Authority is not to give its consent within the twenty–one day period, and if a request is made to the Secretary of State within the period, and notice of the request is served upon the Authority by the person making it, the Authority is not to give its consent unless the Secretary of State has served a notice on the Authority stating that he declines to comply with the request.[83]

Reference of applications for consent to the Secretary of State

The Secretary of State is empowered, either in consequence of representations or objections made to him or otherwise, to direct the Authority to transmit to him for determination specified kinds of applications for discharge consent. Where a direction is given to the Authority referring an application for consent to the Secretary of State, the Authority is bound to comply with the direction and inform the applicant of the transmission of the application to the Secretary of State. In the event of an application being transmitted to the Secretary of State for determination, the general provisions relating to publicity and notification in relation to applications will have effect subject to prescribed modifications.[84]

Where an application is transmitted to the Secretary of State for determination he may cause a local inquiry to be held with respect to the application or afford the applicant and the Authority an opportunity of appearing before, and being heard by, a person appointed by the Secretary of State for that purpose. This power is to be exercised by the Secretary of State in any case where a request to be heard is made in the

---

[83] Sch.10 para.3(1) to (4).

[84] Sch.10 para.4(1) to (3). Ancillary provisions relating to the various powers of the Secretary of State to direct applications to be referred to him, to provide exemptions from publicity requirements and to hear appeals from determinations of the Authority are set out in the Control of Pollution (Consents for Discharges etc.) (Secretary of State Functions) Regulations 1989, S.I. 1989 No.1151 (Sch.10 para.4(9)).

prescribed manner by the applicant or the Authority. In that case an opportunity of being heard is to be afforded to any person who has made representations or objections to the Secretary of State with respect to the application. It is then for the Secretary of State to determine the application by directing the Authority to refuse its consent or to grant consent either unconditionally or subject to conditions.[85]

Consents without application

Consents without application may be granted by the Authority where a person has caused or permitted trade or sewage effluent or other matter to be discharged into any controlled waters, or from land into the sea outside the seaward limits of controlled waters,[86] or in contravention of a notice of prohibition prohibiting the discharge.[87] Where contraventions of these kinds arise, and a similar contravention is likely, the Authority may serve an instrument in writing on the discharger giving its consent, subject to any specified conditions, for the discharge. In a situation of this kind, however, a consent granted without application is not to relate to any discharge which occurred before the consent was served.[88] The conditions to which a consent may ordinarily be subject,[89] are to have effect in relation to a consent granted without application in the same way as for consent granted after an application has been made. Analogous provisions also apply in relation to publicity, so that the fact of the consent having been granted is to be published in local newspapers and the *London Gazette*, and notification of the consent is to be sent to local authorities and, where relevant, the Secretary of State and the Minister, as would an application for consent.[90]

Revocation of consents and alteration and imposition of conditions

The Authority is placed under a duty to review the consents which are granted as a result of applications and consents granted without applications, and the conditions to which they are subject. Subject to

---

[85] Sch.10 para.4(4) to (7) Water Resources Act 1991.

[86] Contrary to s.85(3).

[87] Under s.86.

[88] Sch.10 para.5(1) and (2).

[89] Under Sch.10 para.2(5) and (6).

[90] para.5(3) and (4).

certain restrictions upon the power of the Authority to review consents it may, as a result of review, revoke a consent, or modify the conditions of a consent or make an unconditional consent subject to conditions. If on review it appears that no discharge has been made in pursuance of a consent during the preceding twelve months, the Authority may revoke the consent by a notice served on the owner or occupier of the land from which the discharge would be made in pursuance of the consent.[91]

The Secretary of State is empowered to direct the Authority to serve a notice revoking a consent or modifying the conditions of a consent, or imposing conditions in the case of an unconditional consent, if it appears appropriate to do so for certain purposes. The purposes are those of enabling the Government to give effect to any Community obligation or international agreement to which the United Kingdom is a party, for the protection of public health or of flora and fauna dependent on an aquatic environment or in consequence of any representations or objections made to the Secretary of State or otherwise.[92]

The Authority may become liable to pay compensation in respect of any loss or damage sustained as a result of the Authority's compliance with a direction given by the Secretary of State in relation to the protection of public health or of flora and fauna dependent on an aquatic environment. The liability to pay compensation arises where the Authority, in complying with the direction, does anything which, apart from the direction, would be precluded under restrictions upon powers of variation and revocation of consents. In addition, the Authority is liable to pay compensation where it is unable to show that a direction was given in consequence of a change of circumstances which could not reasonably have been foreseen at the beginning of the period to which the restriction relates. Alternatively, the liability to pay compensation will arise where the Authority is unable to show the direction to have been given after consideration by the Secretary of State of material information which was not reasonably available to the Authority at the beginning of the period. For the purposes of the Authority's liability to pay compensation, information is material in relation to a consent if it relates to any discharge made, or to be made by virtue of the consent, to

[91] para.6(1) to (3).

[92] para.6(4).

the interaction of any such discharge with any other discharge, or to the combined effect of the matter discharged and any other matter.[93]

Restriction on variation and revocation of consents

Where consent is given by the Authority for a discharge, either on application or without application, the instrument signifying the consent of the Authority is to specify a period during which no notice of revocation or modification will be served in respect of the consent. Notices modifying a consent are also to specify a period during which a subsequent notice altering the terms of the consent is not to be served. The period during which revocation or variation of a consent is precluded, without the consent of the person making the discharge, is stated to be not less than a two–year period beginning with the day on which a consent takes effect or the day on which the notice specifying the period is served.[94]

The restrictions upon variation and revocation of a consent by the Authority do not prevent the Authority serving a notice revoking or modifying a consent which has been given without application in certain circumstances. Variation or revocation of a consent which has been granted without application is permitted if the notice is served in consequence of any representations or objections made in relation to the consent, and not more than three months after the beginning of the period during which representations and objections may be made concerning the consent.[95]

Appeals

Provision is made for an appeal to the Secretary of State where the Authority has made certain kinds of adverse determination in relation to discharge, and other kinds of, consents otherwise than in pursuance of a direction of the Secretary of State. These are, where the Authority has refused a consent application; given a consent subject to conditions; revoked or modified a consent or made an unconditional consent subject to conditions; specified a period during which variation or revocation of

[93] para.6(5) and (6).
[94] para.7(1) to (3).
[95] para.7(4).

a consent is not to take place;[96] refused a consent for any deposit of solid refuse of a mine or quarry;[97] or refused a consent[98] in relation to deposits and vegetation in rivers. In any of these cases the person applying for the consent, or whose conduct would be authorised by the consent, may appeal against the decision of the Authority to the Secretary of State.[99]

On appeal, the Secretary of State may give the direction requiring the Authority to give consent, either unconditionally or conditionally, to modify the conditions of a consent or to make an unconditional consent conditional, or to modify the period during which variation or revocation of a consent is not to take place. In the event of the Secretary of State giving a direction that the determination of the Authority should be modified or reversed, the Authority is bound to comply with the direction.[100]

Charges in connection with discharge consents

Where an application is made to the Authority for a discharge consent or other consent relating to the control of pollution,[101] or the Authority gives a consent otherwise than when an application for consent has been made,[102] or a consent is for the time being in force, the Authority may require the payment to it of such charges as may be specified in, or determined under, a charging scheme. Charges are liable to be paid by the person making the application, or the person authorised to do anything by virtue of the consent and on whom the consent is served, or in the case of consents presently in force, the person who makes a discharge in pursuance of the consent. Provision may be made under a charging scheme to impose a single charge in respect of the whole period for which the consent is in force, or separate charges in respect of different parts of that period, or both a single charge and separate charges. It is the duty of the Authority to take appropriate steps

---

[96] For the purposes of Sch.10 para.7(1) or (2).

[97] Under s.89(4)(a).

[98] Under s.90.

[99] s.91(1) and (2).

[100] s.91(5).

[101] Under Part III Water Resources Act 1991. That is, consents under ss.88(1)(a), 89(4)(a) or 90.

[102] Under Sch.10 para.1 Water Resources Act 1991.

to bring the provisions of any charging scheme which is for the time being in force to the attention of persons likely to be affected by it.[103]

Before submission to the Secretary of State for approval, the Authority is to publish a proposed charging scheme, in a manner appropriate to bring it to the attention of persons likely to be affected, specifying a period within which representations or objections may be made to the Secretary of State. It is then the duty of the Secretary of State, in determining whether or not to approve the scheme or to approve it subject to modifications, to consider any representations or objections made to him and not withdrawn, and to have regard to specified matters.[104] The matters to which he is to have regard are the desirability of ensuring that the amount recovered by the Authority by way of charges under the scheme does not exceed an amount reasonably attributable to the expenses incurred by the Authority in carrying out its functions under the consent provisions[105] and otherwise in relation to discharges into controlled waters. In addition, he is to have regard to the need to ensure that no undue preference is shown, and that there is no undue discrimination, in the fixing of charges by or under the scheme.[106]

Discharge consents and powers of the authority to discharge water

In relation to discharges made by the Authority, special provision is made for regulations to be made by the Secretary of State to modify the water pollution provisions of the Water Resources Act 1991 in relation to consents which, under Chapter II of Part III of the Act, are required by the Authority. Regulations of this kind may make prescribed modifications to the general provisions on discharge consents and may provide for consents to be required to be given by the Secretary of State,

---

[103] s.131(1) to (3) and (6).

[104] s.132(1) and (2).

[105] "Consent provisions" means the provisions of Sch.10 to the Act, together with the provisions of s.91 (appeals to the Secretary of State) and s.131 (power to make charges) (s.132(5)).

[106] s.132(3). The details of the present scheme are set out in *Schemes of Charges in Respect of Applications and Consents for Discharges to Controlled Waters*, (1991) National Rivers Authority.

instead of the Authority, or in certain cases be deemed to have been so given.[107]

Where the Authority is carrying out, or is about to carry out, the construction, alteration, repair, cleaning, or examination of any reservoir, well, borehole or other work belonging to the Authority, or it is exercising or about to exercise specified powers,[108] it may cause water in any relevant pipe,[109] or the other waters mentioned, to be discharged into any available watercourse. However, this power is stated not to authorise any discharge which damages or injuriously affects the works or property of any railway company[110] or navigation authority or floods or damages any highway. If the Authority fails to take all necessary steps to secure that any water discharged by it in accordance with this power is as free as may be reasonably practicable from mud and silt, solid, polluting, or injurious substances, and any substances prejudicial to fish or spawn, or spawning beds or food of fish, it will be guilty of an offence and liable, on summary conviction, to a fine not exceeding £400.[111]

A limitation upon the power of the Authority to discharge for works purposes is that, except in an emergency, no discharge through any pipe the diameter of which exceeds 229 millimetres may be made except with a prescribed consent. Application for a consent of this kind involves an application being made by the Authority to the Secretary of State and served upon specified persons who may be affected by the proposed discharge. The consent may relate to a particular discharge, or to discharges of a particular description, and be made subject to reasonable conditions, but consent may not be unreasonably withheld. If the Authority contravenes, without reasonable excuse, any condition of

---

[107] s.99, and see Control of Pollution (Discharges by the National Rivers Authority) Regulations 1989, S.I. 1989 No.1157.

[108] The specified powers concerned relate to laying of pipes in streets (s.159), laying of pipes on other land (s.160), and the power to carry out works in a street or on other land to deal with foul water and pollution (ss.162(2) and (3) and 163(1)(b) Water Resources Act 1991).

[109] "Relevant pipe" means a resource main or discharge pipe (s.159(5)).

[110] "Railway company" mean the British Railways Board, London Regional Transport or any other person authorised by any enactment, or by any rule or regulation made under any enactment, to construct, work or carry on a railway (s.163(4)).

[111] s.163.

the consent, it will be guilty of an offence and liable, on summary conviction, to a fine not exceeding £400.[112]

Integrated pollution control and water pollution law

Amongst the defences for authorised discharges available to the principal water pollution offences under the Water Resources Act 1991, it is a defence to show that an entry of matter into waters or a discharge was under and in accordance with an authorisation for a prescribed process designated for central control under Part I of the Environmental Protection Act 1990.[113] This is a reference to the separate system of authorisations provided for in relation to the implementation of the system of integrated pollution control imposed upon certain prescribed processes and substances under Part I of the 1990 Act.

General nature of integrated pollution control

The theoretical justification for integrated pollution control arose from criticisms, registered by the Royal Commission on Environmental Pollution, of the limitations of administrative jurisdiction placed upon bodies regulating pollution of the different environmental media failing to reflect the complexities of effective overall pollution control. The Royal Commission drew attention to the links between pollution of air, water and land, and proposed that there should be a unified inspectorate to ensure an integrated approach to difficult industrial pollution problems. It was suggested that these problems should be tackled at source so that damage to the total environment should be kept to a minimum. The aim of the inspectorate should be to achieve the "best practicable environmental option" (BPEO) taking into account the entire pollution from a process and the technical possibilities for dealing with it.[114]

---

[112] s.164.

[113] s.88(1)(b) Water Resources Act 1991.

[114] See Fifth Report of the Royal Commission on Environmental Pollution (1976 Cmnd.6371) and also Twelfth Report (1986 Cm.301).

Authorisations for prescribed processes

Part I of the Environmental Protection Act 1990 provides for the establishment of integrated pollution control. In so far as it relates to the aquatic environment this is achieved, first, by enabling the Secretary of State to introduce regulations prescribing processes the carrying on of which, or substances the release into the environment of which, will be subject to special authorisation.[115] A second key feature of integrated pollution control is the criminalisation of prescribed processes, except where they are conducted under an authorisation granted by the "enforcing authority", Her Majesty's Inspectorate of Pollution (HMIP), and in accordance with the conditions to which the authorisation is subject.[116] Specifically, all authorisations are to include an implied general condition that the person carrying on the process must use "the best available techniques not entailing excessive cost", termed "BATNEEC", for preventing or reducing the release of prescribed substances into any environmental medium, including the aquatic environment, and for rendering harmless any other substances which might cause harm if released.[117] A notable feature in relation to the BATNEEC requirement is the onus of proof involved in relation to it. A person who is accused of failing to adhere to BATNEEC must show that there was no better available technique not entailing excessive cost than that which was in fact used to satisfy the condition.[118]

In addition to the generally implied BATNEEC condition, authorisations are also to include such specific conditions as the enforcing authority considers appropriate for achieving stated objectives. The objectives to be sought through the imposition of conditions in authorisations include compliance with quality standards or objectives established under certain "relevant enactments". These include the water quality objectives to be set under Chapter I of Part III of the Water

[115] s.2 Environmental Protection Act 1990. See also the Environmental Protection (Prescribed Processes and Substances) Regulations 1991, S.I. 1991 No.472. Other matters are provided for under the Environmental Protection (Authorisation of Processes) (Determination Periods) Order 1991, S.I. 1991 No.513; and the Environmental Protection (Applications, Appeals and Registers) Regulations 1991, S.I. 1991 No.507.

[116] s.6 and Sch.1 Environmental Protection Act 1990.

[117] s.7(4).

[118] s.25(1).

Resources Act 1991.[119] Consequently, in the determination of conditions in an authorisation concerning a discharge to controlled waters, HMIP will be bound to impose conditions designed to achieve or maintain the water quality objectives which have been set for the receiving waters concerned. Where a process is likely to involve the release of substances into more than one environmental medium, the BATNEEC strategy will be applied to the environment as a whole, having regard to "the best practicable environmental option available".[120]

Offences

It is an offence to conduct a prescribed process otherwise than under and in accordance with the conditions of an authorisation, and special enforcement powers are given to the enforcing authority in relation to this offence. Where HMIP is of the opinion that a person operating a prescribed process under an authorisation is contravening any condition of the authorisation, or is likely to do so, the authority may serve an "enforcement notice" upon him specifying, amongst other things, the matter constituting the contravention and the steps that must be taken to remedy it. If HMIP is of the opinion that the conduct of a prescribed process under an authorisation involves "an imminent risk of serious pollution of the environment" then a "prohibition notice" may be served specifying the risk involved, the steps which must be taken to remove it and a direction that the authorisation will cease to have effect to authorise the process until the prohibition notice is withdrawn.[121]

The offences of conducting a prescribed process otherwise than under and in accordance with an authorisation, or the failure to comply with the requirements of an enforcement or prohibition notice, are punishable by the imposition of a fine of £20,000, on summary conviction, and a fine of unlimited amount, or to imprisonment for a term not exceeding two years or both where the conviction is brought on

---

[119] s.7(2)(c) and (12)(e) Environmental Protection Act 1990, and on water quality objectives under the Water Resources Act 1991 see p.294 above.

[120] s.7(7) Environmental Protection Act 1990. In addition to the general implied condition, and the specific conditions imposed by the enforcing authority, a power is given to the Secretary of State to issue directions to the enforcement authority as to conditions which are, or are not, to be included in all authorisations, in authorisations of any specified description, or in any particular authorisation (s.7(3)).

[121] s.13 and 14.

indictment. Offences concerning the failure to afford an inspector facilities and assistance when required to do so, failure to provide information or intentionally to make a false entry in any record required to be kept as a condition of an authorisation are punishable with a lower fine of £2,000 on summary conviction.[122] In relation to the more serious offences the court may, in addition to or instead of imposing any punishment, order the convicted person to take specified steps for remedying any matters which it appears to be in his powers to remedy,[123] and an offence is committed by a failure to comply with a court order of this kind.[124]

Information provisions

The Environmental Protection Act 1990 imposes a range of obligations in relation to environmental information. Specifically, a duty is imposed upon HMIP to maintain a register containing particulars relating to applications for authorisations; authorisations granted; variation, enforcement and prohibition notices; revocations of authorisations; appeals to the Secretary of State concerning authorisations; convictions for offences; information provided in pursuance of authorisations; directions given to HMIP by the Secretary of State; and any other matters which may be prescribed. It is the duty of HMIP to secure that the registers maintained by them are available, at all reasonable times, for inspection by the public free of charge and to afford members of the public facilities for obtaining copies of entries on payment of a reasonable charge.[125]

Two exceptions exist to the requirement that information about the operation of integrated pollution control authorisations is to be included in HMIP's public register. First, information is not to be included if, in the opinion of the Secretary of State, its inclusion would be contrary to the interests of national security.[126] Second, information is excluded if it is determined by HMIP, or on appeal the Secretary of State, to be

---

[122] s.23(1) to (3).
[123] s.26(1).
[124] s.23(1)(l).
[125] s.20(1) and (7).
[126] s.21(1).

commercially confidential.[127] In the latter case, however, information is to cease to be commercially confidential after the expiry of a period of four years from the date of the determination unless, on application from the person who furnished the information, HMIP determines that the information remains commercially confidential.

Relationship between HMIP and the National Rivers Authority

Certain overlaps of responsibility exist between HMIP and the National Rivers Authority in relation to the implementation of integrated pollution control in relation to the aquatic environment. In respect of applications, the appropriate body for a discharger to approach is primarily determined by the nature of the process in which he is engaged and the nature of the substances which he intends to discharge to the aquatic environment. The overriding obligation is that a prescribed process is conducted with the necessary authorisation under Part I of the 1990 Act, as that authorisation serves as an explicit defence to any proceedings for the water pollution offence under the Water Resources Act 1991.[128] The converse is not the case, that is, it would be no defence to the offence of conducting a prescribed process without authorisation, contrary to the 1990 Act for the accused to show that he was in possession of a discharge consent under the 1991 Act.

In relation to authorisations, the 1990 Act has explicitly formulated the duty of HMIP to impose conditions in prescribed process authorisations so that the duty of the National Rivers Authority to realise water quality objectives under the 1991 Act will not be impeded. Hence, as has been noted, the specification of objectives to be achieved in a prescribed process authorisation includes compliance with water quality objectives under the 1991 Act. Moreover, the 1990 Act prevents HMIP granting a prescribed process authorisation if the National Rivers authority certifies its opinion that the discharge proposed will result in or contribute to a failure to achieve any water quality objective under the 1991 Act, and any authorisation that is granted is to include such conditions as appear to the Authority to be appropriate for integrated pollution control purposes.[129]

---

[127] s.22.

[128] s.88(1)(b) Water Resources Act 1991.

[129] s.28(3) Environmental Protection Act 1990.

The monitoring of water quality in controlled waters remains the principal duty of the National Rivers Authority as provided for under the 1991 Act.[130] However, powers are provided to HMIP inspectors to enter premises, conduct examinations and to take water samples in the capacity of HMIP as the enforcement authority in respect of prescribed process authorisations.[131]

In respect of the exchange of information between the two bodies enabling access to that information by the public, HMIP is under a duty to furnish the National Rivers Authority with the particulars contained in the HMIP register[132] to permit the Authority to discharge its duty to keep corresponding particulars in its registers.[133]

Waste disposal

Amongst the defences to the principal water pollution offences, under Chapter II of Part III of the Water Resources Act 1991, is the defence that a person will not be guilty of the offences in relation to any entry of matter or discharge which is under and in accordance with a waste management licence, granted under Part II of the Environmental Protection Act 1990, or a disposal licence, issued in pursuance of s.5 of the Control of Pollution Act 1974.[134] The defence in relation to disposal licences is limited in its application to the two principal offences of, first, causing or knowingly permitting the entry of poisonous noxious or polluting matter or solid waste matter to enter any controlled waters and, second, causing or knowingly permitting matter to enter inland freshwaters so as to tend to impede the proper flow of the waters in a manner leading to pollution.[135] Generally, this exception relates to the system of controls applicable to waste disposal sites provided for under Part I of the Control of Pollution Act 1974, and to be provided for in future under Part II of the Environmental Protection Act 1990.

---

[130] s.84(2)(a) Water Resources Act 1991.

[131] s.17 Environmental Protection Act 1991.

[132] s.20(9).

[133] s.190(1)(f) Water Resources Act 1991, and on registers kept by the Authority generally see p.224 above.

[134] s.88(1)(c) and (4) Water Resources Act 1991.

[135] That is, the defence concerning disposal licences does not apply to the principal water pollution offences provided for under s.85(2) to (4), see s.88(3).

Waste management licensing

Under the new law, a waste management licence is required to authorise the treatment, keeping or disposal of any specified description of controlled waste[136] in or on specified land. A licence is to be granted on such terms and subject to such conditions as appear to the waste regulation authority[137] to be appropriate. Conditions may relate to the activities which the licence authorises and to the precautions to be taken and works to be carried out in connection with, or with the consequences of, those activities. Accordingly, requirements may be imposed in the licence which are to be complied with before the activities which the licence authorises have begun or after the activities which the licence authorises have ceased. A licence will continue in force until revoked or surrendered.[138] Where an application is made to a waste regulation authority, the authority may not reject it if it is satisfied that the applicant is a fit and proper person,[139] unless it is satisfied that its rejection is necessary for the purpose of preventing pollution of the environment,[140] harm to human health or serious detriment to the amenities of the locality.[141]

---

136 "Waste" is stated to include any substance which constitutes a scrap material or an effluent or any other unwanted surplus substance arising from the application of any process, and any substance or article which requires to be disposed of as being broken, worn out, contaminated or otherwise spoiled. "Controlled waste" is defined to mean household, commercial and industrial waste, and these terms are further defined (s.75 Environmental Protection Act 1990).

137 The "waste regulation authorities" are, in England, county councils, except for Greater London and the metropolitan areas, where the authority is either a statutorily constituted waste authority or the district council, and in Wales, district councils (s.30(1) Environmental Protection Act 1990).

138 s.35.

139 The meaning of "fit and proper person" is described in s.74.

140 "The environment" is stated to consist of all, or any, of the following media, namely land, water and the air. "Pollution of the environment" means pollution of the environment due to the release or escape into any environmental medium from, amongst other things, land on which controlled waste is treated, kept or deposited of substances or articles constituting or resulting from the waste and capable, by reason of the quantity or concentrations involved, of causing harm to man or any other living organisms supported by the environment (s.29(1) and (2)).

141 Rejection for the purpose of preventing serious detriment to the amenities of the locality will be inapplicable where planning permission is in force in relation to the use to which the land will be put under the licence (s.36(3)).

Where the waste regulation authority proposes to issue a licence, the authority must, before it does so, refer the proposal to the National Rivers Authority and consider any representations about the proposal which the Authority makes during the period allowed.[142] If the National Rivers Authority requests that the proposed licence should not be issued, or disagrees about the conditions of the licence, the matter may be referred to the Secretary of State and the licence may not be issued except in accordance with his decision.[143]

The duty of care

The licensing system for waste provided for under Part II of the Environmental Protection Act 1990 is underpinned by a duty of care[144] in relation to the keeping, treatment or disposal of controlled waste and a criminal offence relating to unauthorised or harmful deposit, treatment or disposal of waste. This provides that no person may deposit controlled waste, or knowingly cause or knowingly permit controlled waste to be deposited in or on any land unless a waste management licence authorising the deposit is in force and the deposit is in accordance with the licence. In addition, it is an offence to treat, keep or dispose of controlled waste, or knowingly cause or knowingly permit controlled waste to be treated, kept or disposed of in or on any land except under and in accordance with a waste management licence, or to treat, keep or dispose of controlled waste in a manner likely to cause pollution of the environment or harm to human health.[145] It is a defence for a person charged with this offence to prove that he took all reasonable precautions and exercised all due diligence to avoid the commission of the offence; or that he acted under instructions from his employer and neither knew nor had reason to suppose that the acts done by him constituted an

[142] The period allowed is twenty one days beginning with the day on which the proposal is received by the National Rivers Authority, or such longer period as the waste regulation authority and the National Rivers Authority may agree in writing (s.36(10)).

[143] s.36(4) and (5).

[144] On the duty of care see s.34.

[145] s.33(1). However, these provisions do not apply to household waste from a domestic property which is treated, kept or disposed of within the curtilage of the dwelling by or with the permission of the occupier of the dwelling, or to cases prescribed by the Secretary of State by Regulations (s.33(2) and (3)).

offence; or that the acts alleged to constitute an offence were done in an emergency in order to avoid danger to the public and that, as soon as reasonably practicable after they were done, particulars of them were furnished to the waste regulation authority in whose area the treatment or disposal of the waste took place. A person who commits the offence will be liable, on summary conviction, to imprisonment for a term not exceeding six months or to a fine not exceeding £20,000 or both, and on indictment to imprisonment for a term not exceeding two years or a fine or both, but in the case of certain kinds of dangerous or intractable waste, termed "special waste", provided for under Regulations, the term of imprisonment which may be imposed on indictment is extended to five years.[146]

In contrast to previous provisions, it is no longer possible for the holder of a waste management licence to surrender it at will. Surrender will only be allowed with the permission of the waste regulation authority, and that permission will only be given by a certificate of completion granted if the authority is satisfied that the condition of the land is unlikely to cause pollution of the environment or harm to human health. A certificate of completion may only be granted after inspection of the land, after reference of the proposal to grant the certificate is made to the National Rivers Authority and consideration is given to any representations made by that Authority about the proposal. If the National Rivers Authority requests that the surrender of the licence should not be accepted, the matter may be referred to the Secretary of State and the surrender may not be accepted except in accordance with his decision.[147]

Other respects in which the National Rivers Authority may be involved in the disposal of waste on land concern discharge consents and planning matters. Although Part II of the Environmental Protection Act 1990 is concerned with the disposal of waste on land, certain kinds of waste disposal operation may involve the discharge of liquid forms of effluent into controlled waters. In such a situation the waste management licensee may also require a discharge consent under Chapter II of Part II of the Water Resources Act 1991. In relation to planning matters, it is a

---

[146] s.33(7) to (9) Environmental Protection Act 1990, and on the meaning of "special waste" see s.62.

[147] s.39(1) to (7).

prerequisite to the grant of a waste management licence that either planning permission or a certificate of established used has been granted.[148] Consequently, the National Rivers Authority will previously have had the opportunity to make representations as to the harmful effects of a proposed waste disposal site in its capacity as a statutory consultee for planning purposes.[149]

Deposit of waste at sea

Amongst the authorisations which serve as a defence to the principal water pollution offences under Chapter II of Part III of the Water Resources Act 1991 is the defence provided for where the entry of matter into waters takes place under and in accordance with a licence granted under Part II of the Food and Environment Protection Act 1985.[150] This exception relates to the system of licensing provided for in respect of the deposit, loading and incineration of waste, and 'scuttling' of vessels at sea provided for under the 1985 Act. Generally, a licence issued by the Minister of Agriculture, Fisheries and Food is required for any of these operations, and in determining applications for such licences the Minister is bound to have regard to the need to protect the marine environment, the living resources which it supports and human health.[151]

A number of criminal offences arise in respect of infringements of the licensing system for deposits of waste in United Kingdom waters and United Kingdom controlled waters[152] provided for under Part II of the 1985 Act. Most significantly, it is an offence for a person to conduct an operation for which a licence is needed otherwise than in pursuance of a licence and in accordance with its provisions, or causing or permitting

[148] s.36(2) Environmental Protection Act 1990.

[149] s.65 Town and Country Planning Act 1990, and Art.18(1) General Development Order 1988, S.I. 1988 No.1813; and see p.333 below on planning law generally.

[150] s.88(1)(d) Water Resources Act 1991.

[151] s.8(1) Food and Environment Protection Act 1985.

[152] "United Kingdom waters" means any part of the sea within the seaward limits of United Kingdom territorial waters, and the sea includes any estuary or arm of the sea and any waters of any river, channel, creek or bay where the tide flows at mean high water springs or any area submerged at that time (s.24(1) Food and Environment Protection Act 1985). The reference to "United Kingdom controlled waters" was added by s.146(2) and (3) Environmental Protection Act 1990.

another person to do so.[153] A person found guilty of this offence will be liable, on summary conviction, to a fine of an amount not exceeding £50,000, or on conviction on indictment to a fine or to imprisonment for a term of not more than two years or to both.[154] This offence is subject to an exception where deposit of waste takes place in order to secure the safety of a vessel or to preserve life and the Minister is informed, within a reasonable time, of the operation, the locality in which it took place and the substances or articles deposited.[155] In addition, the Minister is empowered to make an order specifying other operations which do not need a licence, and this power has been exercised by the making of the Deposits at Sea (Exemptions) Order 1985.[156]

POLLUTION PREVENTION

Anti–pollution works and operations

Amongst the land and works powers of the Authority, provided for under Chapter I of Part VII of the Water Resources Act 1991, are significant pollution prevention powers authorising the Authority to take action by embarking upon various kinds of anti–pollution works. These provisions allow the Authority to undertake specified works and operations where it appears that any poisonous, noxious or polluting matter or any solid waste matter is likely to enter, or to be or to have been present in, any controlled waters. In a case where the matter appears likely to enter any controlled waters, works and operations may be carried out for the purpose of preventing it from doing so. In a case where the matter appears to be, or to have been, present in any controlled waters, works and operations may be conducted for the purpose of removing or disposing of the matter, or remedying or mitigating any pollution caused by its presence in the waters. In so far as reasonably practicable to do so, the Authority may also carry out works or operations for the purpose of restoring the waters, including flora and

---

[153] s.9(1).

[154] s.21(1) and (2) Food and Environment Protection Act 1985, as amended by s.146 Environmental Protection Act 1990.

[155] s.9(3).

[156] S.I. 1985 No.1699.

fauna dependent on the aquatic environment, to their state immediately before the matter became present in the waters. In no case, however, will the Authority be entitled to impede or prevent the making of any discharge in pursuance of a discharge consent.[157]

Where works or operations of the kinds provided for are carried out by the Authority, it is entitled to recover the expenses reasonably incurred in doing so from any person who caused or knowingly permitted the matter in question to be present at the place from which it was likely to enter the controlled waters, or caused or knowingly permitted the matter to be present in the waters. By way of exception to this general power to recover expenses, the Authority is not able to recover in respect of waters from an abandoned mine which are permitted to be present at a place from which they are likely to enter controlled waters, or where they enter controlled waters. These powers do not derogate from any right of action or other remedy, whether civil or criminal, in proceedings instituted otherwise than in accordance with these powers, and do not affect any restriction imposed by or under any other enactment, whether public, local or private.[158]

Other powers to deal with foul water and pollution

Without prejudice to the power of the Authority to undertake anti–pollution works and operations, as described above, the Authority has the power to undertake various kinds of work to deal with foul water and pollution on any land which it owns or over which it has acquired the necessary easements or rights.[159] Specifically, the works authorised are

---

[157] s.161(1) and (2) Water Resources Act 1991, and see p.304 above on discharge consents.

[158] s.161(3) to (5).

[159] The kinds of water in relation to which these powers may be exercised are specified in s.159(6)(b) as surface or underground water which belongs to the Authority or any water undertaker or from which the Authority or any water undertaker is authorised to take water; water of any reservoir which belongs to or is operated by the Authority or any water undertaker or which the Authority or any water undertaker is proposing to acquire or construct for the purpose of being so operated; or any underground strata from which the Authority or any water undertaker is for the time being authorised to abstract water in pursuance of a licence under Chapter II of Part III of the Water Resources Act 1991 (s.162(1)).

the construction and maintenance of drains, sewers, watercourses, catchpits and other works for the purpose of intercepting, treating or disposing of any foul water arising or flowing from that land or of otherwise preventing pollution of specified kinds of water. However, this power will not authorise the Authority, without the consent of a navigation authority, to intercept or take any water which the navigation authority are authorised to take for the purposes of their undertaking. Other powers to deal with foul water and pollution allow the Authority to carry out all such works in a street, and otherwise than in a street, as are required to secure that the water in any relevant waterworks[160] is not polluted or otherwise contaminated, and incidental works thereto.[161]

Requirements to take precautions against pollution

Provision is made for precautionary measures to prevent water pollution under the Chapter III of Part III of the Water Resources Act 1991 allowing the Secretary of State to make preventative regulations in relation to water pollution. Specifically, he is empowered to prohibit a person from having custody or control of any poisonous, noxious or polluting matter unless prescribed works and precautions and other steps have been taken for the purpose of preventing or controlling the entry of the matter into any controlled waters. In addition, he may make regulations requiring a person who already has custody or control of, or makes use of, poisonous, noxious or polluting matter to carry out works and take precautions for the same purpose.[162]

Certain matters are explicitly provided for in relation to the power of the Secretary of State to make precautionary regulations. Regulations may confer power on the Authority to determine the circumstances in which a person is required to carry out works or take precautions or other steps, and to specify the works, precautions or other steps which are required to be undertaken. Another matter which may be provided for in

---

160 "Relevant waterworks" means any waterworks which contain water which is or may be used by a water undertaker for providing a supply of water to premises (s.162(6)).

161 s.162. See also the power of the Authority to discharge water in relation to works under s.163 discussed at p.313 above.

162 s.92(1).

precautionary regulations is a facility for appeals to the Secretary of State against notices served by the Authority in pursuance of its power to determine what preventative measures are required. The regulations may also provide that contravention of precautionary requirements is to be an offence the maximum penalty for which is not to exceed the penalties provided for in relation to the principal offences of polluting controlled waters described above.[163]

The power of the Secretary of State to make precautionary regulations[164] has been exercised in an agricultural context by the enactment of the Control of Pollution (Silage, Slurry and Agricultural Fuel Oil) Regulations 1991.[165] These Regulations require persons with custody of a crop being made into silage, livestock slurry or certain fuel oil storage facilities to carry out works and take precautions and other steps for preventing pollution of controlled waters. The Regulations provide for exemptions from these requirements in certain circumstances, but also for the loss of exemptions where the Authority is satisfied that an otherwise exempt structure under the Regulations poses a significant risk of pollution of controlled waters. Rights of appeal to the Secretary of State are conferred where notices requiring work to be done, or precautions taken, are served by the Authority. Contravention of the Regulations, by having custody or control of facilities which fail to meet specifications set out in Schedules to the Regulations, is punishable, on summary conviction, by a fine not exceeding £2,000 and, on conviction on indictment, by a fine.

Water protection zones

Under Chapter III of Part III of the Water Resources Act 1991 provision is made for the designation of water protection zones as areas in which activities likely to result in pollution of controlled waters may be prohibited or restricted. The designation of a water protection zone is made by the Secretary of State in Wales, or by the Secretary of State in consultation with the Minister of Agriculture, Fisheries and Food in the

---

[163] s.92(2).

[164] As previously provided for under ss.110 and 185(2)(c) to (e) of the Water Act 1989, now repealed.

[165] S.I. 1991 No.324.

case of an area wholly or partly in England. Designation is provided for where it is appropriate, with a view to prohibiting or restricting the carrying on in the designated area of specified activities. In particular, designation is brought about with a view to preventing or controlling the entry of any poisonous, noxious or polluting matter into controlled waters, where it is appropriate to prohibit or restrict the carrying on of activities which are likely to result in the pollution of those waters. The effect of designation is to enable the prohibition or restriction in the designated area of activities specified or described in the order.[166]

Without prejudice to the generality of the Secretary of State's power to designate water protection zones, a number of particular matters may be provided for in an order designating a zone. Specifically, a designation order may confer power on the Authority to determine the circumstances in which an activity is prohibited or restricted and to determine the activities to which a prohibition applies.[167] Alternatively, an order may apply a prohibition or restriction in respect of any activities which are carried on without the consent of the Authority or in contravention of any conditions subject to which consent is given. An order may also provide that contravention of a prohibition or restriction or of a condition of a consent, is to be an offence the maximum penalty for which is not to exceed those provided for in relation to the principal offences of polluting controlled waters, described above. Anything falling to be determined by the Authority under a water protection zone designation order may be determined in accordance with a procedure and by reference to matters and the opinion of persons specified in the order.[168]

The Secretary of State may not make an order for the creation of a water protection zone except on the application of the Authority, and detailed procedural matters relating to orders designating zones are set out in Schedule 11 to the Act.[169] Schedule 11 provides that where the Authority applies for an order designating a water protection zone, a

---

[166] s.91(2) and (3) Water Resources Act 1991.

[167] The Secretary of State is empowered to make regulations with respect to any order which requires the consent of the Authority for the carrying on of any activities (s.96(1)).

[168] s.93(4)(a) to (d), and see p.295 above on the principal offences.

[169] s.93(5).

copy of the order is to be submitted to the Secretary of State and published in the locality of the proposed zone and in the *London Gazette*. Publication in newspapers in the locality is to state the general effect of the order, a place where a draft of the order may be inspected, and that any person may object within a twenty–eight day period. The Authority is obliged, at the request of any person, and on payment of a reasonable charge, to furnish a copy of the draft submitted to the Secretary of State. The Secretary of State may make an order on the same terms as the draft order, or in those terms modified as he may think fit, or he may refuse to make an order, and he may hold a public inquiry before making an order designating a water protection zone.[170]

Nitrate sensitive areas

Water protection zones may not be designated in order to prevent the entry of nitrate into controlled waters as a result of anything done in connection with the use of land for agricultural purposes.[171] This is because the problem of nitrate contamination of water supplies has been separately provided for under the 1991 Act by provision for the designation of nitrate sensitive areas. Accordingly, a nitrate sensitive area may be designated, in order to prevent or control the entry of nitrate into controlled waters as a result of, or of anything done in connection with, the use of any land for agricultural purposes. Designation for these purposes is brought about where it is considered appropriate to do so by the relevant Minister.[172]

Where an area is designated as a nitrate sensitive area, in addition to entering into compensation agreements, the relevant Minister may make an order in respect of a designated area for the imposition of requirements, prohibitions or restrictions to prevent the entry of nitrate into controlled waters in relation to the carrying on, on agricultural land, of specified activities. The order may provide for specified or determined

---

[170] Sch.11.

[171] s.93(3).

[172] s.94(1) and (2). "The relevant Minister" for the purposes of an order of this kind is the Secretary of State in relation to an area which is wholly in Wales, and in relation to land which is wholly in England, or partly in England and partly in Wales, the expression means the Minister and the Secretary of State acting jointly (s.94(7)).

amounts of compensation to be paid, if any, in respect of the obligations imposed under the order.[173]

Alongside the general power to impose restrictions and make payments under an order relating to a nitrate sensitive area, a range of more particular powers is provided for in relation to orders of this kind. Hence, the appropriate Minister may determine the circumstances in which the carrying on of any activity is required, prohibited or restricted and determine the kinds of activity concerned. Similarly, the Minister may give consent for a requirement not to apply, or to apply only subject to conditions, or to apply prohibitions or restrictions only where consent is not granted, or where the conditions imposed in a consent are not complied with.[174] Penalties may be imposed for contravention of restrictions, or breaches of consent conditions, subject to the maximum levels provided for in relation to the principal offences of polluting controlled waters, described above.[175]

The detailed procedural provisions relating to the designation of nitrate sensitive areas are set out in Schedule 12 to the Act.[176] This provides for the relevant Minister to make an order designating an area on application by the Authority. An application by the Authority for an order designating a nitrate sensitive area is not to be made unless pollution is likely to be caused by the entry of nitrate into controlled waters as a result of anything done in connection with the use of the land for agricultural purposes, and existing provisions are not sufficient to prevent or control the entry of nitrate into those waters. Before making the order, the relevant Minister is to publish a notice with respect to the order in local newspapers and in the *London Gazette*. The notice published in the local newspapers is to state the general effect of the proposed order, a place where the order can be inspected and that any person may object to the order within a period of forty–two days. A copy of the order is to be furnished to any person on payment of a reasonable charge. After expiry of the period for objections, the relevant Minister

---

[173] s.94(3).

[174] The Ministers may, by regulations, make provision for the purpose of any order which requires consent to the carrying on of any activities or to any failure to carry on any activity (s.96(2)).

[175] s.94(5).

[176] Effective under s.94(6).

may make the order on the terms proposed, or in a modified form, or he may decide not to make any order. A public inquiry may be held before deciding whether to make the order or to make it with modifications.[177] These powers have been exercised in the creation of the Nitrate Sensitive Areas (Designation) Order 1990 which designates ten areas in England as nitrate sensitive areas.[178]

Where an area has been designated as a nitrate sensitive area, the relevant Minister may enter into agreements in relation to the land for the purpose of preventing or controlling the entry of nitrate into controlled waters as a result of anything done in connection with the use of land for agricultural purposes. Under agreements of this kind the owner of the freehold interest in the land, or any person having an interest in the land where the consent of the freeholder has been given, accepts such obligations in respect of the management of land, or otherwise, as may be imposed by the agreement. Beyond the original parties, the effect of the agreement will be to bind all persons deriving title from the person originally entering into the agreement with the relevant Minister to the extent of the agreement.[179]

Codes of good agricultural practice

The Secretary of State and the Minister of Agriculture, Fisheries and Food, acting jointly, are empowered to make a statutory instrument approving any code of practice for the purpose of giving practical guidance to persons engaged in agriculture with respect to activities that may affect controlled waters, and promoting what appear to them to be desirable practices for avoiding or minimising the pollution of controlled waters. The Secretary of State and the Minister are not to make an order creating a code of agricultural practice unless they have first consulted the Authority.[180]

---

[177] Sch.12.

[178] S.I. 1990 No.1013, as amended by S.I. 1990 No.1187.

[179] s.95 Water Resources Act 1991.

[180] s.97(1) and (3), and see *Code of Good Agricultural Practice for the Protection of Water* (July 1991) Ministry of Agriculture, Fisheries and Food, and Water (Prevention of Pollution) (Code of Practice) Order 1991, S.I. 1991 No.2285.

Contravention of a code of agricultural practice is not of itself to give rise to any criminal or civil liability, but the Authority is to take into account whether there has been, or is likely to be, any contravention of this kind in determining when and how it should exercise its powers. Specifically, a contravention of this kind is to be taken into account in relation to the exercise of the Authority's power to impose a notice of prohibition prohibiting certain kinds of discharge,[181] or any powers conferred on the Authority by regulations[182] requiring precautions to be taken against pollution.[183]

Water pollution prevention and planning law

Although outside the provisions of the Water Resources Act 1991, another significant legal mechanism for the preventative control of water pollution is the use of planning law to restrict developments which are likely to cause pollution. In the most general terms, the Town and Country Planning Act 1990 defines "development" to mean the carrying out of building, engineering, mining or other operations in, on, over or under land, or the making of any material change in the use of any buildings or other land, and requires planning permission for the carrying out of any development of land.[184] On application, and after having regard to material considerations such as matters relating to pollution control,[185] planning permission may be granted by the local planning authority[186] and may be granted either unconditionally or subject to such conditions as the authority thinks fit, or refused.[187]

---

[181] Under s.86(1) Water Resources Act 1991.

[182] Under s.92.

[183] s.97(2).

[184] ss.55(1) and 57(1) Town and Country Planning Act 1990. See also s.13 Planning and Compensation Act 1991, extending the meaning of "building operations" in the definition of development to encompass demolition and other operations.

[185] See *Hoveringham Gravels v. Secretary of State for the Environment*, [1975] Q.B. 754.

[186] The council of a county is the county planning authority for the county and the council of a district is the district planning authority for the district, subject to express provisions to the contrary in relation to non-metropolitan counties, and all functions conferred upon local planning authorities are to be exercisable both by county planning authorities and district planning authorities (s.1(1) and (3) Town and Country Planning Act 1990).

Although it is accepted as a matter of planning policy that the withholding of development consent, or the granting of consent subject to conditions, should not be used as a means of securing objects that can be achieved under other legislation,[188] the facility for the creation of structure and local plans to which regard is to be had in determining applications for development consent,[189] and formulating policy and general proposals for development of land in the area of local planning authorities, may be an effective mechanism for the protection of watercourses from pollution. Accordingly, it has been stated that local planning authorities should have regard to the impact that their planning policy will have on the environment and matters of pollution control.[190]

Before individual applications for development consent of a kind which have the potential to cause pollution are determined provision is made for publication of notices of application,[191] and consultation with specified authorities in relation to particular categories of development. In particular, the National Rivers Authority is a statutory consultee in relation to developments involving or including mining operations; the carrying out of works or operations in the bed of or on the banks of a river or stream; for the purpose of refining or storing mineral oils and their derivatives; involving the use of land for the deposit of refuse or waste; or relating to the use of land as a cemetery. In these cases the local planning authority are required to consult with the National Rivers Authority before granting planning permission, to take into account any representations made by it, and not to determine an application until at

---

[187] ss.58, 62 and 70.

[188] Planning Policy Guidance Note 1 para.22, and Department of the Environment Circular 1/85 para.18; and see *Hereford and Worcester County Council v. Dubberley*, (1985) 1 P.A.D. 85.

[189] Provided for under ss.31 and 36 Town and Country Planning Act 1990, and see s.26 Planning and Compensation Act 1991 on the status of development plans.

[190] Department of the Environment Circular 22/84 para.4.34. See also ss.31(3)(b) 36(3)(b) Town and Country Planning Act 1990, as amended by Sch.4 Planning and Compensation Act 1991, which require structure and local plans to include policies for the improvement of the physical environment.

[191] s.65 Town and Country Planning Act 1990.

least 14 days after the date on which the Authority has been served a copy of the application.[192]

SUPPLEMENTAL PROVISIONS ON WATER POLLUTION

Application to radioactive substances

Except as provided for by regulations made by the Secretary of State, nothing amongst the control of pollution provisions of the Water Resources Act 1991 is to apply to radioactive waste within the meaning of the Radioactive Substances Act 1960. As a counterpart to this, however, the Secretary of State is empowered to make regulations to provide for prescribed provisions to have effect with such modifications as he considers appropriate for dealing with radioactive waste. Similarly, regulations may modify the 1960 Act, or any other Act in relation to radioactive waste, in consequence of the control of pollution provisions of the Water Resources Act 1991.[193]

Civil liability, savings and limitation for summary offences

Subject to provisions relating to offences under two or more laws,[194] nothing in Part III of the Water Resources Act 1991, concerned with the control of pollution, confers a right of action in any civil proceedings, other than proceedings for the recovery of a fine, in respect of any contravention of that part of the Act or subordinate legislation, unless expressly provided for within the control of pollution provisions of the Act. Nothing in Part III of the Act derogates from any right of

---

[192] Art.18 Town and County Planning General Development Order 1988, S.I. 1988 No.1813. See also Sch.1 and 2 Town and Country Planning (Assessment of Environmental Effects) Regulations 1988, S.I. 1988 No.1199.

[193] s.98(1) Water Resources Act 1991. The Secretary of State has exercised his power, under previous legislation, to make regulations in this respect by creating the Control of Pollution (Radioactive Waste) Regulations 1989, S.I. 1989 No.1158, which have the effect of bringing radioactive waste within the scope of the control of pollution provisions of the Act, but in such a manner that no account will be taken of the radioactive properties of the substance concerned. On pollution of water by radioactivity see p.342 below.

[194] Provided for under s.18 Interpretation Act 1978.

action or other remedy, whether civil or criminal, in proceedings instituted otherwise than under that part of the Act. Similarly, nothing in the pollution control provisions of the Act affects any restriction imposed by or under any other enactment, whether public, local or private.[195]

A general procedural stipulation imposed in relation to offences under Part III of the Water Resources Act 1991 is that a magistrates' court may try any summary offence under that part of the Act, or subordinate legislation, if the information is laid not more than twelve months after the commission of the offence.[196] This power applies notwithstanding other general provisions concerning the time limit for summary proceedings to be brought,[197] but may be of limited application since most of the offences provided for in relation to the control of pollution are hybrid offences to which the time limit for summary proceedings would not apply.[198]

International obligations and transitional provisions

The Secretary of State has the power to provide by regulations that the water pollution provisions of the 1991 Act are to have effect with prescribed modifications for the purpose of enabling the Government of the United Kingdom to give effect to any Community obligations,[199] or to any international agreement to which the United Kingdom is for the time being a party.[200]

The provisions of Part III of the 1991 Act are to have effect subject to Schedule 13 which reproduces transitional provisions originally made in connection with the coming into force of the Water Act 1989 and have the general effect of allowing certain consents and other provisions to continue in force under the 1991 Act.[201]

---

[195] s.100 Water Resources Act 1991. On civil liability for water pollution generally see Ch.3 above.

[196] s.101.

[197] Under s.127 Magistrates' Courts Act 1980.

[198] See *R. v Dacorum Magistrates' Court, ex parte Michael Gardiner Ltd.*, (1985) 149 J.P. 677.

[199] On European Community obligations in relation to water quality generally see p.355 below.

[200] s.102 Water Resources Act 1991.

[201] s.103.

WATER POLLUTION UNDER MISCELLANEOUS LEGISLATION

Discharges to sewers

A person will not be guilty of any of the principal water pollution offences under the Water Resources Act 1991 in respect of a discharge made into a sewer or works vested in a sewerage undertaker if the undertaker was bound to receive the discharge. As a counterpart of this, a sewerage undertaker will not be guilty of an offence in relation to the contravention of a discharge consent due to a discharge by another person into a sewer or works of the undertaker which the undertaker was not bound to receive and could not reasonably have been expected to prevent.[202] These provisions relate to a separate system of authorisations for discharges to sewers which is provided for under Part IV of the Water Industry Act 1991.

Notably, under the Water Industry Act 1991, it is an offence for a person to throw, empty or turn, or suffer or permit to be thrown or emptied or to pass specified matter and substances, into any public sewer, or into any drain or sewer communicating with a public sewer. In particular the offence arises in respect of (a) any matter likely to injure the sewer or drain, to interfere with the free flow of its contents or to affect prejudicially the treatment and disposal of its contents; (b) any chemical refuse or waste steam, or any liquid of a temperature higher than one hundred and ten degrees Fahrenheit which is a prohibited substance; or (c) any petroleum sprit[203] or carbide of calcium. The reference to a "prohibited substance" in relation to chemical refuse, waste steam or heated liquids means that the substance, either alone or in combination with the contents of the sewer or drain in question, is dangerous, the cause of a nuisance or injurious or likely to cause injury to health. A person contravening these provisions will be guilty of an

---

[202] s.87(2) and (3), see p.299 above.

[203] "Petroleum spirit" means such (a) crude petroleum; (b) oil made from petroleum or from coal, shale, peat or other bituminous substances; or (c) product of petroleum or mixture containing petroleum, as, when tested in the manner prescribed by or under the Petroleum (Consolidation) Act 1928, gives off an inflammable vapour at a temperature of less than seventy–three degrees Fahrenheit (s.111(5) Water Industry Act 1991).

offence and liable, on summary conviction, to a fine not exceeding £2,000 and to a further fine not exceeding £50 for each day on which the offence continues after conviction and, on conviction on indictment, to imprisonment for a term not exceeding two years or to a fine or both.[204]

Separate provision is made under the Water Industry Act 1991 for controls upon the discharge of trade effluent into public sewers.[205] Thus, the occupier of any trade premises in the area of a sewerage undertaker may discharge any trade effluent proceeding from those premises into the undertaker's public sewers if he does so with the undertaker's consent. The power to grant discharges for the entry of effluent into a public sewer will not authorise the discharge of effluent other than by means of a drain or sewer. However, the prohibition upon the discharges of matter likely to injure a sewer or drain and chemical and other refuse, except for petroleum spirit and calcium carbide, described above, will not apply to discharges of effluent which are lawfully made in accordance with a consent. The counterpart of the power to grant authorisations for discharges of trade effluent is that, if effluent is discharged without a consent or other authorisation, the occupier of the premises will be guilty of an offence and liable, on summary conviction, to a fine not exceeding £2,000 or, on conviction on indictment, to a fine.[206]

The requirement that trade effluent is discharged into public sewers in accordance with a consent granted by a sewerage undertaker is underpinned by an analogous system of authorising discharges to that operative in relation to discharges into controlled waters and described above. Provision is made for applications to sewerage undertakers for

---

[204] s.111(1) to (4) Water Industry Act 1991.

[205] "Trade effluent" is defined for these purposes to mean (a) any liquid, either with or without particles of matter in suspension in the liquid, which is wholly or partly produced in the course of any trade or industry carried on at trade premises; and (b) in relation to any trade premises, means any such liquid which is so produced in the course of any trade or industry carried on at those premises, but does not include domestic sewage. "Trade premises" means any premises used or intended to be used for the carrying on of any trade or industry, and for these purposes land or premises used or intended for use, in whole or in part and whether or not for profit (a) for agricultural or horticultural purposes or for the purposes of fish farming; or (b) for scientific research or experiment, are to be deemed to be premises used for carrying on a trade or industry (s.141(1) and (2) Water Industry Act 1991).

[206] s.118.

consents, applications for the discharge of special categories of effluent, conditions of consents, appeals against decisions of the sewerage undertaker, variations and review of consents, and payment of compensation in certain circumstances.[207] In addition, particular provision is made in relation to applications for consent for discharges containing "special category effluent" requiring these applications to be referred to the Secretary of State on the questions of whether the discharge concerned should be prohibited or whether requirements should be imposed as to the conditions on which a discharge may be allowed.[208]

Public health law and water pollution

Part III of the Environmental Protection Act 1990 imposes responsibilities upon local authorities in respect of matters which fall within the definition of "statutory nuisance" provided for under that Act.[209] Procedures are laid down for the removal of this kind of nuisance and criminal offences provided for in relation to it. Accordingly, it is the general duty of every local authority to cause their area to be inspected from time to time for the detection of statutory nuisances and to take reasonably practicable steps to investigate complaints.[210] Amongst the listed statutory nuisances are included any dust, steam, smell or other effluvia arising on industrial, trade or business premises and which are prejudicial to health or a nuisance, any accumulation or deposit which is prejudicial to health or a nuisance, and any other matter declared by any

---

[207] Generally see Chapter III of Part IV Water Industry Act 1991.

[208] ss.120 and 138. See also Trade Effluents (Prescribed Processes and Substances) Regulations 1989, S.I. 1989 No.1156, as amended by the Trade Effluents (Prescribed Processes and Substances) (Amended) Regulations 1990, S.I. 1990 No.1629.

[209] Formerly provisions relating to statutory nuisance were provided for under Part III Public Health Act 1936 and the Public Health (Recurring Nuisances) Act 1969, now repealed.

[210] The area of a local authority which includes part of the seashore will also include for these purposes the territorial sea lying seawards of that part of the shore, and provisions are to have effect in relation to this area as if references to premises and the occupier of premises included respectively a vessel and the master of a vessel (s.79(11) Environmental Protection Act 1990).

enactment to be a nuisance.[211] The last category encompasses matters relating to watercourses provided for under former legislation. These include, first, any pond, ditch, gutter or watercourse which is so foul or in such a state as to be prejudicial to health or a nuisance and, second, a watercourse, not being ordinarily navigated by vessels employed in the carriage of goods by water, which is so choked or silted as to obstruct or impede the proper flow of water and thereby to cause a nuisance, or to give rise to conditions prejudicial to health.[212]

Where a local authority is satisfied that a statutory nuisance exists, or is likely to occur or recur, in the area of the authority, it is to serve a notice, termed an "abatement notice", imposing any or all of certain requirements. The requirements are that the abatement of the nuisance is to be prohibited or restricted in its occurrence or recurrence and that necessary works should be executed and steps taken for any of those purposes within specified times. The abatement notice is to be served on the person responsible for the nuisance, or where the nuisance arises from any defect of a structural character, on the occupier of the premises, or where the person responsible for the nuisance cannot be found or the nuisance has not yet occurred, on the occupier or owner of the premises. The person served with the notice may appeal against the notice to a magistrates' court within twenty–one days of its service. If that person, without reasonable excuse, contravenes or fails to comply with any requirement imposed by the notice, he will be guilty of an offence and liable, on summary conviction, to a fine not exceeding £2,000 together with a further fine of £200 for each day on which the offence continues after the conviction. In relation to industrial, trade or business premises, the maximum fine is £20,000 without provision for a daily fine to be imposed.[213]

Where more than one person is responsible for a statutory nuisance, proceedings may be brought against each of them whether or not any one of them is responsible for what would by itself constitute a nuisance. Where a statutory nuisance affects the area of a local authority but is caused by some act or default committed or taking place outside the area, the local authority may act as if the act or default were wholly

---

211 s.79(1) Environmental Protection Act 1990.

212 s.259(1)(a) and (b) Public Health Act 1936.

213 s.80(1) to (6) Environmental Protection Act 1990.

within their area, except that any appeal is to be heard by a magistrates' court having jurisdiction where the act or default took place. If an abatement notice has not been complied with, the local authority may abate the nuisance and do whatever may be necessary in execution of the notice. Expenses reasonably incurred in abating or preventing the recurrence may be recovered from the person causing the nuisance or the owner of the premises concerned, and a court may apportion the expenses between persons causing the nuisance in such a manner as the court considers fair and reasonable. Detailed matters relating to procedures for appeals, powers of entry and related powers, offences of obstruction, procedures where a local authority is in default of its duties in relation to a statutory nuisance, and the protection of officers against personal liability are provided for under Schedule 3 to the Environmental Protection Act 1990.[214]

Magistrates' courts are also empowered to act on a complaint made by any person on the ground that he is aggrieved by the existence of a statutory nuisance. Analogous provisions provide that if a court is satisfied that an alleged nuisance exists, or is likely to recur, the court may make an order requiring the defendant to abate the nuisance within a specified time and to execute works necessary for that purpose, and prohibiting a recurrence of the nuisance by requiring the defendant, within a specified time, to execute any works necessary to prevent the nuisance. Before proceedings of this kind are instituted, however, the person aggrieved by the nuisance must give the defendant notice of his intention to bring the proceedings and specify the matter complained of. In addition to an abatement order of this kind, the court may also impose a fine upon the defendant not exceeding £2,000. A person who, without reasonable excuse, contravenes any requirement or prohibition imposed as a consequence of these proceedings will be guilty of an offence and liable, on summary conviction, to a fine not exceeding £2,000 and a further daily fine of £200 for each day on which the offence continues after conviction. The court may also direct the local authority for the area in which the nuisance occurred to do anything which the person convicted was required to do by the court under the order to which the conviction relates.[215]

---

[214] s.81(1) to (4) and (7).

[215] s.82.

Radioactive pollution

As previously noted, nothing in the control of pollution provision of the Water Resources Act 1991 is to apply to radioactive waste, though by regulations radioactive waste may be the subject of a water pollution offence providing that no account is taken of the radioactive properties of the substance concerned.[216] This is because radioactive pollution of the environment, including the aquatic environment, is separately provided for under the Radioactive Substances Act 1960, concerned with the safe disposal of radioactive wastes, and the Nuclear Installations Act 1965, providing the statutory basis for the processing, storage and disposal of wastes generated by the nuclear power programme undertaken by the United Kingdom Atomic Energy Authority.

Controls arising under the Radioactive Substances Act 1960 were formerly exercised directly by the Secretary of State, but a recent amendment has empowered him to appoint inspectors to assist him, one of whom is to be the "chief inspector", for the purposes of integrated pollution control, of Her Majesty's Inspectorate of Pollution.[217] Controls under the 1960 Act concern, amongst other matters, the accumulation and disposal of radioactive waste.[218] Subject to specified exceptions for

---

[216] s.98(1) Water Resources Act 1991 and Control of Pollution (Radioactive Waste) Regulations 1989, S.I. 1989 No.1158; and see p.335 above. Similarly, in relation to a range of other enactments, no account is to be taken of any radioactivity possessed by any substance or article or by any part of any premises (s.9(2)(a) and Sch.1 Radioactive Substances Act 1960).

[217] s.11A(1) to (3), as inserted by s.100(1) Environmental Protection Act 1990. On integrated pollution control see p.315 above. The Radioactive Substances Act 1960 has been extensively amended by Part V Environmental Protection Act 1990, and particularly s.105 and Sch.5 to that Act.

[218] "Radioactive waste" is stated to mean waste which consists wholly or partly of: (a) a substance or article which, if it were not waste, would be a radioactive material, or (b) a substance or article which has been contaminated in the course of the production, keeping or use of radioactive material, or by contact with or proximity to other specified waste. "Radioactive material" means anything which, not being waste, is either a *specified substance* or an article made wholly or partly from or incorporating such a substance. The specified substances referred to here are (a) a substance containing an element specified in the Third Schedule to the Radioactive Substances Act 1960, in such a proportion that the number of microcuries of that element contained in the substance, divided by the number of grammes which the substance weighs, is a number greater than that specified in relation to that element

the nuclear power industry, defence purposes and certain hospitals, persons keeping radioactive material must be registered with the chief inspector, and registration can be refused or made subject to such limitations or conditions as are thought fit, the details of which are to be specified in a registration certificate.[219]

The basic prohibition upon the disposal of radioactive waste is that no person may, except in accordance with an authorisation, dispose of any radioactive waste on or from any premises which are used for the purposes of an undertaking[220] carried on by him, or cause or permit any radioactive waste to be so disposed of, if he knows or has reasonable grounds for believing it to be radioactive waste. A similar prohibition is imposed on the unauthorised disposal of radioactive waste received for the purpose of disposal, so that no person who receives any radioactive waste for disposal, knowing or having reasonable grounds for believing it to be radioactive, may dispose of it or cause or permit it to be disposed of except in accordance with an authorisation. Exceptions to this general prohibition are provided for in relation to the disposal of clocks or watches containing radioactive material, and under a range of particular exemption orders made by the Secretary of State.[221]

Authorisation for the disposal of radioactive waste may be provided by the chief inspector, and in some circumstances by the chief

---

in the appropriate column of that Schedule; (b) a substance possessing radioactivity which is wholly or partly attributable to a process of nuclear fission or other process of subjecting a substance to bombardment by neutrons or to ionising radiations, not being a process occurring in the course of nature, or in consequence of the disposal of radioactive waste, or by way of contamination in the course of the application of a process to some other substance (s.18(1) and (2) Radioactive Substances Act 1960).

[219] s.1(3) to (5) Radioactive Substances Act 1960, as amended by s.100 Environmental Protection Act 1990.

[220] "Undertaking" includes any trade, business or profession, and, in relation to a public or local authority, includes any of the powers or duties of that authority, and, in relation to any other body or person, whether corporate or incorporate, includes the activities of that body. "Disposal" includes the removal, deposit or destruction of any waste, or the discharge thereof, whether into water or into the air or into a sewer or drain or otherwise, or the burial thereof, whether underground or otherwise (s.19(1) Radioactive Substances Act 1960).

[221] s.6(1), (3) and (5). See, for example, Radioactive Substances Exemption Order S.I. 1962 No.2648, concerned with luminous articles; S.I. 1962 No.2712, concerned with geological specimens; and S.I. 1980 No.953, concerned with smoke detectors.

inspector and the Minister of Agriculture, Fisheries and Food.[222] Authorisations may be granted in respect of radioactive waste generally, or in respect of waste of a description specified in the authorisation, and may be granted subject to such limitations or conditions as the chief inspector may think fit. Authorisations may be revoked at any time, or varied by attaching limitations or conditions, or by revoking or varying conditions or attaching further conditions to an authorisation.[223] By recent amendments to the 1960 Act provision is also made for the chief inspector to serve enforcement and prohibition notices similar to those provided for under the general regime of controls applicable in respect of integrated pollution control.[224]

Offences are created in relation to the contravention of requirements relating to the registration of premises used for the keeping of radioactive material, authorisation for the keeping of radioactive materials, and for the disposal of radioactive waste. Specifically, offences arise in relation to failure to register unexempt premises where radioactive material is kept or used; causing unauthorised disposal of radioactive waste, and such waste received for disposal in the course of an undertaking; failure to comply with a limitation or condition governing the keeping or use of radioactive material by a person registered or exempted from registration; and non–compliance with an authorisation, or a limitation or condition in an authorisation, granted for the disposal of radioactive waste.[225] However, proceedings for these offences are not to be instituted except by the Secretary of State or by, or with the consent of, the Director of Public Prosecutions. On summary conviction an offender will be liable to a fine not exceeding £2,000, or imprisonment for a term not exceeding three months, or both, and on

---

[222] The latter case arises in relation to premises used for the purposes of an undertaking by the United Kingdom Atomic Energy Authority, premises in respect of which a nuclear site licence under the Nuclear Installations Act 1965 is in force, or premises for which the period of responsibility under such a licence has not come to an end (s.8(1) Radioactive Substances Act 1960, as amended).

[223] s.8(3), (4) and (7).

[224] s.11B and 11C, inserted by s.102 Environmental Protection Act 1990. On integrated pollution control generally see p.315 above.

[225] s.6 Radioactive Substances Act 1960.

conviction on indictment, a fine or imprisonment for a term not exceeding five years or both.[226]

The Nuclear Installations Act 1965 is concerned with the regulation of radioactivity originating from nuclear energy installations, and subjects such installations to a system of licensing. The 1965 Act also creates criminal offences relating to radioactive pollution from such installations and, most significantly, imposes civil liability upon the licensees of nuclear installations for causing radioactive pollution. Liability arises in relation to injury or damage resulting from exposure to nuclear matter[227] in relation to licensed nuclear sites.

Alongside the provision made for licensing and inspection of nuclear installations imposed by the 1965 Act, the operator of an installation of this kind is placed under a strict duty to prevent occurrences involving radioactive pollution causing injury to any person or damage to any property either on or off the licensed site.[228] However, in most instances, situations involving a breach of duties under the Act, and giving rise to civil liability on the part of the licensee, will be actionable only under the Act, and not upon other bases of liability outside the Act such as in tort.[229] Otherwise than where injury or damage is the result of hostile action in the course of armed conflict,[230] a claimant will be able to recover compensation under the Act for a breach of the duty of a licensee of a nuclear installation where the claim is brought within a thirty year limitation period from the time of the occurrence which gave rise to the claim.[231] The liability of a licensee to pay

---

226 s.13(2) and (7).

227 "Nuclear matter" means (a) any fissile material in the form of uranium metal, alloy or chemical compound (including natural uranium) or of plutonium metal, alloy or chemical compound, and any other fissile material which may be prescribed; and (b) any radioactive material produced in, or made radioactive by the exposure to the radiation incidental to, the process of producing or utilising any such fissile material (s.26(1) Nuclear Installations Act 1965).

228 s.7.

229 s.12(1) and (2).

230 s.13(4)(a).

231 s.15(1). A twenty year limitation period is provided for in respect of claims arising from nuclear matter which has been stolen from, or lost, jettisoned or abandoned by the person whose breach of duty gave rise to the claim (s.15(2)).

compensation under the Act is subject to financial limits,[232] and in order for claims of specified or determined magnitude to be met, nuclear site licensees are bound to make such provision by insurance, or other means, as the Secretary of State for Trade and Industry, with the consent of the Treasury, may approve.[233]

Oil and other pollution from ships

Although criminal liability for an escape or discharge of oil from land is capable of falling within the general law of water pollution, discussed previously, to a great extent the law relating to oil pollution from ships, and controls upon other kinds of pollution from ships, has developed from international conventions to which the United Kingdom is a party. Of greatest importance in this respect is the 1973 International Convention for the Prevention of Pollution from Ships, "MARPOL",[234] which establishes controls for oil, noxious liquid substances, packaged goods, sewage and garbage, though not all of its provisions have yet been implemented. In relation to oil, MARPOL requires oil tankers over a certain size to be fitted with segregated ballast tanks; specified equipment to be installed on certain vessels to monitor and control oily discharges; certain regions to be designated "special areas" in which oily discharges are absolutely prohibited; and states given increased powers to inspect and detain foreign ships suspected of violating the Convention. The implementation of these obligations, and an extension of the law to cover the bulk carriage of noxious liquid substances, in the domestic law of the United Kingdom was brought about through the amendment of the Prevention of Oil Pollution Act 1971 by the Merchant Shipping (Prevention of Oil Pollution) Regulations 1983.[235]

---

[232] s.16(1).

[233] s.19(1).

[234] Cmnd.5748, as amended by the 1978 Protocol Cmnd.7347.

[235] S.I. 1983 No.1398, as amended by S.I. 1985 No.2040. See also, Merchant Shipping (Reporting of Pollution Incidents) Regulations 1987, S.I. 1987 No.586. The Prevention of Oil Pollution Act 1971 has been amended by the Prevention of Oil Pollution Act 1986 to cover discharges of oil from vessels into waters which are on the landward side of the baselines for measuring the breadth of the territorial waters of the United Kingdom, and are navigable by sea–going vessels. In relation to substances other than oil, see Merchant Shipping (Control of Pollution by

In general terms, the Prevention of Oil Pollution Act 1971 establishes criminal offences in a range of offences in a range of situations where oil is discharged into navigable waters, and provides extensive powers of intervention by the Secretary of State in the event of shipping casualties. The Act also imposes requirements in relation to the keeping of records relating to transfers of oil and empowers officials to inspect records and ensure that recording duties have been complied with. The most general prohibition upon the discharge of oil into United Kingdom waters is that an offence which is committed where any oil,[236] or mixture containing oil, is discharged under specified circumstances into certain waters. Hence, if the discharge is from a place on land, an offence is committed by the occupier of that place, unless he proves that the discharge was caused by the act of a person who was in that place without the express or implied permission of the occupier. The waters in respect of which the offence may arise are stated to be the whole of the sea within the seaward limits of the territorial waters of the United Kingdom and all other waters, including inland waters, which are within those limits and are navigable by sea–going ships. A person found guilty of the offence is liable on summary conviction to a fine not exceeding £50,000, or on conviction on indictment to a fine.[237]

Noxious Liquid Substances In Bulk) Regulations 1987, S.I. 1987 No.551; and Merchant Shipping (Prevention of Pollution by Garbage) Regulations 1989, S.I. 1989 No.2292. In relation to the provision of reception facilities, see Prevention of Pollution (Reception Facilities) Order 1984, S.I. 1984 No.862; Control of Pollution (Landed Ships' Waste) Regulations 1987, S.I. 1987 No.402; Merchant Shipping (Reception Facilities for Garbage) Regulations 1989, S.I. 1989 No.2293.

236 "Oil" is defined to mean oil of any description and includes spirit produced from oil of any description and coal tar (s.29(1) Prevention of Oil Pollution Act 1971). This definition encompasses vegetable as well as mineral oils (*Cosh v. Larsen*, [1971] 1 Lloyd's Rep.557).

237 s.2 Prevention of Oil Pollution Act 1971. See *Rankin v. De Coster*, [1975] 2 All E.R. 303, where it was held that waters contained in a 'dry dock' were navigable waters for these purposes. See also *Federal Steam Navigation Co. Ltd. v. Department of Trade and Industry*, [1974] 2 All E.R. 97, which establishes that the offence is one of strict liability. But see also s.2(1) which provides that it is a defence for the occupier of a place on land to prove that neither the escape of oil nor any delay in discovering it was due to any want of reasonable care, and that as soon as practicable after it was discovered all reasonable steps were taken for stopping or reducing it.

Specific restrictions are imposed under the Prevention of Oil Pollution Act 1971 in relation to the transfer of oil at night. Thus, no oil may be transferred between sunset and sunrise to or from a vessel in any harbour in the United Kingdom unless the requisite notice has been given to the harbour master or the operation is conducted for the purposes of a fire brigade.[238] If any oil or mixture containing oil is discharged or escapes into the waters of a harbour from a ship or a place on land it must be reported at once to the harbour master or harbour authority, and failure to do so is an offence.[239]

The Merchant Shipping (Prevention of Oil Pollution) Regulations 1983, as amended, apply to United Kingdom ships wherever they are, and to other ships while they are within United Kingdom territorial waters, other that United Kingdom warships and certain other state–owned vessels used for non–commercial service. The 1983 Regulations impose requirements in respect of the surveying and certification of oil tankers and other ships above specified sizes along with regulations as to the keeping of oil record books in a specified form. In the event of a discharge of oil or an oily mixture which is not within specified exceptions, a full statement is to be made in the oil record book for the vessel of the circumstances of, and the reasons for, the discharge. Otherwise than in accordance with provisions relating to discharges for safety purposes or discharges resulting from damage to a ship or its equipment, controls are imposed upon operations involving pollution through the discharge of oil.

In respect of civil liability for oil pollution, liability may arise as a matter of common law in respect of an escape or discharge which falls within various parts of the law of tort.[240] However, civil liability for oil pollution from ships has also been the subject of special legislation, in the form of the Merchant Shipping (Oil Pollution) Act 1971,[241] which

---

[238] s.10.

[239] s.11.

[240] *Esso Petroleum v. Southport Corporation*, [1956] A.C. 218.

[241] See Merchant Shipping Act 1974, which is amended by the Merchant Shipping Act 1988.

was enacted in order to allow the United Kingdom to ratify the 1969 International Convention on Civil Liability for Oil Pollution Damage.[242]

The basic principle of strict civil liability for accidental or intentional oil pollution from ships undertaking bulk carriage of persistent oil is provided for under the 1971 Act. This is to the effect that where, as a result of any occurrence taking place while a ship is carrying a cargo of persistent oil in bulk, any oil carried by the ship, whether as part of the cargo or otherwise, is discharged or escapes from the ship, the owner will be liable for specified kinds of loss except as otherwise provided for by the Act. The losses for which liability is imposed are any damage caused in the area of the United Kingdom by contamination resulting from the discharge or escape; the cost of measures reasonably taken for the purpose of preventing or reducing such damage; and any damage caused by any measures so taken.[243] Exceptions to the general regime of strict civil liability for oil pollution from ships within these provisions provide that the owner of the vessel concerned will not be liable in respect of acts of war and certain other hostilities, and an exceptional, inevitable and irresistible natural phenomenon; discharges due wholly to acts or omissions of other persons with intent to do damage; and negligence or wrongful acts of government or other authorities responsible for maintaining lights or other navigational aids.[244] However, the extent of liability under these provisions may be limited to an amount related to the ship's tonnage, subject to a maximum amount.[245] Provision to meet claims is made through the imposition of compulsory insurance liability for pollution upon ships carrying a bulk cargo of more than a stated amount.[246] An international fund has also been established enabling shipowners to secure contributions, in respect of claims against them, from major importing companies, in the event of liability exceeding a specified sum.[247]

---

[242] Cmnd.4403. See also the 1971 International Convention on the Establishment of an International Fund for Compensation for Oil Pollution Damage (Cmnd.5061, as amended by 1970 Protocol (Cmnd.7029), and 1984 Protocol).

[243] s.1 Merchant Shipping (Oil Pollution) Act 1971.

[244] s.2.

[245] s.4(1).

[246] s.10.

[247] The fund is provided for under Part I Merchant Shipping Act 1974.

Water supplies

Formerly, an offence was provided for under the Water Act 1945 in relation to the pollution of water to be used for water supply purposes.[248] This is now provided for under the Water Industry Act 1991 which provides that a person will be guilty of an offence by any act or neglect whereby the water in any waterworks which is used or likely to be used for human consumption or domestic purposes, or for manufacturing food or drink for human consumption, is polluted or likely to be polluted. The offence is qualified, however, by the stipulation that it is not to be construed as restricting or prohibiting any method of cultivation which is in accordance with the principles of good husbandry. Further qualification provides that the offence is not to be construed as restricting or prohibiting the reasonable use of oil or tar on any highway maintainable at public expense so long as the highway authority take all reasonable steps for preventing the oil or tar, and any liquid or matter resulting from the use of the oil or tar, from polluting the water in any waterworks. A person guilty of the offence will be liable, on summary conviction, to a fine not exceeding £2,000, and, in the case of a continuing offence, a further fine not exceeding £50 for every day on which the offence continues after conviction. On conviction on indictment, the maximum penalties are imprisonment for a term not exceeding two years or a fine or both.[249]

Public order offences also arise in relation to the contamination or interference with water used for water supply purposes. Thus, it is an offence to contaminate or interfere with water, or make it appear that water has been contaminated or interfered with where this is done with the intention of causing public alarm or anxiety, or causing injury to members of the public using or consuming water, or causing economic loss to a water undertaker or supplier because of people using less water

---

[248] s.21 Water Act 1945, as amended by Sch.25 para.7(4) Water Act 1989, now repealed.

[249] s.72 Water Industry Act 1991. For these purposes "waterworks" includes any spring, well, adit, borehole, service reservoir or tank, and any main or other pipe or conduit of a water undertaker (s.72(5)). "Domestic purposes" is a reference to the supply of water to any premises, or to drinking, washing, cooking, central heating and sanitary purposes for which water supplied to those premises may be used (s.218(1)).

or due to the remedial measures that are necessary to avoid public injury or alarm. Similarly, it is an offence for a person to threaten that he or another will contaminate or interfere with water, or claim that he or another has contaminated or interfered with water with intent to cause alarm, injury or economic loss. A person convicted of these offences will, on summary conviction, be liable to a fine not exceeding £2,000 and a maximum of six months' imprisonment or both, and on conviction on indictment to a maximum of ten years' imprisonment and a fine or both.[250]

Other miscellaneous provisions

Gas

Specific controls apply to the pollution of watercourses as a consequence of the manufacture or supply of gas. Under Public Health Law an offence is committed where a person engaged in the production of gas causes or suffers to be brought or to flow into specified waters any washing or other substance produced in making or supplying gas, or wilfully does any act connected with the making or supplying of gas by which such waters are fouled. The waters specified are any stream, reservoir, aqueduct, pond or place for water, or any communicating drain or pipe. A manufacturer found guilty of this offence will be liable to forfeit £200 for each offence, and will be liable for a penalty of £20 per day for each day on which the offence continues or water is fouled commencing from 24 hours after a notice is served by a local authority.[251]

Under the Gas Act 1972 special provision is made where gas which is stored underground pollutes any water or interferes with the flow of any water, or displaces water located in or percolating through an underground stratum, and as a result a person is prevented from effectively exercising or enjoying a protected right[252] which was exercisable at the time when the storage authorisation order came into force. In such circumstances, the public gas supplier operating the underground gas storage is obliged to cleanse the water if it is practicable and economical to do so, unless the holders of the right are a water

[250] s.38 Public Order Act 1986.

[251] s.68 Public Health Act 1868, as amended ss.38 and 46 Criminal Justice Act 1982.

[252] On protected rights, see s.26 Water Resources Act 1963.

undertaker or the National Rivers Authority, in which case the gas supplier must pay compensation for the costs of cleansing the water. Compensation is also payable for any loss or damage occasioned by the pollution.[253]

Pipelines

Pollution prevention duties are imposed upon the owner of a pipeline, so that it is the duty of the owner to make, and to ensure the efficient carrying out of, arrangements whereby, in the event of an accidental escape or the ignition of anything in the line, immediate notice of the event is given to certain bodies. The bodies to be notified are the National Rivers Authority and water undertakers who will have, in consequence of the happening of the event, to take steps to prevent or combat pollution of water or flooding. Similarly, sewerage undertakers will have to be informed where they may have to take steps to prevent injury to sewers or sewage disposal works, interference with the free flow of the contents of sewers, or prejudicial effects upon the treatment and disposal of sewer contents.[254]

Fisheries

A number of water pollution offences arise in connection with the protection of fisheries. Under freshwater fishery law, it is an offence for any person to cause or knowingly permit to flow, or put or knowingly permit to be put, into any waters containing fish, or into any tributaries of water containing fish, any liquid or solid matter to such an extent as to cause the waters to be poisonous or injurious to fish or the spawning grounds, spawn or food of fish.[255] In addition, subject to certain exceptions, it is an offence to use in or near any inland or coastal waters any poison or other noxious substance with intent to take fish.[256]

Under sea fisheries legislation, local fisheries committees are given the power to create byelaws for the purpose of prohibiting or regulating the deposit or discharge of any solid or liquid substance

---

[253] s.15 Gas Act 1965, as amended by Sch.25 para.32(3) Water Act 1989.
[254] s.37(1) Pipelines Act 1962, as amended by Sch.25 para.30 Water Act 1989.
[255] s.4(1) Salmon and Freshwater Fisheries Act 1975, and see p.426 below.
[256] s.5(1).

detrimental to sea fish or sea fishing.[257] In relation to shellfish, a power is provided for Ministerial orders to be made for the regulation of fisheries for shellfish and specifically the protection of such fisheries from certain kinds of pollution. Accordingly, provision is made for an offence where a person knowingly deposits any ballast, rubbish or other substance within the limits of regulated and certain other kinds of shellfisheries.[258]

Animal health

An offence is created under animal health legislation where any person without lawful authority or excuse, proof of which shall lie on him, throws or places, or causes or suffers to be thrown or placed, into any river, stream, canal, navigation, or other water, or into the sea within 4.8 kilometres of the shore, the carcase of an animal which has died of disease, or has been slaughtered as diseased or suspected of being diseased.[259]

Cemeteries and Harbours Clauses Acts

Provisions for particular kinds of pollution offences were made in various "Clauses Acts" passed in 1847. Hence, where a company or local authority provides a cemetery which is authorised by a special Act incorporating the Cemeteries Clauses Act 1847, this will incorporate provision for a special offence relating to fouling of water. This provides that if the cemetery company at any time cause or suffer to be brought or to flow into any stream, canal, reservoir, aqueduct, pond or watering place, any offensive matter from the cemetery, whereby the water therein is fouled, they will forfeit £50. In addition, provision is made for any person having the right to use the water fouled to sue the company for any damage sustained.[260]

Where the Harbours, Docks and Piers Clauses Act 1847 is incorporated into a local harbour Act, provision is made that, where any person throws or puts any ballast, earth, ashes, stones or other thing into

---

[257] s.5(1)(c) Sea Fisheries Regulation Act 1966, and Sea Fisheries (Byelaws) Regulations 1985, S.I. 1985 No.1785, and generally see p.457 below.

[258] ss.1 and 7(4)(c) Sea Fisheries (Shellfish) Act 1967.

[259] s.35(4) Animal Health Act 1981.

[260] ss.2 and 22 Cemeteries Clauses Act 1847, and on the position of a local authority see s.214(3) and Sch.26 para.14 Local Government Act 1972.

a harbour or dock, a criminal offence will be committed, and the person will be liable to a penalty not exceeding £25. The offence is made subject to the provision that it is not to interfere with any land preservation or reclamation works, and will not prejudice or prevent any person from adopting any measure which he would otherwise be lawfully entitled to adopt.[261]

Pesticides

The control of pesticides is provided for under Part III of the Food and Environment Protection Act 1985, which has as its objective the protection of health of human beings, creatures and plants, safeguarding the environment, and securing safe, efficient and humane methods of controlling pests.[262] These purposes are to be achieved, amongst other means, by requiring Ministerial approval[263] for pesticides in accordance with regulations, and the imposition of prohibitions upon the sale and use of specified pesticides. The general mechanism for the control of pesticides is through a system of Ministerial authorisation whereby approval is given for sale, use and other matters in relation to the handling of pesticides.[264] Detailed effect is given to the pesticides approval scheme by the Control of Pesticides Regulations 1986,[265] which impose specific prohibitions upon pesticides and substances used for pesticidal purposes relating to the advertising, sale, supply, storage and use of pesticides. In respect of the use of pesticides, no person may use a pesticide unless Ministerial approval has been given for it, by way of an experimental permit or provisional or full approval, and the conditions relating to its use are complied with. Infringement of these provisions is an offence, and a person found guilty of this offence is liable, on

---

[261] s.73 Harbours Docks and Piers Clauses Act 1847. The amount of the penalty was substituted by s.31(5), (6) and (9) Criminal Law Act 1977.

[262] For these purposes a "pest" is defined as any organism harmful to plants or to wood or other plant products, any undesired plant and any harmful creature. A "creature" means any living organism other than a human being or a plant. A "pesticide" is any substance, preparation or organism prepared or used for destroying a pest (ss.16(15) and 24(1) Food and Environment Protection Act 1985).

[263] The Ministers concerned are the Minister of Agriculture, Fisheries and Food in England and the Secretary of State for Wales.

[264] s.16(1) and (2) Food and Environment Protection Act 1985.

[265] S.I. 1986 No.1510.

summary conviction, to a fine not exceeding £2,000, or on conviction on indictment to a fine.[266]

A particular problem existed until recently in relation to the use of anti-fouling paints, containing the substance tributyltin, used to protect boats and to prevent the accumulation of algal growth on aquaculture equipment. Tributyltin was found to have seriously toxic effects upon shellfish and other forms of aquatic life. In addition to controls under Part II of the Food and Environment Protection Act 1985, it was thought necessary to exercise powers under the Control of Pollution Act 1974 to regulate the importation, use and supply of any substance to prevent damage to persons, animals or plants, or pollution of air, water or land.[267] Accordingly, the Control of Pollution (Anti-fouling Paints and Treatments) Regulations 1987[268] were made, making it unlawful to supply for retail sale, or by way of retail sale, any anti-fouling paint, or anti-fouling treatment, containing a tri-organotin compound, subject to the defence that the person charged can show that he took all reasonable steps, and exercised all due diligence, to avoid committing the offence. The punishment for contravention of the Regulations is a fine not exceeding £2,000 on summary conviction, or a fine of unlimited amount on indictment.

WATER QUALITY UNDER EUROPEAN COMMUNITY LEGISLATION

The constitution and legislation of the European Community

The United Kingdom's membership of the European Economic Community has had a dramatic effect upon national law in general and environmental law in particular. The final sections of this Chapter seek to outline the status of Community provisions relating to water quality, and

---

[266] Under ss.16(12) and 21(3) and (4) Food and Environment Protection Act 1985.

[267] s.100 Control of Pollution Act 1974, repealed, now see s.140 Environmental Protection Act 1990. Another instance of this power being exercised in relation to the protection of the aquatic environment is the Control of Pollution (Anglers' Lead Weights) Regulations 1986, S.I. 1986 No.1992.

[268] S.I. 1987 No.783, replacing S.I. 1987 No.783 and S.I. 1986 No.2300.

to indicate some of the general features of water quality Directives and their implications for the law of England and Wales.

The objectives of the European Economic Community, as originally specified in the Treaty of Rome of 1957, were stated to be the establishment of a common market and a progressive approximation of the economic policies of the Member states to promote a harmonious development of economic activities, a continuous and balanced expansion, an increase in stability, an accelerated raising of the standard of living, and closer relations between the states belonging to the Community.[269] However, it later became apparent that harmonious expansion and development of economic activities could not be imagined in the absence of an effective campaign to combat pollution and nuisances, and improvement in the quality of life and the protection of the environment.[270] Accordingly, a series of Action Programmes were embarked upon with the aim of bringing about improvements in the state of the environment of the Community involving, amongst other things, the prevention, reduction and, as far as possible, the elimination of pollution and nuisances.

Initially, the Action Programmes on the environment were given legal effect through the enactment of Community legislation based upon the original provisions of the 1957 Treaty. The Treaty provided for measures directly affecting the establishment or functioning of the common market, and for legal action where necessary to attain, in the course of operation of the common market, an objective of the Community for which the Treaty had not provided the necessary powers.[271] Much of the early environmental legislation of the Community is based upon one or other, or both, of these justifications. However, explicit provision for Community environmental legislation was later provided for through the amendment of the 1957 Treaty by the enactment of the Single European Act.[272] The Single European Act made explicit provision for environmental measures based upon the objectives of preserving, protecting and improving the quality of the environment,

---

[269] Cmnd.7480.

[270] Declaration of the Council of Ministers, of 22 November 1973, on the Programme of Action of the European Communities on the Environment.

[271] Arts.100 and 235.

[272] Bull. EC Supp 2/86. The Single European Act entered into force on 1 July 1987.

contributing towards the protection of human health, and ensuring a prudent and rational utilisation of natural resources. Community environmental action taken in furtherance of these objectives is now to be based upon the principles that preventative action should be taken wherever possible, that environmental damage should as a priority be rectified at source, and that the polluter should pay.[273]

The original Treaty provisions, and the extension of powers brought about under the Single European Act, enable the Community to enact legislation covering a wide range of environmental matters, including measures for the protection of the aquatic environment. The Community legislation which has been enacted by the Council of Ministers of the member states of the Community in relation to water quality has taken the form of Directives. Directives are stated to be binding as to the result to be achieved, but are to leave to the national authorities of the Member states the choice of form and methods of legislation.[274] As a consequence of this, Directives approved by the Council oblige each member state to enact national legislation giving effect to the objectives of the Directive within its area and within the time period stipulated for implementation by the Directive.

The measures of domestic law which are introduced within a member state must be of a binding legal character, rather than a mere administrative direction.[275] In some circumstances it may be possible for a Directive to be legally actionable within a member state, despite the failure of the government of that state to enact implementing legislation. This possibility arises under the principle of "direct effect" whereby a Directive is capable of giving rise to rights and duties within a member state, despite the absence of implementing legislation, if it is sufficiently clear and unambiguous, unconditional and not dependent upon further action being taken either by the Community or the member state.[276] It is

---

[273] Art.130R 1957 Treaty of Rome 1957, as amended by the Single European Act 1986.

[274] Art.189.

[275] *Re the EEC Directive Concerning the Quality of Bathing Water: EC Commission v. Kingdom of the Netherlands*, Case 96/81 [1982] E.C.R. 1791.

[276] *Van Duyn*, 41/74 [1974] E.C.R. 1337; and *Molkerei–Zentrale Westfalen/Lippe GmbH v. Hauptzollamt*, 28/67 [1968] E.C.R. 143; *Marshall v. Southampton Area Health Authority*, [1986] 2 W.L.R. 780; *Foster v. British Gas PLC*, (1990) *The Times* 13 July 1990 E.C.J.

presently unclear, however, to what extent water quality Directives will meet the criteria for direct effect.

Amongst the powers and duties of the executive body of the European Community, the European Commission, is that of the enforcement of Community legislation.[277] Where a member state fails to fulfil an obligation under a Community Directive, the Commission is empowered to institute proceedings in the European Court of Justice. The procedure leading to litigation involves the Commission reminding the member state in default of its duties under Community law and inviting it to take measures necessary to conform to those duties. If neither an acceptable action or explanation is forthcoming from the member state, the Commission delivers a reasoned opinion on the matter specifying a time limit for compliance. Finally, if the time limit for compliance is not met, the Commission may bring the matter before the Court of Justice.[278] If the Court of Justice finds that the member state has failed to fulfil its obligations under Community law, the state is then required to take the necessary steps to comply with the judgment of the Court.[279] Final compliance, however, rests with the defaulting state in that the Treaty does not provide for any coercive means by which adherence to the obligations imposed upon a member state may be secured.

In addition to the European Court considering matters brought before it at the instigation of the Commission or a member state, the Court has the capacity to give preliminary rulings on matters of Community law at the request of national courts in the Member States. Where the invocation or interpretation of Community law is contested in a national court of a member state, the national court *may*, or when there is no judicial remedy against its decision it *must*, request a ruling from the Community Court. Where this is done, the national court is obliged to suspend its proceedings in order for the issue of Community law to be resolved.[280] The competence of the Community Court in relation to preliminary rulings is such that it is able to give declarations upon the

277 Art.155 Treaty of Rome.

278 Art.169.

279 Art.171.

280 Art.177.

validity of statutory enactments passed by the parliaments of member states according to their conformity with Community law.[281]

The water quality directives

The following is a chronological list of all the Community Directives that have matters of water quality as their principal concern:[282]
75/440/EEC: Council Directive of 16 June 1975 concerning the quality required of surface water intended for the abstraction of drinking water in the Member States.[283]
76/160/EEC: Council Directive of 8 December 1975 concerning the quality of bathing water.[284]
76/464/EEC: Council Directive of 4 May 1976 on pollution caused by certain dangerous substances discharged into the aquatic environment of the Community.[285]
79/869/EEC: Council Directive of 9 October 1979 concerning the methods of measurement and frequencies of sampling and analysis of surface water intended for the abstraction of drinking water in the Member States.[286]
79/923/EEC: Council Directive on the quality required of shellfish waters.[287]

---

[281] See *Factortame Ltd. v. Secretary of State (No.2)*, [1991] All E.R. 70.
[282] Note: this list is based upon the information contained in the *Official Journal of the European Community Directory of Community Legislation in Force* (16th Ed – as at 1 December 1990) and subsequent enactments. It does not include Directives which relate more directly to other areas such as those concerning detergents (73/404/EEC), waste from the titanium dioxide industry (78/176/EEC), the use of sewage sludge in agriculture (86/278/EEC) and Directives with a general environmental objective such as the freshwater fish Directive (78/659/EEC). Note also: this list does not include various Council decisions and resolutions in relation to water covering matters such as the exchange of information on water quality (77/795/EEC), action programmes on sea pollution by hydrocarbons (79/869/EEC), and co-operation between Member States in the sphere of water (OJ C 272, 12 October 1984 p.2).
[283] OJ L 194, 25 July 1975 p.26.
[284] OJ L 031, 5 February 1976 p.1.
[285] OJ L 129, 18 May 1976 p.23.
[286] OJ L 271, 29 October 1979 p.44.
[287] OJ L 281, 10 November 1979 p.16.

80/68/EEC: Council Directive of 17 December 1979 on the protection of groundwater against pollution caused by certain dangerous substances.[288]
80/778/EEC: Council Directive of 15 July 1980 relating to the quality of water intended for human consumption.[289]
82/176/EEC: Council Directive of 22 March 1982 on limit values and quality objectives for mercury discharges by the chlor–alkali electrolysis industry.[290]
83/513/EEC: Council Directive of 26 September 1983 on limit values and quality objectives for cadmium discharges.[291]
84/491/EEC: Council Directive of 9 October 1984 on limit values and quality objectives for discharges of hexachlorocyclohexane.[292]
86/280/EEC: Council Directive of 12 June 1986 on limit values and quality objectives for discharges of certain dangerous substances included in List I of the Annex to Directive 76/464/EEC.[293]
91/271/EEC: Council Directive of 21 May 1991 concerning urban waste water treatment.[294]
Council Directive of 14 June 1991 concerning the protection of fresh, coastal and marine waters against pollution caused by nitrates from diffuse sources.[295]

Whilst each of these Directives has its own distinctive features, and particular implications for the domestic law of the Member States, some generalisations can be drawn in relation to the general legal structure of water Directives and the pollution control strategy which underlies them. In general terms, the Directives may be grouped under three headings. First, there are those Directives which are concerned with the contamination of water by particular pollutants, such as the Dangerous Substances Directive (76/464/EEC) and various subsidiary Directives enacted under it to tackle pollution caused by specified kinds

[288] OJ L 020, 26 January 1980 p.43.
[289] OJ L 229, 30 August 1980 p.11.
[290] OJ L 081, 27 March 1982 p.29.
[291] OJ L 291, 24 October 1983 p.1.
[292] OJ L 274, 17 October 1984 p.11.
[293] OJ L 181, 4 July 1986 p.16.
[294] OJ L 135, 30 May 1991 p.40.
[295] This Directive has not yet been published in its final form but it is based upon a proposal by the Commission of 5 January 1989, COM(88) 708 final, OJ C 54, 3 March 1989 p.4.

of harmful substance. Second, are those Directives which are concerned with the quality of water required for particular uses, such as drinking water (75/440/EEC) or bathing water (76/160/EEC). Third, are those Directives which seek to regulate activities which constitute a source of water pollution, and this approach is best illustrated in the recent Directives concerning urban waste water treatment (91/271/EEC) and water pollution by nitrates from diffuse sources.

Directives concerned with particular pollutants

Amongst the group of Directives which are concerned with the contamination of water due to specific pollutants, the key provision is the Dangerous Substances Directive (76/464/EEC) which constitutes a "framework directive" establishing the general legal mechanism for the reduction and elimination of water pollution caused by specified dangerous substances. Hence, the Directive envisages the enactment of subsequent implementing directives, or "daughter directives", which will provide for the specific control of individual substances. The Directive applies to the pollution[296] of inland surface waters, territorial waters, internal coastal waters[297] and ground waters.[298]

---

[296] "Pollution" means the discharge by man, directly or indirectly, of substances or energy into the aquatic environment, the results of which are such as to cause hazards to human health, harm to living resources and to aquatic ecosystems, damage to amenities or interference with other legitimate uses of water. "Discharge" means the introduction into inland surface waters, territorial waters, inland coastal waters or ground water of any substance listed in List I or List II of the Annex to the Directive, with the exception of discharges of dredgings, operational discharges from ships in territorial waters, and dumping from ships in territorial waters (Art.1 Dangerous Substances Directive 76/464/EEC).

[297] "Inland surface water" means all static or flowing fresh water situated in the territory of one or more Member States. "Internal coastal waters" means waters on the landward side of the base line from which the breadth of territorial waters is measured, extending, in the case of watercourses, up to the fresh–water limit. "Fresh–water limit" means the place in the watercourse where, at low tide and in a period of low fresh–water flow, there is an appreciable increase in salinity due to the presence of sea water (Art.1 Dangerous Substances Directive 76/464/EEC).

[298] In relation to groundwater, however, the Dangerous Substances Directive has ceased to apply on the implementation of a separate Directive on groundwater (Art.4(4) Dangerous Substances Directive), see Groundwater Directive (80/68/EEC).

In relation to the waters to which the Dangerous Substances Directive applies, a distinction is drawn between the most harmful substances, in terms of their toxicity, persistence and bioaccumulation, and less harmful substances which may still have a deleterious effect upon the aquatic environment in certain circumstances. The most harmful substances feature on List I of the Annex to the Directive, known as the "black list", and the less harmful substances appear on List II, the "grey list". As an initial measure, however, black list substances are regarded as featuring in the grey list until limit values or quality objectives for these substances have been established.

Ultimately, the objective of the Directive is to eliminate pollution by List I substances and to reduce pollution by List II substances. This is to be done by means of a system of prior authorisation of discharges of substances in both Lists by the competent authority in the member state concerned. For the List I substances, authorisations must contain emission standards not exceeding limit values laid down by the European Council on the basis of the "best technical means available", or alternatively, the discharge must be prohibited where the discharger is unable to comply with the established emission standard. In respect of the List II substances, the Directive obliges member states to establish programmes of quality objectives in order to reduce pollution from these substances.[299]

The strategy of controlling water pollution by the imposition of emission standards has been the source of much disagreement between member states as to the relative appropriateness of emission standards as opposed to quality standards for receiving waters. On the one hand it has been argued that excessive concern with the imposition of emission standards may overlook and fail to utilise the assimilative capacity of ambient waters to disperse and neutralise pollutants. Whilst on the other hand it has been maintained that quality objectives place insufficient emphasis upon the need to prevent pollution at source through regulation of identifiable points of origin. Generally, the United Kingdom has expressed a preference for the quality objective approach whilst the other member states have preferred emission standards.

---

[299] Arts.2, 5, 6 and 7 Dangerous Substances Directive (76/464/EEC).

The differences in pollution control strategy have resulted in the compromise solution of a "parallel approach" found in the Dangerous Substances Directive, whereby, though priority is given to the application of emission standards, the option remains for a member state to adopt a quality objective approach if it sees fit to do so. Thus, member states can comply with ambient water quality objectives established by the European Council if it can be shown that these are being met and continuously maintained throughout the area affected by a discharge.[300] This is the approach preferred by the United Kingdom whereas the rest of Europe favours the emission standard approach.

Because the Dangerous Substances Directive is a framework directive, it is dependent upon subsequent measures, specifying limit values and quality objectives for particular substances, in order to realise its ultimate objectives. Accordingly, subsidiary Directives have been adopted determining these parameters for mercury (82/176/EEC), cadmium (83/513/EEC) and hexachlorocyclohexane (84/491/EEC). Despite these measures, progress in the specification of limit values and quality objectives for List I substances has been slow due to the requirement of unanimity between member states before the adoption of subsidiary directives can be brought about. To some extent these delays have been tackled by means of a special Directive on limit values and quality objectives (86/280/EEC) which seeks to codify general provisions relating to adoption and methods of measurement and procedures for monitoring compliance with quality objectives allowing the future addition of further List II substances to the Annex of the Dangerous Substances Directive. Under the 1986 Directive and later amendments to it (88/347/EEC and 90/415/EEC), a number of new substances have been added to List II of the Annex of the Dangerous Substances Directive.

Directives concerned with water for particular uses

Whilst the Dangerous Substances Directive places emphasis upon particular kinds of pollutant, a number of other Directives are primarily concerned with the quality of water which is required for particular kinds

---

[300] Art.6(3).

of water use. Examples of this kind of Directive are the Drinking Water Directive (75/440/EEC), the Bathing Water Directive (76/160/EEC), the Shellfish Waters Directive (79/923/EEC) and the Directive on Water for Freshwater Fish (78/659/EEC).[301] Although each of these differ in their objectives and the detailed requirements which they impose, a number of general characteristics may be discerned in the water use Directives.

First, the water use Directives contain Annexes setting out parameters relating to G, or *Guide*, values and I, or *Imperative* values. Member states are to establish parameters for the waters concerned which are to be no less stringent than the mandatory I values, and must endeavour to respect the stricter G values. Second, member states are required to designate or identify the waters within their area to which the directives apply, though in some instances the rather unspecific criteria which are to be used for this purpose leave member states with a considerable degree of discretion. Third, all the directives incorporate a non–degradation principle whereby implementation of the Directives may not directly or indirectly lead to deterioration of the waters at issue. Fourth, the Directives allow for derogation from their requirements by member states in exceptional circumstances. Fifth, the competent authorities in the member states are made responsible for sampling, analysis and inspection in accordance with the provisions of each Directive. Sixth, a simplified procedure is provided for to allow the Directives to be adapted in the light of technical progress. Seventh, the Directives make provision for reporting back to the European Commission on the operation of each Directive within the different member states and for communication to the Commission as to the provisions of national law which have been adopted in the sphere of each directive.

Directives concerned with particular polluting activities

Amongst the most recent Directives on water quality adopted by the European Council, the emphasis has shifted from specific pollutants and water uses towards a concern to regulate water polluting activities. This new focus of attention is evident in the Commission's Fourth Action

---

[301] OJ 1978 L 291 p.1.

Programme on the Environment,[302] which envisages combating fresh water and marine pollution from specific and diffused sources and encouraging the development of improved waste management in relation to waste water. The two latest Directives, concerning urban waste water treatment (91/271/EEC) and pollution caused by nitrates from diffuse sources, closely follow this new strategic emphasis.

The Urban Waste Water Treatment Directive

The urban waste water Directive recognises the need to prevent the environment from being adversely affected by the disposal of insufficiently treated urban waste water and recognises the need for secondary treatment of such water along with the need for similar treatment for industrial discharges of biodegradable industrial waste water which does not enter urban waste water treatment plants before being discharged to receiving waters. Accordingly, the Directive is primarily concerned with the collection, treatment and discharge of urban waste water, and the treatment and discharge of waste water from specified industrial sectors, in order to protect the environment from the adverse effects of these kinds of effluent.[303]

The central obligation imposed under the Directive is that all member states are to ensure that all urban areas, or agglomerations, are provided with collecting systems for urban waste water,[304] at the latest by the end of the year 2000 for those with a population equivalent[305] of more

---

302 Covering the period 1987 to 1992 (OJ C 328, 7 December 1987 p.1).

303 Art.1 Urban Waste Water Treatment Directive (91/271/EEC).

304 "Urban waste water" means domestic water or the mixture of domestic waste water with industrial waste water and/or run–off rain water. "Domestic waste water" means water from residential settlements and services which originates predominantly from the human metabolism and from household activities. "Industrial waste water" means any waste water which is discharged from premises used for carrying on any trade or industry, other than domestic waste water and run–off water. "Agglomeration" means an area where the population and/or economic activities are sufficiently concentrated for urban waste water to be collected and conducted to an urban waste water treatment plant or to a final discharge point. "Collecting system" means a system of conduits which collects and conducts urban waste water (Art.2 Urban Waste Water Directive (91/271/EEC)).

305 "1 p.e. (population equivalent)" means the organic biodegradable load having a five–day biochemical oxygen demand (BOD5) of 60g of oxygen per day (Art.2 Urban Waste Water Directive (91/271/EEC)).

than 15,000 and the end of 2005 for those with a population between 2,000 and 15,000. For urban waste water discharging into receiving waters which are considered to be "sensitive areas", member states are to ensure that collection systems are provided by the end of 1998 for agglomerations of more than 10,000. These general obligations arise unless the establishment of a general collecting system is not justified either because it would produce no environmental benefit or because it would involve excessive cost. In these cases individual, or other appropriate systems of collection which achieve the same level of collection, are to be used.[306] In addition to the obligation to provide urban waste collecting systems, member states are to ensure that water entering these systems is subject to secondary or equivalent treatment by the year 2000 for discharges from areas of a population equivalent of more that 15,000, by 2005 for areas of population between 10,000 and 15,000, and by 2005 for discharges to freshwater and estuaries for areas of population between 2,000 and 10,000.[307]

Exceptions to the obligations imposed by the Directive are provided for where, in exceptional cases, due to *technical problems* for geographically defined population groups, member states may submit a request to the Commission for a longer period for compliance with the requirement of ensuring that urban waste water entering collection systems is subjected to secondary treatment. Where this is done, however, the request must set out the technical difficulties experienced and propose an action programme with an appropriate timetable for its implementation.[308]

Emphasis is also placed upon the operational aspects of urban waste water treatment through an obligation that treatment plants are to be built to comply with appropriate Articles of the Directive and are to be designed, constructed, operated and maintained to ensure sufficient performance under all normal local climatic conditions taking into account seasonal variations in the effluent load. Before the end of 1993

---

306 Art.3.

307 Art.4. "Secondary treatment" means treatment of urban waste water by a process generally involving biological treatment with a secondary settlement or other process in which the requirements established in Table 1 of Annex 1 to the Directive are respected (Art.2).

308 Art.8.

the discharge of industrial waste water into collecting systems is subject to prior regulations and/or specific authorisations by the competent authority. By the end of 2000, biodegradable industrial waste water from certain industrial sectors which does not enter urban waste water plants before discharge to receiving water is to be subject to conditions in regulations or prior authorisation by the competent authority in relation to discharges from plants representing a population equivalent of 4,000 or more. Treated waste water is to be reused wherever possible, and disposal routes are to minimize the adverse effects upon the environment. This obligation is specifically stated to apply in relation to sludge arising from waste treatment and, whilst the disposal of sludge is to be subject to regulations or authorisation, it is reaffirmed that by the end of 1998 the disposal of sludge to surface waters by dumping from ships, or discharge from pipelines, is to be phased out.[309]

The Directive on Pollution by Nitrates from Diffuse Sources

The encouragement of agricultural practices which are environmentally beneficial and, in particular, the reduction at source of fresh water and marine pollution from diffused sources including products used in agriculture, also features within the Community's Fourth Action Programme on the environment. This policy has been given particular effect by the Directive on the protection of fresh, coastal and marine waters against pollution caused by nitrates from diffuse sources.[310]

Water pollution caused by nitrates, originating from farming practices such as the excessive application of nitrogen fertiliser and the spreading of animal manure, has been a continuing problem in several areas of the Community. Despite a requirement in the Drinking Water Directive (80/778/EEC) that drinking water should not exceed the limit of 50 mg/l, this parameter has been exceeded in certain areas and there is the prospect of several member states being subject to legal proceedings brought by the European Commission.[311]

---

309 Arts.10, 11 and 13.

310 Set out in proposal COM(88) 708 final, and approved by the Council of Ministers of 14 June 1991.

311 OJ 1989 C324/6.

The new Nitrates Directive tackles this form of water pollution by imposing a requirement upon member states to designate all zones vulnerable to water pollution from nitrate compounds according to specified criteria. The criteria make explicit reference to areas in which surface waters intended for the abstraction of drinking water contain more than the 50 mg/l concentration of nitrate.[312] After a further period, member states are to take the necessary measures to ensure that, for each farm or livestock unit in a vulnerable area, the amount of livestock manure applied to the soil is not to exceed the amount produced by specified numbers of animals. In effect, therefore, the animal holding capacity of farms under the Directive will be dictated by their capacity effectively to dispose of the manure produced without producing water contamination. Further rules will cover permissible methods of disposal of manure to land, matters such as the minimum distance to be left between watercourses and the area to which manure is applied and the suitability of storage facilities for manure. Likewise, in relation to nitrogen fertilisers, rules will establish maximum land application rates based on the uptake of nitrogen by crops and the amount of nitrogen already present in the soil concerned. Records are to be kept concerning the application of nitrogen in vulnerable zones, and member states are to consider incorporating certain matters concerning the application of fertilisers and manure in guidelines on good agricultural practice.[313] Member states are to monitor their waters in respect of nitrate content, and publish periodic reports on the basis of the monitoring programmes.[314]

Community water law and national legislation

Community water Directives are principally addressed to member states, and consequently impose a primary obligation on national governments to ensure that obligations under each Directive are fully implemented in domestic law by the time required by the Directive. However, in certain respects, Directives are explicit in imposing water quality monitoring, discharge authorising and other duties upon the

---

[312] Art.3 Nitrates Directive.

[313] Art.4.

[314] Arts.5 and 10.

competent authorities within each member state. The competent authority in relation to the implementation of water quality Directives in England and Wales is the National Rivers Authority and, accordingly, it is charged with the duty of ensuring that water quality in England and Wales meets Community requirements in so far as its legal powers enable it to do so.

In general terms, the duty of the Authority is to ensure that Community water quality objectives are realised through the system of water classification, the specification of water quality objectives for particular waters and the legal duty to achieve and maintain those objectives at all times, which are imposed upon the Authority under the Water Resources Act 1991.[315] It is envisaged that the water quality objectives which are set for particular waters will reflect the standards required by any Community Directives within which they fall, and the Secretary of State will be obliged to set objectives which serve to implement Directives by this mechanism. In addition, the duty of the Authority to exercise any of the powers conferred upon it under the 1991 Act to ensure that water quality objectives are achieved at all times means that powers such as those relating to bringing proceedings for pollution offences and the granting of discharge consents are to be used purposively with the object of meeting Community obligations.

In relation to particular Community Directives, the existing powers of the Authority may not be adequate to ensure full implementation and additional powers may be needed. For example, full implementation of the Directive on pollution by nitrates from diffuse sources may require powers to regulate land use which are not presently provided for.[316] Although, in most instances, it may be possible to secure complete implementation of Directives by the use of existing powers allowing the enactment of delegated legislation, provision is made in the Water Resources Act 1991 for modifications of the provisions of the Act concerned with the control of pollution to be brought about by

[315] ss.82 to 84 Water Resources Act 1991. For a discussion of these provisions, see p.292 above.

[316] See the discussion of nitrate sensitive areas under s.94 Water Resources Act 1991 and the Nitrate Sensitive Areas (Designation) Order 1990, S.I. 1990 No.1013, as amended by S.I. 1990 No.1187, at p.330 above.

Ministerial regulations where this is necessary in order for the United Kingdom to give effect to Community obligations.[317]

[317] s.116 Water Resources Act 1991, and see also, s.2(2) and (4) European Communities Act 1972.

Chapter 12

FLOOD DEFENCE AND LAND DRAINAGE

Introduction

Traditionally, the main purposes of flood defence and land drainage have been the protection of land in rural and urban areas from flooding and inundation by fresh or sea water, the improvement of agricultural land and the conservation of water in watercourses for riparian owners and other users. Alongside these may be added the recent concern that land drainage activities should be undertaken with proper concern for the state of flora and fauna which are dependent on the aquatic environment provided by watercourses. Accordingly, land drainage operations will be subject to the general environmental and recreational duties provided for under the Water Resources Act 1991, and corresponding duties provided for under the Land Drainage Act 1991.[1]

In practice, the objectives of flood defence and land drainage are achieved by periodic cleansing, scouring and improvement operations upon the channels of watercourses, including the removal of obstructions, the maintenance and erection of structures for controlling the flow of water, the execution of land drainage and flood relief schemes and the provision of flood warning systems. Drainage work is carried out under the overall supervision of the Minister of Agriculture, Fisheries and Food,[2] by the "flood defence authorities", that is, the

---

[1] See s.17 Water Resources Act 1991, discussed at p.211 above, and s.12 Land Drainage Act 1991 discussed at p.389 below.

[2] Although Ministerial responsibility for flood defence rests primarily with the Minister of Agriculture, Fisheries and Food and the Secretary of State for Wales in relation to Wales, in some instances the Minister is empowered to act jointly with the Secretary of State. Hence, under the Land Drainage Act 1991, "the Minister" means the Minister of Agriculture, Fisheries and Food, and "the Ministers" means the Minister and the Secretary of State, and anything which falls to be done by the Ministers means those Ministers acting jointly. "The relevant Minister" (a) in relation to internal drainage districts which are neither wholly nor partly in Wales or to the boards for such districts, means the Minister; (b) in relation to internal drainage districts which are partly in Wales or to the boards for such districts, means the Ministers; and (c) in relation to internal drainage districts which are wholly in

National Rivers Authority which conducts its flood defence function through regional and local flood defence committees, and internal drainage boards. Additionally, land drainage and flood defence work may be undertaken by local authorities exercising a power to maintain the flow of watercourses in their area and carry out drainage works,[3] or by private landowners such as farmers or riparian owners who possess various common law rights in respect of drainage and flood prevention.[4] Coast protection works, usually taking the form of sea walls or flood embankments, are executed either by the National Rivers Authority or by maritime local authorities under the Coast Protection Act 1949.[5]

As has been noted previously,[6] the public duty to protect land from inroads by the sea or other inundation by water, has been exercised through a series of enactments providing for different administrative arrangements over the years. Bills of Sewers of 1427 and 1531 gave rise to Commissioners with responsibility for flood defence, and counterparts of these officials were provided for under subsequent legislation. The modern law, however, can be identified in the Land Drainage Act of 1930 and the subsequent consolidating Act of 1976 which repealed most of the previous legislation.[7] The Land Drainage Act of 1976 was extensively amended by provisions under the Water Act 1989.[8] In particular, the 1989 Act introduced the systematic terminological change of substituting the expression "flood defence" in most instances where "land drainage" had previously been employed, though "flood defence" was stated to mean the drainage of land within the meaning of the 1976

Wales or the boards for such districts, means the Secretary of State (s.72(1) Land Drainage Act 1991).

[3] See p.391 below.

[4] See Ch.3 above.

[5] See p.59 above on the Coast Protection Act 1949.

[6] See p.59 above.

[7] Although regulations and orders made under the repealed legislation remained in force unless expressly repealed (s.117(1) and Sch.6 paras.6 and 9 Land Drainage Act 1976).

[8] In particular, Part III Chapter III (ss. 136 to 140) and Schedule 15 Water Act 1989. Subordinate legislation made under the Land Drainage Act 1976 continued to have effect under the Water Act 1989 unless expressly revoked (Sch.26 para.36(2) Water Act 1989).

Act and the provision of flood warning systems.[9] The water consolidation legislation of 1991 replaced the 1976 Act, as amended, with the Land Drainage Act 1991, and this is now the principal enactment,[10] though most of the provisions concerning the flood defence functions of the National Rivers Authority are included in the Water Resources Act 1991.[11]

FLOOD DEFENCE AND THE NATIONAL RIVERS AUTHORITY

The flood defence and land drainage functions

Flood defence and land drainage are stated to be functions of the National Rivers Authority by virtue of Part IV of the Water Resources Act 1991, the Land Drainage Act 1991 and functions transferred to the Authority by the Water Act 1989 including land drainage functions under local statutory provisions and subordinate legislation.[12] The flood defence function of the Authority is stated to extend to the territorial sea adjacent to England and Wales so far as the area of any regional flood defence committee of the Authority includes any area of the territorial sea or provision is made for the exercise of any power in relation to the territorial sea.[13] Where any function of the Authority falls to be carried out at a place beyond the seaward boundaries of a regional flood defence committee, that place is assumed to be within the area of the committee

---

[9] s.136(9) Water Act 1989, and s.221(1) Water Resources Act 1991.

[10] Although subordinate legislation made under Acts repealed by the water consolidation legislation is to continue to have effect under the corresponding provisions of the consolidation Acts (Sch.2 para.1 Water Consolidation (Consequential Provisions) Act 1991).

[11] In particular, Part IV Water Resources Act 1991.

[12] s.2(1)(c) Water Resources Act 1991, and see Sch.15 para.1(3) Water Act 1989. In relation to the flood defence functions of the Authority, "drainage" includes defences against water, including sea water, irrigation other than spray irrigation and warping (the fertilisation of land by inundation by water). "Flood defence" means the drainage of land and the provision of flood warning systems (s.113(1) Water Resources Act 1991).

[13] s.2(5). Provision for the exercise of flood defence functions in relation to the territorial sea is made under s.165(2) and (3).

whose area is adjacent to the area of sea where the place is situated.[14] For the purpose of carrying out the flood defence function, the Authority is from time to time to carry our surveys of the areas in relation to which this function is carried out, and in the exercise of its powers is to have due regard to the interests of fisheries including sea fisheries.[15]

Flood defence committees

The general function of the National Rivers Authority in relation to flood defence is subject to an obligation placed upon it to arrange for flood defence functions to be carried out by regional flood defence committees. Regional flood defence committees may, in turn, delegate duties to local flood defence committees for districts within their region, or in some instances to local authorities, or other bodies with land drainage interests such as the conservators or commissioners with special responsibility for a particular watercourse.

The overall duty upon the Authority to exercise a general supervision over all matters relating to flood defence is subject to the obligation of the Authority to carry out this function, under both the Water Resources Act 1991 and the Land Drainage Act 1991, through committees. Specifically, in relation to the area of each regional flood defence committee, the flood defence functions of the Authority are to be carried out by the regional flood defence committee for that area, and in cases involving the areas of more than one regional flood defence committee by a committee, or jointly by committees, determined in accordance with arrangements made by the Authority. The Authority may give a regional flood defence committee directions of a general or specific character as to the carrying out of its flood defence functions, other than internal drainage functions[16] if the carrying out of that function

---

[14] s.9(2).

[15] s.105(1).

[16] "Internal drainage functions" means the functions of the Authority under ss.108, 139 and 140 of the Water Resources Act 1991, and ss.2 to 9 (concerned with transfer to and supervision by the Authority of internal drainage boards), 38, 39 and 47 (concerned with differential drainage rates and exemptions from such rates), and 57 and 58(1) (concerned with provisions with respect to contributions by the Authority to the expenses of internal drainage boards and the expenses of the Authority as such a board), Land Drainage Act 1991 (s.106(7) Water Resources Act 1991).

is likely materially to affect the Authority's management of water for purposes other than flood defence. However, the Authority is not to make arrangements for the carrying out by any other body or committee of any of its functions with respect to the issuing of levies or the making of drainage charges,[17] and the Authority may not authorise any other body or committee to borrow money for purposes connected with the Authority's flood defence function.[18]

Regional flood defence committees

As a consequence of terminological amendments brought about by the Water Act 1989, the functions previously carried out by regional land drainage committees are to be carried out by regional flood defence committees, and provision is made under the Water Resources Act 1991 for the continuance of these committees for the purposes of carrying out functions under that Act.[19] Accordingly, each area which formerly had a regional land drainage committee will have a regional flood defence committee subject to provisions which are made for the alteration of boundaries and the amalgamation of committees.[20] The Authority is to maintain a principal office for the area of each regional flood defence committee.[21]

A regional flood defence committee is to consist of a chairman and a number of other members appointed by the relevant Minister,[22] two members appointed by the Authority and a number of members appointed by or on behalf of the constituent councils of the region. No

---

17 Levies are provided for under the Local Government Finance Act 1988, and the making of charges is provided for under Chapter II of Part VI Water Resources Act 1991.

18 s.106 Water Resources Act 1991.

19 s.137(1) Water Act 1989, and s.9 Water Resources Act 1991.

20 s.137(2) and Schedule 16 Water Act 1989. Now see Sch.3 to Water Resources Act 1991 on the alteration of boundaries and the amalgamation of areas of regional flood defence committees.

21 s.9(3) Water Resources Act 1991.

22 The "relevant Minister" for these purposes is, in relation to the regional flood defence committee for an area the whole or the greater part of which is in Wales, the Secretary of State; and in relation to any other regional flood defence committee, the Minister of Agriculture, Fisheries and Food (s.10(6) Water Resources Act 1991).

member of a regional flood defence committee is to be a member of the Authority. Subject to provisions for the amalgamation of regional flood defence committees, the total number of members of a committee and the members appointed on behalf of constituent councils is to be the same as provided for under previous legislation.[23] In relation to the appointment of a person as a chairman or member of a committee by the Minister, or as a member appointed on behalf of the constituent councils, the Minister or the council making the appointment is to have regard to the desirability of appointing a person who has experience of, and has shown capacity in, some matter relevant to the functions of the committee.[24]

The Authority may from time to time make a determination varying the number of members of a regional flood defence committee, and it is to submit any determination of this kind to the relevant Minister. However, the total number of members of a regional flood defence committee may not be less than eleven and may not consist of more than seventeen members unless a Ministerial order to that effect has been made.[25] Detailed matters relating to the membership and procedure of regional flood defence committees are provided for under Schedule 4 to the Water Resources Act 1991.[26]

Local flood defence schemes and committees

The arrangements for local land drainage schemes, as provided for under the Land Drainage Act 1976,[27] continued in force under the amendments introduced under the Water Act 1989, subject to their being retitled "local flood defence schemes" administered by a "local flood defence committee".[28] Similarly, under the Water Resources Act 1991, it

---

[23] s.10(1) and (2) Water Resources Act 1991, and see s.138(1) Water Act 1989.

[24] s.10(4) Water Resources Act 1991.

[25] s.11.

[26] Effective under s.14.

[27] s.4 Land Drainage Act 1976.

[28] Similarly, existing local land drainage schemes continued to have effect under the Water Act 1989 as if they are local flood defence schemes, and local land drainage districts and local land drainage committees continued to be treated as if they are local flood defence districts and local flood defence committees, and the membership of local flood defence committees were to consist of the members of the previous local land drainage committees (s.139(2) and (4) Water Act 1989).

is provided that a local flood defence scheme may be made for the creation, in the area of a regional flood defence committee, of one or more districts, to be known as "local flood defence districts", and for the constitution, membership, functions and procedure of a committee for each district, to be known as the "local flood defence committee" for that district.[29]

The mechanism for the creation of local flood defence schemes involves a regional flood defence committee submitting to the Authority a local flood defence scheme for an area in which there is no such scheme in force or a scheme varying a local flood defence scheme and replacing it with another scheme. Before submission of the scheme, the regional flood defence committee is to consult every local authority whose area falls within the area of the scheme and organisations representing persons interested in flood defence or agriculture. The Authority is to send the proposed scheme to one of the Ministers, and he may approve it with or without modifications and fix a date for it to come into force.[30]

A local flood defence committee is normally to consist of not less than eleven and not more than fifteen members. However, a recommendation may be included by a regional flood defence committee in proposing a local flood defence scheme that the committee should contain a greater number of members than fifteen. In that case, the Minister is empowered to direct that the membership may be a number greater than fifteen. A local flood defence committee is to consist of a chairman and members appointed from the regional flood defence committee and members appointed on behalf of constituent councils, but the number of members appointed by the constituent councils is to be one more than the number of members appointed by the regional flood defence committee.[31] Detailed matters relating to the membership and procedure of local flood defence committees are provided for under Schedule 4 to the Water Resources Act 1991.[32]

---

[29] s.12(1) Water Resources Act 1991, formerly provided for in s.139(1) Water Act 1989.

[30] s.12 Water Resources Act 1991.

[31] s.13.

[32] Effective under s.14.

Main river functions of the Authority

The powers exercisable as functions of internal drainage boards under the Land Drainage Act 1991, are conferred upon the National Rivers Authority in relation to main rivers.[33] As has already been noted, a "main river map" means a map relating to the area of a regional flood defence committee which shows by a distinctive colour the extent to which any watercourse in that area is to be treated as a main river, and indicates which watercourses are designated in a special drainage scheme.[34] Main river maps are to be conclusive evidence for the purposes of the Land Drainage Act 1991, and all other purposes, of what is a main river.[35] The Authority is bound to keep the main river map for the area of a regional flood defence committee at the principal office of the Authority for that area and to provide public access to it at all reasonable hours. Main river maps are subject to amendment by either of the Ministers by the substitution of the whole or part of an existing map.[36]

The functions of the Authority in relation to main rivers include all the powers which are exercisable otherwise than in relation to a main river by a drainage board under the Land Drainage Act 1991, including powers to require works for securing the maintenance of flow of a watercourse under that Act.[37] Provisions under that Act relating to the commutation of obligations,[38] having effect where a person is under an obligation imposed upon him by reason of tenure, custom, prescription or otherwise to do any work in connection with the drainage of land in connection with a main river, are to operate as if the Authority were

[33] 107(1). "Main river" means a watercourse shown as such on a main river map and includes any structure or appliance for controlling or regulating the flow of water into, in or out of the channel which is situated in the channel or in any part of the banks of the channel and is not vested in or controlled by an internal drainage board (s.113(1) Water Resources Act 1991).

[34] See p.226 above.

[35] However, if any question arises whether any work, or proposed work, is drainage work in connection with a main river, the question is to be referred to one of the Ministers for decision or, if either of the parties so requires, to arbitration (s.73(1) Land Drainage Act 1991).

[36] On main river maps generally see ss.193 and 194 Water Resources Act 1991.

[37] That is, powers provided for under s.25 Land Drainage Act 1991.

[38] Under ss.33 and 34 Land Drainage Act 1991.

under a duty to commute the obligation. The exercise of powers in relation to a main river is to encompass the exercise of that power in relation to the banks of the river or in connection with the river.[39]

Schemes for transfer of functions to the Authority

The National Rivers Authority may at any time prepare, and submit to either of the Ministers for confirmation, a scheme making provision for the transfer from any drainage body[40] to the Authority of all rights, powers, duties, obligations and liabilities, including liabilities incurred in connection with works, over or in connection with a main river, and of any property held by the drainage body for the purpose of, or in connection with, any functions transferred. The Minister to whom a scheme is submitted may confirm the scheme by order made by statutory instrument in accordance with the procedure to be followed in connection with the making of an order of this kind and set out in Schedule 14 to the Water Resources Act 1991. Where liabilities are incurred in connection with a scheme of this kind by the transfer of liabilities from a local authority to the Authority, the Authority may require the local authority to contribute towards the discharge of those liabilities.[41]

Structures in, over or under a main river

No person may erect any structure in, over or under a watercourse which is part of a main river except with the consent of the Authority and in accordance with plans and sections approved by the Authority. Without the consent of the Authority, no person is permitted to carry out

---

[39] s.107 Water Resources Act 1991. "Banks" means banks, walls or embankments adjoining or confining, or constructed for the purposes of or in connection with, any channel or sea front, and includes all land and water between the bank and low-watermark (s.113(1) Water Resources Act 1991). On the meaning of "banks" under previous legislation see *Jones v. Mersey River Board*, [1957] 3 All E.R. 375; and *Oakes v. Mersey River Board*, (1957) J.P.L. 824.

[40] "Drainage body" means an internal drainage board or other body having power to make or maintain works for the drainage of land (s.108(9) Water Resources Act 1991).

[41] s.108.

any work of alteration or repair on any structure in, over or under a watercourse which is part of a main river if the work is likely to affect the flow of water in the watercourse or to impede drainage work. Likewise, no person may erect or alter any structure designed to contain or divert floodwaters of any part of a main river except with the consent of the Authority and in accordance with plans and sections approved by the Authority. Work carried out in contravention of these provisions may be removed, altered or pulled down by the Authority, and it may recover from the person in default the expenses incurred in so doing. However, the prohibitions upon erection and alteration of structures are not to apply to work carried out in an emergency providing the person carrying out the work informs the Authority that it has been carried out and the circumstances in which it was carried out.[42]

In relation to the consent of the Authority for the erection or alteration of structures in, over or under a main river and the erection of structures to contain or divert floodwaters, the Authority may require the payment of an application fee by a person who applies for consent. The amount of the fee is to be £50 or a sum specified by an order made by the Ministers. The consent of the Authority is not to be unreasonably withheld, and is deemed to have been given if it is neither given nor refused within a period of two months after the day on which the application for consent was made, or two months after the liability to pay an application fee is discharged, whichever of these is the later. The consent may be given subject to any reasonable condition as to the time at which and the manner in which work is to be carried out.[43]

Arrangements with certain authorities

The Authority, with a view to improving the drainage of any land, may enter into an arrangement with a navigation or conservancy authority for a range of purposes where the agreement is approved by the Ministers. The purposes are, (a) the transfer to the Authority of the whole or part of the undertaking of the navigation or conservancy authority or of any part of the rights, powers, duties, liabilities and obligations of that authority or any property vested in the authority as such; (b) the

---

[42] s.109.

[43] s.110.

alteration or improvement by the Authority of any of the works of the navigation or conservancy authority; or (c) the making of payments by the Authority to the navigation or conservancy authority, or by that authority to the Authority, in respect of any matter for which provision is made by the arrangement.[44]

Flood defence and drainage works

The Authority has a range of powers to carry out flood defence and drainage works in connection with main rivers. The powers of the Authority are, (a) to cleanse, repair or otherwise maintain existing drainage works in an efficient state; (b) to improve existing works by deepening, widening or otherwise improving any existing watercourse or removing or altering mill dams, weirs or other obstructions to watercourses, or raising, widening or otherwise improving any existing drainage work; and (c) to construct new works by making any new watercourse or drainage work or erecting any machinery or doing any other act required for the drainage of land. Irrespective of whether the works are in connection with a main river, the Authority has the power to maintain, improve, or construct drainage works for the purpose of defence against sea water or tidal water, and that power may be exercised above and below the low–water mark. The Authority may also construct works and do all things in the sea or any estuary which are necessary to secure an adequate outfall for a main river. However, none of these provisions authorises any entry on the land of any person except for the purpose of maintaining existing works.[45]

The Authority may by agreement with any person carry out, improve or maintain, at that person's expense, any drainage works which that person is entitled to conduct subject to a grant being paid in relation to the expense involved.[46] The Authority may also enter into an agreement with any local authority or navigation authority for the carrying out by that authority, on such terms as to payment or otherwise

[44] s.111.

[45] s.165(1) to (3) and (6).

[46] Grants may be paid under s.149(3).

as may be specified in the agreement, of any work in connection with a main river which the Authority is authorised to carry out.[47]

For the purposes of planning law, the classes of permitted development within the Town and Country Planning General Development Order 1988 encompass certain land drainage developments by the Authority. Thus, a development by the Authority in, on or under a watercourse, or land drainage works required in connection with the improvement, maintenance or repair of the watercourse, are granted planning consent under the Order without the need for the Authority to apply for consent.[48]

The Authority may, without making payment for it, appropriate and dispose of any matter removed in the course of carrying out work for the widening, deepening or dredging of any watercourse and deposit any matter removed on the banks of the watercourse or a width of land adjoining the watercourse which is sufficient to enable the matter to be removed and deposited by mechanical means in one operation. However, this power does not authorise the deposit of any matter in such a manner as to constitute a statutory nuisance within the meaning of Part III of the Environmental Protection Act 1990.[49] The Authority and the council of any district or London borough may enter into an agreement providing for the disposal by the council of any matter removed in connection with flood defence works and for the payment by the Authority to the council of a specified sum in respect of the disposal of the matter by the council.[50]

Flood warning systems

The Authority is empowered to provide and operate flood warning systems, to provide, install and maintain apparatus required for the purposes of such systems, and to carry out any other engineering or building operations so required.[51] A "flood warning system" is any

---

[47] s.165(4) and (5).

[48] Art.3 and Sch.2 para.15 Town and Country Planning General Development Order 1988, S.I. 1988 No.1813.

[49] On statutory nuisance in relation to water pollution see p.339 above.

[50] s.167 Water Resources Act 1991.

[51] s.166(1).

system for the purpose of providing warning of any danger of flooding, whereby information with respect to (a) rainfall, including any fall of snow, hail or sleet, as measured at a particular place within a particular period; (b) the level of flow of any inland water, or part of an inland water at a particular time; or (c) other matters appearing to the Authority to be relevant for that purpose, is obtained and transmitted, whether automatically or otherwise, with or without provision for carrying out calculations based on such information and for transmitting the results of those calculations.[52]

Flood defence regulations and byelaws

The Ministers are empowered to make provision by regulations generally for the purpose of carrying into effect the provisions of Part IV of the Water Resources Act 1991, concerning flood defence, and other flood defence provisions of the Act.[53]

The Authority is empowered to make byelaws for the purpose of carrying out its function in relation to flood defence and land drainage.[54] Hence, the Authority may make byelaws in relation to any particular locality or localities as it considers necessary for securing the efficient working of any drainage system including the proper defence of land against sea or tidal water. In particular, byelaws may be made for the purposes of (a) regulating the use, and preventing the improper use, of any watercourses, banks or works vested in the Authority or under its control or for preserving them from destruction; (b) regulating the opening of sluices and flood gates in connection with any works under (a); (c) preventing the obstruction of any watercourse vested in the Authority or under its control by the discharge into it of any liquid or solid matter or by reason of such matter being allowed to flow or fall into it; and (d) compelling persons having control of any watercourse vested in the Authority or under its control, or of any watercourse flowing into

---

[52] s.148(5).

[53] s.112.

[54] s.210 and Schs.25 and 26, and generally see p.235 above on the power of the Authority to make byelaws.

it, to cut the vegetable growths in or on the bank of the watercourse and, when cut, to remove them.[55]

INTERNAL DRAINAGE BOARDS

A "drainage body" is defined, under the Land Drainage Act 1991, as the National Rivers Authority, an internal drainage board or any other body having the power to make or maintain works for the drainage of land.[56] As has been described, the drainage powers of the Authority relate primarily to those functions which are exercisable in relation to main rivers. In relation to other, or "ordinary", watercourses and land which will derive benefit or avoid danger as a result of drainage operations, drainage functions are exercised in respect of internal drainage districts by internal drainage boards in accordance with the Land Drainage Act 1991.

It is provided that, for the purposes of drainage of land, there are to continue to be internal drainage districts, which are to be areas within the areas of regional flood defence committees which derive benefit, or avoid danger, as a result of drainage operations, and internal drainage boards, each of which is to be the drainage board for an internal drainage district.[57] An internal drainage board is to exercise a general supervision over all matters relating to the drainage of land within its district and to have such other powers and perform such other duties as are conferred or imposed under the Land Drainage Act 1991. An internal drainage board is to be a body corporate consisting of members elected and holding office in accordance with Schedule 1 to the Act and its members are to be appointed in accordance with those provisions by charging authorities.[58] The proceedings of internal drainage boards are governed by Schedule 2 to the Act.[59]

---

[55] Sch.25 para.5(1) and (2).

[56] s.72(1) Land Drainage Act 1991.

[57] See s.6 Land Drainage Act 1976 and s.140 Water Act 1989 on the previous provisions.

[58] "Charging authorities" has the same meaning as in the Local Government Finance Act 1988 (s.72(1) Land Drainage Act 1991). See Internal Drainage Boards (Finance) Regulations 1990, S.I. 1990 No.72, as amended by S.I. 1991 No.523.

[59] s.1 Land Drainage Act 1991.

Where a petition for the alteration of the boundaries of an internal drainage district is made to the Authority by a sufficient number of qualified persons or by a qualified authority,[60] and the boundaries of the district have not been altered or reviewed for a period of ten years, the Authority is bound to review those boundaries. The process of review involves the Minister being informed,[61] and the publication of a notice concerning the review and a statement that representations may be made to the Authority within thirty days. The Authority is bound to consider any representations made and to consult the drainage board for the internal drainage district concerned. The Minister is then to be informed whether the Authority proposes to submit a scheme for the reorganisation of the internal drainage district. Where the Authority does not propose to submit a scheme for reorganisation of internal drainage districts but considers that an order subdividing a district for the purposes of raising expenses should be made by the drainage board in question,[62] the Authority may direct that board to make an order on specified terms,

---

[60] Subject to Sch.2 para.19 of the Water Consolidation (Consequential Provisions) Act 1991, which makes provision with respect to qualification by reference to drainage rates levied on land in respect of years beginning before 1993, "qualified persons" are persons who are the owners and occupiers of any land in the district in respect of which a drainage rate is levied. "A sufficient number of qualified persons" means not less than forty; or not less than one–fifth of the number of persons who are qualified; or persons for whom the assessable value of their land, for the purposes of the last drainage rate levied in the district, is not less than one–fifth of the assessable value of all the land in respect of which that rate was levied (s.72(2) Land Drainage Act 1991). "Qualified authority" in relation to an internal drainage district, means a charging authority for an area wholly or partly included in that district, and "charging" authority has the same meaning as in the Local Government Finance Act 1988 (s.72(1)).

[61] "The Minister" for the purposes of the Land Drainage Act 1991 means the Minister of Agriculture, Fisheries and Food. "The Ministers" means the Minister and the Secretary of State, and in relation to anything which falls to be done by the Ministers, means those Ministers acting jointly. "The relevant Minister" (a) in relation to internal drainage districts which are neither wholly nor partly in Wales or to the boards for such districts, means the Minister; (b) in relation to internal drainage districts which are partly in Wales or to the boards for such districts, means the Ministers; and (c) in relation to internal drainage districts which are wholly in Wales or to the boards of such districts means the Secretary of State (s.72(1) Land Drainage Act 1991).

[62] An order sub–dividing a district may be made under s.38.

but the direction will not come into effect unless confirmed by the Minister if the internal drainage board objects to the direction.[63]

Schemes for the reorganisation of internal drainage districts are provided for whereby the Authority may, and must if directed by the Minister, submit to him for confirmation a scheme for the constitution of new internal drainage districts and boards and other matters. The other matters which such a scheme may concern include the alteration of boundaries of any internal drainage board; the amalgamation of the whole or any part of an internal drainage district with another district; the abolition of Commissioners of Sewers; the abolition or reconstruction of any internal drainage district and drainage board; the constitution of new internal drainage districts; the constitution of internal drainage boards for all or any of the separate internal drainage districts constituted by the scheme; the amendment of the method of constituting an internal drainage board; the making of alterations in or additions to local Acts and awards; and any supplemental or consequential matters. Provision is made for a reorganisation scheme to be submitted to the relevant Minister and a copy to every internal drainage board, local authority, navigation, harbour and conservancy authority affected by it, and for publication in newspapers allowing for representations to be made within one month of publication. The Minister may confirm the scheme, with or without modifications, in accordance with the detailed provisions of Schedule 3 to the Land Drainage Act 1991.[64]

On petition by the Authority presented to the Minister, he may by order transfer to the Authority the powers, duties, liabilities, obligations and property, including maps, deeds and other documents, of the drainage board of any internal drainage district. Where this is done, the Authority becomes the drainage board for that district.[65] The converse provision is that where, by virtue of a scheme for the reorganisation of internal drainage districts, or an order for the transfer of functions to the Authority, the Authority is the drainage board of an internal drainage

[63] s.2. These provisions do not require the Authority to carry out a review or publish any notice on a petition which, in the opinion of the Minister, is frivolous (s.2(7)).

[64] See also Reg.7 Land Drainage (General) Regulations 1932, S.R. and O. 1932 No.64, and Reg.6 Land Drainage (River Authorities) General Regulations 1965, S.I. 1965 No.443.

[65] s.4 Land Drainage Act 1991.

district, the Minister may constitute an internal drainage board for that district and transfer to it the property and liabilities of the Authority as the drainage board for that district. An order of this kind requires a petition for constituting an internal drainage board for that district to be made to the Authority by a sufficient number of qualified persons, or by a qualified authority. The Authority must send a copy of the petition to the Minister, who is bound to consider the views of the Authority before making an order of this kind.[66]

Supervision of drainage boards by the Authority

The National Rivers Authority may, for securing the efficient working and maintenance of existing drainage works and the construction of new drainage works, give general or special directions for the reasonable guidance of internal drainage boards with respect to their powers and duties. The consent of the Authority is required, and may be given subject to reasonable conditions but may not be unreasonably withheld, for an internal drainage board to construct drainage works, or alter existing drainage works, if they will affect the interests of, or the working of, any drainage works belonging to another internal drainage board. Questions as to whether the consent of the Authority is unreasonably withheld, or whether a condition subject to which it is given is unreasonable, must be referred to the Minister. An internal drainage board may not, otherwise than by maintaining an existing work, construct or alter any structure, appliance or channel for the discharge of water from their district into a main river except by agreement with the Authority or, in default, by determination of the Minister. In the event of an internal drainage board acting in contravention of these provisions, the Authority may execute any works and do anything necessary to prevent or remedy any damage resulting from the action of the internal drainage board and recover from that board summarily, as a civil debt, the expenses reasonably incurred in exercising that power.[67] The Authority has certain powers in relation to the prohibition of obstructions

[66] s.5.
[67] s.7.

in watercourses and contravention of those prohibitions[68] which are exercisable concurrently with the powers of an internal drainage board.[69]

Where the Authority is of the opinion that land is injured or likely to be injured by flooding or inadequate drainage which might be remedied wholly or partially by an internal drainage board exercising its powers, and which are either not being exercised at all, or are not being exercised to the necessary extent, the Authority may exercise all or any of those powers. Before exercising default powers in this manner, the Authority is required to give thirty days' notice of their intention to do so. If the drainage board object, the Authority must obtain the consent of the relevant Minister before exercising the powers. The Minister may hold a public local inquiry with respect to the objection.[70]

In exercising the powers of an internal drainage board, the Authority is entitled to inspect and take copies of any deeds, maps, books and other documents in the possession of the internal drainage board relating to land drainage in the district of the board. Any person who intentionally obstructs or impedes any person authorised for this purpose will be liable, on summary conviction, to a fine not exceeding £1,000.[71]

The Authority may, on application of the council of any county, metropolitan district or London borough, direct that the power to act in default of an internal drainage board is to be exercised by that council instead of the Authority. If the Authority refuse the application, the council may appeal to the relevant Minister, who may require the Authority to comply with the application.[72]

The Authority may enter into an agreement with any internal drainage board for the carrying out by the board of any work in connection with a main river which the Authority is authorised to carry out. The Authority, with the consent of an internal drainage board, may carry out and maintain works which the board is authorised to carry out or maintain on such terms as are agreed, or the Authority may agree to contribute to the expense of carrying out maintenance of any works by an internal drainage board. An internal drainage board may, with the

---

68 Under ss.23 and 24.

69 s.8.

70 s.9(1) to (4).

71 s.9(5) and (6).

72 s.10.

consent of an internal drainage board for another district, carry out or maintain works in the other district on such terms as may be agreed between the boards, or agree to contribute towards the expense of works by the internal drainage board for another district.[73]

Environmental and recreational duties

It is the general environmental duty of each of the Ministers, the National Rivers Authority and every internal drainage board, in formulating or considering any proposals relating to any functions of the board, so far as may be consistent with the purpose of any enactment relating to the functions of the board,[74] to exercise their powers so as to further the conservation and enhancement of natural beauty and the conservation of flora, fauna and geological or physiographical features of special interest. Similarly, they are to have regard to the desirability of protecting and conserving buildings, sites of and objects of archaeological, architectural or historic interest, and to take into account any effect which proposals would have on the beauty or amenity of any rural or urban area or on those flora, fauna, features, buildings, sites or objects.[75]

The general recreational duty of the Ministers, the Authority and internal drainage boards requires them, in formulating or considering any proposals relating to their functions, to have regard to the desirability of preserving for the public any freedom of access to areas of woodland, mountains, moor, heath, down, cliff or foreshore and other places of natural beauty. Similarly, they are to have regard to the desirability of maintaining the availability to the public of any facility for visiting or inspecting any building, site or object of archaeological, architectural or historic interest, and to take into account any effect which proposals would have on freedom of access or on the availability of that facility.[76]

In relation to an internal drainage board, the general environmental and recreational duties apply in respect of any proposals relating to the

---

[73] s.11.

[74] In the case of the Secretary of State, so far as may be consistent with his duties under s.2 Water Industry Act 1991.

[75] s.12(1) Land Drainage Act 1991.

[76] s.12(2).

functions of the Authority or a water or sewerage undertaker, proposals relating to the management of land held by a water or sewerage undertaker, and proposals relating to the disposal of protected land by a water or sewerage undertaker.[77] These proposals are to be treated as proposals relating to the functions of the internal drainage board for the purposes of the environmental and recreational duties. Subject to obtaining the consents of navigation, harbour and conservancy authorities before doing anything which obstructs or interferes with water under the control of those authorities, it is the duty of an internal drainage board to take steps which are reasonably practicable and consistent with the functions of the board for securing that the rights of the board are exercised so as to ensure that water or land is made available, in the best manner, for recreational purposes. In so doing, it is the duty of the internal drainage board to take into account the needs of persons who are chronically sick or disabled, but none of the provisions relating to recreational duties require facilities to be made available free of charge.[78]

Where the Nature Conservancy Council for England or the Countryside Council for Wales are of the opinion that any area of land is of special interest by reason of its flora, fauna or geological or physiographical features, and may be affected by schemes, works, operations or activities of an internal drainage board, the appropriate Council is to notify that fact to every internal drainage board whose works, operations or activities may affect the land. Where a National Park authority or the Broads Authority[79] is of the opinion that land in a National Park or in the Broads is land in relation to which the environmental or recreational duties are of particular importance, and may be affected by schemes, works, operations or activities of an internal drainage board, the appropriate authority is to notify that fact, and the reasons for it, to every internal drainage board whose works, operations or activities may affect the land. Where notification has been received, the board is bound to consult the notifying body before carrying out any

---

[77] Protected land is provided for under ss.3 and 156(7) Water Industry Act 1991.

[78] s.12(3) to (6) Land Drainage Act 1991.

[79] "National Park authority" means a National Park Committee of a joint or special planning board for a National Park, and "the Broads" has the same meaning as in the Norfolk and Suffolk Broads Act 1988 (s.13(5) Land Drainage Act 1991).

works, operations or activities which are likely to destroy or damage any of the flora, fauna, or geological or physiographical features by reason of which the land is of special interest, or significantly to prejudice anything which makes the application of the environmental or recreational duties of particular importance in relation to that land. However, this duty is not to apply in relation to anything done in an emergency where particulars of what has been done are notified to the appropriate body as soon as practicable afterwards.[80]

POWERS TO FACILITATE OR SECURE THE DRAINAGE OF LAND

General powers of internal drainage boards and local authorities[81]

A range of general powers in relation to the drainage of land are given to internal drainage boards acting within their internal drainage districts, and local authorities carrying out drainage of small areas,[82] or acting to prevent flooding or to mitigate any damage caused by flooding of their areas. Specifically, the powers provided to drainage boards and local authorities are the following: (a) to maintain existing works, that is to say, to cleanse, repair or otherwise maintain in a due state of efficiency any existing watercourse or drainage work; (b) to improve any existing works, that is to say, to deepen, widen, straighten or otherwise improve any existing watercourse or remove or alter mill dams, weirs or other obstructions to watercourses, or raise, widen or otherwise improve any existing drainage work; and (c) to construct new works, that is to say, to make any new watercourse or drainage work or erect any machinery or do any other act (other than an act referred to in (a) or (b) above) required for the drainage of any land. In addition, where a drainage board or local authority desires to carry out any drainage works, otherwise than in relation to a main river, for the benefit of their district or area, in land outside that district or area, they will have the same powers for that

---

[80] s.13. See *Nature Conservancy Council v. Southern Water Authority*, (1991) *The Times* 17 June 1991 D.C.

[81] See also the miscellaneous powers of internal drainage boards described at p.412 below.

[82] As provided for under s.18 Land Drainage Act 1991.

purpose as are conferred under the Land Drainage Act 1991 on persons interested in land which is capable of being drained or improved.[83]

Notably, these powers do not impose any *duty* upon internal drainage boards and authorities to carry out drainage works, but merely confer a power to do so, and whether this power is exercised in a particular case is a matter entirely within their own discretion. If a drainage authority decide not to exercise their powers they are not liable to a member of the public for damage sustained by reason of the failure to exercise the powers. If the discretion to exercise powers is exercised, however, the duty owed to a member of the public is the duty not to exacerbate the damage that person would have suffered if the authority had done nothing.[84]

None of the powers of a drainage board or local authority authorises any person to enter on the land of any person except for the purpose of maintaining existing works, or authorises a county council to exercise any power except in accordance with further provisions.[85] It has been held that an authority requiring entry on land for improving existing works need not obtain the consent of persons having only an incorporeal right in the water and not in the bank.[86]

Where injury is sustained by any person by reason of the exercise by a drainage board or local authority of any of their powers, the board or authority will be liable to make full compensation to the injured person, and in a case of dispute the matter is to be determined by the Lands Tribunal.[87] The extent of the duty to compensate in these

---

[83] s.14(1), (2) and (3).

[84] Generally, see *East Suffolk Catchment Board v. Kent*, (1941) 105 J.P. 129; *Smith v. Cawdle Fen Commissioners*, [1938] 4 All E.R. 64; and *Gillett v. Kent Rivers Catchment Board*, [1938] 4 All E.R 810.

[85] s.14(4) Land Drainage Act 1991. Further powers of local authorities are provided for under s.16.

[86] *Proctor v. Avon and Dorset River Board*, [1953] C.P.L. 562.

[87] s.14(5) and (6) Land Drainage Act 1991; and see *Marriage v. East Norfolk Rivers Catchment Board*, (1949) 113 J.P. 362. Where a claim for compensation is referred to the Lands Tribunal, it is for the arbitrator to determine not only the amount of compensation, but also the issue of whether the claimant is entitled to compensation (*Rhodes v. Airedale Drainage Commissioners*, (1876) 35 L.T. 46), and a right to compensation may be barred unless a claim is brought within the appropriate limitation period (*Vincent v. Thames Conservators*, (1953) 4 P. & C.R. 66; and *Robson v. Northumberland and Tyneside River Board*, (1952) 3 P. & C.R. 150).

circumstances has been the subject of a considerable amount of litigation under previous legislation.[88] Past decisions have indicated that if damage is caused by work done in pursuance of the general drainage powers which is performed in a negligent or unreasonable manner, or where the damage is caused by work which is outside the scope of those powers, the appropriate remedy may be through an action based on negligence rather than the statutory claim for compensation.[89] Conversely, providing a drainage board or local authority act within the scope of their general drainage powers, a riparian owner whose legal rights are violated as a consequence will be unable to gain a remedy in the absence of negligence on the part of the board or authority.[90] An agreement to pay compensation for injury to a landowner is not to be a condition precedent of a drainage board or local authority exercising its powers, nor may it be made a condition of entry upon land.[91]

Notably for the purposes of planning law, the classes of permitted development within the Town and Country Planning General Development Order 1988 encompass developments by drainage bodies. Hence, a development by a drainage body in, on or under a watercourse or land drainage works in connection with the improvement, maintenance or repair of the watercourse or works is granted planning

---

[88] For cases under the Land Drainage Act 1930, see *Scutt and Screeton v. Lower Ouse Internal Drainage Board*, (1953) 4 P. & C.R. 71; *Lovegrove v. Isle of Wight River Board*, (1956) J.P.L. 221; *Jones v. Mersey River Board*, [1957] 3 All E.R. 375; *Oakes v. Mersey River Board*, (1957) J.P.L. 824; *Birch v. Ancholme Drainage Board*, (1958) J.P.L. 257; *Rippingale Farms Ltd. v. Black Sluice Internal Drainage Board*, [1963] 1 W.L.R. 1347; *Glazebrook v. Gwynedd River Board*, (1964) 15 P. & C.R. 75; *Burgess v. Gwynedd River Authority*, (1972) 24 P. & C.R. 150; *Welsh National Water Development Authority v. Burgess*, (1974) J.P.L 665; *Thameside Estates v. Greater London Council*, (1977) 249 E.G. 347. For cases under the Land Drainage Act 1976 see *Steel Stampings v. Severn Trent Water Authority*, (1982) 263 E.G. 359; *Andrew v. Cod Beck Internal Drainage Board*, (1983) 23 R. & V.R. 270; *Day & Sons v. Thames Water Authority*, (1984) 270 E.G. 1294; *Marine Industrial Transmissions v. Southern Water Authority*, (1989) 29 R.V.R. 221.

[89] See *Ash v. Great Northern Railway Co.*, (1903) 67 J.P. 417; *Roberts v. Charing Cross Railway*, (1903) 87 L.T. 732; *R. v. Darlington L.B.*, (1865) 29 J.P. 419; *Coe v. Wise*, (1886) 30 J.P. 484.

[90] *Proctor v. Avon and Dorset Rivers Board*, [1953] C.P.L. 562; *Marriage v. East Norfolk River Catchment Board*, (1949) 113 J.P. 362.

[91] *Symes v. Essex Rivers Catchment Board*, (1937) 101 J.P. 179.

consent under the Order without the need for the drainage body to apply for consent.[92]

Disposal of spoil

An internal drainage board or a local authority may, without making payment, appropriate and dispose of any matter removed in the course of the execution of any work for widening, deepening or dredging any ordinary watercourse.[93] The board or authority may also deposit any matter removed on the banks of the watercourse, or on such a width of land adjoining the watercourse as is sufficient to enable the matter to be removed and deposited by mechanical means in one operation. These powers are not to be exercised by a local authority except for the purpose of drainage of small areas,[94] and so far as is necessary for preventing flooding or mitigating any damage caused by flooding in their area.[95]

Generally, the powers relating to the disposal of spoil will not authorise the deposit of any matter if the deposit would constitute a public nuisance within the meaning of Part III of the Environmental Protection Act 1990.[96] Where injury is sustained by a person by reason of the exercise of these powers, the internal drainage board or local authority *may* pay such amount of compensation as they may determine, and if the injury could have been avoided if the powers had been exercised with reasonable care, a *liability* to pay compensation arises and must, in a case of dispute, be determined by the Lands Tribunal.[97] An internal drainage board or local authority may enter into an agreement with the council of any district or London borough for the disposal by

---

[92] Art.3 and Sch.2 para.14 Town and Country Planning General Development Order 1988, S.I. 1988 No.1813. But see also Town and Country Planning (Assessment of Environmental Effects) Regulations 1988, S.I. 1988 No.1199; and Land Drainage Improvement Works (Assessment of Environmental Effects) Regulations 1988, S.I. 1988 No.1217.

[93] An "ordinary watercourse" means a watercourse which does not form part of a main river (s.72(1) Land Drainage Act 1991).

[94] Provided for under s.18.

[95] s.15(1) and (2).

[96] On statutory nuisance generally see p.339 above.

[97] Liability arises in accordance with s.14(4) and (5) Land Drainage Act 1991.

the council of spoil and for the payment by the board or authority to the council of a sum provided for by the agreement.[98]

Exercise and supervision of drainage powers

Where general drainage powers or powers to dispose of spoil which are conferred upon a non–metropolitan district council are not exercised by that council, they may be exercised by a county council at the request of the district council. Alternatively, the general drainage powers may be exercised by the county council on its own initiative after not less than six weeks' notice have been given by the county council to the district council. Where the powers are conferred upon a metropolitan district council or London borough council or the Common Council of the City of London and are not exercised, they may be exercised by the National Rivers Authority, at the request of the council, or after six weeks' notice from the Authority to the council. Provision is made for an appeal to the Secretary of State in either instance, in which case the powers are not to be exercised unless the notice from the county council, or the Authority as the case may be, is confirmed by the Secretary of State.[99]

Supervision of the exercise of powers by a local authority is provided for by the National Rivers Authority, so that a local authority may not exercise general drainage powers or powers in relation to the disposal of spoil except with the consent of, and in accordance with any reasonable conditions imposed by, the Authority. Before giving consent for these purposes, the Authority is to consult with any internal drainage board for the area concerned. The consent of the Authority is not to be unreasonably withheld and is deemed to be given if neither given nor refused within two months after the application for it is made, subject to provision for disputes to be determined by the Ministers. Consent of the Authority is not required for work carried out in an emergency, but a local authority conducting emergency work is required, as soon as practicable, to inform the Authority of the carrying out of the work and the circumstances under which it was carried out.[100]

---

[98] s.15(3) to (5).
[99] s.16.
[100] s.17.

Drainage of small areas

Where the National Rivers Authority considers that any land is capable of improvement by drainage works, but that the constitution for that purpose of an internal drainage board would not be practicable, or a local authority other than a district council is of that opinion in relation to land in their area, either authority may, in accordance with a scheme for the drainage of a small area, enter the land and carry out drainage work which is considered desirable. A scheme of this kind is to state the works proposed to be executed; the area to be improved; the estimated expenses of carrying out the works;[101] the maximum amount recoverable by the authority; and the manner in which the expenses of executing and maintaining the works are to be apportioned amongst the lands in the area to be improved. Expenses incurred by either authority in carrying out drainage works up to the maximum amount recoverable, and expenses in maintaining the works, are to be recoverable by the authority from the several owners of the land to which the scheme relates. A scheme of this kind is to be registrable as a local land charge.[102]

The detailed provisions relating to the making of schemes for small drainage works are provided for under Schedule 4 to the Land Drainage Act 1991. This provides that, before a scheme for the drainage of a small area is made, the local authority is to consult the National Rivers Authority. Either authority is to give owners and occupiers of land within the area, and other persons affected by the scheme, notice of its intention to make the scheme, and of the place where a draft of it can be inspected, and state a time of not less that thirty days in which objections can be made. In the event of objections, the scheme is not to be made unless a draft is confirmed by the Minister, with or without modifications. Before confirming the draft, the Minister must either cause a public inquiry to be held or give the authority and the person by whom objections have been made an opportunity of being heard before a person appointed by the Minster for that purpose. When made, the

---

[101] Subject to Ministerial exemption for public works which are urgently required in the public interest, the estimated expenses, including the administrative expenses, of carrying out the works are not to exceed £50 per hectare of the land to be improved (s.18(4) and (6)).

[102] s.18.

authority is to send copies of the scheme to the owners and occupiers of land to which it relates, and notify certain local authorities for the land concerned.[103]

Arrangements as to works

An internal drainage board, with a view to improving the drainage of any land in its district, may enter into an arrangement with a navigation or conservancy authority for the transfer to the board of any part of the undertaking of the navigation or conservancy authority and any property vested in it, for the alteration or improvement by the board of any works of the authority, or the making of payments to the authority in respect of any matter provided for in the agreement. However, no agreements of this kind may be made in relation to any main river, and the exercise of the power to enter into an agreement will require the approval of the relevant Minister and the Secretary of State.[104]

Other agreements are provided for whereby an internal drainage board may, by agreement with any person and at that person's expense, carry out and maintain, whether within or outside their district, any drainage works which that person is entitled to carry out and maintain on an ordinary watercourse. Similarly, a local authority, other than the council of a non–metropolitan district may, by agreement with any person, and at that person's expense, carry out within the authority's area any drainage work which that person is entitled to carry out.[105]

Obligations to repair watercourses and bridges

Nothing in the Land Drainage Act 1991 or previous legislation operates to release any person from any obligations to which that person was subject by reason of any tenure, custom prescription or otherwise.[106] Accordingly, if a person by reason of any pre–existing obligation is

---

[103] See Drainage Schemes (Notices) Regulations 1965, S.I. 1965 No.445.

[104] s.19(1) to (3). On the meanings of "navigation authority" and "conservancy authority" see p.253 above.

[105] s.20 Land Drainage Act 1991.

[106] *North Level Commissioners v. River Welland Catchment Board*, (1938) 102 J.P. 82; and *Attorney–General v. St. Ives R.D.C.*, [1961] 1 All E.R. 265.

liable to do any work in relation to a watercourse, bridge or drainage work, whether by way of repair, maintenance or otherwise, and fails to do that work, the internal drainage board concerned may serve a notice on that person requiring him to do the necessary work with all reasonable and proper dispatch. If that person fails to comply with the notice within seven days, the drainage authority may do the work and recover the reasonable expenses so incurred.[107]

Ministerial authorisation for landowners to carry out works

Where any persons interested in land are of the opinion that it is capable of improvement but works cannot be carried out because of the objection or disability of any person whose land would be entered upon, cut through or interfered with for the purpose of the works, those persons may present an application to the appropriate Minister for an order authorising them to carry out the works. An application for these purposes is to be in a prescribed form, and notice is to be given to persons whose lands are to be entered, the National Rivers Authority and any internal drainage board for the area concerned. Provision is made for objections to be made and for the payment of compensation for injury suffered in relation to the works.[108]

Obstructions in watercourses

No person may erect a mill dam, weir or other like obstruction to the flow of any watercourse or raise or otherwise alter any such obstruction, or erect any culvert that would be likely to affect the flow of any watercourse or alter any culvert in a manner that would be likely to affect the flow, without the consent of the internal drainage board concerned. The drainage board may require the payment of an application fee of £50, or another sum specified in an order made by the Ministers. Consent is not to be unreasonably withheld, and if the board fail, within two months of receiving an application and application fee, to notify the applicant of their determination, the application consent is deemed to have been given. Any question as to whether consent is

---

[107] s.21 Land Drainage Act 1991.

[108] s.22.

unreasonably withheld is to be referred to arbitration. These provisions do not apply to works under the control of a navigation, harbour or conservancy authority, or to works executed or maintained under statutory powers.[109]

If an obstruction which is erected or altered in contravention of the requirement to obtain consent is deemed to be a nuisance, the drainage board may serve a notice on the person by whom the obstruction has been erected, where he has the power to remove the obstruction, or otherwise upon any person who has that power, requiring that person to abate the nuisance within a specified time. If the person acts in contravention of, or fails to comply with, the notice he is guilty of an offence and liable, on summary conviction, to a fine not exceeding £2,000, and a further daily fine not exceeding £40 for each day on which the contravention or failure continues after the conviction. The drainage board may take action to remedy the effect of the contravention or failure and recover the expenses reasonably incurred by them from the person in default.[110]

Works for maintaining the flow of a watercourse

Where an ordinary watercourse is in such a condition that the proper flow of water is impeded, then, unless the condition is attributable to subsidence due to mining operations, including brine pumping, the internal drainage board or local authority concerned may require a person on whom notice is served to remedy that condition. For these purposes, the drainage board concerned is the board for the district in which the watercourse is situated, and the local authority is the authority for the area in which the powers are to be exercised. However, where the watercourse is not in the area of an internal drainage board, the powers may be exercised by the National Rivers Authority. The person on whom a notice is to be served is to be any person having control of the part of the watercourse where the impediment occurs, or any person owning or occupying land adjoining that part, or any person to whose act or default the condition is due.[111]

---

[109] s.23.

[110] s.24.

[111] s.25(1) to (3).

A notice requiring works for maintaining the flow of a watercourse is not to be served on any person requiring him to carry out work on land not owned by him without the consent of the owner and the occupier of that land, except where it is not practicable, after reasonable inquiry, to ascertain the name and address of the owner or occupier. The notice is to indicate the nature of the works to be carried out and the period within which they are to be carried out, and the existence of a right of appeal to a magistrates' court.[112] Subject to an appeal, if the person upon whom a notice is served fails to carry out the works within the specified period, the drainage board or local authority may themselves carry out the works, and recover from that person the expenses reasonably incurred in so doing. In addition, the person will be guilty of an offence and liable, on summary conviction, to a fine not exceeding £1,000.[113]

Before exercising its powers to require works for maintaining the flow of a watercourse, a local authority is to notify the internal drainage board for the district concerned, or if none exists, the National Rivers Authority. Where a local authority has other powers for securing the appropriate flow of water in a watercourse under their jurisdiction, the power to require works for maintaining the flow of a watercourse is not to be exercised by any other body except by agreement with the local authority or where, after reasonable notice from that body, the local authority fails to exercise its powers or exercises them improperly. Where a watercourse is under the jurisdiction of a navigation, harbour or conservancy authority or board of conservators, the consent of that body will be required before the power to require works for maintaining the flow of a watercourse is exercised. However, these restrictions do not to apply in relation to main rivers in relation to which the National Rivers Authority may exercise corresponding powers as a part of their main river functions.[114]

---

[112] Provision for appeals is made under s.27.

[113] s.25(4) to (6).

[114] s.26. The main river functions of the National Rivers Authority are provided for under s.107 Water Resources Act 1991.

Restoration and improvement of ditches

Where a ditch[115] is in such condition as to cause injury to any land or to prevent the improvement of drainage of any land, the Agricultural Land Tribunal may, on the application of the owner or occupier of the land, make an order requiring the person or persons named in the order to carry out work for cleansing the ditch, removing from it any matter which impedes the flow of water, or otherwise putting it in proper order, and for protecting it as specified in the order. An order with respect to a ditch may name any person who is the owner or occupier of land through which the ditch passes or which abuts on the ditch and any person who has a right to carry out the work specified in the order. Where an Agricultural Land Tribunal makes an order requiring persons jointly to carry out any work, the Tribunal may specify the proportions in which those persons are to contribute to the cost of carrying out the work.[116]

An order requiring remedial work to be carried out on a ditch is sufficient authority for the named person to do the work specified and, so far as may be necessary for that purpose, to enter land specified by the order. Where work specified in an order has not been carried out after three months, or any longer time specified in the order, the appropriate Minister or a drainage body authorised by him may carry out the work, and enter any land which it is necessary to enter for that purpose. The Minister or the body authorised to carry out the work in default may then recover from the person named in the order reasonable expenses incurred in doing the work which ought to have been done by him.[117]

A person entitled to enter land by virtue of a default order of this kind may take with him other persons and equipment, but if the land is unoccupied he must leave it as effectually secured against trespassers as he found it. Not less than seven days' notice is to be given of the entry on land to the occupier. Where any person sustains injury by reason of the exercise of any power conferred by a default order then, unless the power was exercised for the purpose of carrying out required work, the person

---

[115] "Ditch" includes a culverted and a piped ditch but does not include a watercourse vested in or under the control of a drainage body (s.28(5) Land Drainage Act 1991).

[116] s.28.

[117] s.29(1) and (2).

sustaining the injury will be entitled to full compensation, which in a case of dispute will be determined by the Lands Tribunal.[118]

Where the drainage of any land requires work to be carried out in connection with a ditch passing through other land, or the replacement or construction of a ditch, or the alteration or removal of any drainage work in connection with such a ditch, the Agricultural Land Tribunal may, on the application of the owner or occupier of the land to be drained, make an order authorising him to carry out work specified in the order and, so far as may be necessary, to enter any specified land.[119]

Powers to modify existing obligations

Variation of awards

Where any award made under a public or local Act contains any provision which in any manner affects or relates to the drainage of land, including a provision affecting the powers or duties of a drainage body or other person as to the drainage of land, the National Rivers Authority may, and must if directed by the Minister, submit to the appropriate Minster for confirmation a scheme for revoking, varying or amending that provision. An application of this kind can be made by any person who is under an obligation imposed by the award or any internal drainage board, providing the applicant has requested the Authority to submit a scheme and the Authority has failed to do so within six months or has submitted a scheme which is different to that requested. In accordance with the detailed provisions set out in Schedule 3 to the Land Drainage Act 1991, the Minster may confirm the scheme with or without modifications.[120]

Commutation of obligations

Where a person is under an obligation imposed on him by reason of tenure, custom, prescription or otherwise[121] to do any work in

---

[118] s.29(3) to (6).

[119] s.30.

[120] s.32.

[121] The obligations concerned do not encompass purely contractual obligations, or voluntary payments paid under a contract, see *Eton R.D.C. v. Thames Conservators*, (1950) 114 J.P. 279; and *Re Fitzherbert Brockhole's Agreement, River Wyre Catchment Board v. Miller*, (1939) 103 J.P. 379.

connection with the drainage of land, whether by way of repairing banks or walls, maintaining watercourses or otherwise in connection with a main river, the National Rivers Authority or the drainage board for the internal drainage district in which the work falls to be done may commute the obligation with the consent of the appropriate Minister. Where commutation of an obligation is proposed, the Authority or the board is to give the Minister, in a manner which he may direct,[122] a notice of any proposal to commute the obligation, the terms on which it is to be commuted and the period within which any objection to the proposal may be made. The person on whom the obligation is imposed may notify the Authority or the board of his objection to the proposal within one month of the notice, and the question whether the Authority or board is to proceed to commute the obligation is then to be referred to the Minster whose decision is final.[123]

Power to vary navigation rights

The power to vary navigation rights is provided for where an application is made to either of the Ministers for that purpose by the National Rivers Authority and, in relation to an ordinary watercourse, the drainage boards for every internal drainage district within which any of the waters are situated. If it appears to the Minister that a navigation authority is not exercising at all, or is not exercising to the necessary extent, the powers vested in it, and it is desirable to do so with a view to securing the better drainage of land, he may revoke, vary or amend the provisions of any local Act relating to navigation rights over any canal, river or navigable waters or the powers and duties of the navigation authority with respect to those waters. In addition, the Minister may extinguish, vary or suspend those rights, powers or duties with a view to securing the better drainage of any land. An order of this kind may only be made after he has consulted the Secretary of State, and may not be made by the Minister so as to affect any waters within the ebb and flow

[122] See the Land Drainage (River Authorities) General Regulations 1965, S.I. 1965 No.443.

[123] s.33 Land Drainage Act 1991. On the financial consequence of commutation see s.34.

of the tide at ordinary spring tides except with the consent of the Secretary of State for Transport.[124]

FINANCIAL PROVISIONS CONCERNING THE NATIONAL RIVERS AUTHORITY

As has previously been noted, the general financial duties concerning the National Rivers Authority specifically provide that, subject to certain exceptions, revenue raised in relation to flood defence functions may only be expended on of the Authority's flood defence functions in or for the benefit of the local flood defence district in which it was raised.[125] Other provisions under the Water Resources Act 1991 concerning the revenue of the Authority allow for levies upon local authorities, the imposition of general and special charges in relation to drainage functions and for revenue from internal drainage boards.[126]

Levies on local authorities

The power of the National Rivers Authority to impose levies upon local authorities, in relation to the flood defence functions of the Authority, is achieved by deeming the Authority to be a levying body for the purposes of the Local Government and Finance Act 1988. This provides the Authority with the power to make regulations for the issuing of a levy upon local authorities.[127]

General drainage charges

The National Rivers Authority is empowered to raise an amount per hectare of chargeable land in a local flood defence district by way of a general drainage charge. This charge is not to be levied, however,

---

[124] s.35. The detailed provisions relating to orders of this kind are provided for under Sch.3.

[125] s.118 Water Resources Act 1991, and p. 240 above.

[126] On the system of financing flood defence generally see *Financing and Administration of Land Drainage, Flood Prevention and Coast Protection in England and Wales* (1985 Cmnd.9449).

[127] s.133, and see s.74 Local Government Finance Act 1988. See National Rivers Authority (Levies) Regulations 1990, S.I. 1990 No.118.

unless it has been recommended by the regional flood defence committee for the district for which it is to be levied. For these purposes, the area of a regional flood defence committee in relation to which no local flood defence scheme is in force is to be treated as a single local flood defence district, and any parts of the area of a regional flood defence district in relation to which no local flood defence scheme is in force are to be treated as a single local flood defence district.[128]

A general drainage charge for a local flood defence district is to be at a uniform amount per hectare of chargeable land in that district. The uniform amount per hectare is ascertained by multiplying the relevant quotient by one penny and by a number specified by either of the Ministers for this purpose. The number specified by the Minister, apart from any adjustment made to take account of rough grazing land, is to be such as to secure, so far as reasonably practicable, that the aggregate amount produced by the charge will be equal to the aggregate amount which, if the chargeable land had been liable to be rated for the financial year beginning in 1989, would have been produced by a rate levied on the land.[129] The "relevant quotient" for the purpose of calculating a general drainage charge is determined by the application of a statutory formula.[130]

Special drainage charges

A special drainage charge may be raised by the Authority where it appears that the interests of agriculture require the carrying out, improvement or maintenance of drainage works in connection with any watercourses in the area of any regional flood defence committee. Where this is the case, the Authority may submit a scheme to the Minister for confirmation designating the watercourses concerned and making provision for the raising of a special drainage charge for the purpose of meeting the expenses of drainage works and any expenses arising from

---

[128] s.134 Land Drainage Act 1991.

[129] s.135. The detailed provisions with respect to assessment, incidence, payment and enforcement of general drainage charges are set out in Sch.15 Water Resources Act 1991. See also Drainage Charges Regulations 1990, S.I. 1990 No.214; and General Drainage Charges (Forms) Regulations 1990, S.I. 1990 No.564.

[130] The formula is set out in s.136 Land Drainage Act 1991.

those works. A scheme of this kind is to designate, for the purposes of the special drainage charge, so much of the area of the regional flood defence committee as consists of land which is agricultural land that would benefit from drainage works in connection with designated watercourses. If the scheme is confirmed, the designated watercourses are to be treated as part of the main river.[131]

A special drainage charge is to be levied by the Authority in respect of relevant chargeable land included in an area designated for the purpose of a scheme. The special drainage charge raised is to be at a uniform amount per hectare of the relevant chargeable land. The uniform amount is to be determined by the regional flood defence committee for the area which includes the relevant chargeable land, but it is not to exceed an amount specified in the scheme as the maximum amount, or a greater amount authorised by one of the Ministers on the application of the Authority, or twenty-five pence or any other amount substituted in an order made by one of the Ministers.[132]

Revenue from internal drainage boards

The Authority is under a duty to require every internal drainage board to make contributions towards the expenses of the Authority, subject to certain qualifications applicable to minor internal drainage districts.[133] However, provision is made for appeals to the relevant Minister to be brought against a resolution of the Authority in this respect within a six week period.[134] The Authority may issue precepts to internal drainage boards requiring payment of any amount required by way of a contribution from an internal drainage board and the board is bound to pay the amount demanded. It is, however, the duty of the Authority to prepare, in a form directed by the Minister, a statement of

---

[131] s.137(1) to (4). "Agricultural land" has the same meaning as in the Agriculture Act 1947, see p.254 above on this. The detailed provisions relating to the making and confirmation of schemes for special drainage charges are set out in Sch.16 Water Resources Act 1991. See also *Alford Drainage Board v. Mablethorpe*, (1986) 227 E.G. 867.

[132] s.138(1) to (3). The detailed provisions relating to assessment, incidence, payment and enforcement of special drainage charges are provided for in Sch.15.

[133] s.139.

[134] s.140.

the purpose to which the amount demanded by the precept is intended to be applied and the basis on which it is calculated, and an internal drainage board will not be liable to pay the amount demanded until they have received a statement of this kind.[135]

FINANCIAL PROVISIONS CONCERNING INTERNAL DRAINAGE BOARDS

Raising and apportionment of expenses

The expenses of internal drainage boards exercising powers under the Land Drainage Act 1991 and other enactments, in so far as they are not met by contributions from the Authority, are to be raised by means of drainage rates and special levies.[136] The expenses of a drainage board which are raised by means of drainage rates in respect of the financial year beginning in 1993 and subsequent years are to be defrayed out of drainage rates without regard to the purpose for which expenses were incurred.[137]

With respect to the raising of expenses of an internal drainage board for the financial year beginning in 1993 and subsequent years, the proportion of the expenses of the board to be raised from the proceeds of drainage rates is to be equal to the agricultural proportion of land values in that district. The proportion of expenses of that board to be raised from the proceeds of special levies is to be such as to raise the balance of expenses of the board remaining after deduction of the amount to be raised for that year from the proceeds of drainage rates. Drainage boards are, before 15 February of each year, to determine, for the financial year following, the "agricultural proportion" as the aggregate annual value of

---

[135] s.141.

[136] Drainage rates are provided for under Chapter II of Part IV of the Land Drainage Act 1991, or in relation to any time before 1 April 1993 by Sch.2 para.15 Water Consolidation (Consequential Provisions) Act 1991. Special levies may be issued under s.75 Local Government Finance Act 1988. See Internal Drainage Boards (Finance) Regulations 1990, S.I. 1990 No.72.

[137] s.36 Land Drainage Act 1991.

chargeable properties in their district divided by the aggregate annual value of all other land in the district.[138]

A drainage board, after consultation with the Authority, may, for the purpose of levying differential drainage rates or issuing differential special levies, divide their district into sub–districts, and may exercise their powers to make and levy differential drainage rates or issue differential special levies. An order made in accordance with this power may determine the proportions of the expenses of the drainage board for that district which are to be raised in the respective sub–districts within that district.[139] Alternatively, a petition may be made for the making, variation or revocation of an order sub–dividing a district by a sufficient number of qualified persons. Where this is done, the board must consider the petition and, if directed by the Authority, they are to make, vary or revoke the order either in accordance with the petition or as modified by the direction. If the Authority acts as the board, it is to do similarly when so directed by either of the Ministers, [140]

Levying of drainage rates

In respect of the financial years beginning in or after 1993, the drainage board for an internal drainage district may make a drainage rate in respect of agricultural land and buildings. Drainage rates are to be assessed and levied upon the occupiers of hereditaments in the district, subject to the proviso that the owner of a hereditament will be deemed to be its occupier during any period when it is unoccupied.[141]

Subject to provisions relating to the subdivision of districts and the power to grant exemptions from rating, a rate made by a drainage board for an internal district is to be assessed at a uniform amount per pound throughout the district on the annual value of the agricultural land or agricultural buildings in respect of which it is made. The annual value of any chargeable property is to be the amount which is equal to the yearly rent of the chargeable property at which the holding might reasonably be

---

[138] s.37(1) and (2).
[139] s.38(1) and (2).
[140] s.39(1) and (2).
[141] s.40(1) and (2). Generally, see Internal Drainage Boards (Finance) Regulations 1990, S.I. 1990 No.72.

expected to have been let, by a prudent and willing landlord to a prudent and willing tenant on specified terms.[142] In accordance with this formula every internal drainage board is to determine, not later than 31 December 1992, the annual value for each chargeable property in their district at that date. Where a determination is made, the board is to serve notice of the determination on the occupier of the property concerned together with a statement of a right of appeal.[143]

A power for an internal drainage board to grant exemptions from rating is provided for whereby, after consultation with the Authority, the board may order that no rates are to be levied on the occupier of hereditaments in any portion of their district. Similarly, an occupier of a hereditament in the district may request the board to exempt his property from rating, and where the request is refused the occupier may appeal to the Authority, or if the Authority is the board, the relevant Minister, who may direct the board to make or amend the order as requested.[144]

MISCELLANEOUS FINANCIAL PROVISIONS AND POWERS

Further financial provisions

Powers to borrow

An internal drainage board may borrow, on the security of their property or income, for the purpose of defraying any costs, charges or expenses incurred by them in the execution of their duties, or for the purpose of discharging any loan contracted by them. Similarly the council of any county or London borough and the Common Council of the City of London may borrow for purposes provided for under the Land Drainage Act 1991. However, the consent of the relevant Minister will be required for any borrowing by a board other than borrowing for

---

[142] s.41(1) and (2) Land Drainage Act 1991. The terms of the lease are set out in s.41(4).

[143] s.42(1) and (3). Rights of appeal against determinations are provided for under ss.45 and 46. On adjustment of annual values to secure a fair distribution of the rating burden see ss.43 and 44. See also Drainage Rates (Forms) Regulations 1990, S.I. 1990 No.173; and Drainage Rates (Appeals) Regulations 1970, S.I. 1970 No.1152.

[144] s.47 Land Drainage Act 1991.

the purpose of discharging a loan previously contracted, and money may not be borrowed for a period exceeding fifty years. Where money is borrowed in respect of which only some part of the district of a board will be liable, repayment may only be made out of rates or special levies or contributions received in respect of that part of the drainage district.[145]

Navigation tolls

The power of the National Rivers Authority to make an application for the imposition of navigation tolls will, in the case of waters within an internal drainage district which do not form a part of a main river, be exercisable by the drainage board for the district concurrently with the Authority. Accordingly, powers of the Authority to apply to the Secretary of State for an order to impose navigation tolls will be similarly exercisable by a board concurrently with respect to ordinary watercourses in their area.[146]

Contributions by the Authority

Where, by reason of the quantity of water which an internal drainage district receives from lands at a higher level, or the period that will elapse before the district obtains any relief from operations of the Authority on a main river, a board considers that contributions towards its expenses should be made by the Authority, the board may make an application to it for that purpose. The Authority may resolve to make a contribution to the board for these reasons. However, if the board is aggrieved by the resolution made by the Authority, or the council of any county or London borough is aggrieved that the contribution is excessive, the board or council may within six weeks of the notice of the resolution to the board appeal to the relevant Minister against the resolution. The Minister may, after considering objections and holding a public enquiry, make such an order as he thinks fit.[147]

---

[145] s.55(1) to (5).

[146] s.56. On the powers of the Authority in this respect see s.143 Water Resources Act 1991.

[147] s.57 Land Drainage Act 1991.

Allocation of Authority revenue

Where the National Rivers Authority is the internal drainage board for an internal drainage district, it may by resolution specify an amount corresponding to the amount of any contribution which, if it were not the drainage board for the district, it would make to that drainage board or require from the board. Accordingly, expenses incurred by the Authority as the drainage board are to be defrayed out of the revenue received by it otherwise than as the board, or expenses incurred by the Authority as such are to be defrayed out of sums received by it as the board.[148]

Ministerial grants

The appropriate Minster may make grants towards the expenditure incurred by internal drainage boards or by other drainage bodies except the Authority in the exercise of their functions in carrying out drainage schemes. Grants are to be of amounts, and subject to conditions, approved by the Treasury. Where a drainage body is about to incur expenditure in respect of any work which, if it is properly carried out, a grant would be payable, the Minister may, with the approval of the Treasury, make advances to that body on account of the expenditure. In addition, grants may be made to internal drainage boards or local authorities in respect of arrangements with other persons for carrying out drainage works.[149]

Local authority contributions and expenses

A local authority may contribute, or undertake to contribute, to the expenses of the carrying out or maintenance of any drainage works by a drainage body, such an amount as, having regard to the public benefit to be derived from the work, appears to the local authority to be proper, and it may borrow for this purpose.[150] Subject to express provision to the contrary, the expenses of the council of a metropolitan district or London borough under the Land Drainage Act 1991 are to be defrayed as general expenses or special expenses charged on such parts of the metropolitan district or borough as the council think fit.[151]

---

[148] s.58.

[149] s.59; and see Land Drainage (Grants) Regulations 1967, S.I. 1967 No.212.

[150] s.60 Land Drainage Act 1991.

[151] s.61.

Miscellaneous powers of internal drainage boards

Powers to acquire and dispose of land

An internal drainage board may, for any purpose in connection with the performance of any of its functions, acquire land inside or outside its district by agreement, or if authorised by the relevant Minister, acquire land compulsorily. The exercise of the powers conferred on local authorities,[152] is to be included in the purposes for which the council of any district or London borough or the common council of the City of London may be authorised by the Secretary of State to purchase land compulsorily. In either instance the Acquisition of Land Act 1981 is to apply to compulsory acquisition of land.[153]

An internal drainage board may dispose of land held by it in any manner it wishes. However, except with the consent of the relevant Minister, a board may not dispose of land otherwise than by way of a short tenancy,[154] for a consideration less than the best that can reasonably be obtained. Except with the consent of the relevant Minister, the board may not dispose of land, otherwise than by way of a short tenancy, which has been acquired by it compulsorily or acquired at a time when it was authorised to acquire it compulsorily.[155]

Powers of entry of internal drainage boards and local authorities

Any person authorised by an internal drainage board or local authority, after producing, if required, a duly authenticated document showing his authority, may exercise the following powers of entry: (a) to enter any land for the purpose of exercising any functions of the board or local authority under the Land Drainage Act 1991; (b) to enter and survey any land, including the interior of any mill through which water passes or in connection with which water is impounded, and take levels of the land and inspect the condition of drainage works on it; and (c) to inspect and take copies of any Acts of Parliament, awards or other documents which are in the possession of any internal drainage board,

[152] Under ss.14 to 17 and 66 Land Drainage Act 1991.

[153] s.62(1) to (3).

[154] "A short tenancy" consists of the grant of a term not exceeding seven years or the assignment of a term which at the date of assignment has not more than seven years to run (s.63(4)).

[155] s.63.

local authority or navigation authority, which relate to the drainage of land and confer any powers or impose any duties on that board or authority.[156]

A person entitled to enter in accordance with these provisions may take with him such other persons and equipment as may be necessary, but if the land is unoccupied he must leave it as effectually secured against trespassers as he found it. Except in an emergency, admission to any land may not be demanded, unless notice of the intended entry has been given to the occupier and, if the land is used for residential purposes or the demand is for admission with heavy equipment, that notice has been given not less than seven days before the demand was made. Where injury is sustained by any person by the exercise of the powers of entry, the board or authority will be liable to make full compensation to the injured person, and in a case of dispute the amount payable will be determined by the Lands Tribunal. If any person intentionally obstructs or impedes any person exercising a power of entry, he will be guilty of an offence and liable, on summary conviction, to a fine not exceeding £1,000.[157]

Regulations and byelaws

Each of the Ministers has the power to make regulations for the purposes of prescribing anything which may be prescribed under the Land Drainage Act 1991 and generally for the purpose of carrying the Act into effect.[158]

An internal drainage board or local authority and, in certain circumstances, a county council may make byelaws necessary for securing the efficient working of the drainage system in their district or area. Without prejudice to the generality of this, byelaws may be made for the purposes of (a) regulating the use and preventing the improper use of any watercourses, banks or works vested in them or under their control or for preserving them from destruction; (b) regulating the opening of sluices and flood gates in connection with works under (a); (c) preventing the obstruction of any watercourse vested in them or under their control by the discharge into it of any liquid or solid matter or by

---

[156] s.64(1).

[157] s.64(2) to (6).

[158] s.65.

reason of that matter being allowed to fall into it; (d) compelling persons having control of any watercourse vested in a board or local authority or under its control, or any watercourse flowing into that watercourse, to cut the vegetable growths in or on the bank of the watercourse and, when cut, to remove them. These powers to make byelaws are not to be exercisable by a board in connection with a main river, the banks of that river or any drainage works in connection with it, and they may be exercised by a local authority only so far as is necessary to prevent flooding or to remedy or mitigate any damage caused by flooding.[159]

Byelaws for these purposes will not be valid until they are confirmed by the relevant Minister, in relation to an internal drainage board, and in the case of byelaws made by a local authority, by the Minister in relation to England or the Secretary of State in relation to Wales in accordance with the detailed procedure set out in Schedule 5 to the Land Drainage Act 1991. A person who acts in contravention of, or who fails to comply with, a byelaw will be guilty of an offence and liable, on summary conviction, to a fine not exceeding £1,000 and to a further daily fine of £40 for every day after conviction on which the contravention or failure continues. Where a person acts in contravention of, or fails to comply with, a byelaw, a board or local authority may take action necessary to remedy the effect of the contravention and recover the expenses reasonably incurred by them in so doing.[160]

---

[159] s.66(1) to (3).

[160] s.66(5) to (7) .

Chapter 13

FISHERIES UNDER STATUTE

THE FISHERIES FUNCTION OF THE NATIONAL RIVERS AUTHORITY

The fisheries function

Amongst the principal functions of the National Rivers Authority is that relating to fisheries, which arises by virtue of Part V of the Water Resources Act 1991, the Diseases of Fish Act 1937, the Sea Fisheries Regulation Act 1966, the Salmon and Freshwater Fisheries Act 1975 and other enactments relating to fisheries.[1] Accordingly, it is stated to be the general fisheries duty of the Authority to maintain, improve and develop salmon fisheries, trout fisheries, freshwater fisheries and eel fisheries.[2]

The area in respect of which the Authority is to carry out its functions relating to fisheries is to be the whole of England and Wales together with (a) such part of the territorial sea adjacent to England and Wales as extends for six nautical miles from the baselines from which the breadth of that sea is measured; and (b) in relation to Part V of the Water Resources Act 1991, the Diseases of Fish Act 1937 and the Salmon and Freshwater Fisheries Act 1975, so much of the River Esk, with its banks and tributary streams up to their source as is situated in Scotland, but excluding the River Tweed.[3]

Ministerial powers and fisheries orders

Previously, the performance of the fisheries function of water authorities had been subject to the overall supervision of the Minister of Agriculture, Fisheries and Food with the Secretary of State for Wales exercising functions in relation to land and waters in the area of the water

---

[1] s.2(1)(d) Water Resources Act 1991.

[2] s.114.

[3] s.2(6). "The River Tweed" means "the river" within the meaning of the Tweed Fisheries Amendment Act 1859, as amended by byelaws (s.2(7) Water Resources Act 1991).

authority for Wales.[4] However, an amendment brought about under the Water Act 1989 provided that where any function of a Minister of the Crown under certain fishery enactments was exercised by different Ministers according to the water authority or water authority area in relation to which it was exercised, in future it was to be exercised concurrently by the Minister of Agriculture, Fisheries and Food and by the Secretary of State.[5] Accordingly, in the discussion which follows, references to "the Ministers" are to be understood as references to the two Ministers acting concurrently in relation to powers and duties under the Diseases of Fish Act 1937, the Sea Fisheries Regulation Act 1966, the Salmon and Freshwater Fisheries Act 1975 and local statutory provisions and subordinate legislation relating to fisheries.

The Ministers are empowered, on application made to them by the Authority, by order made by statutory instrument, to make provision in relation to fisheries in an area defined by the order for the modification (a) of any provisions of the Salmon and Freshwater Fisheries Act 1975 relating to the regulation of fisheries; (b) of the powers of the Authority relating to the acquisition of land for fisheries purposes;[6] and (c) of any provisions of a local Act relating to fisheries in that area. A Ministerial order of this kind may contain such supplemental, consequential and transitional provision, including payment of compensation to persons injuriously affected by the order, as is necessary or expedient in connection with the order, but no order is to apply to waters in respect of which a licence has been granted for the rearing of fish.[7]

Before an order is made the Ministers are to send the Authority a copy of the draft of the order and notify the Authority of the time within which, and the manner in which, objections to the draft order may be made to the Ministers. No order is to be made unless the Authority has caused notice of the Minister's intention to make the order, the place

---

[4] s.41(1) Salmon and Freshwater Fisheries Act 1975 defines "the Minister" to mean the Minister of Agriculture, Fisheries and Food, but the Transfer of Functions (Wales) (No.1) Order 1978, S.I. 1978 No.272, transferred functions to the Secretary of State for Wales in relation to land or waters in the area of the Welsh Water Authority.

[5] Sch.17 para.1(3) and (4) Water Act 1989.

[6] Under s.156 Water Resources Act 1991.

[7] s.115(1) and (2) Water Resources Act 1991. Licences for the rearing of fish are provided for under s.29 Salmon and Freshwater Fisheries Act 1975.

where copies of the draft may be inspected and obtained and notification of the time and manner in which objections may be made to be published in the *London Gazette* or any other manner which is best adapted for informing the persons affected. The Ministers are to consider any objections made and may cause a public local inquiry to be held with respect to them, and a statutory instrument containing the order will be subject to an annulment procedure in pursuance of a resolution of either House of Parliament.[8]

Where any fishery, land or foreshore proposed to be comprised under a Ministerial order, or any fishery proposed to be affected by the order, or any land over which it is proposed to acquire an easement, belongs to Her Majesty in right of the Crown or forms part of the possessions of the Duchy of Lancaster or Cornwall or belongs to, or is under the management of any government department, the order will require the consent of the appropriate authority. The "appropriate authority" means, in relation to the foreshore, the Crown Estate Commissioners; in the case of any foreshore, fishery or land forming part of the possessions of the Duchy of Lancaster, the Chancellor of the Duchy; in relation to any foreshore, fishery or land forming part of the possession of the Duchy of Cornwall, the Duke of Cornwall or persons empowered to dispose of land of the Duchy; in the case of any foreshore, fishery or land which belongs to or is under the management of a government department, that government department.[9]

Each of the Ministers has the power to provide by regulations that the provisions of Part V of the Water Resources Act 1991, or any other enactment relating to the carrying out by the Authority of its fisheries functions, are to have effect with modifications prescribed for the purpose of enabling the government of the United Kingdom to give effect to any Community obligations or any international agreement to which the United Kingdom is for the time being a party.[10]

---

[8] s.115(3) to (6) Water Resources Act 1991.

[9] s.115(7) and (8). For these purposes, the "foreshore" is defined to include the shore and bed of the sea and of every channel, creek, bay, estuary and navigable river as far as the tide flows (s.115(9)).

[10] s.116.

Regional and local fisheries advisory committees

The Authority is bound to establish and maintain advisory committees of persons who are not members of the Authority but appear to it to be interested in any fisheries of this kind in different parts of the area of the Authority, and to consult those committees as to the manner in which the Authority is to perform its duty to maintain, improve and develop fisheries. The duty to establish and maintain advisory committees requires the Authority to establish and maintain a regional advisory committee for each area of the Authority which it considers appropriate to regard as a region, and such local advisory committees as it considers necessary to represent the interests of persons interested in fisheries in the different parts of the region. It is the duty of the Authority, in determining the regions for which regional advisory committees are established and maintained, to ensure that one of those regions consists wholly, or mainly, of Wales.[11]

Fisheries contributions

Each of the Ministers has the power, on application to him by the Authority, to make provision by order for the imposition, on the owners and occupiers of fisheries in an area, of requirements to pay contributions to the Authority. Contributions are to be of amounts determined under the order in respect of the expenses of carrying out the Authority's functions in relation to fisheries in that area. Fisheries contributions are to be paid or recovered in a manner specified in the order, and are to be refundable in such circumstances as are specified in the order. The provisions relating to Ministerial orders, described above, are to have effect in relation to the power to create an order for fisheries contributions in the same way as they have effect for the purpose of modifying provisions of the Salmon and Freshwater Fisheries Act 1975 and other statutory provisions.[12]

---

[11] s.8(1) and (2).

[12] s.142, and see s.155 on Ministerial orders generally. The reference to owners and occupiers of fisheries is to have the same meaning as in the Salmon and Freshwater Fisheries Act 1975. Hence, "owner" includes any person who is entitled to receive rents from a fishery or premises, and "occupier", in relation to a fishery or premises,

Land acquisition for fisheries purposes

In accordance with the general power of the Authority to do anything which is incidental to its primary functions,[13] and particular powers which are given to it in relation to the compulsory purchase of land,[14] express powers are provided for the purchase or lease of land by agreement or, if authorised, compulsorily in relation to fisheries purposes. These powers relate to (a) any dam, fishing weir, fishing mill dam, fixed engine or other artificial obstruction and any fishery attached to or worked in connection with the obstruction; (b) so much of the bank adjoining a dam as may be necessary for making or maintaining a fish pass;[15] and (c) for the purpose of erecting and working a fixed engine, any fishery land or foreshore together with any easement over any adjoining land necessary for securing access. The Authority may either alter or remove an obstruction acquired in exercise of these powers, or by itself or its lessees use or work the obstruction for fishing purposes and exercise the right of fishery acquired in any lawful manner, subject to the provisions of any lease under which an obstruction is acquired.[16]

The power to make fishery byelaws

A power is given to the Authority to make byelaws for a range of purposes connected with its fishery functions.[17] A person who contravenes a byelaw made in accordance with these powers will be guilty of an offence and liable, on summary conviction, to a fine not

---

includes any person for the time being in actual possession of the fishery or premises (s.41(1) Salmon and Freshwater Fisheries Act 1975). On the ownership of fisheries generally see Ch.8 above.

[13] Under s.4 Water Resources Act 1991.

[14] Under s.154.

[15] The power of the Authority to construct and alter fish passes is provided for under s.10 Salmon and Freshwater Fisheries Act 1975.

[16] s.156 Water Resources Act 1991. Expressions used in relation to this power have the same meanings as under the Salmon and Freshwater Fisheries Act 1975 and are defined below.

[17] Under s.210 and Schs.25 and 26 Water Resources Act 1991. A water undertaker also has powers, subject to confirmation by the Secretary of State, to create byelaws regulating fishing, with respect to any waterway or associated land owned or managed by it (s.157(1) and (3) and Sch.10 Water Industry Act 1991).

exceeding £1,000. Similarly, provisions for byelaw offences under the Salmon and Freshwater Fisheries Act 1975 are to have effect so that any offence is punishable to the same extent.[18]

In relation to certain fisheries byelaws, special provision is made for the payment of compensation to persons adversely affected by them. Thus, where the owner or occupier of a fishery claims by notice to the Authority that the fishery is injuriously affected by a byelaw made for specified purposes, and that claim is made before the end of twelve months after the confirmation of the byelaw, the claim and the amount of compensation to be paid, by way of annual payment or otherwise, for the damage to the fishery is to be determined in default of agreement by a single arbitrator appointed by one of the Ministers. The purposes in relation to which compensation claims may be made relate to byelaws (a) prohibiting the use for taking salmon, trout, or freshwater fish of any instruments other than a fixed engine in waters, and at times, prescribed by the byelaw; (b) specifying the nets and other instruments other than fixed engines, which may be used for taking salmon, trout, freshwater fish and eels and imposing requirements as to the use of those nets and instruments; and (c) imposing requirements as to the construction, design, material and dimensions of any nets or instruments used for taking those fish including, in the case of nets, the size of mesh. Where compensation is payable by way of an annual payment under a compensation agreement, the Authority or the person entitled to the payment, may at any time after the end of five years from the date of the award require it to be reviewed by an arbitrator appointed by one of the Ministers. The compensation to be paid after the review is to be the amount determined by the arbitrator.[19]

Fishery byelaw purposes

The Authority has the power, in relation to any part or parts of the area in relation to which it carries out fisheries functions under Part V of the Water Resources Act 1991, to make byelaws generally for the purposes of the better execution of the Salmon and Freshwater Fisheries Act 1975 and the better protection, preservation and improvement of any

---

[18] s.211(3) and (6) Water Resources Act 1991.
[19] s.212.

salmon fisheries, trout fisheries, freshwater fisheries and eel fisheries. In addition to the general power to make byelaws, a range of specified powers allow byelaws to be made for particular purposes. These purposes are: (a) prohibiting the taking or removal from any water, without lawful authority, of any fish, whether alive or dead; (b) prohibiting or regulating (i) the taking or trout or any freshwater fish of a size less than prescribed by the byelaw, or (ii) the taking of fish by any means within a specified distance above or below any dam or other obstruction, whether artificial or natural; (c) prohibiting the use for taking salmon, trout or freshwater fish of any instrument other than a fixed engine in prescribed waters and at prescribed times; (d) specifying the nets and other instruments other than fixed engines which may be used for taking salmon, trout, freshwater fish and eels, imposing requirements as to the use of those nets and instruments and regulating the use, in connection with fishing with rod and line, of any specified lure or bait; (e) authorising the placing and use of fixed engines at prescribed places, and in a prescribed manner;[20] (f) imposing requirements as to the construction, design, material and dimensions of nets, instruments or engines mentioned in (d) to (e) above, including in the case of nets the size of mesh; (g) requiring and regulating the attachment to licensed nets and instruments of marks, labels or numbers, or the painting of marks or numbers or the affixing of labels or numbers to boats, coracles or other vessels used in fishing; (h) prohibiting the carrying in any boat or vessel whilst being used in fishing for salmon or trout of any net which is not licensed, or which is without a prescribed mark, label or number; and (i) prohibiting or regulating the carrying in a boat or vessel during the annual close season for salmon of a net capable of taking salmon, other than a net commonly used in the area for sea fishing and carried in a boat or vessel commonly used for that purpose.[21]

---

[20] The Authority may not make any byelaws by virtue of this provision in relation to any place within a sea fisheries district of a local fisheries committee except with the consent of that committee (Sch.25 para.6(7)). On local fisheries committees see p.457 below.

[21] Sch.25 para.6(1) and (2). In relation to these powers, and other powers to make byelaws under Sch.25 para.6, byelaws may be made to apply to the whole or any parts of the year, and expressions used have the same meanings as under Salmon and Freshwater Fisheries Act 1975 (Sch.25 para.6(6) and (7) Water Resources Act 1991).

Subject to provisions under the Salmon and Freshwater Fisheries Act 1975 providing for a *duty* upon the Authority to make byelaws about the close season for fishing,[22] the Authority has the *power,* in relation to any part or parts of its fishery area, to make byelaws (a) fixing or altering any close season under the 1975 Act; (b) dispensing with a close season for freshwater fish or rainbow trout; (c) determining for the purposes of the 1975 Act the period of the year during which gratings need not be maintained; (d) prohibiting or regulating fishing with rod and line between the end of the first hour after sunset on any day and the beginning of the last hour before sunrise on the following morning; (e) determining the time during which it is lawful to use a gaff in connection with fishing with rod and line for salmon or migratory trout; (f) authorising fishing with rod and line for eels during the annual close season for freshwater fish.[23]

The Authority has the power, within any part or parts of its fishery area, to make byelaws for the purpose of regulating the deposit or discharge in any waters containing fish of any specified liquid or solid matter which is detrimental to salmon, trout or freshwater fish, or to the spawn or food of fish. In relation to this power, however, the Authority may not make a byelaw so as to prejudice any powers of a sewerage undertaker to discharge sewage in pursuance of any power given by public general Act, a local Act or a provision confirmed by Parliament.[24]

The Authority also has the power, in relation to its fishery area, to make byelaws for the purpose of requiring persons to send to the Authority returns, in such form, giving specified particulars at specified times (a) of the period or periods during which they have fished for salmon, trout, freshwater fish or eels; (b) of whether they have taken any; and (c) if they have, of what they have taken.[25]

---

[22] Under Sch.1 Salmon and Freshwater Fisheries Act 1975.

[23] Sch.25 para.6(3) Water Resources Act 1991.

[24] Sch.25 para.6(4) and (7).

[25] Sch.25 para.6(5).

THE SALMON AND FRESHWATER FISHERIES ACT 1975

The Salmon and Freshwater Fisheries Act 1975 came into force on 1 August 1975,[26] and has been amended by subsequent provisions under the Salmon Act 1986 and the Water Act 1989, with the Water Act amendments consolidated under the Water Resources Act 1991 along with other presentational changes in the law. However, despite the amendments, the 1975 Act remains the most important provision in relation to the fisheries function of the Authority. The Act deals with prohibition of certain modes of taking or destroying fish, under Part I; obstructions to the passage of fish, under Part II; times of fishing and selling and exporting fish, under Part III; fishing licences, under Part IV; administration and enforcement, under Part V; and miscellaneous and supplemental matters, under Part VI. These matters are considered under the following sections of this work.

Prohibition of certain modes of taking or destroying fish

Prohibited implements

No person may use any of the following instruments for the purpose of taking or killing salmon, trout or freshwater fish:[27] (1) a firearm within the meaning of the Firearms Act 1968;[28] (2) an otter lath or jack, wire or snare;[29] (3) a crossline or setline;[30] (4) a spear, gaff,

---

[26] s.43(2) Salmon and Freshwater Fisheries Act 1975. Certain parts of the 1975 Act contain provisions re-enacted from earlier legislation including Salmon and Freshwater Fishery Acts of 1972 and 1923, and Salmon Fishery Act 1861.

[27] s.1(1)(a) Salmon and Freshwater Fisheries Act 1975. "Salmon" means all fish of the salmon species and includes part of a salmon. "Trout" means any fish of the salmon family commonly known as trout and includes migratory trout and char. "Migratory trout" means trout which migrate to and from the sea. "Freshwater fish" means any fish living in fresh water exclusive of salmon and trout and of any kinds of fish which migrate to and from tidal water and of eels, and "eels" includes elvers and the fry of eels (s.41(1)).

[28] "Firearm" means a lethal barrelled weapon of any description from which any shot, bullet or other missile can be discharged (s.57(1) Firearms Act 1968).

[29] "Otter lath or jack" includes any small boat or vessel, board or stick, or other instrument, whether used with a hand line, or as an auxiliary to a rod and line, or otherwise for the purpose of running out lures, artificial or otherwise (s.1(3) Salmon

stroke–haul, snatch or other like instrument;[31] (5) a light. It is also an offence for a person to have in his possession any of these instruments intending to use it to take or kill salmon, trout or freshwater fish, or to throw or discharge any stone or other missile for the purpose of taking or killing, or facilitating the taking or killing of any salmon, trout or freshwater fish.[32] A person who contravenes these provisions is guilty of an offence unless he proves to the satisfaction of the court that the act was done for the purpose of the preservation or development of a private fishery and with the previous written consent of the Authority. By way of exception, however, no offence is committed where a person uses a gaff consisting of a plain metal hook without a barb, or a tailer, as auxiliary to angling with rod and line, or has in his possession a gaff or tailer intending to use it for that purpose.[33]

Roe, spawning and unclean fish

Any person who, for the purpose of fishing for salmon, trout or freshwater fish, uses any fish roe, or buys, sells, or exposes for sale, or has in his possession any roe of salmon or trout is guilty of an offence.[34] A person who knowingly[35] takes, kills or injures, or attempts to take, kill or injure salmon, trout or freshwater fish which is unclean or immature,[36]

---

and Freshwater Fisheries Act 1975). On the meaning of "otter" see *Allen v. Parker*, (1891) 30 L.R. Ir. 87.

30 "Crossline" means a fishing line reaching from bank to bank across water and having attached to it one or more lures or baited hooks, and "setline" means a fishing line left unattended in water and having attached to it one or more lures or baited hooks (s.1(3)). On "night lines" see *Barnard v. Roberts*, (1907) 71 J.P. 277.

31 "Stroke–haul or snatch" includes any instrument or device, whether used with a rod and line or otherwise, for the purpose of foul hooking any fish (s.1(3) and see *Prescott v. Hutin*, (1966) 110 S.J. 905). On the meaning of "instrument" see *Jones v. Davies*, (1902) 86 L.T. 447; *Maw v. Holloway*, [1914] 3 K.B. 594.

32 s.1(1)(b) and (c) Salmon and Freshwater Fisheries Act 1975.

33 s.1(4), and see *Wedderburn v. Duke of Atholl*, (1900) A.C. 403.

34 s.2(1) Salmon and Freshwater Fisheries Act 1975.

35 Although ignorance of fact may amount to a defence, see *Hopton v. Thirwell,* (1863) 9 L.T. 327, and on evidence of intention, see *Davies v. Evans,* (1902) 86 L.T. 419.

36 "Immature" in relation to salmon means that the salmon is of a length less than twelve inches measured from the tip of the snout to the fork or cleft of the tail, and in relation to any other fish means that the fish is of a length less than that, if any, prescribed by byelaw. "Unclean" in relation to any fish means that the fish is about

or who buys, sells or exposes for sale, or has in his possession any such fish or part of such fish is guilty of an offence. This offence is subject to the exception that it will not apply to any person who takes a fish accidentally and returns it to the water with the least possible injury.[37] The wilful disturbance of any spawn or spawning fish, or the bed of any bank or shallow on which any spawn or spawning fish may be is an offence subject to the exercise of a legal right to take materials from any waters.[38] In respect of the offences concerning roe, unclean or immature fish, and disturbing spawning fish, a person will not be guilty of the offences if he does an act for the purpose of the artificial propagation of salmon, trout or freshwater fish or for some scientific purpose or for the purpose of the preservation or development of a private fishery and he has obtained the previous permission of the Authority.[39]

Nets

It is an offence for a person to shoot or work a seine or draft net for salmon or migratory trout in any waters across more than three-fourths of the width of those waters. It is also an offence for a person, except in a place where smaller dimensions are authorised by byelaws, to take or attempt to take salmon or migratory trout with any net having a mesh of less dimensions than two inches in extension from knot to knot, with the measurement being made on each side of the square, or eight inches measured round each mesh when wet. This offence does not arise in relation to a landing net which is used as an auxiliary to angling with rod and line. The placing of two or more nets one behind the other or

---

to spawn or has recently spawned and has not recovered from spawning (s.41(1) Salmon and Freshwater Fisheries Act 1975). In *Pyle v. Welsh Water Authority*, ((1986) unreported Carmarthen Crown Court 17 March 1986) the court held that a gravid fish, which an expert thought might be up to 10 days before spawning, was "about to spawn" for the purposes of this offence. See *Wells v. Hardy*, ([1964] 1 All E.R. 953) on the meaning of "taking" in relation to this offence.

[37] s.2(2) and (3) Salmon and Freshwater Fisheries Act 1975.

[38] s.2(4). However, s.42(8) states that nothing in the Act is to affect the legal right of persons to dredge, scour, cleanse or improve any navigable river, canal or other inland navigation. See *Proctor v. Avon and Dorset River Board*, (1953) C.P.L. 562. On the disturbance of spawning fish by canoeists see *Welsh Water Authority v. Crowther*, (1988) unreported Chester Crown Court 4 November 1988.

[39] s.2(5) Salmon and Freshwater Fisheries Act 1975.

near to each other in such a manner as practically to diminish the mesh of the nets used, or the covering of the nets used with canvas, or the using of any other device so as to evade the minimum mesh size will amount to a contravention of that prohibition.[40]

Poisonous matter and polluting effluent

It is an offence for a person to cause or knowingly permit to flow,[41] or to put or knowingly permit to be put, into any water containing fish, or into any tributaries of those waters,[42] any liquid or solid matter to such an extent as to cause the waters to be poisonous or injurious to fish or the spawning grounds, spawn or food of fish. However, no offence is committed by the exercise of any legal right or the continuation of a method in use in connection with the same premises prior to 18 July 1923 if the best practicable means have been used within a reasonable cost to prevent such matter from doing injury to fish or to the spawning grounds, spawn or food of fish.[43] In addition, proceedings in relation to this offence may only be instituted by the Authority or by a person who has first obtained a certificate from the Minister that he has a material interest in the waters alleged to be affected. Moreover, no person will be guilty of an offence of causing pollution under these provisions in respect of any entry of matter into any controlled waters which occurs under and in accordance with a consent under Chapter II of Part III of the Water Resources Act 1991 or as a result of any act or omission under and in accordance with that consent.[44]

---

[40] s.3. On the use of nets see *Davies v. Evans*, (1902) 86 L.T. 419; *Dodd v. Armor*, (1867) 31 J.P. 773; *Moses v. Raywood*, [1911] 2 K.B. 271; *Alexander v. Tonkin*, [1979] 2 All E.R. 1009.

[41] On "cause or knowingly permit" see *Alphacell Ltd. v. Woodward*, [1972] 2 All E.R. 1475, distinguishing *Moses v. Midland Rly. Co.*, (1915) 84 L.J.K.B. 2181; *Price v. Cromack*, [1975] 2 All E.R. 113; on "knowingly permit" see *West Riding of Yorkshire Council v. Holmfirth*, [1894] 2 Q.B. 842; and generally see p.297 above.

[42] For cases on the meaning of "tributary" see *Merricks v. Cadwallader*, (1881) 46 L.T. 29; *Hall v. Reid*, (1882) 48 L.T. 221; *Harbottle v. Terry*, (1882) 47 J.P.136; *George v. Carpenter*, [1893] 1 Q.B. 505; *Evans v. Owen*, [1895] 1 Q.B. 273; *Stead v. Nicholas*, [1901] 2 K.B. 163; *Cook v. Clareborough*, (1903) 70 J.P. 252; *Moses v. Iggo*, [1906] 1 K.B. 516.

[43] s.4(1) and (2) Salmon and Freshwater Fisheries Act 1975.

[44] Sch.1 para.30(1) Water Consolidation (Consequential Provisions) Act 1991. On discharge consents generally see p.304 above.

Explosives, poisons, electrical devices and destruction of dams

No person may use in or near any waters, including waters adjoining the coast of England and Wales to a distance of six nautical miles measured from the baselines from which the breadth of the territorial sea is measured, any explosive substance, any poison or other noxious substance, or any electrical device, with intent thereby to take or destroy fish.[45] A person who contravenes these provisions or who, for the purpose of doing so, has in his possession any explosive or noxious substance or any electrical device is guilty of an offence.[46]

Exceptions to this offence arise where a person uses a substance or device for a scientific purpose or for protecting, improving or replacing stocks of fish and with the permission of the Authority. In respect of the use of a noxious substance, the permission of the Authority may not be given otherwise than with the approval of the Minister.[47] Where this permission is given it will also serve as a defence to the offences relating to the entry of matter which is poisonous or injurious to fish,[48] contravention of fishery byelaws[49] and also the general pollution control offence[50] of causing or knowingly permitting the entry of polluting matter into controlled waters.[51] It is an offence for a person, without lawful excuse, to destroy or damage any dam,[52] flood-gate or sluice with intent to take or destroy fish.[53]

---

[45] s.5(1) Salmon and Freshwater Fisheries Act 1975, as amended by s.9(1) and Sch.2 para.20 Fishery Limits Act 1976. On the meanings of "baselines" and "territorial sea" see p.26 above.

[46] s.5(4) Salmon and Freshwater Fisheries Act 1975.

[47] s.5(2). "Poison or noxious material" has been held to encompass anything put into water which was injurious to the health or life of fish or which rendered their capture more easy (*R. v. Antrim Justices*, [1906] 2 I.R. 298).

[48] Under s.4(1) Salmon and Freshwater Fisheries Act 1975, see above.

[49] Under s.210 and Sch.25 para.6(4) Water Resources Act 1991, see p.235 above.

[50] Under s.85(1) Water Resources Act 1991, see p.295 above.

[51] s.5(5) Salmon and Freshwater Fisheries Act 1975.

[52] "Dam" includes any weir or other fixed obstruction used for the purpose of damming up water (s.41(1)).

[53] s.5(3).

Obstructions to the passage of fish

Fixed engines

A person who places or uses an unauthorised fixed engine in any inland or tidal waters[54] will be guilty of an offence.[55] "Fixed engine" is defined to include (a) stake net, bag net, putt, putcher; (b) any fixed implement or engine for taking or facilitating the taking of fish; (c) any net secured by anchors and any net or other implement for taking fish fixed to the soil, or made stationary in any other way; and (d) any net placed or suspended in any inland or tidal waters unattended by the owner or a person duly authorised by the owner to use the same for taking salmon or trout, and any engine, device, machine or contrivance, whether floating or otherwise, for placing or suspending that net or maintaining it in working order or making it stationary.[56] An "unauthorised fixed engine" means any fixed engine other than (a) a fixed engine certified in pursuance of the Salmon Fishery Act 1865 to be a privileged fixed engine; (b) a fixed engine which was in use for taking salmon or migratory trout during the open season of 1861, in pursuance of an ancient right or mode of fishing as lawfully exercised during that open season, by virtue of any grant or charter or immemorial usage;[57] (c) a fixed engine the placing and use of which is authorised by byelaws made by the Authority or local fisheries committee by virtue of the

---

[54] On "tidal waters" see *Ingram v. Percival*, [1968] 3 W.L.R. 663; and see p.25 above.

[55] s.6(1), as amended by s.33(1) Salmon Act 1986.

[56] s.41(1) Salmon and Freshwater Fisheries Act 1975. On fixed engines generally see *Holford v. George*, (1868) 32 J.P. 468; *Thomas v. Jones*, (1864) 29 J.P. 55; *Birch v. Turner*, (1864) 29 J.P. 37; *Percival v. Stanton*, [1954] 1 All E.R. 392; *Gore v. Special Commissioners for English Fisheries*, (1871) 33 J.P. 405; *Vance v. Frost*, (1894) 58 J.P. 398; *Lyne v. Leonard*, (1868) 32 J.P. 422; *Watts v. Lucas*, (1871) 35 J.P. 579; *Champion v. Maughan*, [1984] 1 All E.R. 680; *Gray v. Blamey*, (1990) *The Times* 4 June 1990.

[57] On the legality of ancient fishing weirs and dams see *Robson v. Robinson*, (1783) 3 Doug. K.B. 306; *Williams v. Wilcox*, (1838) 8 Ad. & El. 314; *Rolle v. Whyte*, (1868) L.R. 3 Q.B. 286; *Leconfield v. Lonsdale*, (1870) L.R. 5 C.P. 657; *Pirie and Sons Ltd. v. Kintore*, [1906] A.C. 468; *Fraser v. Fear*, (1912) 107 L.T.423. On "immemorial usage" see *Bevins v. Bird*, (1865) 12 L.T. 304; *Olding v. Wild*, (1866) 14 L.T. 402.

Salmon Act 1986;[58] or (d) a fixed engine which is placed and used by the Authority with the consent of, or in accordance with a general authorisation given by, the Minister or the Secretary of State.[59] A person acting under directions given by the Authority may take possession of or destroy an engine placed or used in contravention of this provision.[60]

Fishing weirs

No unauthorised fishing weir may be used for taking or facilitating the taking of salmon or migratory trout. "Unauthorised", for these purposes, means that the weir was not lawfully in use on 6 August 1861 by virtue of a grant or charter or immemorial usage. A fishing weir extending more than halfway across a river at its lowest state of water must not be used for taking salmon or migratory trout unless it has a free gap or opening in the deepest part of the river between the points where it is intercepted by the weir and (a) the sides of the gap are in line with and parallel to the direction of the stream at the weir; (b) the bottom of the gap is level with the natural bed of the river above and below the gap; and (c) the width of the gap in its narrowest part is not less than one–tenth part of the width of the river. A free gap must not be more than 40 feet wide and must not be less than 3 feet wide. A person using a weir in contravention of this provision or making any alteration in the bed of a river in such a manner as to reduce the flow of water through a free gap is guilty of an offence.[61]

---

[58] s.6(3) Salmon and Freshwater Fisheries Act 1975, as amended. (d) was added by s.33(2) Salmon Act 1986. s.33(3) Salmon Act 1986 enabled byelaws to be made by the Authority authorising the placing of certain fixed engines (now see Sch.25 para.6(2)(e) Water Resources Act 1991). s.37(2) Salmon Act 1986 provided local fisheries committees with the power to make byelaws to authorise the placing and use of certain fixed engines (amending s.5 Sea Fisheries Regulation Act 1966). See p.457 below on the powers of local sea fisheries committees.

[59] Added by Sch.17 para.7(3) Water Act 1989.

[60] s.6(2) Salmon and Freshwater Fisheries Act 1975.

[61] s.7. "Fishing weir" means any erection, structure or obstruction fixed to the soil either temporarily or permanently, across or partly across a river or branch of a river, and used for the exclusive purpose of taking or facilitating the taking of fish (s.41(1)).

Fishing mill dams

No unauthorised fishing mill dam may be used for taking or facilitating the taking of salmon or migratory trout.[62] "Unauthorised", for these purposes, means a fishing mill dam which was not lawfully in use on 6 August 1861 by virtue of a grant or charter or immemorial usage. A fishing mill dam must not be used for taking salmon or migratory trout unless it has a fish pass of such form and dimensions as approved by the Minister and is maintained in such a condition, and has constantly running through it a flow of water, that will enable fish to pass up or down. A person who uses an unauthorised fishing mill dam, or attempts to use a dam without a fish pass as described, is guilty of an offence. If a fishing mill dam does not have a fish pass attached to it as required by law, the right to use the dam for taking fish is deemed to have ceased and is forever forfeited, and the Authority may remove from it any cage, crib, trap, box, cruive or other obstruction to the free passage of the fish.[63]

Duty to make and maintain fish passes

Under certain circumstances a duty to make and maintain a fish pass may arise in relation to waters frequented by salmon or migratory trout. Specifically, this duty arises where (a) a new dam is constructed or an existing dam is raised or otherwise altered so as to cause increased obstruction to the passage of those fish, or any other obstruction to their passage is created, increased or caused; or (b) a dam, which from any cause has been destroyed or taken down to the extent of one half of its length, has been rebuilt or reinstated. In these circumstances the owner or occupier of the dam or obstruction, on being required to do so by the Authority, must make and maintain a fish pass for those fish of such form and dimensions as the Minister approves. Failure to do so renders the owner or occupier guilty of an offence. In the event of default by the owner or occupier the Authority is empowered to do any work required,

---

[62] s.8(1). "Fishing mill dam" means a dam used or intended to be used partly for the purpose of taking or facilitating the taking of fish, partly for the purpose of supplying water for milling or other purposes. "Mill" includes any erection for the purpose of developing water power, and the expression "milling" has a corresponding meaning (s.41(1)). For cases on the meaning of "fishing mill dam" see *Garnett v. Backhouse*, (1867) 8 B. & S. 490; *Pike v. Rossiter*, (1877) 37 L.T. 635; *Moulton v. Wilby*, (1863) 2 H. & C. 25; *Rossiter v. Pike*, (1878) 4 Q.B.D. 24.

[63] s.8(2) to (5) Salmon and Freshwater Fisheries Act 1975.

and for that purpose may enter upon the dam or obstruction and recover its expenses from the person in default.[64]

Power of the Authority to construct and alter fish passes

The Authority may, with the consent of the Minister, construct and maintain a dam, or in connection with a dam, a fish pass of a form and dimensions approved by the Minister. This power is exercisable subject to the proviso that no injury is done to the milling power, or water supply of or to any navigable river, canal or other inland navigation. The Authority may, with Ministerial consent, abolish or alter, or restore to its former state of efficiency, any existing fish pass or free gap, or substitute another fish pass or free gap, providing that no injury is done to the other water users described. If any person injures a new or existing fish pass constructed or altered by the Authority, he will be bound to pay expenses incurred by the Authority in repairing the injury.[65]

Minister's consents and approvals for fish passes

Any approval or consent which may be given by the Minister to or in relation to a fish pass may be given provisionally until he notifies the applicant that the fish pass is functioning satisfactorily. The Minister may revoke a consent or approval which has been given provisionally after giving the applicant not less that 90 days' notice of his intention to do so. Where the Minister approves a fish pass and does not revoke his approval, the fish pass is deemed to be in conformity with the requirements of the Salmon and Freshwater Fisheries Act 1975.[66]

Injuring or obstructing a fish pass or free gap

Various activities involving the injury or obstruction of a fish pass or free gap amount to an offence. These are if a person (a) wilfully alters or injures a fish pass; (b) does any act whereby salmon or trout are obstructed or liable to be obstructed in using a fish pass or whereby a fish pass is rendered less efficient; (c) alters a dam or the bed or banks of the river so as to render a fish pass less efficient; or (d) uses any contrivance or does any act whereby salmon or trout are in any way liable to be

---

[64] s.9.

[65] s.10.

[66] s.11.

scared, hindered or prevented from passing through a fish pass. In any of these cases a person guilty of the offence will be bound to pay any expenses which may be incurred in restoring the fish pass to its former state of efficiency. The owner or occupier of a dam will be deemed to have altered it if it is damaged, destroyed or allowed to fall into a state of disrepair and, if after notice is served on him by the Authority, he fails to repair or reconstruct it within a reasonable time so as to render the fish pass as efficient as before the damage or destruction. Similarly, if any person (a) does any act for the purpose of preventing salmon or trout from passing through a fish pass, or takes, or attempts to take, any salmon or trout in its passage through a fish pass; or (b) places any obstruction, uses any contrivance or does any act whereby salmon or trout may be scared, deterred or in any way prevented from freely entering and passing up and down a free gap at all periods of the year, he will be guilty of an offence.[67]

Sluices

Any sluice for drawing off water which would otherwise flow over any dam in waters frequented by salmon or migratory trout is to be kept shut on Sundays, and at all times when the water is not required for milling purposes, in such a manner as to cause the water to flow through any fish pass in or connected with the dam or, if there is no fish pass, over the dam. It is an offence to fail to shut a sluice in this manner unless permission to keep it open is granted by the Authority. However, the requirement to shut sluices will not prevent a person opening a sluice for the purpose of letting off water in cases of flood or for milling purposes or when necessary for the purpose of navigation or, subject to previous notice having been given to the Authority, for cleaning or repairing the dam or mill or its appurtenances.[68]

Gratings

Where water is diverted from waters frequented by salmon or migratory trout by means of a conduit or artificial channel, and the diverted water is used for the purpose of a water or canal undertaking or

---

[67] s.12, and see *Devonshire v. Drohan*, [1900] 2 I.R. 161 on the nature of a "free gap".
[68] s.13.

for the purpose of any mill, the owner of the undertaking or the occupier of the mill is bound to place and maintain a grating or gratings across the conduit or channel for the purpose of preventing the descent of salmon or migratory trout. This requirement is subject to the exception that exemption from the obligation may be granted by the Authority. Again subject to the power of the Authority to grant an exemption, gratings must also be placed and maintained across conduits or channels to prevent salmon or migratory trout entering the outfall from a water diversion. In either case, failure to place or maintain a grating is an offence, subject to the suspension of this obligation during any period which may be prescribed by byelaw. Gratings are to be constructed and placed in a manner and position approved by the Minister, and are not to be placed in such a manner as to interfere with the passage of boats on any navigable canal.[69]

Boxes and cribs in weirs and dams

No fishing weir or fishing mill dam may be used for taking salmon or migratory trout by means of cribs or boxes unless these comply with the requirements of the Salmon and Freshwater Fisheries Act 1975. These require that (a) the upper surface of the sill of a box or crib must be level with the bed of the river; (b) the bars or inscales of the heck or upstream side of the box or crib (i) must not be nearer than two inches; (ii) must be capable of being removed; and (iii) must be placed perpendicularly; and (c) there must not be attached to any such box or crib any spur or tail wall, leader or outrigger of a greater length than 20 feet from the upper or lower side of the box or crib.[70]

Restrictions on taking salmon or trout above or below an obstruction

It is an offence to take or kill, or to attempt to take or kill, except with rod and line, or to scare or disturb any salmon or trout within certain proximities of obstructions or mill races. Specifically this offence is committed (a) at any place above or below any dam or any obstruction, whether artificial or natural, which hinders or retards the passage of salmon or trout, being within 50 yards above or 100 yards below the dam or obstruction, or within such other distance from the dam or obstruction

[69] s.14, and see *R. v. Recorder and Justices for Londonderry*, [1930] N.I. 104.
[70] s.16.

as may be prescribed by byelaws; (b) in any waters under or adjacent to any mill, or in the head race or tail race of any mill, or in any waste race or pool communicating with a mill; or (c) in any artificial channel connected with any such dam or obstruction.[71] These prohibitions do not apply to any legal fishing mill dam not having a crib, box or cruive, or to any fishing box, coop, apparatus, net or mode of fishing in connection with, and forming part of, the dam or obstruction for purposes of fishing. Where a fish pass approved by the Minister is for the time being attached to a dam or obstruction, these provisions are not to be enforced in respect of the dam or obstruction until compensation has been made by the Authority to the persons entitled to fish in the waters for that right of fishery.[72]

Times of fishing and selling and exporting fish

Close seasons and times: salmon

Subject to any byelaws to the contrary, the general annual close season for salmon is the period between 31 August and 1 February; the period between 31 October and 1 February for angling with rod and line; and for fishing with putts and putchers, the period between 31 August and 1 May. The weekly close time for salmon is from 6 a.m. on Saturday to 6 a.m. on Monday.[73] Any person fishing for, taking, killing or attempting to take or kill salmon (a) except with a rod and line or putts and putchers, during the annual close season or weekly close time; (b) with a rod and line during the annual close season for rod and line; or (c) with putts and putchers during the annual close season for putts and putchers, is guilty of an offence. By way of exception, however, no offence is committed in respect of any act done for the purpose of artificial propagation of fish, or for some scientific purpose, if the previous permission of the Authority has been obtained.[74] It has also been established that an intention to catch salmon must be shown for this

---

[71] On "adjacent" see *Wellington Corp. v. Lower Hutt Corp.*, [1904] A.C. 775, and generally see *Moulton v. Wilby*, (1863) 27 J.P. 536; *Onions v. Clarke*, (1917) 81 J.P. 77.

[72] s.17 Salmon and Freshwater Fisheries Act 1975.

[73] s.19(1) and Sch.1 para.6, and see *Ruther v. Harris*, (1876) 40 J.P. 454.

[74] s.19(2) and (3).

offence to be committed. Hence, where a fisherman staked out nets to catch sea fish, during the close season for salmon, but later found salmon had been caught in the net, he was found not guilty of the offence of fishing for salmon during the close season.[75]

Fixed engines must be removed or rendered incapable of taking or obstructing the passage of salmon during the annual close season and during the close season for putts and putchers, and also during the weekly close time except in the case of putts and putchers. No obstructions may be placed in a river during the annual close season or weekly close time, or any contrivance used or any act done, for the purpose of deterring salmon or migratory trout from passing up the river. In relation to the placing of obstructions, however, it is a defence for a person to show that the obstruction, contrivance or act, as the case may be, was undertaken in the course of legally fishing for fish other than salmon or migratory trout.[76]

Close seasons and times: trout

Subject to any byelaws to the contrary, the annual close season for trout other than rainbow trout is the period between 31 August and 1 March, and the annual close season for rod and line fishing is the period between 30 September and 1 March. The weekly close time for trout is from 6 a.m. on Saturday until 6 a.m. on the following Monday. Any person who fishes for, takes, kills or attempts to take or kill trout other than rainbow trout (a) except with a rod an line, during the annual close season or weekly close time for trout; or (b) with a rod and line during the annual trout close season for rod and line will be guilty of an offence.[77] This offence is subject to the exception that it will not be committed in respect of any act done for the purpose of the artificial propagation of fish or the stocking or restocking of waters, or for some scientific purpose,[78] if he has obtained the previous permission of the Authority.[79] As in relation to salmon, the placing of any obstruction in a

---

[75] *Cain v. Campbell,* [1978] Crim L.R. 292.

[76] s.20 Salmon and Freshwater Fisheries Act 1975, and see *Hodgson v. Little*, (1864) 143 E.R. 1101; *Bell v. Wyndham*, (1865) 29 J.P. 214.

[77] s.19(1) and (4) and Sch.1 para.6.

[78] See *Price v. Bradley*, (1885) 50 J.P. 150.

[79] s.19(5) Salmon and Freshwater Fisheries Act 1975.

river during the close season or weekly close time for the purpose of deterring migratory trout from passing up a river is an offence.[80]

Sale, export and consignment of salmon and trout

It is an offence for a person to buy, sell or expose for sale, or to have in his possession for sale,[81] salmon between 31 August and 1 February. However, this offence is subject to the exceptions that no offence is committed if the salmon has been (a) canned, frozen, cured, salted, pickled, dried or otherwise preserved outside the United Kingdom; (b) so treated in the United Kingdom between 1 February and 31 August; (c) caught outside the United Kingdom; or (d) caught as a clean salmon within such limits if its capture by net, instrument or other device was lawful at the time and in the place where it was caught. The burden of proving that any salmon bought, sold, exposed for sale or in the possession of any person for sale comes within one of the exceptions will lie on the person buying, selling or exposing it for sale, or having it in his possession for sale.[82]

The sale of trout other than rainbow trout is subject to the restriction that it is an offence for a person to buy, sell or expose for sale or to have in possession for sale any trout between 31 August and 1 March. As with salmon, however, this offence is subject to the exceptions that no offence is committed if the trout has been (a) canned, frozen, cured, salted, pickled, dried or otherwise preserved outside the United Kingdom; (b) so treated in the United Kingdom between 1 March and 31 August; (c) caught outside the United Kingdom; or (d) caught as a clean trout within such limits if its capture by net, instrument or other device was lawful at the time and in the place where it was caught. Again, the burden of showing any of these exceptions lies upon the person so claiming. Specifically in relation to trout, however, a person will not be guilty of the offence in respect of any act done for the artificial propagation of fish, or the stocking or restocking of waters, or for some scientific purpose.[83]

---

[80] s.20(3).

[81] Actual physical possession is not necessary, see *M'Attee v. Hogg*, (1903) 5 F. (Ct. of Sess.) 67; see also *Birkett v. McGlassons Ltd.*, [1957] 1 All E.R. 369.

[82] s.22(1) to (4) Salmon and Freshwater Fisheries Act 1975.

[83] s.22(1) to (4).

It is unlawful for unclean salmon or trout, or salmon or trout caught during the time when their sale is prohibited, to be exported or entered for export. Salmon and Trout intended for export between 31 August and 1 May must be entered for that purpose with the proper officer of customs before shipment.[84] It is an offence for a person to consign or send a package containing salmon or trout by any common or other carrier unless the outside of the package containing it is conspicuously marked "salmon" or "trout" as the case may be. An authorised officer may open any package suspected to contain salmon or trout and detain it if not so marked, or where a marked package is being dealt with contrary to law.[85]

Close seasons: freshwater fish

The annual close season for freshwater fish is the period between 14 March and 16 June except in those waters for which a close season is dispensed with or a different season is specified by byelaws. The annual close season for rainbow trout, if any, is that fixed for those waters by byelaws.[86] Any person who during the annual close season for freshwater fish or rainbow trout fishes for, takes, kills, or attempts to take or kill any freshwater fish or rainbow trout in any inland water, or who fishes for eels by means of a rod and line in any inland water will be guilty of an offence. This prohibition does not apply, however, (a) to the removal by the owner or occupier, from any several fishery where salmon or trout are specially preserved, of any eels, freshwater fish or rainbow trout not so preserved; (b) to any person fishing with rod and line in any specially preserved fishery with the previous permission of its owner or occupier; (c) to any person fishing with rod and line for eels in any waters in which such fishing is authorised by a byelaw; (d) to the taking of freshwater fish or rainbow trout for scientific purposes; or (e) to the taking of freshwater fish for bait in a several fishery with the permission of its owner or occupier or in any other fishery, unless the taking would contravene a byelaw.[87]

---

[84] s.23(1) and (2).
[85] s.24(1) to (3).
[86] s.19(1) and Sch.1 paras.4 and 5.
[87] s.19(6) to (8). On specially preserved fisheries see *Thames Water Authority v. Homewood*, (1981) *The Times* 25 November 1981.

Before 25 June in any year it is unlawful to hang, fix or use in any waters frequented by salmon or migratory trout any baskets, nets, traps or other devices for catching eels, or to place[88] in any inland water any device to catch or obstruct any fish descending the river. Between 1 August and 1 March it is an offence to place on the apron of any weir[89] any basket, trap or device for taking fish, except wheels or leaps for taking lamperns (lampreys). However, these prohibitions do not apply to the use of eel baskets not exceeding ten inches in diameter constructed so as to be fished with bait, and not used at any dam or other obstruction or in any conduit or artificial channel by which water is diverted from a river, or to any device for taking eels authorised by the Authority with the consent of the Minister.[90]

Fishing licences

Licences to fish

The National Rivers Authority is bound to regulate fishing for salmon and trout by means of a system of licensing and, unless excused by the Minister, must regulate fishing for freshwater fish of any description and eels by licensing. A licence entitles the person to whom it is granted, and no other, to use an instrument specified in the licence to fish for any fish of a description, in an area and for a period so specified.[91]

A fishing licence for the use of an instrument other than a rod and line to fish for salmon or trout will also authorise the use of the instrument for that purpose by the authorised servants or agents of the person to whom it is granted, but not exceeding the specified number.[92] A fishing licence for the use of a rod and line will entitle the licensee to use as an ancillary to that use a gaff, consisting of a plain metal hook without a barb, or a tailer or landing net. A licence to use any instrument to fish for salmon authorises the use of that instrument to fish for trout,

---

[88] On the meaning of "place", see *Briggs v. Swanwick*, (1883) 47 J.P. 564.

[89] On the meaning of "apron of a weir", see *Maw v. Holloway* [1914] 3 K.B. 594.

[90] s.21(1) and (2) Salmon and Freshwater Fisheries Act 1975.

[91] s.25(1) and (2).

[92] s.25(3) and Sch.2 para.13, and see s.36(2) Salmon Act 1986 limiting the circumstances in which a person may be duly authorised as a servant or agent of the licensee for these purposes. See *Lewis v. Arthur*, (1871) 35 J.P. 35.

and a licence to use any instrument for fishing for salmon or trout authorises the use of that instrument for fishing for freshwater fish and eels.[93] However, a licence to fish with rod and line authorises only the use of a *single* rod and line,[94] and will not authorise a person to fish with any other instrument,[95] or retrospectively authorise a person for previous unlicensed use of a rod and line.[96]

A general licence may be granted to any person or association entitled to an exclusive right of fishing in any inland waters to fish in those waters subject to any conditions agreed between the Authority and the licensee. The general licence then entitles the licensee and any undisqualified person authorised by him in writing or, in the case of an association by its secretary, so to fish.[97]

Limitation of fishing licences

The Authority may by order confirmed by the Minister limit for a period not exceeding ten years from the coming into operation of the order the number of fishing licences to be issued in any year for fishing in any part of its area for salmon or trout, other than rainbow trout, with any specified instrument other than rod and line. An order of this kind may provide for the selection of the applicants to whom licences are to be issued where the number of applications exceeds the number of licences which may be granted.[98] An order may be revoked by the Minister, or by an order made by the Authority and confirmed by the Minister.[99]

---

[93] s.25(4) to (6) Salmon and Freshwater Fisheries Act 1975.

[94] s.41(1), and see *Combridge v. Harrison*, (1895) 59 J.P. 198.

[95] *Williams v. Long*, (1893) 57 J.P. 217. On the meaning of "instrument" see *Gibson v. Ryan*, [1967] 3 All E.R. 184, and the taking of fish without the use of an instrument *Gazard v. Cooke*, (1890) 55 J.P. 102; and *Stead v. Tillotson*, (1900) 64 J.P. 343.

[96] *Wharton v. Taylor*, (1965) 109 S.J. 475.

[97] s.25(7) Salmon and Freshwater Fisheries Act 1975. See *Mills v. Avon and Dorset River Board*, [1955] 1 All E.R. 382.

[98] s.26(1). See *R. v. South West Water Authority ex parte Cox*, (1981) *The Times* 2 January 1981; *R. v. Minister of Agriculture, Fisheries and Food ex parte Wear Valley District Council*, (1988) *Local Government Review* p.849; *R. v. Minister of Agriculture, Fisheries and Food, ex p. Graham*, (1988) *The Times* 16 April 1988.

[99] s.26(7).

Unlicensed fishing

A person in any place in which fishing for fish of any description is regulated by a licensing system who fishes for or takes fish of that description otherwise than by means of an instrument which he is entitled to use for that purpose by virtue of a licence, or otherwise than in accordance with the conditions of the licence, is guilty of an offence. A person is also guilty of an offence if he has an instrument in his possession, with intent to use it for fishing or taking fish, other than an instrument which he is authorised to use for that purpose by virtue of such a licence.[100]

The prohibition upon taking of salmon or trout otherwise than by means of a licensed instrument applies to the taking of live or dying fish but not to dead fish.[101] A person fishing with no intention of catching the species of fish for which a licence is required does not require a licence for that species.[102] Where the licence is for the use of a single instrument, a licensee must not use more than one such instrument at the same time, thus a licence to fish with a single rod and line has been held not to authorise the holder to fish with three rods and lines.[103]

Duty on licences

Other than where the Authority grants an exemption in a special case, a duty will be payable in respect of a licence. The duty payable is fixed by the Authority, but will require the approval of the Minister if written objection is made to a proposed duty by an interested person. Different duties may be fixed depending on the instrument, period, parts of the area, descriptions of fish and classes of licence holder. The Authority may grant a temporary licence for up to 14 days. In respect of general licences, there will be payable such a sum as may be agreed by the Authority and the licensee.[104]

A fishing licence must be granted by the Authority to every applicant who at the time of the application is not disqualified from

---

[100] s.27.

[101] *Gazard v. Cook*, (1890) 55 J.P. 102; and *Stead v. Tillotson*, (1900) 64 J.P. 64.

[102] *Marshall v. Richardson*, (1889) 60 L.T. 605; *Watts v. Lucas*, (1871) 24 L.T.128; but see *Hill v. George*, (1880) 44 J.P. 424; *Short v. Bastard*, (1881) 46 J.P. 580; *Moses v. Raywood*, [1911] 2 K.B. 271.

[103] *Combridge v. Harrison*, (1895) 72 L.T. 592.

[104] s.25(8) and Sch.2 paras.1 to 8 Salmon and Freshwater Fisheries Act 1975.

holding a fishing licence, on payment of the appropriate duty in respect of the instrument to which the licence relates. However, a fishing licence will not confer any rights to fish at a place or a time at which the licensee is not otherwise entitled to fish,[105] nor will the licence authorise the erection of any structure or the use of any installation or instrument, for or in connection with fishing, which would otherwise be illegal.[106]

Power to require production of fishing licences

A water bailiff appointed by the Authority, or any constable, may require any person who is fishing, or whom he reasonably suspects of being about to fish, or to have within the preceding half hour fished in any area, to produce his licence or other authority to fish and to state his name and address. A person holding a fishing licence for any area may, on production of his licence, require any person who is fishing in that area to produce his licence or other authority to fish and to state his name and address. If any person required to produce his fishing licence or other authority, or to state his name and address, fails to do so he will be guilty of an offence. If, however, within 7 days after the production of his licence was required he produces the licence or other authority at the appropriate office of the Authority, he may not be convicted of the offence of failing to produce it.[107]

Introduction of fish into inland waters

A person will be guilty of an offence if he introduces any fish or spawn of fish into an inland water, or has in his possession any fish or spawn of fish intending to introduce it into an inland water, unless he first obtains the consent of the Authority. However, this general prohibition has been amended to allow an exception where the inland water is one which consists exclusively of, or of part of, a fish farm and

[105] On rights to fish generally see Ch.8 above.

[106] s.25(8) and Sch.2 paras.15, 16 and 17.

[107] s.35, as amended by Sch.17 para.7 Water Act 1989.

which, if it discharges into another inland water, does so only through a conduit constructed or adapted for this purpose.[108]

Powers of water bailiffs

Powers of search

In addition to the general powers of entry possessed by persons designated by the Authority,[109] water bailiffs and persons appointed by the Minister are given special powers in respect of the enforcement of the Salmon and Freshwater Fisheries Act 1975 and the Salmon Act 1986.[110] Specifically, a water bailiff appointed by the Authority is given a power of search whereby (a) he may examine any dam, fishing weir, fishing mill dam, fixed engine or obstruction, or any artificial watercourse, and for that purpose enter on any land; (b) he may examine any instrument or bait which he has reasonable cause to suspect of having been or being used or likely to be used in taking fish in contravention of the Act,[111] or any container[112] which he has reasonable cause to suspect of having been used or likely to be used for holding any such instrument, bait or fish; (c) he may stop and search[113] any boat or other vessel used in fishing in the area of the Authority or any vessel or vehicle which he has reasonable cause to suspect of containing (i) fish which have been caught in contravention of the Act; (ii) any such instrument, bait or container as aforesaid; and (d) he may seize any fish and any instrument, vessel, vehicle or other thing liable to be forfeited in pursuance of the Act.[114]

---

[108] s.30 Salmon and Freshwater Fisheries Act 1975, as amended by s.34 Salmon Act 1986. "Fish farm" has the same meaning as in the Diseases of Fish Act 1937, see p.456 below.

[109] Under Chapter II of Part VII Water Resources Act 1991, see p.218 above.

[110] On the Salmon Act 1986 generally see p.448 below.

[111] The words "in contravention of the Act" here and in the following clause are to include reference to salmon in relation to which a relevant offence has been committed under s.32 of the Salmon Act 1986 (s.32(6)(a) Salmon Act 1986, and see p.450 below).

[112] A similarly worded provision has been held to include pockets in clothing *Taylor v. Pritchard,* [1910] K.B. 320.

[113] In *Jones v. Owens,* (1870) 34 J.P. 759 a person was convicted although illegally searched.

[114] s.31(1) Salmon and Freshwater Fisheries Act 1975. The things liable to forfeiture under the Act are set out in Sch.4 para.5, and see p.446 below.

If any person refuses to allow a water bailiff or a person appointed by the Minister to make any entry, search or examination which he is authorised to make, or to seize anything which he is so authorised to seize, or resists or obstructs a water bailiff or a person so appointed in any such entry, search, examination or seizure, he will be guilty of an offence.[115]

Power to enter lands

Again, in addition to any other powers that a water bailiff may have to enter lands in his general capacity as a person designated by the Authority,[116] specific powers to enter land are provided for under the Salmon and Freshwater Fisheries Act 1975. This provides that any water bailiff or other officer of the Authority, under a special order in writing from the Authority, and any person appointed by the Minister under a special order in writing from him, may at all reasonable times, for the purpose of preventing any offence against this Act, enter, remain upon and traverse any lands adjoining or near to any waters other than a dwelling house or the curtilage of a dwelling house or decoys or lands used exclusively for the preservation of wild fowl.[117]

Orders and warrants to enter suspected premises

A Justice of the Peace may authorise a water bailiff or other officer of the Authority to enter and remain on any land situated on or near any waters for not more than twenty–four hours where an offence against the Act is suspected of being or is likely to be committed to detect the persons committing the offence.[118] In addition, a water bailiff or other officer of the Authority or a constable may be authorised by warrant to enter suspected premises to detect any offence against the Act[119] and

[115] s.31(2). See also Sch.20 para.7 Water Resources Act 1991.

[116] Generally see Chapter II of Part VII Water Resources Act 1991, discussed at p.218 above.

[117] s.32(1) Salmon and Freshwater Fisheries Act 1975. See *Heseltine v. Myers*, (1894) 58 J.P. 689.

[118] s.33(1).

[119] This power may also be exercised in relation to s.32 Salmon Act 1986, concerned with handling salmon in suspicious circumstances (s.32(6)(b) Salmon Act 1986), see p.449 below.

seize all illegal nets or other instruments and fish on the premises suspected to have been illegally taken.[120]

Power to apprehend persons fishing illegally at night

A water bailiff, or any person appointed by the Minister, with assistants, may seize without warrant any person illegally taking or killing fish by night, or found on or near any waters with intent illegally to take or kill fish or having in his possession any instrument prohibited by the Act for the capture of fish, and deliver the offender into the custody of a police officer. "By night" for the purposes of this provision means between the expiration of the first hour after sunset, on any day, and the beginning of the last hour before sunrise on the following morning.[121]

The water bailiff as a police constable

A water bailiff, or a person appointed by the Minister, is deemed to be a police constable for the purpose of enforcement of the Salmon and Freshwater Fisheries Act 1975, or any order or byelaw under it. Accordingly, he will have the same powers and privileges, and be subject to the same liabilities as a constable has or is subject to by virtue of the common law or any statute.[122] This provision allows water bailiffs to exercise the powers of arrest provided for under the Police and Criminal Evidence Act 1984. These confer powers to arrest for "arrestable offences" and a power to arrest for "non–arrestable offences" where the "general arrest conditions" are satisfied.[123]

---

[120] s.33(2) Salmon and Freshwater Fisheries Act 1975. See also Sch.20 para.2 Water Resources Act 1991 on warrants to exercise entry.

[121] s.34 Salmon and Freshwater Fisheries Act 1975. In *MacKinnon v. Nicolson*, ([1916] S.C. 6) it was held that the times of sunset and sunrise are the times at which the sun sets and rises in the locality of the offence.

[122] s.36(1). The reference to the Salmon and Freshwater Fisheries Act 1975 is to include reference to s.32 Salmon Act 1986, concerned with handling salmon in suspicious circumstances, by virtue of s.32(6)(b) Salmon Act 1986, see p.449 below.

[123] Under s.24 Police and Criminal Evidence Act 1984 "arrestable offences" are defined to include those for which, amongst other things, a person of 21 years of age or over, not previously convicted, may be sentenced to imprisonment for a term of five years. "Non–arrestable offences" are those less serious offences, including offences under the Salmon and Freshwater Fisheries Act 1975. The "general arrest conditions" cover, amongst other things, a situation where the name of the relevant

The production by a water bailiff, or a person appointed by the Minister, of evidence of his appointment will be a sufficient warrant for him exercising the powers conferred on him by the Salmon and Freshwater Fisheries Act 1975. The significance of this is that it may become unlawful for a bailiff to exercise other powers under the Act if no evidence of authority is shown. Hence in *Barnacott v. Passmore*[124] the accused, who had threatened a water bailiff who sought to exercise his power to search a boat which he suspected to contain salmon, was acquitted because it was held that the bailiff's failure to produce his instrument of appointment provided a justification for the accused's resistance to the search. In *Cowler v. Jones*[125] however, it was held to be sufficient production of authority for a bailiff to hold up his warrant of authority, despite the fact that it was too dark for the document to be read. It has been held also that a bailiff will not step outside his authority by not producing evidence of appointment in circumstances where no occasion to do so arises.[126] A bailiff is entitled to take legal proceedings without being specially authorised to do so by his employers.[127]

The Authority is empowered to obtain the services of additional constables under s.15 of the Police Act 1964.[128] Where this is done, a police constable whose services are provided will have all the powers and privileges of a water bailiff.[129]

Offences and penalties

Punishments

The penalties in relation to the various offences arising under the Salmon and Freshwater Fisheries Act 1975 are set out in the form of a

---

person is unknown to, and cannot be readily ascertained by, the constable (s.25 Police and Criminal Evidence Act 1984).

124 (1887) 19 Q.B.D. 75.

125 (1890) 54 J.P. 660.

126 *Edwards v. Morgan,* [1967] Crim. L.R. 40.

127 *Pollock v. Moses,* (1894) 70 L.T. 378.

128 s.28(6) and Sch.3 para.39(1)(c) Salmon and Freshwater Fisheries Act 1975.

129 s.36(3).

table in Part I of Schedule 4 to the Act.[130] This provides that, for the most serious offences under the Act, such as the use of prohibited instruments for the purpose of taking or killing fish,[131] on summary conviction, the maximum penalty will be a period of three months' imprisonment or a fine of £2,000, or both. On conviction on indictment, the maximum penalty for the offence will be two years' imprisonment or a fine of unlimited amount or both.[132] Corresponding maximum penalties are allocated by the table in Schedule 4 to the various offences under the Act previously described. A person guilty of an offence against any of the provisions of the Act not specified in the table will be liable on summary conviction to a fine not exceeding £1,000.[133]

Forfeiture

The court by which a person is convicted of an offence against the Act may order the forfeiture of (a) any fish illegally taken by him or in his possession at the time of the offence; (b) any instrument, bait or other thing used in the commission of the offence; (c) in the case of an offence of unlawful possession of any substance or device in contravention of s.5 of the Act,[134] that substance or device; and (d) on conviction on indictment, any vessel or vehicle used in or in connection with the commission of the offence or in which any substance or device unlawfully in his possession was contained at the time of the offence. The court may order any object so forfeited to be disposed of as the court thinks fit.[135]

---

[130] Effective under s.37, as amended by Sch.6 Criminal Law Act 1977, s.46 Criminal Justice Act 1982, s.32(2) and (3) Magistrates' Courts Act 1980, and s.35 Salmon Act 1986.

[131] Under s.1 Salmon and Freshwater Fisheries Act 1975, see p.423 above.

[132] Sch.4 table, as amended by s.35(1) Salmon Act 1986.

[133] Sch. 4 para.1(2), and see also s.211(3) Water Resources Act 1991.

[134] s.5 Salmon and Freshwater Fisheries Act 1975 is concerned with the prohibition of use of explosives, poisons or electrical devices and the destruction of dams, see p. 427 above.

[135] s.37 and Sch.4 para.5. In *R. v. Williams*, ((1991) *The Times* 4 July 1991) it was held that in relation to the forfeiture of vehicles or vessels the *use* of the item in relation to the offence was sufficient to justify forfeiture and it did not need to be shown that the accused was the *owner* of it.

In addition to the items mentioned previously, an authorised officer of the Authority may seize any salmon, trout or freshwater fish bought, sold or exposed for sale, by, or in the possession for sale of, any person in contravention of the Act. Where any fish or other thing of a perishable nature is seized as liable to forfeiture, the person by whom it is seized may sell it, and the net proceeds of sale will be liable to forfeiture in the same manner as the fish or other thing sold. If and so far as the thing is not forfeited, the proceeds of sale are to be paid on demand to the owner. However, no person will be subject to any liability on account of his neglect or failure to exercise the power to sell the seized item.[136]

Licence forfeiture and disqualification

If a person is convicted of an offence under the Act, the court may also order that any fishing or general licence held by him is to be forfeited, and he will be disqualified from holding and obtaining a fishing or general licence or having his name entered as a servant or agent of a licensee[137] or from fishing by virtue of a fishing or general licence for such period not exceeding five years, as the court thinks fit.[138] A person who is prosecuted for an offence against the Act and who is the holder of a fishing or general licence must either (a) cause it to be delivered to the clerk of the court not later than the day before the date appointed for the hearing, or (b) post it, at such a time that in the ordinary course of post it would be delivered not later than that day, in a letter addressed to the clerk and either registered or sent recorded delivery service, or (c) have it with him at the hearing. If he is convicted of the offence and the court makes an order for the forfeiture of the licence, the court must order the licence to be surrendered. If the offender has not posted the licence or caused it to be delivered, and does not surrender it as required, then he will be guilty of an offence and the licence will be revoked from the time when its surrender was ordered. Where a court orders a licence to be surrendered, or where a person is disqualified from holding a licence, the court must (a) send notice of the order to the Authority, unless the Authority prosecuted in the case, and (b) if the

---

[136] s.37 and Sch.4 para.7 and 8.

[137] Under Sch.2 paras.9 to 14.

[138] s.37 and Sch.4 para.9, as amended by s.141 and Sch.17 para.15 Water Act 1989.

licence has been surrendered, forward it to the Authority who may dispose of it as they think fit.[139]

Magistrates' powers

Any offence committed against the Act on the sea–coast or at sea beyond the ordinary jurisdiction of a court of summary jurisdiction will be deemed to have been committed in any place abutting on that sea–coast or adjoining that sea, and may be tried and punished accordingly.[140]

A Justice of the Peace will not be disqualified from hearing any case under the Act by reason only of being a subscriber to any society for the protection of fish, but a Justice will not be entitled to hear any case in respect of an offence committed on his own land or in relation to any fishery of which he is the owner or occupier.[141] A magistrate will be disqualified from adjudicating if he was present at a meeting which authorised the prosecution,[142] unless it can be shown that he took no part in the decision to prosecute.[143] On conviction of an offence against the Act, the clerk of the court must forward a certificate of conviction to the Authority within one month.[144]

THE SALMON ACT 1986

Although the extensive provisions of the Salmon and Freshwater Fisheries Act 1975 regulate the activities of angling, commercial fishing and various activities relating to fisheries, the Act provides limited powers in relation to the possession and trade in unlawfully taken salmon. This limitation in the law was rectified by Part III of the Salmon Act 1986 which introduced two additional measures concerning provision for a salmon dealer licensing scheme and a new offence of handling salmon in suspicious circumstances.

---

[139] s.37 and Sch.4 paras.10 and 11 Salmon and Freshwater Fisheries Act 1975.

[140] s.37 and Sch.4 para.2.

[141] s.37 and Sch.4 para.4.

[142] *R. v. Henley,* [1892] 1 Q.B. 504; and *R. v. Huggins,* [1895] 1 Q.B. 563.

[143] *R. v. Pwllheli JJ., Ex p. Soane,* [1948] 2 All E.R. 815.

[144] s.37 and Sch.4 para.12 Salmon and Freshwater Fisheries Act 1975.

Dealer licensing

The Minister and the Secretary of State are empowered to make provision by order for the purpose of prohibiting persons from (a) dealing in salmon[145] otherwise than under and in accordance with a licence issued in pursuance of the order by specified persons, or (b) buying salmon from a person who is not licensed to deal[146] in salmon.[147] An order of this kind may (a) prescribe the manner and form of an application for a licence to deal in salmon and the sum, or maximum sum, to be paid on the making of an application; (b) specify the circumstances in which an application is to be granted or refused and the conditions that may be incorporated in a licence; (c) authorise the amendment, revocation or suspension of a licence; (d) create criminal offences consisting in the contravention of, or failure to comply with provisions relating to the dealer licensing scheme;[148] (e) provide for matter to be determined for the purposes of any provision by a person authorised to issue a licence; and (f) make provision, whether by applying the Salmon and Freshwater Fisheries Act 1975 or otherwise, for the purpose of facilitating the enforcement of any provision relating to the dealer licensing scheme.[149] It has been indicated by the Ministry of Agriculture, Fisheries and Food, however, that no dealer licensing scheme in accordance with these provisions is presently envisaged.

Handling salmon in suspicious circumstances

The offence of handling salmon in suspicious circumstances is committed by a person if, at a time when he believes or it would be

[145] "Salmon", for the purposes of the Salmon Act 1986, means all migratory fish of the species *Salmo salar* and *Salmon trutta* and commonly known as salmon and sea trout respectively and part of any such fish (s.40(1) Salmon Act 1986).

[146] "Deal" in relation to salmon, includes selling any quantity of salmon, whether by way of business or otherwise, and acting on behalf of a buyer or seller of salmon (s.31(6) Salmon Act 1986).

[147] s.31(1) Salmon Act 1986.

[148] Provided for under s.31.

[149] s.31(2).

reasonable for him to suspect that a relevant offence[150] has at any time been committed in relation to any salmon, he receives the salmon, or undertakes or assists in its retention, removal or disposal by or for the benefit of another person or if he arranges to do so.[151] An offence is a "relevant offence" for these purposes if (a) it is committed by taking, killing or landing that salmon either in England and Wales or in Scotland; or (b) that salmon is taken, killed or landed, either in England and Wales or in Scotland, in the course of commission of the offence. For the purposes of the offence of handling salmon in suspicious circumstances, it is immaterial that a person's belief or the grounds for suspicion relate neither specifically to a particular offence that has been committed nor exclusively to a relevant offence or to relevant offences. However, it will be a defence in proceedings for an offence to show that no relevant offence had in fact been committed in relation to the salmon in question. It will also be a defence for a person to show that the conduct which is alleged to constitute a relevant offence is anything done in good faith for purposes connected with the prevention or detection of crime or the investigation or treatment of disease.[152]

For the purpose of enforcement of the offence of handling salmon in suspicious circumstances certain amendments were made to the Salmon and Freshwater Fisheries Act 1975. These allow the 1975 Act to have effect as if (a) in relation to the powers of search of bailiffs,[153] the references to a fish taken in contravention of the 1975 Act included reference to a salmon in relation to which a relevant offence has been committed; and (b) in relation to warrants to enter suspected premises,[154] water bailiffs being constables for the purpose of enforcing the 1975

[150] "Offence", in relation to the taking, killing or landing of a salmon either in England and Wales or in Scotland, means an offence under the law applicable to the place where the salmon is taken, killed or landed (s.32(7) Salmon Act 1986).

[151] s.32(1) Salmon Act 1986. A person guilty of this offence will be liable (a) on summary conviction, to imprisonment for a term not exceeding three months or to a fine not exceeding the statutory maximum or to both; (b) on conviction on indictment, to imprisonment for a term not exceeding two years or to a fine or to both (s.32(5)).

[152] s.32(2) to (4).

[153] Under s.31(1)(b) and (c) of the Salmon and Freshwater Fisheries Act 1975.

[154] Under s.33(2).

Act,[155] border rivers,[156] prosecution by the Authority,[157] and procedure on prosecutions,[158] the references to the 1975 Act are to have effect as if they included reference to s.32 of the Salmon Act 1986 which provides for the offence of handling salmon in suspicious circumstances.[159]

THE THEFT ACT 1968

Theft of fish

At common law fish in a running water are *ferae naturae* and cannot be stolen or become the property of an owner of a private fishery until they have been caught and so appropriated into the possession of the captor.[160] However, after appropriation or when placed in an enclosed water, fish become the subject of property and so may be the subject of theft. A person is guilty of theft if he dishonestly appropriates property belonging to another with the intention of permanently depriving the other of it.[161] For these purposes wild creatures, tamed or untamed, will be regarded as property, but a person cannot steal a wild creature not tamed or ordinarily kept in captivity, or the carcase of any such creature, unless either it has been reduced into possession by or on behalf of another person and possession of it has not since been lost or abandoned, or another person is in the course of reducing it into possession.[162] Accordingly, it has been held that it is an offence to steal fish from a private pond,[163] and fish which have been taken and captured in a net may be stolen,[164] as may fish caught at sea and deposited in the hold of a vessel.[165]

---

155 Under s.36(1).
156 Under s.39(1).
157 Under Sch.3 para.39(1)(a).
158 Under Part II of Sch.4.
159 s.32(6) Salmon Act 1986.
160 See p.196 above, and *R. v. Hundsdon,* (1781) 3 East P.C. 611. Contrast the position in Scots law, see *Valentine v. Kennedy,* (1985) S.C.C.R. 88.
161 s.1(1) Theft Act 1968.
162 s.4(4).
163 *Gray's Case,* (1594) Owen 20; *Gray v. Trowe,* (1601) 75 E.R. 1043; and *R. v. Steer,* (1704) 6 Mod. Rep. 189.
164 *Young v. Hitchens,* (1844) 6 Q.B. 606.
165 *R. v. Mallison,* (1902) 86 L.T. 600.

Taking or destroying fish

Although the offence of theft is inapplicable to the taking of fish from an unenclosed water, such an action is capable of amounting to the distinct offence of taking or destroying fish provided for under para.2 of Sch.1 to the Theft Act 1968. This provides that a person who unlawfully[166] takes[167] or destroys, or attempts to take or destroy, any fish[168] in water[169] which is private property or in which there is any private right of fishery will commit an offence.[170] This provision will not apply to taking or destroying fish by angling during the daytime,[171] but a person who by angling in the daytime unlawfully takes or destroys, or attempts to take or destroy, any fish in water which is private property or in which there is any private right of fishery will commit an offence.[172] The court by which a person is convicted of either of these offences may order the forfeiture of anything which, at the time of the offence, the offender had with him for use for taking or destroying fish. Any person may arrest without warrant anyone who is, or whom he, with reasonable cause, suspects to be committing the offence of taking or destroying fish other than by angling during the daytime. Any person may seize from any person who is, or whom he with reasonable cause suspects to be, committing either offence, anything which on that person's conviction would be liable to be forfeited.[173]

---

[166] On the meaning of "unlawfully" see *R. v. Stimpson,* (1863) 27 J.P. 678; *Halse v. Alder,* (1874) 38 J.P. 407; and *Smith v. Andrews,* [1891] 2 Ch.678.

[167] Catching fish with the intention of eventually returning them to the water may constitute "taking" for these purposes (*Wells v. Hardy,* [1964] 1 All E.R. 953).

[168] The offence may be committed in relation to any kind of fish including shellfish (*Caygill v. Thwaite,* (1885) 49 J.P. 614; *Leavett v. Clark,* [1915] 3 K.B. 9).

[169] The offence may be committed in either tidal or non–tidal waters (*Paley v. Birch,* (1867) 8 B. & S. 336).

[170] Sch.1 para.2(1) Theft Act 1968. A person committing this offence will, on summary conviction, be liable to imprisonment for a term not exceeding three months or to a fine not exceeding £400.

[171] "Daytime" means the period beginning one hour before sunrise and ending one hour after sunset at the times at which sunrise and sunset occur locally (*MacKinnon v. Nicholson,* [1916] S.C. 6).

[172] Sch.1 para.2(2). A person committing this offence will, on summary conviction, be liable to a fine not exceeding £50.

[173] Sch.1 paras.2(3) and (4).

THE DISEASES OF FISH ACTS 1937 AND 1983

The Diseases of Fish Act 1937 was enacted with the principal objective of preventing the spread of the fish disease furunculosis amongst salmon and freshwater fish. The Act incorporated a mechanism for the application of controls in relation to other fish diseases by allowing for the extension of its provisions in relation to other prescribed diseases.[174] Accordingly, this power has been exercised on a number of occasions to modify the list of "prescribed" diseases under the Act.[175]

The Diseases of Fish Act 1937, as amended by the 1983 Act, imposes prohibitions and restrictions upon the import of live fish.[176] Hence, the importation of fish of the salmon family into Britain is prohibited and the importation of live freshwater fish or live eggs of salmon and freshwater fish may only be brought about under and in accordance with a licence issued by the Minister of Agriculture, Fisheries and Food.[177]

---

[174] s.13(1) Diseases of Fish Act 1937, as amended by Diseases of Fish Order 1973, S.I. 1973 No.2093.

[175] See, Diseases of Fish Orders S.I. 1966 No.944, S.I. 1973 No.2093, S.I. 1978 No.1022, S.I. 1984 No.301, S.I. 1988 No.195, and S.I. 1990 No.616. The combined effect of these Orders is that the list of prescribed diseases under the Act includes the following: bacterial kidney disease (BKD), furunculosis of salmon, gyrodactyliasis caused by *Gyrodactylus salaris*, infectious haematopoietic necrosis (IHN), infections pancreatic necrosis (IPN), spring viraemia of carp (SVC), viral haemorrhagic septicaemia (VHS) and whirling disease (*Myxosoma cerebralis*).

[176] Although the Acts concern only imports of *live* fish, the importation of dead fish may be restricted for disease control purposes by the Animal Health Act 1981, s.10(1) of which empowers the Minister of Agriculture, Fisheries and Food and the Secretary of State to impose controls upon the import of live or dead fish. This power has been exercised under the Salmonid Viscera Order 1986 (S.I. 1986 No.2265) to prevent the import into Britain of ungutted salmonids except under the order of a licence.

[177] s.1 Diseases of Fish Act 1937, and see Diseases of Fish Regulations 1984 S.I. 1984 No.455 and Importation of Live Fish of the Salmon Family Order 1986 S.I. 1986 No.283. "Fish" does not include shellfish but otherwise means fish of any kind. "Fish of the salmon family" includes all fish of whatever genus belonging to the family *Salmonidae*. "Freshwater fish" does not include fish of the salmon family, or any kinds of fish which migrate to and from tidal waters, but otherwise includes any fish living in freshwater. "Shellfish" includes crustaceans and molluscs of any kind (s.10(1)).

If the Minister has reasonable grounds to suspect that any waters are, or may become, infected waters,[178] he may declare the waters concerned, and such land adjacent to them as appropriate in the circumstances, as a "designated area" for the purposes of taking a range of measures to prevent the spread of disease. Specifically, he may prohibit or regulate the taking into or out of the designated area any specified or described live fish, eggs of fish and foodstuff of fish and regulate the movement within the area of any of the things specified or described.[179] Where an order of this kind has been made, he may serve a notice on any occupier of inland waters[180] situated in the designated area, or any person carrying on the business of fish farming in marine waters[181] within the area, directing the person to take practicable steps to secure the removal of dead or dying fish from the waters and regulate the manner in which the fish are to be disposed of.[182]

Where the National Rivers Authority has reasonable grounds for suspecting that any inland waters, which are not a fish farm,[183] are infected waters it must report the facts forthwith to the Minister, and it is empowered to take any practicable steps for the removal of dead or dying fish from the water. Where an order designating infected waters is in force, the Minister has a power to authorise the Authority to remove any fish, or fish of a specified description from any inland water other than a fish farm, and to use such methods, including methods which are otherwise illegal, as he considers most expedient for the purpose. The Authority is then to destroy or dispose of all fish removed and send the

---

[178] "Infected waters" means waters in which any of the prescribed diseases exist among fish, or in which the causative organisms of any of those diseases are present (s.10(1) as amended by the Diseases of Fish Order 1973 S.I. 1973 No.2093).

[179] s.2(1) and (2) Diseases of Fish Act 1937.

[180] "Inland waters" means waters within Britain which do not form part of the sea or of any creek, bay or estuary or of any river as far as the tide flows (s.10(1)).

[181] "Marine waters" means waters, other than inland waters, within the seaward limits of the territorial sea adjacent to Britain (s.10(1)).

[182] s.2A.

[183] "Fish farm" means any pond, stew, fish hatchery or other place used for keeping, with a view to their sale or to their transfer to other waters, including any other fish farm, live fish, live eggs of fish, or foodstuff of fish, and includes any buildings used in connection therewith, and the banks and margins of any water therein (s.10(1)).

Minister a return stating the numbers of fish at such times as he may direct.[184]

If a Ministry Inspector suspects that any inland fish farm waters are infected, he is empowered to serve a notice upon the occupiers, and where this is done the facts are to be reported to the Minster. The effect of service of a notice of this kind is that no live fish, or live eggs of fish, may be taken into or out of the fish farm, and no foodstuff of fish may be taken out of the farm, without the permission of the Minister. This prohibition applies for a thirty day period from the service of the notice, unless the occupier receives intimation from the Minister that permission is no longer required. The initial period during which movements are prohibited may be extended by another thirty day period if the Minister thinks it desirable to do so. Analogous provisions in relation to preliminary precautions against fish disease also apply in relation to fish cages in marine waters. More generally, if any person entitled to take fish from any inland waters, or employed for the purpose of having the care of any inland waters, has reasonable grounds for suspecting that the waters are infected waters, it is his duty forthwith to report the facts to the Minster or, if the waters are not a fish farm, to the National Rivers Authority. Failure to do so without reasonable excuse is an offence.[185]

Any person guilty of an offence under the 1937 Act, as amended, will be liable on summary conviction to a fine not exceeding £1,000, and the court by whom any person is convicted of an offence under the Act may order to be forfeited any fish, eggs of fish, foodstuff of fish or article in respect of which the offence was committed.[186] The National Rivers Authority has power to take legal proceedings to enforce the provisions of the Act in respect of inland waters in its area.[187]

Registration of fish farms

Whilst a principal objective of the Diseases of Fish Act 1983 was to amend the 1937 Act, it also introduced new powers providing for a scheme for the registration of fish farms and the collection of information

---

[184] s.3(1) to (3).

[185] ss.4 and 4A.

[186] s.8(1).

[187] s.8(2), and see s.141 and Sch.17 para.3 Water Act 1989.

with a view to the prevention of fish disease. Hence, the Minister[188] may exercise a power to require information about various forms of fish farming[189] if it appears necessary to obtain the information for the purpose of preventing the spread of disease among fish.[190] In relation to an inland fish farm[191] occupied for the purpose of fish farming, a Ministerial order may require the occupier (a) to register the business in a register kept for the purpose by the Minister; (b) to furnish in writing to the Minister such information as may be specified in the order in relation to the fish farm and to fish, eggs of fish and foodstuff for fish; (c) to compile such records as may be so specified in relation to the matters mentioned under (b) above; and (d) to retain for such period, not exceeding three years, as may be specified any record compiled in accordance with (c) above.[192] Analogous provisions apply in relation to persons who own or possess any cage, pontoon or other structure which is anchored in marine waters[193] and is used for the purposes of a business of fish farming. Similar information may also be required in respect of a person carrying on a business of shellfish farming.[194] Failure to provide this information without reasonable excuse, knowingly furnishing false information, failing to comply with a requirement by an authorised person to produce the information, or obstructing such a person in the exercise of his powers is an offence. A person found guilty of this

---

[188] "The Minister" means, in relation to England, and any marine waters adjacent to England, the Minister of Agriculture, Fisheries and Food, and in relation to Wales, and adjacent marine waters, the Secretary of State for Wales (s.7(8) Diseases of Fish Act 1983).

[189] "Fish farming" means the keeping of live fish with a view to their sale or to their transfer to other waters (s.7(8)).

[190] s.7(1).

[191] "Inland fish farm" means any place where inland waters are used for the keeping of live fish with a view to their sale or to their transfer to other waters, whether inland or not. "Inland waters" means waters within Britain which do not form part of the sea or of any creek, bay or estuary or of any river so far as the tide flows (s.7(8)).

[192] s.7(2). See the Registration of Fish Farming Businesses Order 1985 S.I. 1985 No.1391.

[193] "Marine waters" means waters within Britain which do not form part of the sea or of any creek, bay or estuary or of any river as far as the tide flows (s.7(8) Diseases of Fish Act 1983).

[194] s.7(3) and (4).

offence will be liable on summary conviction to a fine not exceeding £1,000.[195]

THE SEA FISHERIES REGULATION ACT 1966

Local fisheries committees

Under the Sea Fisheries Regulation Act 1966, the Minister[196] may, on the application of a county or metropolitan district council, (a) create a sea fisheries district comprising any part of the sea[197] within the national or territorial waters of the United Kingdom adjacent to England or Wales,[198] either with or without any part of the adjoining coast; (b) define the limits of the district, and the area chargeable with any expenses under the Act; and (c) provide for the constitution of a local fisheries committee for the regulation of the sea fisheries carried on within the district.[199] If a county or metropolitan council refuses or neglects to apply for an order after an application has been made to it by not less than twenty persons who are ratepayers and inhabitants of the county or district and interested in sea fisheries, the ratepayers may themselves apply to the Minister for an order. In that case the Minister will be bound to proceed as if the application had been made by the council unless the council can satisfy the Minister that the order should not be made.[200]

The local fisheries committee for a sea fisheries district is a committee of the county or metropolitan district council, or a joint committee of councils, as determined by the order creating the district.

---

[195] s.8(1).

[196] Functions of a Minister of the Crown under the Sea Fisheries Regulation Act 1966 are to be exercisable concurrently by the Minister of Agriculture, Fisheries and Food and the Secretary of State (s.20(1) Sea Fisheries Regulation Act 1966, as amended by the Transfer of Functions (Wales) (No.1) Order 1978 S.I. 1978 No.272 and s.141 and Sch.17 para.1(3) Water Act 1989).

[197] "Sea" includes the coast up to high water mark (s.20(1) Sea Fisheries Regulation Act 1966).

[198] On territorial waters see p.26 above.

[199] s.1(1) Sea Fisheries Regulation Act 1966, and s.272(1) and Sch.30 Local Government Act 1972 and s.16 and Sch.8 para.19(2) Local Government Act 1985.

[200] s.3 Sea Fisheries Regulation Act 1966. On the publication of draft orders, see s.4.

The committee is to consist of members appointed by the council, or by the constituent councils in such proportions as so determined, and additional members, not exceeding the number of members required to be appointed by the council or constituent councils. The additional members of the committee are to include one person appointed by the National Rivers Authority and the rest are to be persons appointed by the Minister as being persons acquainted with the needs and opinions of fishing interests of that district.[201]

An order constituting a local fisheries committee may contain regulations as to the number and mode of appointment of the members of the committee, and other expedient matters relating to the constitution of the committee.[202] The expenses of a local fisheries committee, so far as payable by a county or metropolitan district council, are according to the order constituting the committee, to be general or special expenses of the council and, if special expenses, are to be chargeable only on that part of the council's area as is directed by the order.[203] Any expense which the committee is required by the Minister to incur in the collection of statistics is to be paid out of moneys provided by Parliament.[204]

Byelaws for the regulation of sea fisheries

Subject to any regulations made by the Minister,[205] a local fisheries committee may make byelaws for the following purposes: (a) for restricting or prohibiting, either absolutely or subject to any exceptions and regulations, the fishing for or taking of all or any specified kinds of sea fish[206] during any period specified in the byelaw; (b) for restricting or

---

[201] s.2(1) and (2), as amended by s.272(1) and Sch.30 Local Government Act 1972 and s.16 and Sch.8 para.19 Local Government Act 1985. "Fishing interests" includes all persons interested in fisheries, either as owners of fisheries or interests therein, fishermen, fishing boat owners, fish curers, fish merchants or otherwise (s.2(2)).

[202] s.2(5) Sea Fisheries Regulation Act 1966.

[203] s.17(1), as substituted by s.16 and Sch.8 para.19 Local Government Act 1985.

[204] s.17(2) Sea Fisheries Regulation Act 1966.

[205] See Sea Fisheries (Byelaws) Regulations 1985, S.I. 1985 No.1785.

[206] "Sea fish" means fish of any description found in the sea including shellfish but does not include (a) fish of the salmon species, or (b) trout which migrate to and from the sea. See also s.37(1) Salmon Act 1986 on the meaning of "sea fish". "Shellfish" includes crustaceans and molluscs of any kind (s.20(1)).

prohibiting, either absolutely or subject to regulations provided by the byelaws, any method of fishing for sea fish or the use of any instrument of fishing for sea fish and for determining the size of mesh, form and dimensions of any instrument of fishing for sea fish; (d) for the regulation, protection and development of fisheries for all or any specified kinds of shellfish, including – (i) the fixing of the sizes and condition at which shellfish may not be removed from a fishery and the mode of determining those sizes; (ii) the obligation to re–deposit in specified localities any shellfish the removal or possession of which is prohibited by or in pursuance of any Act; (iii) the protection of shellfish laid down for breeding purposes; (iv) the protection of culch and other material for the reception of the spat or young of any kinds of shellfish; and (v) the obligation to re–deposit culch and other material in specified localities; (e) for constituting within their district any district of oyster cultivation[207] for the purpose of prohibiting the sale of oysters between certain dates; (f) for directing that a defence[208] to the offence of selling oysters between certain dates will not apply; (g) for revoking or amending any order[209] prohibiting the taking of crabs and lobsters in certain areas; (h) for revoking or amending any byelaw made in accordance with these powers.[210]

In addition to these matters, additional byelaw–creating powers have been provided for under the Salmon Act 1986. These allow byelaws to be made for the purposes of protecting salmon and preventing any interference with their migration and are to be exercisable as if the above references to sea fish included references to salmon.[211] Also local fisheries committees have the power to make byelaws for the purposes of authorising the placing and use of fixed engines[212] in their district, at such times and in such a manner as may be prescribed, and to impose requirements as to the construction, design, material and dimensions of fixed engines, including in the case of nets the size of mesh. In either of

---

[207] Provided for under s.16(2) Sea Fisheries (Shellfish) Act 1967.

[208] Under s.17(2) Sea Fisheries (Shellfish) Act 1967.

[209] Under s.10 Sea Fisheries (Shellfish) Act 1967.

[210] s.5(1) Sea Fisheries Regulation Act 1966, as amended. Purpose (c) for which regulations could formerly be made was repealed by the Water (Consequential Amendments) Regulations 1989, S.I. 1989 No.1968.

[211] s.37(1) Salmon Act 1986.

[212] Under s.6 Salmon and Freshwater Fisheries Act 1975, and see p.428 above.

these cases, however, the local fisheries committee is not to make byelaws for these purpose unless the National Rivers Authority has consented to the byelaws being made by the committee.[213]

Certain general restrictions are imposed upon the powers of local fisheries committees to make byelaws and they are not authorised to make byelaws which (a) prejudicially affect any right of several fishery, or any right on, to or over any portion of the sea shore, where that right is enjoyed by any person under any local or special Act of Parliament, or any Royal charter, letters patent, prescription, or immemorial usage, except with the consent of that person; (b) affect any byelaw made by the National Rivers Authority or restrict the power of the Authority to make any byelaw; or (c) affect any power of a local authority to discharge sewage in pursuance of any power conferred by a general or local Act of Parliament or by a provisional order confirmed by Parliament.[214]

No byelaw made by a local fisheries committee under the Sea Fisheries Regulation Act 1966 will have effect until it is confirmed by the Minister.[215] He may, before confirming a byelaw, cause a local inquiry to be held with respect to the byelaw and may, in any case, confirm the byelaw without modification or with such modifications as may be assented to by the local fisheries committee.[216] The Minister may revoke any byelaw made by a local fisheries committee if this is necessary or desirable for the maintenance or improvement of fisheries after having given notice to the committee and after having considered any objections raised by them and, if so required by them, after holding a public inquiry.[217]

Any person who contravenes any byelaw of a local fisheries committee will be guilty of an offence and liable on summary conviction to a fine not exceeding £2,000.[218] Where any vessel is used for fishing in a manner constituting a contravention of any byelaw restricting fishing for specified kinds of fish or restricting any method of fishing, the

---

[213] s.37(2) and (3) Salmon Act 1986.

[214] s.6 Sea Fisheries Regulation Act 1966.

[215] s.7(1), and see above p.416 on the meaning of "the Minister".

[216] s.7(2).

[217] s.8.

[218] s.11(5) Sea Fisheries Regulation Act 1966, as amended by ss.38 and 46 Criminal Justice Act 1982.

skipper and the owner of the vessel will be guilty of an offence and liable on summary conviction to a fine not exceeding £2,000.[219] The court by which the skipper and owner is convicted may also order the forfeiture of any net or other fishing gear used in committing the offence and any fish in respect of which the offence was committed.[220] However, in proceedings taken against the owner of a vessel in respect of an offence committed by the skipper, it will be a defence for the owner to prove that he exercised all due diligence to prevent the commission of the offence.[221]

Where an offence under the 1966 Act is committed on the sea coast or at sea beyond the ordinary jurisdiction of a magistrates' court and not on or from a ship or boat, it is deemed to have been committed within the body of any county which abuts the sea coast or adjoins that sea, and may be tried and punished accordingly.[222]

Fishery officers

A local fisheries committee may appoint fishery officers[223] for the purpose of enforcing the observance within their district of byelaws made by the committee. For the enforcement of byelaws, a fisheries officer will be deemed to be a constable and to have the same powers and privileges and be subject to the same liabilities as a constable has and is subject to at common law or by statute.[224] A local fisheries committee may, with the consent of the National Rivers Authority, appoint as an officer of the committee any officer of the Authority, and conversely the

[219] s.11(2) Sea Fisheries Regulation Act 1966, as amended by ss.38 and 46 Criminal Justice Act 1982.

[220] s.11(2A) Sea Fisheries Regulation Act 1966, inserted by s.5 and Sch.1 Fishery Limits Act 1976.

[221] s.11(3) Sea Fisheries Regulation Act 1966.

[222] s.11(7).

[223] Fishery officers must be distinguished from British sea fishery officers appointed for the purposes of the Sea Fisheries Acts, see s.7 Sea Fisheries Act 1968.

[224] s.10(1) and (3) Sea Fisheries Regulation Act 1966, and see s.36(1) Salmon and Freshwater Fisheries Act 1975 discussed above at p.444.

National Rivers Authority may appoint as an officer of the Authority any officer of the committee.[225]

For the purposes of enforcing byelaws made by a local fisheries committee, a fishery officer may, within the limits of the district, or of any adjoining sea fisheries district or district under the jurisdiction of the National Rivers Authority or a harbour authority, (a) stop and search any vessel or vehicle used within the district in fishing or in conveying either fish or any substance the deposit or discharge of which is prohibited or regulated by byelaw; (b) examine any instrument used in fishing for fish and search any container used in carrying fish; and (c) seize any sea fish or instrument taken or used in contravention of any byelaw.[226] If any person, without reasonable excuse, proof of which will lie on him, refuses to allow a fishery officer to exercise the powers conferred on him under the Sea Fisheries Regulation Act 1966, or resists or obstructs an officer in the performance of his duty, he will be guilty of an offence and liable on summary conviction to a fine not exceeding £2,000.[227]

Other powers of local fisheries committees

Local fisheries committees are given a range of miscellaneous powers. These allow the committee to stock or restock any public fishery for shellfish and for that purpose they may incur any expenses sanctioned by the Minister.[228] Subject to the approval of the Minister, a committee may undertake or cause to be undertaken, the destruction of predatory fish, predatory marine animals, predatory birds and eggs of predatory birds, if and so far as that destruction appears to the committee to be desirable for the preservation and improvement of the fisheries within their district and is not illegal under any Act other than the Sea Fish Industry Act 1938.[229]

---

[225] s.10(4) Sea Fisheries Regulation Act 1966, and s.141 and Sch.17 para.1 Water Act 1989.

[226] s.10(2) Sea Fisheries Regulation Act 1966.

[227] s.11(1), as amended by ss.38 and 46 Criminal Justice Act 1982.

[228] s.13(1) Sea Fisheries Regulation Act 1966.

[229] s.13(2). Provisions for the protection of seals are enacted by the Conservation of Seals Act 1970 and wild birds, their nests and eggs are protected by the Wildlife and Countryside Act 1981.

A local fisheries committee may contribute or undertake to contribute to the expenses of a harbour authority constituted under the Fishery Harbours Act 1915 for a harbour to which that Act applies situated wholly or partly in the district of the committee.[230] A committee may also contribute to the payment of the cost of executing works for the maintenance or improvement of any small harbour situated wholly or partly in their district which is a harbour which the Minster is satisfied is used principally by persons engaged in the sea fishing industry.[231]

Any local fisheries committee may, within their district, enforce any Act relating to sea fisheries.[232] In addition, the committee may institute proceedings for any offence under the Prevention of Oil Pollution Act 1971 which is committed within the district of the committee.[233]

Areas of local fisheries committees and the National Rivers Authority

Where a proposed sea fisheries district will adjoin or overlap the area of the National Rivers Authority, the Minister is required to define the limits of the sea fisheries district by drawing a line at or near the mouth of every river or stream flowing into the sea or into any estuary within those limits, or near the mouth of any estuary within those limits, and the sea fisheries district will not extend above that line. A Ministerial order of this kind, however, may provide that the National Rivers Authority is to have the powers of a local fisheries committee with respect to the river, stream or estuary.[234]

Where an area is under the jurisdiction of the National Rivers Authority or a harbour authority, and a sea fisheries district has not been created for the area, the Minister may confer on the National Rivers

---

[230] s.13(3) Sea Fisheries Regulation Act 1966.

[231] s.13(4). In either case, "harbour" includes any haven, cove or other landing place and "works" includes any slipways, capstans and other works facilitating the landing, launching or beaching of vessels in any harbour (s.13(4)).

[232] s.13(5).

[233] s.19(6) Prevention of Oil Pollution Act 1971.

[234] s.18(1) Sea Fisheries Regulation Act 1966.

Authority, or the harbour authority,[235] the powers of a local fisheries committee with respect to that area.[236] Where the National Rivers Authority or a harbour authority have the powers of a local fisheries committee, those powers are to be exercised subject to the same conditions as if exercised by a local fisheries committee. Likewise, the provisions of the Sea Fisheries Regulation Act 1966 will apply in relation to byelaws made, or officers appointed, in exercise of those powers as if the byelaws were made or the officers appointed by a local fisheries committee.[237] A county or metropolitan council may pay, or contribute to, any expenses incurred by the National Rivers Authority in exercise of their powers in accordance with these provisions.[238]

---

[235] "Harbour authority" means any person or persons being or claiming to be the owner or owners of a harbour or having the duty of improving, managing, maintaining or regulating a harbour (s.20(1)).

[236] s.18(2).

[237] s.18(3) Sea Fisheries Regulation Act 1966. The making of byelaws by the National Rivers Authority is subject to s.210 and Schs.25 and 26 Water Resources Act 1991, see p.235 above.

[238] s.19 Sea Fisheries Regulation Act 1966, as amended by s.16 and Sch.8 para.19 Local Government Act 1985.

INDEX

Note: in the entries which follow, where two numbers are separated by the letter "n" the first number refers to a page in the text and the second to the relevant footnote.

A

Page

abstraction, ...2, 13
- defined, ...250
- easements of, ...106–7
- evidence of, ...235
- extraordinary use of water, ...73–5
- licence requirement *see* licence to abstract and obstruct
- National Rivers Authority and water undertakers, by, ...269–70
- ordinary use of water, ...72–3
- percolating water, ...123–4, 126
- riparian rights, ...14, 66, 69–70, 72–7, 248
- statutory restrictions on, ...201, 207, 218, 229, 230, 237, 248–251
- statutory rights to, ...253–7, 260–1, 263, 266–8
- underground water, .. 122–3, 216n52, 249–51, 254, 257, 258, 261, 266, 272

access
- licence to abstract and impound and, ...258
- navigable rivers, ...149–51
- obstruction interfering with right of, ...141
- over foreshore, ...50–2
- riparian rights, ...67–8, 69

accretion and encroachment, ...21, 46–50, 151, 215

act of God, ...64, 86, 167, 298

Advisory Committee for Wales, ...209

agricultural pollution, ...328, 350
- codes of good agricultural practice, ...332–3
- nitrates, ...30–2, 360, 361, 367–8

agriculture
- abstraction for, ...254–5, 272
- drainage charges and rates, ...405–6, 408–9

aircraft, ...56

amenities, ...2, 321

anchorage rights, ...136–7, 139

Angell, ...2–3

animal health and pollution, ...353

anti–fouling paints, ...355

archaeological sites, ...31n44, 211, 212, 389

arm of the sea, ...5, 26, 31n45, 42

armed conflict *see* wartime exigency

Page

artificial watercourses, ... 5, 10–11, 115–121
 distinction between natural and, ... 115–16
 easement to receive water, ... 111
 permanent, ... 116–18
 pollution of, ... 91, 120–121, 291
 powers of water bailiffs, ... 442
 riparian rights and duties, ... 10, 14, 71–2, 114, 116–18, 120
 temporary, ... 101, 118–19
Attorney–General, ... 61, 98–9, 141

B

ballast as obstruction, ... 149
bank(s), ... 1, 7
 definition, ... 12–13, 379n39
 deposit of material on, ... 13, 383, 394
 erections on, ... 152–3
 fishing from, ... 195
 included in National River Authority's powers relating to main rivers, ...379
 ownership, ... 134, 154–5
 raising, ... 82
 repair of, ... 62–5
 works or operations on, ... 334
 see also embankment
bathing, ... 50
bathing water quality, ... 294n19, 359, 361, 364
bay, ... 5
bed, ... 1, 11–12
 alterations
  affecting flow near a mill, ... 82–3
  reducing flow, ... 429
 erections on, ... 78–80, 141–3, 152–3, 154, 190
  unauthorised, on foreshore, ... 43
 obstructions which have become part of, ... 82
 ownership
  artificial watercourse, ... 118
  navigable river, ... 154–5
  non–tidal, ... 17–20, 70, 78, 182, 184
  sea *see* under Crown
  tidal, ... 16, 20–21, 46
  type of fishery related to, ... 175
  where channel alters, ... 20–21, 70, 139
  works or operations on, ... 334
"best available techniques not entailing excessive cost" (BATNEEC), ... 316

Page
"best practicable environmental option" (BPEO), ...315
boats, boating, ...52, 160, 161
  beaching or mooring on non-tidal watercourse, ...134
  control of pollution from, ...160
  see also fishing boats and vessels; vessels
boreholes, ...124, 219, 229, 232, 250, 251, 255, 256, 257, 350n249
boundaries, ...18
  accretion and, ...48
  fisheries, ...191–3
  lying at obtuse angle to bank, ...19–20
  seaward, ...52–3
  see also medium filum aquae
bridges, ...148, 166, 168, 169
  construction, ...169–72
  floating, ...163
  maintenance, ...172–4, 397–8
British Coal Corporation, ...38
British Waterways Board, ...250, 258
Broads Authority, ...213, 390
byelaws
  bathing, ...50
  fishery, ...188, 237, 419–422, 425, 427, 434
    sea, ...352–3, 458–461, 464
  flood defence and land drainage, ...383, 413–14
  National Rivers Authority's powers to make, ...235–7, 383
  navigation, ...138, 154, 158, 159–160, 161

C

cadmium, ...360, 363
calcium carbide, ...337, 338
canals, ...8, 12, 115, 120, 138, 148, 353
  easements, ...101, 110, 112
  fisheries, ...194, 431, 432, 433
  medium filum rule, ...19
canoes
  disturbance of fish, ...140, 196, 425n38
catchment area, ...1–2
catchpits, ...327
cattle washing and watering, ...23, 72, 75, 92, 105, 106
cemeteries, ...334, 353
cesspools, ...121, 129
channel, ...5, 7
  alteration of, ...20–1, 70, 139, 193

channel – *continued* Page
clearing, 81–2, 156
operations on for flood defence and land drainage, 371
underground watercourse, 9, 126–7
charter
fishery rights, 187, 188, 428, 429, 430
chemicals
refuse, as, 337, 338
storage, 87, 129–130
Cinque Ports, 58
"civil emergency", 233
civil engineers
"independent", 284n159
maintenance and construction of reservoirs, 282–7
"supervising engineer", 285–6
coast protection and sea defence, 59–65, 381
coast protection authorities, 60
licence to take materials from seashore, 55
order to prohibit removal of materials from foreshore, 61
coast protection works, 61–2, 83, 146, 372
coastal states
contiguous zone and, 27–8
continental shelf, and, 36–7, 38
criminal jurisdiction in relation to foreign ships, 27
exclusive economic zone and, 33
sovereignty, 26, 28
coastal waters, 24–65
defined, 25, 291, 292
discharges into, 305
"relevant river or watercourse", 291–2
"coastline", 42
Code of Practice on Conservation, Access and Recreation, 214
codes of good agricultural practice, 332–3
colliery refuse as obstruction, 149
"collision regulations", 158–9
Commissioners of sewers, 59, 372, 386
common fishery, 175
common of fishery, 175, 176, 183–4
commons, 194
consents for discharges *see* discharge consents
conservancy authorities, 153–161, 223, 240, 397
consultee, 212, 245, 386, 390, 400
duty to maintain navigation, 146, 147, 156–8
National Rivers Authority as, 159–60, 206, 208, 380–1
regulation of navigation, 157, 158–9

conservancy authorities – *continued* Page
rights to abstract or impound, 253, 257, 259
conservation *see* environmental
conservators, 137–8
Conservators of the River Thames, 138, 155, 157
contamination *see* pollution
contiguous zone, 27–8
continental shelf
domestic law, 38–9
international law, 36–8
"controlled waters" in Water Resources Act 1991, 290–2
Convention on Fishing and Conservation of Living Resources of the High Seas (1966), 24
Convention on the Continental Shelf (1964), 24, 37n77
Convention on the High Seas (1963), 24, 38, 41n95
Convention on the Territorial Sea and Contiguous Zone (1965), 24
conveyancing
and accretion of land, 48–9
and *medium filum* rule, 18–19, 183
cooling purposes, use of water for, 2, 69
corporeal fishery, 175, 185
Countryside Council for Wales, 213, 390
crabs, 459
creek, 5, 163
Crown
coast protection duties, 59
conservancy duties, 153–4
exemption from payment of tolls, 165
grant of bed and soil of estuary or tidal water 131, 180–1
grant of fishery rights, 176, 180–1
jurisdiction over "royal rivers", 154
jurisdiction over territorial waters, 28
licence for ferry, 163, 166, 169
ownership of bed of inland lake, 21–2, 193
ownership of bed of navigable watercourse, 139
ownership of bed of non–tidal river, 182
ownership of bed of tidal watercourse, 15, 16, 20, 176
ownership of foreshore, 42–3, 49, 178, 190
ownership of islands, 30–1, 47
ownership of sea bed, 29–31, 38, 41, 46, 136, 179
rights relating to wreck and royal fish, 50, 55–8
Crown Estate Commissioners, 30, 43, 53, 417
"Crown land", 60n239
culvert, 3, 398

Page

custom
acquisition of water easements, ... 105, 125
common of piscary appurtenant, ... 184
digging ballast, sand and shingle, ... 54
drying nets on private land, ... 179
embank against flood, to, ... 83–4
permissible pollution, ... 92–3, 108
repair banks, to, ... 62
right over foreshore, ... 50, 51
several fishery in tidal watercourse, ... 186
taking "wreck of the sea, flotsam and jetsam", ... 45
towing rights, ... 137
cut, ... 3, 115
cutting, ... 133

D

dam, ... 73, 76–7, 80, 81, 398
fisheries, ... 215, 419, 421, 427, 430–2, 433, 442
fishing mill, ... 215, 419, 430, 434, 442
see also impounding
dangerous substances Directive, ... 293n19, 359, 360
deckchairs, ... 50n173, 51
deed
for creation and extinguishment of easements, ... 101, 102, 113
transfer of ferry, ... 163
transfer of fishery rights, ... 185, 186, 191
definitions
"abstraction", ... 250
"agglomeration" (Directive 91/271/EEC), ... 365n304
"agricultural land", ... 406n131
"agriculture", ... 254n46
"arrestable offences", ... 444n123
"banks", ... 12–13
of main rivers, ... 379n39
"bed", ... 11–12
"by night", ... 444
"causing and knowingly permitting", ... 297–8
channel, ... 127
"charging authorities" (land drainage), ... 384n58
"coastal waters"
for water pollution purposes, ... 291, 292
in Water Resources Act 1991, ... 25
"coastline", ... 42

definitions – *continued* Page
"collecting system" (Directive 91/271/EEC), ... 365n304,
"compensation water", ... 277n136
"consent provisions", ... 313n105
"conservancy authority", ... 253n42
"consumer", ... 221n68
"continental shelf", ... 36
"controlled waste", ... 321
"crossline", ... 424n30
"Crown land", ... 60n239
"daytime", ... 452n171
"derelict", ... 57
"development", ... 333
"discharge" (Directive 76/464/EEC), ... 361n296
"discharge pipe", ... 227n101
"discrete waters", ... 6, 228n105, 249
"disposal" of radioactive substances, ... 343n220
"disposal licence", ... 303n63
"ditch", ... 4, 401n115
"domestic purposes", ... 350n249
"domestic waste water" (Directive 91/271/EEC), ... 365n304
"drain", ... 3–4
"drainage", ... 373n12
"drainage body", ... 379n40, 384
"eels", ... 423n27
"effluent", ... 296n27
"environment", ... 321n140
"exclusive economic zone", ... 32
"existing ferry", ... 164n18
"exploration", ... 39n84
"firearm", ... 423n28
"fish", ... 453
"fish farm", ... 442n108, 454n183
"fish farming", ... 456n189
"fishing boat", ... 34n64
"fishing interests", ... 458n201
"fishing mill dam", ... 430n62
"fishing weir", ... 429n61
"fixed engine", ... 428
"flood", ... 83
"flood defence", ... 372, 373n12
"flood warning system", ... 241n150, 382–3
"flotsam", ... 56
"foreign fishing boat", ... 34n65
"foreshore", ... 41–2, 417n9

definitions – *continued* Page

"freshwater fish"

under Diseases of Fish Acts, ... 453n177

under Salmon and Freshwater Fisheries Act 1975, ... 423n27

"fresh–water limit" (Directive 74/464/EEC), ... 361n297

"general arrest conditions", ... 444n123

"ground waters", ... 292

"harbour authority", ... 253n42, 464n235

harbour works, ... 463n231

high seas, ... 39, 40–1

"immature salmon", ... 424n36

"impounding works", ... 251–2

"independent" civil engineer, ... 284n159

"industrial waste water" (Directive 91/271/EEC), ... 365n304

"infected waters", ... 454n178

"inland fish farm", ... 456n191

"inland freshwaters", ... 5–6, 291–2

"inland surface water" (Directive 76/464/EEC), ... 361n297

"inland waters"

Diseases of Fish Acts, ... 454n180, 456n191

Water Resources Act 1991, ... 5–6, 249

"internal coastal waters" (Directive 74/464/EEC), ... 361n297

"internal drainage functions", ... 374n16

"jetsam", ... 56

"lagan", ... 56–7

"lake", ... 21n120

"land drainage", ... 246n14, 255n54

"licence of right", ... 267

"main river", ... 378n33

"marine waters", ... 454n181, 456n193

"migratory trout", ... 423n27

"miles"

Fishery Limits Act, ... 33n58

Water Resources Act 1991, ... 207n20

"mill", ... 430

"mine", ... 302n57

"National Park authority", ... 390n79

"nautical miles", ... 29n32

"navigation", ... 135

"navigation authority", ... 253n42

"non–arrestable offences", ... 444n123

"non–natural" land use, ... 86–7

"nuclear matter", ... 345n227

"occupier" (fishery), ... 418n12

"offence" of taking, killing or handling salmon, ... 450n150

definitions – *continued* Page
"offshore installation", 39n84
"oil", 347n236
"1 p.e." (population equivalent) (Directive 91/271/EEC), 365n305
"ordinary watercourse", 394
"otter lath or jack", 423n29
"owner" (fishery), 418n12
"pest", 354n262
"pesticide", 354n262
"petroleum spirit", 337n203
"poisonous, noxious or polluting", 295–6, 427n47
"pollution", 91–2, 361n296
"pollution of the environment", 321n140
"public sewer", 4n5
qualification (land drainage), 385n60
"quarry", 302n57
"radioactive material", 342n218
"radioactive waste", 342n218
"Railway Company", 314n110
"relevant lake or pond", 5–6, 291–2
"relevant Minister"
Land Drainage Act 1991, 371n2, 385n61
nitrate sensitive areas, 330n172
Water Resources Act 1991, 236n132, 241n149, 375n22
"relevant offence" (taking, killing or handling salmon), 450
"relevant pipe", 314n109
"relevant river or watercourse"
inland freshwaters, 5–6
pollution control, 291–2
"relevant territorial waters", 290–1
"relevant waterworks", 327n160
"relevant works power" of National Rivers Authority, 219n59
reservoir, 280
"resource main", 221n67, 227n101
"riparian rights", 66
"river", 3
"River Tweed", 415
"road–ferry", 164n21
"salmon"
Diseases of Fish Acts, 453n177
Salmon Act 1986, 423n27, 449n145
"sea beach", 42
"sea fish, fishing", 34n63, 458n206
"seashore", 41, 145n105
"secondary treatment" (Directive 91/271/EEC), 366n307

definitions – *continued* Page

"service pipe", 221n68
"setline", 424n30
"sewage effluent", 296n27
"sewer", 3–4
"shellfish", 453n177, 458n206
"source of supply" for water resources purposes, 249
"spray irrigation", 254n47
"spring", 125
"statutory order", 303
"stopcock", 221n68
"stroke–haul or snatch", 424n31
"substance" for water pollution purposes, 296n27
"supervising engineer", 285–6
"taking" salmon, trout or freshwater fish, 425n36
"territorial waters", 28
"the Broads", 390n79
"the Minister(s)"
Diseases of Fish Acts, 456n188
for fishery legislation, 34n61, 416
Land Drainage Act 1991, 371n2, 385n61
Water Resources Act 1991, 205n10
"the sea", 26, 31n45
Sea Fisheries Regulation Act 1966, 457n197
"tidal waters", 15, 25–6
"trade effluent", 296n27, 338n205
"trade premises", 338n205
"trout", 423n27
"unauthorised" fishing mill dam, 430
"unauthorised" fishing weir, 429
"unauthorised" fixed engine, 428
"unclean" fish, 424n36
"underground strata", 249
"undertaker(s)" (Reservoirs Act 1975), 280–1
"undertaking" (disposal of radioactive substances), 343n220
"underwater exploitation, exploration", 39n84
"United Kingdom waters", 31n45, 323n152
"urban waste water" (Directive 91/271/EEC), 365n304
"vessel", 302n55
"waste", 321n136
"waste management licence", 303n63
"waste regulation authorities", 321n137
"watercourse", 2–5, 6, 249n28, 291
"waterworks", 350n249
"wreck", 56–7

Page
Department of the Environment, ...199
"derelict", ... 55, 56, 57
"dereliction", ...46
Director General of Water Services, ... 198, 201, 231
Director of Public Prosecutions, ...251n34, 252n39, 344
discharge consents, ...297n32, 304–15, 319, 326, 426
 appeals to Secretary of State, ... 311–12
 applications, ...299, 305–7
 charges, ...312–13
 consents without application, ... 309, 311
 drought orders and, ... 275, 278
 notification of proposal to give consent, ... 307–8
 reference of applications to Secretary of State, ... 308–9
 restrictions on variation and revocation of, ...311
 revocation of, alteration and imposition of conditions, ... 309–11
 trade effluent, for, ... 338–9
 waste disposal, for ...323
discharge pipe, ...227
discharge(s)
 authorised, ... 303–25
  under integrated pollution control, ... 315–20
 byelaws relating to fisheries, ...422
 coastal waters, into, ...305
 consents for *see* discharge consents
 defences to principal water pollution offences, ...303
 drought orders and, ... 275, 277, 279
 easements to, ... 110–111
  effluent, of, ...2, 96, 234–5, 323
  public sewers, into and from, ... 299–300, 337–9
  trade effluent, of, ... 104–5, 296, 338–9
 European Community Directives on *see under* European Community
 polluting matter, of, *see* pollution
 prohibitions of certain, ... 298–9
 sampling, ...234–5, 307
 sewage, of, *see* sewage discharge
 vessels, from, ... 299, 302
 water, of,
  foul water, ...5
  land, from, ... 87–9, 116
  mines, from, ...88–9, 90, 110, 302
  National Rivers Authority for works purposes, by, ...18, 226, 313–15
 see also escapes
"discrete waters", ... 6, 228, 249

Page

ditch, ...3, 133, 401–2
- definition, ...4, 401n115

diversion
- action for diverting water from a mill, ...81
- of artificial watercourse, ...118
- easements of, ...106–7
- extraordinary use of water, ...72–3
- in general, ...76–7
- ordinary use of water, ...72–3
- riparian rights and, ...71, 72–7
- River Thames, ...147
- of specified navigable watercourse for bridge construction, ...170–1
- taking water at spring head as wrongful, ...7–8, 123
- *see also* abstraction

dock, ...5, 148, 354

doctrine of accretion, ...21, 46–50

"domestic purposes"
- defined, ...350n249
- use of water for *see under* water
- *see also* water supply

drain, ...103, 119, 121, 125, 128, 216n52, 302, 327
- defined, ...3–4
- *see also* land drainage

drainage boards, and coastal protection, ...59

drainage charges and rates, ...404–6, 407–9

dredging operations, ...146, 154, 155, 425n38

drinking water quality, ...293n19, 359, 361, 364, 367

drought orders, ...273–280
- emergency, ...274, 276–7, 279n142
- offences under, ...279–280
- ordinary, ...273–6
- provisions, works and compensation under, ...277–9

dry watercourse, ...4, 7

Duchy of Cornwall, ...417

Duchy of Lancaster, ...417

Dyers Company, ...58

dykes, ...3

E

easements
- acquisition, ...101–5
  - custom, ...105
  - grant, ...101–2

easements, acquisition – *continued* Page
prescription, ... 103–5
statute, ... 105
extinguishment of, ... 112–14
nature and characteristics of, ... 100–1
secondary, ... 111–12
specific, ... 106–12
easements (particular)
abstraction, diversion and obstruction, ... 79, 106–7
acquired by National Rivers Authority, ... 326
artificial watercourse, of, ... 116, 117–18
discharging flood water, ... 83
discharging or receiving water, ... 110–11
diverting flood water, ... 85
erecting obstruction, ... 79
fisheries, ... 417, 419
navigation, ... 137, 154
pollute, to, ... 93, 107–9, 114
preventing flood damage, ... 83, 101
protecting house from the sea, ... 62
repairing banks of a river, ... 63
spraying crops and water cattle, ... 23, 75
taking water from a spring, ... 9
taking water for domestic purposes, ... 23, 105, 125
on tidal navigable watercourses, ... 149
underground and percolating water, ... 110
eel fisheries, ... 210, 415, 421, 422, 437–8, 439
"eels" defined, ... 423n27
electricity industry, ... 246, 272
embankment, ... 79, 83–4
see also bank(s)
emergency
civil, ... 233
defence to pollution offences, ... 301–2
discharges for works purposes by National Rivers Authority, ... 314
land drainage work, ... 380, 391, 395
encroachment *see* accretion and encroachment
"environment" defined, ... 321n140
environmental duties
National Rivers Authority, of, ... 14, 229, 246, 310, 325–6, 389–91
Water Resources Act 1991 and Land Drainage Act 1991, in, ... 371, 389–91
environmental information, ... 318–19, 320
environmental policy, ... 198, 199
European Economic Community, ... 356–7

Page

environmental pollution, ... 321, 322, 323
    defined, ... 321n140
escapes of polluting matter *see* pollution
escapes of water, ... 84–9
    civil liability of National Rivers Authority for, ... 233–4
    from reservoirs, ... 86, 287, 289
    rule in *Rylands v. Fletcher*, ... 86–7
Esk, river, ... 207, 415
estuaries, ... 1, 5, 26, 31n45, 42, 192, 193, 463
European Community
    constitution and legislation, ... 209, 231, 310, 336, 355–9, 417
        "direct effect" principle, ... 357–8
    Directives
        concerned with particular polluting activities, ... 200 364–8
        concerned with water quality, ... 357, 358, 359–361, 363–4
        75/440/EEC on quality of drinking water, ... 293, 359, 361, 364
        76/160/EEC concerning bathing water, ... 294n19, 359, 361, 364
        76/464/EEC on pollution caused by dangerous substances, ... 293, 359, 360, 361–3
        78/659/EEC on water for freshwater fish, ... 359n282, 364
        79/923/EEC on the quality required of shellfish waters, ... 359, 364
        80/68/EEC on protection of groundwater against pollution by certain dangerous substances, ... 360, 361n298
        80/778/EEC on quality of water intended for human consumption, ... 360, 367
        82/176/EEC on limit values and quality objectives for mercury, ... 360, 363
        83/513/EEC on limit values and quality objectives for cadmium discharges, ... 360, 363
        84/491/EEC on limit values and quality objectives for discharges of hexachlorocyclohexane, ... 360, 363
        86/280/EEC on limit values and quality objectives for List I substances, ... 360, 363
        88/347/EEC amending 86/280/EEC, ... 363
        90/415/EEC amending 86/280/EEC, ... 363
        91/271/EEC concerning urban waste water treatment, ... 360, 361, 365–7
        Directive on pollution by nitrates from diffuse sources, ... 360, 361, 367–8, 369
    fisheries policy, ... 35–6, 177
    pollution legislation, ... 200, 290, 350–70
        emission standards, ... 362–3
    Regulation 101/76, ... 36n69
    water legislation, ... 199, 290, 293

European Community – *continued* Page
and national legislation ... 368–370
European Court of Justice, ... 358
exclusive economic zone
domestic law, ... 33–6
international law, ... 32–3

F

factory legislation, ... 14
ferries, ... 104
"existing ferry", ... 164n18
extinguishment, ... 169
legal character of, ... 162–5
rights and obligations of owner, ... 165–9
terminals, ... 144–5
firefighting, ... 256
fish
byelaws relating to taking, ... 420, 421, 427
causing or knowingly permitting pollution of, ... 304n72, 426, 427
defined in Diseases of Fish Acts, ... 453n177
diseases, ... 453–7
"designated area", ... 454
import restrictions, ... 453
interfering with free passage of, ... 79, 196, 428–34, 435, 436, 438
introduction into inland waters, ... 441–2
prohibition of certain modes of taking or destroying, ... 423–7, 446
sale of forfeited, ... 447
taking above or below obstruction, ... 433–4
taking or destroying under Theft Act 1968, ... 452
taking with nets, ... 189, 420, 421, 425–6, 428
theft, ... 196, 451
times of fishing, selling, exporting, ... 434–8
fish farming
inland waters, ... 455, 456
licence, ... 416
marine waters, ... 454, 455, 456
fish farms, ... 441
registration, ... 455–7
fish pass, ... 215, 419, 430–1, 434
fish ponds, ... 193–4, 196, 451
fisheries, ... 2, 201, 265n89
byelaws, ... 188, 237, 419–22, 425, 427, 434
change of course in navigable river and, ... 139
common law, ... 175–197

fisheries – *continued* Page
compensation for injury by byelaw of National Rivers Authority, ...237
compensation for restrictions on taking salmon and trout, ...434
navigation right takes precedence over fishery right, ...139–140
non–tidal watercourses, in, ...176, 181, 182, 186, 187, 190–1, 194
pollution of, ...93–4, 197, 352–3, 426, 427
private, ...176, 178, 181, 182–197, 439, 452
boundaries of, ...191–3
canals and reservoirs, ...194
claims to, ...184–7
disturbance of, ...140, 196–7, 425
evidence of title to, ...187–190
lakes and ponds, ...22, 193–4
paths, ...194–5
presumptions as to ownership of, ...190–1
weirs, ...147, 195–6
public *see under* public rights
regional and local fisheries advisory committees, ...418
sea *see* sea fisheries
statutory provisions, ...415–464
contributions of fisheries to National Rivers Authority, ...418
land acquisition, ...419
ministerial powers and fisheries orders, ...415–17
provisions of Diseases of Fish Acts, ...453–7
provisions of Salmon Act 1986, ...448–451
provisions of Salmon and Freshwater Fisheries Act 1975, ...423–448
in tidal waters, ...176–182, 184, 187
see also sea fisheries
types, ...175–6
fisheries advisory committees, ...210
fisheries functions of National Rivers Authority,
....206, 207, 209, 236, 246, 374, 415–23
acquisition of land and obstructions, ...419
fisheries contributions to, ...418
infected waters, ... 454, 455
power to make fishery byelaws, ...237, 419–422
regional and local fisheries advisory committees, ...418
sea fisheries, ...458, 460, 461, 462, 463–4
fishery limits, ...19, 33–6, 177
"miles" defined for, ... 33n58
fishery officers, ...461–2
fishing boats and vessels, ...56, 446, 460–1, 462
defined, ... 34n64
fishery byelaws, ...421
foreign, ...34–5, 177

fishing boats and vessels – *continued* Page
powers of water bailiffs concerning, 442
fishing licences, 182, 438–41
forfeiture and disqualification, 447–8
fishing mill dam, 215, 419, 430, 434, 442
defined, 430n62
fishing paths, 194–5
fishing weir, 215, 419, 429, 433, 442
fishing with rod and line, 425, 433, 434, 435, 437, 438, 439, 452
byelaws, 421, 422, 434
fixed engines, 147, 180, 189, 215, 237, 419, 421, 428–9, 435, 442, 459
floating bridge, 163
floating structure in navigable river, 152
flood
damage to bridge, 173
defined, 83
opening sluices to let off water in cases of, 432
see also escapes of water
flood defence, 201–2, 238, 371–414
definition of watercourse for, 4
regulations and byelaws, 383–4
rights to protection against flood, 82–4, 372
flood defence functions of National Rivers Authority,
59–60, 205, 206, 207, 209, 222, 236, 237, 239–240, 241, 372, 373–7
byelaws, 383–4
financial provisions, 375, 404–7
flood warning systems, 282–3
powers to carry out works in connection with main rivers, 381–2
flood defence committees, 374–5
see also local flood defence committees; regional flood defence committees
flood–gates, 427
flood warning systems, 371, 373, 382–3
"flotsam", 55, 56
flowing water, 1, 7–8, 13–14
accretion of land abutting, 47
interference with, 70–1, 124
rights to use *see* riparian rights
footpath *see* public footpaths
foreign fishing boats, 34–5, 177
defined, 34n65
foreshore
access over, 50–2
accretion and encroachment, 46–50
defined, 41–2, 417n9

foreshore– *continued* Page
fishing on, 177–180, 192, 195
jurisdiction over, 52–3
landing and embarkation, 137, 178
limits and ownership, 41–6, 56, 178, 190, 460
moorings on, 136, 178–9
order to prohibit removal of materials from, 61
ownership of natural products on, 53
rights over, 50
works on as obstruction to navigation, 145–6
foul water, 216n52, 314n108, 326–7
freedom of the seas, 33, 39–41, 132
fresh waters
fishery rights, 176
freshwater fish, 422, 423, 424, 439, 447, 453
close seasons, 437–8
defined, 423n27, 453n177
Directive 78/659/EEC, 359n282, 364
freshwater fisheries, 210, 352, 415, 421
provisions of Salmon and Freshwater Fisheries Act 1975, 423–48
fresh–water limits, 25, 226, 292, 361n297

G

gas manufacture and supply, 305n73, 351–2
gas refuse pollution, 94
Geneva Convention on the Law of the Sea, 24
goits, 112, 115, 120
grant
easements of water, 100, 101–5, 106, 116
exclusive right to cut seaweed, 53–4
ferry, 163
fishery rights, 176, 180–1, 183–9, 191, 428, 430
navigation on non–tidal waters, 134
ownership of foreshore, 44–6, 56, 179
oyster bed, 139
right to pollute, 93
riparian rights, 69, 117
weirs, 195, 429
gratings, 432–3
byelaws, 422
gravel, taking, 50, 55
gravel pits, 84, 128
Grotius, 39
"ground waters" defined, 292

Page

grounding rights, ...135

H

Hale, ...20, 58, 180, 193n120
harbour
    floating, ...138
    pollution, ...354
harbour works, ...463
    erection, ...49
harbour authority, ...146, 147, 240
    abstracting or impounding rights, ...253, 257, 259
    consultee, ...212, 245, 386, 390, 400
    contributions by local fisheries committees, ...463
    National Rivers Authority as, ...159–160, 206, 208
    oil pollution and, ...348
    powers of local fisheries committee, ...463, 464
    rights to divert, ...223
Health and Safety Commission, ...231
Health and Safety Executive, ...231
heated liquids, discharge of, ...337
Her Majesty's Inspectorate of Pollution (HMIP), ...316, 317, 318, 319, 320, 342
    relationship with National Rivers Authority, ...319–320
hexachlorocyclohexane, ...360, 363
high seas
    "collision regulations", ...158
    domestic law, ...40–1
    freedom of, ...27, 33, 39–41, 132
    international law, ...39–40
highway, ...151, 314, 350
    across dock, ...148
    along sea wall, ...62, 65
    as towpath, ...137
    bridges and, ...169–170, 172–3
    ferry and, ...164–5
    fishing from, ...195
highway authority, ...55, 65, 111, 164, 165, 169–170, 172–4, 302

I

impounding
    licence requirement *see* licence to abstract and obstruct
    National Rivers Authority and water undertakers, by, ...269–270
    statutory restrictions on, ...207, 218, 237, 251–2

impounding – *continued* Page
statutory rights, 253–7
impounding works defined, 251–2
see also dams; reservoirs
inclosure of waste, 19
incorporeal fishery, 140, 175, 176, 183, 185, 196
industrial pollution, 315
industrial waste water, 365, 367
infected waters, 454–5
injunction
disturbance of fishery, 140, 196–7
encroachment on exclusive right of access, 150
extraordinary use of water, 74
ferry, relating to, 166, 169
obstruction of towpath, 138
pollution, 90, 94, 95–7, 99
polluting underground percolating water, 129
preventing water flowing to a mill, 81
taking stones from foreshore, 54
unlawful obstruction and diversion, 79
unreasonable interference with use of water, 71
inland freshwaters
defined, 5–6
for pollution control purposes, 291–2
pollution offences, 302, 320
"relevant lake or pond", 5–6, 291–2
"relevant river or watercourse", 5–6, 291–2
inland navigation, 431
drought orders and, 277
see also canals; navigable rivers
inland waters
byelaws, 236
fish farming, 455, 456
fishery rights, 190
flood defence, 59–60, 82–3
gauge for measuring, 229–230
minimum acceptable flows, 245–7, 261
minimum acceptable level or volume, 247–8
public right of navigation, 134, 140, 158–9, 160
statutory definitions, 5–6, 249, 454n180, 456n191
inspection chambers, 235, 307
integrated pollution control, 315
authorisations for prescribed processes, 316–17
information provisions, 318–19, 320
offences under, 317–18

Page

internal drainage boards, ...372, 384–414
 arrangements as to works, ...397
 consent for obstructions, ...398–9
 consultee, ...222, 245, 260, 398
 contributions to expenses of National Rivers Authority, ...406–7
 disposal of spoil, ...394–5
 environmental and recreational duties, ...389–391
 financial provisions, ...407–10
 general powers, ...391–4, 398
 miscellaneous powers, ...412–14
 powers to modify existing obligations, ...402–3
 repair of watercourses and bridges, ...171, 173–4, 397–8
 supervision by National Rivers Authority, ...387–9
 works for maintaining flow of watercourse, ...399
internal drainage districts, ...384–7
International Convention for the Prevention of Pollution from Ships 1973 (MARPOL), ...346
International Convention on Civil Liability for Oil Pollution Damage 1969, ...349
International Convention on the Establishment of an International Fund for Compensation for Oil Pollution Damage, ...349
international law and agreements, ...24, 209, 417
 "collision regulations", ...158–9
 continental shelf, ...36–8
 exclusive economic zone, ...32–3
 high seas, ...39–40
 on pollution, ...310, 336, 346, 349
 territorial sea, ...26–8
 see also European Economic Community
International Regulations for Preventing Collisions at Sea 1972, ...158, 159
irrigation, ...73, 74–5, 104
 see also spray irrigation
islands
 medium filum rule, ...19
 at sea, ...30–1, 47

J

"jetsam", ...55, 56
joint planning board, ...216
Justice of the Peace *see* magistrate

L

laches, ...97

Page

"lagan", ... 55, 56–7
lake, ... 5, 6, 291–2
  defined, ... 21n120
  fishery, ... 22, 193–4
  ownership of lake bed, ... 21–2, 193
  pollution, ... 91
lampreys, ... 438
land
  acquisition and disposal of, ... 50, 164, 214–16, 219, 258–9, 412, 419
  powers of entry
    internal drainage boards and local authorities, by, ... 412–13
    water bailiff's, ... 443
    Water Resources Act 1991, under, ... 218–221
  reclamation *see* reclamation
land charges, ... 216
land drainage, ... 59, 115, 198, 246, 371–414
  abstraction for, ... 255
  agricultural purposes, for, ... 85, 128
  "banks" defined for, ... 13
  disposal of spoil, ... 394–5
  drainage of small areas, ... 396–7
  environmental and recreational duties, ... 389–391
  finance, ... 404–411
  general powers of internal drainage boards and local authorities, ... 391–4
  Ministerial authorisation for landowners to carry out works, ... 398
  powers to modify existing obligations, ... 402–4
  repair of sea walls and river banks, ... 64
  restoration and improvement of ditches, ... 401–2
  schemes for transfer of functions to National Rivers Authority, ... 379, 386–7
  support of subterranean water, ... 126–7
  "watercourse" defined for, ... 4
  works for maintaining flow of watercourse, ... 399–400
land drainage charges and rates, ... 404–6, 407–9
land drainage functions of National Rivers Authority, ... 206, 207, 209, 222, 246, 373–411
  acquisition of accretions of land, ... 50, 215
  arrangements with certain authorities, ... 380–1
  boundaries of internal drainage districts and, ... 385–7
  byelaws, ... 236, 237, 383
  consultee, ... 398, 408
  drainage of small areas, ... 396–7
  financial provisions, ... 241, 404–7, 410–11
  powers in connection with main rivers, ... 378–80, 381–2
  powers to maintain flow of watercourse, ... 399

land drainage functions of National Rivers Authority – *continued* Page
powers to modify existing obligations, 402–4
supervision of drainage boards and local authorities, 387–9, 395
transfer of functions to, 379, 386–7
land preservation works, 354
land use, 2
"non–natural", 86–7
landing rights, 134, 136–7, 162, 178
landowner
drainage works, 398, 401–2, 402–3
duties to repair sea walls and river banks, 62–5
escape, overflow and discharge of water, 84–9
right to discharge dirty water, 121
rights relating to land adjoining sea, 51, 54–5, 83
rights relating to surface water, 14, 128
rights to underground percolating water, 14, 124
use of water by non–riparian, 69–70
see also riparian owner; riparian rights
Lands Tribunal, 392, 394, 402, 413
Law Commission, 201, 202
lease, of fishery, 185–6, 190, 191
licence
abstract and obstruct, to, 78, 107, 124, 224–5, 248–52, 269
applications, 257–263
charges, 266, 270–3
civil liability, 268–9
derogation from protected rights, 266–8
form and content of, 263–5
registers, 273
revocation and variation of, 265–6
succession to, 264
combined abstraction and impounding, 259
extinguish easements, to, 113
ferry, for, 163, 166, 169
fish, to, 182, 438–441
fishery, of, 185–6, 190, 191
import fish, to, 453
"licence of right", 267
navigation, relating to, 154, 155
rearing of fish, 416
salmon dealer, for, 448–9
livestock *see* cattle
lobsters, 459
local authority
coastal protection powers, 59, 60

local authority – *continued* Page
easements, ... 105
entitlement to main river maps, ... 227
ferries, ... 164
foreshore, powers relating to, ... 43, 50–1, 52–3
land drainage and flood defence, and,
.... 372, 374, 377, 379, 381, 382, 388, 391–7, 399
disposal of spoil, ... 394–5
drainage of small areas, ... 396–7
financial provisions, ... 409, 411
levies on, for flood defence, ... 404
powers of entry to land, ... 412–13
powers relating to acquisition of land, ... 412
powers to make byelaws, ... 413, 414
works for maintaining flow of watercourse, ... 399–400
navigation, and, ... 158
pollution, and, ... 96, 97, 98
public health law, ... 339–341
reservoirs, powers relating to, ... 281–8
sea fisheries district, and, ... 457, 464
water resource management, ... 216, 231
local fisheries advisory committees, ... 418
local fisheries committees, ... 352, 421n20, 457–464
byelaws, ... 352, 428, 458–461
fishery officers, ... 461–2
other powers, ... 462–3
local flood defence committees, ... 210–11, 372, 376–7
local flood defence districts, ... 377, 404–5
local flood defence schemes, ... 210, 376–7
local inquiries, under Water Resources Act 1991, ... 237–8, 262
local land drainage schemes, ... 376
local planning authorities and pollution, ... 333–5
locks, ... 147, 154, 156
London Gazette, ... 259, 260, 305, 306, 309, 330, 331, 417
lord of the manor
ownership of fishery, ... 45, 191
ownership of foreshore, ... 43–5
right to cut seaweed, ... 53–4
wreck, and, ... 55, 56, 57
loss of amenity, ... 95

M

magistrate
fisheries, and, ... 443, 448

magistrate – *continued* Page
warrant to enter under Water Resources Act 1991, ...220
magistrates' court, ...336, 341, 400
main river, ...60, 226–7
bridge over, ...171
flood defence and drainage works, ...381–2
maps, ...226–7, 378
riparian rights in relation to lateral tributaries, ...68–9
structures in, over or under, ...379–80
main river functions of National Rivers Authority, ...378–9
arrangements with navigation or conservancy authorities, ...380–1, 400
structures in, over and under, ...379–380
transfer of functions to, ...379
mandamus, prerogative writ of, ...96, 141
manholes, ...235, 307
maps
fresh–water limits, ...25, 226, 292
main rivers, ...226–7, 378
waterworks, ...227–8
marine fish farming, ...454, 455, 456
marine nature reserves, ...31n44
medium filum aquae, ...17–20, 22, 70, 183, 190, 194
tidal watercourse, ...192–3
Medway, river, ...195
mercury, ...360, 363
migratory fish
diversions interfering with movements of, ...77
migratory trout, ...423n27, 425, 428, 429, 430, 433, 435, 436
mill
artificial watercourse, and, ...115, 119, 120
defined, ...430n62
easements, ...106–7, 114
pollution of percolating water, ...129
power to enter, ...412
taking of salmon or trout above or below, ...434
milling
use of water for, ...80–1, 82, 431, 432, 433
mineral oils *see* oil
mineral rights, ...215
acquisition by National Rivers Authority, ...223
exploration of continental shelf, ...38
minerals
exploitation, ...31n44, 55, 123, 229
mines
customary use of water, ...105

mines – *continued* Page
drainage, ...118
easement to receive water, ...111
pollution and, ...90, 92–3, 108, 302, 312, 326
water discharging from, ...88–9, 110, 302, 326
mining operations, ...122, 229, 334
Minister of Agriculture, Fisheries and Food, ...324, 344, 371, 415, 453
Minister of Transport, ...52–3, 145–6
Monopolies Commission, ...231
mooring(s)
rights, ...134, 135, 136–7, 151–2
seabed, ...43, 136, 178–9
vessels as obstruction, ...149
mooring anchor as obstruction, ...149
mooring buoys, ...158

N

National Parks, ...213, 390
National Rivers Authority, ...199, 201, 202
acquisition of land resulting from drainage work, ...50, 215
bridges, ...170, 171, 173–4
charges, ...240–1
coast protection powers, ...59–60, 381
codes of practice for, ...214
committees with functions in relation to, ...209–11
compulsory works, ...217–18, 219, 303
constitution, ...204–6
directions in interest of national security, ...233, 242
discharge consents *see* discharge consents
environmental duties *see* under environmental
financial provisions, ...239–42
flood defence functions *see* flood defence functions of National Rivers Authority
gas pollution and, ...352
general duties relating to water industry, ...211
incidental functions and powers, ...207–8
information provisions, ...224–232
land and works powers, ...214–223, 314n108
licence to abstract or obstruct *see* licence to abstract or obstruct
management of reservoirs, ...280
Ministerial directions to, ...208–9
navigation functions *see* navigation functions of National Rivers Authority
pollution prevention and control *see* pollution functions of National Rivers Authority

National Rivers Authority – *continued* Page
powers of entry, ... 218–221
principal functions, ... 206–7
protection of water quality, ... 200, 206, 294, 295, 319–320, 369
relationship with Her Majesty's Inspectorate of Pollution, ... 319–320
"relevant works power", ... 219n59
National Rivers Authority, The, ... 199
national security, ... 233, 242, 318
Natural Environment Research Council, ... 229, 232
Nature Conservancy Council for England, ... 213, 390
navigable watercourses, ... 15, 16, 132, 236, 425n38
bridges, ... 169–171
change of channel, ... 139
fish passes, ... 431
obstruction *see* obstruction
oil pollution *see* oil pollution
ownership, ... 154–5
riparian rights, ... 68, 149–151
weirs, ... 195
navigation, ... 2, 131–161, 432
defined in Merchant Shipping Act 1894, ... 135
freedom of, ... 27, 33, 37, 41
non–tidal watercourses, ... 133–5
public right of *see* public right of navigation
tidal watercourses, ... 131–3
navigation authorities, ... 146, 153–161, 240, 327, 381, 397, 413
abstracting and impounding rights, ... 253, 257, 259
consultee, ... 170, 212, 245, 386, 390, 400
drought orders and, ... 277
duty to maintain navigation, ... 156–8
powers relating to towpaths, ... 137, 138
powers to divert watercourses, ... 223
regulation of navigation, ... 139, 157, 158–9
navigation commissioners, ... 139
duty to repair sea walls, ... 64
navigation functions of National Rivers Authority,
.... 139, 159–160, 206, 208, 246, 314, 380–1, 402–3, 410
navigation rights
anchoring, mooring and landing, ... 134, 135, 136–7, 139, 178
extinguishment of, ... 139
passage and grounding, ... 135–6, 433
precedence over right of fishery, ... 139–140
towing, ... 137–9
navigation tolls, ... 410

Page

negligence
abstraction of water, ... 126, 265
drainage work, ... 393
failure to maintain river wall, ... 64
ferries, ... 167
obstruction of vessels, ... 153
pollution, ... 75, 90, 129
nets, ... 179, 189, 425–6, 428, 444, 451
fishery byelaws, ... 420, 421, 425
sea fishing, ... 459
"night lines", ... 424n30
nitrate pollution, ... 330–2, 360, 361, 367–8
nitrate sensitive areas, ... 209, 330–2
"relevant Minister", ... 330n172
nitrates Directive, ... 360, 361, 367–8, 369
non–riparian owner *see* landowner
non–tidal watercourses, ... 16–20
fishery rights, ... 176, 181, 182, 186, 187, 190–1, 194
ownership of bed, ... 17–20, 70, 78, 182, 184
nuclear power, ... 342–6
nuisance
obstruction erected in contravention of consent requirement, ... 399
pollution, ... 90, 109, 129
public *see* public nuisance
right to abate, ... 79–80, 141
statutory, under Environmental Protection Act 1990, ... 339–341, 382
weirs as, ... 147–8

O

obstruction
byelaws to prevent, ... 413–14
common law, ... 78–84, 171, 215
easements of, ... 106–7
fisheries, to, ... 419, 442
flood defence, ... 82–4, 391, 398–9
National Rivers Authority's powers to prevent or alter
on main rivers, ... 381, 383–4, 387–8
navigable watercourses, ... 140–9, 154, 156, 157, 212–13
passage of fish, to, ... 79, 196, 428–34, 435, 436, 438
offshore installation, ... 38–9
defined, ... 39n84
oil
defined, ... 347n236

oil – *continued* Page
storage, ...334
oil pollution, ...337, 338, 346–9, 350, 463
overflow, ...128, 197
see also escapes
oyster beds, ...30n42, 109, 139–140, 192
oysters, ...183, 459

P

passage rights, ...135–6, 433
see also under public rights
percolating water, ...14, 91
easements regarding, ...110
pollution, ...129–130
surface water, ...8, 128
underground, ...88, 121–6, 351
absence of riparian rights, ...71, 121–3
abstraction, ...123–4
support from, ...126–7
pesticides
pollution, ...354–5
"petroleum spirit", ...337, 338
piers, ...52
pipe–laying powers of National Rivers Authority, ...216–17, 314n108
pipelines
pollution by, ...352
pipes
easements relating to, ...112
interference with, ...221–2
piracy, ...40
planning control
bridge construction, ...171–2
developments below limit of foreshore, ...53n186
drainage development, ...382, 393–4
mooring of vessels, ...152
National Rivers Authority works, ...223, 382
pollution prevention, ...333–5
removal of sand and gravel, ...55
waste management licensing and, ...321n140, 323–4
police *see* water bailiffs
pollution
action in negligence for, ...75
artificial watercourses, ...91, 120–1, 291
common law, ...89–99

pollution – *continued* Page
environmental, ... 321, 322, 323
defined, ... 321n140
fisheries, ... 93–4, 197, 352–3, 426, 427
percolating water, ... 129–30
underground water, ... 87
pollution control, ... 2, 198, 201, 238, 239
animal carcases, ... 353
"coastal waters" defined for, ... 25
"controlled waters" defined for ... 290–2
discharges to sewers, ... 299–300, 337–9
European Community legislation *see under* European Community
gas, ... 351–2
"inland freshwaters" defined for, ... 5–6
international obligations and transitional provisions, ... 336
pesticides, ... 354–5
public health law, ... 339–341
radioactive substances, ... 335, 342–6
riparian rights and, ... 67
statutory provisions, ... 290–370
vessels, ... 160, 346–49
"watercourse" defined for, ... 5
water supply, ... 350–1
pollution functions of National Rivers Authority,
... 4, 208, 216n52, 218, 220, 230–1, 234–5, 236–7, 295
anti–pollution works and operations, ... 325–6
consent for cutting vegetation, ... 301
consultees, ... 322, 323, 324, 334–5, 352
nitrate sensitive areas, ... 331
other powers to deal with foul water and pollution, ... 314n108, 326–7
prohibition notices for discharges, ... 298–9, 302, 309, 317, 333
register, ... 225–6
requirement to take precautions against, ... 327–8
water protection zones, ... 327–8
pollution offences, ... 239, 295–302
civil liability, savings and limitations for summary, ... 335–6
controlled waters, ... 295–8
defences to, ... 301–2
deposits and vegetation in rivers, ... 301
discharges into and from public sewers, ... 299–300
gas, ... 351
integrated pollution control, under, ... 316, 317–18
Prevention of Oil Pollution Act 1971, under, ... 347–8
prohibitions of discharges, ... 298–9
public health law, under, ... 339–41

pollution offences – *continued* Page
radioactive substances, ... 342, 344–5
Water Industry Act 1991, under, ... 337–8
water supply, ... 350–1
pollution prevention, ... 325–335
codes of good agricultural practice, ... 332–3
pipelines, ... 352
planning law and, ... 333–5
precautionary regulations, ... 327–8
nitrate sensitive areas, ... 209, 330–2
water protection zones, ... 200, 328–330
pond, ... 5, 6, 91, 111, 291–2, 353
fisheries in, ... 193–4, 196, 451
port authority, ... 158
Port of London Authority, ... 144
power generation, ... 2, 80–1
prescriptive liability
maintain bridge, to, ... 172
repair walls and banks, ... 63, 64
prescriptive rights
abstraction, diversion and obstruction, ... 106–7
acquisition of easement of, ... 75, 85, 103–5, 110, 111, 112
affect volume and flow of water, to, ... 80
artificial watercourse, ... 116–19
extinguishment of easement of, ... 113–14
ferry, ... 163
fishery, ... 184, 186–7, 194–5
foreshore, to, ... 45–6, 50, 53, 54
pollution, ... 93, 108–9
taking stones from waste land, ... 54
towing, ... 137
towpath, ... 138
wreck, ... 55
private nuisance, ... 141
Privatisation of Water Authorities in England and Wales 198, 199
profit a prendre, ... 54, 125, 175, 180, 186–7, 196
profit of piscary, ... 175
public access to information about water regulation, ... 200, 224–7
public footpath, ... 62, 65
public health
injury to, ... 109
protection of, ... 310, 321, 322, 323, 339–341, 351, 357
public highway *see* highway
public inquiry
drainage of small areas, ... 396

public inquiry – *continued* Page
nitrate sensitive areas, ...332
reservoirs, ...281
water protection zones, ...330
public landing places, ... 134, 137
public local inquiry
drainage, ...388
fisheries, ...417
public navigable rivers *see* navigable watercourses
public nuisance
drainage works, ...394
encroachment on soil of foreshore, ...43
obstruction of public navigable river, ... 140–1, 142, 145, 153
pollution, ... 98–9
sea wall as, ...63
public right of way, ... 62, 137
public rights
fish, to, ...15, 16–17, 42, 43, 46, 50, 134, 139, 176–182, 195
floating seaweed, ...53
foreshore, to, ...50–2, 178
navigation, of 15, 16, 17, 22–3, 43, 46, 50, 68, 131, 178
extinguishment, ...139
fishing and, ...139–40
high seas, ...27, 33, 37, 41
incidents of, ...135–9
inland waters, ... 134, 140, 158–9, 160
non–tidal watercourses, ...133–5
tidal watercourses, ...131–3
shooting, ...134
tidal watercourses, to, ...15, 16
pump, ...111

Q

quia timet action, ...98
quo warranto, writ of, ...163

R

radioactive substances, ...335, 342–6
railways, ... 143, 148, 155, 168, 171, 314
rainbow trout, ...437
reclamation, ...215
works, ... 151, 354

Page

recreational duties
National Rivers Authority, of, ...211–14, 223, 246, 389–391
statutory, ...371, 389–391
regional fisheries advisory committees, ...418
regional flood defence committees,
205, 207, 210–11, 227, 239–40, 372, 373, 375–6, 377, 405–6
regional land drainage committees, ...375
regional rivers advisory committees, ...209
Report on the Consolidation of Certain Enactments Relating to Water, ...202
reservoir, 5, 6, 208, 216, 219, 223, 244, 280–9, 291, 292n13, 326n159, 353
certification, ...282–3
criminal and civil liability of undertakers, ...288–9
definitions, ...280–1
discontinuance, ...286
"enforcement authority", ...281
escapes of water from, ...86
fisheries, ...194
inspections and monitoring, ...284–6
qualification of engineers, ...282
registration by local authorities, ...281–2
"resource mains", ...221–2, 227
riparian owner, ...69–70
alteration to depth of water, ...144
consent to land or moor to bank, ...137
damage from drainage works, ...393
evidence of possession of fishery, ...190
pollution of artificial watercourse, ...120
riparian rights and duties, ...1, 13–14, 21, 22, 70–2
abate obstruction, to, ...79–80
abrogation by local statutes, ...77
absence in underground percolating water, ...121–3
abstraction *see* under abstraction
access to watercourse, ...67–8, 69, 149–51
artificial watercourses, ...10, 14, 71–2, 114, 116–18, 120
classification, ...72
construct erection on land, to, ...141
drainage and flood prevention, ...372
easements *see* easements
escape, overflow and discharge of water, ...84–9
fishery, ...190–1
interference with flow and, ...67
interference with use of water, ...71
nature of, ...66–9
navigable watercourses, on, ...137, 149–53

riparian rights and duties – *continued* Page
non–tidal watercourses, ... 17, 134, 190
obstruction *see* obstruction
pollute, to, ... 89, 93, 107–9
towpath, to, ... 138
water flowing in defined channel, ... 122,127
water quality, ... 60, 70, 71, 76, 89–91
water quantity, ... 60, 70, 71, 74, 76–7
river, ... 1
alterations to level, ... 82
offences concerning deposits of vegetation in, ... 301
prescriptive right to pollute, ... 109
Woolrych's definition, ... 3
see also watercourse
river authorities, ... 243
river purification authorities (Scotland), ... 295
road–ferries, ... 164
Royal Commission on Environmental Pollution, ... 315
royal fish and fowl, ... 50, 58, 181

S

salmon
byelaws, ... 459
close seasons and times, ... 434–5
defined, ... 423n27, 449n145, 453n177
"immature", ... 424n36
"unclean", ... 424n36
handling in suspicious circumstances, ... 443n119, 444n122, 449–451
"offence", ... 450n150
"relevant offence", ... 450
importation, ... 453
provisions of Salmon Act 1986, ... 448–51
sale, export and consignment, ... 436–7
salmon dealer licensing scheme, ... 448–9
salmon farming, ... 30
salmon fisheries, ... 210, 415, 421, 422, 447
provisions of Salmon and Freshwater Fisheries Act 1975, ... 423–45
offences under, ... 445–8
sand, taking, ... 46, 50, 53–5
sand–banks and *medium filum* rule, ... 19
Sark, river, ... 207
Scotland
application of National Rivers Authority to, ... 207
royal fish, ... 58

Scotland – *continued* Page
theft of fish, 451n160
sea, 24–65
definitions, 26, 31n45, 457n197
fishery rights, 176, 178
pollution *see* under pollution control
territorial *see* territorial sea
sea banks, 60, 61–2
sea beach, 19–20
defined, 42
sea bed
mooring rights, 43, 136
ownership *see* under Crown
works obstructing navigation, 146
sea fish, fishing
defined, 34n63, 458n206
destruction of predators, 462
sea fisheries, 457–64
byelaws, 352–3, 458–61, 464
fishery officers, 461–2
local fisheries committees, 457–8
pollution, 352–3
sea walls, 60, 61–2, 151
repair, 62–5
"seashore", 41
see also foreshore
seaweed, taking, 46, 50, 53–5
Secretary of State for Wales, 415
sequestration of assets, 98
several fishery,
94, 175, 176, 180–1, 183, 186, 187, 189, 190, 191, 193, 196, 437, 460
sewage
discharge, 10–11, 104, 109, 113–14, 296, 422, 460
disposal, 87
pollution by, 93, 96, 98, 121
fisheries, 93–4
prescriptive right to transmit, 111
treatment and purification, 4–5, 198, 200
sewerage services, 199, 201
sewerage undertakers, 201, 204, 211, 212, 216, 231, 234, 390,
consultees, 352
drought orders, and, 274, 275, 276, 278, 279
liability for discharges into and from public sewers, 299–300, 337
sewers, 3–4, 10, 115, 123, 216n52, 291, 327
discharges into and from, 299–300, 337–9

Page
shellfish, ...452n168, 453n177, 458n206
    public right to, ...179
shellfish farming, ...456
shellfish waters
    Directive 79/923/EEC, ...359, 364
shellfisheries, ...353, 459, 462
shells, taking, ...50, 53–5
shingle, taking, ...49, 50, 53–5, 61
ships *see* vessels
shooting over foreshore, ...51, 134
shore, ...11
silting, ...139
    works causing, on navigable watercourse, ...144–5
Single European Act, ...356, 357
sites of special scientific interest, ...213, 214, 246
sludge disposal, ...367
sluices, ...3, 427, 432
soil of watercourse *see* bed
spray irrigation, ...75, 106, 254, 265, 266, 272–3
springs, ...88, 110, 111, 115, 123, 125, 350n249
stand–pipes, ...276
statutory nuisance *see* nuisance
steam, waste, ...337
stillwaters, ...21–3, 47–8
stones, taking, ...46, 54
stream *see* river; watercourse
street works, ...217, 327
surface water, ...110
    landowners' rights, ...14, 85, 111, 123–4
    powers of National Rivers Authority to undertake
        anti–pollution operations, ...326
swans, ...58

T

tempest, extraordinary, ...63
territorial fishery, ...175, 185
territorial sea
    domestic law, in, ...28–32, 207, 373
    international law, in, ...26–8
territorial waters, ...25, 28–32
    fishery rights, ...177
    "relevant" for water pollution, ...290–1
Thames, river, ...58, 144, 147, 195

Page

tidal lands
National Rivers Authority works, ...223
"tidal navigable rivers", ... 16, 132
ownership of bed, ...42
tidal river, ...11, 20
limits of tidal part, ... 181–2
weirs, ...148
see also tidal watercourse
tidal watercourse, ...15
ascertaining *medium filum*, ...20, 192–3
fishery rights, ... 181–2
navigation, ... 131–3
ownership of bed of, ...16, 20–1, 46
pollution, ...91
riparian rights, ...68
see also tidal river
tidal waters,
defined, ...15
domestic law, in, ... 25–6
fisheries, ... 176–82, 184, 187, 190
medium filum rule and, ...19, 20
minimum acceptable flows, ...246
rights of navigation and fishing, ... 139–40
tolls, ... 154, 156, 157, 159, 164, 165
towing rights, ... 137–9
towpath, ...12, 137–9, 157
fishing from, ...195
trade effluent, ... 104–5, 296, 338–9
Treaty of Rome, ...356, 357, 358
trespass, ...90, 121, 140, 155, 189, 197, 298
tributyltin, ...355
trout
close seasons and times, ... 435–6
defined, ... 423n27
sale, export and consignment, ...436–7, 447
trout fisheries, ...210, 415, 421, 422
provisions of Salmon and Freshwater Fisheries Act 1975,
..........423, 424, 428, 431–2, 438, 439, 440
tunnels *see* bridges
Tweed, river, ... 207, 415

U

UNCLOS, ...24, 26–8, 32–3, 36–7, 38, 39–40, 41n95

Page

underground river *see* underground watercourse
underground strata, ...249
water in, ...2, 208, 245, 249n29, 292, 326, 351
underground water, ...8, 9–10, 115–30
abstraction *see* under abstraction
easements regarding, ...110, 326
percolating underground, ...121–6, 129–30
pollution, ...87, 129–30
water flowing in a defined channel *see* underground watercourse
underground watercourse, ...5, 9, 71, 126–7, 291
riparian rights, ...71
United Kingdom Atomic Energy Authority, ...342, 344n222
"United Kingdom Waters" defined, ...31n45
United Nations Conference on the Law of the Sea *see* UNCLOS
urban waste water treatment
Directive 91/271/EEC, ...360, 361, 365–7

V

vessels
discharges from, ...299, 302
navigation rights *see* navigation rights
obstruction by, ...147, 149, 151–2
oil and other pollution from, ...160, 346–9
powers of entry to, ...218, 442–3
"scuttling" at sea, ...324
statutory nuisance under public health law, ...339n210
sunken *see* wreck
theft of, ...159
theft of fish from, ...451
Vintner's Company, ...58
vis major, ...86

W

Wales
fisheries, ...415–16, 418
wall(s), ...12, 13
flood, ...84, 85
retaining, as evidence of title to seashore, ...45
sea *see* sea walls
wartime exigency, ...97, 345
waste discharge, ...115
waste disposal sites, ...320, 324

Page

waste land, inclosure, ...19
waste management and disposal, ... 303, 334
 at sea, ...324–5
 offences, ...320, 322–5
 radioactive *see* radioactive substances
 "special waste", ...323
waste management licence, ...321–4
 defined, ... 303n63
 duty of care, ...322–4
waste regulation authorities, ... 321, 323
 defined, ...321n137
waste surface water, ... 8–9
water
 distinction between use and ownership of, ...67
 larceny and theft of, ...14
 ownership of, ... 14, 155
 quality *see* water quality
 quantity *see* water quantity
 rights, ...1, 351
  acquired rights, ...100–14
  natural rights, ...66–99
 use of, ...2
  cooling purposes, ...2, 69
  domestic purposes, ...23, 72–3, 87, 105, 125, 254–5
  extraordinary, ...73–5
  manufacturing purposes, ... 73, 118
  ordinary, ...72–3
  right to use, ...67
water authority, ... 198, 199, 204n8, 209, 243
 negligence for contaminating water supply, ...75
water bailiffs, ...441, 442–5, 450
Water Environment: the Next Steps, ...199
water industry *see* water regulation; water undertaker
water mains, ...3, 115, 221, 350n249
water protection zones, ...200, 328–30
water quality, ...66, 70, 71, 76, 89–91
 drinking, ... 293n19, 359, 361, 364, 367
 EEC legislation, ...355–70
 meaning of pollution and, ...92
 National Rivers Authority and, ...200, 206, 294, 295, 319–20, 369
 sampling, ...218, 219, 220, 234–5, 307, 320
water quality classification, ... 292–3, 294, 306, 369
water quality objectives, ...225, 238, 246, 293, 294–5, 316, 319, 362–3, 369
water quantity, ...66, 70, 71, 74, 76–7

water quantity– *continued* Page
abstraction licences, ...263–4, 265, 266
water regulation, ...198–242
background to Water Act 1989, ...198–201
"consumer", ...221n68
customer services committees, ...198, 201
evidence of samples and abstractions, ...234–5
financing and charging systems, ...200
information provisions, ...224–32
offences under Water Resources Act 1991, ...238–9
"service pipe", ...221n68
"stopcock", ...221–2
"the relevant Minister", ...236n132, 241n149
water consolidation legislation, ...201–42
water resource management, ...2, 198, 243–89
definition of "inland waters" for, ...5
water resources functions of National Rivers Authority, ...208, 216, 243–80
charges, ...270–3
general management functions, ...244–5
licences *see* licences
"source of supply", ...249
Water Services Public Limited Companies, ...198–9, 200, 201
water supply, ...3, 73–4, 105, 198, 199, 200, 201, 208, 244, 291
"domestic purposes" defined, ...350n249
pollution of, ...327, 350–1
water undertakers, ...201, 204, 211, 212, 216, 231, 244–5, 352, 390
abstraction and impounding by, ...269–70
consultees, ...245, 260, 352
drought orders, ...274, 275, 276, 278, 279
easements, ...105
information rights and duties, ...228, 230–1
powers to create byelaws regulating fishing, ...419n17
prohibition on using sewers or drains to convey
foul water without treatment, ...5
regulation of navigation by, ...161
reservoirs, ...280
watercourse
common law, ...6–11
constituents, ...11–14
definitions, ...2–3
statutory, ...3–5, 249n28, 291
in general, ...1–3
maintenance related to land drainage, ...397–400
statutory definitions, ...3–5, 249n28, 291
temporary, ...107

Page

waterworks, ...327
    defined, ...350
    maps of, ...227–8
weir, ...154, 398, 438
    fishing weir, ...215, 419, 429, 433, 442
    navigable watercourse, on, ...147–8
    obstructing fisheries, ...147, 195–6
well, ...91, 121, 122, 123–4, 127, 129, 257, 350n249
    easements, ...109, 110, 111, 125
    sinking, ...229, 232, 250, 251, 255, 256
wharf, ...142, 143, 151, 153
Woolrych, ...3
wreck, ...31–2, 50, 55–7
    custom to take, ...45
    obstruction, as, ...146–7
    prohibited area, ...32
    restricted area, ...31